THE *OLD ENGLISH HEPTATEUCH*
AND
ÆLFRIC'S *LIBELLUS DE VETERI TESTAMENTO ET NOVO*

———

EARLY ENGLISH TEXT SOCIETY
No. 330

Ðis synd þa bebodu 7 domas 7 laga þe a*lmihten* gesette betwyx him 7 israhela folce on sinai dune.
Her onginð seo boc þe ys ge nemned on
ebreisc. uagedaber. þys on greden numerus.
7 on englisc ge tel. for þam þe israhela bearn
wæron on þære getealde.

DRIHTEN SPRÆC PI TO DRICE TO MOISE ON SINAI
dune on þære halgan stowe on þa forman
dæg þæs æfteran monðes. on þa oðrum geare þe
his folon of egypta lande. Nim 7 tell þa israhela folc swa hwæt swa ri wæpned hæver fra
twentig wintrum 7 forð þralle þa fejengercan
of israhela folce. telle þu 7 aaron heap mælum
7 þæra mægða ealdoras beoð inc mid hyra hywoð
þe his sint hyra naman. Of ruben elisur sede ures
sunu. Of simeon salamiel surisaddais sunu. Of
iuda nason aminadabis sunu. Of isachar nathana-
el suares sunu. Of zabulon heliab elonis sunu. Iosepes bearna. Of ephraim elisama amuiudes sunu.
Of mannase gamliel phadasures sunu. Of beniamin
abidan gedeonis sunu. Of dana ahiezes amisaddages
sunu. Of aser phegiel ochranes sunu; Of gad elia-
saphadueles sunu. Of neptalim ahyra enananis sunu.
Ðis sind þe wæron þa æðolestan ealdoras geond þa-
reisa israhela heapoð men. Moises 7 aaron
gegaderodon ealle þas on þam forman dæge þæs

THE *OLD ENGLISH HEPTATEUCH* AND ÆLFRIC'S *LIBELLUS DE VETERI TESTAMENTO ET NOVO*

EDITED BY

RICHARD MARSDEN

VOLUME ONE
INTRODUCTION AND TEXT

Published for
THE EARLY ENGLISH TEXT SOCIETY
by the
OXFORD UNIVERSITY PRESS

OXFORD
UNIVERSITY PRESS

Great Clarendon Street, Oxford OX2 6DP
United Kingdom

Oxford University Press is a department of the University of Oxford.
It furthers the University's objective of excellence in research, scholarship,
and education by publishing worldwide. Oxford is a registered trade mark of
Oxford University Press in the UK and in certain other countries

© The Early English Text Society 2008

The moral rights of the authors have been asserted

Database right Oxford University Press (maker)

First Edition published in 2008

All rights reserved. No part of this publication may be reproduced,
stored in a retrieval system, or transmitted, in any form or by any means,
without the prior permission in writing of Oxford University Press,
or as expressly permitted by law, or under terms agreed with the appropriate
reprographics rights organization. Enquiries concerning reproduction
outside the scope of the above should be sent to the Rights Department,
Oxford University Press, at the address above

You must not circulate this book in any other form
and you must impose this same condition on any acquirer

Published in the United States of America by Oxford University Press
198 Madison Avenue, New York, NY 10016, United States of America

British Library Cataloguing in Publication Data
Data available

Library of Congress Cataloging in Publication Data
Data available

Original Series, 330

ISBN 978-0-19-956143-8

PREFACE

The work of preparing this edition has been spread over many years, interrupted several times by other projects. Research leave funded by the Arts and Humanities Research Council of Great Britain and by the University of Nottingham enabled me to complete volume 1 and begin work on the projected volume of commentary and glossary. Both the Council and the University, along with the University's School of English Studies, contributed towards travel and other expenses, which I acknowledge gratefully. I would like to record here also my thanks to the staff of the Bodleian Library, the British Library, the Cambridge University Library, the Parker Library, the Hallward Library of the University of Nottingham (where the Lincoln Cathedral Library fragment has been housed), and the Pierpont Morgan Library in New York for their cooperation and kindness in facilitating my work during numerous visits. I am indebted to Kevin Kiernan for supplying me with digitized ultraviolet images of London, British Library, Cotton Otho B. x, which enabled me to decipher additional readings.

R.M.

CONTENTS

ILLUSTRATION	viii
ABBREVIATIONS	ix
BIBLIOGRAPHY	xii
INTRODUCTION	
I. Previous Editions	xix
II. The Present Edition	xxxii
III. The Manuscripts	xxxiv
IV. The Relationships between the Manuscripts	lxix
V. Editorial Procedures and Conventions	clxxv
THE TEXTS	1
Prefatio to Genesis	3
Genesis	8
Exodus	89
Leviticus	129
Numbers	138
Deuteronomy	154
Joshua	177
Judges	190
Libellus de ueteri testamento et nouo	201

ILLUSTRATION

Oxford, Bodleian Library, Laud Misc. 509, f. 72^r (actual size). Reproduced by permission of the Bodleian Library. *frontispiece*

ABBREVIATIONS

MANUSCRIPT SIGLA

The following sigla are used to refer to the manuscripts discussed in the Introduction:

B London, British Library, Cotton Claudius B. iv
B^t Cambridge, Corpus Christi College 379, ff. 10^r–12^v (Talbot's transcription of part of a leaf since lost from B)
Bo Oxford, Bodleian Library, Bodley 343
C Cambridge, University Library, Ii. 1. 33
Co Cambridge, Corpus Christi College 201, pp. 151–160
H Oxford, Bodleian Library, Hatton 115
L Oxford, Bodleian Library, Laud Misc. 509
Ln Lincoln, Cathedral Library 298, no. 2
N Nicholson's readings from a lost manuscript fragment, cited by Thwaites
O London, British Library, Cotton Otho B. x
O^w Wanley's transcription in his *Catalogus* of the incipit and explicit of O, now destroyed
P New York, Pierpont Morgan Library, G. 63

In references to manuscript contents, figures following a forward slash after a folio number indicate line numbers (e.g. f. 24^v/1 refers to line 1 on the verso of f. 24).

SHORT TITLES

Bosworth Toller   J. Bosworth and T. N. Toller, *An Anglo-Saxon Dictionary* (Oxford, 1882–98); with T. N. Toller, *An Anglo-Saxon Dictionary: Supplement* (Oxford, 1908–21); and A. Campbell, *Enlarged Addenda and Corrigenda to the Supplement* (Oxford, 1972)
DOE   *Dictionary of Old English in Electronic Form A–F*, ed. A. Cameron *et al.*, Dictionary of Old English

ABBREVIATIONS

	Project, Centre for Medieval Studies, University of Toronto (2003 release)
Gneuss, *Handlist*	Helmut Gneuss, *Handlist of Anglo-Saxon Manuscripts* (Tempe, Ariz., 2001)
Hall and Meritt	John R. Clark Hall, *A Concise Anglo-Saxon Dictionary*, 4th edn. with suppl. by H. D. Meritt (Cambridge, 1969)
Ker	N. R. Ker, *Catalogue of Manuscripts Containing Anglo-Saxon* (Oxford, 1957; reissued with suppl., 1990)
OE Corpus	*The Old English Corpus in Machine Readable Form*, Database of the Dictionary of Old English Project, ed. Antonette Di Paolo Healey, Centre for Medieval Studies, University of Toronto (2004 release)
Wanley, *Catalogus*	Humphrey Wanley, *Antiquæ Literaturæ Septentrionalis Liber alter, seu Humphredi Wanleii Librorum Vett. Septentrionalium qui in Angliæ Biblioth. extant, Catalogus Historico-Criticus; nec non multorum Vett. Codd. Septentrionalium alibi extantium notitia, cum totius operis sex Indicibus* (Oxford, 1705) [Part 2 of George Hickes's *Linguarum Vett. Septentrionalium Thesaurus Grammatico-Criticus et Archæologicus*]

OTHER ABBREVIATIONS

add.	added
alt.	altered
CSASE	Cambridge Studies in Anglo-Saxon England
del.	deleted
EETS	Early English Text Society (old series)
eras.	erased, erasure
illus.	illustration
Lat.	Latin
NS	new series
OE	Old English
OEH	*Old English Heptateuch*
om.	omits, omitted
ss	supplementary series

supp.	supplied
var(s).	variant reading(s)
Vulg.	the Latin Vulgate (see note, p. xvii)

BIBLIOGRAPHY

EDITIONS

Ælfric de veteri et novo Testamento, Pentateuch, Josua, Buch der Richter und Hiob, ed. Christian W. M. Grein, Bibliothek der angelsächsischen Prosa, 1 (Kassel, 1872; repr. Hamburg, 1921).
Ælfric's Catholic Homilies: The Second Series. Text, ed. M. R. Godden, EETS ss 5 (London, 1979).
Ælfric's Lives of Saints, ed. W. W. Skeat, 2 vols., EETS os 76/82 and 94/114 (London, 1881–1900, repr. 1966).
Ælfric's Prefaces, ed. Jonathan Wilcox, Durham Medieval Texts, 9 (Durham, 1994).
Alt- und mittelenglische Anthologie, ed. Rolf Kaiser (Berlin, 1954); 3rd edn. rev. as Medieval English: An Old English and Middle English Anthology (1958; 5th edn. 1961).
Altenglisches Lesebuch (Prosa), ed. Josef Raith (Munich, 1940; 2nd edn. 1958); 3rd edn., as part of his Altenglisches Wörterbuch zum altenglischen Lesebuch (Prosa und Poesie) (1967).
Altenglisches Übungsbuch zum Gebrauche bei Universitäts-Vorlesungen, mit einem Wörterbuche, ed. Julius Zupitza (Vienna, 1874).
Altsächsische und angelsächsische Sprachproben, herausgegeben und mit einem erklärenden Verzeichniss der angelsächsischen Wörter, ed. Heinrich Leo (Halle, 1838).
Analecta Anglo-Saxonica: A Selection in Prose and Verse from Anglo-Saxon Authors of Various Ages, with a Glossary, Designed Chiefly as a First Book for Students, ed. Benjamin Thorpe (London, 1834).
Analecta Anglo-Saxonica: Selections in Prose and Verse from the Anglo-Saxon Literature: With an Introductory Ethnological Essay, and Notes, Critical and Explanatory, ed. Louis F. Klipstein, 2 vols. (New York, 1849; 2nd edn. 1871).
An Anglo-Saxon Book of Verse and Prose, ed. W. J. Sedgefield (Manchester, 1928).
The Anglo-Saxon Chronicle: A Collaborative Edition, vi: MS. D, ed. G. B. Cubbin (Cambridge, 1996); vii: MS. E, ed. Susan Irvine (Cambridge, 2004).
An Anglo-Saxon Reader in Prose and Verse, with Grammatical Introduction, Notes, and Glossary, ed. Henry Sweet (Oxford, 1876; and many editions).
Angelsächsische Chrestomathie, oder Sammlung merkwürdiger Stücke aus den Schriften der Angelsachsen . . . mit beigefügter hochdeutschen Uebersetzung und einem Kupfer, ed. Johann Oelrichs (Hamburg and Bremen, 1798).

BIBLIOGRAPHY

Angelsächsische Homilien und Heiligenleben, ed. Bruno Assmann, Bibliothek der angelsächsischen Prosa, 3 (Kassel, 1889; repr. with an introduction by P. A. M. Clemoes, Darmstadt, 1964).
Angelsächsische Sprachproben zum Gebrauch seiner Zuhörer, ed. Heinrich Leo (Halle, 1835).
Anglo-Saxon Bibles and 'The Book of Cerne', ed. A. N. Doane, Anglo-Saxon Manuscripts in Microfiche Facsimile, 7 (Tempe, Ariz., 2002).
The Cambridge Old English Reader, ed. Richard Marsden (Cambridge, 2004; repr. with corr. 2007).
'Catalogus Librorum Manuscriptorum Bibliothecae Wigorniensis' made in 1622–23 by Patrick Young, Librarian to King James I, ed. I. Atkins and N. R. Ker (Cambridge, 1944).
Chase, Frank H., 'A New Text of the Old English Prose *Genesis*', *Archiv für das Studium der neueren Sprachen und Literaturen*, 100 (1898), 241–66.
The Chronicle of England or a Compleat History, Civil, Military and Ecclesiastical, of the Ancient Britons and Saxons from the Landing of Julius Caesar in Britain, to the Norman Conquest, ed. Joseph Strutt, 2 vols. (London, 1777–8).
Cox, R. S., 'The Old English Dicts of Cato', *Anglia*, 90 (1972), 1–42.
Crawford, S. J., 'The Lincoln Fragment of the Old English Version of the Heptateuch', *Modern Language Review*, 15 (1920), 1–6.
De Bonis, Maria C., 'La versione in prosa della "Genesi" in inglese antico del ms Cambridge, Corpus Christi College, 201' (Ph.D. thesis, Università degli Studi di Firenze, 1998/99).
Eadwine's Canterbury Psalter Edited with Introduction and Notes from the Manuscript in Trinity College, Cambridge, Pt. 2: *Text and Notes*, ed. Fred Harsley, EETS os 92 (London, 1889).
Early English Homilies from the Twelfth Century MS. Vesp. D XIV, ed. Rubie D.-N. Warner, EETS os 152 (London, 1917).
Exameron Anglice or The Old English Hexameron, ed. S. J. Crawford, Bibliothek der angelsächsischen Prosa, 10 (Hamburg, 1921; repr. Darmstadt, 1968).
First Readings in Old English, ed. P. S. Andern (Wellington, 1948; 2nd edn. 1951).
Grein, Christian W. M. 'Ælfric's metrischer Auszug aus dem "Buch der Richter"', *Anglia*, 2 (1879), 141–52.
The Handbook of Specimens of English Literature, Selected from the Chief British Authors, and Arranged Chronologically, ed. Joseph Angus (London, n.d.; repr. 1866, 1867).
Heptateuchus, Liber Job, et Evangelium Nicodemi; Anglo-Saxonice. Historiae Judith Fragmentum; Dano-Saxonice, ed. Edward Thwaites (Oxford, 1698).
Judith, ed. Mark Griffith (Exeter, 1997).
An Old and Middle English Reader on the Basis of Professor Julius Zupitza's

Alt- und Mittelenglisches Übungsbuch with Introduction Notes and Glossary, ed. George Edwin MacClean (Boston, 1886; 2nd edn. New York and London, 1893).
An Old English Anthology, ed. Whitney F. Bolton (London, 1963; repr. Evanston, Ill., 1966).
Old English Homilies from MS Bodley 343, ed. Susan Irvine, EETS 302 (Oxford, 1993)
The Old English Illustrated Hexateuch: British Museum Cotton Claudius B. IV, ed. C. R. Dodwell and Peter Clemoes, Early English Manuscripts in Facsimile, 18 (Copenhagen, 1974).
The Old English Version of the Gospels, ed. R. M. Liuzza, 2 vols., EETS 304 and 314 (Oxford, 1994–2000).
The Old English Version of the Heptateuch, Ælfric's Treatise on the Old and New Testament and his Preface to Genesis, ed. S. J. Crawford, EETS 160 (London, 1922; repr. with the text of two additional manuscripts transcribed by N. R. Ker, 1969).
The Salisbury Psalter, ed. C. Sisam and K. Sisam, EETS 242 (London, 1959).
A Saxon Treatise concerning the Old and New Testament Written about the Time of King Edgar (700 yeares agoe) by Aelfricus Abbas, ed. William L'Isle (London, 1623). Reissued in 1638 as *Divers Ancient Monuments in the Saxon Tongue.*
Sweet's Anglo-Saxon Reader in Prose and Verse, ed. Dorothy Whitelock (Oxford, 1967).
Two of the Saxon Chronicles Parallel, with Supplementary Extracts from the Others, ed. John Earle and Charles Plummer, 2 vols. (Oxford, 1892–9).
Ussher, Jacob, *Historia dogmatica controversiae inter orthodoxos et pontificios de scripturis et sacris vernaculis* (London, 1690).

STUDIES AND WORKS OF REFERENCE

An Anglo-Saxon Primer, with Grammar, Notes, and Glossary, ed. Henry Sweet (Oxford, 1882).
Apthorp, G. F., *A Catalogue of the Books and Manuscripts in the Library of Lincoln Cathedral* (Lincoln, 1859).
Assmann, Bruno, 'Abt Ælfric's angelsächsische Bearbeitung des Buches Hiob', *Anglia*, 9 (1886), 39–42.
Baker, Peter S. 'The Old English Canon of Byrhtferth of Ramsey', *Speculum*, 55 (1980), 22–37.
Barnhouse, Rebecca, and Withers, Benjamin C. (eds.), *The Old English Hexateuch: Aspects and Approaches* (Kalamazoo, Mich., 2000).
Bishop, T. A. M., *English Caroline Minuscule* (Oxford, 1971).

BIBLIOGRAPHY

Budny, Mildred, 'The Biblia Gregoriana', in Richard Gameson (ed.), *St Augustine and the Conversion of England* (Thrupp, Glos., 1999), 237–84.
Bright's Old English Grammar and Reader, ed. Frederic G. Cassidy and Richard N. Ringler, 3rd edn. (New York, 1971).
Carley, James P., *The Libraries of King Henry VIII*, Corpus of British Medieval Library Catalogues, 7 (London, 2000).
Clemoes, Peter, 'The Chronology of Ælfric's Works' [corr. repr.], *Old English Newsletter*, Subsidia, 5 (Binghamton, NY, 1980).
Cockayne, T. O., *The Shrine: A Collection of Occasional Papers on Dry Subjects* (London, 1864–70).
Crawford, S. J., 'The Dialect of the Cambridge Manuscripts of the Old English Prose Genesis', *Transactions of the Philological Society* 1917–20 (1932), 41–7.
—— 'The Late Old English Notes of MS. (British Museum) Cotton Claudius B. iv', *Anglia*, 47 (1923), 124–35.
Förster, Max, 'Ælfric's s. g. Hiob-Übersetzung', *Anglia*, 15 (1893), 473–7.
Franzen, Christine, *The Tremulous Hand of Worcester: A Study of Old English in the Thirteenth Century* (Oxford, 1991).
Godden, Malcolm, *Ælfric's Catholic Homilies: Introduction, Commentary and Glossary*, EETS ss 18 (Oxford, 2000).
Graham, Timothy, 'Early Modern Users of Claudius B. iv: Robert Talbot and William L'Isle', in Barnhouse and Withers (eds.), *The Old English Hexateuch*, 271–316.
—— (ed.), *The Recovery of Old English: Anglo-Saxon Studies in the Sixteenth and Seventeenth Centuries* (Kalamazoo, Mich., 2000).
Hill, Joyce, 'The "Regularis Concordia" and its Latin and Old English Reflexes', *Revue bénédictine*, 101 (1991), 299–315.
Irvine, Susan, 'The Compilation and Use of Manuscripts Containing Old English in the Twelfth Century', in Mary Swan and Elaine M. Treharne (eds.), *Rewriting Old English in the Twelfth Century*, CSASE 30 (Cambridge, 2000), 41–61.
James, M. R., *The Ancient Libraries of Canterbury and Dover: The Catalogues of the Libraries of Christ Church Priory and St Augustine's Abbey at Canterbury and of St Martin's Priory at Dover. Now first collected and published with an introduction and identifications of the extant remains* (Cambridge, 1903).
—— *A Descriptive Catalogue of the Manuscripts in the Library of Corpus Christi College, Cambridge*, 2 vols. (Cambridge, 1909–12).
Jost, Karl, 'Wulfstan und die angelsächsische Chronik', *Anglia*, 47 (1923), 105–23.
—— 'Unechte Ælfrictexte', *Anglia*, 51 (1927), 82–103 and 177–219.
Keefer, Sarah Larratt, 'Assessing the Liturgical Canticles from the Old

English Hexateuch', in Barnhouse and Withers (eds.), *The Old English Hexateuch*, 109–43.

Ker, N. R., 'Membra Disiecta', *British Museum Quarterly*, 12 (1938), 130–5.

Lutz, Angelika, 'The Study of the Anglo-Saxon Chronicle in the Seventeenth Century and the Establishment of Old English Studies in the Universities', in Graham (ed.), *The Recovery of Old English*, 1–82.

Marsden, Richard, 'Ælfric as Translator: The Old English Prose Genesis', *Anglia* 109, (1991), 319–58.

—— 'Old Latin Intervention in the Old English *Heptateuch*', *Anglo-Saxon England*, 23 (1994), 229–64.

—— *The Text of the Old Testament in Anglo-Saxon England*, CSASE 15 (Cambridge, 1995).

—— 'Translation by Committee?: The "Anonymous" Old English Heptateuch', in Barnhouse and Withers (eds.), *The Old English Hexateuch*, 41–89.

—— 'Latin in the Ascendant: The Interlinear Gloss of Laud Misc. 509', in Katherine O'Brien O'Keeffe and Andy Orchard (eds.), *Latin Learning and English Lore: Studies in Anglo-Saxon Literature for Michael Lapidge*, 2 vols. (Toronto, 2005), i. 132–52.

—— 'Ælfric's Errors: The Evidence', in Mary Swan (ed.), *Essays for Joyce Hill on her Sixtieth Birthday = Leeds Studies in English*, 38 (2006), 135–60.

Mitchell, Bruce, *Old English Syntax*, 2 vols. (Oxford, 1985).

—— and Robinson, Fred C., *A Guide to Old English*, 6th edn. (Oxford, 2001).

Müller, L. C., *Collectanea Anglo-Saxonica maximam partem nunc primum edita et vocabulario illustrata* (Copenhagen, 1835; repr. Amsterdam, 1970).

Murphy, Michael, 'Edward Thwaites, Pioneer Teacher of Old English', *Durham University Journal*, 73 (1981), 153–9.

Nehab, J., *Der altenglische Cato* (diss., University of Göttingen, 1879).

Pons-Sanz, Sara, 'A Paw in Every Pie: Wulfstan and the Anglo-Saxon Chronicle Again', *Leeds Studies in English*, 38 (2007), 31–52.

Pulsiano, Phillip, 'William L'Isle and Editing of Old English', in Graham (ed.), *The Recovery of Old English*, 173–206.

Rask, Rasmus K. *Angelsaksisk Sproglære tilligemed en kort Læsebodg* (Stockholm: Wiborg, 1817).

—— *A Grammar of the Anglo-Saxon Tongue with a Praxis by Erasmus Rask. A New Edition Enlarged and Improved by the Author. Translated from the Danish*, trans. Benjamin Thorpe (Copenhagen, 1830; 2nd edn. London, 1865; 3rd edn. 1879).

Reinsma, Luke M., *Ælfric: An Annotated Bibliography* (New York and London, 1987).

Schipper, W., 'A Composite Old English Homiliary from Ely: Cambr. Univ. Libr. MS Ii. 1. 33', *Transactions of the Cambridge Bibliographical Society*, 8 (1983), 285–98.
Smith, A. B., *The Anonymous Parts of the Old English Hexateuch: A Latin-Old English, Old English–Latin Glossary* (Cambridge, 1985).
Swaen, A. E. H. 'Ælfric's *Prefatio Genesis Anglice*', *Englische Studien*, 67 (1932), 318.
Sweet's Anglo-Saxon Primer, rev. Norman Davies, 9th edn. (Oxford, 1953).
Temple, Elżbieta, *Anglo-Saxon Manuscripts 900–1066*, A Survey of Manuscripts Illuminated in the British Isles, 2 (London, 1976).
Thomson, R. M., *Catalogue of the Manuscripts of Lincoln Cathedral Chapter Library* (Cambridge, 1989).
Traxel, Oliver M., *Language Change, Writing and Textual Interference in Post-Conquest Old English Manuscripts: The Evidence of Cambridge, University Library, Ii. 1. 33* (Frankfurt am Main, 2004).
Treharne, Elaine M., 'The Dates and Origins of Three Twelfth-Century Old English Manuscripts', in Philip Pulsiano and Elaine M. Treharne (eds.), *Anglo-Saxon Manuscripts and their Heritage* (Aldershot, 1998), 227–53.
Vernon, E. J., *A Guide to the Anglo-Saxon Tongue: A Grammar after Erasmus Rask, Extracts in Prose and Verse . . .* (London, 1846).
White, C. L., *Ælfric: A New Study of his Life and Writings with a Supplementary Classified Bibliography Prepared by M. R. Godden* (Hamden, Conn., 1974).
Withers, Benjamin C., *The Illustrated Old English Heptateuch, Cotton Claudius B.iv: The Frontier of Seeing and Reading in Anglo-Saxon England* (London, Toronto and Buffalo, 2007).
Woolley, R. M., *Catalogue of the Manuscripts of Lincoln Cathedral Chapter Library* (Oxford, 1927).
Wormald, Francis, *English Drawings of the Tenth and Eleventh Centuries* (London, 1952).
Wormald, Patrick, *The Making of English Law: King Alfred to the Twelfth Century*, i: *Legislation and its Limits* (Oxford, 2000).

VULGATE CITATIONS

Latin Vulgate citations are taken from *Biblia Sacra iuxta Latinam vulgatam versionem ad codicum fidem, cura et studio monachorum Abbatiae pontificiae Sancti Hieronymi in Urbe O.S.B. edita*, ed. H. Quentin et al., 18 vols. (Rome, 1926–95):

I *Liber Genesis* (1926)
II *Liber Exodi–Levitici* (1929)

III *Libri Numerorum–Deuteronomii* (1936)
IV *Libri Iosue–Iudicum–Ruth* (1939)

Division of the Latin text in citations is by colon (with colon breaks indicated by a forward slash), as in the above volumes, and references to textual variation are based, without further comment, on their editors' critical apparatus. For Genesis, supplementary information is taken from *Vetus Latina: Die Reste der altlateinischen Bibel nach Petrus Sabatier neu gesammelt und herausgegeben von der Erzabtei Beuron* (Freiburg, 1949–), ii: *Genesis*, ed. B. Fischer (1951–4).

Modern English translations of the Latin are given only where interpretation may be an issue; they are the present editor's.

INTRODUCTION

I. PREVIOUS EDITIONS

Since the seventeenth century, there have been three complete editions of the *Old English Heptateuch*, based on the two major manuscripts, L and B. Both of these begin with Ælfric's *Prefatio* to Genesis, but only the former has the complete Heptateuch (i.e. including Ælfric's homiletic version of Judges), along with Ælfric's *Libellus de ueteri Testamento et nouo*; it includes also his letter to Wulfgeat, which is not edited in the present volume. B contains Genesis–Joshua only and is the so-called 'illustrated Hexateuch'. Some of the material from other extant manuscripts, which transmit only parts of the *OEH*, has been edited separately; so too have Ælfric's *Prefatio* and his *Libellus*. In this Introduction, the abbreviation *OEH* is used to designate the complete Heptateuch compilation; when only the Hexateuch is meant, this is made clear.

1. Complete Editions and Facsimiles

The first complete edition of the *OEH* was published in 1698 by Edward Thwaites (1667–1711), one of a group of prominent Anglo-Saxonists associated with the Queen's College, Oxford.[1] Thwaites printed the text of L, using C and B to fill in gaps. The title page of his volume reads:

Heptateuchus, Liber Job, et Evangelium Nicodemi; Anglo-Saxonice. Historiae Judith Fragmentum; Dano-Saxonice. Edidit nunc primum ex MSS codicibus Edwardus Thwaites, è Collegio Reginae. Oxoniae, è Theatro Sheldoniano. An. Dom. MDCXCVIII. Typis Junianis.

The last digit of MDCXCVIII on the title page does not match the font used for the rest of the date, which suggests a late change, presumably from MDCXCVII. On the reverse of the title page the imprimatur, given by John Meare, Vice-Chancellor of Oxford University, is dated 27 Dec 1697. However, Thwaites's dedication

---

[1] For a survey of the Oxford Anglo-Saxonists, see Angelika Lutz, 'The Study of the Anglo-Saxon Chronicle in the Seventeenth Century and the Establishment of Old English Studies in the Universities', in Timothy Graham (ed.), *The Recovery of Old English: Anglo-Saxon Studies in the Sixteenth and Seventeenth Centuries* (Kalamazoo, Mich., 2000), 1–82 at 48–64.

of the work to George Hickes—'viro summo . . . Literaturæ Anglo-Saxonicæ Instauratori'—provoked Meare to impound it. He feared offending members of the government, for Hickes had been deprived of the deanery of Worcester and proscribed for refusing to swear allegiance to the new king, William of Orange, in 1690. This seems to have been an overreaction on Meare's part, however, and the decision was soon reversed.[2] Thwaites's text is set in the Old English font developed by Franciscus Junius. The volume has an engraved frontispiece, head-pieces, and initials by Michael Burghers, engraver to the University of Oxford. There are 206 pages, with the pagination restarting for the last three sections ([i–vi], 1–168, 1–32), and the contents are as follows:

1. Six unnumbered pages of prefatory material. The last includes a citation from Ælfric's *Libellus*: 'Fif bec he (Moyses) awrat mid wunderlicum dihte . . . on Englisc sumne cwide in' [ellipsis original].
2. The Pentateuch, plus Joshua and Judges, all ascribed by Thwaites, in his preface, to Ælfric (pp. 1–163).
3. Job. A pared-down version of a homily from Ælfric's second series, as transcribed by William L'Isle in Oxford, Bodleian Library, Laud Misc. 381 (pp. 164–8).[3]
4. *Evangelium Nicodemi, Anglo-Saxonice*, based on a transcript by Junius (pp. 1–20).
5. *Fragmentum historiae Judith*. The first printing of the poem preserved in the *Beowulf* manuscript (British Library, Cotton Vitellius A. xv), set out continuously, as in the manuscript, and based again on a transcript by Junius (pp. 21–6).[4]
6. *Notae* (pp. 27–32).

The first of Thwaites's *notae* deal with parallel readings in other texts and the rubrics which punctuate the Pentateuch, and he prints (pp. 29–30) an OE version of Exodus 15, the first 'song of Moses',

---

[2] Michael Murphy, 'Edward Thwaites, Pioneer Teacher of Old English', *Durham University Journal*, 73 (1981), 153–9 at 155.

[3] The full text of the homily is printed in *Ælfric's Catholic Homilies: The Second Series. Text*, ed. M. R. Godden, EETS ss 5 (London, 1979), no. 30, pp. 260–7; and see Max Förster, 'Ælfric's s. g. Hiob-Übersetzung', *Anglia*, 15 (1893), 473–7. The first part of Laud Misc. 381 contains L'Isle's translation of the *Prefatio* and Heptateuch into contemporary English.

[4] On this printing of the poem, see *Judith*, ed. Mark Griffith (Exeter, 1997), 8–11 and n. 30.

because, as he points out, it is absent from L; the text is derived from an unpublished transcription by William L'Isle of the interlined version of the canticle as given in the Eadwine Psalter (Cambridge, Trinity College, R. 17. 1).[5] Then, on p. 32, Thwaites prints variant readings taken, he explains, from a manuscript fragment of Exodus given by William Nicholson to Edmund Gibson, who passed the readings to him. This is our only evidence for a lost witness to the *OEH*, which is given the siglum N in the present edition.[6]

The next edition of the *OEH*, this time with only Job added, was that of Christian Wilhelm Michael Grein, state archivist and Privatdocent at the University of Marburg in Hesse: *Ælfric de veteri et novo Testamento, Pentateuch, Josua, Buch der Richter und Hiob* (Kassel and Göttingen: Georg H. Wigland, 1872). This volume (iv + 272 pages) was the first in Grein's 'Bibliothek der angelsächsischen Prosa in kritisch bearbeiteten Texten'. A few emendations and problematical readings appear in footnotes. For the Heptateuch, Grein includes a Latin Vulgate text, in the Clementine version, below the Old English. He records in his Vorrede (pp. iii–iv) that he has been unable to fulfil his desire to consult the manuscripts themselves and has therefore restricted himself to tidying up (*säubern*) the texts of Thwaites, for the Heptateuch, and of 'De L'Isle', for the *Libellus* (see below). He expresses the hope of being able to supply an edition of collations of the other manuscripts among forthcoming volumes of the Bibliothek der angelsächsischen Prosa, though in fact this was never to happen. Thus Grein's edition is essentially a reprint of those of Thwaites and L'Isle. He uses his own orthographical conventions, however; thus, for example, Genesis 1:9, which is printed in the present edition as 'God þa soþlice cwæð: "Beon gegaderode þa wæteru" ', is presented by Grein as 'God þâ sođlîce cvæđ: Beón gegaderode þä väteru'. Grein,

---

[5] L'Isle's copy is in Bodleian Library, Laud Misc. 201, ff. 241ᵛ–245ʳ. The Exodus canticle belonged to his edition of 'The Saxon-English Psalter', which formed part of a project to print all 'the remaines of the Saxon-English Bible'. On this, see Phillip Pulsiano, 'William L'Isle and Editing of Old English', in Graham (ed.), *The Recovery of Old English*, 173–206 at 198–205. For the canticle text, see *Eadwine's Canterbury Psalter Edited with Introduction and Notes from the Manuscript in Trinity College, Cambridge*, Pt. 2: *Text and Notes*, ed. Fred Harsley, EETS os 92 (London, 1889), 248–50. L'Isle makes a few modifications to the text and gives alternative readings (apparently from other manuscript versions of the gloss), which Thwaites reproduces also.

[6] See below, p. lx. Nicholson subsequently criticized Thwaites's edition for its lack of an introduction, the absence of a parallel Latin text, and the inclusion of the apocryphal gospel of Nicodemus; see Murphy, 'Edward Thwaites', 156, and, on the possible use of the edition for learners of Old English, p. 157.

following Thwaites, does not always reproduce accurately the manuscript usage of thorn and eth. His edition was reprinted unaltered in Hamburg by Henri Grand in 1921.

Meanwhile, however, at the instigation of Richard Wülker, Grein had reissued his version of L's text of Judges separately, in 480 metrical lines: 'Ælfric's metrischer Auszug aus dem "Buch der Richter"', *Anglia*, 2 (1879), 141–52. Only two Vulgate citations within the text, and the OE translation of the first of them, were left out of the metrical scheme.[7]

The last complete edition was that by Samuel J. Crawford, head of the department of English Language, University College, Southampton, in the late 1920s, and afterwards Professor of English Philology at the Madras Christian College: *The Old English Version of the Heptateuch, Ælfric's Treatise on the Old and New Testament and his Preface to Genesis Edited together with a Reprint of 'A Saxon Treatise concerning the Old and New Testament: now first published in print with English of our times by William L'Isle of Wilburgham (1623)' and the Vulgate text of the Heptateuch*, EETS os 160 (London: Oxford University Press, 1922). The edition (ix + 442 pages) includes facsimiles of pages from B (ff. 11^r and 38^r) and from C (f. 24^r). There are three appendices. In the first, Crawford prints the late OE notes to be found in Claudius B. iv and 'the early English glosses and marks' found in the text of Judges in Hatton 115; in the second, he discusses the relationship between C and the other manuscripts and analyses the dialect of C; and in the third, he tackles the provenance of B and L.

Crawford based his text on B, noting in his preface (p. vii) that this was the first time that its text had been printed in full; he gave no other reason for preferring B to L. In his critical apparatus, Crawford collated the readings of L in Genesis to Joshua and, where available, of C and Co in Genesis, N in Exodus and Ln in Numbers; for Judges, he printed the text of L, collated with that of H. As the first item in his volume, he printed the *Libellus de ueteri testamento et nouo* from L, with the text of Bo in parallel, where available (i.e. for most of the Old Testament section). Crawford's edition contains a fair number of inaccuracies throughout, but they are especially notable in his collations of Ln and parts of Co and in the *Libellus*.

---

[7] The exercise had little point; the use of rhythmical effects by Ælfric, especially frequent alliteration, is an important aspect of his style, but it is not consistent and large numbers of Grein's discrete 'lines' have no special metrical character at all.

Furthermore, the integrity of the OE as narrative is persistently undermined by the draconian imposition of the modern system of division by chapter and verse, which sometimes involves making a break between clauses in a sentence. Crawford prints a corresponding Latin version at the bottom of each page of the Heptateuch text. Anachronistically (as in Grein's edition), it is the sixteenth-century Clementine revision of the Vulgate. Crawford was not averse to emending this occasionally (sometimes apparently following Grein), to suit the Old English version, but without authority from any extant Vulgate manuscripts.

An expanded reprint of Crawford's edition was issued by the Early English Text Society in 1969: *The Old English Version of the Heptateuch, Ælfric's Treatise on the Old and New Testament and his Preface to Genesis . . . with the Text of Two Additional Manuscripts transcribed by N. R. Ker* (London: Oxford University Press). The edition itself is unaltered, but on twenty additional pages Ker edits the texts of two manuscripts unknown to Crawford, Co and P.

A black-and-white facsimile of B was published in 1974 by C. R. Dodwell and Peter Clemoes: *The Old English Illustrated Hexateuch: British Museum Cotton Claudius B. IV*, Early English Manuscripts in Facsimile, 18 (Copenhagen: Rosenkilde). An introduction (pp. 13–73) has the following sections: 'The history and probable origins of the manuscript' (by Dodwell and Clemoes); 'The physical structure and contents of the manuscript' (by Dodwell and Clemoes); 'The composition of the Old English text' (by Clemoes); 'The production of an illustrated version' (by Clemoes); 'The technique and style of the illustrations' (by Dodwell); and 'The basic originality of the illustrations' (by Dodwell). The introduction includes five plates in colour. Black-and-white facsimiles of both L and B are included also in A. N. Doane, *Anglo-Saxon Bibles and 'The Book of Cerne'*, Anglo-Saxon Manuscripts in Microfiche Facsimile, 7 (Tempe, Ariz., 2002).

A complete digitized reproduction of B is now available on a CD-ROM in Benjamin C. Withers, *The Illustrated Old English Heptateuch, Cotton Claudius B.iv: The Frontier of Seeing and Reading in Anglo-Saxon England* (London: The British Library, and Toronto and Buffalo: University of Toronto Press, 2007).

2. EDITIONS OF PARTIAL VERSIONS AND FRAGMENTS

Parts of four portions of the Heptateuch, extant in manuscripts C, Ln, Co, and P, have been edited separately:

C: Frank H. Chase, 'A New Text of the Old English Prose *Genesis*', *Archiv für das Studium der neueren Sprachen und Literaturen*, 100 (1898), 241–66. Chase prints only the chapters of Genesis in which C departs radically from the text in B (i.e. Genesis 4–5, 10–11, and 22–4); he presents C and B in parallel columns (pp. 252–66).

Ln: Samuel J. Crawford, 'The Lincoln Fragment of the Old English Version of the Heptateuch', *Modern Language Review*, 15 (1920), 1–6. After a brief introduction, including some notes on the phonology and orthography of this fragment of Numbers, Crawford gives a transcription, without apparatus; he fills gaps caused by damage to the manuscript with text from L. He integrates Ln's readings in the critical apparatus of his EETS edition of the complete *OEH*.

Co: As noted above, the Genesis text of Co was appended by Ker to the 1969 reprint of Crawford's edition (pp. 444–56); there is a facsimile of Co's p. 159 (facing p. 454). A full critical edition of Co has been produced by Maria C. De Bonis: 'La versione in prosa della "Genesi" in inglese antico del ms Cambridge, Corpus Christi College, 201' (Ph.D. thesis, Università degli Studi di Firenze, 1998/99). This includes a comprehensive analysis of the language of Co in relation to the other manuscripts.

P: As noted above, the Exodus text of P was appended by Ker to the 1969 reprint of Crawford's edition (pp. 458–60), with a facsimile of f. 3^v (facing p. 460).

3. Published Extracts

The earliest use of an extract from the *OEH* appears to have been in an antiquarian survey of 'ancient' texts by Joseph Strutt: *The Chronicle of England or a Compleat History, Civil, Military and Ecclesiastical, of the Ancient Britons and Saxons from the Landing of Julius Caesar in Britain, to the Norman Conquest, with a Compleat View of the Manners, Customs, Arts, Habits, &c, of those Peoples*, 2 vols. (London: ptd. by Joseph Cooper and Thomas Jones for Walter Shropshire, 1777–8; repr. 1779). In the appendix to vol. 2 (pp. 279–83) is a transcription of Genesis 1: 1–8 (*On angynne . . . mergen oðer dæg*) from B, with an interlined modern translation.[8]

---

[8] Strutt includes also, among his 'specimens of Anglo-Saxon language', the Lord's Prayer, an extract from the Old English Gospels (John 5), the Creed, and *Cædmon's Hymn*.

By the end of the eighteenth century, an interest in promoting the study of Old English was well established, and the *OEH* became a frequently mined source of edited extracts for language primers and reading books. The earliest example seems to have been that of Johann Oelrichs in Germany, with his *Angelsächsiche Chrestomathie, oder Sammlung merkwürdiger Stücke aus den Schriften der Angelsachsen . . . mit beigefügter hochdeutschen Uebersetzung und einem Kupfer* (Hamburg and Bremen: Hofmann, 1798). Oelrichs included (on pp. 19–21) the following extracts: Genesis 9:1–17, 22–4, 45:1–16, 24–6; Exodus 20:1–17, 23–6; Deuteronomy 1:6–21, 28–30; Leviticus 19:3–37, 31–3; Numbers 16:1–35, 33–40; Deuteronomy 32:1–43, 40–2; and Judges 7:2–25.

In England, Benjamin Thorpe published his *Analecta Anglo-Saxonica: A Selection in Prose and Verse from Anglo-Saxon Authors of Various Ages, with a Glossary, Designed Chiefly as a First Book for Students* (London: John and Arthur Arch, 1834). Thorpe's second group of OE texts is headed 'from the Heptateuch' and includes (on pp. 25–31) Ælfric's *Prefatio* to Genesis (see below) and Genesis 1:1–31. In his own preface (p. iv), Thorpe notes that the texts are taken from Thwaites's edition of the Heptateuch, 'corrected, in one or two instances, from De Lisle's transcript [of B] in the Bodleian Library'. However, both texts are absent from the second edition of the *Analecta*, published 'with corrections and improvements', with the same title, in 1846 (London: Smith, Elder and Co.).

E. J. Vernon followed with his *A Guide to the Anglo-Saxon Tongue: A Grammar after Erasmus Rask, Extracts in Prose and Verse . . .* (London: John Russell Smith, 1846), which (on pp. 109–16) includes Genesis 45:1–28 and Exodus 23:1–29, 31–3, 'taken with some alterations from Thwaites's Heptateuchus'. Rask's work had not included the biblical pieces but did have extracts from Ælfric's *Libellus* (see below).

In Germany, in about 1855, Theodor Müller included extracts from Genesis in an *Angelsächsisches Lesebuch*, which C. L. White reports as being 'not all printed . . . but well known'.[9] Julius Zupitza soon followed, with his *Altenglisches Übungsbuch zum Gebrauche bei*

---

[9] C. L. White, *Ælfric: A New Study of his Life and Writings with a Supplementary Classified Bibliography Prepared by M. R. Godden* (Hamden, Conn., 1974), 205. The report (in item 56 of White's bibliography) is in fact a quotation of the words of Edward Dietrich; Gen. 42–5 is said to have been printed. The present editor has been unable to trace the *Lesebuch*.

Universitäts-Vorlesungen, mit einem Wörterbuche (Vienna: Wilhelm Braumüller, 1874). This included 'Jacob und Esau', i.e. Genesis 27:1–45 (text IX), and 'Samson', i.e. Judges 13:2–16:27, in the *OEH*'s abbreviated version (text X). Both texts were based on Grein (see above) and were ascribed to Ælfric. Zupitza's work was reissued by the same publisher in 1882 as *Alt- und Mittelenglisches Übungsbuch zum Gebrauche bei Universitäts-Vorlesungen, mit einem Wörterbuche*, with 'Jacob und Esau' at pp. 45–7 and 'Samson' at pp. 47–9. An American version of Zupitza's work was then prepared by George Edwin MacClean: *An Old and Middle English Reader on the Basis of Professor Julius Zupitza's Alt- und Mittelenglisches Übungsbuch with Introduction, Notes and Glossary* (Boston: Ginn, 1886; 2nd edn. New York and London: Macmillan, 1893). The two Old Testament pieces appeared as texts XIII and XIV.

Meanwhile, Henry Sweet had published in England the first edition of his *An Anglo-Saxon Primer, with Grammar, Notes, and Glossary* (Oxford: Clarendon Press, 1882). This contained, as text III, five 'Old Testament Pieces', the first two of which were extracts from the *OEH* in L's version, namely the stories of the tower of Babel in Genesis 11:1–7[10] and of Abraham's offering of Isaac in Genesis 22:1–19; the other three pieces were taken from various Ælfrician homilies. Sweet's text IV was the 'Samson' episode from Judges which Zupitza had used. The extracts were included in each edition of this popular primer up to the eighth (1905), but for the ninth, issued in 1953, the reviser, Norman Davis, omitted them to make room for other material, including Ælfric's *Prefatio* to Genesis (see below).

Further reading books in Old English appeared in the closing decades of the nineteenth century, mostly in Germany and America. Others, including British ones, followed regularly during the twentieth century and continue to do so in the early twenty-first. Most have at least one passage from the *OEH*, usually from Genesis.[11]

---

[10] Sweet begins his text with the last two words of 10:32 (*æfter þam*) prefixing 11:1 (*soþlice ealle menn spræcan*). Lack of punctuation at this point in L makes the conflation plausible.

[11] For such publications up to about 1983, see Luke M. Reinsma's invaluable *Ælfric: An Annotated Bibliography* (New York and London, 1987).

4. ÆLFRIC'S *PREFATIO* TO GENESIS

Ælfric's *Prefatio* to his translation of Genesis is included in all the editions of the complete *OEH* listed above—namely, those of Thwaites (1698), Grein (1872 and 1921), and Crawford (1922 and 1969); but it has often been printed separately, too, and was indeed the first part of the *OEH* to be published. This was in a collection of the works of James Ussher, Archbishop of Armagh and Primate of All Ireland (1625–56), published in 1690 by Henry Wharton, chaplain to Archbishop Sancroft and an avid historian of the archbishops and bishops of the Anglican Church:

Iacobi Usserii, Armachani Archiepiscopi, Historia dogmatica controversiae inter orthodoxos et pontificios de scripturis et sacris vernaculis. Nunc primum edita. Accesserunt ejusdem dissertationes II. de pseudo-Dionysii scriptis, et de epistola ad Laodicenos; antehac ineditae. Descripsit, digessit, et notis atque auctario locupletavit Henricus Wharton, A.M. Reverendissimo in Christo Patri ac Domino, Archiepiscopo Cantuariensi, a sacris domesticis.

The volume is in two sections, the first of ten chapters and the second (a 'supplement') of eight, but with continuous pagination. The second part has its own title page: *Auctarium Historiæ dogmaticæ Jacobi Usserii Armachani de Scripturis et Sacris Vernaculis Auctore Henrico Wharton*, and Ælfric's *Prefatio* is in this part, on pp. 380–6, in a section headed '*1000. Elfricus Abbas, & Anglosaxonum Ecclesia*'. Wharton prints the Old English text and, in parallel columns, a Latin translation of this, which he attributes to George Hickes. The Old English is taken from L and is transcribed with fair accuracy, except for regular changes of þ to ð, and some unhappy word division (such as *ond ræde* for *ondræde*). The transcription was made after L had been annotated (mainly by William L'Isle: see p. xliii), as is clear from its use of *be Paulo* in place of the original (and correct) *be Petre* (line 31 in the present edition). There is a handful of footnotes by Wharton, several of which are textual. In introducing the *Prefatio* (p. 379), Wharton notes that Ælfric wrote for Sigeweard a tract on the Old and New Testaments published by L'Isle in 1638, and cites from it Ælfric's statement of the necessity of Scripture for all Christians, and he gives the list of biblical books which Ælfric says he has put into the vernacular. Genesis, writes Wharton, is preceded by a preface which

answers objections to the vernacularization of Scripture, which he will give, as it has not previously been published.

The first leaf of B, carrying the first half of Ælfric's *Prefatio*, is now missing, but much of the text was transcribed into his diary by an early Old English enthusiast, Robert Talbot (see pp. xlvi–xlvii), in about 1620, and this has been edited by Timothy Graham in his 'Early Modern Users of Claudius B. iv: Robert Talbot and William L'Isle', in Rebecca Barnhouse and Benjamin C. Withers (eds.), *The Old English Hexateuch: Aspects and Approaches* (Kalamazoo, Mich., 2000), 271–316 at 315–16, with a facsimile of f. 10^r on p. 277.

During the nineteenth century, the *Prefatio* became established as a staple text in grammars and readers aimed at students of the language. The first such use was by Benjamin Thorpe, in his *Analecta Anglo-Saxonica* of 1834, noted above, with the *Prefatio* at pp. 25–8. It was omitted, however, from the second edition of 1846. Meanwhile, it had appeared, under the title 'Älfric's Vorrede zur Genesis', in an Old English reader published in Germany by Heinrich Leo, his *Angelsächsische Sprachproben zum Gebrauch seiner Zuhörer* (Halle: an der Saale, 1835), 11–15.[12] It was reprinted in the enlarged *Altsächsische und angelsächsische Sprachproben, herausgegeben und mit einem erklärenden Verzeichniss der angelsächsischen Wörter* (Halle: Eduard Anton, 1838), 15–18. Leo based his edition on Thorpe's and noted that Thorpe had used that of Thwaites; Leo used the latter's orthography.

The use of the *Prefatio* in readers and primers continued through the twentieth century and into the twenty-first. The following list includes only works in which the complete text is edited:[13]

1. *Altenglisches Lesebuch (Prosa)*, ed. Josef Raith (Munich: Hueber, 1940); 2nd edn. 1958; 3rd edn., as part of his *Altenglisches Wörterbuch zum altenglischen Lesebuch (Prosa und Poesie)* (1967), 45–8. Uses L.
2. *Alt- und Mittelenglische Anthologie*, ed. Rolf Kaiser (Berlin, 1954); 3rd edn. rev. as *Medieval English: An Old English and Middle English Anthology* (1958; 5th edn. 1961), 134–5. Uses L and B from Crawford's edition.

[12] This information comes from White, *Ælfric*, item 31, p. 202; the present editor has been unable to trace and examine a copy of this earlier of Leo's works, which perhaps circulated privately.

[13] For details of readers and anthologies printing extracts, see Reinsma, *Annotated Bibliography*.

3. *Sweet's Anglo-Saxon Primer*, rev. Norman Davies, 9th edn. [1st edn. 1882] (Oxford: Clarendon Press, 1953), 79–80. Uses L.
4. *Bright's Old English Grammar and Reader*, ed. Frederic G. Cassidy and Richard N. Ringler, 3rd edn. [1st edn. 1891] (New York: Holt, Rinehart and Winston, 1971), 250–4. Uses L and B, with reference also to Talbot's transcription (B^t).
5. Bruce Mitchell and Fred C. Robinson, *A Guide to Old English*, 6th edn. (Oxford: Blackwell, 2001), 190–5. Uses L and B.
6. *The Cambridge Old English Reader*, ed. Richard Marsden (Cambridge: Cambridge University Press, 2004; repr. with corr. 2007), 122–9. Uses L, with reference to B^t.

All Ælfric's prefaces, including that to Genesis, have been edited in a single volume, with introduction, notes and glossary, by Jonathan Wilcox: *Ælfric's Prefaces*, Durham Medieval Texts, 9 (Durham, 1994). The Genesis preface is at pp. 116–19, with notes on pp. 178–80. Wilcox uses L.

5. ÆLFRIC'S *LIBELLUS*

Ælfric's *Libellus de ueteri testamento et nouo* has been printed infrequently. It was, nevertheless, the earliest of the texts edited in the present volume to appear, in William L'Isle's *A Saxon Treatise concerning the Old and New Testament* (London, 1623), 1–43. L'Isle printed the OE text on the left page and a contemporary English translation opposite;[14] the translation is serviceable but contains inaccuracies. The work's title page reads as follows:

A Saxon Treatise concerning the Old and New Testament written about the time of King Edgar (700 yeares agoe) by Aelfricus Abbas, thought to be the same that was afterward Archbishop of Canterburie. Whereby appeares what was the Canon of Holy Scripture here then receiued, and that the Churche of England had it so long agoe in the Mother-tongue. Now first published in print with English of our times, by William L'isle of Wilburgham, Esquier for the Kings Bodie: The Originall remaining still to be seene in Sr Robert Cottons Librarie, at the end of his lesser Copie of the Saxon Pentateuch. And hereunto is added out of the Homilies and Epistles of the fore-said Ælfricus, a second Edition of A Testimonie of Antiquitie, &c. touching the Sacrament of the Bodie and Bloud of the Lord, here publikely preached and receiued in the Saxons time, &c.

---

[14] Left and right pages carry the same number, but the printed numbers in fact only begin on the right-hand p. 12; the earlier ones are pencilled in on the right-hand pages only.

Extera quid quærat sua qui uernacula nescit?

London. Printed by John Haviland for Henrie Seile, dwelling in Pauls Church-yard at the Signe of the Tygers head. 1623.

The 'lesser Copie of the Saxon Pentateuch' referred to by L'Isle is L, which was once owned by Sir Robert Cotton (see p. xxxviii). The contents of the *Treatise* are as follows:

1. 'The Saxon Characters or Letters'; some errata; a quotation from Jeremiah 6.
2. Thirty-nine verse stanzas entitled 'To the prince his hignes, welcome-home and dedication'.
3. A list of contents, followed by an address 'To the Readers'.
4. The *Libellus*, with the OE version on the left page and a translation on the facing page.
5. Title page for 'A Testimony of Antiquitie'.
6. Preface, and a declaration of endorsement by named archbishops and bishops.
7. Title page for 'Sermon of the Pascall Lambe', followed by the sermon itself.
8. Some more extracts from the homiletic works of Ælfric.
9. Title page for 'The Lords Prayer, the Creed, and the Commandments in the Saxon and English Tongue', followed by these texts.

The work was reissued in 1638 by L'Isle, using the same printed sheets, under the title *Divers Ancient Monuments in the Saxon Tongue: Written seven hundred years agoe* . . . The items were, however, reordered thus: 5, 7, 1, 2, 3, 4, 8, 9, and so the *Libellus* now appeared later in the volume.

The text of the *Libellus*, as transmitted in Bo (i.e. the Old Testament section only), was printed by Bruno Assmann as item VII in a volume of Old English homilies, sermons, and saints' lives, half of them by Ælfric: *Angelsächsische Homilien und Heiligenleben*, Bibliothek der angelsächsischen Prosa, 3 (Kassel: Georg H. Wigand, 1889), 81–91. Assmann collated his text with Grein's edition of L and gave variations in an apparatus. His volume was reprinted in 1964, with an introduction by Peter Clemoes (Darmstadt: Wissenschaftliche Buchgesellschaft).

The *Libellus*, in the version from L, was included as the first item of his edition of the *Heptateuch* by Grein (pp. 1–21; i.e. not in its manuscript place), in 1872 and 1921; see above. Crawford, too,

included the *Libellus* as the first item in his edition (pp. 15-75), in 1922; see above. He printed L'Isle's seventeenth-century English translation at the bottom of the page, although it cannot have escaped his attention that it is defective in places.[15] Crawford considered that there was sufficient variation between the version of the Old Testament section in L and that in Bo to warrant printing both in full and in parallel. The variation is in fact largely limited to orthographical and phonological, rather than textual, features; thus, in the present edition, only L's text is printed in full, with Bo's variations given in the critical apparatus.

Several grammars, readers, and anthologies have included extracts from the *Libellus*. The earliest seems to have been Danish, Rasmus K. Rask's *Angelsaksisk Sproglære tilligemed en kort Læsebodg* (Stockholm: Wiborg, 1817). Rask printed two sections, lines 28-83 on the Old Testament and lines 701-814 on the New. He took his extracts from L'Isle and, rather oddly, prefixed them with the words of the title page of L'Isle's *A Saxon Treatise*. Rask produced a second edition, which was translated by Benjamin Thorpe, as *A Grammar of the Anglo-Saxon Tongue with a Praxis by Erasmus Rask. A New Edition Enlarged and Improved by the Author. Translated from the Danish* (Copenhagen: Møller, 1830; 2nd edn. London: Trübner, 1865; 3rd edn. 1879). On pp. 193-201, Thorpe gave the same *Libellus* extracts as Rask, but he printed them all in half-lines, in two columns (i.e. the half-lines must be read in sequence down each column in turn).[16] The same extracts, printed in the same manner, were included by Louis F. Klipstein in his *Analecta Anglo-Saxonica: Selections in Prose and Verse from the Anglo-Saxon Literature: With an Introductory Ethnological Essay, and Notes, Critical and Explanatory*, 2 vols. (New York: George P. Putnam, 1849; 2nd edn. 1871), 74-88.

In his *The Handbook of Specimens of English Literature, Selected from the Chief British Authors, and Arranged Chronologically* (London: The Religious Tract Society, n.d.; repr. 1866, 1867), Joseph Angus included a very short extract from the beginning of the *Libellus*, based on L'Isle.

The complete Old Testament portion of the *Libellus* was chosen by Henry Sweet for the reader which most British students of Old English were to use for almost a century: *An Anglo-Saxon Reader in*

---

[15] For instance, *on last* is translated as 'at last' (line 643).
[16] Rask had done this only with a group of eight half-lines in the Old Testament extract (p. 195).

INTRODUCTION

Prose and Verse, with Grammatical Introduction, Notes, and Glossary (Oxford: Clarendon Press: 1876). It was his text XII, pp. 56–74, with notes on pp. 196–7. In his headnote, Sweet states that 'De Lisle's' text, used by Grein as the basis of his own edition, is full of omissions and wanton alterations, which I have carefully supplied and corrected'. The *Libellus* remained in the second to the sixth editions of *An Anglo-Saxon Reader* (1879, 1881, 1884, 1885, and 1888), but was omitted from the seventh edition of 1894, which had been 'enlarged and partly rewritten' and was now called *An Anglo-Saxon Reader in Prose and Verse, with Grammar, Metre, Notes and Glossary*. Sweet wanted to introduce texts to illustrate dialectal varieties of Old English, including the Vespasian Hymns. He explains in his preface: 'To make room for this additional material, I have cut out *Ælfric on the Old Testament* on account of its disproportionate length and want of interest.'[17]

There was a similar lack of enthusiasm for the *Libellus* in the twentieth century from the compilers of readers and anthologies. Only two seem to have chosen extracts, very short in each case: W. J. Sedgefield, *An Anglo-Saxon Book of Verse and Prose* (Manchester: Manchester University Press, 1928), 313–14 (lines 4–21 and 924–33);[18] and Whitney F. Bolton, *An Old English Anthology* (London: Arnold, 1963; repr. Evanston, Ill.: Northwestern University Press, 1966), 19–20 (lines 56–83).[19]

II. THE PRESENT EDITION

The present edition of the *OEH* and the *Libellus* is the first to collate all the available manuscript material and to present variations in a single critical apparatus. Each manuscript has been examined anew. The apparatus includes many new readings in Genesis recovered from the fire-damaged O, some of them from a leaf of this manuscript not identified by Crawford, others from leaves not exhaus-

---

[17] Sweet's *Reader* went through a series of further editions. The ninth (1922) was a revision by C. T. Onions, the fifteenth (1967) was another by Dorothy Whitelock; this edition, retitled *Sweet's Anglo-Saxon Reader in Prose and Verse*, is still available in its 1975 corrected impression.

[18] Sedgefield includes part of the *Prefatio* also, and the epilogue to Judges.

[19] The *Libellus* is now the subject of a comprehensive study by Larry J. Swain at the University of Illinois at Chicago.

tively deciphered by him. There are new readings, too, in Exodus, taken from two fragmentary leaves of P, which were not printed by Ker. The base text used in this edition of the Heptateuch translations, including Ælfric's *Prefatio*, and of the *Libellus* is that carried by L. For part of the *Prefatio* and for the Hexateuch, B is used to supply readings when L is defective. For Judges, H is so used, and for the *Libellus*, Bo.

In the biblical books, modern chapter and verse division, which is indispensable for ease of reference within scriptural texts, is indicated in superscript in a way which, it is hoped, will not cause undue disruption to the Old English narrative, which is without any divisions in L, except those few indicated by large initial capital letters (see pp. xli–xlii). The decision to omit a parallel Latin text from the present edition, thus rejecting the precedent set by earlier editors, was not taken lightly, but it was ultimately judged necessary on the grounds of practicality. Unless an artificial, hybrid 'Vulgate' were to be created for the occasion, tailored, by the selection of variant readings from random sources, to bring it into the closest possible correspondence with the Old English version, it would be necessary to present a critical Latin text with its own extensive apparatus. This would have to show the numerous variant readings found in early medieval Vulgate manuscripts, many of which are, or may be, relevant to an understanding of the Old English translator's version. Instead of this, the Latin text is dealt with extensively, with important variations displayed, in the commentary volume.

In the Introduction, reference to the Old English texts of the books of the Hexateuch is made by chapter and verse numbers. In the case of Judges, however, extensive use of homiletic material interwoven with scriptural translation and paraphrase makes this system impractical. Thus, for Judges, as for the *Prefatio* and the *Libellus*, line numbers are provided and are used for reference purposes.

III. THE MANUSCRIPTS

There are nine extant manuscript witnesses to all or part of the *OEH* and/or the *Libellus de ueteri testamento et nouo*; a tenth was extant until at least the seventeenth century but is now known by report only. This, a bifolium, may originally have been part of the same volume from which the fragments in P derive. Further witnesses are a sixteenth-century transcription by Robert Talbot of part of the *Prefatio* to Genesis that is now wanting in B, and the transcription by Humphrey Wanley of the incipit and explicit of O. In the present edition, the well-established manuscript sigla used by Crawford or, in the case of the two manuscripts which he did not see, by Ker, are retained—with one exception. In accordance with the logical procedure of choosing sigla which are recognizable for their relationship to library names or shelf-marks, the siglum for Bodley 343 is here Bo, not X, as Crawford had it. The transcription of B by Talbot, just noted, which was not used by previous editors, is designated B^t, and that of O by Wanley is O^w.

In the descriptions which follow, a 'Ker number' after shelf-marks directs attention to the relevant entry in N. R. Ker's *Catalogue*. The detailed collation data which Ker gives for some of the manuscripts are not repeated here. Assessments of dating, origin, and provenance are Ker's, unless otherwise indicated. Data relating to page size and written text area have been checked and occasionally modified, though in any case the figures can usually only be approximate or average. Tabular summaries of manuscript contents and statistics are given in Tables 1–3 on pp. xxxvi–xxxviii.

L
Oxford, Bodleian Library, Laud Misc. 509
(Ker 344)

Ff. iv + 143; foliated, in black ink, i–iv, 1–142, (143). Ff. i–iv, 142, and 143 are post-medieval binding leaves (with 142 turned back to front and upside down since the foliation was made, so that the number is now at the bottom left of the present verso). A separate sequence of individual page numbers, also in black ink, had already been inserted continuously (i.e. on both the rectos and the versos) on the pages containing the *Libellus*, starting at what is now f. 120^v (which is thus designated '1')

and ending on f. 141ᵛ (designated '42'). When the second, overall, foliation took place, the numbers on the rectos of these pages were crossed out and the new folio numbers were written immediately below them, but the page numbers on the versos were left untouched. However, between the first and second foliations, one leaf of the *Libellus* section became misplaced; thus the present f. 133, as its original page numbering reveals (38–9), belongs between the present f. 139 (with page numbers 36–7) and f. 140 (numbered 40–1). Page size is $c.211 \times 138$ mm, with a written area of $c.155 \times 90$–6 mm, in twenty-nine lines per page on ff. 1–33 and twenty-six lines thereafter. See also Wanley, *Catalogus*, 67–9; Gneuss, *Handlist*, no. 657.

L is a compact volume, copied in the second half of the eleventh century, containing Ælfric's *Prefatio Genesis anglice*, the Heptateuch, Ælfric's letter to Wulfgeat, and his *Libellus de ueteri testamento et nouo*.[20] A further part of this manuscript, containing a translation of Felix's *Vita S. Guthlaci*, is now British Library, Cotton Vespasian D. xxi, ff. 18–40. The last two leaves of L (ff. 140 and 141) were the opening leaves of an eight-leaf quire of which the last six leaves are now ff. 18–23 in Vespasian D. xxi.[21] Although no convincing evidence clarifying the origin of the manuscript has been found, M. R. James tentatively attributed a twelfth-century hand responsible for some of the Latin material in it to Christ Church, Canterbury, and this prompts speculation that the whole volume belonged to that house.[22] This was certainly the provenance of many manuscripts in the old Royal Library, to which L belonged. As recorded at the top of f. 2ʳ (though much of the inscription has been trimmed away), it was once no. 159 in the Royal collection. An entry in the 1542 inventory of King Henry VIII's books which had been in the 'Upper Library' at Westminster reads: 'Bookes written in tholde Saxon tong two, thone of the Pentatiuk and sanctes lyues, thother of

---

[20] The letter to Wulfgeat is the only item from L not edited in the present volume. It was edited by Assmann, as no. 1 in his *Angelsächsische Homilien und Heiligenleben*, 1–12. L has the only complete copy of the letter, but a version of it appears also in Oxford, Bodleian Library, Junius 121 (Ker 338), ff. 124ʳ–130ᵛ. Wulfgeat of Ilmingdon, in Mercia, was a nobleman who had taken much interest in Ælfric's works; Ælfric had promised him more, and the letter (a homily) was the result.

[21] See N. R. Ker, 'Membra Disiecta', *British Museum Quarterly*, 12 (1938), 130–5 at 131–2.

[22] *The Ancient Libraries of Canterbury and Dover* (Cambridge, 1903), 525.

TABLE 1. *Manuscript contents*

Siglum	Shelf-mark	Date[a]	Contents
L	Oxford, Bodleian Library, Laud Misc. 509	s. xi²	Ælfric's *Prefatio*, the Heptateuch (one leaf lost after f. 5ᵛ), Ælfric's letter to Wulfgeat and his *Libellus de ueteri testamento et nouo*.
B	London, British Library, Cotton Claudius B. iv	s. xi¹	Illustrated Hexateuch, with text of Ælfric's *Prefatio* (two leaves wanting) and Genesis–Joshua.
Bᵗ	Cambridge, Corpus Christi College 379, ff. 10ʳ–12ᵛ	s. xvii¹	Talbot's transcription of much of B's first leaf of Ælfric's *Prefatio*.
C	Cambridge, University Library, Ii. 1. 33	s. xii²	Ælfric's *Prefatio* and Gen. 1–24:26 are item 1 (ff. 2ʳ–24ᵛ) in a compilation of devotional material.
Co	Cambridge, Corpus Christi College 201, pp. 1–178	s. xi^med	Gen. 37:2–end is item 56 (part B, pp. 151–60) in a compilation of religious and legal texts; three leaves lost (with 41:2–42:20 and 47:18–50:25).
O	London, British Library, Cotton Otho B. x	s. xi¹	Fire-damaged fragments of Gen. 40:18–47:24 (ff. 57, 33, 31, 32, 34, 35).
Oʷ	Wanley, *Catalogus*, 192 [Lost bifolium]	1705 ?s. xi	Transcription of lost incipit and explicit of O.
N			Readings from Exod. 9:20–10:9 and 13:19–14:23 reported by Nicholson and printed by Thwaites, 1698.
P	New York, Pierpont Morgan Library, G. 63	s. xi²	Parts of Exod. 16–17, 19–20, 23–32 on two leaves and two fragments.
Ln	Lincoln, Cathedral 298, no. 2	s. xi²	Num. 10:28–16:3 on a damaged bifolium.
H	Oxford, Bodleian Library, Hatton 115	s. xi^ex	Ælfric's version of Judges is item 30 (ff. 108ʳ–116ʳ) in collection of homilies, etc.
Bo	Oxford, Bodleian Library, Bodley 343	s. xii²	Ælfric's *Libellus*, OT section only, is item 65 (ff. 129ʳ–132ʳ) in collection of homilies, etc.; several lacunae.

[a] In the case of C and H, which are chronologically extended compilations, the dates indicated are for the specific biblical items.

TABLE 2. *Manuscript location and status of texts edited in this volume*

Text	MS	Status
Prefatio to Genesis	L	Complete.
	B	First half wanting, owing to loss of leaf.
	B^t	Transcription of much of B's missing leaf.
	C	Complete.
Genesis	L	Complete, except 3:20–5:12.
	B	Complete.
	C	1:1–24:26.
	Co	37:2–41:2, 42:19–47:19.
	O	Fragments of 42:18–47:24.
Exodus	L	Complete.
	B	Complete.
	N	Readings from 9:20–10:9 and 13:19–14:23.
	P	Parts of 16:16–17:14, 19:6–20:21, 23:8–29:12, 29:46–32:24.
Leviticus	L	Complete.
	B	Complete.
Numbers	L	Complete.
	B	Complete.
	Ln	10:28–16:3; lacunae, owing to damage.
Deuteronomy	L	Complete.
	B	Complete.
Joshua	L	Complete.
	B	Complete.
Judges	L	Complete.
	H	Complete, with interpolations.
Libellus de ueteri testamento et nouo	L	OT and NT complete.
	Bo	OT only, several lacunae.

TABLE 3. *Page size, lineation, and word count in the manuscripts of the* OEH

MS	Page size	Written area	Lines per page	Words per page
L	211 × 138 mm	155 × 90 mm	26 or 29	240–330
B	328 × 217 mm	267 × 167 mm	38	420
C	222 × 158 mm	75 × 110 mm	21–26	240–80
Co	280 × 162 mm	250 × 122 mm	41	520
O	195 × 140 mm	175 × 115 mm	29	250
N	*unknown*	*unknown*	*unknown*	280
P	281 × 189 mm	210 × 164–70 mm	25	270
Ln	300 × 209 mm	277 × 189–97 mm	37	595

NOTE. The dimensions of pages and written areas are approximate. Page size has sometimes been affected by trimming, notably in the case of the Lincoln fragment. Word counts are rounded figures and, where possible, are averages derived from an exact count of a sample of ten pages. The figures for lines and words in the case of B are for a full page, though on most of the pages the text is in fact interrupted by illustrations. On the large variation in word count for L, see pp. xxxix–xl; on the estimated count for N, see p. lx.

medicine'.[23] The first of these is L, and clearly the *Vita* was still with the rest at this time. The volume subsequently passed into the possession of Sir Robert Cotton, and presumably this is when it was divided. The section which is now Laud Misc. 509 is no. 81 in Cotton's 1621 catalogue, preserved in British Library, Harley 6018; the section which is now Vespasian D. xxi is part of no. 80.[24] Cotton's table of the contents of what is now Laud Misc. 509 is still to be found on the verso of the first leaf of the volume (bound upside down); curiously, Ælfric's letter to Wulfgeat, written continuously between Judges and the *Libellus*, is overlooked:

Catalogus Tractatuū in isto Volumine.

1 Alfrici ad Ædelwardum Aldermanū, Genesos, Exodi, Numerorū, Deutronomij, et Iosuæ versio Saxonica. fol. 1.

2 De Libro Iudicum, Saxonice, eodem Autore. fol. 113.

3 Libellus eiusdem authoris de veteri Testamento et Nouo: fol. 130. 141.

---

[23] See James P. Carley, *The Libraries of King Henry VIII*, Corpus of British Medieval Library Catalogues, 7 (London, 2000), 120.

[24] Both on f. 53ʳ. Extracts copied from the manuscript when it was in the Cottonian collection are in Oxford, Bodleian Library, James 18 (3855), f. 66.

Cotton lent the manuscript to William L'Isle before 23 April 1621, for this is the date on one of the lists of lent volumes written at the end of his catalogue, which includes the entry 'Liber Genesis et pentatuchum Saxonice bound with my armes and claspes in 4to—Mr Lyll of Cambrig'.[25] The next owner was Archbishop Laud, who presumably had it, along with other manuscripts, direct from L'Isle. His ownership is confirmed by a partly damaged inscription at the bottom of f. 1^r: 'Liber Guil: Laud Archiēpi Cant[. . .] & Cancellae: Universitati Oxon. 1638'. But in 1639, he gave the volume to the Bodleian Library, where it at first bore the shelf-mark Laud E. 19. On the recto of the first leaf (whose verso carries the 'upside down' list noted above), L'Isle's list of contents (on five lines) reads 'The Saxon Pentateuch. &ct. / Josuah / Judges / Ælfricus de Mysterijs Testamenti Veteris. Testamenti Novi / &.t'. Again, the letter to Wulfgeat is ignored.

The text of L is mainly in one hand, dated by Ker to the second half of the eleventh century. Notable are an open-bowled *e*, both low and long *s*, the latter (not used at end of word) having a 'broken' shaft made in two strokes, and an ð in which the long curving upstroke is tagged to the left at the top and the cross-stroke does not transect the upstroke. There is a tendency for the ends of the descenders to turn to the left; *y* is always dotted. A second hand wrote ff. 15^r/8–21 and 15^v/1–10, and a third f. 17^r/11–23. The change at 15^r/8 is very marked, the second script being smaller, less condensed, and less consistent; notable in it are a *g* with a closed bowl beneath, and a þ whose cross-stroke does not end (as it does in the main script) with a tag. The third script is different again: there is more compression, a finer pen is used, and there are serifs on the ascenders. When the main scribe writes Latin (most often in the *Libellus*), the most significant difference is the use of a caroline *g*. Abbreviation is confined largely to the Tironian *et* for *and* (almost invariably),[26] the crossed thorn for *þæt*, and *cw̄* for *cwæð*; *m* is sometimes suspended, other letters more rarely. The number of lines per page is twenty-nine on ff. 1–33^v, i.e. the first four quires (which consist of nine, eight, eight, and eight leaves), and on these leaves there is pricking in the outer margins. Thereafter, there are

---

[25] London, British Library, Harley 6018, f. 148^v.
[26] In about 5,450 occurrences of the conjunction in L (excluding the letter to Wulfgeat), it is written unabbreviated only 100 times. The abbreviation is used for the first element of nouns such as *andgit* and parts of the verb *andswarian* about a dozen times in all.

twenty-six lines per page and the leaves are without pricking. There is also a tendency to get in a few more letters per line in the earlier pages (up to 10 per cent more). The total writing area per page, however, remains more or less the same throughout. As a consequence of these differences, the writing looks rather more dense on the earlier pages than the later ones, and, while a page in the first four quires typically carries 320–30 words, in the rest of the manuscript, 240–60 is the norm. Punctuation is mainly by a punctus on the line (but sometimes slightly raised), less frequently by a punctus versus (usually marking a section end), and occasionally by a punctus elevatus.[27]

Decoration is simple, consisting of red, green, or purple initials, usually plain but occasionally embellished; titles are in red, in the script and hand of the main scribe, and sometimes the lines of rubrics are alternately bright red and metallic red (which has dulled to a muddy purple). The coloured initial letters are used thirty-one times, distributed as shown below, with most in Genesis (ten) and Exodus (thirteen). Typically, the enlarged letters fill a vertical space approximately equivalent to that taken up by three lines of script; a few are larger, as indicated in the list below. Often they project into the left margin. Each starts a fresh line, so that space is sometimes left after the text on the previous line ends; in four of such cases (ff. 45^v, 48^v, 49^v, and 72^r), a decorative flourish is added in the space. Red is the most frequently used colour for the initials (nineteen occurrences), followed by green (eleven); one letter is in purple. There are also two in black. The enlarged initials are indicated here in bold type.

1^r	Prefatio	**Æ**LFRIC MUNUC (red, very faded; preceded by title, appar. in red and metallic red)
3^r	Gen. 1:1	**O**n anginne (green)
4^v	Gen. 2:4	**D**as sind (black; 1-line round Ð)
6^r	Gen. 5:32	**N**oe soðlice (green; preceded by rubric in red)
9^r	Gen. 12:1	**G**od cwæð (red; preceded by rubric in red)
17^v	Gen. 23:1	**S**ARRA LEOFODE (red)
24^v	Gen. 37:2	**Ð**a iosep (green; preceded by rubric in red)
28^r	Gen. 41:15	**P**HARAO cw̄ (purple; 4-line p, bottom of page)
30^r	Gen. 42:36	**Ð**a cw̄ iacob (red)

---

[27] None occurs in the *Prefatio*, Genesis, or Leviticus. The highest concentration is in the *Libellus*, where seven out of eleven occurrences are in Latin citations.

33ʳ	Gen. 46:8	*Soðlice þis* (green)
36ʳ	Gen. 49:1	*Soþlice iacob* (red)
37ʳ	Exod. 1:1	Þʏs sʏɴᴅ (green; 5-line letter, bottom of page; preceded by rubric in red)
43ᵛ	Exod. 7:7	*Soþlice moises* (red)
44ʳ	Exod. 7:20	*Soðlice moises* (red)
45ᵛ	Exod. 8:28	*Ða cw̄ pharao* (red)
46ʳ	Exod. 9:1	*Soþlice drihten* (green)
46ᵛ	Exod. 9:13	*Witodlice drihten* (red; 5-line letter)
48ᵛ	Exod. 10:21	*Soðlice drihten* (red)
49ᵛ	Exod. 12:1	*Witodlice drihten* (green; 5-line letter, top of page)
56ᵛ	Exod. 20:1	*God spræc* (black; 2-line letter)
60ʳ	Exod. 29:9	*Siððan þu* (red)
62ʳ	Exod. 32:7	*Drihten spræc* (red)
63ʳ	Exod. 32:30	*Æfter opron* (green, with red decoration within the top part of the *E*)
63ᵛ	Exod. 33:1	*Drihten cw̄* (red)
65ᵛ	Lev. 1:1	Dʀɪʜᴛᴇɴ ᴄʟɪᴘoᴅᴇ (4-line round-backed *D* in red, with red and green decoration; preceded by 5 lines of rubric in alternate metallic red and red)
72ʳ	Num. 1:1	Dʀɪʜᴛᴇɴ sᴘʀᴀ̃ᴄ (green; preceded by 4-line rubric in alternate metallic red and red)
76ʳ	Num. 13:1	*Æfter þam* (red)
82ᵛ	Deut. 1:1	Ðɪs sɪɴᴛ (red; preceded by 3-line rubric in alternate metallic red and red)
95ᵛ	Deut. 31:22	*Moises wrat* (green)
97ᵛ	Deut. 32:49	Dʀɪʜᴛᴇɴ ᴡᴀ̃s (red)
108ʳ	Judg. [*prol.*]	Æꜰᴛᴇʀ Ðᴀᴍ (red; preceded by title in metallic red)
115ᵛ	Letter	*Ic ælfric* (green; preceded by preamble in metallic red)
120ᵛ	Libellus	Æʟꜰʀɪᴄ ᴀʙʙoᴅ (red; preceded by incipit in red, preamble in black)

In Genesis, three of the initials come at those main divisions of the book which are also marked by rubrics in L (at 5:32, 12:1, and 37:2). Many of the other initials, in each book, come at traditional points of Vulgate *capitulum* division. That at Genesis 46:8 is echoed in the

copies of Genesis in Co and O, and two of those in Exodus (at 29:9 and 32:9) are paralleled by enlarged letters in P in the same places.[28] Throughout the manuscript (though their concentration varies), sentences often begin with a more or less 'bold' capital letter (in black); this is especially the case if the first word refers to the deity. In a few places, the copyist himself seems to have been responsible for putting a bold capital over what had first been written as a small letter. Occasionally these capitals are enlarged also, though they are not usually as prominent as the coloured initials (with the notable exception of the *G* on f. 56^v, which is listed above); examples are *W* on *Witodlic*e on both f. 49^v and f. 50^r, and *7* on ff. 82^v and 83^r.

A few corrections were made to L by the main copyist himself, but the text acquired several further layers of correction, emendation, or annotation, in various stages:

1. One to two generations after its copying, an extensive but intermittent interlinear Latin gloss, supplying a Vulgate text, was added to ninety-three of the 144 pages of the OE text of the Heptateuch, and glosses were added also to three pages of the *Libellus*.[29] About one-third of the pages involved in the Heptateuch are heavily glossed, often continuously for long stretches; on the others, as few as only two or three glosses may appear per page. The gloss was probably the work of one person, writing a hand dated by Ker to the later eleventh or earlier twelfth century. The purpose of the gloss is not entirely clear, but it may in some sense be a reassertion of the authority of the Vulgate text. In general, error or omission in the OE version, which the Latin tends to highlight, has been ignored (and perhaps not noticed), but in about a dozen cases, it seems to be the glossator who has in fact made changes to the Old English text (in a larger script than that used for the Latin gloss and quite like the original one), introducing corrections. (These are noted in this edition's critical apparatus, though certainty is not always possible.) The glossator also added a single OE gloss, *bæcelinge*, to a Latin word, *clibano*,

---

[28] See R. Marsden, 'Translation by Committee?: The "Anonymous" Old English Heptateuch', in Barnhouse and Withers (eds.), *The Old English Hexateuch*, 41–89 at 47–8, where, however, several of the initials were inadvertently omitted from the discussion. See also vol. 2.

[29] See R. Marsden, 'Latin in the Ascendant: The Interlinear Gloss of Laud Misc. 509', in Katherine O'Brien O'Keeffe and Andy Orchard (eds.), *Latin Learning and English Lore: Studies in Anglo-Saxon Literature for Michael Lapidge*, 2 vols. (Toronto, 2005), i. 132–52.

which itself was part of the Latin gloss of OE *ofenbacene* (Lev. 2:4, f. 66ᵛ).

2. A few corrections were made, in a small neat hand, in black ink, which are very hard to date; they may be of the twelfth century.
3. Reading marks occur sporadically, though they are rare in the first thirty folios. Long vowels in names such as *ááron*, *pharaó* and *rubén* attract them regularly; so do the words *eá*, *sǽ*, *ǽ*, and *án*, and sometimes other monsyllables, such as *mín*, *lá*, and *dǽg*. On some pages, the accenting becomes more intense, as on f. 99ᵛ, where *út*, *lóca*, and *fár* are among the accented words. None of the accents appears to have been added by the copyist, and they are not reproduced in this edition.
4. Various other interventions were made in or around the text in the thirteenth or fourteenth centuries, including the addition of chapter numbers to the biblical books (i.e. the numbers of the 'modern' system of division, widely introduced in the thirteenth century), running titles for the books, and various marginalia in Latin, in pencil or ink. Curiously, these additions do not start until f. 61ᵛ, where *Exodus* is written at the top of the page, *oblit*[*us*] in the margin, to mark a point at which the Old English translation has omitted some of the Vulgate narrative, and *xxxii* also in the margin, to show the start of Exodus 32. Thereafter, these three strands of information are provided more or less continuously up to and including Judges.
5. Finally, while the manuscript was in his possession in the 1620s, William L'Isle added a large number of corrections and annotations throughout, during a process of comparing the text with that in B, which he also annotated.[30]

Collation of text of L:

f. 1ʳ/1	[Prefatio *begins*] ÆLFRIC MUNUC GRET
f. 3ʳ/18	[Prefatio *ends*] nele his woh | gerihtan.
f. 3ʳ/18	[*rubric*] INCIPIT LIBER. GENESIS ANGLICE
f. 3ʳ/19	[Gen. 1:1] ON ANGINNE GESCEOP GOD
f. 37ʳ/23	[Gen. *ends*] on his stowe of egipta lande.
f. 37ʳ/24–5	[*rubric*] Ellesmoth on hebreisc . . . ut færeld on englisc.

---

[30] On L'Isle's activities with L and B, including his close comparison of the OE text with the Vulgate, see Graham, 'Early Modern Users', 287–312.

f. 37ʳ/26	[Exod. 1:1] ÞYS SYND ISRAELA BEARNA NAMAN ÐE MID IACOBE
f. 65ᵛ/12	[Exod. ends] nan fŷr on þā | dæge.
f. 65ᵛ/12–16	[*rubric*] Her onginneð seo þridde boc . . . sind þar awritene.
f. 65ᵛ/17	[Lev. 1:1] DRIHTEN CLIPODE TO MOISE on þære halgan
f. 72ʳ/2	[Lev. ends] 7 israhela folce on sinai dune.
f. 72ʳ/3–6	[*rubric*] Her onginð seo boc þe ẏs ge nemned on ebreiscū. uagedaber . . . on þære ge tealde.
f. 72ʳ/7	[Num. 1:1] DRIHTEN SPREC WITODLICE TO MOISE
f. 82ᵛ/2	[Num. ends] swa swa hī dihte iosue.
f. 82ᵛ/3–5	[*rubric*] Her onginð seo boc þe is genemned on ebreiscū . . . seo æftre æ.
f. 82ᵛ/6	[Deut. 1:1] ÐIS SINT ÐA WORD ÐE MOISES SPRæc
f. 98ᵛ/11	[Deut. ends] þe moises worhte. ætforan israela folce.
f. 98ᵛ/12	[*new line but no division signalled*; Josh. 1:1] Hit wæs æfter moyses forðsiþe
f. 107ʳ/27	[Josh. ends] wæs ḡseald on | ephraim dune. [*bottom of page*]
f. 107ᵛ	[*blank page*]
f. 108ʳ/1	[*heading*] DE LIBRO IUDICUM ANGLICE
f. 108ʳ/2	[Judg. *starts*] ÆFTER ÐAM ÐE MOYSES SE MÆRA HERETOGA
f. 115ᵛ/10	[Judg. ends] se ðe æfre rixað on ecnisse. AMEN.
f. 115ᵛ/10–11	[*rubric*] Nis þis gewrit be anum | men awriten ac is be eallum. [*gap*]
f. 115ᵛ/12	[Letter to Wulfgeat *starts*] Ic ælfric abbod on ðisū englisc̄u ge write freondlice
f. 120ᵛ/1	[Letter ends] 7 rixað a to worulde. AMEN.
f. 120ᵛ/2	[*rubric*] Incipit libellus de u`e´teri testamento et nouo
f. 120ᵛ/3–4	[*heading*] Ðis gewrit wæs to anū men gediht ac hit mæg swa ðeah manegum fremian. [*gap*]
f. 120ᵛ/5	[Libellus OT *starts*] ÆLFRIC ABBOD GRET FREONDLICE SIGWERD
f. 131ᵛ/21	[Libellus OT *ends*] eow sẏlfū to ræde.

f. 131ᵛ/21–2   [rubrics] EXPLICIT DE VETERI TESTA |
              MENTO. INCIPIT DE NOVO TESTAMENTO.
f. 131ᵛ/23   [Libellus NT starts] IC SECGE ÐE NV SIWERD
              ÐÆT ic her gesett hæbbe
f. 141ᵛ/21   [Libellus NT ends] beo þam writere to plihte 7 me
              to tale. [blank space]

B

London, British Library, Cotton Claudius B. iv (Ker 142)

Ff. iv + 156 + iv; foliated (i–iv), 1–156, (157–60). The eight flyleaves are modern paper. Ff. 74, 147, and 156 are twelfth-century parchment insertions, bearing extended commentary (see below). A first foliation missed out 32, so that the original numbers after 31 are all one too high; each incorrect figure was subsequently crossed out and the appropriate lesser one added underneath. In addition, the present ff. 152 and 153 had become misordered and thus bore the numbers, respectively, 154 (corrected to 153) and 153 (corrected to 152). At the top of the former leaf is written 'read this leaf after the next' in a hand of the sixteenth century, and thus the manuscript must have been bound already at this time. The two leaves were reordered at or before a nineteenth-century binding (made by Charles Tuckett, senior, between 1825 and 1865), after which their numeration was altered yet again, this time to the correct 152 and 153. Crawford's note about the leaves implies wrongly that the transposition persists.[31] In 2006, the manuscript was disbound at the British Library, to facilitate digital filming, and then rebound in-house in dark green calfskin.[32] Page size is c.328 × 217 mm, with a written area of c.267 × 167 mm, and thirty-eight lines per page. See also Wanley, *Catalogus*, 253–4; Gneuss, *Handlist*, no. 315; Dodwell and Clemoes, *Illustrated Hexateuch*; Elżbieta Temple, *Anglo-Saxon Manuscripts 900–1066, A Survey of Manuscripts Illuminated in the British Isles*, 2 (London, 1976), no. 86.

---

[31] *Heptateuch*, 394.
[32] The results are available on a CD-ROM of the complete manuscript issued by the British Library and the University of Toronto Press to accompany Withers, *The Illustrated Old English Heptateuch* (see p. xxiii).

B is a carefully planned and magnificently illustrated Hexateuch. Genesis is preceded by Ælfric's *Prefatio*, but this is incomplete owing to the loss of the first leaf (before the present f. 1). Ker placed the production of B in the first half of the eleventh century; Wormald was more specific, suggesting the second quarter of the century, on art-historical grounds, a view endorsed by Dodwell and Clemoes.[33] In a catalogue of the library of St Augustine's, Canterbury, made between 1491 and 1497, is the entry *Genesis anglic' 2° fo. and sylð us d. 1. G. 1.*[34] This clearly refers to our manuscript, for *and sylð us* are indeed the words which begin what was f. 2 (but is now f. 1, owing to the loss of the first leaf). The Canterbury habit when cataloguing books was to use the opening words on the recto of the second folio. The reference simply to *Genesis anglice* is not of significance; as Dodwell and Clemoes point out, this description was no doubt picked up from the the rubric *Incipit prefatio genesis anglice* which headed the lost f. 1, according to the transcription of Robert Talbot (see below).[35] The Kentish dialect of the English notes which were added to the manuscript in the mid-twelfth century (see below) indicates that it was at Canterbury, or at least in the south-east of England, by then. Dodwell and Clemoes argue further that the style of the illustrations has affiliations with that of work in other manuscripts with known Canterbury connections, and they are confident that, unless contrary evidence surfaces, St Augustine's may be assumed to be the place of origin.[36]

After the dissolution of St Augustine's in 1538, Robert Talbot (?1505–58), prebendary of Norwich, sometime chaplain to Thomas Cranmer and an enthusiastic student of Old English, appears to have been the first private owner of B.[37] As part of his study of the

---

[33] Francis Wormald, *English Drawings of the Tenth and Eleventh Centuries* (London, 1952), 67; Dodwell and Clemoes, *Illustrated Hexateuch*, 16.

[34] James, *Ancient Libraries*, 201, no. 95. This entry, along with several others, was added after the main entries.

[35] *Illustrated Hexateuch*, 15.

[36] Ibid. 16. Mildred Budny notes that one of the artists responsible for the illustrations is the same who added a Mark evangelist portrait to f. 30^v of London, British Library, Royal 1 E. vi, a Bible made at St Augustine's, of which only the gospels and part of Acts survive (mostly in Royal 1 E. vi, but with fragments in Canterbury, Cathedral Library and Archives, Add. 16, and Oxford, Bodleian Library, Lat. Bibl. b. 2 (P)). See her 'The Biblia Gregoriana', in Richard Gameson (ed.), *St Augustine and the Conversion of England* (Thrupp, Glos., 1999), 237–84 at 269.

[37] On Talbot's use of B, see Graham, 'Early Modern Users', 271–82; Ker, *Catalogue*, l. On the post-medieval history of B, see also Dodwell and Clemoes, *Illustrated Hexateuch*, 13–15.

manuscript, Talbot transcribed much of Ælfric's *Prefatio* to Genesis; the transcription is designated B^t in the present edition. B's immediate fate after Talbot's death is unknown, but it was acquired at some time between 1603 and 1621 by Sir Robert Cotton. The inscription *Ro: Cotton Bruceus* appears in the upper right margin of the present f. 1^r, showing that the original first leaf, carrying the earlier part of Ælfric's preface, had already been lost.[38] Cotton lent both B and L to William L'Isle in about 1621, after which L'Isle collated the two texts and made extensive emendations and annotations throughout both manuscripts.

Two scribes were responsible for the original text of B, both of them using what Ker called 'heavy uncalligraphic, round hands' of the first half of the eleventh century. Scribe 1 copied ff. 1^r–20^v, 56^v–73^v, 75^r–146^v, and 148^v–155^v, and scribe 2 ff. 21^r–56^v. Scribe 1 wrote more spaciously in his first stint than subsequently, and used almost no abbreviations, other than 7; he often put hyphens at the ends, and sometimes the beginnings, of lines. Scribe 2 wrote a more compressed hand and used more abbreviations and suspensions, including ꝥ and cw̄; occasionally he used a flat-topped *a* and high *e*-ligature; and he extended the upstroke on ð higher than scribe 1 did and made the fine cross-stroke transect it, rather than merely touch it. In both hands, *y* is regularly dotted. Punctuation is by punctus, often placed medially, and punctus versus, usually at more pronounced sense breaks; sentences following the latter usually start with a capital letter. A few stress marks may be contemporary with the copying, but most were added in the twelfth century (see below). Titles are in red, in either rustic capitals or the script of the text.

The text is broken up by a total of 394 coloured illustrations, many of them subdivded into individual scenes. Often there are two, and sometimes three, per page, with only a few lines of text separating them; some take up the whole of a page. Sections of text following an illustration usually begin with a two-line capital in green or red, which sits partly in the margin. The largest continuous stretch of unillustrated text is the sixteen pages which give Deut. 1–31:8 (ff. 128^v–136^r). Most of the illustrations are literal interpretations of events told in the OE text immediately preceding them. They were made by several different artists, and some of those towards the end of the codex were left unfinished. On two pages,

---

[38] Graham, 'Early Modern Users', 284.

149^v and 150^r, space was left for drawings not begun, but it is clear that, in some cases at least, the drawings were made before the text was written. A detailed catalogue of the contents of the illustrations, page by page, with interpretation, is given by Dodwell and Clemoes.[39] In his analysis of the step-by-step production of B, Clemoes argues that the apparent process of the preparation of pages by the artist, including the pricking out at one time of two pages of a bifolium, when they would not eventually be adjacent, suggests that he was following an existing model, and that therefore B was not the first manuscript in which the text had been combined with illustrations.[40] It does nevertheless seem that the illustrations were first prepared in close relation to the specific text transmitted in B, for Dodwell points to a number of illustrations which interpret passages according to B's unique OE versions of the relevant biblical passages, which had been corrupted by omission. Thus, in an account of 'four kings against five', i.e. a total of nine kings, in Genesis 14, the text of B omits the phrase 'wið fif ciningas', and the illustration which follows the passage duly shows us only four kings.[41]

In three places, before Gen. 5:31 (f. 12^v), Gen. 12:1 (f. 21^r) and Gen. 37:2 (f. 53^r), much larger initial capitals are used (on *Noe*, *God*, and *Ða*, respectively). These represent main divisions of the Genesis text. They are preceded by rubrics in the case of the second and third divisions, as in L; at the first, however, a two-line space has been left but the rubric itself was never written in, though it is present in L. The third rubric is in Co, too, and was also in O (see below). B has no rubric preceding Gen. 1:1, as both L and C do, but a blank half-line at the end of the *Prefatio* (f. 1^v) was probably intended for one.

A notable feature of B is the extensive additions made apparently by two annotators. The first, working in the mid-twelfth century and using a brown ink, added notes in Latin and in an English which shows Kentish dialectal forms;[42] he made a few additions to the main text also, and inserted numerous accents (some in odd places),

---

[39] *Illustrated Hexateuch*, 17–42. [40] Ibid. 53–8, esp. 57–8.
[41] Ibid. 71. For other apparent cases of the influence of the specific text of B on the illustrators, see Dodwell's notes to the illustrations on ff. 9^v, 20^r, 21^v, 22^v, 67^r, 126^v, 127^v, 128^r, and 152^r.
[42] Printed by Crawford, *Heptateuch*, 419–22, and also, with an analysis of phonology and grammar, in his 'The Late Old English Notes of MS. (British Museum) Cotton Claudius B. iv', *Anglia*, 47 (1923), 124–35.

mostly acute accents but also ones shaped like a *c* on the *o* of *God* and on some other short vowels. The second annotator, working a little later in the twelfth century and using a much blacker ink, added numerous exegetical and other notes in Latin in a protogothic script in the margins and in blank spaces, often within illustrations; they extend also onto two extra supplied leaves, ff. 74 and 147, and the last leaf of the codex, f. 156 (now badly damaged, with much of the upper right part torn away). The sources of the added material, as identified by name in the text, are works by Josephus, (pseudo-)Methodius, Hrabanus, Jerome, and a certain 'Normannus' ('Norman' in one of the English notes), along with the Latin text of the pseudepigraphal story of Joseph and his wife Asenath.[43] However, the material has recently been under scrutiny and these sources have been questioned.[44] The twelfth-century contributions include an 'OE' text of 140 words summarizing Genesis 34 (along with 33:18–2 and 35:8), which recounts the rape of Dina, an episode left untranslated in the original version.[45]

A further layer of additions or emendations was added to B by William L'Isle in the early seventeenth century, who compared the text of B with that of L. Ker identified the addition of 'ca. XXXVII' at the top of f. 53 as being in the hand of Robert Talbot.

On f. 155^v, the text of Joshua ends at the end of 24:32, with only the last word, *lande*, on an otherwise blank sixth line, the rest of the page being taken up with an illustration. Clemoes has speculated that the last verse of Joshua, consisting of twenty-six words in L, may have been on a subsequent leaf, since lost.[46] The last quire has suffered considerable damage, and it is quite possible that an extra leaf was originally inserted before the present f. 156 (which is filled with some of the twelfth-century annotations).

Collation of text of B:

f. 1^r/1   [*was* f. 2; Prefatio *starts line* 62] 7 sylõ us sinna forgyfnysse

---

[43] See Dodwell and Clemoes, *Illustrated Hexateuch*, 15, and Crawford, 'The Late Old English Notes', 124–5.

[44] A. N. Doane and William P. Stoneman will challenge them in an edition of all of B's notes and glosses, in English and Latin, which is in preparation (personal communication from Doane).

[45] Crawford (*Heptateuch*, 422 n. 1) noted that the style of the summary suggests Ælfric as its author, but Doane and Stoneman (see previous note) have concluded that it is a 12th-c. composition, and it is therefore not evidence that the annotators had available another, longer version of the OE text, now lost, from which to copy.

[46] *Illustrated Hexateuch*, 15 n. 8.

INTRODUCTION

f. 1ᵛ/33   [Prefatio *ends*] nele his gewrit gerihtan.
f. 1ᵛ/34   [Gen. 1:1] On angynne gesceop god
f. 72ᵛ/13 [Genesis *ends*] of egypta lande.
f. 72ᵛ/13 [Exod. 1:1] Ðis synd israhela bearna naman [*enlarged cap.* Ð]
f. 105ᵛ/1 [*after illus.* Lev. 1:1] Drihten clypode to moyse
f. 110ᵛ/21 [Leviticus *ends*] hela folce on sinai dune. [*illus. follows*]
f. 111ʳ/1 HER ONGYNÐ SEO BOC ÐE IS GENEMNED ON EBREISC. UALEDABER
f. 111ʳ/5 [Num. 1:1] [ ]rihten spræc witodlice to moyse[47]
f. 128ʳ/9 [Numbers *ends*] swa swa him dihte iosue. [*two illus. follow*]
f. 128ᵛ/1 HER ONGYNÐ SEO BOC ÐE IS GENEMNED ON EBREISC HELLE ADABARIM
f. 128ᵛ/4 [Deut. 1:1] Ðis synd ða word ðe moyses spræc
f. 139ʳ/38 [Deuteronomy *ends*] worhte ætforan israhela folce. [*two pages of illus. follow*]
f. 140ᵛ/1 [Josh. 1:1] Hit wæs geworden æfter moyses forðsiðe
f. 155ᵛ/7 [Joshua *ends*] to iosepes bearna lande. [*illus. follows*]

Bᵗ

Cambridge, Corpus Christi College 379,
ff. 10ʳ–12ᵛ

Corpus 379 is a notebook belonging to Robert Talbot (see B, above), into which, in the mid-sixteenth century, he transcribed a large part of Ælfric's *Prefatio* to Genesis. He also compiled there a list of thirty-two words or phrases in Old English, the first twenty-four taken from Genesis 37 and 38.[48] The transcription is now our only evidence for the text on B's original first leaf, containing the first half of the *Prefatio*, which was subsequently lost. The transcription is of about two-thirds of this, and is writtten in a very large and clear sixteenth-century hand at the rate of fifteen to seventeen lines per page (*c*.208 × 147 mm). It opens with 'Incipit prefatio Genesis anglice' and ends '7 well bysnian to godum weorcum, &c', thus

---

[47] The space for a three-line capital *D* in *Drihten* has been left but not filled.
[48] The text of the *Prefatio* (ff. 10ʳ–12ᵛ of Talbot's diary) is edited by Graham, 'Early Modern Users', 314–16, with a facsimile of f. 10ʳ on p. 277. Graham prints Talbot's Latin and Old English list (f. 13ʳ⁻ᵛ of the diary) on p. 280, with facsimile of f. 13ʳ on p. 278. In all but one case, Talbot gives the Latin equivalent of the words or phrases, and in five cases a contemporary English equivalent also.

breaking off at the start of Ælfric's account of the spiritual and symbolic interpretation of the events of Scripture. Talbot then records nineteen words of a sentence from the conclusion to the *Prefatio*, as extant on B's f. 1^v ('ic cweðe nu . . . on englisc awendan &c'), introducing it with 'Item in fine eiusdem epistolę dedicatoriæ sic ait'. In his edition of Talbot's transcription, Graham describes its faults as 'characteristic of sixteenth-century work on Old English'.[49] These include uncertainty about final *e*, which is either omitted, where it must have been in the original, or added, where it would not have occurred. Graham suggests that there is faulty word separation, too, indicating, in his view, that Talbot did not fully understand the text. It is worth noting, however, that the section of the *Prefatio* which is extant in B does itself show some fairly erratic, though not unusual, word presentation (e.g., *onðam*, *ðafor gyfnysse*, *forus*, which may be compared with Talbot's *forðanðe*, *fulsoð*, etc.). In the critical apparatus of the present edition of the *Prefatio*, readings from B in the missing earlier part are given from Talbot's transcription, labelled B^t. As in Graham's edition, instances of the omission of final *e* (e.g. *ðær* for *ðære*) and incorrect addition of *e* (e.g. *twelfe* for *twelf*) are taken to be transcription errors by Talbot, not errors by the scribe of B, and so are ignored in the apparatus. However, the few other errors or variations (including a case of homoeoteleuton in line 23) are given. Certainly, as Graham notes, Talbot could have been responsible for these himself; on the other hand, examples of carelessness are frequent in the work of B's scribe.

C

Cambridge, University Library Ii. 1. 33, ff. 2^r–24^v (Ker 18)

Ff. v + 226 + ii; foliated (i–iv), 1–227, (228, 229). Ff. i–ii and 228–9 are paper flyleaves, supplied at binding; ff. iii–iv were supplied by J. M. Kemble; f. 1 is a sixteenth-century parchment flyleaf, on which a contents list has been written. Ff. 2–227 were formerly paginated incorrectly 1–449 in red pencil on rectos. Several leaves are missing. Page size is *c*.222 × 158 mm, with a writing area of *c*.175 × 110 mm, in twenty-one to twenty-six lines per page (and rarely 29), but consistently twenty-four in the Genesis text. Bound in the seventeenth century. See also Wanley, *Catalogus*, 162–3.

---

[49] Graham, 'Early Modern Users', 279.

The manuscript is a collection of forty-four items, including homilies, saints' lives, and other devotional material, copied during an extended period in the second half of the twelfth century. Thirty-six of the items are from Ælfric's two series of *Catholic Homilies* and his *Lives of Saints*. Item 1, on ff. 2^r–24^v/8, is the *Prefatio* to his translation of Genesis, followed by the translation itself (i.e. Gen. 1–24:26).[50] The manuscript was no. 10 in the list of those given by Archbishop Parker to the Cambridge University Library in 1574; hence the sixteenth-century heading above the opening of the *Prefatio*: 'Genesis in Englishe. Matthæus Cantuar: dedit. 1574'.[51] The same hand wrote below the text on the first page: 'Continet paginas 450'. There is some evidence that the manuscript may have reached Ely (see below), in which case it is likely that Parker acquired it while he was a canon there.

Ker recognized that the manuscript had been written over an extended period, mainly in the second half of the twelfth century, and he identified two main hands: the first wrote ff. 2^r–36^v and 220^v–227^v, and the second ff. 37^r–120^v. Other scholars, alerted by changes in the appearance of the scripts which Ker himself had noted, have deduced more complexity. William Schipper distinguishes a third hand, which he believes wrote ff. 37^r–52^v, while Oliver Traxel claims to be able to identify a fourth, responsible for most of quires 1–4, that is, ff. 2^r–24^v and 25^r–28^v.[52] However, an authoritative study by scholars in the Leeds- and Leicester-based research project, 'The Production and Use of English Manuscripts 1060 to 1220', has endorsed Ker's original view: it concludes that there were only two different hands, displaying 'the natural changes of a script which has evolved over time'.[53] As for the origin of the manuscript, Schipper uses the arrangement of the contents, especially the prominence of

---

[50] The end of C's Genesis has traditionally been given as 24:22 (including by the present editor), but there is no doubt that the closing two words, 'god heriende', paraphrase the Latin words which end 24:26, *et adorauit dominum*; 24:23–5 and the first part of 26 are not translated.

[51] It was also listed as having been bequeathed to Corpus Christi College, though it was never there. See M. R. James, *A Descriptive Catalogue of the Manuscripts in the Library of Corpus Christi College, Cambridge*, 2 vols. (Cambridge, 1909–12), i, p. xxxvii.

[52] Schipper, 'A Composite Old English Homiliary from Ely: Cambr. Univ. Libr. MS Ii. 1. 33', *Transactions of the Cambridge Bibliographical Society*, 8 (1983), 285–98; and Traxel, *Language Change, Writing and Textual Interference in Post-Conquest Old English Manuscripts: The Evidence of Cambridge, University Library, Ii. l. 33* (Frankfurt am Main, 2004), with the evidence set out on pp. 46–53 and a summary on p. 221.

[53] See <www.le.ac.uk/ee/em1060to1220/catalogue/CULIi.1.33>.

Ælfric's homily on St Æthelthryth, to suggest that part of it, at least, was copied at Ely.[54] Traxel believes that the compilation may have been begun at St Augustine's, Canterbury, and then been continued at Ely. Elaine Treharne discounts the Ely connection but accepts a south-eastern origin, though perhaps at Rochester or Christ Church, Canterbury, rather than St Augustine's; she has identified the scribe who copied ff. 2–36^v and 120^v–227^v of C as the same who wrote a few folios in Cambridge, Corpus Christi College 367 (Ker 63), containing parts of Ælfric's *De temporibus*.[55]

The scribe of ff. 2^r–24^v, the leaves containing the *Prefatio* and Genesis, writes a very untidy hand, with much inconsistency in the size of letters, which show a mixture of caroline and insular features. Some three-quarters of proper names and words starting a new sentence have their first letter highlighted, either by simple enlargement of the minuscule form, as with *a*, *l*, *b*, tall *s*, and *þ*, or by the use of a 'capital' form, as with *N*, *R*, *M*, and *S*, and occasionally *B* and *Ð*. However, *N* is always, and *R*, *N*, and *S* usually, written within the same vertical space as a minuscule letter without an ascender, and it is not always clear whether an initial letter has in fact been deliberately enlarged or whether it falls within the scribe's normal range of variation. Suspension of *n* and *m* is very frequent, often in the middle of words, and is marked by a tagged bar. Other abbreviations abound, such as $\bar{g}$- for *ge*-, and are sometimes radical, as in $\bar{r}.\bar{w}.\bar{m}.$ for *rihtwisramanna* (Gen. 21:14). Large, elaborately decorative initials in red begin *Ælfric* at the start of f. 2^r and *IN principio* on line 3 of f. 3^r; in the latter case, the *I* sits in the left margin and stretches up to above line 1 and down to below line 8. Throughout the text, the initial letters of the words which begin sentences, and a few letters elsewhere, are filled out in red. At the bottom of f. 4^r, in about one-third of a line of space left at the end of the *Prefatio*, the rubric *INCIPIT LIB[ER] GENESIS.* is written in now fading red ink.[56] The *I* of *IN angynne* at the top of 4^v, also in the margin, starts well above line 1 but reaches only as far as line 4, and is black.

---

[54] 'A Composite Old English Homiliary', 291–2.
[55] Elaine M. Treharne, 'The Dates and Origins of Three Twelfth-Century Old English Manuscripts', in Philip Pulsiano and Elaine M. Treharne (eds.), *Anglo-Saxon Manuscripts and their Heritage* (Aldershot, 1998), 227–53 at 339–44.
[56] In the critical apparatus of his edition (p. 81), Crawford indicates that C shares with L the additional word *anglice*, but there is no trace of this. The rubric already intrudes a little into the right-hand margin, ending with a punctus.

A large number of emendations was made to the text of the *Prefatio* and Genesis in at least two phases, to judge by the evidence of the ink used. Both scribes may have been involved. The emendations encompassed the correction of obvious error, the provision of words originally omitted from the source, and linguistic updating. A later Latin glossator of the manuscript made one contribution to our text, on f. 7ʳ, where he glossed *yrmþa* with *erumpnas*.[57]

Relevant contents of C:

f. 2ʳ/1 [*Prefatio starts*] Ælfric munuc gret æþelweard ealdorman
f. 4ʳ/24 [*Prefatio ends*] writere gif he nele his woh gerihtan.
f. 4ʳ/24 [*rubric fills out the line*] INCIPIT LIB[ER] GENESIS.
f. 4ᵛ/1 [Gen. 1:1] IN ANGẏnne gesceop god heofonan 7 eorþan.
f. 24ᵛ/8 [*Genesis ends* (24:26)] 7 gildene biagas god herieNDE.

Co
Cambridge, Corpus Christi College 201, pp. 1–178
(Ker 49)

Ff. ii + 89 + ii; paginated (i–ii), 1–177, (i–ii), with large figures in red pencil on rectos only (1, 3, 5, etc.); the opening flyleaves are modern paper, those at the end sixteenth-century parchment; several leaves are missing. Page size is *c*.280 × 162 mm, with a written area of *c*.250 × 122(–140) mm. Severe trimming of the pages has reduced the width of the margins considerably. There are forty-one lines per complete page, except for p. 153, which has forty lines, and pp. 171–8, with twenty lines. Rebound in 1948. See also Wanley, *Catalogus*, 137–48; Gneuss, *Handlist*, no. 65.5.

Corpus 201 is a miscellaneous collection of sixty regulatory, homiletic, devotional, and legal items, two of which were copied at the opening of the eleventh century, constituting Ker's 'part A' (pp. 1–7 and 161–7), and the rest, pp. 8–160 and 167–76, in three separate hands, in the mid-eleventh century, Ker's 'part B'. Item 56 in part B, pp. 151–60, the only contribution of 'scribe 3', is a translation of the latter part of Genesis in the *OEH* version, but with

---
[57] Traxel, *Language Change*, 126–7 and 152–3.

many revisions.[58] It is preceded (on pp. 147–51) by two items on 'English' saints, including St Alban, and followed (as part of the original 'A' contribution) by 418 lines of alliterative homiletic verse, the OE *Judgement Day II* (pp. 161–7). T. A. M. Bishop identified one of the hands in part B, the one responsible for pp. 170–6, as that of a New Minster, Winchester, scribe.[59] There are a number of other pointers to Winchester also, as the origin of the volume, including evidence of the use of a local feature of the liturgy in its version of the *Regularis Concordia*.[60] Patrick Wormald, describing the volume as 'a manual for the drilling of a Christian society', has speculated that its exemplar may have come from York.[61]

There is no reason to doubt that Co's text of Genesis consisted originally of the whole of 37:2 to 50:25 (i.e. to the end of the book), which is the story of Joseph. The text of 37:2 is preceded by the rubric which appears also in L and B at this point (*Her cydde . . . Abrahames ofsprincge*), though in a slightly erroneous form. It starts on p. 151, at the beginning of the fourth line, with a large *H*, but with no break. There are now two lacunae in Co's text: a leaf is missing between pp. 154 and 155, with the text of Gen. 41:2 (*and hig man læswode*) to 42:20 (*eowerne gingstan broðor*), and two leaves after p. 160, with the text of Gen. 47:18 (*þæt we nan þing*) to the end (which would probably have filled the lost two leaves completely). Thus three of an original nine leaves are wanting, carrying just under 40 per cent of the text of Gen. 37:2–50:25. In the description in his *Catalogus* (p. 146), in which our text is item lxxviii, Wanley notes the loss after 47:18 but not the earlier lacuna; there is no way of knowing whether he overlooked it or whether the leaf was still in place in his time. He gives the opening rubric, and the incipit and the explicit of the text.

Matthew Parker, who probably obtained the manuscript from Edward Cradock, Lady Margaret Professor of Divinity in Cambridge (1575–94), bound it with another manuscript, consisting of a copy of the *Capitula* of Theodulf of Orléans in Latin, a homily in OE, and an OE translation of the *Capitula*. These constitute pp. 179–272 of

[58] It is item 86 in James, *A Descriptive Catalogue*, i. 485–91.
[59] *English Caroline Minuscule* (Oxford, 1971), p. xv n. 2.
[60] See Joyce Hill, 'The "Regularis Concordia" and its Latin and Old English Reflexes', *Revue bénédictine*, 101 (1991), 299–315 at 311.
[61] *The Making of English Law: King Alfred to the Twelfth Century*, i: *Legislation and its Limits* (Oxford, 2000), 206–10, with a useful table showing the make-up of the manuscript on pp. 204–5.

Corpus 201 (Ker 50). Ker notes that 201 apparently did not reach Corpus Christi College at the same time as the bulk of Parker's manuscripts, for it appears only as an addition ('Miscellan. Saxonice'), both to the list of his gifts extant in the Parker Library and to that in the library of Trinity Hall, Cambridge, and it is not in a copy of the list preserved in London, Lambeth Palace Library 723 at all. It is, however, likely to be the 'Miscellan. Saxonice' in John Parker's booklist in Lambeth Palace Library 737 (f. 163ᵛ). The manuscript was at Corpus Christi College by 1600, when it bore the shelf-mark S 18, as it does in Wanley's *Catalogus*. The present binding was made in 1948, to replace one made in the eighteenth century.

The text of Genesis is written without any breaks and is completely without decoration (thus contrasting with all the other sections of the manuscript); the large, three-line *H* which begins the rubric on p. 151 is black. The very regular round hand which copied Genesis does not occur elsewhere in the manuscript; Ker described it, curiously, as 'beautiful' and dated it to the mid-eleventh century.[62] It took over from the main hand, which had finished art. 55 in line 3 on the third leaf of quire 11. On some pages, the many occurrences of ð, on which the long upstroke curves back at an angle of 45 degrees and is crossed by a long slash, are sufficient to produce an odd patchwork effect. The scribe often writes *u* for *f*. Capitals are used initially for many (but by no means all) of the names; when this letter is *e*, a tall minuscule version is used. In *iacoB*, a small capital is used only at the end of the name. A facsimile of part of p. 159 is given in Ker's supplement to Crawford's edition.[63]

O

London, British Library, Cotton Otho B. x, ff. 31, 32, 33, 34, 35, 57 (Ker 177, art. 19)

Badly damaged by fire in the Cotton library in London in October 1731. The main manuscript, Ker's 'A', appears to have consisted originally of 171 leaves, of which fifty-four survive. All but one are bound, but disordered, in a volume in the British Library (in which fifty-four separately mounted fragments represent fifty-three original leaves); the exception is a single leaf in Bodleian Library, Rawlinson Q. e. 20. The London volume has a further thirteen fragments, making sixty-seven in all; one is from Ker's 'manuscript

---

[62] In the supplement to Crawford, *Heptateuch*, 444.   [63] *Heptateuch*, 455.

C' (see below), two are unidentified, and ten are from various other identified manuscripts.[64] Page size was $c.195 \times 140$ mm, with a written area of $c.175 \times 115$ mm.

Manuscript A, which included the Genesis extract (of which five leaves survive, mounted as six fragments), probably had 171 leaves (ff. '1–142' and '166–194', using Wanley's numbering) and was a collection of saints' lives and homilies, copied in the eleventh century. Ker's 'B', with perhaps originally twelve leaves (Wanley's ff. '155–164'), and 'C', with an unknown number of leaves (starting at Wanley's f. '195'), 'may or may not' have been originally part of the same manuscript as A. Ker based his analysis of what remains on the description made by Wanley in his *Catalogus*; apparently some items were misordered already. Otho B. x belonged to John Joscelyn, Matthew Parker's Latin secretary, as can be deduced by various notes made in other manuscripts by him and by Cotton; these show also that there were nine more leaves at the beginning of the volume when Joscelyn possessed it than when Wanley catalogued it.[65]

Wanley lists the Genesis extract as his item no. xxviii, starting on f. 166: 'Fragmentum libri Geneseos, cap. 37, ad finem libri, continens historiam Josephi Patriarchæ, ex Ælfrici versione Desumptum'. He gives an incipit of twenty-nine words (the fourteen-word rubric beginning 'Her cydde' and the first fifteen words of 37:2, ending 'his gebroðrum') and an explicit of sixty words (all of Gen. 50:25 and a twenty-eight-word amplification); both are used in the collation of the present edition (with the modified siglum O^w), since neither of the leaves carrying them, the first and the last, survives. Preservation work on the fragments of O was apparently done in the 1860s and they were mounted separately on the sixty-seven 'folios' of the present volume, which underwent further preservation work in the 1960s. The Genesis fragments are ff. 31–5 and 57 of the volume, an apparent total of six folios. Crawford missed out f. 57 when preparing his edition, no doubt because its identity had not yet been established; Ker presumably made the identification. The leaf is thus collated in the present edition for the first time, but it is one of the most damaged leaves, consisting now of just a jagged elongated fragment, carrying small segments from about twenty-two lines of text. The other leaves have fared rather better, though none is complete, or completely legible. The best preserved is f. 32. The

---

[64] See Ker, *Catalogue*, nos. 168, 175, 178, 179, 180, and 181.   [65] Ibid. 228–9.

fragments are now bound out of order; f. 57 is in fact the earliest in the sequence, followed by ff. 33, 31, 32, 34, and 35. However, the fragments on the latter two folios do not represent the remains of two separate leaves of the original manuscript but are the upper and lower halves of a single leaf; furthermore, the fragment on f. 34 is mounted back to front. Thus, f. 34^v must be read first, then f. 35^r, followed by ff. 34^r and 35^v. In the table below, the fragments are presented in their original order.

As noted, Wanley records the start of the Genesis text as being on f. 166 (presumably the recto) of the volume he saw; the next item, the *Depositio Sancti Suuithuni Mitissimi Episcopi*, is given as beginning on f. 181^v. The implication is that the Genesis text was on ff. 166^r–181^r, which is thirty-one sides, covering fifteen complete leaves and the recto of a sixteenth. Ker indeed gives the notional ending place of Genesis as 181^r. However, an estimate of the amount of missing text, based on the space taken up by what survives, suggests that it is more likely that the completion of Gen. 37:2–50:25 needed at least part of f. 181^v also. Wanley's description (which follows his habit of giving the starting page of each text without qualification) does not preclude this possibility; the *Depositio Sancti Suuithuni* may have begun some way down f. 181^v. Like the other leaves, f. 57 will no doubt have carried twenty-nine lines originally, but as neither of the leaves adjacent to it survives, it is impossible to tell exactly what proportions of the missing seven lines were above and below the twenty-two lines for which, however minimally, there is evidence on the fragment. The best estimate, based on an approximate calculation of how much text will have filled the three leaves between the present ff. 57 and 33, is that the distribution was about even; hence the start and end points conjectured in the following table (where letters in the OE between square brackets are illegible or missing).

Original foliation	Present foliation	Text of Genesis
166^r–169^v		[37:2–?40:18]
170^r	57^r	?40:18–?41:9 (. . . windlas. þæt – [gesawe] cuman . . .)
170^v	57v	?41:9–?16 (. . . þa ð[ohte] – [mæg ic] don . . .)
171^r–173^v		[41:16–43:11]
174^r	33^r	43:11–23 (Nimað eac – mid eow)

174^v	33^v	43:23–44:4 (ne ondræde – far æfter)
175^{r-v}		[44:4–45:3]
176^r	31^r	45:3–16 (hym for ege – iosepes b[roðru])
176^v	31^v	45:16–46:1 (comon to – he com)
177^r	32^r	46:1–16 (to aðsware – 7 areli)
177^v	32^v	46:17–34 (þis wæron Asseres – eardige[an on gessen lande])
178^r top	34^v	46:34–47:6 (for ðan ðe – [hym gessen])
178^r bott.	35^r	47:6–14 (land gif – iosep hæfde)
178^v top	34^r	47:14–19 ([ge]gaderod eal – [licge weste])
178^v bott.	35^v	47:19–24 ([7 we forw]urðon – þa feow[er])
179^r–181^v		[47:24–50:25]

Thus, what has survived from the Genesis text in Otho B. x, with varying degrees of completeness, is ff. 170, 174, and 176–8. A total of eleven of the sixteen original leaves is missing, including four at the beginning and three at the end. Three sections of Genesis are represented on the surviving leaves: 40:18–41:16, 42:11–44:4, and 45:3–47:24. These amount to about 30 per cent of the text of Joseph's story, but substantial parts of several of the leaves have been destroyed, and scorching or distortion of the remaining parchment has rendered much of the surviving text illegible. Only about one-third of the text of the sections can be recovered with any certainty, and thus Otho B. x supplies us with collatable material for little more than 10 per cent of Gen. 37:2–50:25. As well as the text from f. 57, the collation in the present edition includes readings from the other leaves which Crawford did not record. On the other hand, in a few cases it has proved impossible to confirm readings apparently seen by Crawford. It is not clear whether this is a consequence of further deterioration of the manuscript after his examination or mistakes by him.

Several hands were used in the manuscript as a whole, one of them being responsible for all the surviving leaves of Genesis. Ker noted the distinctive *e*, formed with an unusually long sloping back. Decoration consists of a dab of red on 7 and on the first letter of each sentence.

N
Nicholson's fragment of Exodus (Ker 404)

On p. 31 of his 1698 edition of the Heptateuch, Edward Thwaites lists variant readings taken, according to the preamble to the list, from a manuscript fragment which was given by William Nicholson, bishop of Carlisle, to Edmund Gibson, later bishop of London, and then shared with Thwaites himself:

Variantes lectiones collectae ab Exodi Fragmento, quod olim casu repertum, amicus noster GUILIELMUS NICOLSONUS dono dedit amico suo nostroque EDMUNDO GIBSONO; qui ipsum lacerum autographum mecum benigne communicauit. Characteres Fragmenti antiquitatem quatuor seculorum prae se ferunt.

All three men were, or had been, members of a group of enthusiasts for Old English at the Queen's College, Oxford. Gibson would go on to publish an edition of the Anglo-Saxon Chronicle in 1692. Nicholson had resigned his fellowship of the college in 1681, before either Gibson or Thwaites (both natives of Westmorland) had arrived, to take a parish in his native diocese of Carlisle, of which he would later become bishop; but he continued to encourage a circle which included also George Hickes.[66] No trace of the Exodus fragment in question can now be found. The readings are variants from the text as transmitted in L, on which Thwaites was basing his edition, and they suggest that the fragment must have contained two continuous portions of text, Exod. 9:20–10:9 and 13:19–14:23. It makes sense further to take it that it was a bifolium, for Thwaites uses the singular when referring to it. In view of the gap in the text, it could not have been the innermost bifolium of a quire. The text on each of the leaves from which citations are taken (assuming that the first and last words given were in each case from near the start and near the end of the leaves) was about 560 words, that is, 280 words per side.[67] But the amount of text separating the two portions of Exodus on the bifolium is some 1620 words; these would thus fill, fairly exactly, not two but three complete leaves (six sides). In terms of the make-up of a quire, therefore, the only way to interpret the

---

[66] See the letters from Nicholson to Thwaites, 29 June 1697, and Gibson to Thwaites, 22 July 1697, in Oxford, Bodleian Library, Rawlinson D. 377, ff. 18 and 122.

[67] The distribution of the lemmata given by Nicholson shows that the leaves were complete, not fragmentary, like some of those in P.

evidence seems to be that the N-fragment came from a quire which was completed by one more bifolium and a half-sheet (in whatever order they were). This might have been planned, or it could be that the scribe made a mess of one half of a bifolium and cut it out.[68] The structure would thus have been, assuming a notional seven-leaf quire:

[f. 1]
f. '2'   Exod. 9:20 (drihten ondræd)–10:9 (wyllað)
[ff. '3–5']   Exod. 10:10–13:18
f. '6'   Exod. 13:19 (moyses)–14:23 (eal)
[f. 7]

The estimated word count for the pages of N is very close to the figure observed for P (see table, p. xxxviii), which has parts of later chapters of Exodus. It is entirely possible, therefore, that N and P derive from the same copy of the *OEH*; nothing in the language of the two witnesses suggests otherwise (see further p. lxxi).

P

New York, Pierpont Morgan Library, G 63 (Ker 418)

Two complete leaves and separate vertical strips from each of the two leaves conjugate with them, copied in the second half of the eleventh century. The dimensions of the two complete leaves (ff. 1 and 3) are *c*.281 × 189 mm and 279 × 188 mm, and of the strips (ff. 2 and 4) 280 × 53 mm and 279 × 62 mm. The writing area on the complete leaves is *c*. 210 × 164–70 mm. All leaves have twenty-five lines of writing. See also Gneuss, *Handlist*, no. 866.

The leaves were found by the dealer Bernard Quaritch of London, loose inside an eighteenth-century atlas, which was among books obtained from Ireland. A mark on f. 3^v shows that they were originally paste-downs in a copy of Sebastian Munster's *Dictionarium Trilingue Lat. Gr. Heb.* (Basle, 1530), in the Diocesan Library of Cashel in Ireland. The leaves were bought by H. P. Kraus of New York, and then by William S. Glazier (1907–62), whose collection was deposited in the Pierpont Morgan Library, New York, by its

---

[68] See Ker's discussion of half-sheets, *Catalogue*, p. xxiv. He suggests that a planned half-sheet would be more likely to be inserted before the central bifolium, because it was easier to make it secure there.

trustees in 1963. The leaves and fragments were then bound in blue morocco by Sangorski and Sutcliffe. Both the complete leaves and the strips have been neatly trimmed, giving them straight edges. There is some creasing on the inner vertical edges of the complete leaves.

The text of Exodus carried by each of the leaves is shown below. It is continuous on ff. 1 and 3, but only three or four words from each line remain on the strips (ff. 2 and 4). It may be noted that Exodus in the *OEH* is a much reduced version of the Vulgate narrative, even in the complete manuscripts; hence the apparently large jumps in the text in places.

f. 1^r 16:16 (fæt ful. þe)–16:35 (to chanaan lande.)
f. 1^v 17:1 (Hi foron of sin)–17:14 (Witodlice ic adilgige)
f. 2^r 19:6 (Ðis synd ða)–19:20 (driht eode u)
f. 2^v 19:21 (n ofer þa ge)–20:21 (þ folc wæs afæ)
f. 3^r 23:8 (þu lac þa)–23:28 (ær þu in fare.)
f. 3^v 23:31 (Ic sette þine gemæro)–29:12 (on þæs weofodes)
f. 4^r 29:46 (dde of Egipta lan)–32:8 (ut alædde of egyp)
f. 4^v 32:10 (hi for do nu hi me)–32:24 (þa cw̄ ic to)

Each folio carries, or carried, between 325 and 365 words on each side, and this enables us to determine the relationship between the surviving leaves. They come from a quire of eight, in a gathering of four bifolia.

Original foliation	*Present foliation*	*Exodus text*
f. '1'	f. 1	16:16–17:14
f. '2'		[17:15–19:6]
f. '3'	f. 2	19:6–20:21
ff. '4–5'		[20:21–23:8]
f. '6'	f. 3	23:8–29:12
f. '7'		[29:12–46]
f. '8'	f. 4	29:46–32:24

Thus each of the two strips was originally conjoint with one of the complete leaves: ff. 1 and 4 formed a bifolium (original ff. '1' and '8'), and so did ff. 2 and 3 (original ff. '3' and '6'). Missing are the second and the inner bifolia.

The script, in dark brown ink, was dated by Ker to the second half of the eleventh century. It is large and rather untidy. All thorns slope

backwards; *a* is sometimes caroline; *s* varies between tall or low at random; and *g* often has a fine stroke added, sloping upwards from the left end of the horizontal top stroke (in nine cases out of forty-one, for instance, on f. 1^r). There is regular contraction, including that of *þæt*, *cwæþ* and *þonne*, and suspension of terminal *m*; *y* is always dotted. Reading marks have been added rarely, at an indeterminate date. There is little decoration. On f. 3^r, *Syþþan* (Exod. 29:9) is given an enlarged (but one-line) *S* and on f. 4^r, *Drihten* (Exod. 32:7) a two-line round *D*; both are in metallic red. On f. 3^v, *H* in *He cwæð* (Exod. 26:1) and *M* in *Moyses* (Exod. 26:3 and 5) are dabbed in the same colour.

Ln
Lincoln, Cathedral Library 298, no. 2 (Ker 125)

Two adjacent leaves, once joined, which survived as binding fragments; copied in the second half of the eleventh century. They are bound now as the second item in a portfolio of twelve flyleaves, wrappers, paste-downs, and loose leaves from manuscripts and printed books, collected early in the twentieth century. The maximum dimensions of the leaves now are 300 × 209 mm, with a written area of 277 × 189–97 mm; each leaf has thirty-seven lines. See also Wanley, *Catalogus*, 305; Gneuss, *Handlist*, no. 276; R. M. Thomson, *Catalogue of the Manuscripts of Lincoln Cathedral Chapter Library* (Cambridge, 1989), 205.[69]

The leaves carry Num. 10:28–16:3, and the continuity of text between the two shows that they formed the central bifolium of a quire. Except on the inner vertical edges of the leaves, where a margin of some 18 mm remains, trimming has been drastic. This affects especially the outer vertical edges and has removed a few letters from the ends of the longer lines. Furthermore, the leaves were mutilated, presumably while they were folded and still joined, by the tearing away of a large jagged section from the bottom right-hand third. The tear, identical on the two leaves, starts some 90 mm up the right-hand side, so that all but a few of the innermost words

---

[69] Thomson designates the various items by letters of the alphabet, so that our fragments are item 'B', rather than '2', but it seems better to retain the established designation.

on each of the last ten lines on each page have been lost. Some creasing has affected the upper parts of the leaves.

The full text of Numbers carried was as follows, though now there are many gaps, for the reasons noted:

f. 1^r 10:28 (Ða hi þa ut foran)–11:19 (flæsc 7 ge etað)
f. 1^v 11:20 (fulne monað oð)–12:12 (ne forwurðe)
f. 2^r 12:12 (nu is healf hire)–14:3 (þæt we forwur)
f. 2^v 14:3 (ofslagene 7 ure)–16:3 (wunað on him)

Wanley never apparently inspected the leaves but records in his catalogue having heard about them from his honoured friend Thomas Tanner of Norwich Cathedral; they had been used as the flyleaves of a manuscript book.[70] The leaves seem to have become lost subsequently. There is certainly no mention of them in a nineteenth-century catalogue of the cathedral's manuscripts,[71] and, writing in 1898, Chase lamented that the cathedral librarian 'knows nothing' of them.[72] However, they were rediscovered, as Crawford reports, by Canon R. M. Woolley, when he was preparing a catalogue of the library a few years later, thus enabling Crawford to publish an edition of their text in 1920.[73]

Ker assigned the copying to the second half of the eleventh century. Crawford observed 'a fine regular hand',[74] but Ker's description 'ill-formed' is nearer the mark. It is rounded but rather squat, with many small irregularities. Ascenders are notably splayed at their tops, sometimes notched quite deeply. A tiny hairline slopes up to the right from the ends of all descenders (including those of the Tironian *et*). The *s* varies between low and caroline, the shaft of the latter being broken to a greater or lesser degree; occasionally it is straight and the letter becomes a 'long' *s*. The *y* has a fine descending stroke, upturned at the end; the back of

---

[70] Wanley, *Catalogus*, 305. 'Fragmenta quaedam Excerptorum Ælfrici ex Pentateucho, Saxonice, ad frontem calcemque cujusdem MS. Codicis compacta ut accepi a D. Tho. Tannero Cancellario Eccl. Norwicensis, amicoque meo plurimum colendo.'

[71] G. F. Apthorp, *A Catalogue of the Books and Manuscripts in the Library of Lincoln Cathedral* (Lincoln, 1859), with the manuscript list on pp. 277–85. There is also no mention of the fragments in earlier catalogues of the cathedral's holdings, made in the 12th and 15th cc.

[72] Chase, 'A New Text', 242.

[73] Crawford, *Heptateuch*, 6; his edition is 'The Lincoln Fragment'. Woolley's catalogue is *Catalogue of the Manuscripts of Lincoln Cathedral Chapter Library* (Oxford, 1927), with the fragment described on p. 183.

[74] *Heptateuch*, 6.

the squat rounded *d* is short; and the *e* is round-backed. The suspension mark for *m* is a zigzag. Sentences begin with a capital letter and there is much variety of form for these; there are, for instance, both minuscule and rustic *D* and three forms of *M*. These initial letters are always filled with red. There is a small amount of correction, most of it apparently contemporary, and possibly by the copyist.

H
Oxford, Bodleian Library, Hatton 115
(Ker 332, art. 30)

Ff. v + 156 + iii; foliated i–v, 1–139, 139a, 140–58. Ff. i–iii and 156–8 are paper flyleaves from the time of binding; ff. iv–v are parchment flyleaves. Several leaves are missing. Page size is $c.268 \times 160$ mm, with a written area of $c.197 \times 100$ mm, in twenty-seven lines. See also Wanley, *Catalogus*, 36–40; Gneuss, *Handlist*, no. 639.

A collection of miscellaneous homilies and other material, copied variously in the second half of the eleventh century and up to the middle of the twelfth. The bulk of the manuscript is made up of three booklets, containing Ælfrician works, mostly copied by one scribe in the second half of the eleventh century:[75]

1. ff. 1–64: General homilies and short admonitory pieces.
2. ff. 68–94 (with Lawrence, Kansas, University of Kansas Library, Y 104): Homilies for various specific occasions.
3. ff. 95–139^r: General homilies and Old Testament pieces.

Item 30, in the third booklet, ff. 108^r–116^r, is headed *Sermo excerptus de libro iudicium* and is a copy of the homily which is found otherwise only in L, built around extensive translation of parts of Judges. There are two more short booklets containing non-Ælfrician material (ff. 140–7, a sermon, and ff. 148–55, various prognostications). The manuscript was in Worcester in the first half of the thirteenth century, as corrections by that centre's scribe with the 'tremulous hand' show, and many of the items in it appear also in other

---

[75] The scheme set out by Christine Franzen in her description of the manuscript in *The Tremulous Hand of Worcester: A Study of Old English in the Thirteenth Century* (Oxford, 1991), 38–44, is followed here.

manusucripts associated with Worcester (including Hatton 116 and the first part of Cambridge, Corpus Christi College 178).[76] There is, however, no evidence that it originated at Worcester. Godden has suggested that it has a common source with Cotton Vespasian D. xiv (Ker 209), which was copied in Rochester or Canterbury in the early twelfth century.[77] The manuscript was no. 317 in Patrick Young's catalogue of the manuscripts of Worcester Cathedral.[78] It was in the possession of Christopher, Lord Hatton, by 4 August 1643, after he had apparently persuaded the Dean and Chapter to allow him to borrow the important group of Anglo-Saxon manuscripts now associated with his name.[79] They were given to the Bodleian Library by the first baron's son, Sir Christopher Hatton, in 1675. Hatton 115 was formerly Junius 23, as in Wanley's *Catalogus*, where Judges is item no. xxviii, which Wanley wrongly gives as beginning on f. 105. He prints the incipit and an extensive excipit.

The script in an upright, round hand which, as Ker noted, is very like that responsible for a copy of Ælfric's *Excerptiones de arte grammatica anglice* in British Library, Cotton Faustina A. x (Ker 154). The overall effect is one of untidiness, owing mainly to variation in the height of the body of the letters. Wedges on ascenders vary from a crude blob to a more or less neat serif, but sometimes the stroke is notched instead. The ascender of ð varies in its angle; its cross-bar may be horizontal or even incline downwards from left to right. The ends of the descenders curve to the left. Ker noted especially the untidiness of *o*, with its crude joins top and bottom. Long *s* is regularly used initially and medially, but not finally. The hand is not found in any other known Worcester manuscripts. The mark of abbreviation is cup-shaped and a triangle of dots is used to signal words omitted in error. Initials are in metallic red or green, and the first letter of sentences is usually dabbed with red. There are many additions to the text, made in the later twelfth or the first half of the thirteenth century, including Latin glosses (such as *reddent*, glossing *ageafon*, f. 112^v), sometimes

---

[76] On this Worcester scribe, see Franzen, *The Tremulous Hand*. She discusses Hatton 116 (Ker 333) and Corpus 178 (Ker 41), which are both books of homilies, mostly by Ælfric, on pp. 44–51.
[77] *Ælfric's Catholic Homilies II*, ed. Godden, p. lxviii.
[78] '*Catalogus Librorum Manuscriptorum Bibliothecae Wigorniensis*' made in 1622–23 by Patrick Young, Librarian to King James I, ed. I. Atkins and N. R. Ker (Cambridge, 1944), 56.
[79] In their account of Hatton's association with Worcester in '*Catalogus Librorum*', 13–17 at 14, Atkins and Ker emphasize that he had no right to keep them.

with contemporary English equivalents, too (such as *piler. colu[m]-na[m]*, written opposite OE *swerum*, f. 114ʳ). Regular emendation includes the modernization of spelling (as when *i*, *o*, and *k* are written above *gefylce* to make *gifolke*, f. 115ᵛ, and *quike* is given in the margin for *cucu*, f. 114ʳ), and sometimes of morphology (as in *leien*, given for *lagon*, f. 115ʳ). Such changes were made by at least two different hands and occur throughout the manuscript.

Bo
Oxford, Bodleian Library, Bodley 343
(Ker 310)

Ff. v + 205; foliated i–xxxix, 1–167, 169–74. F. 173 is a medieval parchment flyleaf; ff. i, ii, iv, v, and 174 are post-medieval paper. Ff. vi–xxxix were formerly paginated 1–59, 58–66. Several leaves are missing. Page size is *c*.310 × 200 mm, with a text area of 253–7 × 160–3 mm and thirty-one lines per page consistently in the *Libellus* but twenty-eight to thirty-six elsewhere. See also Wanley, *Catalogus*, pp. 36–4.

A collection of eighty-five items in OE, mostly homilies, forty-eight of them from Ælfric's two series of *Catholic Homilies*, copied in the second half of the twelfth century. Various items in Latin were added later in the late twelfth or early thirteenth centuries in the manuscript's originally blank spaces. The items are arranged in no special order.[80] Item 65, on ff. 129ʳ–132ʳ/26, is the Old Testament portion of the *Libellus de ueteri testamento et nouo*. A leaf is missing between ff. 130 and 131. Ker noted some internal evidence that the manuscript originated in the West Midlands. Irvine agrees, adding linguistic evidence, and suggests that the scribe was probably writing near Worcester, but not at Worcester itself.[81] She believes that he relied on many small collections of homiletic material ('booklets'), rather than a single large one, and that his efforts illustrate a process of multiple copying of homilies which was a feature of the eleventh and twelfth centuries. The manuscript falls into seven sections of varying length, formed by groups of quires. Each section ends with blank space before the next section starts on a fresh quire. The

---

[80] For a comprehensive description of the manuscript and its contents, see *Old English Homilies from MS Bodley 343*, ed. Susan Irvine, EETS 302 (Oxford, 1993), pp. xviii–liv. Much of the brief description here is based on Irvine's.

[81] Ker, *Catalogue*, 375; *Old English Homilies*, ed. Irvine, pp. li–lii.

Libellus is the first of twelve items (nos. 65–76) in the sixth section ('f' in Irvine's scheme). Six of the other items are also by Ælfric, including two letters for Wulfstan of York, and four are by Wulfstan himself; the last item, added much later on blank space, consists of three lines on the age of the Virgin Mary.[82] In his *Catalogus*, p. 22, Wanley makes our text item no. lxiv; he gives the incipit and explicit (which contains the error *bed* for *beo*).

The bulk of the manuscript (ff. 1–170) is written by a single scribe, though with some changes in style. Ker dated the hand to the second half of the twelfth century and characterized it as 'skilful, small but clear, fluent and well-spaced'. The *r* is usually caroline but sometimes has the reverse-*s* form; *g* is caroline (for the stop) or insular (for the spirant); *s* is caroline and sometimes extends below the line. The ends of descenders usually turn to the left. There is frequent suspension by means of a straight, or sometimes hooked, bar; a hooked *d* is often used for *de*. A four-line green Ð in green and a rubric in red begin the text. Some initial letters are shadowed in red, green, or black on ff. 129^r, 131^{r-v}, and 132^r only.

An additional witness
British Library, Cotton Vespasian D. xiv,
ff. 7^r–11^v (Ker 209)

Vespasian D. xiv is a compilation of mainly homiletic and exegetical material, copied in Ker's estimation in the middle of the twelfth century, probably at Rochester or Canterbury. Ker speculated that it might later have been in female ownership, on the evidence of some prayers added at the end of the twelfth century.[83] The third item in the compilation, on ff. 7^r–11^v, is a copy of the free OE translation of parts of the *Disticha Catonis*. Following the dicts, on f. 11^v, are two precepts, about bribery and witchcraft, which are clearly derived from the *OEH* version of Deut. 16:19 and 18:11–12. The first is almost exactly similar, while the second is partly paraphrased. Their source was first identified by J. Nehab, in *Der altenglische Cato* (diss., University of Göttingen, 1879), 71.[84] They have been printed several

---

[82] For the full contents of section f, see *Old English Homilies*, ed. Irvine, pp. xliii–xlvii.

[83] On the issues of the Rochester origin and the use by females, see especially Susan Irvine, 'The Compilation and Use of Manuscripts Containing Old English in the Twelfth Century', in Mary Swan and Elaine M. Treharne (eds.), *Rewriting Old English in the Twelfth Century* CSASE 30 (Cambridge, 2000), 41–61 at 48–54.

[84] At 53/19–54/10, according to Ker, *Catalogue*, 134; unseen by the present editor. Ker

times since, including by Rubie D.-N. Warner, in her *Early English Homilies from the Twelfth Century MS. Vesp. D XIV*, EETS os 152 (London, 1917), with the text of the two scriptural precepts on p. 7. The most recent edition of the OE dicts is by R. S. Cox, 'The Old English Dicts of Cato', *Anglia*, 90 (1972), 1–42, with the two precepts on p. 16.

Copies of the OE version of the *Disticha Catonis* are also in British Library, Cotton Julius A. ii, ff. 141^r–144^v (Ker 159; mid-twelfth century), and Cambridge, Trinity College R. 9. 17 (819), ff. 1–48^v (Ker 89; end of eleventh or beginning of twelfth century), the latter being the copy on which Cox based his edition. Both are of undetermined origin. Neither has the precepts from Deuteronomy, but the text in Julius is truncated, through the loss of a leaf, and so we cannot know whether the addition was made uniquely in the Vespasian copy. The Trinity copy has its own unique appendage to the main text, some lines of unknown origin which begin 'Ac sanctus Agustinus sæde swiðe bispell by ðy'.[85] The texts of the precepts are cited in this edition's apparatus for Deut. 16:19 and 18:11–12. The closer correspondence of the Vespasian text to that of L, rather than B, is clear, notably in Deut. 16:19, where L and Vespasian share 'wendað rihtwisra word', against B's 'awendaþ rihtwisnessa word' (Lat. *mutant uerba iustorum*).

IV. THE RELATIONSHIPS BETWEEN THE MANUSCRIPTS

1. Overview

In the following pages, the evidence of the extant manuscripts relating to the textual transmission of the *OEH* and the *Libellus de ueteri testamento et nouo* is set out in detail. Here, a brief overview of that evidence, with a summary of conclusions, is given.

---

also reports that the lines were printed by T. O. Cockayne, in *The Shrine: A Collection of Occasional Papers on Dry Subjects* (London, 1864–70), 162. However, this is incorrect; what Cockayne prints is some lines from f. 47^r of Trinity College R. 9. 17, and they have no connection with the text of the *OEH*. The earliest printing of the precepts, though without scriptural identification, appears to have been by L. C. Müller, in *Collectanea Anglo-Saxonica maximam partem nunc primum edita et vocabulario illustrata* (Copenhagen, 1835; repr. Amsterdam, 1970), 47.

[85] Ker, in his *Catalogue*, omits mention of the added scriptural precepts in his description of Vespasian D. xiv and instead, mistakenly, reports that they are in Trinity College R. 9. 17.

There are compelling reasons (including the unifying use of rubrics) to see the *OEH* as a composite work, compiled from various sources after a decision had been made to gather a significant portion of Old Testament Scripture in OE in a single volume. The compilation drew on the following. First, there were identifiable pre-existing translations, not produced with the compilation in mind. These included at least the translations of Gen. 1–24:26 and of Joshua, both of which Ælfric made for his patron Æthelweard, as recorded in the *Prefatio* (lines 2–4) and the *Libellus* (line 230) respectively. Stylistic evidence shows convincingly that the second half of Numbers is also the work of Ælfric.[86] In the absence of any hint (in references within his own works) of Ælfric's having been involved in the *OEH* compilation process, it must be assumed that these translations were made independently of, and indeed before, that process. Second, use may have been made of other pre-existing translations by unnamed translators. In the *Prefatio* (lines 6–7), Ælfric himself mentions that 'some other person' has already translated Genesis 'from Isaac to the end of the book' for Æthelweard, and it is likely that this, too, found its way into the hands of the compiler(s) of the *OEH*.[87] This translation cannot logically be identified with the surviving version of Gen. 37:2–50:25 in Co and O, for that, as discussed below, is a revision of the one used in the *OEH*. Third, after such material as pre-existed had been gathered, further translations may have been prepared specifically to complete a Hexateuch for the compilation project. It seems reasonable to identify the translator or translators of such material at this stage with the compiler or compilers, though this cannot be proved.

The original compilation almost certainly did not include the version of Judges which appears in L. This is indicated, for one thing, by its absence from B, which in concept appears to be a purpose-made 'edition' of the Hexateuch only. Furthermore, Judges is begun on a fresh sheet of parchment in L, rather than following on without a break from the preceding book (in this case, Joshua), which was the procedure followed in the copying of all the other books. This suggests that the sequence Genesis–Joshua was copied from a discrete manuscript, a booklet, of the Hexateuch, and that Judges was taken, albeit by the same main scribe, from a separate exemplar.

---

[86] See the overview by Clemoes, *Illustrated Hexateuch*, 43–8.

[87] The possibility that Æthelweard himself was involved in the compilation is discussed in vol. 2.

L may have been the first (and possibly the only) manuscript in which the seventh book of the Old Testament was added to the first six. Judges stands out from the Hexateuch books as having a different purpose, being cast as a homily; there is much direct translation but it is accompanied by a considerable volume of explication. Ælfric's letter to Wulfgeat and his *Libellus* were copied into L immediately after Judges, without breaks. It is thus likely that these three works were already collected in their own booklet, perhaps a volume dedicated to works by Ælfric.

The text of the Hexateuch (preceded by the *Prefatio* to Genesis) survives more or less complete only in L and B, which were apparently copied during the first and second halves of the eleventh century respectively. The two texts are sufficiently close to show that they derive from a common source, an archetype which may be labelled *LB*. The pattern of unique error in the two versions indicates that neither can have been copied, or directly derived from, the other.

Three eleventh-century fragments, P and N, both with parts of Exodus, and Ln, with parts of Numbers, are extant or, in the case of N, known by report. P and Ln are too different in their presentation to have belonged originally to a single volume. On the other hand, N, to judge from an estimate of the number of words carried by each page of the lost bifolium, could have been part of the same volume as P; this possibility is not contradicted by anything in its language (as known from Nicholson's list of readings), though this evidence does little more than confirm the relative linguistic, as well as textual, closeness of the members of the group BNPLn against L.[88] The possibility that N, P, and Ln belonged to manuscripts (whether two or three) of independently circulating parts of the *OEH* cannot be ruled out; Æthelweard presumably received his copies of Ælfric's Genesis and Joshua in discrete manuscripts, and we know from the evidence of the reported work of 'some other man' and from Co and O that later parts of Genesis had a separate circulation. However, the close textual affinities between each of the fragments and B makes it probable that they, too, come from Hexateuchs.

Co is a far more substantial manuscript witness. It transmits the last part of Genesis, the story of Joseph (Gen. 37–50), in a text which is clearly based on that of *LB*, but in a revised form. Another

[88] The comparative orthography and phonology of the manuscripts are discussed in vol. 2.

manuscript, O, catastrophically damaged by fire in the eighteenth century, likewise transmitted the last part of Genesis, in the same revised text which appears in Co, though with some significant variation.

Thus we know of a total of seven manuscripts with texts deriving from the archetype *LB*, belonging to seven original volumes or possibly only six, if N and P derive from the same one. There are sufficient agreements between the texts of CoO and B, even after revision, as well as those of PNLn and B, to show that all are textually closer to B than to L, and therefore that they are part of a group deriving from what we may label *B*, a line of transmission which diverged from *LB*. Thus, a curiosity of the extant manuscript record of the *OEH* is that L stands apart from all the other surviving witnesses, as sole evidence for a branch which we may label *L*; there is no indication that this led anywhere beyond L itself. There is evidence that L's text gives us, overall (but not consistently), a rather more accurate picture of the text of *LB* than B does, especially in the *Prefatio* and Genesis. This is despite the fact the L seems to have been copied later than B, and probably later than Co and O also. However, the imprecision of dating by palaeographical criteria allows for the possibility that the chronological distance between L and B was in fact quite small.

There is one further important manuscript, C, copied long after any of the others (in the later twelfth century), which transmits the *Prefatio* and the translation of Genesis up to 24:26, within a collection of other texts. There is good reason to identify this, not as a late copy of the version of the *Prefatio* and Genesis transmitted in the witnesses detailed above (i.e. derived from the *OEH* archetype *LB*), but as a late copy of the precursor of this version. Thus, C seems to bear witness, at some remove, to the oldest extant text associated with the *OEH*. This conclusion is bolstered by the fact that, even allowing for some evolution and much corruption consequent on many generations of copying, it presents a translation which is consistently close to the Vulgate, whereas, in the version in the compilation (i.e. *LB*, represented by L and B), three extended sections have been revised in ways which distance them from the Vulgate, even though their debt to the ancestor text of C (which we may label *C*) remains apparent (see below, pp. lxxxiv–xcvi). It thus seems logical to take the version of the early part of Genesis in C to be derived, albeit over a considerable period of time, from Ælfric's

original translation; the fact that, in the Cambridge manuscript, it is transmitted among what are mostly other Ælfrician works strengthens that case. The alternative explanation, that the text of Gen. 1–24:26 used in the compilation, witnessed now by L and B, with its three passages translated in a radically different way from the rest, was Ælfric's original translation, and that subsequently this was edited and revised, with 'back translation' of the three passages noted, is hardly credible.[89]

The fact that Ælfric states in the *Prefatio* that he has translated Genesis 'to Isaace Abrahames suna' may be taken as further corroboration of the status of C as giving us the nearest we have to Ælfric's text. That designation 'to Isaace Abrahames suna' is in fact far from precise. The climactic moment of Isaac's story is of course his father's willingness to sacrifice him, and any casual reference to Isaac as 'Abraham's son' automatically brings the incident first to mind, but that ends in Genesis 22, whereas at Gen. 24:26 we are midway through the narrative of the fetching of Rachel to be Isaac's wife. Thereafter, Isaac continues to feature quite prominently until Genesis 27 (in which, as an old man, he is deceived by Jacob), after which little is heard of him until his death in Genesis 35. Certainly 24:26 is a rather odd place to stop, and it could be that C gives us an incomplete version of Ælfric's Genesis, which might have gone originally as far as chapter 35. In the *Prefatio*, Ælfric tells his patron that he will translate no more of Genesis than up to Isaac, because, as noted above, someone else had translated the book for him 'from Isaac to the end' ('sum oðer man þe hæfde awend fram Isaace þa boc oþ ende'). The implication is that Æthelweard would now, with Ælfric's latest contribution, be in possession of a complete translation of Genesis. A logical way to interpret 'from Isaac', therefore, would be 'from the death of Isaac', and the existence of two witnesses (Co and O) to a discrete translation of 37:2–50:25, seems to confirm that natural break in the overall Genesis narrative. This, however, is a false trail, for the CoO version post-dates the version in the *OEH* (see pp. cxxxvi–clii). If the latter is indeed the 'other man's' work alluded to by Ælfric, there is no reason to assume that he, like the author of the revised version in CoO, did not start until 37:2. The Genesis text in LB after 24:26 is certainly not, on stylistic grounds, attributable to Ælfric. If there had indeed been an Ælfrician version which went beyond

[89] The authorship of the various parts of the *OEH* is discussed fully in vol. 2.

24:26, and perhaps as far as Genesis 35 or 36, and if the compiler had it, he must have decided not to use it. This certainly appears to be what happened in three extended passages in the earlier part of Genesis (discussed in the next section), the last of which in fact extends to Genesis 24; but in those passages the compiler's new version is distinct in its paraphrastic style, whereas his Gen. 24:60–36 is largely a close translation of the Vulgate (though in the earlier part of Genesis 25 and in Genesis 26 it is much curtailed). If Ælfric did indeed translate beyond 24:26 (and the oddity of breaking off at this point remains inescapable), perhaps as far as the death of Isaac, we might conjecture that an imperfect copy reached the *OEH* compiler, one ending at Genesis 24:26. This of course is where the copy in C ends, the (unremarkable) conclusion thus being that the C derives from the same incomplete copy of Ælfric's Gen. used by the compiler.[90]

As indicated above, neither the homiletic version of Judges, nor the *Libellus de ueteri testamento et nouo*, which (along with Ælfric's letter to Wulfgeat) are added to the translation of the Hexateuch in L only, seems to have been part of the original compilation. Each item is extant otherwise only in single copies, in both cases among collections of homiletic material. L thus represents a second phase of compilation, perhaps, as suggested, a 'one-off' product; there is no evidence that more copies of the whole extended compilation were ever made.

In the pages which follow, the evidence on which the above statements are based is presented and analysed, and the textual relationships between the manuscript witnesses are investigated. Although L and B are the most important of these, and this edition is based on their evidence, C, as a witness to the precursor of half of LB's Genesis text, has a logical claim to receive attention first.

2. THE TEXT OF C

Cambridge, University Library, Ii. 1. 33 is a composite manuscript of homiletic works mostly by Ælfric. It was copied late in the twelfth century, over a period of several decades, and the text of the *Prefatio* and Gen. 1–24:26, on ff. 2^r–24^v, was subject to contemporary

[90] Faced with the incomplete narrative in 24:15–26 (which ends with the marriage of Rachel and Isaac not actually accomplished, though it is clearly to happen), the compiler might be expected to eschew it for a brief summary.

emendation in two or more phases. Given that at least 150 years, and perhaps nearer 200, separate this copy from Ælfric's work of translation (done, in the estimation of Clemoes, between about 992 and 1002),[91] and that a considerable number of other copies may have intervened during the transmission process, it is not surprising that the text should have been subject to omissions, additions, and other corruptions. Evaluating these, and thus understanding the obscured textual relationship between C and LB, is difficult. Our only reference points are the Vulgate exemplar from which Ælfric translated, of which the textual details are of course unknown, and the derived versions of the translation in L and B themselves. But two points may be made. First, all the evidence we have suggests that Ælfric usually translated the Latin fully and closely;[92] second, except in the three anomalous passages discussed below, and in spite of its obvious defects, the coincidence of the text of C with that of LB remains remarkable, if phonological and orthographical developments are ignored.

The many corruptions in C's text may have been established cumulatively, unnoticed, over several or many generations of copying. On the other hand, the bulk of them could result from one particularly disastrous copying stint, perhaps the one which produced C itself; it is hard to see why copies would continue to be made if the text were not being read and, if this were indeed the case, it is likely that the most glaring of the problems would have been spotted and dealt with. There are errors of spelling throughout, such as *oðsloh* for *ofsloh* (4:23), *feofon* for *seofon* (5:25), *mætþum* for *mægþum* (10:20), and *him snipað* for *emsnidað* (17:11). Most striking is the number of omissions. The more substantial, involving whole phrases or clauses, occur at 1:7 (16 words), 2:3 (10 words), 2:5 (7 words), 2:20 (5 words), 4:5 (9 words), 4:7 (10 words), 7:24 (3 words), 11:3–4 (23 words), 11:27 (11 words), 13:10 (10 words), 13:14 (8 words), 14:12 (5 words), 14:13 (9 words), 17:8 (4 words), 18:31 (4 words), 18:32 (4 words).[93] Homoeoteleuton clearly explains the omissions in 1:7, 2:3, 2:20, 4:7, 11:3–4, and 11:27, which are disruptive. Curiously,

---

[91] 'The Chronology of Ælfric's Works', *Old English Newsletter*, Subsidia, 5 (Binghamton, NY, 1980), 34–5. Clemoes uses circumstantial and stylistic evidence to assign Genesis and Joshua to this period, with Numbers and Judges following in the period 1002–5.

[92] For an assessment of Ælfric's translation technique in Genesis, see R. Marsden, 'Ælfric as Translator: The Old English Prose Genesis', *Anglia*, 109 (1991), 319–58.

[93] The omissions in 4:7 and 11:3–4 and 27 are in sections in which the text of LB was substantially revised, and so the wording in C's original version may have varied.

however, none of the omissions from 13:10 to 18:32 substantially affects the integrity of the narrative, and a deliberate attempt to cut down the text might be suspected. Yet no consistent pattern of 'editing' is discernible in C's Genesis as a whole, and so these omissions were presumably accidental, too.

There are many further losses, of only one or two words, affecting the coherence of the narrative, such as those of *teon* in 1:20, *fultum* in 2:20, *heortena* in 6:5, *and seofen* in 7:2, *se eard* in 13:10, *bæftan* in 16:13, *gingran* in 19:31, and *lecgan* in 21:7. However, some fifty other small omissions in C (in relation to LB) create no obvious problems and there is thus no way of knowing whether they are in fact omissions from C or amplifications in LB; it is probable that both processes are represented. No useful comparison with the Vulgate text can be made in most cases (not least because more than half of the occurrences are in paraphrased clauses), but there are a few exceptions. In the following examples, the given words, which are in LB but are omitted from C, do have equivalents in the Vulgate, and so there is a good case for assuming that LB accurately preserves Ælfric's translation.

1:21	god (Lat. *Deus*)
8:8	eft (Lat. *post eum*)
8:11	to noe (Lat. *ad eum*)
12:1	ða (Lat. *autem*)
13:12	soðlice (Lat. *uero*)
13:16	eac swilce (Lat. *quoque*)
19:16	hand (Lat. *manum*)
20:5	and (Lat. *et*)

As well as the very many omissions, there are some additions and amplifications in C, in relation to the text of LB. A few are clearly erroneous. Examples are:

6:3	gast] þæt his min yrre *add.* (*with h erased*)[94]
9:23	on hira sculdra (heora sculdrum B)] ofer him and ofer his sculdra (Lat. *humeris suis*)
14:21	þæt he hæfde eall þæt] hee hefde þæt *add.*

Most of the amplifications in C are unexceptional, however. Examples are:

---

[94] This peculiar addition may be the remnant of an annotation or gloss.

1:12   gehwilc] an gehwylc
3:22   nu] efne nu
13:9   færst] fram me *add.*
13:15 on ecnisse] Amen *add.*
15:5   locian] up *add.*
18:24 forweorðan] forspillan and forweorþan
18:31 rihtwisra] manna *add.*
18:32 yrsige] wið me *add.*
22:5   wile] þæt *add.*

How many of these were in Ælfric's original text but were dropped during transmission to LB, and how many were originally absent but were added during that transmission, it is impossible to say. The addition of *amen* in 13:15, after *on ecnisse*, looks very like the reflex of a scribe familiar with the liturgy, or at least some prayers, in the vernacular. The expanded translation of Lat. *peribunt* with a doublet of verbs in 18:24—'forspillan and forweorþan' for L's simple 'forweorðan (forwurþan B)'—is characteristic of Ælfric's style, but also that of other homilists.[95]

In a section of C which is not rendered in LB, Crawford identified a problem of what he thought was accidental transposition. A sentence based on the Vulgate of 10:7 ('Chuses suna Remgma gestrynde .ii. sunu Sabba and Dadan'), is placed after 10:12, and Crawford moved it back in his edition. However, in its manuscript position, the sentence comes before a modified OE version of 10:13 ('Mesraim Cames oþer sunu'), and this suggests that the repositioning was intentional: Cham's son Chus had these two sons, and Cham's other son Mesraim had these. 'Correction' thus seems inappropriate.

As well as addition and loss, and occasional muddle, there is a certain amount of further textual variation between LB and C, where both variants are appropriate and often are simply synonyms. Examples are the following; here, and in the following two lists, LB's reading is given first:

19:3 (*interp.*)   swa] swiþe
9:27   gemenigfilde] tobrede
12:5, 13:1–5   comon] becomon
12:19   intingan] þingum (Lat. *causam*)
13:6   ætgædere] togadere

[95] The verb *forspillan* was highlighted by Clemoes, *Illustrated Hexateuch*, 45, as a 'non-Ælfrician' word. It is used in Exod. 12:13, Lev. 26:22, and Deut. 9:26.

13:7	intingan] þingan (þing *app. on eras.*, intinga *in margin*)
13:16	geriman] ariman (*twice*)
18:16	wera] manna
19:37	oð] on (Lat. *in*)
20:13	ferdon] foran
21:5	hundwintre] hund wintra eald
21:30	pytt] wæterpytt
22:13	lace] ansægednysse

It is easy to see how, perhaps at the compilation stage, a copyist might substitute words or idioms which he was more accustomed to use. *þing* in the sense of 'cause', as in 12:19, is much favoured by Ælfric in his works. The contemporary marginal addition of *intinga* in 13:7 raises the question of whether the text of C was revised, using another exemplar. Because 13:7 is paraphrased, there is no direct Latin equivalent for OE *intingan/þingan*, but *intinga* has been used, as we have seen, in 12:19, and this could have prompted the marginal addition.

In a handful of cases, LB have an OE version which is more faithful to the Vulgate than that in C:

1:11	æppelbære treow] æppeltreow (Lat. *lignum pomiferum*)
3:21	eac] þa (Lat. *quoque*)
7:19	ealre] þære (Lat. *uniuerso*)
13:7	wunedon] wære (wunedon *add. above*) (Lat. *habitabant*)
13:11	his breðer] oðer (Lat. *a fratre suo*)

In these cases, LB's version is likely to be the original one, which has been modified in transmission to C.

Elsewhere, however, and more often, it is C which has the closer translation, as in these examples:

2:17	on swa hwylcum dæge] for þan on hwilcum dæge (Lat. *in quocumque enim die*)
3:19	to duste wyr[þ]st (gewyr[þ]st B)] to duste gewendst (Lat. *in puluerem reuerteris*)
9:24	awoc of þam slæpe] awoc on þam wine (Lat. *euigilans . . . ex uino*)

The change of nouns in 9:24 is especially notable, but the process by which *slæpe* might be substituted for *wine*, perhaps unconsciously,

simply because it was logical, is straightforward; this is one of the archetypal *LB* errors (see below). It is curious that both L and B appear to have an error in the writing of the second-person singular form of *weorþan*; *(ge)wyrst* it is not a verbal form recorded anywhere else in the *OE Corpus* (except once as an error for *wyrcst*).

There are further cases where amplifications in LB's version leave C closer to the Vulgate. They include 'hungergear' for 'hunger' (12:10; Lat. *fames*), 'on þære birig sodoma' for 'on sodoma' (13:12; Lat. *in Sodomis*) and 'on ærne mergen' for 'on morgen' (21:14), the addition of 'geond eall' (13:10), 'on eornoste' (14:15), and 'furðon' (14:23), and the explanatory addition of 'for þan þe god him arode' (19:17). The sort of glossing seen in the latter is done by Ælfric occasionally, and this might be a case, not of amplification in LB, but of loss from C. In 3:10, LB add *leof*, echoing an Old Latin variant addition, *domine*, which is used by several patristic writers but is not in any of the collated Vulgate manuscripts. We cannot know whether Ælfric used *domine*, after which it was lost in transmission to C, or whether it was a spontaneous addition to the LB tradition. Omissions from LB of words with Vulgate equivalents include *ac* (15:11; Lat. *et*), *þa* (17:19; Lat. *et*), and *twa* (19:15; Lat. *duas*).

Some variations between C and LB are particularly hard to assess. In the following, neither version follows the Vulgate's order of elements:

12:16 *oues et boues et asini et serui et famulae et asinae et cameli*[96]
LB   on orfe and on þeowum on olfendum and on assum
C   on orfe and on olfendum and on assun and on þeowum

The two versions seem to be interdependent, for they have the same reduction of the diffuse Latin sentence, whose distinction between the sexes, as far as both asses and servants are concerned, has been eliminated. LB's version remains more faithful to the Vulgate, inasmuch as it puts the servants next to the cattle and before the camels. But it is notable how the metrical possibilities of the alliterating nouns are optimized in C. This rearrangement could have been made at any time during transmission, but it does suggest Ælfrician style, in which case C's version is original and LB's is a modification, either accidental or deliberately made by reference to a Latin text.

[96] '(And he had) sheep and oxen and he-asses, and male servants and female servants, and she-asses and camels.'

The latter possibility raises the whole question of whether the text of the archetype of LB was revised at the time of the compilation of the *OEH* by reference to the Vulgate. This is considered again below in a discussion of the much-modified portions of LB. Here it will be sufficient to ask whether there is any persistent evidence for such revision in the bulk of LB's text of Genesis 1–24:26. If C as we have it were a faithful reproduction of Ælfric's original translation, and the only version of it available to the *OEH* compiler, then clearly revision with reference to a Latin text would have been inevitable, if only to make good some obvious losses. However, with such a long period intervening between Ælfric's work of translation and the copy we have in C, the differences between LB and C, both where LB supplies text absent from C and where its version appears to be closer to the Vulgate than that of C, can be explained easily enough, not as evidence of gain by LB with reference to the Latin, but as loss from C in the copying generations after its ancestor text separated from that which led to *LB*. Thus, for example, the best explanation for LB's *æppelbære treow* in 1:11 (see the above list), which clearly translates Lat. *lignum pomiferum* more closely than C's *æppeltreow*, is that *æppelbære treow* was indeed Ælfric's translation but that it became abbreviated during copying. We would need many more examples of closer LB readings before we could make a good case for deliberate revision. Closeness to the Latin is a hallmark of Ælfric's Genesis, as is especially notable in the passages discussed below, where LB's version differs substantially from his. However, even Ælfric did not maintain total fidelity, and thus there can be no complete certainty on this issue.[97]

An interesting disparity between the versions occurs in 12:15. The context is the observation by the Egyptians of the attractiveness of Sarah, newly arrived with Abraham:

Vulgate	C	LB
et nuntiauerunt principes Pharoni et laudauerunt eam apud illum / et sublata est mulier in domum Pharonis	and þas cynges ealdormen spræcon be hure wlite to þam. cynge farao. and gelæddon hi beforan him	and þæs cininges ealdormen spræcon be hire wlite to þam cininge farao. and heredon hig beforan him. þæt wif wearþ þa læht and gelæd to þam cininge

---

[97] See Marsden, 'Ælfric as Translator', especially pp. 333–40.

In the first part of the passage, LB and C share an amplified version of the Latin *nuntiauerunt* (picking up the theme of Sarah's attractiveness from the previous verse). C's version of the rest of the passage, however, is much reduced by omission of half of the information (*laudauerunt eam*), though the result is perfectly adequate, as the praising of Sarah has already been implied. Conceivably, this is how Ælfric rendered the text; but in that case, the version in LB could only have been produced by retranslation after independent consultation of a Vulgate text, where the missed *et laudauerunt eam apud illum* would have been found. In fact, however, it seems unlikely that Ælfric would have omitted to translate this clause, in an otherwise full rendering of the narrative. LB's version may thus be a faithful reproduction of that of Ælfric, in which it will be noted that the use of the passive in the last clause is close to the Vulgate. One way to account for C's version, if we accept LB's as the original one, is by assuming a deliberate summarizing reduction at some stage in transmission to C. The alliterating doublet of past participles in the longer LB version, *læht and gelæd* (*gelæht and gelædd* B), looks at first sight rather like an Ælfrician touch. However, the participles are not by any means synonyms, and *læht* ('seized') is a dramatic amplification not authorized by the Vulgate text. Thus, embellishment by the *OEH* compiler seems the more likely explanation. It is entirely possible that a Latin text was indeed consulted by the compiler when preparing his Genesis text, but clearly, if it were used, it was in an oddly selective manner; Ælfric's paraphrase of the opening part of the above passage has not been emended.

This same reservation applies to the few other cases (such as the variation in word order in 12:16, noted above) where one explanation for the differences between LB and C versions could be revision of LB against a Latin text. Such revision is not precluded, and we can scarcely doubt that any monastery where work on the *OEH* was being done would have possessed a complete Vulgate, or at the very least part-Bibles of the most important Old Textament books.[98] Yet it would be strange for minor concessions to the Latin to be made but no overall attempt to bring the Old English into line with it.

[98] On the form in which biblical texts circulated in Anglo-Saxon England, see R. Marsden, *The Text of the Old Testament in Anglo-Saxon England*, Cambridge Studies in Anglo-Saxon England, 15 (Cambridge, 1995), 39–49.

LC *and* BC *variants*

As well as the many differences which have been highlighted between LB on the one hand and C on the other, there are some readings shared by L and C but not B, and others shared by B and C but not L. These may be of significance in establishing the relative distance of L and B from C and from each other. Overt copying errors are excluded from the following discussion; clearly, for instance, B's *gehyrdes* in 3:17, where LC correctly have *gehirdest*, tells us something about the work of B's scribe (or that of the copyist responsible for his exemplar) but nothing reliable about textual relationships. Assessment of the readings is, as always, complicated by the lateness and relatively poor quality of C's text, but there seems no reason to question the fundamental integrity of C as a transmitter of Ælfric's original translation.

In the *Prefatio* and in Gen. 1–24:26, correspondences between L and C are more frequent than between B and C, in the proportion two to one, an assessment based on about 110 variants. Gen. 3:20–5:12 cannot be included in the comparison, owing to the loss of a leaf from L. Even where a variant text 'makes sense', there is no way of distinguishing between deliberate variation and accidental alteration. Many of the variations involve very small matters, such as the use or otherwise of a conjunction or a verbal prefix, and they could have become established casually at any and every stage of transmission. Other variants are rather more 'positive', in the sense that they are more likely to have been chosen than to have occurred accidentally.

In the following representative cases, the readings in LC are clearly more faithful to the Vulgate than those in B; in each case, B offers slight modifications (mostly amplifications), which might have been made unconsciously:

2:2	weorce LC	weorcum B	Lat. *opere*
2:23	þeos bið geciged LC	beo heo geciged B	Lat. *haec uocabitur*
2:23	of were genumen LC	of hyre were genumen B	Lat. *de uiro sumpta est*
8:12	seo ne gecirde LC	swa heo ne gecyrde B	Lat. *quae non est reuersa*
9:6	mannes blod LC	ðæs mannes blod B	Lat. *humanum sanguinem*
19:2	nateshwon LC	nelle we nateshwon B	Lat. *minime*

LC/B variations in the *Prefatio*, which has no Latin source, and those in paraphrased or amplified passages of Genesis, cannot be compared to a Latin model. They include:

Pref. 75	leohtlicum LC	leohtum B
Pref. 84	god bebead LC	seo æ bebead B
Pref. 114	to urum LC	on urum B
Pref. 122	woh gerihtan LC	gewrit gerihtan B
1:12	forþ ateah LC	forð teah B
6:2	þa þe (þa ða C) LC	ðe B
12:4	bebead (bebiæd C) LC	bead B
15:15	se (þe C) tima LC	ðin tima B
17:3	cwæþ to LC	to cwæð B
18:33	ferde þa LC	þa ferde B
20:5	cwæð sylf LC	sylf cwæð B
20:15	ætforan LC	beforan B

As noted, overall instances where BC share a variant which is not in L are 50 per cent fewer. They include:

1:24	gedon BC	geworden L	
3:11	ne ete BC	of ne ete L	Lat. *de quo . . . ne comederes*
6:5	awend BC	gewend L	
6:6	man BC	mannan L	
9:23	his næcednysse BC	heora fæder nacednisse L	Lat. *uerenda patris sui*
9:25	chanaan BC	cham L	Lat. *Chanaan*
12:18	swa wið me BC	wið me swa L	
18:9	þin wif sarra BC	sarra þin wif L	

There are three instances in the *OEH*, as here in 6:6, where L prefers the weak form of *mann* and C the strong form; in the two others (in the *Prefatio* and Gen. 20:4), unlike here, B shares L's weak form.[99] In 9:25, though *cham* for *chanaan* may have been written in error, it is not wrong, as 'Chanaan' describes the stock of 'Ham' and the substitution occurs occasionally in Vulgate manuscripts also. In 9:23, it is L which transmits the more faithful version of the Latin (*patris sui*); copyists in the lines of transmission to C and B might well have adopted the perfectly reasonable substitution of *his* for

---

[99] Ælfric frequently uses the weak form, as well as the strong, in his writings.

heora fæder independently. Overall, the differences are minor, and many of them probably arose as simple errors in L or in a predecessor of L; others may have arisen as a result of coincidental changes in B and C.

On the evidence of these two groups of variants, and following the assumption that the archetype of LB was based on a text of Ælfric's Genesis much younger than the defective version in C, we are bound to identify L's text as nearer to that archetype than the text of B, in this opening part of the *OEH* (i.e. Gen. 1–24:26). If we were to restrict our analysis to just the *Prefatio* and Genesis 1–4, L's dominance over B would be by a ratio of more than three to one. Fewer differences are to be seen the later chapters, however. The lowest number is in Genesis 16–22, though even here a slightly higher rate of LC correspondences is apparent. Nevertheless, given the number of readings in which C agrees with neither L nor B (see above, *passim*), many of which are likely to have become established in C arbitrarily over several copying generations, it must be probable that some at least of the LC and BC coincidences arose by chance.

Rubrics

C lacks the rubrics which are in L before 5:32 ('Her swutelað þas ælmihtigan Godes mildheortnisse and his wundru hu he Noe bearh and his wife and his teame æt þam miclan flode') and in LB before Gen. 12:1 ('Her swutelað þas ælmihtigan Godes mildheortnysse and his wundru hu he Abraham geceas and his bletsunga him sealde and his ofspringe'). These appear to be the work of the *OEH* compiler in a move to give some useful structure to the Genesis narrative; a similar rubric precedes Gen. 37:2 in L, B, Co, and O ('Her cydde God ælmihtig his mildheortnysse þe he Abrahame behet on Iosepe Abrahames ofspringe'). The absence from B of the rubric before 5:32 is presumably owing to accidental loss in the process of transmission.

3. The Sections of Genesis Revised in LB

In most of Genesis, our three main witnesses, L, B, and C, transmit the same OE text, with the sort of mainly minor differences which are consistent with normal copying variation. There are three passages, however, in which LB and C diverge considerably:

(a) 4:1–5:31
(b) 10:1–11:32
(c) 22:20–24:26

The identification of the extent of passage (a) given here differs slightly from that made by Crawford, who has it finishing at 5:32. It is more likely, in fact, that 5:32 marks the return to a shared text, not least because, as noted above, in L (but not in B, which is thus defective in this respect) a new section of the narrative is signalled here (i.e. before 5:32, not after it) by a rubric. The only textual difference between L and C in 5:32 is a minor syntactical one, consistent with normal variation between the two versions:

L Noe soðlice ða ða he wæs fif hund geara þa gestrinde he þri suna

C Noe soðlice ða ða he wæs v. hund geare eald þa gestrinde he þri sunus

B is defective in this passage, with *ða ða he* omitted.

In general, C's version of the rendered text in the sections under review is much fuller than that in LB. Moreover, in each section there are long passages which are retained in C but are not rendered at all in LB, namely, (a) 4:23–4 and 5:1–4; (b) 10:3–31 and 11:10–26; and (c) 22:20–4, 23:14–15, and 24:11–14, 16–26. In section (c), C's version of 22:20–4 is in fact just a twenty-four-word summary, which rounds off the preceding narrative by noting that twelve sons were born to Abraham's brother Nachor and that their names may be read 'on þære ledenrace'. Presumably, the *OEH* compiler considered this summary to be unnecessary. In chapter 24, C translates vv. 1–26, though with abbreviation in vv. 16–26, and this is where its version of Genesis ends, in the middle of the story of how Abraham's servant goes to fetch Rebecca for Isaac. LB has a full translation only as far as v. 10; it omits vv. 11–14 and then gives what is in effect a summary, in thirty-four words, of parts of vv. 15–26, telling the interested reader that further information may be found 'on þære ledenbec'. LB has no version of the subsequent thirty-four verses (24:27–60), but restarts its narrative at 24:61.

Several questions arise in connection with these three distinct sections of translation. Why are these particular passages treated differently in the two textual traditions? Are the large gaps in LB's version the result of deliberate editing? Do the two traditions still derive from a common original, or has there been retranslation from a Latin source for the later one (i.e. LB)? It will be convenient to treat the sections separately.

(a) Genesis 4–5

In this section, the most fully rendered of the three in LB, C's approximately 980 words are reduced to about 780 in B. The opening lines of Genesis 4 will serve to illustrate the sorts of differences characteristic of each of the sections under review. Capitalization and punctuation of the OE texts are given as in the manuscripts; L is absent here (the leaf bearing 3:20–5:12 having been lost), but there is no reason to doubt that it carried substantially the same text as B.

Vulgate	C	(L)B
Adam uero cognouit Heuam uxorem suam / quae concepit et peperit Cain dicens / possedi hominem per dominum / rursusque peperit fratrem eius Abel / fuit autem Abel pastor ouium et Cain agricola / factum est autem post multum dies / ut offeret Cain de fructibus terrae munera domino	Adam soðlice æfter þisum breac his wiues and heo eacnode and acende cain and cwæð. Ic æfde mannan þurh god. Eft heo acende his broðor abæl. Abel wæs þa sciephirde and Cain hirðling. Hit wæs þa æfter manegum dagum þæt Caim ofrode gode lac of þare eorþ an wæstmum	Soðlice adam gestrynde cain be euan his gemæccan. and ðus cwæð. ðisne man me sealde drihten. Eft he gestrynde abel. abel wæs sceaphyrde. and cain eorðtilia. Ða wæs hit geworden æfter manegum dagum ðæt cain brohte drihtne lac of eorðan tilingum

C always follows closely the Vulgate, with only the filler adverbial phrase *æfter þisum* added and two small syntactical changes made (i.e. the subordinate clause beginning *quae concepit* replaced by the coordinated *and heo eacnode*, and *dicens* rendered by *and cwæð*; both changes accord with Ælfric's translation style). B's version conveys the same information as C's in these verses but uses paraphrase in four of the five main statements; the exception is the one about the occupations of Cain and Abel, which it would be hard to paraphrase. There has been some abbreviation of the narrative, from forty-eight words in C to forty-one in B, but this does not seem to be the only motive of B's reviser; there is an apparent desire to do it differently. Perhaps 'ðisne man me sealde drihten' has more clarity

than the literal (yet scarcely obscure) 'ic æfde mannan þurh god', but no such logic can be claimed for the other changes. Where C, with the Vulgate, has Eve 'bearing' sons, B has Adam 'begetting' them, and where C has Cain 'offering' a sacrifice, in B he 'brings' it. Synonymous (or near-synonymous) alternative vocabulary is frequently used in B, not only in this passage but throughout the section. Examples are:

4:1	wiues C	gemæccan B	Lat. *uxor*
4:2	hirðling C	eorðtilia B	Lat. *agricola*
4:11	underfeng C	onfeng B	Lat. *suscepit*
4:25	gecigde C	nemde B	Lat. *uocauit*

Two of B's words may be said to be 'non-Ælfrician'; Ælfric never uses *eorðtilia* in his works (though the word is rare anyway), and *gemæcca* appears only three times. Change for change's sake seems to have been made by the reviser also in 4:5 and 4:8. In the former, B's 'wearð . . . yrre' is substituted for C's 'hirsode' (Lat. *iratus . . . est*), but in the latter, B uses 'yrsode . . . wið' for C's 'aras togeanes' (Lat. *consurrexit . . . aduersus*). In 4:5 and 6, B eschews the Vulgate's 'falling face' idiom altogether.[100]

Apparent anomalies in this relationship between the two versions can usually be explained in terms of corruption of the late copy in C. There is an example in 4:7:

Vulgate	C	(L)B
nonne si bene egeris recipies / sin autem male statim in foribus peccatum aderit / sed sub te erit appetitus eius et tu dominaberis illius	gif þu ðonne yfel dest. þærrihte bið þeo syn æt þam ingange. ac his gewilnung bið under þe and þu wylst hine	Gyf ðu god dest hit ðe bið mid gode forgolden. Gyf ðu ðonne yfel dest sona hit byð ðe mid yfele forgolden

Given the fidelity of the rest of C's version of this passage to the Latin, it need not be doubted that the first 'gyf þu' clause in B, i.e. the rendering of *nonne si bene egeris recipies*, was originally in Ælfric's translation also but became lost in transmission to C, by simple homoeoteleuton. B's version is a rather inadequate paraphrase, for in

---

[100] E.g. Gen. 4:5 *iratusque est Cain uehementer et concidit uultus eius*: C 'þa hirsode Caim þearle and his nebwlite ætfeol'; B 'þa wearð cain ungemetlice yrre'.

its rendering of the second Latin colon, it fails to convey the point that evil is not simply requited with evil but begets even more evil; and it omits the important positive corollary in the third colon.

B makes subsequent omissions in the section under discussion. The first is of 4:23–4, an obvious passage for deletion, given the obscurity of its content, an allusion by Lamech to his killing of a man. The omission of 5:1–4 is again justifiable, as the passage consists of repetitive references to Adam and his descendants. Thereafter, B's version is full but still consistently paraphrased. Notably, the expansive Vulgate formula for announcing the age and then death of each of Adam's descendants in turn is given literally in C but more directly and succinctly in B. Thus, in 5:20:

Vulgate	C	(L)B
et facti sunt omnes dies Iared nongenti sexaginta duo anni et mortuus est	wæron þa gewordene ealle iaredes dagas .ix. hund geara 'and' twa and syxti and he forðferde	and he forðferde ða he wæs nigonhundwintre and fif and sixtigwintre

There is a further apparent anomaly in 4:16:

Vulgate	C	(L)B
egressusque Cain a facie domini habitauit profugus in terra ad orientalem plagam Eden	Cain ferde þa fram godes ansine to eastdæle. and wunede flyma on þam lande. Eden	Cain eode fram drihtnes ansyne. and he wunode flyma on ðam eastdæle ðæs landes. ðe is genemned eden

Strictly speaking, C's version is incorrect, for it seems to imply that Cain will live as a fugitive *in* Eden. Jerome's Latin is ambiguous, though he was certainly trying to convey the sense of the Hebrew here, which is that Cain flees to a place 'east of Eden', i.e. outside Eden in an easterly direction.[101] It is curious that *to eastdæle* has been put so early in the sentence, and it may be that there has been some corruption in this passage during transmission to C. But the important question here is whether B's version could be derived

---

[101] The Douay translators of the Vulgate faithfully (if perhaps unintentionally) retain the ambiguity: 'And Cain went forth from the face of the Lord and dwelt as a fugitive on the earth, at the east side of Eden.'

from C's or must have been made with reference back to the Latin text. It will be noted, first, that B's version commits the same error as C's, for it too implies that Cain will be a fugitive *in* (the eastern part of) Eden. Furthermore, in its use of both *wunode flyma* and *eastdæle*, it closely echoes C. Only in its collocation of *eastdæle* and *lande* does B seem to be nearer to the Vulgate. The error in the location of the exile could have been made by the two translators independently, but on balance it seems likely that B's version is a paraphrase and rationalization of C's (which, as already suggested, may have been in a slightly different form originally), complete with explanatory amplification before *Eden*. This does not rule out the possibility that the compiler did look back at the Vulgate text of this rather awkward passage. If this were the case, however, his diligence still did not keep him from error.

There are four occasions in section (a) where B's version uses the adverb *witodlice*, apparently translating a Latin adverb or conjunction, where C is without. In 4:17 and 5:15, the Latin has *autem*, in 4:11, *igitur*, and in 4:13, simply *-que*. Again, there is probably no need to posit reference to a Vulgate text here; it is hard to see why such minor emendation would be the result. The reviser may have had a predilection for *witodlice*, or C may have lost one or more adverbs in these positions. It should be noted that, in 4:19, B has *witodlice*, where it is inappropriate in respect of the Vulgate, whose syntax C reproduces exactly; and in 5:21, C has *witodlice* for Latin *porro*, where LB have nothing.

A more puzzling passage is 4:20–1, where B's version is confused:

Vulgate	C	(L)B
genuit Ada Iabel	þa acende ada iabel	be adan. he
qui fuit pater	þe wæs fæder þare	gestrynde iabal. and
habitantium in	þe wunedon on	iubal. and iubal wæs
tentoriis atque	geteldum. and hirda	hyrda fæder. and
pastorum / et	his broþor hatte	þara manna ðe on
nomen fratris eius	iubal þe wæs fæder	geteldum wunedon.
Iubal ipse fuit pater	hea'r'pera and þæra	and sangera fæder.
canentium cithara et	þe organan macodan	and hearpera. and
organo		organystra

C is accurate, except for the unexpected use of the verb *macodan*, and sufficient of its wording recurs to make it the likely basis of B's version. However, in its use of *sangera*, B must have taken its cue

from Lat. *canentium*—unless this word (or perhaps a form of the related verb) was in *C* originally but became lost. If the reviser did make reference to the Vulgate, however, he misunderstood the verbal function of *canentium*: it is not singers who are being described but those who 'sing' upon instruments, i.e. 'make music' upon them. Yet the earlier parallel phrase *habitantium in tentoris* should have alerted a competent translator to the meaning. The explanation for B's version, then, seems to be either the use of a defective *C* text or partial, and ineffective, recourse to the Vulgate.

Twice, in 5:7 and 20, the reviser (or possibly an early copyist of his text) has made errors in rendering complex numbers, though they are correct in C. These are dealt with, along with a handful of other such errors in the three sections, in discussions of archetypal errors below (pp. c–cxiii).

(b) Genesis 10–11

This is the most abbreviated of the sections in LB, with C's approximately 800 words reduced to about 290, owing largely to the omission of two big sections in LB, namely 10:3–31 and 11:10–26, both of which consist of genealogies. Although the 'joins' in LB's truncated version are not always smooth, there is no serious narrative disruption. Elsewhere in the section, LB's version is fairly full, although there is some reduction in 10:6–9. As in section (a), so in this one, LB consistently provide a paraphrased version of material which is translated closely in C.

This section is notable for anomalies which appear at first reading to disrupt the general pattern of revision. In three passages, it is LB which have the fuller text and follow more closely the Vulgate. However, in the first two cases, the omissions in C of twenty-two words in 11:3–4 ('uton wyrcean . . . and cwædon', in LB's version) and eleven words in 11:27 ('ðis ys thares . . . and nachor and aran') are easily explicable. In 11:3–4, Lat. *uenite faciamus* occurs twice and will certainly have been rendered originally both times by Ælfric as 'cumað and utan wircan', but the eye of the copyist of C (or of an ancestor manuscript) slipped straight to the second.[102] Similarly, the long omission in C from 11:27, ending with 'and nachor and aran', can be explained as eyeslip from the end of 11:26 (not rendered in LB), which also ends with 'and nachor and aran'. It is quite possible,

---

[102] In the *LB* tradition, this is less likely to have happened, for the reviser has varied his translation: first *uton wircean* but then *uton timbrian*.

however, that these words were omitted deliberately. Whatever the case, C's rendering of the next sentence, Lat. *porro Aran genuit Lot*, without the adverb ('se Aran gestrinde Lot'), is not surprising; LB, which has no immediately preceding reference to Aran, retains it ('Witodlice aran gestrinde loth').

The case of 11:28–31, the passage immediately following the one just discussed, is trickier. The Latin and the two OE versions are here given in full. Where C or LB are notably closer to the Vulgate, the relevant words are underlined; error is indicated by italics.

Vulgate	C	LB
²⁸ mortuusque est Aran ante Thare patrem suam in terra nauitatis suae in Ur Chaldeorum /	²⁸ and <u>he wæs dead</u> ær his fæder *fære* <u>on þam lande his acennednyss on þære chaldeiscre hur.</u>	²⁸ aran forðferde ær þonne <u>thare</u> his fæder <u>on ur chaldea.</u>
²⁹ duxerunt autem Abram et Nachor uxores / nomen uxoris Abram Sarai et nomen uxoris Nachor Melcha filia Aran patris Melchae et patris Ieschae /	²⁹ Abram þa and nachor wifedon. Abrames wif hatte Sarai. and nachores wif <u>hatte</u> Melcha. <u>aranes dohter. and hire swister hatte iesah.</u>	²⁹ Soðlice abram. and nachor. wifudun. Abrames wif hatte sarai. and nachores wif melcha.
³⁰ erat autem Sarai sterilis nec habebat liberos / ³¹ tulit itaque Thare Abram filium suum et Lot filium Aran filium filii sui / et Sarai nurum suam uxorem Abram filii sui /	³⁰ Abrames wif sarai was untumende. ³¹ Hwæt þa Thare genam *his tweigen sunu mid heora twam wifum.* and Loth his sune suna	³⁰ Sarai wæs untymende <u>næfde heo nan bearn.</u> ³¹ Witodlice thare nam <u>abram. his sunu</u> and loth his suna sunu
et eduxit eos de Ur Chaldeorum ut irent in terram Chanaan / ueneruntque usque Haran et habitauerunt ibi	and gelædde hig of þare chaldeisre hur to þam lande *Aran* and hig wunedon þa on Aran	and gelædde hig <u>on</u> <u>ur chaldea.</u> þæt hig ferdon to chanaan lande. <u>hig foron oð hig comon to aran.</u> and hig wunedon þær

To a large extent, in 11:28–9, C continues to present a close translation: typically, it is fuller than that in LB, including a translation of *in terra nauitatis suae*, and the information that Melcha is Aran's daughter and has a sister (though this reference is paraphrased); these details are omitted from LB's account. The rendering of *mortuusque est* by the very literal 'and he wæs dead' is also characteristic of C. In their repetition (from the previous sentence) of *Aran*, on the other hand, LB are closer to the Latin. This appears to be the case also in their 'ær þonne thare his fæder' for Lat. *ante Thare patrem suam*, but it is almost certain that, in C's 'ær his fæder fære' (which might be interpreted as 'before his father's journey/death'), *fære* is simply a corruption of *Thare*. Only in LB's rendering of *in Ur Chaldeorum* ('in Ur of the Chaldeans') in 11:28 (and also in 11:31) by 'on ur chaldea', where C conveys the ethnic identity of the city with an adjective, 'on þære chaldeiscre hur', do we see in LB the sort of literalism which we usually associate with C.

It is in 11:30–1 where we find a consistently closer, and more accurate, version in LB, rather than C. First, C amplifies simple 'Sarah' to 'Abrames wif sarai'; it then omits a translation of *nec habebat liberos* (though it is no surprise that this redundant statement should have been dropped). Next, in place of the simple statement that Terah took Abraham, his son, there is a curious addition of spurious detail, namely, that Terah took his two sons plus Lot. As the Vulgate makes quite clear, there was only one son on the journey: 'and Terah took Abraham his son, and Lot the son of Aran, [that is,] his son's son'. The passage appears to have been reworked by some one using the information about Terah's second son Nachor and his wife, which was given (in C only) in 11:29, and making the assumption that they, too, were part of the group; but this is incorrect, as an understanding of the whole episode will make clear. It is hard to believe that Ælfric would have made this error, and LB's version is thus likely to represent his translation, more or less. The best explanation for C's version is that a copyist, at some stage in transmission, tried to improve a corrupt text, in which the triple use of 'son' may have caused confusion. The probability of such corruption is strengthened by the accumulation of other errors in this part of the chapter—homoeoteleuton in the sentence immediately preceding the passage cited, *fære* for *thare* in 11:28, and *Aran* for *Chanaan* in 11:31. It seems unlikely that the LB reviser

RELATIONSHIPS BETWEEN THE MANUSCRIPTS xciii

had recourse to a Vulgate text here; if so, it would be odd that he did not provide a translation of the clarifying colon following the corrupt one (*et Sarai nurum suam uxorem Abram filii sui*), which is absent from both OE versions. But in the rest of 11:31, LB again give us a fairly close rendering of the Latin (though *ueneruntque* is amplified into a clause with two verbs), whereas C abbreviates, in the way that LB normally does. Whatever the explanation for this anomalous passage (11:28–31), it may be noted that, in 11:32, in which Tara's age at death is recorded, LB reverts to its usual habit of paraphrasing the literal rendering in C (see above).

As in section (a), so also in (b) there are many changes in vocabulary. Notable are:

11:4	burh C	ceastre LB	Lat. *ciuitatem*
11:4	mærsian C	wyrðian LB	Lat. *celebremus*
11:6	gereord C	leden LB	Lat. *labium*
	ongunnon C	begunnon LB	Lat. *coeperunt*
11:7	towendon C	todælan LB	Lat. *confundamus*
	gereord C	spræce LB	Lat. *linguam*
11:9	burh C	stowe LB	(*no Latin*)

While in 11:4, LB use *ceastre* (a word which Ælfric uses rarely) for C's *burh*, in 11:5, both versions have *burh* (Lat. *ciuitas*).

(c) Gen. 22:20–24:22

C's version of this section of about 865 words is reduced in LB to about 475 words. The main omissions are 22:20–4 (which even in C is a summary), 23:4, 14–15, and 18, and 24:11–14. Only a brief paraphrase of 24:15–26 is given, and other verses are much condensed, such as 23:5–6 and 11–13, and 24:7 and 8. The remaining material in LB is clearly based on that of C, as is especially obvious in 23:1–3, 9, 16, 19–20, 24:1–2, 5–6, 9–10. A comparison of the versions of 23:1–3 illustrates this:

Vulgate	C	LB
uixit autem Sara centum uiginti septem annis / et mortua est in ciuitate Arbee quae est Hebron in terra Chanaan / uenitque Abraham ut plangeret et fleret eam / cumque surrexisset ab officio funeris / locutus est ad filios Heth dicens	Sarra soðlice lifede hund tweontig geara and .vii.xx gear. and heo siððan forðferde. Abraham bestod hi on ða ealdan wisan. and siððan wolde bicgan heore byrgene. þa spæc he to þam mannum þe he mid wunedun þæt wæron hethes sunu. and hi þises bæd and cwæð	Sarra leofode hundtenontig geara and seofon and twentig geara. and heo syþþan forþferde. and abraham hig bestod on þa ealdan wisan. and wolde bicgan hire birgene æt þam mannum þe he mid wunude. þæt wæron hethes suna

In C, Ælfric departs notably from the Vulgate after the first two clauses. He omits altogether the second part of the second colon (*in ciuitate . . . Chanaan*), then radically paraphrases and amplifies the material of the third colon, in anticipation of the request for a tomb which Abraham is to make in 23:4, which Ælfric then translates in full (not given above). LB omit v. 4 but give a version of vv. 1–3 which relies almost totally on Ælfric, including the paraphrased material. An independent retranslation of this passage from the Latin would surely have resulted in something different. This close use of Ælfric's version in LB, combined with paraphrase and summary, is maintained throughout the section.

There is in fact one apparent anomaly, the omission from C of 24:4, where LB have 'ac far to þam lande þe ic of com and nim him þær wif' (Lat. *sed ad terram et cognationem meam proficiscaris et inde accipias uxorem filio meo Isaac*). The sentence is essential for narrative coherence and the omission must be due to loss during transmission to C. Ælfric's version of 24:4 no doubt repeated the name Isaac at the end, following the Latin (perhaps 'nim þær wif Ysaace', where LB has only the pronoun 'him'), in which case homoeoteleuton could easily have occurred, as *Ysaace* ends v. 3 also in C's version (unlike that of LB, which puts the name earlier).

The LB reviser's penchant for different vocabulary is again evident, though to a smaller extent than in the previous two sections. Notable are:

23:17 lande C   æcere LB   Lat. *ager*
24:3   halsie C   swera LB   Lat. *adiurem*
24:8   gewendan C   faran LB   Lat. *sequi*

However, like C, LB use *land* in 23:20, again translating Lat. *ager*. All of these words are used frequently both by Ælfric and by other writers.

Assessment

Allowing for transmissional errors (especially omissions) in C, which is a very late copy of Ælfric's Genesis, there is almost nothing in the LB version of any of the three sections of text under discussion which could not have been composed by someone in possession of a copy of that original OE translation; and so we do not have to posit wholesale retranslation from the Vulgate. The direct debt to Ælfric's version is especially obvious in section (c). We have noted a possible exception in section (a), Gen. 4:20, where B's *sangera* apparently echoes the Vulgate's *canentium*, though a loss from C's version of an OE word which would have explained *sangera* cannot be ruled out. Reference by the reviser or revisers to a Vulgate may indeed have been made regularly during the revision, but there is no other evidence that such reference prompted changes; in general, the revisions take the OE version farther from the Latin.

Yet the question remains why these three sections should have been re-rendered. The hypothesis that the compilers of the *OEH* had a damaged copy of Ælfric's Genesis, and were thus forced to supply the extra text, would neatly answer the question, but it is not convincing. For one thing, it is hard to imagine what sort of damage would be so selective as to affect seriously these three discrete parts of the manuscript, coinciding with natural breaks in the narrative, and leaving the intervening text apparently unaffected. The intermittent loss of whole leaves from the compiler's exemplar cannot, as far as may be judged, account for the replacement of chapters 4–5, 10–11, and 23–4. An estimation of the relative space taken up by these sections on manuscript pages shows that, while one might fit onto complete leaves, i.e. with an even number of written sides, the other two would not, requiring as they would an odd number of written sides. Loss of a leaf from the end of a booklet might have explained conveniently the need to resupply the text of 22:20–24:6 (the end of Ælfric's Genesis as we know it, though this,

as we have noted, leaves the narrative suspended), but this is in fact the section where the debt of the LB version to Ælfric's is at its most obvious.

It seems, then, in the absence of a convincing explanation in terms of accidental loss or damage to an exemplar (at least before 24:26), that we must be dealing with a deliberate editing procedure. Whoever produced the revised versions of the three passages appears, first, to have been keen to reduce their length considerably. LB's version of the three sections taken together is only just over half the length of the comparable sections of C. As we have seen, several longish passages have been omitted altogether, and throughout there is a tendency to pare down and simplify. Second, in the first two sections especially, but also to some extent in the third, there seems to have been a wilful intention to paraphrase, rather than to translate closely, and almost an obsession with finding alternative vocabulary. This distinct character of the three sections further lessens the plausibility of the theory that loss or damage to the compiler's exemplar had made restoration necessary. It would be hard to explain why the new translator, filling the gaps, would have chosen to paraphrase, reduce, and often omit, when the remaining original translation was so full and so close to the Latin.

Yet why a deliberate (and apparently unnecessary) revision process should have been applied so selectively, to three unconnected sections, remains a puzzle. It hardly seems likely that three different revisers (or even a single one), began the task of revision at different points but never completed it, their (or his) efforts nevertheless being incorporated in the compilation. It may be that what seems to us to be an arbitrary choice of sections was indeed just that. As we have seen, many passages in the sections, though surely based on Ælfric's version, are so consistently and predictably paraphrased, or rendered with alternative vocabulary, that we might almost imagine a monk responding to a set task: 'Reproduce this OE translation of part of Genesis in your own words.' Perhaps, then, we are seeing the results of a pedagogical exercise in the abbreviation and summary, in the vernacular, of Latin Scripture; or perhaps the revisions are simply the product of an enterprising monk with time on his hands and a desire to practise his vernacularizing skills. Yet quite why these versions of the three sections, not the originals, would then have been chosen for the compilation, remains a mystery.

4. THE TEXTS OF L AND B IN THE HEXATEUCH

The two main witnesses to the Hexateuch portion of the *OEH*, L and B, are copies derived from the archetype, *LB*. The text runs to some 60,000 words and, if the many simple orthographical and phonological differences (to be expected in copies written probably one or two generations apart and, again probably, in different centres), as well as what are clearly careless copying errors, are ignored, the overall closeness of the two versions is notable. Nevertheless, there are more than three hundred textual variations between the two texts, and these provide the bulk of our raw material for tracing the history of the *LB* text, both in L and B and in the associated manuscripts N, P, Ln, Co, and O. Many variations certainly originate in errors, but many of them are viable, and some of them perhaps deliberate, alternative readings.

A number of errors or apparent textual errors are shared by L and B (and the manuscripts associated with them) and were thus in the archeype *LB*. They may be divided, notionally at least, into two categories: translation errors and transmission errors. Translation errors will have resulted from misunderstanding of the original Latin text by the OE translators, or possibly from corruption of that text in the exemplar used, resulting in the wrong Latin being rendered faithfully by an unsuspecting translator. Transmission errors are distinct from these, and will have arisen from the misunderstanding or miscopying of the OE English text after the initial translation. Three points of origin for these are possible: they may have been made before the preparation of *LB*, in copies of parts of the Hexateuch intervening between the translator's original versions and the exemplars used for the compilation, where these were not the translator's original manuscripts (and this was presumably the case with those parts of the Hexateuch prepared by Ælfric for Æthelweard, to whom we may assume the original copy was sent); or they may have been made at the time of the preparation of *LB*, when material from various sources (including probably translations made specifically for the compilation) was being assembled and integrated; or they may have been made in derived copies of *LB* (if there were any), before the *L* and *B* branches, as we now identify them, separated. Each type of error may be represented in the copies we have.

Distinguishing between errors of translation and errors of transmission is not always easy, however, for all our manuscript witnesses

are comparatively remote both from the original translators and their exemplars and from the compiler or compilers. Deciding which type of error is in question is usually a matter of assessing probabilities, rather than establishing certainties. The position of C, derived from Ælfric's translation, *C*, is in theory pivotal. If LB share errors with C, then that is prima facie evidence that the error pre-dates the compilation and may have been made at the point of translation, not during subsequent transmission. If C does not share an LB error, then this should help to confirm the error as one of transmission. In practice, however, there are anomalies. An example of the problems faced in making assessments is the rendering of part of Gen. 16:4:

    Lat. *at illa concepisse se uidens despexit dominam suam*
    LB   and agar þa geeacnode. and eac forseah hire hlæfdian

As a consequence of finding herself pregnant, Hagar despises her barren mistress, a sequence of cause and effect which is clear in the Latin but broken by the OE conjunctive phrase 'and eac'. It seems unlikely that a close and careful translator such as Ælfric would have made such an error, so perhaps *eac* was inserted almost unconsciously, as a metrical embellishment by a copyist during transmission of the text. However, the error is in C as well as LB. The same embellishment could have been established independently in this textual tradition, but it may be that the addition of *eac* was made in the line of transmission which led from *C* to both C itself and the compilation which produced *LB*.

The errors in the *OEH* most likely to be those of translation are those which involve the syntax of a clause or phrase, where misunderstanding of the Latin may easily have occurred. A classic case of the misunderstanding of the Latin ablative absolute construction is found in Gen. 47:10:

    Lat. *benedicto rege*
    LB   and se cining hine bletsode

The subject of the clause is indeed *rege*, but *benedicto* is a passive perfect infinitive: 'the king having been blessed'. At a defining moment in his story, the venerable Jacob, as he parts from Pharaoh, blesses him. The OE version, which transposes the roles, is quite inappropriate. In other cases, aural or visual confusion between similar Latin words may be detected. For example, in

Gen. 32:4, Jost's suggestion that the translator read, or heard, Lat. *fugi* for *fui*, remains the most obvious explanation for an odd rendering:[103]

Lat. apud Laban peregrinatus sum et fui usque in praesentem diem
LB   ic wracnode mid labane and fleah hine oþ þisne dæg

In view of the instability of the Vulgate text in the early medieval period, we would expect to find some errors, or apparent errors, attributable to corruption in the translator's Vulgate exemplar (of the sort which might produce ostensibly plausible variation). Sometimes the critical edition of the *Biblia Sacra* provides us with evidence of such corruption or variation, but errors in the translators' exemplar or exemplars, which may have enjoyed limited circulation in the earlier Middle Ages, but of which no record remains, can never be ruled out. Only a tiny proportion of the Old Testament Vulgate manuscripts used in the later tenth and earlier eleventh centuries in England has survived, and so there is almost no first-hand evidence.[104] Ælfric's translation of Josh. 11:19 offers an example of the probable influence of Vulgate corruption:

Lat. non fuit ciuitas quae se traderet filiis Israhel praeter Eueum qui habitabat in Gabaon
LB   and ælc burhwaru wæs bugende to him. buton Eueum ana. þe eardode on Gabaon

In the context of Joshua's campaign against disobedient cities, the OE version is illogical: none of them capitulates *except* 'the Hevite' (i.e. the city of the Hevites), which is why Joshua goes on to defeat them, one by one. However, most medieval Vulgate manuscripts have a double negative version of the passage: *non fuit ciuitas quae se non traderet filiis Israhela*. This version must explain Ælfric's error, though it is perhaps surprising that he did not notice the problem.[105]

Original translation errors, whether attributable to misunderstanding of the Latin or to a faulty Vulgate text, cannot be emended.[106]

---

[103] Karl Jost, 'Unechte Ælfrictexte', *Anglia*, 51 (1927), 82–103 and 177–219 at 204; also Clemoes, *Illustrated Hexateuch*, 48.
[104] See Marsden, *Text of the Old Testament*, 39–54 for an overview of the problem.
[105] See Richard Marsden, 'Ælfric's Errors: The Evidence', in Mary Swan (ed.), *Essays for Joyce Hill on her Sixtieth Birthday* = *Leeds Studies in English* 38 (2006), 135–60 at 153–4.
[106] The relationship between the *OEH* and the Vulgate and the methods and problems of translation are analysed in vol. 2.

Transmission Errors in the Archetype LB

The archetype *LB*, however, had already incorporated a number of transmission errors, made subsequent to the translation process. These are thus shared by all manuscripts derived from *LB*. They are errors arising from the misunderstanding or miscopying of an OE English text. It has been noted that such transmission errors cannot always be distinguished from translation errors, but they may be identified with relative confidence when there are obvious mechanisms by which they could have occurred, such as when aurally or visually similar OE words or phrases have been confused, or when the text contains repetitions which might trigger eyeslip. Transmission errors may have occurred at any or all stages leading to the establishment of the archetype. As we have seen, a good deal of the translation was already circulating before the *OEH* was compiled. This included Ælfric's version of Gen. 1–24:26 and of Joshua, but we do not know whether Ælfric retained a copy of each, from which further copies were made, or sent the only copies to Æthelweard, who then allowed copies of these to be made. We do know that one copy of the Genesis translation, *C*, became the precursor of the extant C. The evidence of this text is a little ambivalent. On the one hand, as we have seen, it shares with LB a few apparent translation errors which it is unlikely that Ælfric would have made; on the other hand, it preserves some obviously correct readings (listed below) which became corrupted in LB.

Each of the errors listed below could have arisen in the copying of the various translations which were circulating, before they came into the hands of the compiler(s). Any idea of a pristine textual form for the compilation is certainly unrealistic; there is no guarantee that the compilation stage included a complete overhaul of the text supplied, of the sort which might have allowed for the detection and correction of error. A big lacuna in Exodus (24:12–29:8; see pp. cvii–cviii) may have been there from the start, in a booklet collected, or specifically produced, for the compilation. The only manuscripts without transmissional errors at this stage would theoretically have been those, if there were any, made by the compilers or their agents specifically to provide the text not yet available. But errors may have been introduced at the first copying of the complete 'new' work (*LB*), or in subsequent copies, if there were any, before the separate *L* and *B* branches diverged. Given the volume of the Hexateuch text,

the number of archetypal errors seems in fact to be quite small, which suggests a relatively small number of copies intervening between the original compilation and the branching of *LB*. Indeed, there might have been none. It is at least clear that neither L nor B is itself the archetypal version of the *OEH* compilation, nor even a first or second copy, as indicated by the large number of unshared errors of transmission which both contain (see pp. cxiii–cxix).

Fifty-two erroneous readings, apparent archetypal errors, shared by L and B (and the other witnesses also, where they are available) are listed below. Not included are minor morphological errors, such as *unwemme* for *unwemne*, used by both L and B in Lev. 1:3. Strictly speaking, the masculine accusative form of the adjective is required before *oxancealf*, but grammatical niceties are frequently ignored in late Anglo-Saxon manuscripts, and the sharing of the 'incorrect' form by L and B may be coincidental. In the citations below, the form of the OE text given is that of L, presented as in the manuscript, with B's version noted only where there are significant differences. Owing to the loss of the leaf in L containing Gen. 3:20–5:12, errors occurring in this section of text in B cannot be confirmed as archetypal, and so they are classified as independent 'B errors' in the next section.

Pref. 100   LB's *fandunge* is awkward in its context, and C's *fadunge*, which is echoed by *gefadian* in 101, doubtless preserves the original Ælfrician reading.

Gen. 1:26   LB's omission of the possessive pronoun before the first noun in 'to andlicnisse and to ure gelicnisse' (translating Lat. *ad imaginem et similitudinem nostram*) is likely to be accidental, not a reversion to extreme literalism (which might also have led to *ure* being placed after *gelicnisse*). C has the pronoun.[107]

Gen. 5:20   For the Lat. *et facti sunt omnes dies Iared nongenti sexaginta duo anni et mortuus est*, LB have 'and he forðferde þa he wæs nigon hund wintre and fif and sixtig wintre' (i.e. 965 years). C has the

---

[107] Cf. Ælfric's *Hexameron*, 332–3: 'to ure anlicnysse and to ure gelicnysse'; *Exameron Anglice or The Old English Hexameron*, ed. S. J. Crawford, Bibliothek der angelsächsischen Prosa, 10 (Hamburg, 1921; repr. Darmstadt, 1968).

correct figure: '.ix. hund geara and twa and syxti' (962). The error could have resulted from a copyist's eyeslip to 'fif and sixtigwintre', which follows after another six words (i.e. in 5:21). We may note L's similar problem in 5:18, where it (but not B) has 65 for 162, and B has its own problem with numbers in 5:6–7.

Gen. 7:11 A translation of Lat. *anno sescentesimo uitae Noe* is omitted, leaving a reference to the time of cessation of the flood unanchored, though at first glance the OE syntax may seem to work. This LB error is shared by C also, yet it is most unlikely that Ælfric would have made it as he translated, and so it was presumably made during the copying of the version of C used for the compilation, or an intervening copy after the text left Ælfric's hands. The same error may have been made independently in C (or an ancestor) and LB.

Gen. 9:24 LB render Lat. *quae fecerat ei filius suus minor* quite wrongly with a plural noun and verb, and have no translation of the crucial *minor*: 'hwæt his suna him dydon'. The reference is to Noah's discovery, on sobering up after his drunkenness, that one of his sons, the youngest (Ham), has drawn attention to his (Noah's) nakedness. The other two sons have behaved respectfully. C makes the same mistake, but again it is difficult to conceive of Ælfric making it (or adopting a vague paraphrase encapsulating the activities of the sons in general), and so it may have arisen in the copy of Ælfric's Genesis used for the compilation, or have been made independently in LB and in C. In the same verse, LB (but not C) have the error *slæpe* for *wine* (see p. lxxviii).

Gen. 10:32 In LB's 'þurh þas wæron þeoda todælede on eorðan æfter þam', the final demonstrative has no antecedent and so is left awkwardly dangling; the use of *æfter þam* as a self-contained temporal reference, 'after that', is unlikely. Thus, the

addition of *flode*, as in C, is necessary (translating Lat. *post diluuium*).

Gen. 10–11 Two large gaps in the LB text of Genesis, 10:3–31 and 11:10–26, were identified by Clemoes as major transmission errors, for the text of each omitted section is translated in full in C.[108] However, it may be that they result from deliberate cutting at the compilation stage. Both sections consist exclusively of the genealogical listing of the descendants of the sons of Noah. The first break is admittedly rather awkward, but that at 11:9 is less so. Conceivably, the cuts could have been made to *LB* after compilation, but it seems far more likely that they were part of the same process by which sections of the C-text were paraphrased. Gen. 24:16–22 were also omitted from the compilation in this way. A more serious lacuna after Exod. 24:11 is discussed below.

Gen. 25:15 In a list of the twelve sons of Ishmael, LB omit a translation of *et Cedma*, the last item. In L, 'and cedma' is inserted above the line in a post-medieval hand.

Gen. 25:23 In their rendering of Lat. *populusque populum superabit* by 'and þæt folc oferswið þæt oþer folc', LB omit the numerical adjective *an*, which is essential to complete a balanced clause. Conceivably, the OE version could be a translator's awkward attempt to deal literally with the very spare Latin.

Gen. 28:21 The subject of a main clause, *drihten*, following a subordinate clause, is left stranded without a verb or complement ('gif ic gesund gecyrre to mines fæder huse drihten'); the Latin of the main clause is *erit mihi dominus in deum*, and Grein supplies 'me bið God'. Crawford chooses 'biþ God min', as added by the post-medieval annotator of B. A lacuna is indicated in this edition.

[108] *Illustrated Hexateuch*, 53.

Gen. 35:28   There is no OE translation of the first five words of Lat. *et completi sunt dies Isaac centum octoginta annorum*. Grein supplies 'Isaac leofode', while Crawford, following the late annotator of B, gives 'and gefillede synd dagas isaac'. In fact, 'and wæron gefillede dagas isaac' is more likely, on the pattern of LB's version of a similar Latin clause in Gen. 9:29. It seems highly probable that there was an original clause ending in *isaac*, for it provides an obvious cue for homoeoteleuton, as the previous clause also ends with the name. A lacuna is indicated in this edition.

Gen. 42:13   It is unlikely that an original translation error produced nonsensical 'and se ginsta ys mid urum fæder and na ma' for Lat. *minimus cum patre nostro est alius non est super* ('the youngest is with our father, another is no longer'); accidental loss of one or two words is more probable. It is a *second* brother (*alius*) who is said to be no longer living. Emendation to 'and oþer na ma' is made in this edition; none is made by Grein or Crawford.

Gen. 42:18   Lat. *die autem tertio eductis de carcere* is translated 'þan (on þam B) þriddan dæge hig man lædde to þam cwearterne'. The preposition *to* is emended to *of* in this edition, as in Crawford's but not Grein's.

Gen. 46:8   OE 'þis synd israhela naman' (in L, B, Co, and O) makes sense, but the Latin has *haec sunt nomina filiorum Israhel*, and in all other occurrences of this or a similar formula in the *OEH* (seven in Exodus, one in Numbers, and one in Deuteronomy; see, for instance, Exod. 9:6, below), *filiorum* or its equivalent is rendered.

Gen. 46:11   In 'and leuies sues suna', which is LB's translation of Lat. *filii Leui*, the name *sues* is clearly an unwanted intrusion. Crawford (attributing the suggestion to his mentor, W. A. Craigie) says that *sues* stands for *sue s[una]* and is a gloss on 'iudas suna her and onam and sela' in 46:12.[109]

[109] *Heptateuch*, 199.

Sue was the wife of Juda (see Gen. 38:2), so that Her, Onam, and Sela are indeed sons of hers also. The hypothetical gloss, in a previous exemplar, would have been on the line immediately below 'and leuies suna' and could have been incorporated accidentally in copying. If such an explanation is valid, perhaps simple *sues* (possessive to match *iudas*) is more likely to have been the gloss, for it is hard to see why *s* should have been interpreted as *suna*. In Co, correct 'and leuies suna' may show that the error was spotted and put right during its textual revision; O's version is not recoverable.

Exod. 3:11   OE 'þæt ic ga to Pharone and ut alædynde israela bearn of egipta lande' has obvious problems in the second verbal phrase; the Vulgate has *ut uadam et educam*. Crawford emends to 'ut alædynde si', but, in the absence of evidence of the use of a present participle construction quite like this elsewhere in the *OEH*, it seems safer to emend to simple 'ut alæde'.

Exod. 8:3   OE *hordclyfan*, translating *cubiculum lectuli* ('bedchamber') is clearly wrong. It may be an error for *hedclyfan*, which in turn is the form occurring erroneously for *bedclyfan* in several manuscripts of the OE version of the Gospels in Matt. 6:6, rendering *cubiculum*.[110] The emendation *bedclyfan* is made in this edition. Grein and Crawford leave it unchanged.

Exod. 9:6   Lat. *de animalibus uero filiorum Israhel nihil omnino* is rendered 'soðlice israhela bearna nytcnu ne forwearð nan þyng'. Clearly OE *nytenu* is wrong, and gen. pl. *nytena* is required.

Exod. 12:27   Lat. *dicetis eis*, which prefixes this verse (*dicetis eis uictima transitus Domini est*), is not translated in LB, though strictly speaking the narrative needs

---

[110] See *The Old English Version of the Gospels*, ed. R. M. Liuzza, 2 vols., EETS 304 and 314 (Oxford, 1994–2000), i, p. xlvii. The word (often in the form *bedcleofa*) occurs almost exclusively in biblical glosses and translations.

	it. A case might be made that the tag is understood without articulation. Perhaps 'secgað him' has been lost; Grein, with Crawford following, chose to prefix with *þonne*, apparently to complete a correlative pair with *þonne* at the start of 12:26, but in the previous sentence the same syntactical structure with opening *þonne* is used without such repetition.
Exod. 12:29	In rendering Lat. *a primogenito Pharaonis* as 'and faraones yltsan sunu', LB ensure that the subsequent clause, 'oð þære gehæftan wylne frumcennedan cild' (Lat. *usque ad primogenitum captiuae*), is meaningless. Clearly, the Latin preposition must be rendered as *fram*.
Exod. 12:37	LB omit *þusend* from 'neh six hundred þusend wæpmanna' (Lat. *sexcenta fere millia*). Emendation is made in this edition.
Exod. 21:8	Both L and B put erroneous 'and' before 'forlæte hig', which makes it appear that the subject and object of the phrase are the same. A literal translation of the Latin has left an awkward sentence, which at a quick reading may seem to need the added conjunction. The supplying of *he* after the verb would have clarified matters.
Exod. 21:20	The sentence 'Se þe his wiel slicþ mid girde oððe his wylne and hig deade beoð þurh his handa' is without the resolution of a main clause; this is provided by *criminis reus erit* in the Latin. Grein and Crawford supply 'hi bið scildig'. The omission, and the subsequent failure to correct it, may be due to the influence of the previous few lines (21:18–19), in which two *gif*-clauses, each with one or more coordinate clauses atttached, have preceded the main clause.
Exod. 22:15	The Latin of this problematical passage, which deals with the law about what happens if a beast borrowed from a neighbour should be injured, is *quod si inpraesentiarum fuit* [var. *fuerit*] *dominus*

non restituet / maxime si conductum uenerat pro mercede operis sui.[111] Both L and B have simply 'swiþust gif hit beforan þam hlaforde wæs for his weorces hire'. Crawford reconstructs the line, transposing *swiþust* and using an annotation supplied, apparently by L'Isle, in B: 'gyf hit beforan þam hlaforde wæs he hit ne gylde, swiþost gyf hit . . . com for his weorces hyre' (Crawford's ellipsis). But the best explanation for the problem is that the phrase 'he hit ne gilde' (rendering Lat. *non restituet*) preceded *swiþust*, prompting eyeslip from the last words of 22:14 ('he hit gilde'); the surviving OE words are a conflated paraphrase of the rest of the Latin. In the present edition, therefore, a lacuna preceding *swiþust* is indicated. Grein suggested one after 'hlaforde wæs'.

Exod. 23:11 Although *swa* has been written on erased *þu* in L (possibly by the eleventh- or twelfth-century Latin glossator), L, B, and P originally shared 'do þu on þinum wingearde', translating Lat. *ita facies in uinea*. An original adverb *swa* is likely to have been lost.

Exod. 23:21 The essential negative particle *ne* is omitted from 'for þam he ne forgifð' in L, B, and P, translating Lat. *quia non dimittet*. A late hand has added *ne* to L.

Exod. 24:10 As a translation of Lat. *quasi opus lapidis sapphirini*, OE 'swilce þæs stanes þe man saphiros on leden nemð' is clearly deficient. Grein and Crawford supply *weorc* after *stanes*. An original nominative form such as *þas stanas* is perhaps possible. A lacuna is indicated in this edition.

Exod. 24:12–29:9 There is a major disjunction in the narrative after 24:11. That the story of Moses and Aaron and the elders of Israel approaching Mount Sinai should

---

[111] 'But if the lord (i.e. owner) be present, he (the borrower) shall not make restitution, especially if it (the beast) had been brought for the hire of its labour.'

be curtailed in the OE version at that point is not in itself a problem, but the restarting at 29:9d (i.e. the fourth colon) is, for we find ourselves in the middle of an account of the consecration process for Aaron and other priests. The jump is disguised by the fact that the pronoun in the phrase *hira handa* in 29:9 appears to have an antecedent, *israhela bearn*, in 24:11. It is interesting that, in L, 29:9 starts with a large coloured initial letter (one of many such letters), and in the fragment P, also, an enlarged letter begins the verse. This indicates that copyists of the *OEH* were aware of a break: but whether they were merely recording a physical break (perhaps a new booklet), or what they thought was a new stage in the narrative, is not clear. Exodus 25–8 describes in elaborate detail the making of the tabernacle and the altar within it, and it is not surprising that a translator or compiler should wish to edit out most or all of it, but the restart at 29:9 does not seem to make sense. We might envisage the loss of leaves, and indeed, the missing text, if translated in full, would fill four complete leaves of L. If copying were done from booklets, it is very plausible that such a loss might occur. However, it is notable also that 24:12 and 29:9d coincide with capitulum divisions regularly used in medieval Vulgate Bibles. Thus we may in fact after all be seeing the results of a deliberate, if clumsy, editing process at the time of translation.[112]

Exod. 29:40 The previous verse has announced that there shall be a morning lamb and an evening lamb for sacrifice; then vv. 40 and 41 tell how each in turn is to be offered, and this pairing ('the one . . ., the other . . .') is conveyed in the Latin by *in agno uno* (at the end of v. 40) and *alterum* (at the start of v. 41). However, while v. 41 in the OE version

---

[112] On the transfer of Vulgate capitulum divisions to the *OEH*, see Marsden, 'Translation by Committee', 53–63.

in L and B is prefixed with 'oðer lamb', v. 40, the description of how the morning lamb is to be prepared, is left hanging without its defining tag. A noun or pronoun before or after the description must have been lost.

Exod. 34:27   LB's 'Drihten cwæð to moise þæt ic behet þe freondscipe' is clearly deficient as a translation of Lat. *dixitque dominus ad Mosen / scribe tibi uerba haec quibus et tecum et cum Israhel pepigi foedus.* Presumably a rendering of *scribe tibi uerba haec* has been lost. Grein simply adds *Vrit* before *þæt*; Crawford, like the present editor, marks a lacuna.

Lev. 1:13   Here, and in 1:17, *swæcce* ('flavour', translating Lat. *odorem*) is misspelled *spæcce* (the meaning of which is hard to fathom). In both L and B there have been post-medieval attempts to make corrections.

Lev. 2:13   LB's translation of Lat. *in omni oblatione tua offeres sal* with 'þu scealt to ælcere offrunga' is deficient. Grein and Crawford make good with the addition of 'bringan sealt' after 'þu scealt'. The fact that OE modal verbs are very often left with the following verb unexpressed may have helped to preserve the omission unnoticed.

Lev. 3:2   LB have *geotaþ*, where *geoton* would be in concord with five other verbs whose plural subject is 'aarones suna' in a succession of parallel instructions in 3:2–9 (which include another occurrence of *geoton*). The mood (with the spelling of the inflection the same in both manscripts) appears to be subjunctive in each case, with optative sense; the Latin has future (*fundent*, etc.).

Lev. 8:31   Lat. *ibi comedite eas* (sc. *carnes*) is translated 'etað þæra'. Conceivably, *þæra* is a partitive genitive, in the plural to translate *eas*, but the OE antecedent, *mete*, is in fact singular and it seems better to assume that an original *þær*, for *ibi*, has been corrupted; the present edition is

	emended accordingly. Grein's emendation, *þær þa*, used also by Crawford, seems awkward.
Lev. 25:22	In 'of þæt nigoðe gear and oþ niwe cumað', both L and B have *of* instead of *oþ* as the first preposition (Lat. *usque ad . . . donec*); L has a late correction. A few words earlier, B alone makes the same mistake. Crawford leaves *of* uncorrected, noting that confusion of the two words occurs 'not infrequently' in early Middle English and citing examples from Morris's *Early English Homilies*;[113] but that does not seem to justify inaction.
Lev. 26:42	*Nyme* (*nime* B) is written for *gyme* in 'ic gyme min wedd' (Lat. *recordabor foederis mei*). In L, there is a late correction. Cf. correct 'ic gime þæs landes' (Lat. *terrae quoque memor ero*) in both manuscripts later in the same verse.
Num. *rubric*	A Greek translation of the book's title is omitted, though the similar rubrics for Leviticus and Deuteronomy include one. It is thus likely that Numbers had such a title which became lost.
Num. 2:32	Both L and B have problems with their versions of Lat. *sexcenta tria milia quingenti quinquaginta* (i.e. 603,550). The element of the OE version which should have been 'þreo þusenda' is inflated by L to 'þreo and hund þusenda' and by B to 'þreo and hundeahtatig ðusenda'. Presumably both versions stem from the same archetypal corruption (or possibly a translation error), the exact form of which cannot now be established. In L, 'and hund' is scored through, but this is probably a late correction. B alone makes a mistake also with the earlier part of the figure, having 'fif hund' for 'six hund'.
Num. 13:8–9	These verses, within a long lists of tribes, are transposed in L, B, and Ln, though with no adverse effect on the narrative.

---

[113] *Heptateuch*, 300. The consonantal confusion occurs often in C; for an example, see above, p. lxxv.

RELATIONSHIPS BETWEEN THE MANUSCRIPTS   cxi

Num. 16:49   In both L and B, Lat. *in seditione core* is rendered as 'on chores ceastre', where the second noun is obviously an error for *ceaste* ('strife'). Presumably, the original translation got it right.

Num. 22:30   Translating the reproach of Balaam's ass to its master (Lat. *dic quid simile unquam fecerim tibi*), the OE renders *fecerim tibi* as 'þe gebude': 'sege hwænne ic æfre ær þillic þe gebude'. *Gebude* may simply be a corruption of *gedyde*, but *gebude* as the preterite of *gebeodan* ('offer') might be thought appropriate, with a sense of 'behaved towards' or even 'threatened'.[114] Grein emends to *gedyde*; Crawford leaves *gebude*, as does the present editor.

Deut. 1:36   In LB's 'he hit gesihð þæt', translating Lat. *ipse enim uidebit eam* [sc. *terram*], the verb has acquired a second object pronoun (omitted in the present edition). Perhaps *þæt* was originally *þa*, rendering Lat. *enim*.

Deut. 1:37   In the amplified translation of Lat. *mihi quoque iratus dominus propter uos*, an essential possessive pronoun, giving the sense of *propter uos*, has been lost: 'þonne he wæs me yrre fore scilde'. Thus *eowre* is added before *scilde* in the present edition, as it has been late in L, probably by L'Isle.

Deut. 5:24   Lat. *de medio ignis* is translated as 'on fyrynes (fyrrines B) midlene'. Crawford cites W. A. Craigie's suggestion of confusion between *fyres* and *brynes*, which is not very convincing. It is tempting to assume that, in *fyrynes*, we are seeing the adjective *fyren* ('of fire', 'fiery') being used as a noun, although the *DOE* offers no evidence of such usage. The scribes of L and B were comfortable enough with the word to give it their own individual forms. Grein and Crawford emend to *fyres*, but the present editor has left the word intact.

[114] See *DOE*, *gebeodan*, sense 3.f, and cf. *beodan*, senses C.4 and C.7.

Deut. 7:11	The conjunction *and* is essential before *bebeode* in 'domas þe ic eow sylle todæg. bebeode þæt ge don', translating Lat. *iudicia quae ego mando tibi hodie ut facias*. The omission may in turn have prompted erroneous elision of subsequent words in B (see p. cxviii).
Deut. 9:24	In 'on þam dæge þe ic eow cuþe', for Lat. *a die qua nosse uos cepi*, the preposition *on* is clearly quite wrong and is unlikely to be a translation error.
Deut. 10:5	As in Lev. 25:22, both L and B have *of* for *oþ* in 'oþ þisne dæg' (Lat. *hucusque*).
Deut. 25:8–9	In Lat. *si responderit nolo eam uxorem accipere / accedet mulier ad eum*, the last clause is the main one, following a subordinate clause of consequence. LB wrongly insert the conjunction *and*: 'gif he þonne cwið nelle ic hig habban to wife and ga þæt wif to him'. This looks more like a spurious addition by an inattentive copyist than an original translation error.
Deut. 27:26	An essential negative particle has been lost in 'ðe wunað' (Lat. *qui non permanet*).
Deut. 28:34	In 'þæt þu gange wasiende (wasigende B)', the present participle, clearly written in both L and B, is of an apparently non-existent verb. The Latin is *stupens*, and Grein's emendation to *wafiende* ('being astonished') makes good sense; in the absence of any other evidence in the corpus for *wasian*, the emendation is adopted for this edition.
Deut. 28:35	As in Lev. 25:22 and Deut. 10:5, both L and B have *of* for *oþ* in 'fram þam fotwolmum oþ þone hneccan' (Lat. *usque ad*).
Deut. 28:61	A negative particle is omitted in 'þe sint awritene on þisse bec' (Lat. *quae non sunt scriptae*). It is essential for the rhetoric of this verse, though the inaccuracy is not immediately obvious. Both Grein and Crawford overlook the omission; the

former nevertheless includes *non* in his illustrative Vulgate text, but Crawford does not.

Deut. 34:6   Lat. *in ualle terrae Moab* ('in the valley of the land of Moab') is rendered 'on þære dene moab lande' in both L and B. Grein and Crawford emend to *moablandes*, but the fact that both copyists accept the dative noun reinforces the probability that the construction may be an example of 'partitive apposition'.[115]

Josh. 8:15–16   The phrase 'andlang þas westenes', translating Lat. *per solitudinis uiam*, has become misplaced. It follows 'him æfter' (in 8:16) in both L and B, but it belongs earlier, at end of 8:15, after 'mid eallum his here', according to the Latin. This indeed is likely to have been its position in Ælfric's original version, for there it suits well the metrical style of the OE passage. The juxtaposition of the adverb *æfter* and preposition *andlang* in the present arrangement is odd.

Independent error in L *and* B

In addition to shared, archetypal errors, both L and B have their own independent errors in their texts of the Hexateuch; presumably they were not in the archetype. They will have been made during the separate stages of transmission from *LB* to L and B, some of them probably during the actual copying of these specific manuscripts. Conceivably, a few of the errors could indeed have been in the archetype and then been corrected by an alert copyist in one of the two lines of transmission. This is perhaps unlikely to have occurred in more than a handful of cases; many of the errors, especially substantial omissions, could have been made good only by recourse to a second exemplar, or to a Vulgate text.

A survey of independent errors is given below, first for L and then for B. In the case of those in the *Prefatio* and most of Genesis 1–24, the correct reading, whether in B or L, is usually that of C also, and this is indicated in the selected examples. Co and O are available intermittently for the later Genesis, N and P for parts of Exodus, and

---

[115] See the discussion of this construction in Bruce Mitchell, *Old English Syntax*, 2 vols. (Oxford, 1985), i, §1455.

Ln for a small section of Numbers; where these witnesses share specific L or B readings, this is indicated, though discussion of the relationships of each to L and B is left until later sections. Latin equivalents are given only when they may be helpful in illuminating the nature of an error.

i. Errors in L

Careless spelling mistakes (often involving a dropped letter) and the garbling of words through visual or aural confusion occur throughout the manuscript. Examples in Genesis are *weallum* for *weall lim* (11:3), *of* for *oð* (11:4), *ginran* for *gingran* (29:18), *dohra* for *dohtra* (31:43), *getaniað* for *getacniað* (41:27), *on* for *of* (44:8); in Exodus, *bernas* for *beras* (9:31), *higrædene* for *hiwrædene* (12:21), *betsan* for *betstan* (12:35), *beod* for *beoð* (18:19), *systð* for *sypst* (29:31); in Leviticus, *þær* for *þæt* (5:1), *hit* for *ytt* (7:25), *þearfan* for *þearfan* (23:22), *of* for *oþ* (26:41); in Numbers, *asingod* for *asindrod* (12:14), *hræder* presumably for *hwæder* (*nawider* BLn) (12:15), *butan eallum* for *butan weallum* (13:20), *gesylle* for *gestille* (17:5), *be næmbe* for *benæmde* (24:11); in Deuteronomy, *geate* for *getele* (1:11), *an* for *on* (1:27), *gegealt* for *gehealt* (7:12), *oþþe* for *oð he* (28:20), *wines* for *win is* (32:33); and in Joshua, *yltran* for *yldran* (7:6), *swiþe* for *friðe* (23:1).

Genesis, taken with the *Prefatio*, has proportionally fewer errors than any of the other books in L. They are evenly distributed and omission accounts for a fifth of them. Homoeoteleuton is responsible for the loss of eleven words in 3:2–3 and of three words in 46:23–4. Other errors include (with B's correct reading on the left):

5:18   hundwintre twa and sixtig (hundteonti ... and twa and sixti C)] fif and sixtig wintre
12:13 þæt] and þæt
21:34 bogode (logode C)] bletsode
23:19 bebyrigde (birigde C)] bebyrge
38:27 his] his his

Exodus has comparatively few omissions, but they include eleven words lost by homoeoteleuton in 9:22, and the losses of *lande* (18:10), *drihten* (32:11), and *getelda* (33:8). Further errors are:

3:8   stowum (swotum B)] stowe
4:15   ætywe] ætywde
12:12 on egypta godum] on egipta lande (Lat. *in ... diis Aegypti*)

In 12:10, the clause 'and ne gebrece ge nan ban' was supplied over an erasure in the sixteenth century by L'Isle. It is highly probable, however, that these correct words were there originally (as in B), and were subsequently erased by someone who noted that they represent an addition to the Vulgate text (probably of liturgical origin).[116]

Omissions account for over half of the errors in Leviticus, including a six-word loss by homoeoteleuton in 25:11. Other errors include:

3:3	oferwrogen] oferwrihð	
8:9	gyldenbende] gildenbeade (Lat. *laminam auream*)	
10:9	druncen] drincan	
26:23	onfon] ongen fon	

In Numbers, only two omissions have been noted, of *mid* (1:4), and *leuies* (3:17). Other errors include:

2:32	and þreo þusenda] þreo and hund þusenda
6:23	bletsion israhela folc] bletsiað on israela folc
12:8	hiw hwi ne] hiwwinge
12:14	asyndrod] asingod (Lat. *separetur*)
16:35	com] swilce færlice *add.*
20:30	daga] wintra
21:5	wæter] win

In 2:32, B has problems with the numbers also, but different ones, and an archetypal error may be the root cause. As is often the case with such errors, the superfluous words have been deleted later in L, probably by L'Isle. In 6:23, L may preserve the anonymous translator's original, literal rendering of Vulgate *benedicetis filiis Israel*; B's *bletsion* presumably derives from this. In 12:8, B appears to have an accurate rendering of Vulgate *non per figuras . . . quare igitur non timuistis*: 'ne þurh hiw hwi ne ondræde ge eow'.[117]

Omissions in Deuteronomy include six words in 3:27 and the losses of *ne wifmannes* (4:16), *fæderum* (4:31), *and brytte* (9:21), *ðyder* (14:24), and *gehyrsumodon and* (34:9). Errors often involve spurious addition:

---

[116] See R. Marsden, 'Old Latin Intervention in the Old English *Heptateuch*', *Anglo-Saxon England*, 23 (1994), 229–64 at 253–6.

[117] Crawford misunderstands and reads *hiwhwine* (actually *hiw. hwine* in the manuscript) as a mistake for *hiwwinge*, the form in L (for the more usual *hiwunge*). Ln, available for much of this section of Numbers, is deficient at this point.

23:24   bergena] nim add.
28:18   landes wæstm] awirged add.
31:17   dæge] fram him add.
31:24   mid þe] æfter þam add.
31:29   on] and on

Others include:

4:26   forwurðað] wurðað (Lat. perituros esse)
31:16   lande] landun

Joshua has two substantial losses by homoeoteleuton, of twenty words in 1:6–7 and nine words in 3:17; otherwise, the only omission is of *and gange* in 7:14. The opening verse of the book is truncated in L's version, but this may be variation, not error; see p. cxxx. Other errors include:

5:1   ondredon] hira add.
8:5   hi] ge
10:40   syttende] wunode
11:6   ealle to wundienne] ealle wundigean (Lat. omnes istos uulnerandos)
11:14   huðe] hu

In 10:40, a paraphrased verse, the copyist has repeated the verb used in the previous clause; a present participle form is required. Conceivably he miswrote *wuniende*.

ii. Errors in B

About 180 errors occur in B, two-fifths of which are omissions, mostly of single words. Careless spelling mistakes and word confusion occur throughout, and with more frequency than in L. Examples are, in Genesis, *eft* for *oft* (*Pref.* 65), *swylce* for *swiþe* (7:19), *betæce* for *betæhte* (9:3), *gehealde* for *gehirde* (17:20), *cydde* for *dyde* (20:5), *ne scyndest* for *gescindest* (20:6), *fæstnysse* for *fætnysse* (27:28 and 39), *swyðe* for *swiþor* (37:4), *wear* for *wearþ* (40:2), *hwæð* for *hwæðer* (42:16); in Exodus, *hreofe* for *hreofle* (4:6), *færed* for *færeld* (12:21), *ðeow* for *ðeod* (19:6), *aðer* for *oðer* (21:18), *beallum* for *be eallum* (24:8); in Leviticus, *fell* for *fet* (1:9), *fæstest* for *fættest* (3:3), *of* for *oð* (25:22), *sleað* for *fleoð* (26:8); in Numbers, *butan* for *bufan* (1:45), *hunige* for *hunies* (16:14), *eorðflihtes* for *eorðslihtes* (22:4); in Deuteronomy, *bearn* for *bern* (28:17), *eardas* for *ealdras* (29:10),

pamtreowa for *palmtreowa* (34:3); and in Joshua, *chores* for *achores* (7:24), *ac heald* for *achialon* (10:12).

Not included in the above total, or in the examples, are some fifty further omissions, mostly of single letters, made by the copyist of B. They were corrected, usually by the insertion of the missing letter above the word, either by the copyist himself, in a few cases, or by what appears to be another early medieval hand. Many of the other errors, including omissions, were corrected by post-medieval hands, mostly that of L'Isle, often using L as his source.

Genesis has a higher number of errors proportionally that any other of the books in B; there are about eighty of them, distributed fairly evenly; a further four are in the *Prefatio*. Over a third are omissions, including those of six words in 4:18 and 48:21, and of three words in 1:16, 5:32, 14:2–9, and 43:32. Four words are lost in the *Prefatio*, also (23). The repetitive structure of 18:31–2 has confused the scribe of B (or a predecessor) and caused him to misplace thirteen words. In 19:33, 'ne hwænne heo aras' has been added in a mistaken attempt to clarify. Figures have caused problems in 5:6 and 18. Other errors include:

2:10   stowe] to stowe *add*.
24:3   heofonlican] heofon
32:11   cume and ofslea] me ofslea and
33:8   freondscipe] gyfan *add*.
37:4   swiþor] swyðe
43:23   to] mid
44:19   broþor] modor (*also* Co; see p. cxliii)
50:23   he] ic

B shares two errors with C, the omssion of *and hire ofspringe* in 3:15 and *ferde* for *ferdon* in 22:19. In the latter case, the sharing is no doubt coincidental, but that in 3:15 may be more complex. Here, L is unavailable; it is perfectly possible that it had things right and that C and B have lost *and hire ofspringe* coincidentally, for in the context it is an easy omission to make. However, it may have been in L also and thus be an archetypal error. Two further errors in B's Genesis, the addition of *þa cwædon hi* to *tunece* in 37:33 and loss of *cyld* from *cyldfære* in 45:19, are shared by Co and so must have arisen in B, the ancestor of both B and Co (see pp. cxliii–cxlv). The addition in 37:33 is a bungled attempt to improve the narrative.

In Exodus, there are almost three times as many errors in the first

half of the book (up to ch. 17) than in the second, and almost half of these are omissions, often of complete phrases. They include three words in 23:31, four words in 3:6 and 12:7, and six words in 14:27. In 21:16–17, there is a disruptive transposition of verses. Among other errors are:

3:8	stowe] swotum (Lat. *ad loca*); L *has* swote
3:9	to me] to gode
5:22	hwi swencst þu þis folc] hwi swincð þis folc
6:6	alæde . . . alyse] alædde . . . alysde (Lat. *educam . . . eruam*)
7:16	gehiran] forlætan (Lat. *audire*)
8:21	cynn] full
9:2	ofhæfst] hæfst
12:14	freolse] lofe
16:18	gegearwode næfde] gaderode næfre (*also* P)
21:9	gif he hig his suna beweddað] gyf heo is beweddað
21:10	he sceal foresceawian þa mædene gyfta and reaf] forgyfe he ðæt mæden and sylle hyre reaf

In 21:10, there may have been an attempt to simplifiy the very literal translation seen in L, and this may also apply to the problem in 21:9.

Leviticus has a handful of orthographical confusions, some of them noted above, and just three omissions, of *sprec* (25:1), *godes* (25:23), and *ne* (26:14).

In Numbers the few omissions include the particle *ne* in 21:22 and, by homoeoteleuton, twelve words in 31:18. There are several small spurious additions, including ðam (3:12), ðe (14:23), ham (21:4), and *ne* (22:33).

In Deuteronomy, half of all errors are omissions, including four words in 6:5, three in 10:14 and three in 10:22; otherwise they are of single words. Examples of other errors, which include several garbled phrases, are:

7:11	ic eow sylle todæg] eow todæg
10:14	sind on him] syndon hi
11:29	sette ge] set he (Lat. *pones*)
28:64	þar] ðam (Lat. *ibi*)
32:12	hira] eowwer
32:18	gestrinde] gestyrde

Joshua has only four errors, proportionally far fewer than any of the other books in B (or L). There is an omission of five words by homoeoteleuton in 8:14, and of *ealle* in 1:7, and two copying problems noted above.

iii. Assessment of error in L and B

The error rate in B (about 180) is 50 per cent higher than in L (about 120), even ignoring the omissions in B which were apparently made good by more or less contemporary hands. The rate is higher in B's Genesis than elsewhere. This contrasts with the situation in L, where the rate of error in Genesis is lower than in any other book and up to three times greater in Exodus–Numbers. Genesis thus shows the biggest difference in error rate between L and B (the ratio being a little higher than 5:2). In Exodus it is also high (about 2:1), but thereafter, the differences are smaller and, in Numbers and Joshua, L actually performs about 50 per cent worse than B. In both manuscripts, omissions account for more than one-third of the errors; they are mostly small, but there is also a regular stream of larger losses by homoeoteleuton.

Variant readings in L *and* B

When the overt errors surveyed above are excluded, there remain more than 300 cases of textual variation between L and B. They encompass alternative vocabulary, word order, syntax, and morphology. It is likely that most were established at some stage through careless copying, not deliberate emendation. Nevertheless, in each case, the alternatives are (arguably) plausible readings, valid in the context of the narratives of which they are a part. Determining with certainty which form is archetypal (i.e. the reading of *LB*) is not always possible, but in about a quarter of cases it can be demonstrated that one or the other version renders more accurately the wording of the Vulgate. In these cases, the general assumption is made that the closer an OE rendering is to the Latin of the Vulgate, the more likely it is to represent the translator's original efforts, which reached *LB*. Conversely, the rendering which is less close is more likely to have arisen through a modification, whether accidental or deliberate, during transmission from one copy to another. In respect of the first twenty-four chapters of Genesis, for which we have in C a late version of Ælfric's translation (a hallmark of which is fidelity to the Vulgate), the general validity of this rule can be

demonstrated; that is, readings shared by C and L but absent from B, or shared by C and B but absent from L, are more likely than not to be closer to the Vulgate.

In the lists of variations in Genesis–Joshua given below, the Latin of the Vulgate is shown, except where the OE is part of a paraphrase or amplification; no significant variations in the Vulgate text occur in the passages involved. In cases where one reading appears to be closer to the Latin than the other, it is highlighted with an asterisk.

i. *Prefatio*

In each of the following cases, L and C agree against B, so it is likely that they transmit Ælfric's version and that of the *LB* archetype.

84	god bebead LC	se æ bebead B
106	swa swa LC	swa B
114	to urum LC	on urum B
122	woh gerihtan LC	gewrit gerihtan B

ii. Genesis

The main variations in Genesis 1–24:26, where three witnesses are available, are listed first.

2:2	þam weorce LC*	þam weorcum B	Lat. *opere*
2:21	þær þær L	þær BC	
2:23	þeos bið LC	beo heo B	
	of were LC*	of hyre were B	Lat. *de uiro*
3:3	swulton LC	sweltan B	
3:7	siwodon LC*	sywodon him B	Lat. *consuerunt*
5:29	geswince L	geswyncum BC*	Lat. *laboribus*
6:2	þam þa þe LC	ðam ðe B	
7:2	þam unclænum LC	unclænum B	
7:19	þa eorðan LC	eorðan B	
8:1	þa wind L	wind BC	
8:4	armenies LC	armenisces B	Lat. *armeniae*
8:12	seo LC*	swa heo B	Lat. *quae*
9:3	betæhte LC*	hi betæce B	Lat. *tradidi*
9:6	mannes blod LC*	ðæs mannes blod B	Lat. *humanum sanguinem*
9:10	eallum þam LC	eallum B	
9:23	sculdra LC	sculdrum B	
9:25	cham L	chanaan BC*	Lat. *Chanaan*

RELATIONSHIPS BETWEEN THE MANUSCRIPTS   cxxi

13:6	ahton L*	om. B	Lat. *capere*
15:8	cwæð LC	cwæð þa B	
	hit witan LC	witan B	
16:2	and heo cwæð L	and cwæð BC	
17:5	gecyðed L	geciged BC*	Lat. *uocabitur*
	abram heononforþ L	heononforþ abram BC	
18:9	sarra þin wif L*	þin wif sarra BC	Lat. *Sara uxor tua*
18:16	þanon LC	ða þanon B	
18:23	þa rihtwisan L	þone rihtwisan BC*	Lat. *iustum*
18:30	ne do ic him na LC	ne do ic him B	
18:33	god ferde þa LC	god þa ferde B	
19:2	nateshwon LC*	nelle we nateshwon B	
	on L*	ut on BC	Lat. *in*
19:15	scildigan LC	forscyldigan B	
19:38	seo L	and seo BC*	Lat. *quoque*
20:5	hyre broðor wære L	wære (wæs C) hyre broðor BC	
20:12	ic genam hig LC	ic hi genam B	
20:15	ætforan eow LC	beforan eow B	
21:6	eac mid me L	mid me BC*	Lat. *mihi* (no adv.)
21:8	fram soce sarra L	fram gesoce BC*	Lat. *in die ablactationis*
21:14	alædde LC	lædde B	
21:16	sarlice wepende LC	wepende B*	Lat. *fleuit* (no adv.)
21:23	nu me L	me nu BC	
21:26	him to LC	to him B	
	hit sylf LC	sylf hyt B	
21:27	heora ægþer LC	ægþer B	
	æfre wurdon LC	wurdon B	
22:12	cwæð ða L*	cwæð BC	Lat. *dixitque*
	ondrætst swyðe L	swyðe ondrætst BC	
	woldest ofslean L	ofslean woldest BC	
22:14	uidit . . . uidebit LC*	uidit . . . uidit B	Lat. *uidet . . . uidebit*
23:16[118]	seolfres be fullon gewihte L	be fullan gewihte seoflres B	

[118] LB's paraphrased version of this passage differs radically from that of C.

INTRODUCTION

In thirty readings, L and C concur against B; in eighteen, B and C concur against L. Among the twenty asterisked readings, L has twelve and B has eight; and in fifteen out of the twenty, the asterisked reading, whether shared with L (eight times) or B (seven times), is the one found in C.

Variations in the rest of Genesis are as follows. In this list and subsequent lists, the reading to the left is that of L, and to the right that of B; variations which are closer to the Latin are again asterisked. Co and O are available intermittently in the later Genesis, as shown; the relationship of their texts to those of L and B is analysed elsewhere (pp. cxxxv–clii).

27:8	sunu min	sunu	
27:20	þæt me hrædlice*	þæt hyt me swa hrædlice	Lat. *ut cito . . . mihi*
27:27	he hyne ongeat*	he him to onleat	Lat. *sensit*
27:45	feccan hider	hider feccean	
28:11	sunne setlgange	sunne setlunge	
28:12	on þære hlædre	on þære*	Lat. *per eam*
29:3	and hi	and	
29:21	ða	ða ða	
29:23	lian his dohtor*	hys dohtor	Lat. *Liam filiam suam*
29:26	gife	forgyfe	
29:27	hafa	hafa ðe	
31:20	nolde na iacob	þa nolde iacob	
31:30	me mine	me	
31:33	nahwær	nahwær þær	
31:44	unc me and þe	me and ðe	
32:18	esauwe his hlaforde	hys hlaforde esauwe	
32:30	ic wæs	wæs	
33:3	oð	oð ðæt	
33:12	togædere	ætgædere	
33:13	ealle drife	drife ealle	
33:14	oþ ic	oð ðæt ic	
37:4	ascunodon	onscunodon Co	
37:8	cwist þu Co	cwyst ðu la	
37:9	abugon	onbugan Co	
37:10	þreatode Co	aðreatode	
37:28	ða	and Co	

38:1	ferde	for Co	
38:13	scep	hys scep	
38:18	æt þam cyrre	æt þam ylcan cyrre Co	
38:19	eode þanon Co	eode ða þanon	
38:21	þæs landes men	ða landes men Co	
38:23	hæbbe hire þæt heo hafað Co[119]	hæbbe hire*	Lat. *habeat sibi*
38:29	com Co	com þa	
39:10	onscunede	ascunode	
39:19	hire wordum wel	swiðe wel hyre wordum	
41:11	anre nihte	on anre nihte	
41:33	gesette hine	gesette	
41:44	bebode	gebode	
42:18	þan þriddan	on þam þriddan	
42:19	on eowrum huse	to eowrum husum*	Lat. *in domos uestras*
42:30	hig cwædon	cwædon Co	
42:31	þence we	þence	
42:34	on bende	on bendum* Co	Lat. *uinculis*
42:35	guton*	tugon Co	Lat. *effunderent*
42:38	mid eow beniamin	beniamin mid eow Co	
	iosep his broþur* Co	iosep	Lat. *frater eius*
44:2	þe he þe	þe he CoO	
44:8	seolfor stælon	stælon ... seolfor Co	
44:15	bedidrian Co	diddrian	
44:16	arasod*	afandod Co	Lat. *inuenit*
44:21	næron sceaweras Co	sceaweras næron	
45:6	naþer ne CoO	ne	
45:12	to eow O (eow to Co)	eow	
45:17	cwæde O	cwæþ Co	
46:21[120]	gera* CoO and hehi	and gera hehi CoO	Lat. *Gera*

[119] Co's version varies slightly from L's: 'habbe þæt þæt heo hauað'.

[120] In respect of *Hehi*, there is much variation in medieval Vulgate manuscripts, both in the form of the name and the use of a conjunction before it.

46:28	þæt* CoO	and	
46:34	secge ge Co	secge O	
47:9	he O	he him Co	
47:15	nabbaþ feoh	feoh nabbaþ CoO	
48:5	þe	ða þe	
48:7	oþre naman	on oþre naman	
48:18	for þam þes ys*	for þam þe he is	Lat. *quia hic est*
49:31	and . . . eac lia	and . . . lia*	Lat. *et Lia*
50:15	dydon	ær didon	

In only fourteen cases in the second half of Genesis may one variant be said to be closer to the Vulgate than the other; in these, L is closer nine times, and B five times. In 27:27, B appears to reinterpret the action, having Jacob bending down to Isaac, rather than Isaac perceiving the odour of Jacob; but presumably the plausible (if pointless) new version arose in error, through the miscopying (or mishearing) of *ongeat* as *onleat*. There are other alterations in B in the same passage, at 27:20 (see above) and 27:16 (an error of omission).

iii. Exodus

Variations in Exodus are as follows:

1:16	si mædencild	mædencyld sy	
2:10	for sunu hyre	hire for suna	
2:20	forleton ge	forlete ge	
2:22	cende sunu	cende him sunu*	Lat. *ei*
2:24	þara getreowþa	þa getreowþa	
3:3	þas*	þa	Lat. *hanc*
3:13	and	and ic	
3:16	com*	eom	Lat *uisitaui*
3:22	and	and on	
4:18	þa git	gyt	
5:10	eow mann	man eow	
5:13	eow man	man eow	
5:18	nan man cef	man nan ceaf	
6:3	and min	min	
6:7	eow me*	eow	Lat. *uos mihi*
6:29	ealle þing	ealle ða þing	
7:20	drihten him	him drihten	
8:6	egipta wætro*	eal egypta wæteru	Lat. *aquas Egypti*

8:9	anne andagan	andagan	
8:9	þegnum	folce	
8:13	hine bead	bead	
8:19	bebead*	him bebead	Lat. *praeceperat*
8:26	egiptisce	egipte	
8:29	offrie gode lac	offrige gode	Lat. *sacrificare domino*
9:2	gif þu þæt git don nelt	gyf þu þæt onscunast*	Lat. *quod si adhuc renuis*
9:14	ofer þin folc*	ofer eal ðin folc	Lat. *super populum tuum*
10:1	ic*	and ic	Lat. *ego*
10:5	on treowe	on treowum	Lat. *ligna*
11:8	þin folc	þis þin folc*	Lat. *serui tui isti*
12:14	to freolse*	to lofe	Lat. *solemnem*
12:42	hig god	god hi	
14:5	faran wyllað	willaþ	
14:28	to laue an	an to lafe	
16:1	þi	on ðam P	
17:5	of*	on P	Lat. *de*
17:9	on minre handa*	on handa P	Lat. *in manu mea*
18:18	þis*	þin	Lat. *iste*
18:25	arwurðe weras	arode weras*	Lat. *uiris strenuis*
19:17	alædde	lædde	
20:7	byð	bið he	
20:11	gehalgode	he gehalgode	
20:24	wyrcað*	ac weorcað	Lat. *facietis*
21:6	beo he	beo	
21:18	hys nextan*	oþerne	Lat. *proximum suum*
21:28	and*	þaet	Lat. *et*
21:30	him man	man him	
22:19	þu	þu hine	
23:12	þæt* P	and	Lat. *ut*
23:25	fram eow	eow fram P	
29:12 cealfes blod	þæs cealfes blod	

29:23	of þæra þeorfra hlafa windle	of ðæra þeorfa windle*	Lat. *de canistro azymorum*
32:1	wæs lange*	wæs to lange	Lat. *moram faceret*
32:5	simbledæg	symbeltid	
32:13	gehete	behete	
32:21	ane þa mæstan synne	þa mæstan synne P	
33:2	drife	adrife	
33:8	þonne	ða	
34:5	þa ... þa*	þa ... and	Lat. *cumque*
34:10	ne on anum lande	ne on nanum lande	
34:12	nyme	ne genime	
34:18	on lengtentide monðes	on lenctenmonþes tide	
34:32	bebead him	him bebead	

Ten of the sixty-two variations in Exodus involve word order, usually simple inversion. In the twenty-two cases where one variant is closer to the Vulgate than the other, it is L's seventeen times, B's five times. The second variation in 8:9 is curious. Twice in the verse, the Vulgate uses a doublet of indirect objects, 'servants' and 'people': *pro seruis tuis et pro populo tuo* and *a seruis tuis et a populo tuo*. L abbreviates in the first instance to 'for þin folc' and in the second to 'fram þinum þegnum', but B has 'for þin folc' and 'fram þinum folce'. It is probable that L's version was archetypal and that B's was levelled to what seemed like a logical repetition of *folc*.

iv. Leviticus

The main variations in Leviticus are as follows:

Rubric	for þam þar	for ðan ðe ðæron	
1:9	forbærnð*	forbærne	Lat. *adolebit*
1:17	ætbred	ætbrede	
4:17	ryft	wahrift	
8:4	bebead	him bebead	
9:3	enitre	anwintre	
18:30	þa þing*	nan dingc	Lat. *quae*
19:26	eton ge	ete ge	
25:4	ne rip	ne ne rip	
25:11	mid ale	mid anum æle	

25:42	alædde	gelædde	
26:7	feallað	hreosað	
26:9	ge beoð*	and ge beoð	Lat. (no conj.)
26:13	raceteagan	racyntan	
26:20	eorðe	seo eorðe	

All three cases where one variant may be said to be (slightly) nearer to the Latin are in L's version.

v. Numbers

The main variations in Numbers are as follows:

Title[121]	uagedaber	ualedaber	
1:2	si wæpnedhades	wæpnedhades sy	
1:3	twentig	twentigum	
1:16	þe	ða þe	
11:6	manna	man Ln	
12:3	wæs soðlice	soðlice wæs Ln	
12:10	swa snaw*	swa hwit swa snaw	Lat. *quasi nix*
13:1	bebead god	god bebead	
13:3	þe*	ðe nu	Lat. (no adverb)
14:3	ure cild Ln	cild	
14:11	nellað hig gelyfan	ne gelyfað hi* Ln	Lat. *non credent*
14:12	fordo	hi fordo Ln	
14:13	cwæð þus	ðus cwæð Ln	
14:32[122]	sweltan	licgan* Ln	Lat. *iacebunt*
14:40	eodon	astigon* Ln	Lat. *ascenderunt*
16:4	sona feoll astreht	feoll astreht sona	
16:32	cynne	geteldum*	Lat. *tabernaculis*
16:49	ær ofslagene	ofslagene*	Lat. *percussi sunt*
17:6–7	him bebead drihten	drihten him bebead	
17:8	wæs þa	þa wæs	
17:10	gehealden þær*	gehealden	Lat. *seruetur ibi*
21:4	him	him ham	
	þa wearð þrit	wearð ða aðryt	
21:7	gebide nu	gebide*	Lat. *ora*

[121] Spellings of the latinized Hebrew name for Numbers both with *uag-* and (more frequently) with *uai-* occur in Vulgate manuscripts (see *Biblia Sacra*, iii. 69); B's *ual-* is strictly speaking an error.

[122] Although BLn clearly transmit the correct reading, *licgan*, L's *sweltan* is not inappropriate.

21:23	seon se cyning	se cyningc	
22:6	awirigenne	wyrigenne	
	awirgest	wyrigst	
22:19	abidað	bidað	
22:27	swiðor	gyt swyðor	
22:32	þæne assan	þinne assan*	Lat. *asinam tuam*
22:34	singie	syngode*	Lat. *peccaui*
	þe ... ænig þing mislicað	ðe ... mislicað*	Lat. *displicet tibi*
Summ.	tæhte swa þeah	swa ðeah tæhte	

In a reversal of the pattern in the first three books, it is B which corresponds more often to the Vulgate, namely, nine times in the twelve cases where comparison can be made. The explanation in four cases is minor amplification in L. It will noted that there is a high proportion of word-order variations.

vi. Deuteronomy

Deuteronomy has proportionally a higher number of variations than the previous books, but eleven of them simply involve verbal prefixes.

1:26	mægðe ungeleafulnysse	geleaflyste	
3:24[123]	þine*	þa	Lat. *tua*
4:1	wyle syllan	syllan wile	
4:2	to eow	eow to	
	ne ge	ne ge ne	
	beode	bebeode	
4:9	bebead	bead	
4:21	me wæs	wæs me	
4:27	þa þeoda	þeoda	
4:39	on heofone*	on heofonum	Lat. *in caelo*
5:22	of	on	
5:29	wisan bebodu	bebodu*	Lat. *mandata*
6:7	on þinum husum	on þinum huse*	Lat. *in domo tua*
9:7[124]	oð þisne dæg	oð þisne andweardan dæg	

---

[123] The last three letters of L's *þine* are written (apparently in a contemporary hand) on an erasure and the original reading cannot be recovered.

[124] In both manuscripts, *dæg* seems to be an original translation error (the Latin being *usque ad locum istum*).

9:27	heardnisse	heardheortnysse	Lat. *duritiam*
10:3	hæbbe*	hæfde	Lat. *habens*
10:19	on	of	
10:22	wæron eowre fæderas	eowre fæderas wæron	
13:1	him mæte	hine mæte	
13:11	natoþæshwon	nateshwon	
14:1	sciron	scerað	
15:7	ænig þinra freonda	ðinra freonda ænig	
15:10	þæt*	and	Lat. *ut*
15:12	ænigne man	ænne mann	
16:19	wendað	awendaþ	
	rihtwisra*	rihtwisnessa	Lat. *iustorum*
17:2–5	to soþe	to soðan	
18:11	wicca	wiccean	
20:23	man hine	hine man	
23:19	þine breþer	ðinum breðer	
25:13–15	ælcum þingum	ælcum þincge	
28:11	swa	swa swa	
28:34	for hire þinge and ege	for hyra ege*	Lat. *ad terrorem eorum*
28:43	utancumene men	utancymene	
28:45	oferhogodon	forhogedon	
28:46	eowrum ofspringum	eowrum ofspryngce	Lat. *in semine tuo*
28:53	besette	besetene	
	þæt ge	oð ge	
	eowre dohtra*	dohtra	Lat. *filiarum tuarum*
28:59	hete	ece	Lat. *plagas*
28:64	todrifþ	adrifð	
	þar*	ðam	Lat. *ibi*
29:6	druncon ge	drunce ge	
31:6	onforhtion	forhtion	
31:9	awrat	wrat	
31:12	gefille	gefyllon	
31:17	onrist	arist	
31:18	hide	behyde	
31:19	to tacne þis leoð	ðis leoð to tacne	

32:5	him singodon unrihtwise	him syngodon on unrihtwisum	
32:24	wildera deora	wildeora	
32:39	slea	ofslea	
32:46	eow nu todæg beodað þa word	eow todæg* beodað þa*	Lat. *uobis hodie* Lat. *mandetis ea*
32:47	wunion don	þurhwunion doð	
34:5	het*	wolde	Lat. *iubente*
34:9	him bebead	bebead	

In the thirteen cases where comparison with the Vulgate indicates that one version is nearer than the other, it is L's eight times and B's five times. The version of 16:19 in a collection of precepts in Cotton Vespasian D. xiv (see pp. lxviii–lxix) has L's *rihtwisra*, which is clearly the original, and correct, reading. In 28:53, OE *besette* (from *besettan*) arguably suits better than *besetene* (from *besittan*) a paraphrase expressing the idea of the affliction of starvation. In 32:5, the Latin has simply *peccauerunt ei*; no antecedent subject is given, but it is understood to be unjust or sinful people in general. Thus L provides what is presumably a plural noun, 'the unjust', which may have been introduced to contrast with *rihtwis* (applied to God) in the previous sentence; B's *on unrihtwisum* appears to produce an adverbial phrase (and this is more likely to have been derived from L's version than the other way round).

vii. Joshua

Like Deuteronomy, Joshua shows a relatively high number of variations The first come in the opening words of the book, where L has an abbreviated version of the translation:

> Lat. *et factum est post mortem Moyse serui domini ut loqueretur dominus*
> L   Hit wæs æfter moyses forðsiþe drihten spræc
> B   Hit wæs geworden æfter moyses forðsiþe drihtnes ðeowan ðæt drihten spræc*

It is difficult to see how the abbreviation could be accidental, although there are no other cases of such deliberate cutting down in L's Joshua. Other variations are as follows:

1:2	aris þu	aris
1:4	þæt ethea land	eðea land

1:5	eallum dagum	on eallum dagum	
2:1	beworht	geworht	
2:11	on eorðan neoþan*	on eorðan	Lat. *in terra deorsum*
2:17	cumað	becumað	
3:3	þære halgan earce*	þære earce	Lat. *arcam foederis*
3:13	swa raðe swa	swa	
4:6	þa	þas*	Lat. *isti*
4:14	mihtiga	ælmihtiga	
5:2	wirc þe nu	wyrc ðe	
5:10	wunudon*	wurdon	Lat. *manserunt*
5:15	sona feoll	feoll sona	
6:3	feohtendas	suwigende	
	swa swa	swa	
6:19	þær	her	
6:23	swa swa	swa	
6:26	gedo edstaþeli[an]*	geedstaðelie	Lat. *suscitauerit et aedificauerit*
7:12	amansumunge	mansumunge	
7:13	þu sege*	ðus secge	Lat. *dic*
8:2	swa swa	swa	
8:18	þa burh*	þas burh	Lat. *urbem*
9:11	comon	comon to eow	
10:12	stira	astyra	
10:18	sette	setton	
10:21	aht cweðan ongean	acweðan ongean*	Lat. *contra . . . mutire*
10:22	teoð	teoð . . . forð	
10:24	gange	gangon	
10:31	mid his folce*	mid his fyrde	Lat. *cum omni Israel*
10:32	acwealde	cwealde	
10:33	on	to	
11:1–3	þa git	ða	
11:6	ne ondræt þu	ne ondræd ðu ðe	
11:19[125]	eardode*	eardodon	Lat. *habitabat*
21:41	ær behet	behet*	Lat. *iurauerat*

[125] The subject of the singular verb (Lat. *habitabat*) is *Eueum* ('the Hevite'), and L translates accordingly, but B legitimately treats it as plural.

21:42	ac*	and	Lat. *sed*
23:6	on sinai dune	on sunai ðam munte	

In the twelve cases where direct comparison with the Vulgate can be made, L is nearer nine times, and B three times. In 6:25, it is very likely that the translator used causative *gedon* plus an infinitve to express the double force of the Latin verbs (*qui suscitauerit et aedificauerit ciuitatem Iericho*), though the infinitive appears as an apparent subjunctive in L (*edstaþelige*); the phrase has been elided in B. Both manuscripts have problems, but different ones, in 6:3. They may have arisen independently, but it is likely that an archetypal corruption prompted both versions. The Latin is *circuite urbem cuncti bellatores semel per diem / sic facietis sex diebus*.[126] L's present text, 'farað nu six dagas simble ymbe þa burh. ælce dæg æne. ealle feohtendras', appears to render this accurately (albeit in a paraphrase). However, *feohtendras* is on an erasure and seems to be in the hand of the late eleventh- or early twelfth-century Latin glossator (see p. xlii). B has the same text as L except that 'and ealle swugiende' is substituted for 'ealle feohtendras'; the addition of the conjunction prevents *swugiende* becoming the subject of *farað*, which is thus without one. Nevertheless, B's phrase seems to anticipate, and appropriately summarize, part of 6:10: *non clamabitis nec audietur uox uestra*. (The rest of 6:10, along with most of 6:4 and 6:5–8 and 11, is otherwise not rendered; abbreviation and omission are frequent in the rendering of Joshua.) It seems very probable that B preserves at least part of the archetypal text, and that L originally had *swugiende* also, until it was erased and *feohtendras* added. Whoever made the alteration in L may have been comparing the Latin text and decided to 'correct' the translation, not realizing that *swugiende* translated some Latin from several lines later.

viii. Assessment of variation in L and B

More than 300 pairs of variant readings have been highlighted above. They are distributed fairly evenly, both among the six books of the Hexateuch and within them. In about a quarter of cases, comparison with the Latin of the Vulgate allows one of a pair of variants to be judged a closer translation. Overall, L's readings are more than half as likely again to be the close ones as those of B (61 readings in L, 35 in B). There is fluctuation, however, between different parts of the

---

[126] 'Go around the city, all you fighting men, once a day; you shall do so for six days.'

Hexateuch in this respect. In Genesis, Exodus, and Leviticus, closer L variants outnumber closer B variants by two to one; in Numbers, that proportion is reversed, but in Deuteronomy and, especially, Joshua it is restored.

In those pairs of variants which cannot usefully be compared with the Latin, there is great similarity between the two versions in respect of the kind of variation involved. For instance, there are twenty cases where L has a clarifying pronoun which is absent from B, and seventeen cases where B has such a pronoun but not L. Thus, in terms of the sort of textual variation which is inevitably established through successive generations of copying from an original archetype, there is no clear evidence that one of our two texts has evolved further than the other.

L and B and the Hexateuch Archetype

L and B, in their texts of the *Prefatio* and Genesis–Joshua, are copies derived from the same archetype of the Hexateuch, *LB*. This was a compilation made from various sources, which included, on the one hand, pre-existing copies of parts of Genesis and Numbers, and Joshua, and on the other hand, translations probably made especially for the compilation. Whether that compilation, in its first complete manuscript manifestation, was itself the archetype is hard to determine. Some of the errors of transmission which have been identified as archetypal may have been in place already in the copies of pre-existing translations used by the compiler(s), and others could have been made in the process of compilation; we do not know how competent and careful the compiler or compilers were. But there are enough archetypal errors to make it likely that some, at least, were made once the compilation itself began to be copied, and thus that the archetype manuscript *LB* from which L and B derive was at least one copying stage away from the compilation. Furthermore, although their texts are remarkably similar overall, there are still sufficient differences between L and B, in the form of independent errors (especially omissions), to indicate that they do not derive directly from *LB* but from two different copies made from it, *L* and *B*.

The question of the length of evolution of each of these independent branches is a difficult one. In the *Prefatio* and Gen. 1–24:26, where L and B may be compared with C's version of Ælfric's text, L shares more readings with C than B does, and is more accurate both overall and in relation to the Vulgate, and thus

seems to be nearer to the archetype. (Implicit in this assessment is of course the assumption that C transmits, albeit rather unevenly, Ælfric's version of Gen. 1–24:26, and that this reached the compilers of the *OEH* basically in the form now extant only in C.) In the Hexateuch overall, the rate of error in B is demonstrably higher than in L. The difference is at its greatest in the *Prefatio*, Genesis, and Exodus, where there are between two and a half and three times more errors in B than in L; in the other books, the rates are more or less equal, or, in a few sections, a little lower in B than in L. When we look at the sorts of error involved in the most unreliable sections of B, we find that a high proportion of them consists of small mistakes made by a careless or ignorant copyist, who arbitrarily omits letters from words; some of the errors have been corrected, possibly by the scribe himself, or at least during the Anglo-Saxon period. It is likely that a high proportion of these errors was made in one bad copying episode. This may have been the copying of B itself. Thus we do not have to see the relatively bad state of B's text as, necessarily, indicative of a longer line of evolution for *B*, with steadily accumulating error, than for *L*; and indeed, we know that B was probably copied some years before L. We may recall here the arguments of Clemoes, that B was not the first copy in the illustrated format, but more likely one of several produced.[127] To call this 'mass production' would clearly be an overstatement, but we certainly might expect to see more careless errors in a situation of repeated and perhaps relatively intense copying.

In the ninety readings where a pair of variants may usefully be compared with the Latin of the Vulgate, L's readings are over 50 per cent more likely to have a closer correspondence than those of B. Taken together with the same relative proportions of overt errors in the two texts, this again points to L as being the more reliable witness to the text of *LB*, even though the evidence is not overwhelming. Thus, the present edition of the *OEH* is based on L. Nevertheless, recourse to B is often necessary to fill lacunae or to correct obvious errors.

The following stemma represents the relationship of C, L, and B to the compilation *LB*; x represents an unknown manuscript or possibly more than one, and y an indeterminate number of manuscripts. The relationship of these manuscripts with the other witnesses to parts of the *OEH* is discussed in subsequent sections.

[127] See p. xlviii.

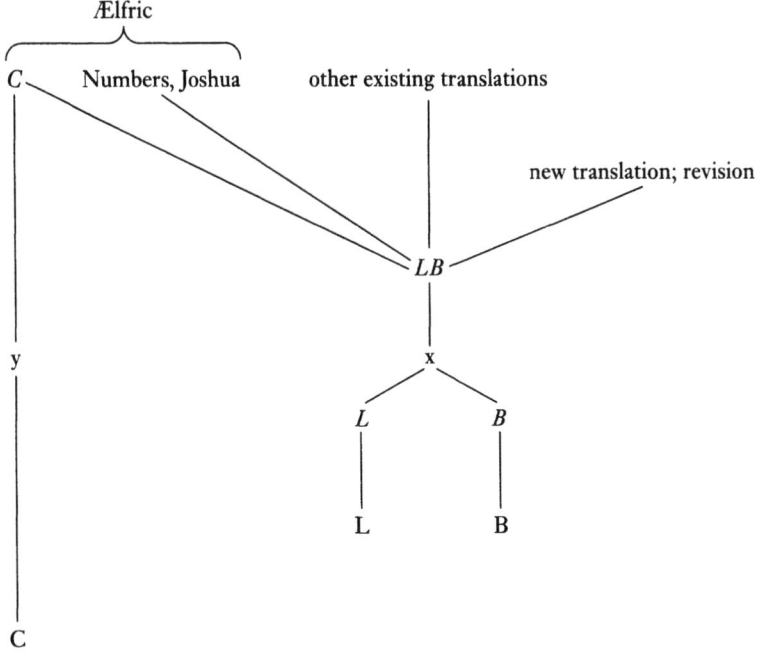

5. The Texts of Co and O

We know from Wanley that Co (Corpus Christi College 201, pp. 151–60) originally contained a complete version of Genesis from 37:2 to the end of the book, preceded by a rubric. This concluding part of Genesis is the story of Joseph's progress from outcast brother to future patriarch, and a major division in both L and B at 37:2 (with the same rubric as in Co) confirms its status as an important narrative in its own right. The loss of three leaves has created two lacunae in Co, the one from 41:2 ('and hig man læswode') to 42:20 ('eowerne gingstan broðor'), and the other from 47:18 ('þæt we nan þing') to the end. Wanley recorded only the latter. The remaining text of Co is notable for regular and often substantial differences from that of LB. There are more than three hundred of them, a figure which excludes purely orthographical and phonological variation. Almost half of the differences involve amplifications to the text as it occurs in LB; none has Vulgate authority.

Where the fire-damaged and fragmentary O (Cotton Otho B. x) is available (i.e. intermittently in Gen. 40:18–41:16, 43:11–44:4, and 45:3–47:24), it shares most of Co's distinctive variants. Neither Co

nor O is now directly available for any of 41:17–42:19 and 47:25–50:25. As recorded by Wanley in his *Catalogus* (p. 192), the opening words of O coincided (with one minor variation) with those of Co; these are the rubric and fifteen words of text, beginning at 37:2. Co and O share an error in the rubric which is absent from LB's version (see below). Wanley also printed the explicit of O, which, like the incipit, is no longer extant in the manuscript. This expands the ending of the text as given in LB (i.e. a translation of the Vulgate's 50:25) and adds a doxology ('to his agenum gecynde . . . aa on ecnysse. amen'). There is no reason to doubt that the same explicit was in Co, though we are now without the manuscript evidence for this as well. It is clear that Co and O transmitted the same version of the text of Genesis 37:2–50:25, a revision of that known in LB; the priority of the latter cannot be doubted, given the evidence which is presented below. There are, however, some differences between the versions in Co and O, which complicate an assessment of the relationship between them and the texts of L and B.

In the analysis of Co which begins this section, the correspondences or otherwise between O's and Co's variants are noted, where they can be ascertained. The absence of information about O in the lists of readings indicates that its text is unavailable or illegible at the point in question. The detailed character of O's text in relation to that of Co is discussed below (pp. cxlv–clii).

The Revised Text in Co *(and* O*)*

As noted above, most of the revision made to the text of Co (and generally of O, where it is available) consists of amplifications. A fifth of these involve the addition of single words, as the following selections illustrate.

Conjunctions and adverbs: *þa* is added twenty-four times (37:2, 12, 17, 28, 34, 38:12, etc.); *and* fifteen times (37:1, 27, 38:16, 20, 40:21, etc.); *nu* eight times (37:30, 32, 38:25, 42:36, etc.); *þæt* three times (40:17, 44:8, 44:12); *þonne* twice (42:38, 43:11); *ac, eac, eft, eal,* and *swa* eight times between them (37:35, 38:22, 29, 40:13, etc.); *þar/þær* and *hider* twice each (39:1, 43:14 and 42:20, 47:4).

Pronouns: *ealle + hig* (37:9), *beo + þu* (38:11), *axaþ + eow* (46:33).

Nouns and names, sometimes substituted for pronouns: *andswarode + iosep* (37:16); *for he > for iudas* (38:12); *chanaan + lande* (47:4).

Adjectives: *on þa tid > on þare ylcan tyde* (38:1), *þræd > wyrmreada þræd* (38:30), *to ðære note > to ðære ilcan note* (40:21).

Other additions and amplifications include the following, in which a few differences between Co and O will be noted; the LB reading is given first:

37:20	secgan] urum uæder *add.*
37:33	iosep] þinne suna *add.*
38:12	þa] sume dæge *add.*
39:16	geþohte] beþohte hyre sylf
40:2	yrre] wið hi *add.*
40:5	binnan firste] þa binnan þam fyrste
42:32	suna] and we him sædon *add.*
42:38	gif] and hu þonne gif
43:1–2	farað] to egipta lande *add.*
43:9	ic] deaðes *add.*
43:14	eac O] min cyld *add.*
43:30	tearas] of his eagan *add.*
	weop] swiðe sare *add.* O
43:32	hi æton] ætsomne *add.* O
44:5	and] sege heom þæt *add.*
45:26	him O] la leof fæder *add.*
46:13[128]	isachares] þis wæron isachares O
46:20	manneses (manases B)] and hi hatton manases O
46:23	danis] þus hatte danis O
47:15	mete O] hlauord *add.*

Many of these seem to be stylistic elaborations, which fill out idiomatically, sometimes dramatically, what were succinct and perfectly adequate renderings of the Vulgate narrative. In 43:9, for instance, nothing in the Latin specifically justifies the insertion of *deaðes* into 'beo ic scyldig' (with the sense 'I shall be liable to die'), even if death might reasonably be predicted as a possible consequence of guilt; the Vulgate has *ero peccati reus in te omni tempore*, which is Juda's declaration of responsibility for his brother Benjamin, whom he is to take from their father, Jacob. The absence from O of Co's additions in 43:14, 45:26, and 47:15 is discussed below.

Co often uses alternative vocabulary, as in the following examples, where again a few differences between Co and O will be noted.

37:11	stille] stillice	(Lat. *tacitus*)
37:28	cypan] cypmen	(Lat. *negotiatioribus*)

[128] The same amplificatory formula is seen in 46:14, 21, and 23.

38:12	dagum] gearum (Lat. *diebus*)
38:15, 21, 22	myltystre] myltresse (Lat. *meretrix*)
38:26	þeah] þeahhwæðere
39:16	unwrenc] wrenc
40:20	gemang] þa amang O
40:21	magister O] ealdor (Lat. *magistri*)
42:22	gehirdun] gelyfdon (Lat. *audistis*)
42:25	feoh] seoluor (Lat. *pecunias*)
42:36	ys on bendum] is gebunden (Lat. *in uinculis*)
43:12	feos O] seolfres (Lat. *pecuniam*)
43:27	arfullice O] arwyrðlice (Lat. *clementer*)
46:29	cræt] carm (Lat. *curru*)
47:6	stowe] healf (Lat. *loco*)

Where the substituted words are not synonyms, they are still quite acceptable alternatives, including *gearum* in 38:12, which is used in an expression of length of life ('æfter manegum dagum/gearum'). Nevertheless, where differences in meaning are apparent, the LB choice remains almost invariably nearer to the Latin. The word *myltresse*, used in 38:15, 21, and 22, is recorded nowhere else in the *OE Corpus*, but it does look like a consciously used alternative form. In 39:16, *unwrenc* ('vile deceit'), which occurs in a paraphrase, is rather more forceful than Co's alternative, *wrenc* ('stratagem', 'deceit'). *Carm* is of interest in 46:29, because the word, presumably derived from Latin *carrus* (perhaps through the oblique *carrum*), has only one other occurrence in the surviving corpus of OE. This is in an interlinear gloss added to the Salisbury Psalter, possibly at Shaftesbury, in the early twelfth century. In Canticle 5 (the first 'song of Moses'), from Exodus 15, the words *cum curribus et aequitibus* are glossed 'mid carman and mid crætan'.[129]

There are many notable alterations of word order and/or syntax in Co's revision, usually accompanied by amplification also. Examples are:

37:15	and axode] þa axode he
38:22	ne mihte ic hig findan] þæt he hig ne mihte nahwar findan
38:26	for þam] þæt is for ðan þe

---

[129] *The Salisbury Psalter*, ed. C. Sisam and K. Sisam, EETS 242 (London, 1959), 290; see also p. 36. The context is Pharaoh's crossing of the Red Sea. The canticle is omitted from the *OEH* translation of Exodus, but in the references to the episode in Exod. 14:7, Latin *currus* is rendered by OE *cræt*.

39:12 and heo teh hine] þa teah hy hine
40:16 þæt ys þæt] me þuhte þæt
43:17 swa him beboden wæs] swa he him beboden hæfde
45:20 forlæte ge nan þing of eowrum yddisce] forlæton (forlæte O) ge eowres ydysces nan ðinc O
47:3   þa he axode] ða axode he hi O

The reviser has a marked liking for periphrastic constructions using auxillary, usually modal, verbs, often as part of wider syntactical change. Examples are:

38:20   þæt he fette] and he scolde feccan
42:36   nymaþ] willað niman
44:5   ge forstælon] hi forstolen habbað
         yfele ge dydon] yuele habbe ge gedon
44:21–31 wistest be þam] woldest witan be þam O
46:28   þæt (and B) he cydde] þæt he sceolde (scolde O) cyðan O

Other small grammatical preferences have been asserted regularly by the reviser. With the verb *(ge)mættan*, for instance, Co has a dative reflexive object, but LB usually an accusative (37:9, 41:1; but in 37:5, B has the dative also). To express motion towards, LB use *on* with the accusative, where Co has *to* with the dative (37:28, 36, 45:4, 5, 46:3, 6, 27); O does not consistently follow Co in this respect (see below). There are several cases where Co substitutes subjunctive verbal forms for indicative, with *-an* as the inflection, as in *willan* for *wyllað* (42:34) and *onscunian* for *onscuniað* (46:34). Co tends also to use imperative forms, where LB has subjunctive; examples are *geðenc* and *lær* for *geþence* and *lære* (40:14), *læd* for *læde* (43:16), and *sec* for *sece* (44:9).

Most of Co's revisions have no obvious purpose. There is nothing to suggest a return to the Vulgate text and an attempt at a more faithful rendering; quite the opposite is usually the case. Thus, in 43:31, Co (with O) replaces LB's 'and þa he þæs geswac' with 'and þa he ðæs wopes geswican hæfde'. In what is already a paraphrase of Lat. *lota facie* ('and when he had washed his face'), the referent of *þæs* in LB's version is totally clear, for Joseph's weeping has been the last thing alluded to in the previous sentence ('and weop'). Nevertheless, the reviser has decided to redefine it, by adding *wopes* (as well as using a periphrastic tense). There are other cases of gratuitous rewriting, as in 42:22:

Lat. *e quibus unus Ruben ait / numquid non dixi uobis nolite peccare in puerum et non audistis me*[130]

LB ða cwæð ruben. cweþe ge. ne sæde ic eow ne singie ge on þam cnapan and ge me ne gehirdun

Co þa cwæð ruben cweþe ge ne sæde ic ær þæt ge syngodon on þam cnapan and ge me ne gelyfdon

LB accurately render the Latin's double envelope structure of speech given within speech, but Co has Ruben reporting on his own words instead of quoting these. Not only the perspective but also the meaning has now changed: 'Did I not say earlier that you sinned against the boy, and you did not believe me?' There is no good reason for the modification, and indeed, something of the dramatic simplicity of the original has been lost.

In 47:15, the drama of a confrontation between the hungry Egyptians and Joseph is considerably weakened in Co, when LB's very literal rendering of the Latin is rewritten and the act of questioning ('Why should we die in front of you?') is removed; O is available also here and shows a slight reduction of Co's version:

Lat. *da nobis panes / quare morimur coram te*
LB syle us mete. hwi swelte we beforan þe
Co syle us mete hlauord elles we sculon swyltan beforan ðe
O syle us mete elles we swylton beforan ðe

In 43:26, there is a rare example of Co's abbreviating the version in LB, part of which is an amplified paraphrase of the Latin description of how Joseph's brothers humbly submit themselves before him; but Co thereby leaves unstated the sense of Lat. *adorauerunt*:

Lat. *et adorauerunt proni in terram*
LB and feollon on þa eorðan and geeaðmeddon wið hine
Co and feollon ealle to his fotum
O and feallon on þa eorðan

O's version again differs. It, too, has a much shortened rendering, but this is obtained merely by omitting the last four words of the LB version, not by substituting a new clause. If we had only O to consider, we would probably evaluate the loss as a simple error (and

---

[130] 'One of them, Ruben, said, "Did I not say to you, 'Do not sin against the boy', and you did not listen to me?"'

one which does not disrupt the sense unduly); but in fact it would be an odd coincidence, given the general close correspondence between Co and O in their variation from LB, if the alterations in this verse in the two manuscripts had no connection. Such differences are discussed further below.

It is clear that Co's additions and amplifications, although in a few cases they perhaps offer more definition, and in a more idiomatic style, are not in general productive of a clearer or more accurate text than the one which we may assume the reviser found in his exemplar (a copy of the *LB* text). In fact, in several further cases, sense is compromised. One comes at the start of the narrative in 37:2, where Joseph is introduced quite abruptly in LB (a large part of the verse having been ignored by the translator). A reason for his brothers' dislike of him is given in the Vulgate, but without elucidation: 'he gewregde his broþru to hira fæder þære mæstan wrohte' (which is an accurate translation of Lat. *accusauitque fratres suos apud patrem crimine pessimo*). The reviser apparently believed this version—in which Joseph accuses his brothers of 'a most wicked crime'—to be incorrect (and it does on a cursory reading seem illogical), and so he transposed subject and object: 'ac hine gewregdon his gebroðra to heora fæder þære mæstan wrohtæ'. Thus it is now the brothers, not Joseph, who do the accusing. Another misunderstanding occurs in 38:12:

Lat.   *ascendebat ad tonsores ouium suarum / ipse et Hiras opilio gregis Odollamites in Thamnas.*[131]

LB   þa for he to his scepscere he and hiras his scephirde se odolamitiscea. on þamnatha.

Co   ða sumne dæge for iudas to his sceapscære and hiras his sceaphyrda and se odolamitisca for to thamnatha.

LB satisfactorily negociate the rather awkward Latin syntax, but Co makes several changes. First, the antecedent of *he* is given (*iudas*), though the name's occurrence a few words earlier makes this unnecessary; second, the first clause has been filled out with an adverbial phrase of time (*sumne dæge*). But then, with the insertion of the conjunction *and* before the phrase *se odolamitisca* and repetition of the verb *for* after it, the sense has been altered: now it seems that

[131] 'And he [Iudas] went up to Thamnas, to the shearers of his sheep, he and Hiras the Odollamite, [who was] the shepherd of his flock.'

Judas goes to his sheep-shearers, along with Hiras his shepherd, while a separate person, 'the Odollamite' (which the reviser seems not to have realized is simply a description of Hiras), goes to Thamnas; there are two journeys instead of one.

A stranger revision occurs in 40:1:

    Lat.   *ut peccarent duo eunuchi . . . domino suo*
    LB   þæt twegen afyryde men agylton wiþ heora hlaford
    Co   þæt .ii. men agylten of hirede wið heora hlauord

The origin of Co's awkward version, the sense of which appears to be that two men 'of the household' (not specified as eunuchs) have sinned, presumably lies in aural or visual confusion between *afyryde* and *of hirede*, but in the two previous references to a eunuch of Pharoah, in 37:36 (*afyredan*) and 39:1 (*afyreda*), there are no problems, and Co's version concurs with that of LB. A misreading of *wunode* as *wuduwe* in 38:11, encouraged by the occurrence of that noun a few words earlier, may account for Co's 'þa for heo wuduwe on hire fæder huse', replacing LB's 'ða for heo and wunude on hire fæder huse' (Lat. *quae abiit et habitauit in domo patris sui*). The resulting statement, that the subject of the verse, Thamar, went in a widowed state to her father's house, is correct, but the essential steps in the narrative are omitted.

Independent Errors in Co

Apart from the problems which have been noted already, Co has a number of clear textual errors, unique to it, as far as we can tell, whether made by the copyist of Co himself or faithfully carried over from his exemplar. Although the material for comparison is limited, it seems that the proportion of independent errors in Co is in fact greater than in O (see below). Homoeoteleuton accounts for losses of six, five, and seven words in 45:22, 46:17, and 47:1 respectively. Other errors include *swegre* for *sweor* (38:13), *genam* for *ne nam* (38:14), *gemacan* for *gemana* (*gemanan* B) (38:16), *seccað* for *secgaþ* (40:8), omission of *hwæþer* (43:27), *beorclyfan* for *beddclyfan* (*bedcleofan* B) (43:30), *eowre* for *ure* O (46:34), and omission of *he lædde* (47:2). In the five cases of error where O is available for comparison (including two of the long omissions), it shares none. Many of Co's errors cause little disruption to the narrative, but they are likely to be accidental, given the tendency for amplification, not simplification.

Overall, Co's independent errors show that the text of O cannot derive from Co itself. This is confirmed by a number of further variants, not obvious errors, which set Co apart from O, as well as from LB; they are listed below.

The Relationship of Co *and* O *to* B

There is a persistent stratum of readings which are shared by Co and O (where available) with B, against L. They are sufficient to show that CoO and B belong on the same branch of transmission from the main *LB* tradition, separating them from L. Among the most positive indications of this shared BCoO tradition are three errors which are not in L:

37:33   tunece L] þa cwædon hi *add.* B, hig cwædon þa *add.* Co
42:35   guton L] tugon BCo (Lat. *effunderent*)
44:19   broþur L] modor BCo (Lat. *fratrem*)

The phrase introduced by B and Co in 37:33 in quite spurious, breaking into a speech by Jacob and attributing the second part of it to his sons; it is the work of an 'improver', not the original translator. Surprisingly, in 42:35, *tugon*, which clearly originated in a copying lapse, makes sense in context.[132] In 44:19, *modor* was an easy enough error to make and is not immediately obvious as such.[133]

Among more than fifty further shared variants, not errors, are the following:

37:3   ofer L] ofer ealle BCo
38:18   þam cyrre L] þam ylcan cyrre BCo
38:21   þæs L] ða BCo
42:38   mid eow beniamin L] beniamin mid eow BCo
43:16   middes dæges L] middæges BCoO
43:23   þæt L] þe BCoO
44:2   þe he þe L] þe he BCoO
44:8   ure saccon L] urum saccum BCo
44:8   we þines hlafordes gold oþþe his seolfor stælon L] we stælon þines hlafordes gold oþþe hys seolfor BCo
46:21   and hehi L] hehi BCoO
47:15   nabbaþ feoh L] feoh nabbaþ BCoO

---

[132] L 'ða hig þus spræcon þa guton hig hira hwæte of hira saccon'.
[133] L 'þu axodest us ær hwæþer we hæfdon fæder oþþe broþur'.

Phonological and orthographical variants are better indicators of local scribal practice, or simply whim, than of textual relationship, but it is worth noting that there is a striking number of cases (some 150) in which B and Co (and O, when available) share such variants; examples are *on middan* for L's *omiddan* (37:7), *nyde* for L's *neade* (43:11), and *leofaþ* for L's *lyfað* (45:26). Both B and Co overwhelmingly (and in the case of Co invariably) prefer *heora* to *hira*, the form used most often in L, and L's *ongen* is always *ongean* in BCo (and in O, in the one available case); B and Co (and usually O) eschew the gemination of final consonants. These features confirm, of course, the independence of L, as much as the interdependence of B, Co, and O.[134]

There is a stratum of readings in B which appear to place it apart both from L and from CoO. However, once we eliminate the effects of the many unique copying errors in B (see pp. cxvi–cxvii), the number of shared LCoO variants is very small and is no challenge to the validity of the BCoO relationship established above.[135] Apart from its copying errors and many small omissions, the idiosyncrasies of B include gratuitous (albeit idiomatic) amplifications, as in *þu la* for LCo's *þu* (37:8) and *þonne þær* for LCo's *þær* (43:5). Contraction of second-person verb and pronoun is characteristic of B, too, as in *sylstu* for *sylst þu* (38:16) and *wenstu* for *wenst þu* (44:8). B's *afandod* for LCo's *arasod* in 44:16 is a more interesting variant. Both verbs offer good translations of Lat. *inuenit* in *Deus inuenit iniquitatem seruorum tuorum*: 'god hæfþ arasod/afandod ure unrihtwisnissa'.[136] The two past participles are similar enough to raise the possibility of graphical confusion at some point in transmission, rather than deliberate variation. In the absence of a substanial number of other readings to suggest a direct connection between L and Co (perhaps arising from a comparison of a manuscript in one textual tradition with a manuscript in the other during a revision process), it is safer to conclude that *arasod* was the archetypal reading, which became *afandod* at quite a late stage in transmission to, or at the copying of, B. There are several variations in B which confirm that modification of at least some of its readings occurred after the CoO line of

---

[134] These matters are discussed in detail in vol. 2.

[135] Cf. the contrary conclusions of De Bonis, 'La versione in prosa', 157, who claims that readings shared by Co and L, against B, are more numerous than those shared by Co and B, against L.

[136] *Afandod*, 'laid open, detected'; *arasod*, 'found out (by testing or experiencing)'.

RELATIONSHIPS BETWEEN THE MANUSCRIPTS

transmission split from *B* itself. In 46:28, for instance, CoO's 'þæt he sceolde cyðan' looks like a modification of the version still in L, 'þæt he cydde', not B's 'and he cydde', which must have been created subsequently. In 39:19, B and Co share a version which varies from that in L ('wel hyre wordum' for 'hire wordum wel'), but B then adds *swiðe*; this is a characteristic amplification, though the possibility that it was in the original BCo version but was then dropped in Co cannot be ruled out.

The Relationship of Co to O

As has been shown, there is ample evidence of the textual closeness of Co and O, setting them apart from B (as well, of course, as L), in the limited amount of text available for study. In the rubric which opens the story of Joseph, Co and O share, or shared, an error, if Wanley's report of O's version is correct. It disrupts the statement that God revealed his mercy to Joseph, as he had promised to Abraham. LB have:

Her cydde god ælmihtig his mildheortnysse þe he abrahame behet on iosepe abrahames ofspringe.

Co renders the last clause, following *behet*, as 'and iosepe and abrahames ofsprincge'. O^w concurs, except that it shares only the first conjunction; the nonsensical effect is the same. Two other major errors, both of omission by homoeoteleuton, are shared by Co and O, of fifteen words (45:19) and two (47:9).

There are about eighty further shared readings, setting CoO apart from B. Most have been noted in the above lists of Co variants. A third of them are substantial amplifications or syntactical changes, involving phrases or clauses of several words. The major examples are in 40:20; 43:26, 30, 31; 45:8, 10, 23, 26; 46:14, 16, 17, 19, 20, 21, 23, 28; and 47:3, 4, 5, 9, 15. In a few cases, while Co and O clearly transmit the same overall modification, there are differences; these are discussed below. Sometimes, the text of the variations is no longer fully recoverable on the relevant leaf of O, but a careful calculation of line length, based on the substantial amount of text which survives adjacent to the locations in question, makes it clear that the variants seen in Co (or at least wording with the same number of characters as they) must have been used in O also; this applies to variants in 43:26, 43:30, and 43:31. In 47:7, where Co has 'se kining' for LB's 'he', an *s* is visible in O, followed by plenty of

space for the amplification, and so it is likely that 'se cynyngc' (for that is O's characteristic spelling of the noun) was there. The remaining shared variants involve minor modifications of LB's text; a third of them are one-word additions.

There are, however, differences between Co and O, and these fall into three categories: those where Co is independent of all other witnesses, through error or unique variation; those where it is O which is independent; and those where Co and O vary from each other but concur with either L or B. The many orthographical or phonological differences between the witnesses are not discussed here.

i. Independence of Co

In those sections where O may be compared, Co has a number of further readings, apart from obvious errors, which set it apart from O, as well as from LB. In the following list (which is selective), LBO share the reading given first:

43:11 stor] and recels *add.*
43:12 feos] seolfres
43:14 þæt he agife] and þæt he gyue
       eac] min cyld *add.*
43:16 his geferan] þan gereuan
43:23 simeon ut] þa ut symeon
43:27 arfullice] arwyrðlice
44:4 birig] þara byrig
       hæfdon] eac *add.*
45:18 þær] *om.*
45:26 him] la leof fæder *add.*
45:27 him (ða O) hira færeld] þa eall of heora færelde eall
46:12 wæron suna] suna wæron
47:15 mete] hlauord *add.*
47:16 þær wiþ mete] mete þar wið
47:17 þæt gear] *om.*

Most of these readings are just the sort of amplifications (or, in 43:27, a word substitution) which are charateristic of Co as a whole. The most obvious explanation for their absence from O must be that they were in the archetype *CoO*, from which both Co and O derive, but that then the text was revised still further in Co (or an intervening copy). However, two of the above variants, those in

43:11 and 43:16, are especially puzzling, because here Co shows itself more faithful to the Latin Vulgate than LBO. In 43:16, LBO's *geferan* ('companion') in 'cwæð he to his geferan' is quite wrong to translate Lat. *praecepit dispensatori* ('he ordered his steward'). Only Co has the appropriate *gereuan*. The error presumably arose in a careless consonantal transposition, which must have taken place in the copying of an exemplar with the spelling *gerefan*. The explanation for the present situation, with LBO sharing the error, might be that it was in the *LB* archetype (having been made either at the point of translation or, more likely, in an early copy), whence it passed into the *B* branch of transmission and thence to *CoO*. O faithfully reproduced it, but at the copying of Co (or an intervening manuscript), the fault was noticed and remedied. The use of *gerefa* several times both earlier in the narrative (in 41:34, 41, and 43) and later (in 43:23 and 44:1 and 4) should indeed have been enough to prompt a correction by any alert reviser, without recourse to the Vulgate.

The other anomalous reading, Co's addition of 'and recels' to 'stor' in 43:11, is harder to explain. Co's list of the six precious substances which Jacob instructs his sons to take as gifts to Joseph is in fact correct: 'tyrwan and hunig and stor and recels and æcerenu and hnyte'. It renders the invariable Lat. *resinae et mellis et storacis stactes et terebinthi et amygdalarum* ('resin and honey and storax, myrrh and terebinth and almonds'). LBO have a truncated version, with only five items: 'tyrwan and hunig and stor and æcirnu and hnite'. It would be somewhat implausible to suggest that the sharing of the omission of *recels* by the three witnesses is a coincidence. L and B could of course derive the error from a shared ancestor, but, once in *B*, it must also have reached the ancestor of Co and O, i.e. *CoO*. In that case, the lost phrase ('and recels' for Lat. *stactes*) must have been reintroduced to Co, or an immediate ancestor. This could only have been done with reference, either to an earlier, uncorrupted OE text, or (more likely) to a Latin text of the Vulgate. There is absolutely no reason, in theory, why such reference should not have been made by any copyist or reviser at any time. What is puzzling, however, is that the reviser should have been alert to this particular omission; there are others in the OE version of Genesis 37–50, transmitted unnoticed (or at least apparently unlamented) in Co. Furthermore, as we have seen, none of the many other emendations in Co brings its version nearer to the Vulgate; the tendency is the opposite. In every case of modification, the reviser's starting point

seems to have been the 'correct' OE of his exemplar text (in the *B* tradition), from which he then parted. There is no obvious reason why a reviser might happen to know the passage under consideration well, and so spot the omission. A further point may be made. If the addition of 'and recels' is indeed a late revision, this reinforces the notion of a second stage of emendation in Co, subsequent to its text's copying from the *CoO* tradition. This issue is taken up again in the concluding remarks below.

Of particular interest also are the further amplifications and emendations in the above list which are so characteristic of the revised text of Co and yet are absent from O. They are the additions in 43:14, 45:26, and 47:15, the reduced paraphrase in 43:26, and the substitution of *arwyrðlice* for *arfullice* in 43:27. It might be suspected that the differences are owing to loss from O, or in the last case corruption, rather than further revision in Co, after it became independent of the ancestry shared with O. This theory is strengthened by further evidence in 47:15, noted already above, where O has Co's revised syntax, turning the Vulgate's question into a subordinate clause, but lacks Co's added *hlauord* and a modal verb (Co 'syle us mete hlauord elles we sculon swyltan beforan ðe', O 'syle us mete elles we swylton beforan ðe'). Such anomalies are considered again below.

ii. Independence of O

In a few cases in the available text, O is independent of L, B, and Co:

43:11   of eowrum LB] eac of eowrum Co, eac eower O
44:1   fylle L, fille B, fyllað Co] fyl O
45:24   and LBCo] he *add.* O
46:6   on LBCo] to O
47:4   to þam LB] hider *add.* Co, þyder *add.* O
47:17   hig þæt gear LB] hi Co, þæt gear hyg O
47:18   þe LBCo] nu *add.* O

In 43:11, O's *eower* (with loss of *of* also) is an error, for it is followed by dative plural adjective and noun. In 46:6, we would expect Co to share O's *to*, for in two other nearby cases CoO have *to* as opposed to LB's *on*, with *land(e)* the object. In 47:4, Co and O share an addition to the LB text but have diverged in respect of the actual adverb used; Co's *hider* seems right in the context, so that O's *þyder* is probably an error. In 47:17, Co, presumably through error (though the sense is

not much affected), omits *þæt gear*, so we cannot know whether or not it shared O's transposition of pronoun and adverbial phrase. There are no further errors unique to O.

In the following four cases, where O amplifies the LB text, Co is not available, but the variants (especially the first) are the sort which we would have expected to be in Co; where both texts are available, there are no cases where O makes substantial independent alterations. The LB reading is given first:

47:19   hwi swelte we] hwi ðuus swyltan we
47:20   ciptun L, cypton B] becypton ða
47:20   pharaone] þa faraone
47:23   nimaþ] nu *add*.

A further interesting aspect of O is the gloss *middangeorde*, which is inserted in 47:13 above *ymbhwyrftum*, in what may be an Anglo-Saxon hand but is not apparently that of the copyist.

iii. Coincidence of O and L

Only in two minor cases does O share a variant with L, and thus differ from B and Co:

45:17   cwæde LO] cwæþ BCo
46:10   sunu LO] suna BCo

In 45:17, both variants are acceptable. In 46:10, *sunu* is strictly speaking an error, for the noun ought to be in the plural, but such levelling of inflection is common enough, especially with this noun, in the eleventh century.

Assessment of the Relationship of Co and O

The evidence presented in the above analyses may be summarized as follows.

1. The text of Co derives from an archetype (*CoO*) which is clearly derived from the *B*-tradition; this is confirmed by some thirty readings in which B and Co (and O, where available) differ from L, including three prominent shared errors. There are, however, many other errors which are unique to B, which indicates some distance beteween it and *CoO*.
2. The *B*-text transmitted to Co has undergone substantial revision, consisting mostly of amplification and paraphrase of the text as

we see it in B itself; the modifications have the overall effect of reducing the OE text's fidelity to the Latin of the Vulgate.

3. Enough of Co's revised readings are shared by O to show that it is in the same textual tradition. However, there are some differences. Independent errors in both show that neither text derives directly from the other. Furthermore, three of Co's characteristic changes are not in O: *seolfres* for *feos* in 43:12, the addition of *la leof fæder* in 45:26, and the transposition of *þær wiþ mete* in 47:16; in 47:15, Co's modifications are only partly transmitted (*hlauord* and *sculon* are not added), and in 43:26, Co and O both abbreviate a passage, but differently.

Accounting satisfactorily for all this evidence is difficult. It might be logical to assume that, in the five instances of difference just cited, O derives from the same, revised, tradition as Co but has suffered from careless copying. Yet, even though only the readings just noted are involved, it would surely be astonishing if they had arisen accidentally. It would mean that, in a copy of Genesis which shows no general problem with copying errors, five were nevertheless made which not only happened to leave the sense of the narrative unaffected, but also restored it (more or less, in the case of the changes in 47:15) to its pre-revision form. Theoretically, a Vulgate text, or even an unrevised OE exemplar, could have been consulted, but then the question would arise, in both events, why only these few out of many inaccuracies were put right.

A further passage where Co and O differ, not yet noted, is worth considering finally. It is in 43:23:

Lat. *nolite timere / Deus uester et Deus patris uestri dedit uobis thesauros in sacculis uestris*

LB   ne ondræde ge eow. eower god and eowres fæder god eow sealde goldhord on eowre saccas

Co   ne ondræde ge eowerne god forðon eower god eow sealde goldhord on eower saccas

O   ne ondræde ge eow. eower[ne] god and eower.. god eow sealde goldhord on eowre saccas

The differences are puzzling. As usual, LB give us an accurate close translation of the Latin ('Fear not; your God, and the God of your father, has given you treasure in your sacks'). Co produces an apparently lucid sentence, which in fact quite alters the dynamics

of the statement; the fearing in question should be absolute, not directed at God. We have seen other instances of the reviser carelessly rewriting and missing the mark (though, as so often, what he produces here is not fundamentally wrong). Yet it is hard to see how O's version could have come about as a copy, even a bad one, of the version in Co. Indeed, it appears rather more like an attempted copy of the LB version, though with *fæder* omitted. The original letters on the erasure, indicated at the end of the second *eower* in O's version, cannot be recovered, but it is tempting to assume that they were *es*. Perhaps a reviser of O (or even the copyist himself) removed them when he realized that, as the text stood, the genitive inflection made no sense. (It is very unlikely that he went to another exemplar of *B* to check his revisions; he would surely then have got things right.) Did he next hope to restore some of that sense by giving the first *eower* a masculine accusative inflection, -*ne*, added above the line (which looks contemporary and could be by the copyist)? The fact that Co also has *eowerne* need not, perhaps, be thought too much of a coincidence. If this is right, then we must see Co's version as having been established, not at the making of *CoO*, but at a subsequent revision. If in this case *fæder* had indeed been missing from the *B*-text which was being used for the first revision, there would have been a good excuse for the further modifications.

Thus, following this thinking, we would have to envisage a minimum two-stage process in the production of Co as we have it. First, a main revision of *B*, which produced *CoO*, containing probably most of the amplifications and other alterations which characterize Co's text, but not all of them. At this stage there would have been no deliberate alteration made to the passage in 43:23, but it was perhaps accidentally corrupted by the omission of *fæder*. Second, *CoO* then became the exemplar both for O, whose scribe tried to be faithful to it throughout, and for Co, whose scribe added another layer of amplifications, and coped with the problem in 43:23 in his own way. This theory does provide an explanation for the fact that O lacks a small but significant number of Co's distinct readings.

However, another possibility is worth putting forward. It is that Co and O derive, not from a 'fair copy' of *CoO*, the revised version of the *B*-text, but from the actual manuscript used for the revision. The process whereby such revisions came to be made is an aspect of textual transmission about which we know little. It would certainly

make sense, however, to assume that, in a revision involving a significant number of changes, some of them quite complex syntactical ones, the reviser would not simply make them up in his head and apply them as he wrote out a copy of his source text, but would first write his proposed revisions interlinearly or marginally in that exemplar. Once this had been done, a first fair copy could be made from the 'marked-up' version. It might seem logical for that first fair copy to become the exemplar for any further copies which were to be made. Yet it is perfectly feasible that, for some practical reason, two fair copies might be made from the one marked-up exemplar. If that were the case, we can envisage easily enough different errors being made at each copying: one copyist might misread or misunderstand a particular annotation; another might carelessly (or even deliberately) ignore one, or part of one. This is conjecture, and variations on the process outlined are possible; but its attraction is that it can explain both the similarities and the differences between Co and O, and it does not require intervening copies after *CoO* to account for the errors in Co and O (though such copies may have existed).[137] It posits, too, a single main revision process, that producing a marked-up *CoO*, and not, as far as Co is concerned, a two-stage one.

The following stemma for Co and O, in relation to LB, based on the above argument and conjecture, is thus suggested.

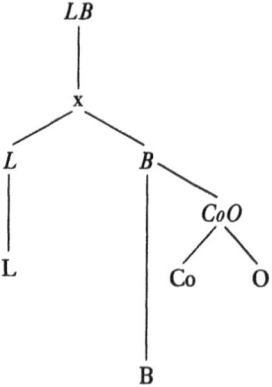

---

[137] Another passage, in which O seems to have a version halfway between that in LB and that in Co, may be considered also in the light of this discussion. In 45:27, LB's 'him hira færeld' becomes 'þa eall of heora færelde eall' in Co and 'ða hira færeld' in O.

6. The Text of N

The bifolium, now lost, whose readings from Exodus 13–14 William Nicholson passed on to Edward Thwaites (see p. lx), may well derive from the same copy of Exodus as the leaves in P, as their page sizes (estimated in the case of N) and the linguistic character of their texts seem to concur. Each witness will, however, be given its own analysis here. We are not offered a complete collation of N by Thwaites, but only, it seems, a record of where the text of N differed from that of L. It is immediately apparent that these differences are often shared by B. Many of them are simply orthographical or phonological; both B and N, for example, invariably use *hi*, not L's *hig*, and *heora*, not *hira*, and both have *ihte*, not *icte*, in 9:24.[138] A few, however, involve errors or textual variants. In four cases, B and N agree simply because of error in L. Thus the latter omits by homoeoteleuton eleven words in 9:22 ('and ofer menn and ofer nytenu and ofer eall egypta land'); in 9:31, it has *bernas* for *beras*, and in 14:7, it omits the preposition *of* before *feohtan* and has *ongen* for *on* before *egipta lande*.[139] Apart from these, there are six shared BN readings (here, and below, L's reading is given first):

9:29 ga ut] ut ga
10:5 þe] *om.*
14:5 faran] *om.*
14:7 feohtan sceal] feohtan mihte
14:16 israhelisce] israhela
14:22 and] ða *add.*

In only one instance does N appear to be closer to L than to B, in a paraphrase of 10:5; both L and N have the clause 'ge on treowe ge on æcron (æcoron N, æcerum B)', whereas B renders the first noun (appropriately, it may be argued) in the plural also, as *treowum* (thus giving the meaning 'in respect both of trees and of fields'). In L, the first *on* has been erased, perhaps by a hasty reader who had not read ahead to see the balanced structure of the double clause.[140]

As noted, it is only divergences of N from L which were recorded by Thwaites, not agreements. Thus there may have been considerably more readings on which LN agreed against B. However, such

---

[138] But there are differences also. For instance, N does not share B's tendency to geminate *n* in *menn* and its compounds.
[139] The erroneous *gen* has been crossed out, but it is not clear when.
[140] Thwaites notes L's erasure in his presentation of the N variants.

cases in the portions of Exodus covered by the fragment would have been few and of minor importance in assessing textual relations. There are two omissions in B, of *on* in 9:26 and *þa* in 9:34, the latter certainly disrupting sense; and in 10:1, B adds *and* before *ic*, but it is of little consequence. Otherwise, the only B variations against L are the contraction *gesihstu* in 10:7 (*gesihst þu* L) and the verb *cyðe* without prefix in 14:4 (*gecyþe* L).

N has only four unique readings:

9:20 se þe drihtnes word (wordes B) ondred] se ðe drihten ondræd
10:1 þe] *om.*
14:5 pharaone] *om.*
14:11 ut] *om.*

In the first case, L is accurate, translating Lat. *qui timuit uerbum domini*, but N's reduction still makes sense. The other three cases involve omissions, and were no doubt scribal errors, though only *pharaone* is essential to meaning.

It seems clear that N was textually in the *B* tradition, quite close to B itself. The evidence, such as it is, would not allow B to be a copy of N, owing to the unique errors in N which did not reach B. There are also sufficient minor problems in B, which are not shared by N (assuming that we can trust Nicholson and Thwaites to have detected and communicated them), to rule out B as the exemplar of N. The two versions appear, therefore, to have derived independently from a common ancestor, perhaps through one or two intermediate stages.

7. The Text of P

The remains of the two bifolia which make up P (Pierpont Morgan G. 63) preserve parts of Exodus 16–17, 19–20, and 23–32. As in the case of N, it is at once clear that there is close textual coincidence between B and P, in readings where they diverge from L. In the following lists, L's readings are given first.

B and P share five corrupt readings:

16:18 gegearwode] gaderode (Lat. *parauerat*)
        næfde] næfre (Lat. *reperit*)
17:5 of] on (Lat. *de*)
19:13 ge gehiron mid þam byman blawan þonne] *om.*
23:31 oþ palastinas sæ] *om.*

P's version of 19:13 is on the first of the parchment strips, f. 2ʳ, where four-fifths of each line is missing, but it is easy enough to calculate that there was no room for the seven words which are also absent from B; they are preceded by another *þonne*, and no doubt the omission was made by homoeoteleuton in an ancestor manuscript.

There are sixteen further instances of BP readings which are absent from L. In three of them, BP clearly give the archetypal reading, and L is in error, though only in the first case is the problem obvious:

24:9   astah] astygon (Lat. *ascenderunt*)
32:4   get] geat þæroff B, ⟨geat þær⟩of P (Lat. *fecit ex eis*)[141]
32:11 cwæð] drihten *add.* (Lat. *domine*)

The remaining BP readings are minor variants, none of which affects the sense of the narrative or can be shown to be closer to the Latin:

16:18   he] *om.*
16:31   manna] man
19:11   sin] beon
23:9 and 21   for þam] þe *add.*
23:25   gebletsie] bletsige B, blætsige P
              fram eow] eow fram
23:33   þi læs] ðe *add.*
24:1   eaðmedað] geeadmedaþ
24:6   hirsume] gehyrsume
29:12   cealfes] þæs cealfes
32:20   þæt] þe
32:21   ane] *om.*

There is a striking coincidence of phonology and orthography in B and P also. In more than sixty cases, a form is shared by BP against L, as in *gegæderodon* for *gaderodon*, *sæternesdæges* for *sæterndæges*, and *healdene* for *healdanne* (twice). In almost thirty cases, however, B goes its own way (with, for example, *undor* for *under*, and *yldestan* for *yltsan*).

Only rarely do LP share a reading absent from B, and in most cases it is the result of corruption in B (whose readings are here on the right):

---

[141] In P, the relevant page (f. 4ʳ) is reduced to a strip, and the verb and all but the last two letters of the adverb have been lost.

17:9 minre] *om.* (Lat. *mea*)
23:12 þæt] and (Lat. *ut*)
      sige] si
32:8 alædde] lædde

Conversely, in one case, LP share the incorrect inflection of a weak noun in the genitive (*wylne* for B's *wylnan*, 23:12) and in another they both lack the conjunction *and*, which is in the Latin, though its loss is not a problem (24:10).

All the cases where P stands apart from LB may be attributed to error by its copyist:

16:20 acreowyd (acreowed B)] creowyd[142]
16:21 genoh] ge
16:25 hit ys drihtnes restedæg] his driht ristendæg
17:8 ongean (ongen B)] on
17:10 stigon uppan] stigon sti uppon
19:19 leng] lenge
23:12 assa] assan (Lat. *asinus*)
23:20 nu] na
23:28 twelf] twel
24:4 mearca] meara

The coincidence of some very positive readings in the text of P is sufficient to show its closeness to B; such are *gaderode* for *gegearwode* and *næfre* for *næfde* in 16:18 and the seven-word and three-word omissions in 19:13 and 23:31. In no important cases do LP coincide against B, and P has no signifcant unique variants. A high incidence of agreement between B and P in their orthographical and morphological forms has been noted also. Neither text can be derived from the other, however, in view of the individual errors which both contain. Although there are no shared idiosyncrasies which might put the case beyond doubt, the origin of P in the same original *OEH* volume as N is likely, as has been shown, in view of a general concurrence of orthography and phonology and volume of text per page.

---

[142] It is possible that *creowyd*, without prefix, is as acceptable as *acreowyd*. Neither word, from hypothetical *(a)creowan* (apparently 'to swarm with', rendering Lat. *scatere*), is recorded elsewhere in the *OE Corpus*.

8. The Text of Ln

The single bifolium Ln (Lincoln Cathedral Library 298, no. 2) carries the text of Num. 10:28–16:3. Like the texts in N and P, this shows clear affinities with B, rather than L.

The main BLn readings are as follows, with L's version given first:

11:6, 9	manna] man	
11:16	læde] læd	
11:24	beforan] *om.*	
11:34	nemdon] genemdon	
12:3	wæs soðlice] soðlice wæs	
12:7	þeowes] ðeowan	
12:14	asingod] asyndrod (Lat. *separetur*)	
13:1	bebead god] god bebead	
	gesette] geset	
	foran] pharan (Lat. *Pharan*)	
13:3	þe] nu *add.*	
13:21	þæt] ðe	
13:24	eallum] ealle	
14:11	nellað hig gelyfan] ne gelyfað hi	
14:12	and] hi *add.*	
14:13	cwæð þus] ðus cwæð	
14:23	ic] ðe *add.*	
14:32	sweltan] licgan (Lat. *iacebunt*)	

Only one of these shared BLn readings, that in 14:23, is an obvious error; the addition of *ðe* before *foreswor* in 'ne geseoð hig þæt land þe ic foreswor heora fæderum' muddles the sense (Lat. *non uidebunt terram pro qua iuraui patribus eorum*). The added word had been crossed out in B, probably by a late corrector. Several of the sharings result simply from error or idiosyncrasy in L; such are its *asingod* in 12:14 and *sweltan* in 14:32. In addition to this small but solid core of positive variants, the reader of B and Ln is at once struck by the frequent coincidence of their orthography and phonology, with some sixty shared forms. These include many spellings of names (as in *osee* for L's *iosee*, Lat. *Osee*; *naabdi* for L's *naabbi*, Lat. *Nahabi*; and *caleph* for L's *calef*, Lat. *Caleb*). L and Ln share only about fifteen such forms, against B. However, in about thirty further cases, Ln is independent of both L and B, a tendency reflected in a number of unique textual variants also (see below).

There are only six cases where L and Ln share variant readings (given here on the left), against B:

11:9	þe þe]	þe
11:11	swenctest]	geswenctest
11:15	and þæt ic]	and ic
11:32	mid micle]	micle
12:10	swa snaw]	swa hwit swa snaw
14:3	ure cild]	cyld

All but one of these result simply from arbitrary variation made by the copyist of B, or his immediate predecessor. The exception is the addition of *mid* before *micle* in 11:32, where LLn are in error. OE 'þa aras þæt folc and gaderode ealne dæg and ealle þa niht micle menio þæra fugela' is a paraphrase of Lat. *surgens ergo populus toto die illo et nocte ac die altero / congregauit coturnicum*; thus, *mid* cannot work, without emendation of the syntax. The sharing of the addition might be explained as independent duplication of a careless assumption that people 'in a great crowd' were collecting the birds; or it might be an archetypal error which was noticed and corrected at the copying of B (or a predecessor) but not of L or Ln.

In proportion to the small amount of text available, there is a comparatively strong independent textual streak in Ln. Seven of the readings involved, however, are clear errors, though we cannot know whether they were lapses by the copyist of Ln or were taken over by him, unnoticed, from his exemplar; here and below, LB share the first reading given:

10:35	seo earc]	se earc
10:35	wæs]	wæs wæs
11:31	eorðan]	*om.*
12:10	hreofnis]	hreofnysse
13:4	þam]	þa
13:10	psalthi]	pilthi
14:33	fædera]	*om.*

The misspelling of *psalthi* was put right by the addition of *s* above, apparently by a contemporary corrector of Ln. There are a further six unique variants in Ln, not overt errors, including two amplifications and two transpositions:

10:28	ut]	þa ut
11:21	flæsc]	to etanne *add.*

12:8   rædelsas] rædels
12:9   gewat] wat
14:3   wurðon gehergode] gehergode wurðon
14:38 iosue and caleph] Caleph and Iosue

The amplification in 11:21 in interesting, because Ln's resulting 'ic sylle him flæsc to etanne' appears to put it closer to Lat. *dabo eis esum carnium* than LB's spare 'ic sylle him flæsc'. However, the addition of *to etanne* could have been triggered at any stage of transmission by the occurrence of the phrase twice previously (in all versions), in 11:4 and 13, where it renders *ad uescendum carnes* and *carnes ut comedamus*, respectively. It seems unnecessary to posit reference back to the Vulgate on the part of Ln's copyist (or an immediate precdecessor). In 14:38, it is LB's word order which follows the Latin.

The score of variants shared with B confirm that Ln belongs in the *B* tradition, though it has a number of its own readings, which set it apart. Certainly, neither B nor Ln is a direct copy of the other; nor is it likely that either is derived from the other, given the absence from Ln of readings such as B's amplification in 12:10, and from B of Ln's comparatively high number of independent readings.

9. A Stemma for L, B, Co, O, N, P, and Ln

On the basis of the evidence examined above, the following scheme of relationship for the two main, two excerpted, and three fragmentary witnesses of the Hexateuch may be suggested. The group BNPLn is clearly distinct from L; overall, both in their patterns of textual variation and error and in their orthographical and phonological characteristics, they show more similarities with each other than with L. However, B, to judge from its comparatively high rate of independent error and emendation, seems to stand at some distance from the others. Similarity of text volume per page (estimated in the case of N) and the lack of any contradictory linguistic features indicate that N and P may derive from a common ancestor manuscript of the Hexateuch, but Ln is certainly not close to them. Co and O both derive from the *B*-stem, through an archetype *CoO*; this was presumably established quite independently of B itself, in view of the changes in B which it lacks. Co and O might both be direct copies (or derived from such copies) of the *CoO* archetype itself, in the form of a *B*-text marked up with modifications. Because no portions of text are shared between

them, the relative positions on the *B*-stem of N and P, Ln, and Co and O cannot be assessed accurately. The text of the fragments of Deuteronomy contained in Cotton Vespasian D. xiv (described on pp. lxviii–lxix) cannot usefully be incorporated in the stemma. The closeness of the manuscript's obviously correct version of Deut. 16:19 to that in L, rather than to B's incorrectly modified version, proves only that the text is in the *LB* tradition. When B's modification was made cannot be ascertained; it could have been at the copying of B itself or at any point on the *B* line of transmission.

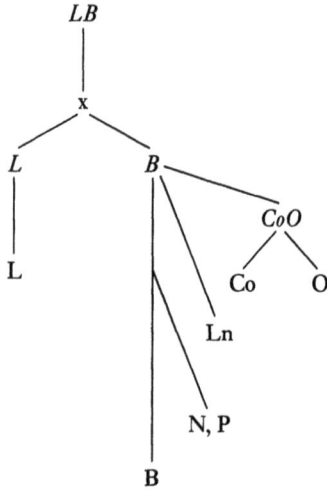

10. The Text of Judges in L and H

Judges stands apart from the other six books of the *OEH*, with a separate textual history. Although it has been copied in L by the same scribe responsible for most of that volume, and presumably at more or less the same time, it begins at the top of a fresh leaf (f. 108^r), the page before it (f. 107^v) having been left blank after Joshua, which ends right at the bottom of f. 107^r. This suggests that Judges was not in the exemplar containing the *Prefatio* plus Genesis–Joshua used by L's copyist; these texts had no doubt been written continuously. However, the two works copied after Judges in L, Ælfric's letter to Wulfgeat and his *Libellus de ueteri testamento et nouo*, follow it without breaks (though each work starts on a fresh line). It is likely, then, that these three texts were already together in

a separate exemplar used by the copyist. Each is an Ælfrician work, which would be enough to explain their collocation in a booklet.

The only other extant witness to Judges is H (Bodleian Library, Hatton 115), which has a text very close in most respects to that in L. Both L and H have been dated to the second half of the eleventh century, and thus the manuscripts may be more or less contemporary, but either could have been copied, conceivably, a generation later than the other. The dating issue is considered further below.

Unlike the books of the OE Hexateuch, which are largely unelaborated translations of Scripture, the version of Judges in L and H has the character of a homily. Selected parts of the Vulgate are translated at length, sometimes quite closely, sometimes more paraphrastically, but they are sandwiched between a prologue of about 200 words and a epilogue of about 1,150 words; there are also three exegetical interpolations in the translated or paraphrased middle section, after 5:32 (156 words), 8:28 (71 words), and 15:19 (91 words). No distinction is made in either manuscript between scriptural passages and the additional material; there are no line breaks or enlarged capitals. Judges is presented as a homily in the present edition and reference to particular readings is made by line number, though chapter and verse numbers are provided in the text also for the sections of translation.

The likelihood that the text of Judges had influenced one of the annals of the *Anglo-Saxon Chronicle* was first raised by John Earle.[143] The annal for 959, as it appears in both the 'D' and 'E' recensions of the *Chronicle*, recounts briefly the death of King Eadwig and accession of his brother Eadgar, and then launches into a euology of the latter, written in a prose with distinct metrical features (and consequently often printed as verse). D (British Library, Cotton Tiberius B. iv, ff. 3–86; Ker 192) was probably copied in the mid-eleventh century or a little later, seemingly at Worcester, and E (Oxford, Bodleian Library, Laud Misc. 636; Ker 346) in the early to mid-twelfth century, at Peterborough. Many of the annals in E are derived from the same source as D, and much of this material seems to have been copied from a northern English exemplar.[144] The lines

---

[143] *Two of the Saxon Chronicles Parallel, with Supplementary Extracts from the Others*, ed. John Earle and Charles Plummer, 2 vols. (Oxford, 1892–9), ii. 152.

[144] See *The Anglo-Saxon Chronicle: A Collaborative Edition*, vi: *MS. D*, ed. G. B. Cubbin (Cambridge, 1996), and vii: *MS. E*, ed. Susan Irvine (Cambridge, 2004), with discussion of the 10th-c. annals at pp. xxxii–xxxix and lviii–lxiv respectively, and the text of the 959 annal at pp. 45 and 56 respectively.

in Judges highlighted by Earle for comparison with the *Chronicle* text come at the very end of the epilogue (331–6), where Ælfric makes allusion to three admirable English kings, Alfred, Æthelstan, and Eadgar, and especially praises the latter. The coincidences of vocabulary and diction between chronicle and homily (the text of which is almost identical in L and H) are indeed remarkable, and can scarcely be coincidental. Here, the relevant lines are compared, with the shared words underlined; the chronicle text is a modernized version of that in E, which is all but identical with D's version:

Judges, 331–6	*Anglo-Saxon Chronicle* (E), 959
Eadgar se æðela and se anræda cining <u>arærde Godes lof</u> on his leode gehwær, ealra <u>cininga swiðost</u> ofer Engla ðeode, <u>and him God gewilde</u> his wiðerwinnan a, <u>ciningas and eorlas</u>, þæt hi comon him to <u>buton</u> ælcum <u>gefeohte</u>, friðes wilniende, him <u>underþeodde</u> to <u>þam þe he wolde. And he wæs gewurðod wide geond land.</u>	He <u>arerde Godes lof</u> wide, and Godes lage lufode, and folces frið bette, swiðost þara cyninga, þe ær him gewurde, be manna gemynde. <u>And God him</u> eac fylste, þæt <u>ciningas and eorlas</u> georne him to bugon, and wurden <u>underþeodde to þam þe</u> he wolde, and <u>butan gefeohte</u> eal he gewilde, þet he sylf wolde. <u>He</u> <u>wearð wide, geond þeodland,</u> swiðe geweorðad.

Karl Jost, rightly concluding that the direction of influence could only be from Ælfric to the chronicler, not the other way round, argued from linguistic evidence that the author of both the 959 annal in D and E and the 975 annal in D (which is also metrical) was Wulfstan, bishop of Worcester and archbishop of York (from 1002), who was intimately familiar with Ælfric's writings and often made use of them. After a more extensive analysis of the language, Sara Pons-Sanz has shown that Wulfstan's authorship is by no means certain.[145] Whatever the case, we can deduce nothing of the textual history of Judges from this borrowing, but it is useful evidence for a slightly wider circulation of Ælfric's Judges than the manuscript evidence otherwise suggests.

---

[145] See 'A Paw in Every Pie: Wulfstan and the Anglo-Saxon Chronicle Again', *Leeds Studies in English*, 38 (2007), 31–52.

Error in L *and* H

Although the two manuscripts carry the same generally good text of Judges, clear errors in L outnumber those in H by about three to one. None of the errors is shared, which indicates that the versions derive independently from a common archetype.

Errors in L

There are about thirty obvious copying errors in L. In the following examples, the correct form in H is given first:

38	moabiscre]	abiscre[146]
70	se sisara]	sesirra
77	behelode]	beheold
82	bufan]	bugan
85	sohte]	*om.*[147]
101	hu him]	halum
102	eargan]	eorgan
128	betæce]	betæhte
136	fynd]	fyrd
147	and heora land]	*om.*
255	benæmde]	benæmbe

In 70, L's *sesirra* seems to be an accidental conflation of *se sisara* (H's reading), rather than a variant spelling, without the preceding demonstrative, of *sisar(r)a*, which is the form used in the other occurrences of the name in L (65, 85, and 87). In another case (135), where Judges 7:16–17 is translated, L's plural verb in 'he todældon hi þa on þrim diglum folcum' works perfectly well as paraphrase, but H's version, with 'he todælde', is closer to the Vulgate (*diuisit*) and may be the original reading.

Several puzzling erasures have been made in L. Where the erased letters can still be read, they seem to be correct, as in H. In two cases, other letters have been added by a late 'corrector', presumably L'Isle, and it is probable that he was responsible for the erasures also, though his reasons are unknown. A bigger erasure may also be by L'Isle and be more justified. The eight words are repetitive, make poor sense, and may be corrupt (*wurdon* for *wurðon*?); perhaps they contain a topical reference. The erasures are as follows:

---

[146] A hand which may be contemporary has added *mo* above.
[147] What looks like L'Isle's hand has written *acsigend embe* above.

73	gehaten > geha*l* (*ten* has been erased and *l* added late)
76	eðode > oðode (*e* has been erased and *o* superimposed late)
89	ofþrihton > ofþri.ton (the erased letter appears to be correct *h*)
93	te extollerunt (extulerunt H) > ... xtollerunt (the erasure is large enough to accommodate three letters)
120	hig (hi H) > ... (there is space for three letters; an initial *h* can be detected under the erasure)

Errors in H

Among clear errors in H are the following, with L's reading given first:

15	langum] langŏum
110	hig²] *om.*
124	folce] afolce
159	þe he] þe ðe
255	we] *om.*
307	him] *om.*
311	an] tyn

Textual Variation in L *and* H

There are about sixty other variations between L and H, where each reading makes good sense, so that error in one or the other witness is not immediately apparent. Even where the readings occur in translated scriptural passages, it is not possible to judge one variation to be the better by virtue of its being more close to the Latin original.

Several single words in L are absent from H: *æfre* (12), *me* (79), *heora* (167), *þa* (211), *sona* (226), *næfre* (230), *eft* (240), *þa* (244), *twam* (248), *eall* (251), *þa* (278). Some of these may be accidental omissions from H; in 251, for instance (Judg. 16:30), the Vulgate passage is paraphrased, but *eall* seems to be needed, and it probably echoes Lat. *super omnes principes*. Other absences in H may of course result from amplification in L of the archetypal text.

In relation to L, H has a few small amplifications:

25	for L	for heora H
77	him L	him þa H
125	geceas L	geceas him H
173	eardigende L	ða eardienne H
290	sende god	sende god to H

Again, these variants may in fact signal loss in L, rather than addition in H to the archetypal text. H has also a substantial addition (as compared with L), which constitutes the only major variation between the two texts. It is in the epilogue, at 279, in a passage in which Ælfric refers to the ruling system of the Romans and explains that a body of senators was appointed to meet daily to administer to the people on the emperor's behalf. H inserts the words which are italicized here:

ðæt synd þeodwitan þe dæghwamlice smeadon on anum sindrian huse embe ealles folces þearfe. *ofer feala þeoda and embe rihtwisnisse.* and heora ræd kyddon siððan þam casere and him gewearð anes.

In some ways it is a rather awkward amplification, adding little to what has already been given, or strongly implied, but the metrical pattern which the addition gives to the passage as a whole (i.e. the alliterating *folces þearfe / feala þeoda* and *rihtwisnisse / ræd*) does suggest Ælfrician style. There is no obvious trigger for eyeslip in the amplified version, of the sort which might explain loss from L of the original words, and yet, if not, it is hard to understand how and why they might have been introduced later to an unamplified version of H (and there are no other such additions). Thus, the two clauses are likely to be part of Ælfric's original homily.

There are several cases of word-order variation betweeen L and H, including:

38	hig ofsloh L	ofsloh hi H
91	nu eac L	eac nu H
246	him macian L	macian him H
280	kyddon siððan L	syððan cyddon H
316	lagon ealle deade L	deade lagon ealle H

Further variations consist mostly the sort of simple substitutions which are common enough in manuscript copying, some of them involving the use of aurally or visually close words. They include:

12	sumne L	fremsumne H
41	swiðe L	syððan H
59	he L	god H
135	folcum L	floccum H
141	stiðlicum L	swiðlicum H
156	þa L	swa H
165	him godes gast on wæs L	him com godes gast on H

181	on L	mid H
190	folce L	laðan flocce H
209	ungeleafulic L	ungeleaffull H
251	afeoll L	offeoll H
282	gebigan L	gewyldon H
319	þeode L	leode H

It might seem likely that H's alliterating *fremsumne* in the prologue (*funde . . . fremsumne fultum*, 12), where L has simply *sumne*, is the original Ælfrician reading, though there is no record of Ælfric using the word, or related ones, in any of his other works.[148] In 41, L's *swiðe* works well, but H's *syððan* may have been Ælfric's original choice, rendering Lat. *postea* (though adverbial *þa* is there also, preceding *swiðe/syððan*). In 135, too, H's *floccum* is probably the original translation of Lat. *partes*. In 190, however, where the Vulgate is paraphrased and both versions are possible, L's *folce* seems rather more appropriate.[149] In 181, L has *l mid* added above, in a contemporary hand responsible for a number of corrections. In 282, *gebigan* and *gewyldon* are not obvious synonyms, but both are appropriate in the context of subduing recalcitrant people to a ruler's will; *gebigan* is perhaps the slightly better choice (and is echoed in the next sentence by the cognate *bugon*), and *gewyldon* might have been introduced subsequently under the influence of the preceding adjective *ungewylde*. On the other hand, the *ungewylde/gewyldon* parallel could well have been part of Ælfric's original rhetoric. In 251, L's apparent use of the preterite of *afeallan* in a transitive sense is unique but is accepted by the *DOE*. It may, however, be a corruption of *offeoll*, the form in H. *Offeallan* is a little-used verb but there are two instances in Ælfric's works, in both of which the idea of something falling onto people (in both cases a tree) is involved, as here in Judges.

One further apparent difference in vocabulary, H's *ofhearmode* for L's *ofearmode* in an amplification in 164, may be merely orthographical. Hall and Meritt list *ofhearmian* (not recorded elsewhere in the OE corpus) as a verb separate from *ofearmian* ('to be pitiful') and with a transitive meaning, 'to cause grief'. Bosworth-Toller are more circumspect and leave open the possibility that the *h*-form is simply a

---

[148] The *OE Corpus* in fact records only seventeen occurrences of the adjective, mainly in psalter glosses. The noun *fremsunes* occurs more frequently but is not used by Ælfric.

[149] Crawford, however, emends L's reading to H's *laðan flocce* in his edition.

variation of *ofearmian*. This seems more probable, so that OE 'ða ofhearmode gode heora yrmða sona' may be interpreted as an impersonal construction; literally, 'it was pitiful to God in respect of their sufferings', i.e. 'their sufferings distressed God'.

A grammatical difference between L and H is seen in the treatment of *wimman*. In each of three relevant occurrences (in 74–5, 80–1, and 85), the word is treated 'correctly' as masculine in H (*se wimman*) but it is given natural gender in L (*seo wimman* or, in one case, *seo wifman*). In all recorded uses of *wimman* in his works, Ælfric is scrupulous in maintaining the masculine gender.[150] A number of further variations between the versions involve the use of verbal or (in one case) nominal prefixes: thus H has *wissunge* for L's *gewissunge* (4), *gefengon* for *fengon* (23), *slean* for *ofslean* (256) and *geendiað* for *endiað* (337). In each case where a *ge*-prefixed verb is involved, L is without the prefix.[151]

Assessment of Judges in L *and* H

Both L and H transmit a reliable text of Ælfric's homiletic paraphrase of Judges. That of H, however, has somewhat fewer errors than that of L. Most of the small textual variations between the two versions, including omissions or additions, must have begun as mistakes also, though there can be no certainty in general about which manuscript is 'correct'. However, in three cases where the Vulgate is being translated directly, the fact that H's variant reading is closer to the Latin than L's is an indication that H more reliably preserves Ælfric's text. In addition, H has a six-word sentence, absent from L, which is easiest explained as being in Ælfric's original text (where it fits into a metrical scheme), but becoming lost accidentally (or even deliberately) in transmission to L.

There is thus good reason to assume that H is closer than L, textually, to Ælfric's version. The occurrence in both manuscripts of independent errors (none is shared) indicates that neither derives in a direct line from the other, but that they descend from a common archetype. We need not envisage a long or complex stemma. The absence of other appearances of the Judges homily in the extensive extant Ælfrician manuscript corpus (the evidence of the *Anglo-Saxon*

[150] The *OE Corpus* lists nine such cases, where gender-specific inflections on *wimman* or associated words occur. The treatment of the noun as feminine is in fact very rare in the corpus as a whole, occurring only in a few late texts.

[151] A search of the *OE Corpus* reveals no useful information about Ælfric's use or otherwise of the prefixed forms in question.

Chronicle notwithstanding) may indicate quite restricted circulation, and so the lines of transmission from Ælfric to L and H may be quite short and simple. Both manuscripts have been dated, mainly on palaeographical evidence, to the second half of the eleventh century. H could date from a little earlier than L during that period, but the fact that it has the better text may simply result from a single careless copying stint in the production of L, or an immediate ancestor of L. Linguistically, both manuscripts show a number of 'late' characteristics, such as the levelling of inflections, but in neither case are they dominant.

11. The Text of the *Libellus* in L and Bo

Ælfric's *Libellus de ueteri testamento et nouo* has only two surviving manuscript witnesses, L and Bo (Bodleian Library, Bodley 343), but the New Testament section is entirely absent from the latter. Moreover, Bo's Old Testament text begins only at L's line 56, and is wanting also from lines 247 to 349, owing to the loss of a leaf. Bo may have been copied up to one hundred years after L, in the second half of the twelfth century. Ælfric's original translation was probably made about 1006, for he introduces himself at the start of the *Libellus* as 'abbod', and thus it must have been written after he became abbot of Eynsham in 1005.[152]

The Text of L

The full text of the *Libellus*, as extant only in L, has approximately 11,500 words but is remarkably free of obvious error. Scribal slips occur at a lower rate than in the books of the Heptateuch; examples are *ecclesiastices* for *ecclesiastes* (307), *eardu* for *eardum* (326), *leasan* for *læssan* (744), and *getacnode* for *getacnodon* (822). There are half a dozen minor omissions, such as those of *and þrittig geara* (101), *hit* (218), and *awrat* (532). Other errors (for which in only one case Bo can be compared) include (with the emended form given first):

275	wunnon]	wunedon
346	gehergodan]	heretogan
427	eorðlice Bo]	eornostlice
821	wuldre]	wundre

In 346, emendation of *heretogan* to the prefixed verb *gehergodan* is made in this edition, for that is the form which occurs several times

[152] See Clemoes, 'Chronology', 33 and 35.

RELATIONSHIPS BETWEEN THE MANUSCRIPTS clxix

later in the narrative. In 427, *eornostlice* seems at first reading to fit the context, but it is clearly wrong, for it is part of the translation of a Latin line which Ælfric has just given, including the phrase *reges terre* ('eorðlice kyngas' in Bo). In 821, *wundre* is not completely out of place, but *wuldre* is more appropriate (and is used five times elsewhere in the tract). Crawford identified several other errors, and emended accordingly. For example, in each of three occurrences of *godcundnysse* in L (in lines 535, 547, and 825), the word is spelled *godgundnysse*, but the consistency suggests that this is a deliberate spelling, and it is preserved in the present edition. An obvious problem occurs in L in a list of the apostles (560-2), where both Matthew and Simon would be expected, in addition to the ten names given. They have been added by a late hand in the manuscript (*Matthæus* after *Thomas*, *Simon Cananeus* after *Tatheus*);[153] Grein and Crawford adopted them without comment but they are omitted in this edition.

There are two examples of dittography in L. In 743, the words 'mildheortnysse and his' are repeated, but in 74 the problem is more substantial. After he has written 'ne he nolde', the scribe's eye has gone back four lines to 'and nolde', and he repeats forty-three words:

wurðian þone þe hine ge worhte and him ðancian æfre ðæs þe he him forgeaf and beon him underðeodd þæs ðe he swiþor geornlice for ðære micclan mærðe þe he hine gemæðegode. He nolde þa habban his scippend hi[m] to hlaforde ne he nolde

Then he continues correctly with 'þurhwunian on ðære soþfæstnisse'. The problem was presumably sparked by the similarity of 'nolde wurðian' and 'nolde þurhwunian', with *nolde* perhaps coming at the end of a line in the exemplar. Comparison of the repeated lines with the first version (used in the edited text) affords us a brief glimpse of routine scribal variation during copying: one punctus (after *forgeaf*) is absent in the repetition, two thorns have been replaced by eths (in *ðancian* and *ðære*), *he* has been added spuriously after *þæs ðe*, and the *m* in *him* (after *scippend*) has been suspended (not obviously for space reasons: the line breaks after the first three letters of *hlaforde*). We cannot, of course, know which forms were in the exemplar. In the case of erroneous *he*, however, it seems unlikely that

[153] In putting Matthew after Thomas, and Simon after Thadeus, the late corrector follows the order given in Matt. 10:2-4, but the overall order of names in the *Libellus* varies from that in the gospel. The corrector has put numbers above the names in the emended list to modify the sequence, but this still is not that of the gospel.

it was there; it would be a strange chance for an unwanted word to have been dropped accidentally in the first copying, and we could not attribute its omission to editorial acumen on the part of the copyist, when he has then repeated forty words without noticing. A late corrector did not cross out the actual added words, but (with the same effect) went back a few words and crossed out the complete sentence, 'He nolde . . . ge mæðegode', adding *sup[er]flua* in the margin.

The Text of Bo

The majority of differences between L and Bo, apart from variations in orthography and phonology, involve morphology and word choice and are consequent on the gap of up to one hundred years which separates the two copies. The language of Bo, as we would expect, reflects many of the changes which were occurring in English during the latter part of the twelfth century. These include the consistent use of *þe* for *se* and *þeo* for *seo*, and the frequent writing of the prefix *ge* as *i*, and the short front vowel *æ* as *a*. There is persistent, but variable, levelling of inflections (about 60 cases), which is especially noticeable in the reduction of dative adjectival and nominal *-um* to *-e* and masculine singular accusative *-ne* to *-e*. Characteristic examples of Bo's forms are seen in *buton ealle synnum* for L's *buton eallum synnum* (59) and *ure hælendes* for L's *ures hælendes* (118).

In the parts of the *Libellus* witnessed by both L and Bo, there are approximately 175 verbs, nouns, adjectives, and adverbs which, in L, are formed with the prefix *ge-*. Just under half of these (74) are without the prefix in Bo, as in *wrohte* for L's *geworhte* (56), *cyndes* for L's *gecindes* (60), and *lomlucor* for L's *gelomlicor* (474). As noted above, in the verbs which in Bo retains the prefix, it becomes *i-* in about half the cases. There is also a tendency (21 cases) for prepositional verb prefixes to disappear in Bo, as in *funde* for L's *afunde* (80) and *burigede* for L's *bebirigde* (223).

Bo's text of the Old Testament section of the *Libellus* (which lacks the opening fifty lines and a page containing lines 247–349) has about twenty clear errors, which is almost three times as many as in the comparable text of L. Several of them seem to reveal a copyist who had little understanding of the text, though others (such as problems of false concord and lack of inflection) must be judged in the context of the general levelling tendency noted above (thus *sunu* for *sunum*, 473, and *heom* for *hig*, 354 and 477). There is only one important

omission, that of *for þære micclan mærðe* in 72–3. Other errors in Bo include:

74	soþfæstnisse]	softnysse
101	on]	oð
109	þæt þæt]	þæt ðer
132	fær witodlice]	fæder witolice
167	norðerne mennisc]	mennisc norðene
170	iapheþes ofspringe]	iapheðes ofsprunges
207	seo boc]	ðeos botū [154]
228	gewann]	he wan
349	iudea]	chaldea
436	god]	gast

In 167, the two words have been marked for transposition with pairs of parallel lines above each, seemingly supplied by the same person (conceivably the copyist himself) who went through the whole text adding fine diagonal strokes both to the descenders of *g*, as decoration, and above many vowels as reading marks. There are no errors shared by L and Bo.

The Texts of L *and* Bo *Compared*

In the following analysis, the text of L is privileged as the notional standard, from which Bo differs. In at least some cases, however, an apparent omission from Bo may result from an amplification in L, so that Bo in fact carries Ælfric's original version.

In the Old Testament section of the *Libellus* in L's version, Ælfric makes ten references to works he has written previously. Seven of these occur in the sections which are extant in Bo, but all except one are omitted. They are:

111–14 We secgað nu mid ofste þas endebirdnisse for þan ðe we oft habbað ymbe þis awriten mid maran andgite. þa þu miht sceawian. And eac ða getacnunga þæt

144–5 swa swa we awriton æror on oðrum larspellum to geleafan trimminge

230–2 Ðis ic awende eac on englisc hwilon æþelwerde ealdormen on þam man mæg sceawian godes micclan wundra mid weorcum gefremode.

407–8 be þam we awriton on englisc on sumum spelle hwilon

---

[154] A hand which may be contemporary has written *boc* above.

449   be þam ic awende on englisc sumne cwide iu
461–2 ða ic awende on englisc on ure wisan sceortlice

The excisions are precise, and therefore deliberate. In the case of the first one, the last word is the demonstrative *þæt*, which strictly speaking belongs with the subsequent clause ('þæt Adam getacnude . . . urne Hælend') but is not essential to it. The one reference to other works of Ælfric which does remain in Bo is at 218–20.[155] Other omissions in Bo, all of them minor and none adversely affecting sense, amount to fewer than a dozen. They include *ðing* (61), *sunu* (75), *furðon* (81), *yðum* (130), *toeacan* (184), *et reliqua* (367), *his* (486), and *twam* (493).

There are two substantial additions to Bo. In neither case does their absence from L cause any obvious disruption to that manuscript's narrative, but it is notable that both are in Ælfric's characteristic rhythmical style. They are shown here, italicized:

116–18   Eua getacnode þe of adames sidan god silf geworhte. godes
         gelaðunge. þe of cristes sidan. siþþan wearð acenned. *his*
         sylfes agen bryd mid his blode aðwogen. Adames slege soðlice
         getacnode ures hælendes slege
134–5   Herto (her L) wæs seo forme yld þissere worulde *and of*
         ðam æhta monnum com eal moncyn syððan. And seo oðer yld
         wæs þissere worulde oð abrahames timan þæs ealdan
         heahfæderes

The idea of the church as Christ's 'agen bryd', alluded to in the first addition, is used by Ælfric in his 'Homily on the Third Sunday after Easter',[156] and he makes several references to the cleansing power of Christ's blood in his hagiographical works.[157] There is, however, no obvious trigger for eyeslip to explain the absence of the words from L, assuming they were in the archetype. The second addition echoes the theme of the 'eight men' (i.e. Noah and his companions), which has been discussed twice in preceding lines. In this case, the repetition of *and* (in the form of the Tironian *et*) might have been

---

[155] 'And we [hit] habbað awend witodlice on Englisc, on þam mann mæg gehiran hu se heofonlica God spræc mid weorcum and mid wundrum him to.' The three references in sections which are in L but are missing from Bo are at 315–16, 407–8, and 665–6.
[156] *Angelsächsische Homilien und Heiligenleben*, ed. Assmann, 93.
[157] For example, 'on his blode ðwogen fram synna horwum' in 'The Forty Soldiers'; see *Ælfric's Lives of Saints*, ed. W. W. Skeat, 2 vols., EETS os 76/82 and 94/114 (London, 1881–1900, repr. 1966), i. 293.

enough to prompt eyeslip and omission. Though both of these clauses are very likely to be Ælfrician, in neither case has L's text been emended in the present edition.

A number of small additions and amplifications are found in Bo also, though some of these may in fact represent archetypal readings which L has lost:

75	gesceop fægerne]	swa fæger isceop Bo
93	æfter]	hæræfter Bo
131	fæder]	oðð̄e *add.* Bo
134	her]	her to Bo
151	ferde]	eft *add.* Bo
180	gehaten]	ihaten ð̄e Bo
189	dyre]	deore and Bo
226	miclum]	his micele Bo
379	þam]	ylcan *add.* Bo
479	abhominatus]	est *add.* Bo

Variations in vocabulary between L and Bo, many of them reflecting later OE or early ME usage in the latter manuscript, include:

90	butu]	ba twa Bo
104	mannan]	man Bo (*acc. sing.*)
121	geciged]	isæd Bo
142	gereordum]	spæce Bo
174	getwisan]	twinnes Bo
182	bearnum]	children Bo
217	racu]	fare Bo
222	gewat]	ferde Bo
368	geciged]	icwædon Bo

In nine occurrences where the present plural of *beon-wesan* is written variously as *sind, synd, syndon,* or *sint* in L, Bo has *beoð* (or once *beð*) in seven cases, and *wurdon* in an eighth. Only in one case (353) is *syndon* preserved. Other minor syntactical and grammatical variations include:

129–30	he getacnode crist þe forð com to us] he tacnode for ð̄i crist ð̄e to us for ð̄i com Bo
146	fulan] fulestan Bo
220	on gewritum] mid write Bo

433   on þæra cininga bocum] on þære kyngbocum Bo
450   witegung] iwitegæd Bo
455   his afandode] hine fandode Bo

In terms of sense, each variation is possible, though one may sometimes be judged more likely to be original than the other. In Bo's version of the clauses in 129–30, for example, we may be seeing the original version, for the complex correlative structure is unlikely to be a modification of the simpler version used in L.[158] In addition, there are a dozen variations between L and Bo in respect of word order.

Assessment of L *and* Bo

The inclusion of cross-references to other Ælfrician works in L, but not (with one exception) in Bo, and the lower error rate in L's text, seem to be good evidence, prima facie, that the version of the Old Testament section of the *Libellus* in L is nearer to Ælfric's composition than that in Bo, and this is of course backed up by the fact that it was copied probably two or three generations earlier. A conscious decision to remove the cross-references must have been taken at some point in transmission, though this is perhaps surprising, when over half the other items in the Bodley volume are Ælfrician homilies. It presumably suggests that the authorship of Ælfric, at least as an integrating factor in a large body of work, was not important by the second half of the twelfth century. Furthermore, given the comparatively high quality of L's text (lacking as it apparently does any major corruptions), it would be reasonable to assume that L is quite close to the original composition. As for Bo, it shares none of L's errors and so cannot derive directly from it and must come from a parallel copy, yet there is very little difference between it and L, if the changes relating to the evolution of the English language are ignored. Thus, a complex line of transmission from the archetype to Bo would seem unlikely. Indeed, the lack of other witnesses to the *Libellus* does suggest that it was not copied widely at all. However, the simple picture thus presented is disrupted by the evidence of the two clauses which are in Bo but absent from L. It is likely that they are Ælfrician, for it is hard to see why two such amplifications would have been made, seemingly arbitrarily but with great stylistic skill, at a later stage of transmis-

---

[158] Crawford emended L's 'forð' to 'for ði com', but it is left in the present edition.

sion. Bo may therefore preserve a text which is, in some ways at least, closer to the original than L's, from which the clauses in question were presumably lost, either by accident or (more likely) deliberately. This could have happened very early in the afterlife of Ælfric's composition; then the text remained more or less unchanged. If this is the case, we should probably assume also that many of the apparent small 'amplifications' in Bo, discussed above, are in fact original Ælfrician readings, subsequently lost, whether from an ancestor of L or L itself.

V. EDITORIAL PROCEDURES AND CONVENTIONS

The texts of the *OEH* and the *Libellus* are based on L. In the *Prefatio* and Genesis to Joshua, the first source for necessary emendations has been B, with C as an additional source in Genesis 1–24. In Judges, H has been used, and in the *Libellus*, Bo. Editorial emendations to L's text are enclosed in square brackets, with the original reading given in the apparatus at the foot of the page. There is no convenient way to show in the text when emendation consists in omitting erroneous original words or letters, but these, too, are shown in the apparatus.

A handful of corrections have been made to L either by the copyist or by what seems to be a contemporary (i.e. Anglo-Saxon) corrector. Most of these consist of a letter, or occasionally a word, added above the line; sometimes a replacement letter is superimposed on the original or squeezed into the body of a word. Such additions are incorporated in the edited text, between primes; they are in italics, if the corrector (as far as can be ascertained) was not the original scribe but was nevertheless operating within the Anglo-Saxon period. A few alterations to the OE text, made apparently by the late eleventh- or early twelfth-century Latin glossator, are noted. Most of the many remaining alterations in L were made in the sixteenth century by William L'Isle. With a few exceptions, such later interventions are ignored in the apparatus. Manuscript deletions are shown, though these can rarely be dated; many are likely to have been made by L'Isle. A wide range of alterations is found in B also, including extensive annotation by L'Isle; very many additions and some corrections were made by annotators in the twelfth century. As with L, in general, only

contemporary emendations in B are indicated in the apparatus, between primes. C has many contemporary (i.e. late twelfth- or early thirteenth-century) alterations, in several phases, added above the line or in the margin; these, too, are indicated in the apparatus (in italics if they are not, apparently, in the hand of the main scribe, though this is not always easy to ascertain).

Throughout the edition, variant readings in the other available manuscripts are noted in the apparatus at the foot of the page. Only variations between þ and ð and *i* and *y* are ignored. The recently renewed interest in the manuscript transmission of Old English in the later eleventh and twelfth centuries justifies the full presentation of all other variants, even though many are purely orthographic. Given that, for the larger part of the *OEH*, there is only one other manuscript witness apart from L, and rarely more than two, even in Genesis, and only one for parts of the *Libellus*, the resulting apparatus is not overburdened.

The aim in the editing of the Hexateuch has been to establish a sound copy of L, which is chosen because, overall, it appears to transmit more accurately than B the archetypal text brought together at the time of the compilation of the *OEH*, of which L and B are copies. No attempt is made to reconstruct that archetype. Similarly, in Judges and the *Libellus*, the aim has been to produce a correct version of L's text of Ælfric's two works, not to try to establish a hypothetical 'autograph' text. Variations in H or Bo, for Judges and the *Libellus* respectively, which may well be the original Ælfrician readings, are not preferred, unless L's text is clearly corrupt.

There has been no attempt to correct what were probably original mistakes of translation, and emendations to the text of L have been made only in the following two circumstances: first, where there is a clear problem of sense in L and a convincing alternative reading or spelling, or an omitted word or phrase, is available in B or another manuscript; and second, where a disruptive mistake in spelling or in grammatical concordance in L (whether shared with other witnesses or not) can be corrected uncontroversially (e.g. *ceastre* emended to *ceaste*, for Lat. *seditione*, in Num. 16:49). Minor mistakes in concordance, such as the omission of the inflection *-n* in the oblique cases of weak nouns, or the use of the inflection *-e* on strong adjectives in the masculine accusative singular, where *-ne* is to be expected, are not normally corrected. Such forms are an accurate illustration of trends in the language during the eleventh century.

This approach differs from that of Crawford, who emended frequently. No other attempt has been made to 'improve' the text of L, even when it can be argued that another version may be a more accurate witness to the archetype (perhaps, in the case of the biblical texts, because it more closely renders a Vulgate passage). Archetypal lacunae (i.e. those shared by each available manuscript) are indicated by ellipses between square brackets. Significant emendations conjectured by previous editors are shown in the apparatus.

For the most part, the texts are written continuously in L. The few breaks which occur at the start of all but one of the seven biblical books and the two succeeding texts, and at various other points in the biblical narratives, are signalled by enlarged, and usually coloured, initial capital letters. These always begin a new line, with space left at the end of the previous line. Only between Joshua and Judges is there a substantial gap, of a whole page, with the latter text starting at the top of a fresh leaf (see pp. lxx–lxxi). The additional paragraph breaks in this edition have been inserted by the present editor for the convenience of modern readers.

In the biblical narratives, modern chapter and verse division is indicated in this edition by superscript numbers, following the precedent set by R. M. Liuzza in his *The Old English Version of the Gospels*. In Genesis to Joshua, textual notes are keyed to these numbers. In Judges, however, the long added homiletic passages make reference by chapter and verse number impractical; this book is therefore provided also with line numbers, as are the *Prefatio* and the *Libellus*, and notes are keyed to these.

The main mark of punctuation in L is the punctus, usually on the line but sometimes raised to roughly medial position. It marks off phrases or clauses, appearing nearly always before the conjunction *and*, and it is used after each item in lists of names; the word *æ* usually has a punctus on each side of it. Sometimes the punctus versus is used, especially when there is a clear break in the biblical narrative; where there is much space at the end of a line, a triangle of punctus may be added. Occasionally (fewer than forty times altogether in the *OEH* and the *Libellus*), the punctus elevatus is used, for no obvious reason and sometimes where a pause is not desirable. Although L's punctuation is consistent, and helpful, some 80 per cent of the time, the contrary cases are sufficient to hamper reading. Consequently, modern punctuation has been introduced in this edition. One result of this is that ambiguities concerning the

clxxviii   INTRODUCTION

distinction between relative and subject pronouns (such as *se* and *þæt*), and between certain adverbs and conjunctions (such as *þa* and *swa*), which are common enough in OE prose, have had to be resolved by the editor. Where this might be contentious, or where other problems concerning the meaning of the OE have arisen in the biblical narratives, Jerome's Vulgate has been consulted for guidance in the first instance; where this itself is not clear (and ambiguities are frequent in the Latin), recourse has been had to the Hebrew text (though the established Masoretic text post-dates Jerome). Modern capitalization has been introduced also. In some 50 per cent of cases, the first letter of a new sentence in L is capitalized. In some parts of the manuscript, it appears that the copyist himself has written capitals over original small letters.

Modern conventions of OE word division are used. The *y* is persistently dotted in the manuscripts, but this is not reproduced in the edited text. Abbreviations are silently expanded. The scribe of L uses crossed thorn for *þæt* and sometimes (not always at or near the end of a line) suspends final *m*, and more rarely *n*, by means of a macron over the penultimate letter of the word; occasionally, *æfter* is abbreviated. *Cwæð* is very often abbreviated to *cw̄*; when written in full, the word more often has *ð* than *þ*, and that is the form used in the edited text. The Tironian *et* is used by the scribe of L (and the scribes of the other manuscripts) almost always, and in a few cases also it is used for the first element in nouns and verbs; it is amplified in the edited text to *and*. Abbreviations are occasionally noted in the apparatus, when this may be useful in understanding an error or variation. Where roman numerals are used in L, however, these are retained, presented (as almost always in the manuscript) between points. Where L spells out a figure but another manuscript uses roman numerals, this is not noted in the apparatus, unless there is an error. Each of the witnesses uses roman numerals at least occasionally, and C nearly always. Reading marks and other accents appear sporadically in L, but all seem to post-date the copying considerably and none is reproduced in the edited text.

The following marks have been used in the text and the apparatus:

[ ]   encloses an editorial alteration to the text as transmitted in L. In the apparatus, the sigla of any manuscripts carrying the emended reading are given first, followed by the actual reading in L and, where applicable, in other manuscripts.

Within longer sections of variant text given in the apparatus, minor variants in specific manuscripts are shown between square brackets.

[. . .] indicates a lacuna in the text, resulting from an omission undetected by the copyist and thus invisible in the manuscript.

` ´ encloses letters or words which were added to the text after it was first written; in all the manuscripts, these are normally interlinear additions. Only emendations which appear to be early medieval are noticed.

italics indicate letters or words added by a hand different from that of the main scribe of the manuscript or the current part of it.

⟨ ⟩ encloses letters or words which are illegible, commonly the result of damage to the manuscript.

... indicates the approximate number of letters lost when a word is illegibly erased or damaged.

. . . within a lengthy lemma indicates editorial omission of text for reasons of space.

THE TEXTS

[*PREFATIO* TO GENESIS]

INCIPIT PREFATIO GENESIS ANGLICE.   f. 1ʳ

ÆLFRIC MUNUC GRET ÆÐELWÆRD EALDORMANN
ead⟨mod⟩lice. Þu bæde me leof þæt ic sceolde ðe awendan of
⟨Ly⟩dene on Englisc þa boc Genesis. Ða þuhte me hefigtime þe to
tiþienne þæs, and þu cwæde þa þæt ic ne þorfte na mar⟨e⟩ awendan   5
þære bec, buton to Isaace, Abrahames suna, for þam þe sum oðer man
þe hæfde awend fram Isaace þ⟨a⟩ boc oþ ende.
   Nu þincð me, leof, þæt þæt weorc is swiðe pleolic me oððe ænigum
men to underbeginnenne, for þan þe ic ondræde gif sum dysig man
ðas boc ræt, oððe rædan g⟨e⟩hyrþ, þæt he wille wenan þæt he mote   10
lybban nu on þære ni⟨wan⟩ æ swa swa þa ealdan fæderas leofodon, þa
on þære tide ær þan þe seo ealde æ gesett wære, oþþe swa swa men
leofodon under Moyses æ. Hwilon ic wiste þæt sum mæssepreost, se
þe min magister wæs on þam timan, hæfde þa boc Genesis and he
cuðe be dæle Lyden understandan. Þa cwæþ he be þam heahfædere   15
Iacobe þæt he hæfde feower wif: twa geswustra and heora twa þinena.
Ful soð he sæde, ac he nyste, ne ic þa git, hu micel todal ys betweohx
þære ealdan æ and þære niwan. On anginne þisere worulde nam se
broþer hys swuster to wife, and hwilon eac se fæder tymde be his
agenre dehter, and manega hæfdon ma wifa to folces eacan. And man 20
ne mihte þa æt fruman wifian, buton on his siblingum. Gyf hwa wyle
nu swa lybban æfter Cristes tocyme swa swa men leofodon ær Moises

---

Damage to the right edge of f. 1 in L has destroyed the ends of the first eleven lines on the recto and their beginnings on the verso; conjectured missing characters are supplied between angle brackets. Lines 1–56 of the Prefatio are wanting in B; some of this text is available in Bᵗ. C is without a heading.

MSS L, Bᵗ, C   2 ÆLFRIC] Alfric Bᵗ   ÆÐELWÆRD EALDORMANN] Æðelweard ealdorman BᵗC   3 awendan] awænden C   4 Lydene] ledene Bᵗ, lædene C   Englisc] ænglis C   5 tiþienne] tiðigenne Bᵗ   cwæde] cweçde Bᵗ   awendan] awænden C   6 buton] butan C   Abrahames suna] habrahames sunu C   þam] ðan BᵗC
9 underbeginnenne] beginnen[e] Bᵗ, underginnenne C   dysig] dusi C   10 rædan] readan Bᵗ   wille] wile Bᵗ   11 fæderas leofodon] fæderes lifedan C   þa] *om.* C
12 þære] þere C   seo] þeo C   gesett] geset BᵗC   men] menn Bᵗ   13 leofodon] lyfedan C   se] þe C   14 þam] ðan C   and] *om.* Bᵗ   15 dæle] dele (e *corr. to* æ) C   Lyden] leden Bᵗ, læden C   16 þinena] þinæna C   17 sæde] sæda C   git] guit C
betweohx] betwux Bᵗ, betwueox C   18 þisere] ðisre Bᵗ, þissere C   worulde] weorlde C
se] þe C   19 broþer] broðor BᵗC   swuster] swustor BᵗC   se] þe C   be] wið C
20 agenre dehter] agene dohtor C   hæfdon ma wifa] ma wif hæfdon C   man] mann Bᵗ
21 buton] butan C   siblingum] siblingan Bᵗ, gesiblingum C

PREFATIO TO GENESIS

æ, oþþe under Moises æ, ne byð se man na cristen, ne he furþo⟨n⟩ wyrðe ne byð þæt him ænig cristen man mid ete.

25 Ða ungelæredan preostas, gif hi hwæt litles understandað of þam Lydenbocum, þonne þingð him sona þæt hi magon mære | lareowas beon, ac hi ne cunnon swa þeah þæt gastlice andgit þærto and hu seo ealde æ wæs getacnung toweardra þinga, oþþe hu seo niwe gecyþnis æft⟨er⟩ Cristes menniscnisse ⟨w⟩æs gefillednys ealra þæra þinga þe seo
30 ealde gecyðnis getacnode towearde, be Criste and be hys gecorenum. Hi cweþaþ eac oft be Petre, hwi hi ne moton habban ⟨w⟩if, swa swa Petrus se apostol hæfde. And hi nellað gehiran ⟨n⟩e witan þæt se eadiga Petrus leofede æfter Moises æ, oþ ⟨þ⟩æt Crist, þe on þam timan to mannum com, began ⟨t⟩o bodienne his halige godspel and
35 geceas Petrum ærest him to `ge´feran. þa forlet Petrus þærrihte his wif, and ealle þa twelf apostolas, þa þe wif hæfdon, forleton ægþer ge wif ge æhta and folgodon Cristes lare to þære niwan æ and clænnisse þe he silf þa arærde. Preostas sindon gesette to lareowum þam læwedum folce. Nu gedafnode him þæt hig cuþon þa ealdan æ
40 gastlice understandan and hwæt Crist silf tæhte, and his apostolas, on þære niwan gecyðnisse, þæt hig mihton þam folce wel wissian to Godes geleafan and wel bisnian to godum weorcum.

We secgað eac foran to, þæt seo boc is swiþe deop gastlice to understandenne and we ne writaþ na mare buton þa nacedan
45 gerecednisse. þonne þincþ þam ungelæredum þæt eall þæt andgit beo belocen on þære anfealdan gerecednisse ac hit ys swiþe feor þam.

23 oþþe under Moises æ] om. B[t]   Moises] moyse C   ne] C f. 2[v]   se] þe C   na] no B[t]   he] om. C   furþon] n lost in hole L, forþon C   24 ete] gereordige C
25 ungelæredan] unigelæredan C   understandað] understandat C   26 Lydenbocum] ledenbocum B[t], lædenbocum C   þingð] ðincð B[t], þinch C   magon mære] magan mæra C   lareowas] lar`þ´eowas C   27 cunnon] cunnan B[t]C   gastlice] gastli`ce´ C   seo] þeo C   28 toweardra þinga] towærdra þincga C   seo] se B[t], ðe C   gecyþnis] gecyðnes C   29 æfter Cristes menniscnisse wæs] wære æfter cristes mennisnesse C   gefillednys] þæs gefyllednesse C   29-30 seo ealde gecyðnis] ðeo ealda gecyðne`s´ C
30 be hys] bi his C   gecorenum] corenum B[t]   31 Petre] LB[t]C (partly del. in L, Paul add. by L'Isle)   hwi] hwig B[t]   32 se[t]] þe C   hæfde] hefde C   se[2]] þe C
33 leofede] leofode B[t], lyfode C   Crist] `crist´ C   34 com] B[t], and add. L, `and´ C   bodienne] bodigenne B[t], bodianne C   halige] halie C   godspel] godspell B[t]
35 Petrum] petrus B[t], þa petrus C   ærest] ærost C   36 hæfdon forleton] hæfdon and forleton B[t], hæddon forletan C   37 folgodon] folgede C   clænnisse] clennesse C
38 þa] om. C   sindon gesette] syndon geset B[t], sindan geset C   lareowum] larðiwum C
39 læwedum] læwedan B[t], læwædum C   gedafnode] gedafonode B[t]   hig] hi B[t]C   ealdan] ealdon C   40 tæhte] tahte C   41 gecyðnisse] ægecyðnesse C   hig] hi B[t]C   mihton] mihtan C   wissian] wisian C   to] om. C   42 wel] well B[t]
43 secgað] segað C   44 buton] butan C   44-5 nacedan gerecednisse] nacedon gerædnusse C   45 eall] al C

PREFATIO TO GENESIS

Seo boc ys gehaten Genesis, þæt ys 'gecyndboc', for þam þe heo ys firmest boca and spricþ be ælcum gecinde. Ac heo ne spricð na be þæra engla gesceapenisse. Heo onginð þus: 'In principio creauit Deus celum et terram.' Þæt ys on Englisc, 'on annginne gesceop God heofenan and eorþan'. Hit wæs soðlice swa gedon þæt God æl | mihtig gewor`h´te on anginne, þa þa he wolde, gesceafta. Ac swa þeah, æfter gastlicum andgite, þæt anginn ys crist, swa swa he sylf cwæþ to þam Iudeiscum: 'Ic eom angin þe to eow sprece.' Þurh þis angin worhte God fæder heofenan and eorþan, for þan þe he gesceop ealle gesceafta þurh þone sunu, se þe was æfre of him accenned, wisdom of þam wisan fæder.

Eft stynt on þære bec on þam forman ferse: 'Et spiritus Dei ferebatur super aquas.' Þæt is on Englisc, 'and Godes gast wæs geferod ofer wæteru'. Godes gast ys se halga gast, þurh þone geliffæste se fæder ealle þa gesceafta þe he gesceop þurh þone sunu. And se halga gast færþ geond manna heortan and silþ us synna forgifenisse, ærest þurh wæter on þam fulluhte and siþþan þurh dætbote. And gif hwa forsihð þa forgifenisse þe se halga gast sylþ, þonne biþ his synn æfre unmyltsiendlic on ecnysse. Oft ys seo halige þrinnys geswutelod on þisre bec, swa swa ys on þam worde þe God cwæþ: 'Uton wircean mannan to ure anlicnisse.' Mid þam þe he cwæð 'uton wircean' ys seo þrinnis gebicnod. Mid þam `þe´ he cwæð 'to ure anlicnisse' ys seo soðe annis geswutelod. He ne cwæð na menifealdlice, 'to urum anlicnissum', ac andfealdlice, 'to ure anlicnisse'.

47 Seo] þeo C   for] C f. 3ʳ   47–8 heo ys firmest boca] hu is boca fyrmest C
48 spricþ be ælcum gecinde] specð be allum gecyndum C   49 þæra] þære C
gesceapenisse] gesceapennesse C   onginð] unginð C   In] *enlarged initial cap.* L
50 Englisc] ænglisc C   annginne] anginne C   51 heofenan] heofonan C
52 geworhte] geweorhte C   anginne] angyn C   53 anginn] angyn C
54 sprece] spece C   55 worhte] weorhte C   heofenan] heofonan C   for þan
þe] þa C   gesceop] gescop C   56 se] þe C   accenned] acenned C   58 stynt]
stent C   bec] boc C   ferse] uerse C   59 is on Englisc and] is þæt C
60 geferod] geferæd C   se] þe C   61 geliffæste se] geliffeste þe C   gesceop]
sccop C   62 se] þe C
MSS L, B, C   62 and silþ] *start of* B   silþ] deþ C   63 forgifenisse] forgyfnysse
B, forgifnesse C   ærest] ærost C   siþþan] siðan C   64 dætbote] dædbote BC   And
gif] *large initial cap.* L, *om.* C   forgifenisse] forgyfnysse B, forgifenesse C   se] ðe C   sylþ]
deð C   65 synn] syn BC   unmyltsiendlic] unmiltsigendlic B, unminsienlic C   Oft]
Eft B   ys] *om.* B   65–6 seo halige þrinnys] þeo halie þrymnys C   66 geswutelod]
geswutelode B, geswutolod C   þisre bec] þissere boc C   worde] weorde C
67 wircean mannan] wyrcan man C   68 wircean] wyrcan C   þrinnis] þrymnys C
69 anlicnisse] anlicnesse C   seo] þeo C   69–70 menifealdlice] menigfealdlice B,
mænigfealdlice C   70 anlicnissum] anlicnesse C   andfealdlice] anfealdlice BC
anlicnisse] anlicnesse C

PREFATIO TO GENESIS

  Eft comon þri englas to Abrahame and he spræc to him eallon þrim swa swa to anum. Hu clipode Abeles blod to Gode, buton swa swa ælces mannes misdæda wregaþ hine to Gode butan wordum? Be þisum litlum, man mæg understandan hu deop seo boc ys on
75 gastlicum andgite, þeah þe heo mid leohtlicum wordum awriten sig. Eft Iosep, þe wæs gesæld to Egipta lande, and he ahredde þæt folc wið þone miclan hunger, hæfde Cristes geta⟨c⟩nunge, þe wæs geseald for us to cwale and us ahredde fram þam ecan hungre helle susle. Ðæt micele geteld þe Moises worhte mid wunderlicum cræfte on þam
f. 2ᵛ westene, swa swa him God | sylf gedihte, hæfde getacnunge Godes
81 gelaþunge þe he silf astealde þurh his apostolas mid menigfældum frætewum and fægerum þeawum. To þam geweorce brohte þæt folc gold and seolfor and deorwirþe gimstanas and menigfælde mærþa. Sume eac brohton gatehær, swa swa God bebead. Ðæt gold getacnode
85 urne geleafan and ure gode ingehid þe we Gode offrian sceolon. Þæt seolfor getacnode Godes spræca and þa halgan lara þe we habban sceolon to Godes weorcum. Ða gimstanas getacnodon mislice fægernissa on Godes mannum. Ðæt gatehær getacnode þa stiþan dædbote þæra manna þe heora sinna behreowsiað. Man offrode eac fela cinna
90 orf Gode to lace binnan þam getelde. Be þam ys swiþe menigfeald getacnung, and wæs beboden þæt se tægel sceolde beon gehal æfre on þam nytene æt þære offrunge, for þære getacnunge þæt God wile þæt we simle wel don oþ ende ures lifes; þonne biþ se tægel geoffrod on urum weorcum.
95   Nu is seo foresæde boc on manegum stowum swiþe nærolice gesett, and þeah swiðe deoplice on þam gastlicum andgite. And heo is swa

  71 comon] coman C   Abrahame] habrahame C   spræc] spec (*corr. to* spæc) C   eallon] eallum BC   72 clipode] clypede C   buton] butan C   73 wregaþ] C *f. 3ᵛ*   butan] buton C   74 litlum] lytlan B   75 leohtlicum] leohtum B   sig] sy BC 76 Iosep] ioseph C   gesæld] geseald BC   ahredde] ahrædde B, aredde C   77 miclan] micelne C   hunger] he *add.* C   getacnunge þe] getacnunga he C   78 ahredde] aredde C   helle susle] *om.* C   79 wunderlicum] wundorlicum B   81 his] is C menigfældum] menifealdum B, mænifealdum C   82 frætewum] fretewungum C þeawum] ..eawum (*parchment damaged*) B   geweorce] weorce B   83 seolfor] seoluer C deorwirþe] deorwurðe B   menigfælde] mænifealde B, mænifealda C   84 Sume] sum⟨e⟩ B   brohton] brohtan C   God bebead] seo æ bebead B   85 sceolon] scoolan (*appar. corr. to* sceolan) C   86 spræca] spæce C   lara] lare BC   87 sceolon] sculon C 87–8 getacnodon mislice fægernissa] getacnode mistlice fægelnyssa C   88–9 dædbote þæra] dedbotæ þara (*corr. to* þæra) C   89 heora] hura C   behreowsiað] bereo`w´siat C 90 menigfeald] mænifeald BC   91 se tægel] se tægl B, þe tægl C   92 offrunge] offrungæ B, ofrunge C   for þære getacnunge] *om.* C   93 simle wel] symble well B   se tægel] se tægl B, þe tægl C   geoffrod] geofrod C   95 seo] þe C   stowum] stowwum C nærolice] nearolice BC   gesett] geset B   95–6 gesett and þeah swiðe deoplice] *om.* C 96 þam] *om.* C   gastlicum] gastlican B   swa] *om.* C

geendebyrd swa swa God silf hig gedihte þam writere Moise, and we ne durron na mare awritan on Englisc þonne þæt Liden hæfþ, ne þa endebirdnisse awendan, buton þam anum þæt þæt Leden and þæt Englisc nabbað na ane wisan on þære spræce fadunge. Æfre se þe awent oþþe se þe tæcþ of Ledene on Englisc, æfre he sceal gefadian hit swa þæt þæt Englisc hæbbe his agene wisan, elles hit biþ swiþe gedwolsum to rædenne, þam þe þæs Ledenes wisan ne can.

Is eac to witanne þæt sume gedwolmen wæron, þe woldon awurpan þa ealdan æ, and sume woldon habban þa [ealdan] and awurpan þa niwan, swa swa þa Iudeiscan doð. Ac Crist sylf and his apostolas us tæhton ægþer to healdenne, | þa ealdan gastlice and þa niwan soþlice mid weorcum. God gesceop us twa eagan and twa earan, twa nosþirlu and twegen weleras, twa handa and twegen fet, and he wolde eac habban twa gecyðnissa on þissere worulde geset, þa ealdan and þa niwan, for þam þe he deþ swa swa hine silfne gewyrð. And he nænne rædboran næfð, ne nan man ne þearf him cweþan to, 'hwi dest þu swa?' We sceolon awendan urne willan to his gesetnissum and we ne magon gebigean his gesetnissa to urum lustum.

Ic cweþe nu þæt ic ne dearr, ne ic nelle, nane boc æfter þissere of Ledene on Englisc awendan. And ic bidde þe, leof ealdorman, þæt þu me þæs na leng ne bidde, þi læs þe ic beo þe ungehirsum, oþþe leas gif ic do. God þe sig milde a on ecnisse. Ic bidde nu on Godes naman, gif hwa þas boc awritan wylle, þæt he hig gerihte wel be þære bysne, for þan þe ic nah geweald, þeah þe hig hwa to wo gebringe þurh lease writeras, and hit byð þonne his pleoh na min. Mycel yfel deð se unwritere, gif he nele hys woh gerihtan.

97 geendebyrd] geendebyrð C   hig] hi B   Moise] moysi C   98 durron] durran C   Englisc] ænglisc C   Liden] leden BC   99 endebirdnisse] C *f. 4ʳ*   buton] butan C   100 wisan] wison C   spræce] *om.* C   fadunge] C, fandunge LB   101 se] þe C   tæcþ] tecð C   103 þe] *om.* C   wisan] wise B   104 witanne] witene B, witone C   woldon awurpan] woldan awirpan C   105 woldon] woldan C   ealdan] *om.* L   awurpan] awyrpan C   106 swa swa] swa B   Iudeiscan] iudeiscean B   109 and¹] *om.* B   twegen] tweigen C   110 gecyðnissa] gecyðnessa C   þissere] ðisre B   geset] gesett B   111 for þam þe] for ðan ðe B, for þam þy C   nænne] nennne C   112 næfð] næf ð' C   dest þu] des'tʹþu C   113 sceolon] sculon C   gesetnissum] gesetnyssae C   114 magon gebigean] magan gebygan C   gesetnissa] gesetnessum C   to] on B   115 þissere] ðisre B   116 Ledene] lædene C   ealdorman] ealdormann C   118 sig] sy BC   119 hig] hi BC   120 hig] hi BC   to] go (g *marked for correction*) B   wo] woge BC   121 pleoh] *om.* C   122 woh] gewrit B

[GENESIS]

INCIPIT LIBER. GENESIS ANGLICE.

¹:¹ ON ANGINNE GESCEOP GOD HEOFENAN AND EORþAN. ² SEO EORÐE soþlice wæs ydel and æmtig and þeostru wæron ofer þære niwelnisse bradnisse, and Godes gast wæs geferod ofer wæteru. ³ God cwæþ þa: 'Geweorðe leoht', and leoht wearþ geworht. ⁴ God geseah þa þæt hit god wæs and he todælde þæt leoht fram þam þeostrum ⁵ and het þæt leoht dæg and þa þeostra niht. Ða wæs geworden æfen and morgen, an dæg. ⁶ God cwæð þa eft: 'Gewurðe nu fæstnis tomiddes þam wæterum and totwæme þa wæteru fram þam wæterum.' ⁷ And God geworhte þa fæstnisse and totwæmde þa wæteru þe wæron under þære fæstnisse f. 3ᵛ fram þam þe wæron bufan þære fæstnisse. Hit wæs þa swa gedon. | ⁸ And God het þa fæstnisse heofenan, and wæs þa geworden æfen and morgen, oþer dæg. ⁹ God þa soþlice cwæð, 'Beon gegaderode þa wæteru þe sind under þeare heofenan and æteowige drignis'. Hit wæs þa swa gedon. ¹⁰ And God gecigde þa drignisse 'eorþan', and þæra wætera gegaderunga he het 'sæs'. God geseah þa þæt hit god wæs, ¹¹ and cwæþ: 'Spritte seo eorðe growende gærs, and sæd wircende, and æppelbære treow, wæstm wircende æfter his cinne, þæs sæd sig on him silfum ofer eorðan.' Hit wæs þa swa gedon. ¹² And seo eorðe forþ ateah growende wirte and sæd berende be hire cinne, and treow wæstm wircende and gehwilc sæd hæbbende æfter his hiwe. God geseah þa þæt hit god wæs. ¹³ And wæs geworden

MSS L, B, C   Rubric, *in red, follows the end of the Prefatio without a line break.*
Rubric INCIPIT LIBER GENESIS ANGLICE] *om.* B (*but an empty half-line preceding the start of the text may have been intended for the rubric*) ANGLICE] *om.* C   1:1 ON] in C; C *f. 4ᵛ*   HEOFENAN] heofonan BC   1:2 SEO] se B, þeo C   æmtig] æmti B þeostru] þeostra B, þustro C   geferod] gefered C   1:3 geweorðe] gewurðe B   wearþ] wæarð B   1:4 þæt²] *om.* B   þeostrum] ðystrum B, þustrum C   1:5 þeostra] ðystru B, þystru C   morgen] merigen B   an] and C   1:6 eft] eft' B   Gewurðe] geweorðe C   fæstnis] fæstnes C   wæteru] wætere C   1:7 fæstnisse¹] fæstnesse C   and totwæmde... bufan þære fæstnisse] *om.* C   þe¹] þa B   1:8 heofenan] heofonan BC   and²] *partly eras.* L   morgen] mergen B   1:9 gegaderode] gegaderade C   þeare] ðære BC heofenan] heofonan B   æteowige drignis] æteo d'r'ygnys C   1:10 gecigde] gecyde C drignisse] drignusse C   þæra wætera] þære wæteru C   sæs] sæ B   1:11 and¹] he *add.* B seo] þu C   wircende] wyrcend C   æppelbære treow] æppeltreow C   cinne] cynde C sæd] sed C   sig] sy BC   silfum] syluum B   1:12 seo] þeo C   forþ] fo`r´ð C   ateah] teah B   wirte] wyrta BC   be] bere (re *subpuncted*) C   hire cinne] heora cynna C gehwilc] an gehwylc C   hæbbende] hebbende C   1:13 mergen] morgen C   se] þe C

GENESIS

æfen and mergen, se þridda dæg. ¹⁴ God cwæð þa soþlice: 'Beo nu leoht on þære heofenan fæstnysse and todælon dæg and nihte, and beon to tacnum and to tidum and to dagum and to gearum, ¹⁵ and hig scinon on þære heofenan fæstnysse and alihton þa eorðan.' Hit wæs þa swa geworden. ¹⁶ And God geworhte twa micele leoht, þæt mare leoht to þæs dæges lihtinge and þæt læsse leoht to þære nihte lihtinge, and steorran he geworhte, ¹⁷ and gesette hig on þære heofenan þæt hig scinon ofer eorðan ¹⁸ and gimdon þæs dæges and ðære nihte, and todældon leoht and þeostra. God geseah þa þæt hit god wæs. ¹⁹ And wæs geworden æfen and mergen, se feorþa dæg.

¹:²⁰ God cwæð eac swilce: 'Teon nu þa wæteru forð swimmende cynn, cucu on life, and fleogende cinn ofer eorþan under þære heofenan fæstnisse.' ²¹ And God gesceop þa þa micelan hwalas and eall libbende fisccinn and stirigendlice, þe þa wæteru tugon forð on heora hiwum, and eall fleogende cinn æfter heora cinne. God geseah þa þæt hit god wæs ²² and bletsode hig, þus cweþende: 'Weaxað and beoð gemenigfilde and gefillaþ | þære sæ wæteru, and þa fugelas beon gemenigfilde ofer f. 4ʳ eorðan.' ²³ And þa wæs geworden æfen and mergen, se fifta dæg. ²⁴ God cwæþ eac swilce: 'Læde seo eorþe forð cuce nitena on heora cinne and creopende cinn and deor æfter heora hiwum.' Hit wæs þa swa geworden ²⁵ and God geworhte þære eorþan deor æfter hira hiwum and þa nitenu and `eall´ creopende cynn on heora cynne. God geseah þa þæt hit god wæs ²⁶ and cwæð: 'Uton wircean man to andlicnisse and to ure gelicnisse, and he sig ofer þa fixas and ofer þa fugelas and ofer þa deor and ofer ealle gesceafta and ofer ealle þa creopende þe stirað on eorþan.' ²⁷ God gesceop þa man to his andlicnisse: to Godes andlicnisse he gesceop hine; werhades and wifhades, he gesceop hig. ²⁸ And God

1:14 todælon] todælan B, todælen C   1:15 hig] hi BC   scinon] scinan C
heofenan] heofonan C   alihton] lihtan C   1:16 þæt mare leoht] *om*. B   þæs] ðes C
lihtinge²] C *f. 5ʳ*   1:17 hig¹] hi BC   heofenan] heofonan C   hig²] hi BC   scinon]
scinan C   1:18 gimdon] gimdan C   todældon] dældon B   þeostra] ðystro B,
ðeostru C   1:19 mergen] morgen C   se feorþa] þe feo`r´ða C   1:20 Teon]
om. C   fleogende cinn] fleohgende cunn C   þære] *om*. B   heofenan] heofonan BC
1:21 God] *om*. C   micelan] miclan B   eall¹] eal BC   fisccinn] fisccyn B
stirigendlice] styrienlice C   eall²] eal C   cinn] cyn B   1:22 hig] hi BC
gemenigfilde¹] gemænifylde BC   gemenigfilde²] gemænifylde B, gemænigfylde C
1:23 mergen] merigen B, morgen C   1:24 seo] þeo C   cuce nitena] cucu nytenu C
cinn] cyn BC   geworden] gedon BC   1:25 God] ða *add*. B   þære] þare C   hira]
heora B, *om*. C   eall] ealle C   cynne] cynnæ C   1:26 cwæð] `c´wæð C   wircean]
wyrcan BC   andlicnisse] anlicnysse B, ure anlicnesse C   sig] sy B, si C   ealle¹] ealla C
ealle²] eall C   þa⁴] *om*. B, þæt C   stirað] styriað B, styreþ C   1:27 andlicnisse¹]
anlicnysse B, anlicnesse C   andlicnisse²] anlicnysse B, anlicnesse C   gesceop¹] gescop C
gesceop²] gescop C   hig] hi BC

hig bletsode and cwæð: 'Wexaþ and beoð gemenigfilde and gefillaþ
þa eorðan, and gewildaþ hig and habbaþ on eowrum gewealde þære
sæ fixas and ðære lyfte fugelas and ealle nytenu þe stiriaþ ofer
eorðan.' ²⁹ God cwæþ þa: 'Efne ic forgeaf eow eall gærs and wyrta,
sæd berende, ofer eorðan, and ealle treowa, þa þe habbaþ sæd on him
silfon heora agenes cynnes, þæt hig beon eow to mete; ³⁰ and eallum
nytenum and eallum fugelcynne and eallum þam þe stiriað on
eorþan, on þam þe ys libbende lif, þæt hig habbon him to
gereordienne.' Hit wæs þa swa gedon, ³¹ and God geseah ealle þa
þing þe he geworhte, and hig wæron swiþe gode. Wæs þa geworden
æfen and mergen, se sixta dæg.

²:¹ Eornostlice þa wæron fullfremode heofenas and eorðe and eall
heora frætewung. ² And God þa `ge´filde on ðone seofeðan dæg hys
weorc þe he geworhte, and he gereste hine on þone seofeðan dæg
fram eallon þam weorce þe he gefremode. ³ And God gebletsode
þone seofeðan dæg and hine gehalgode, for þon þe he on þone dæg
geswac hys weorces þe he gesceop to wirceanne. |

f. 4ᵛ ²:⁴ Ðas sind þære heofenan and þære eorðan cneornisse, þa þa hig
gesceapene wæron on þam dæge þe God geworhte he`o´fenan and
eorðan; ⁵ and ælcne telgor on eorðan, ær þam þe he upp asprunge on
eorðan, and eall gærs and wyrta ealles eardes, ær þan þe hig upp
aspritton. God soðlice ne sende nanne ren ofer eorþan þa git, and
man næs þe þa eorþan worhte, ⁶ ac an wyll asprang of þære eorþan
wætriende ealre þære eorþan bradnysse. ⁷ God gesceop eornostlice
man of ðære eorþan lame and on ableow on hys ansine lifes orþunge
and se mann wæs geworht on libbendre sawle. ⁸ God þa aplantode

1:28 hig¹] hi BC   Wexaþ] weaxað BC   gemenigfilde] gemenifylde B, gemanifealde C
hig²] hi BC   eowrum] heo`w´rum C   1:29 forgeaf] forgyfe B   eow¹] C f. 5ᵛ   eall]
ealle C   ofer] of C   ealle] ealla C   silfon] sylfum B, silfum C   heora] heore C   hig] hi B,
hit C   eow²] heow C   1:30 þe ys] his þe C   hig] hi BC   habbon] habban C
gereordienne] gereordigenne B, gereordiende C   1:31 ealle] ealla C   þing] ðingc B,
þincg C   geworhte] worhte C   hig] hi BC   wæron] wæran C   mergen] merien B,
morgen C   se sixta] þe sixte C   2:1 fullfremode] fulfremode BC   heofenas] heofonas
B, hefonas C   eorðe] eorðan C   2:2 seofeðan¹] seofoðan B, seofanþan C   geworhte]
worhte B, geworuhte C   seofeðan²] seofoðan BC   eallon] eallum BC   weorce] weorcum B
gefremode] gefremeda C   2:3 seofeðan] seofoðan BC   and hine . . . þone dæg] om. C
þon] ðan B   geswac] `and´ gescwac C   gesceop] gescop C   wirceanne] wyrcenne B,
wircanne C   2:4 Ðas] enlarged black initial cap. L   þære¹] ðæra B   heofenan¹]
heofonan C   þære²] ðæra B, þare C   eorðan cneornisse] orþan cneornessa C   hig] hi BC
heofenan²] heofonan BC   2:5 þam] ðan BC   upp¹] up BC   hig] hi BC   upp²] up BC
aspritton] asprutan C   nanne] nænne BC   and man . . . worhte] om. C   man] mann B
2:6 wyll] wyl B, wil C   asprang] asp`r´ang C   wætriende] wæterigende B, wæteriende C
ealre] ealle BC   þære] þare C   bradnysse] bradnesse C   2:7 ðære] þare C   lifes]
liue`s´ C   se] þe C   mann] man B   geworht] geworuht C   sawle] saule C

GENESIS

wynsumnisse orcerd fram frimðe, on þam he gelogode þone man þe he geworhte. ⁹ God þa forð ateah of þære moldan ælces cynnes treow fæger on gesihþe and to brucenne wynsum; eac swilce lifes treow omiddan neorxenawange and treow ingehydes godes and yfeles. ¹⁰ And þæt flod eode of stowe þære winsumnisse to wætrienne neorxenawang. Ðæt flod ys þanon todæled on feower ean. ¹¹ An ea of þam hatte Fison, seo gæþ onbutan þæt land þe ys gehaten Euilaþ, þær þær gold wixt, ¹² and þæs landes gold ys golda selost; þar beoð eac gemette þa gimstanas dellium and honychinus. ¹³ Ðære oþre ea nama ys Gion, seo ys eac gehaten Nylus, seo imbgæð eall þæra Silhearwena land. ¹⁴ Ðære þriddan ea nama ys Tigris, seo gæð ongean þa Assiriscan. Seo feorðe ea ys gehaten Eufrates.

²:¹⁵ God genam þa þone man and gelogode hine on neorxenawange, þæt he þær wircean sceolde and þær begiman, ¹⁶ and bebead him, þuss cweþende, 'Of ælcum treowe þises orcerdes þu most etan. ¹⁷ Soþlice of þam treowe ingehides godes and yfeles ne et þu. On swa hwilcum dæge swa þu ets[t] of þam treowe, | þu scealt deaþe sweltan.' f. 5ʳ ¹⁸ God cwæð eac swilce: 'Nis na god þisum men ana to wunienne. Uton wircean him sumne fultum to his gelicnisse.' ¹⁹ God soþlice gelædde þa nitenu þe he of eorþan gesceop, and þære lyfte fugolas, to Adame, þæt he foresceawode hu he hig gecigde. Soðlice ælc libbende nyten, swa swa Adam hit gecigde, swa ys hys nama. ²⁰ And Adam þa genamode ealle nytenu heora namum and ealle fugelas and ealle wilddeor. Adam soþlice ne gemette þa git nanne fultum his gelican. ²¹ Ða sende God slæp on Adam and þa þa he slep, þa genam he an ribb of his sidan and gefilde mid flæsce þær þær þæt ribb wæs,

2:8 wynsumnisse] wynsumne B, winsumne C   man] mannan C   2:9 gesihþe] sihðe C   brucenne] brucene C   lifes] liues C   omiddan] on middan B, on miden C   neorxenawange] neorxnawange B, neorxenewange C   godes] C f. 6ʳ   2:10 of stowe] to stowe *add.* B   winsumnisse] winsumnesse C   wætrienne] wæterigenne B, wæteriende C   neorxenawang] neorxnawang B, on neorxnewang C   ys] his C   2:11 seo] þeo C   onbutan] onbuton C   gehaten] gehaton C   Euilaþ] euilat C   wixt] wyxð B, wexð C   2:12 þæs] þas C   selost] selæst C   þar] ðær B   gemette þa gimstanas] gemete gymstanes C   honychinus] hon'y'nchinus B, honichilus C   2:13 seo¹] þe C   eac] *om.* C   gehaten] gehaton C   seo²] þe C   þæra Silhearwena] þare Silhearwene C   2:14 þriddan] 'þriddan' C   seo] þe C   Assiriscan] asciriscan C   Seo] þeo C   2:15 neorxenawange] neorxnawange B   wircean] wircen C   þær begiman] þas begymon C   2:16 þuss] ðus BC   etan] eten C   2:17 Soþlice] butan *add.* C   þu] for þan *add.* C   swa²] *om.* C   etst] B, ets L, est C   2:18 þisum] þissum C   ana] anum C   wunienne] wunigenne B   wircean] wircen C   gelicnisse] gelicnesse C   2:19 fugolas] fugelas BC   foresceawode] forsceawode C   hig] hi BC   libbende] libende C   2:20 genamode] 'na'mode C   ealle¹] eallæ C   nytenu . . . and ealle] *om.* C   namum] naman B   ealle³] eallæ C   wilddeor] wildeor B, wilde deor C   Adam²] þa *add.* C   nanne] nænne C   fultum] *om.* C   2:21 ribb¹] rib BC   þær²] *om.* BC   ribb²] rib BC

GENESIS

²² and geworhte þæt ribb þe he genam of Adame to anum wifmen and gelædde hig to Adame. ²³ Adam þa cwæð: 'Ðis ys nu ban of minum banum and flæsc of minum flæsce. þeos bið geciged fæmne, for þam þe heo ys of were genumen. ²⁴ For þam forlæt se man fæder and moder and geþeot hine to his wife, and hig beoð butu on anum flæsce.' ²⁵ Hi wæron þa butu, Adam and his wif, nacode and him þæs ne sceamode.

³:¹ Eac swilce seo næddre wæs geappre þonne ealle þa oðre nytenu þe God geworhte ofer eorðan, and seo næddre cwæþ to þam wife: 'Hwi forbead God eow þæt ge ne æton of ælcum treowe binnan paradisum?' ² Þæt wif andwirde: 'Of þæra treowa wæstme þe synd [on paradisum we etað, ³ and of ðæs treowes wæstme þe stent] omiddan neorxenawange, God bebead us þæt we ne æton, ne we þæt treow ne hrepodon, þy læs þe we swulton.' ⁴ Ða cwæð seo nædre eft to þam wife: 'Ne beo ge nateshwon deade, þeah þe ge of þam treowe eton; ⁵ ac God wat soþlice þæt eowre eagan beoð geopenode on swa hwilcum dæge swa ge etað of þam treowe and ge beoþ þonne englum gelice, witende ægðer ge god ge yfel.' ⁶ Ða geseah þæt wif þæt þæt treow wæs god to etanne, be þan þe hire þuhte, and wlitig on eagum and lustbære on gesihðe, and genam þa of þæs treowes wæstme | and geæt and sealde hire were; he æt þa. ⁷ And heora begra eagan wurdon geopenode. Hig oncneowon þa þæt hig nacode wæron and siwodon ficleaf and worhton him wædbrec.

³:⁸ Eft þa þa God com and hig gehirdon hys stemne, þær he eode on neorxenawange ofer middæg, ða behidde Adam hyne, and his wif eac swa dide, fram Godes gesihþe, onmiddan þam treowe neorxenawanges. ⁹ God clipode þa Adam and cwæþ: 'Adam, hwar eart þu?'

2:22 ribb] rib BC   genam] nam C   hig] hi BC   2:23 minum banum] mine bane C   and] C f. 6ᵛ   þeos bið] beo heo B   þam] ðan BC   were] hyre were B   2:24 þam] ðan BC   moder] modor BC   geþeot] geþeod C   wife] wiuum C   hig] hi BC   butu] buta B, buton C   flæsce] f'l'æsce C   2:25 butu] buta B, buton C   sceamode] scæmede C   3:1 wæs] was C   geappre] geapre B   wife] wifum C   forbead] bebead C   ælcum] ælcon B   treowe] treowum C   3:2 þæra treowa] þære treowe C   synd] sindon C   3:2–3 on paradisum . . . þe stent] om. L   3:3 ðæs] þas C   wæstme] wæstm C   þe stent] C, om. B (þe is add. by late hand)   omiddan] on middan BC   neorxenawange] neorxnawange B   æton] æto C   hrepodon] repodon B, repoden C   swulton] swelton B   3:4 seo nædre] þe næddre C   3:5 geopenode] geoponode C   dæge] dage C   and] om. C   3:6 geseah] geseach C   etanne] etenne B, etene C   þan] ðam B   geæt] æt C   3:7 wurdon geopenode] wordun geoponode C   Hig¹] hi BC   hig²] hi BC   siwodon] sywodon him B, siwedon C   worhton] woruhton C   wædbrec] wadbrec C   3:8 hig] hi BC   stemne] stæmne C   on neorxenawange] on neorxnawange B, oneoxenawange C   middæg] midne dæg B   behidde] beh`y´dde (alt. fr. behedde) C   neorxenawanges] neorxnanwonges B, oneo`r´xenawange C   3:9 hwar] hwær B

GENESIS 13

¹⁰ He cwæð: 'þine stemne ic gehirde, leof, on neorxenawange and ic ondred me, for þam þe ic eom nacod, and ic behidde me.' ¹¹ God cwæð: 'Hwa sæde þe þæt þu nacod wære, gif þu ne æte of þam treowe, þe ic þe bebead þæt þu of ne æte?' ¹² Adam cwæþ: 'þæt wif þæt þu me forgeafe to geferan sealde me of þam treowe and ic æt.' ¹³ God cwæð to þam wife: 'Hwi didest þu þæt?' Heo cwæð: 'Seo næddre bepæhte me and ic æt.' ¹⁴ God cwæð to þære næddran: 'For þan þe þu þis dydest, ðu byst awirged betwux eallum nitenum and wilddeorum. Ðu gæst on þinum breoste and etst þa eorðan eallum dagum þines lifes. ¹⁵ Ic sette feondrædene betweox þe and þam wife, and þinum ofspringe and hire ofspringe. Heo tobryt þin heafod and þu syrwst ongean hyre ho.' ¹⁶ To þam wife cwæð God eac swilce: 'Ic gemenigfilde þine yrmða and þine geeacnunga; on sarnysse þu acenst cild and þu bist under weres anwealde. and he gewild ðe.' ¹⁷ To Adame he cwæð: 'For þan þe þu gehirdest þines wifes stemne and þu æte of þam treowe þe ic þe bebead þæt þu ne æte, ys seo eorðe awirged on þinum weorce. On geswincum þu etst of þære eorðan eallum dagum þines lifes. ¹⁸ Ðornas and bremelas heo a⟨sp⟩rit þe and þu ytst þære eorðan wyrta. ¹⁹ On swate þines andwlitan þu bricst þines hlafes, oþ þæt ðu gewende to eorþan, of þære þe ðu genumen wære, for þan þe ðu eart dust and to duste wyr[þ]st.' ²⁰ Ða gesceop Adam naman his | wife   B f. 7ᵛ
Eua, ðæt is 'lif', for ðan ðe heo is ealra libbendra modor. ²¹ God worhte eac Adame and his wife fellene reaf, and gescrydde hi, ²² and cwæð: 'Nu Adam can yfel and god, swa swa ure sum. Ðe læs he astrecce his hand and nime eac swylce of lifes treowe and ete, and libbe on ecnysse.' ²³ Adræfde hine ða of neorxnawange, ðæt he ða eorðan worhte and him

3:10 stemne] stefne C   gehirde] gehire B   leof] *om.* C   on neorxenawange] on neorxnawange B, oneo`r´xenewange C; C*f.* 7ʳ   ondred] ondræde BC   þam] þan C   þe] *om.* C   eom] heom C   behidde] behyde B   3:11 bebead] forbead C   of²] *om.* BC   3:12 þæt²] ðe BC   æt] ætt B   3:13 didest þu] dydestu B   næddre] nædre B, næddra C   æt] ætt B   3:14 betwux] betweox B   wilddeorum] wildeorum BC   gæst] gest C   lifes] liues C   3:15 betweox] betwux BC   þam] þum *corr. to* þam C   wife] *om.* C   and hire ofspringe] *om.* BC   tobryt] tobrytt B   3:16 wife cwæð God] wiue god cwæð C   gemenigfilde] gemænifylde B, gemanifylde C   geeacnunga] geacnunga C   acenst] BC, acents L   þu²] *om.* C   gewild] gewylt B, gewilt C   3:17 gehirdest] gehyrdes B   wifes] wiues C   bebead] bebiead C   þære] þare C   lifes] liues C   3:18 bremelas] bræmlas C   asprit] sp *lost in hole* L   ytst þære] etst þare C   3:19 þines andwlitan] þine awlitan C   hlafes] `h´laues C   þære] þare C   þan] þā C   wyrþst] wyrst L, gewyrst B, gewendst C   3:20 naman] name C   his] *End of f.* 5ᵛ *in* L; *next leaf lost. The text of 3:20–5:12 in now given from* B; *it is interrupted by illustrations, as shown.*
MSS B, C   wife] wiue C   is²] his C   modor] *illus. follows* B   3:21 worhte] woruhte C   eac] þa C   wife] wiue C   fellene] fellenne C   hi] mid *add.* C   3:22 Nu] efne nu C   can] can`st´ C   Ðe læs] þi les þe C   astrecce] arecce C   lifes] liues C   ecnysse] ecnesse C   3:23 neorxnawange] neo`r´xenewange C   worhte] woruhte C   and] C*f.* 7ᵛ

ðæron tilode, of ðære ðe he genumen wæs. ²⁴ Ða ða he adræfed wæs of neorxnawanges myrhðe, | ða gesette God æt ðam infære engla hyrdrædene and fyren swurd to gehealdenne ðone weg to ðam lifes treowe.

MSS (L), B

⁴:¹ Soðlice Adam gestrynde Cain be Euan his gemæccan and ðus cwæð: 'Ðisne man me sealde Drihten.' ² Eft he gestrynde Abel. Abel wæs sceaphyrde and Cain eorðtilia. | ³ Ða wæs hit geworden æfter manegum dagum ðæt Cain brohte Drihtne lac of eorðan tilingum. ⁴ Abel brohte to lace ða frumcennedan of his heorde. Ða beseah Drihten to Abele and to his lacum ⁵ and ne beseah to Caine, ne to his lacum. Ða wearð Cain ungemetlice yrre, ⁶ and Drihten cwæð to him: 'Hwi eart ðu yrre? ⁷ Gyf ðu god dest, hit ðe bið mid gode forgolden. Gyf ðu ðonne yfel dest, sona hit byð ðe mid yfele forgolden.' ⁸ Ða cwæð Cain to Abele his breðer: 'Uton gan ut.' Ða hi ut agane wæron, ða yrsode Cain wið his broðor Abel and ofsloh hine. ⁹ Ða cwæð Drihten to Caine: 'Hwær is Abel ðin broðor?' Ða andswarode he and cwæð: 'I[c] nat. Segst ðu, sceolde ic minne broðor healdon?' ¹⁰ Ða cwæð Drihten to Caine: 'Hwæt dydest ðu? þines broðor blod clypað up to me of eorðan. ¹¹ Witodlice ðu byst awyrged ofer eorðan, for ðan ðe seo eorðe onfeng þines broðor blodes, ðe ðu mid ðinum handum agute. ¹² þonne ðu tilast ðin on eorðan, ne sylð heo ðe nane wæstmas. Ðu færst worigende and bist flyma geond ealle eorðan.' ¹³ Witodlice Cain cwæð to Drihtne: 'Min unrihtwisnys is mare ðonne ic forgyfenysse wyrðe sy. ¹⁴ Nu todæg ðu me aflymst and ic me behyde fram ðinre ansyne, and ic worige and beo aflymed geond ealle eorðan. Ælc ðæra ðe me gemett me ofslyhð.' ¹⁵ Ða cwæð Drihten to Caine: 'Ne bið hit na swa. Ac ælc ðara ðe ofslihð Cain onfehð seofonfeald wite.' And God him sealde tacn, ðæt nan ðæra ðe hine gemette hine ne ofsloge. | ¹⁶ Cain eode fram Drihtnes ansyne, and he wunode flyma on ðam eastdæle ðæs landes, ðe is genemned Eden.

⁴:¹⁷ Witodlice Cain nam wif, be ðære he gestrynde Enoch. And he getimbrode ceastre and nemde hi be his suna naman, Enoch. ¹⁸ Soðlice Enoch gestrynde [Irad, and Irad gestrynde] [M]aui[a]hel,

---

3:23 tilode] þa tilede C   3:24 neorxnawanges] neo`r´xenawange C   infære] infare C   swurd] swird C   gehealdenne] gehealdene C   lifes] liues C   treowe] *illus. follows* B
MS B   4:2 eorðtilia] *illus. follows*   4:8 hine] *illus. follows*   4:9 Ic] in (c *add. above by late hand*)   4:15 ðara] *alt. to* ðæra   Cain] caiN   4:16 Cain] *illus. precedes*   4:17 Enoch] *illus. follows*   4:18 Irad and Irad gestrynde] *om.*   Mauiahel] nauihel

GENESIS [C]

MS C

⁴:¹ Adam soðlice æfter þisum breac his wiues and heo eacnode and acende Cain and cwæð: 'Ic æfde mannan þurh God.' ² Eft heo acende his broðor Abæl. Abel wæs þa sciephirde and Cain hirðling. ³ Hit wæs þa æfter manegum dagum þæt Caim ofrode Gode lac of þare eorþan wæstmum, ⁴ and Abel ofrode of þam frumcænnedum sceapum his heowodum and of hire fætnesse. Þa beseah God to Abele and to his lacum ⁵ [and ne beseah to Caine ne to his lacum]. Þa hirsode Caim þearle and his nebwlite ætfeol. ⁶ God cwæð þa to Caime: 'Hwi eart þu hirre and hwi ætfeol þin ansin? ⁷ Gif þu ðonne yfel dest, þærrihte bið þeo syn æt þam ingange, ac his gewilnung bið under þe and þu wylst hine.' ⁸ Cain cwæð þa to Abele his broþer: 'Uton gan ut on feld.' Hwæt þa Cain aras togeanes his broðor Abele, þa ða hi on æcere wæron, and hine ofsloh. ⁹ God cwæð þa to Cain: 'Hwær is Abel þin broðor?' He andwirde: 'Ic nat. Eom ic mines broþor hyrde?' ¹⁰ God cwæð to him: 'La hwæt dydest þu? Seo stemn þines broðor blodes clipoð to me of eorþan. ¹¹ Nu þu bist awirged ofer eorþan, þeo þe oponode hire muð and underfeng þines broðor blod of þinre handa. ¹² Þonne wircst þa eorþan, ne silð heo þe hyre wæstmas. Woriende and flyma þu bist ofer eorþan.' ¹³ Cain cwæð to Gode: 'Mare is min unryhtwisnyss þonne ic mage miltsunge geearnian. ¹⁴ Efne | þu adræ`f´st me todæg fram þære eorþan ansine and ic beo   f. 8ʳ behyd fram þinre ansine and ic beo woriende and flyma ofer eorþan. Eal þare þe me gemeteð wile me ofslean.' ¹⁵ God cwæð þa to him: 'Ne bið hit nateshwon swa, ac swa hwa swa ofslicð Caim bið gewitnod beo seofonfealdum', and sette þa mirceals on Cain þæt hine ne ofsloge þe ðe hine gemette. ¹⁶ Cain ferde þa fram Godes ansine to eastdæle and wunede flyma on þam lande Eden.

⁴:¹⁷ Cain breac his wiues and heo geacnode and acende Enoh. Cain þa geworhte him ane burh and genamode þa burh be his sune naman Enoh. ¹⁸ Witodlice Enoh gestrinde Irad and Irad gestrinde Mauihel. Mauihel gestrinde Matusahel and Matusahel gestrinde Lamech, ¹⁹ þe

---

4:5 and ne ... lacum] *om. (supp. by editor from* B)

16   GENESIS [B, L]

     and Maui[a]el gestrynde Matusael, and Matusael gestrynde
B f. 9^v Lamech. | ¹⁹ Witodlice Lamech nam twa wif; oðer wæs genemned
     Ada and oðer Sella. ²⁰ Be Adan he gestrynde Iabal and Iubal. ²¹ And
     Iubal wæs hyrda fæder and þara manna ðe on geteldum wunedon,
B f. 10^r and sangera fæder, and hearpera and organystra. | ²² Be Sellan he
     gestrynde Tubalcain, se wæs ægðer ge goldsmið ge irensmið, and ane
     dohtor, seo hatte Noema.

     ^{4:25} Eft Adam gestrynde sunu, ðone he nemde Seth, and ðus cwæð:
     'Drihten me sealde ðisne sunu for Abel, ðe Cain ofsloh.' ²⁶ Seth
     gestrynde sunu and nemde hine Enos. Se Enos ongan ærest clypian
     Drihtnes naman. |

B f. 10^v ^{5:5} Soðlice Adam leofode nigon hund wintra and ðritig wintra, and he
     forðferde on godre ylde. ⁶ Seth wæs [hundwintre and .v.] ða he
     gestrynde Enos; ⁷ ymb seofan and hundeahtatigwintre æfter ðam, he
     gestrynde suna and dohtra, ⁸ and he forðferde þa he wæs nigon-
     hundwintre and twelfwintre. Ðis is adames cneores. ⁹ Enos gestrynde
     Cainan ða he wæs hundnigontigwintre. ¹⁰ Æfter ðam he gestrynde
     suna and dohtra; ¹¹ and Enos forðferde ða he wæs nygonhundwintre
B f. 11^r and fifwintre. | ¹² Cainan gestrynde Malaleel ða he wæs
L f. 6^r hundseofontig | wintre. ¹³ And æfter þam he gestrinde suna and
     dohtra, ¹⁴ and he forðferde þa he wæs nigonhundwintre and tynwin-
     tre. ¹⁵ Witodlice Malelehel gestrinde Iared þa he wæs fif and
     sixtigwintre, ¹⁶ and siþþan he gestrinde suna and dohtra, ¹⁷ and he
     forðferde þa he wæs eahtahundwintre and fif and hundnigontig-
     wintre. ¹⁸ Iared gestrinde Enoch þa he wæs [hundwintre twa] and

---

    4:18 Mauiael] mauiel   Lamech] *illus. follows*   4:20 Iubal] *illus. follows*
4:21 organystra] *illus. follows*   4:22 Noema] *illus. follows*   4:25 ofsloh] *illus.*
follows   4:26 naman] NamaN; *illus. follows*   5:5 ylde] *illus. follows*   5:6 hundwintre
and .v.] *written on eras. by 12th-c. hand*   5:8 twelfwintre] *illus. follows*   5:11 fifgwintre]
illus. follows
       MSS L, B   5:12 wintre] L *restarts*   5:15 Malelehel] malaleel B
5:18 hundwintre twa] fif L   hundwintre twa and sixtig] *written on eras., 12th c.* B

genam twa wif; an hatte Ada, oþer Sella. ²⁰ Þa acende Ada Iabel, þe wæs fæder þare þe wunedon on geteldum and hirda. ²¹ His broþor hatte Iubal, þe wæs fæder hea[r]pera and þæra þe organan macodan. ²² Þæt oþer wif Sella acende Tubalcain, þe wæs slecgwirhta and smið on eallum weorcum ærest and ysene[s]. His swistor hatte Nohema. ²³ Lameh cwæð þa to his wiuum, Ada and Sella: 'Gehyrað myne stemne, Lameh wif. Hlistað mine spræce, for þan þe ic o[f]sloh wer on minre wunde and iunglincg on minum handan. ²⁴ Seofonfeald wracu bið geseald for Cain and hundseofontig seofonfeald for Lamech.'

⁴:²⁵ Adam soðlice briac his wiues and heo acende sunu and gecigde hine Sech, þus cweþende: 'God forgeaf me oþerne ofspring for Abel, þone Cain ofsloh.' ²⁶ Eac swilce þa Sech wæs sunu acened, þone he het Enos. | Þes ongan to clipienne Godes naman. f. 8ᵛ

⁵:¹ Þis his seo boc Adames mægrace on þone dæg þe God gesceop man to Godes gelicnesse. He geworhte hine ² wer and wif. He gesceop hii and geble`t´sode hi and het his naman Adam, on þam dæge þe hi gesceapene wæron. ³ Adam soðlice leofode hunteonti geare and þritti geare and gestrinde sunu to his gelicnesse and anlycnysse and het hine Seth. ⁴ Þa wæron Adames dages siððan he gestrinde Sech .viii. hund geara and he gestrindæ suna and dohtra. ⁵ Wæs þa geworden eal þe timæ þe Adam leofode nigon hund geara and .xxx. geare and he þa forðferde. ⁶ Sech leofode fif and hundteontig geara and gestrinde Enos. ⁷ He lyfede seðen he gestrinde Enos .viii. hund geare and seofon gear and gestrynde sunu and dohtra. ⁸ Wæron þa gewordene ealle Sethes dagas .ix. hund geare and .xii. gear and he forðferde. ⁹ Enos soðlice leofode hundnygontyg geare and he gestrynde Cainan. ¹⁰ Æfter þes upspringe he leofode .viii. hund geare and .xv. gear and gestrinde suna and dohtra. ¹¹ Wæron þa gewordene ealle Enoses dagas .ix. hund gear and .v. gear; he forðferde. ¹² Cainan lyfode hundsefontig geare and gestrinde Malaleel. ¹³ He lefeode siððan he `ge´strinde Malaleel .viii. hund geara and gestrynde sunu and dohtra. ¹⁴ Wæron þa gewordene ealle Cainanes dagas .ix. hund geare and .x. gear and he forðferde. ¹⁵ Maleleel leofode .v. and sixti geare and gestrinde Iared. ¹⁶ He lifode siððan he gestrinde Iared .viii. hund geare and .xxx. geare and gestrinde sunu and dohtra. ¹⁷ Wæron þa gewordene ealle Maleleelas dagas .viii. hund geare | and .v. and hundnigontig geare and he f. 9ʳ fo`r´ðferde. ¹⁸ Iared leofode hundteonti geare and twa and sixti and

---

4:21 hearpera] heapera   4:22 ysenes] `of´ ysene   4:23 ofsloh] oðsloh
5:3 geare¹] *corr. from* geure

GENESIS [L]

sixtig, and æfter þam he gestrinde suna and dohtra, [20] and he forðferde þa he wæs nigonhundwintre and fif and sixtigwintre. [21] Enoch gestrinde Mathusalam þa he wæs fif and sixtigwintre, [22] and siþþan he gestrinde suna and dohtra; [23] and he wæs on þisum life þreohundwintre and fif and sixtigwintre, [24] and he ferde mid Gode and hine nan man siþþan ne geseah, for þam þe Drihten hine nam, mid sawle and mid lichaman. [25] Witodlice Matusalem gestrinde Lamech þa he wæs [hund and] seofon and hundeahtatigwintre, [26] and æfter þam he gestrinde suna and dohtra, [27] and he forðferde þa he wæs nigonhundwintre and nigon and sixtigwintre. [28] Lamech gestrinde sunu þa he wæs an hund wintra and twa and hundeahtatigwintre, [29] and nemde hine Noe and þus cwæð be him: 'Ðes man us afrefrað fram urum weorcum and fram urum geswince on þam lande þe Drihten wirigde.' [30] Æfter þam he gestrinde suna and dohtra, [31] and he forðferde þa he wæs seofonhundwintre and seofon and hundseofontigwintre.

Her swutelað þas ælmihtigan Godes mildheortnisse and his wundru, hu he Noe bearh and his wife and his teame æt þam miclan flode.

MSS L, B, C

[5:32] NOE SOÐLICE, ÐA ÐA HE wæs fif hund geara, þa gestrinde he þri suna, Sem and Cham and Iafeth. [6:1] Men wurdon þa gemenigfilde ofer eorþan and dohtra gestrindon. [2] Þa gesawon Godes bearn, þæt wæron gode men, manna dohtra, þæt hig wæron wlitige, and namon him wif of eallum þam þa þe hig gecuron. [3] And f. 6ᵛ God cwæð þa: 'Ne þurhwunað na min gast | on menn on ecnisse, for þan þe he ys flæsc.' [4] Entas wæron eac swilce ofer eorðan on ðam dagum, æfter þam þe Godes bearn tymdon wið manna dohtra and hig cendon. Ða sind mihtige fram worulde and hlisfulle weras. [5] Þa

---

5:23 þisum] ðison B   sixtigwintre] sixtiwintre BC   5:24 nam] genam B
5:25 hund and] *om*. LB   5:28 wintra] wintre B   5:29 geswince] geswyncum B
5:30 þam] þe *add*. L   5:31 seofon] seofan B   hundseofontigwintre]
hundseofantiwintre B   Her swutelað . . . miclan flode] *rubric in red* L, *om*. B (*but a space of two lines was left for it*)
      MSS L, B, C   5:32 NOE] *3-line green initial cap*. L; *7-line red initial cap*. B; *no division indicated in* C   ÐA ÐA HE] *om*. B   geara] geare 'eald' C   suna] sunus C   Cham]
Cam C   Iafeth] IAPHET B, Iapheð C   6:1 wurdon þa gemenigfilde] þa wurdon
gemanifilde C   ofer] C *f*. 9ᵛ   gestrindon] gestrinde C   6:2 bearn] biarn C   hig¹] hi BC
þa þe] ðe B, þa ða C   hig²] hi BC   6:3 gast] þæt his (*h eras*.) min yrre *add*. C   on menn]
on men B, omen C   ys] his (*h eras*.) C   6:4 Entas] entos C   æfter þam] æfter þan B,
Efter þan C   bearn] biarn C   hig] hi BC   cendon] cenden C   hlisfulle] hlisfulla C

gestrinde Enoh. ¹⁹ He leofede siððan he gestrinde Enohc .viii. hund geare and gestrinde sune and dohtra. ²⁰ Wæron þa gewordene ealle Iaredes dagas .ix. hund geara `and´ twa and syxti and he forðferde. ²¹ Witodlice Enohc lyfode .v. and sixti geare and gestrinde Matusalam, ²² and Enoch ferde `to heofone´ mid Gode. He leofode siððan he gestrinde Matusalam .iii. hund geare and gestrynde sune and dohtra. ²³ Wæron þa gewordene ealla Enoches dagas .iii. hund geare and .v. and syxti geare. ²⁴ And he ne fo`r´ðferde na, ac ferde mid Gode and næs gesewen siððan mid mannum, for þan þæ God hine genam. ²⁵ Matusala þa leofode hundteontig geara and [s]eofon and hundeahtatig geare and gestrinde Lamech. ²⁶ He leofode siððan he gestrinde Lamech .vii. hund geare and .ii. and hundeahtatig geare and gestrinde sunu and dohtra. ²⁷ Wæron þa gewordene ealle Matusalames dagas .ix. hund geare and .ix. and sixti geare and he forðferde. ²⁸ Lamech þa leofode hundteontig geare and .ii. and hundeahtatig geare and gestrynde sunu ²⁹ and gecigde hine Noe, and cwæð: 'þes gefrefað us fram weorcum and geswincu[m] ure handan ofer eorþan, þe God awirigde.' ³⁰ Lamech leofode þa siððan he gestrinde Noe .v. hund geare and .v. hundnigontig geare and gestrinde sunu and dohtra. ³¹ Wæron þa gewordene ealla Lameches dagas .vii. hund geare and .vii. and hundseofeontig and he forðferde.

⁵:³² Noe soðlice, þa ða he wæs .v. hund geare `eald´, þa gestrinde he þry sunus, Sem, Cam and Iapheð.

5:25 seofon] feofon   5:29 geswincum] geswincu

geseah God þæt micel yfelnys manna wæs ofer eorþan and eall geþanc manna heortena wæs gewend on yfel on eallum timan. ⁶ Gode þa ofþuhte þæt he man geworhte ofer eorðan. He wolde þa warnian on ær and wæs gehrepod mid heortan sarnisse wiðinnan ⁷ and cwæð, 'Ic adilige þone mannan þe ic gesceop fram þære eorðan ansine, fram þam men oþ þa nytenu, fram þam slincendum oð ða fugelas. Me ofþincð soðlice þæt ic hig worhte.'
⁶:⁸ Noe soþlice wæs Gode gecweme and gife ætforan him gemette. ⁹ Das sind Noes cneornissa. Noe wæs rihtwis wer and fulfremed on his mægþum; mid Gode he ferde ¹⁰ and gestrinde þri suna, Sem and Cham and Iafetð. ¹¹ Ða wæs eall seo eorðe gewemmed ætforan Gode and afylled mid unrihtwisnysse. ¹² Ða geseah God þæt seo eorðe wæs gewemmed, for þan þe ælc flæsc gewemde his weg ofer eorðan. ¹³ And God cwæþ þa to Noe: 'Geendung ealles flæsces com ætforan me. Seo eorþe ys afylled mid unrihtwisnysse fram heora ansine and ic fordo hig mid þære eorðan samod. ¹⁴ Wirc þe nu ænne arc of aheawenum bordum, and þu wircst wununge binnan þam arce and clæmst wiþinnan and wiðutan mid tyrwan. ¹⁵ And þu wircst hine þus: Ðreo hund fæþma bið se arc on lenge and fiftig fæðma on bræde and þritig on heahnisse. ¹⁶ Ðu wircst þæron ehþirl and þu getihst his heahnisse togædere on ufeweardum to anre fæðme. Duru þu setst be þære sidan wiðneoðan, and þu macast þreo fleringa binnan ðam arce. ¹⁷ Efne ic gebringe flodes wæteru ofer eorðan, þæt ic of⟨sl⟩ea eall flæsc on ðam þe ys lifes gast under heofenum, and ealle þa þing þe on eorðan synd beoþ fornumene. ¹⁸ Ic sette min wedd to þe, and þu gæst into þam arce, and þine suna, ðin wif and þinra suna wif mid

6:5 geseah] seah C   yfelnys] yuelnis mid C   eall] eal B, ealle C   geþanc manna] manna geþanc C   heortena] om. C   gewend] awend BC   yfel] yuel C   6:6 þa ofþuhte] ofðuhte ða BC   man] mann B   ofer] of C   gehrepod] gerepod C   heortan sarnisse] heortsarnysse C   6:7 adilige] adylgie B, adilegige C   mannan] man BC   gesceop] gescop C   nytenu] nytena C   ofþincð] ofðingð B   hig] hi BC   worhte] geworhte C   6:8 soþlice] om. C   gemette] gemæte C   6:10 suna] sunus C   and²] om. C   Cham] Cam C   Iafetð] iaphet B, Iapheð C   6:11 eall] eal C   unrihtwisnysse] unrihtwisnesse C   6:12 wæs] was C   6:13 Seo] se C   unrihtwisnysse] unrihtwisnesse C   hig] hi B   þære] þeʾrʾ C   6:14 ænne] ane B   aheawenum] aheawʾeʾnum] C   wununge] wununga BC   arce] earce C   clæmst] ʾhineʾ add. C   wiðutan] wiðuton C   6:15 hine] Cf. 10ʾ   arc on lenge] arca an længe C   fæðma] om.   and³] ʾandʾ C   þritig] þrittig C   6:16 ehþirl] egðyrl B, eahþirle C   getihst] tihst B, getigst C   togædere] togadere C   ufeweardum] ufewerdum C   fæðme] fæðma C   Duru] dura C   þære] þara C   wiðneoðan] wiðniođan B   þu³] om. C   macast] macost C   fleringa] fleringe C   arce] ærce C   6:17 gebringe] bringe C   wæteru] wætʾrʾu C   eorðan¹] heorðan C   ofslea] sl lost in hole L   eall] ealla C   lifes] liues C   heofenum] heofonum B, heofonan C   and] om. B   þe²] þe ðe C   eorðan²] eorþen C   beoþ] beo þ C   fornumene] fornumen C   6:18 arce] arca C   suna¹] sunus C   ðin] and ðin B   suna²] sune C

GENESIS

þe. ¹⁹ And of eallum nytenum ealles flæsces | twegen gemacan þu f.7ʳ
lætst into ðam arce mid þe, þæt hig libban magon. ²⁰ Eac of fugelum
be heora cinne, and of eallum orfcinne and of eallum creopendum
cinne, twam and twam faran in mid þe, þæt hi magon libban. ²¹ Ðu
nimst witodlice of eallum mettum þe to mete magon into þe, þæt hig
beon ægðer ge þe ge him to bigleofan.' ²² Noe soþlice dide ealle þa
þing þe him God bebead.
⁷:¹ And God cwæð to him: 'Gang into ðam arce, and eall þin
hiwræden; þe ic geseah soþlice rihtwisne ætforan me on þissere
mægðe. ² Nim into þe of eallum clænum nitenum seofen and seofen
ægþres gecyndes, and of þam unclænum twam and twam, ³ and of
fugelcinne seofen and seofen ægþres gecindes, þæt sæd sige healden
ofer ealre eorðan bradnisse. ⁴ Ic soþlice sende ren nu ymbe seofon
niht ofer eorðan feowertig daga and feowertig nihta togædere and ic
adilegie ealle þa edwiste þe ic geworhte ofer eorðan bradnisse.' ⁵ Noe
ða dide ealle þa þing þe him God bebead. ⁶ And he wæs þa six hund
geara on ylde, ða þa þæs flodes wæteru yþedon ofer eorðan. ⁷ Hwæt
ða Noe eode into þam arce, and his ðri suna and his wif and his suna
wif, for þæs flodes wæterum. ⁸ Eac swilce þa nitenu of eallum cinne
and of eallum fugelcynne ⁹ comon to Noe into þam arce, swa swa
God bebead. ¹⁰ Ða on ðam eahtogan dæge, þa þa hig inne wæron and
God hig belocen hæfde wiðutan, þa yþode þæt flod ofer eorðan.
¹¹ On þam oþrum monðe, on ðone seofenteoðan dæg þæs monðes, ða
asprungon ealle wyllspringas þære micclan niwelnisse, and þære
heofenan wæterþeotan wæron geopenode, ¹² and hit rinde þa ofer
eorðan feowertig daga and feowertig nihta on an. ¹⁷ Wæs þa
geworden micel flod, and þa wæteru wæron gemenigfilde and

6:19 gemacan] gemacon C   lætst] læst C   hig] hi BC   6:20 be] beo C   eallum¹]
alle C   in] ʻin' B   6:21 mettum] mete C   ægðer] ætþer C   bigleofan] bilifan C
6:22 þing] þincg C   bebead] bebiad C   7:1 God] om. C   Gang] gange C   eall] eal B
geseah] geseach C   þissere] þisre B   7:2 seofen¹] seofan B, seofon C   and seofen]
om. C   seofen²] seofan B   ægþres] aiðres C   þam] om. B   unclænum] unclæne C
7:3 seofen¹] seofan B, .vii. C   seofen²] seofan B, .vii. C   þæt sæd] and sæd B, þæt þæt
sæd C   healden] gehaldon C   ealre eorðan] ealle eorþe C   7:4 ymbe seofon] embe
seofan B, ybe .vii. C   niht] nihte C   ealle] nu ealle C   geworhte] worhte B, geworuhte C
7:5 ealle] eall C   þing] ðingc B, þinc C   7:6 geara] gear C   ða þa þæs] þa ðas C
7:7 Hwæt] C f. 10ᵛ   Noe] ʻNoe' C   arce] arca B   suna¹] sunu C   suna²] sunu B
wæterum] wæteru C   7:8 of²] om. B   fugelcynne] fugolcynne B   7:9 comon]
cōman C   bebead] bebiad C   7:10 eahtogan] eahtoðan B, eahteþū C   dæge] dage C
hig¹] hi BC   hig²] hi BC   belocen] belocene C   wiðutan] wiðuton C   7:11 oþrum
monðe] oðre monða C   seofenteoðan] seofenteoðan BC   monðes] monðas C   asprungon]
asprungan C   ealle] eall C   þære] þare C   micclan] miclan BC   þære heofenan] þare
heofonan C   geopenode] geoponode C   7:17 gemenigfilde] gemenifylde B,
gemanifilde C

GENESIS

ahefdon upp þone arc ¹⁸ and yþedon swiþe and gefyldon þære eorðan bradnisse. Witodlice se arc wæs geferud ofer ða wæteru. ¹⁹ And þæt wæter swiðrode swiþe ofer þa eorðan; wurdon þa behelede ealle þa | hehstan duna under ealre heofenan, ²⁰ and þæt wæter wæs fiftyne fæðma deop ofer þa hehstan duna. ²¹ Wearþ þa fornumen eall flæsc þe ofer eorðan styrode, manna and fugela, nytena and creopendra, ²² and ælc þing þe lif hæfde wearþ adyd on þam deopan flode, ²³ buton þam anum þe binnan þam arce wæron. ²⁴ Ðæt flod stod þa swa an hund daga and fiftig daga.

⁸:¹ And God þa gemunde Noes fare and þæra nitena ðe him mid wæron and asende þa wind ofer eorðan, and þa wætera wurdon gewanode ² and þa wilspringas þære miclan niwelnisse wurdon fordytte and þære heofenan wæterþeotan and se ren wearþ forboden. ³ Ða wætera ða gecirdon of þære eorðan, ongean farende, and begunnon to wanigenne æfter oþer healfhund daga. ⁴ Ða ætstod se arc on þam seofeðan monþe ofer þa muntas Armenies landes. ⁵ And þa wætera toeodon and wanedon o[þ] þæne teoðan monð, and on þam teoðan monþe æteowodon þæra munta cnollas. ⁶ Ða æfter feowertigum dagum undyde Noe his ehþirl, þe he on þam arce gemacode, ⁷ and asende ut ænne hremn. Se hrem fleah þa ut and nolde eft ongean cirran, ær þan þe þa wæteru adruwedon ofer eorðan. ⁸ He asende þa eft ut ane culfran, þæt heo sceawode gif þa wætera þa git geswicon ofer þære eorþan bradnisse. ⁹ Heo þa fleah ut and ne mihte findan hwær heo hire fot asette, for þan þe þa wætera wæron ofer ealle eorðan, and heo gecirde ongean to Noe and he genam hig into þam arce. ¹⁰ He abad ða git oðre seofon dagas and

---

7:17 ahefdon] ahefde B upp] up BC 7:18 yþedon] yðodon BC þære] þare C geferud] geferod BC wæteru] wateru C 7:19 swiþe] swylce B þa¹] om. B wurdon] wæron C behelede ealle] geheledon ealla C hehstan] heahstan B, hyhstan C duna] dune C ealre] þære C 7:20 fiftyne fæðma] .xv. fædma C hehstan] heahstan BC 7:21 Wearþ þa] wearþa C eall] eal B styrode] stiredon C fugela] fugelum C nytena] nytenu C 7:22 þing] ðingc B hæfde wearþ] hæfdon weare C 7:23 buton] boton C anum] ane C binnan] binnon C 7:24 and fiftig daga] om. C 8:1 þæra nitena] þare nytenu C him mid] mid him C þa²] om. BC wætera] wæteru B 8:2 wilspringas] wylspringa B, wyllspringas C þære¹] þara C niwelnisse] niwwelnesse C þære²] þare C heofenan] heofonan B 8:3 wætera] wæteru BC þære] þare C wanigenne] wanienne C 8:4 Ða] C f. 11ʳ seofeðan] seofoðan BC Armenies] armenisces B 8:5 wætera] wæteru BC toeodon] toeodan B wanedon] wanodon B, wanenedon (first ne subpuncted) C oþ] þ corr. fr. f (probably by late hand) L, of BC þæne] ðone BC monð] monþe C æteowodon] æteowedon B þæra] þare C 8:6 ehþirl] eahðyrl B, eghþirl C 8:7 hremn] remm C hrem] rem C wæteru] wætero C adruwedon] adruwodon B 8:8 eft] om. C geswicon] teswicon C þære] þare C 8:9 hire] heore C ealle] alle C gecirde] cyrdo C hig] hi BC 8:10 seofon] seofan BC

asende ut eft culfran. ⁱⁱ Heo com þa on æfnunge eft to Noe and brohte an twig of anum elebeame mid grenum leafum on hire muþe. Đa undergeat Noe þæt þa wætera wæron adruwode ofer eorðan, ¹² and abad swa þeah seofon dagas and asende ut culfran, seo ne gecirde ongean him. ¹³ Đa geopenode Noe þæs arces hrof and beheold ut and geseah | þæt þære eorðan bradnis wæs adruwod.   f. 8ʳ

⁸:¹⁵ God þa spræc to Noe, þus cweþende: ¹⁶ 'Gang ut of þam arce, [ðu] and þin wif, þine suna and hira wif, ¹⁷ and eall þæt þærinne ys mid þe, læd ut mid þe ofer eorðan, and weaxe ge and beoð gemenigfilde ofer eorðan'. ¹⁸ Noe þa ut eode of ðam arce, and hig ealle, ofer eorðan. ²⁰ And he arærde an weofod Gode and genam of eallum þam clænan nytenum and clænum fugelum and geoffrode Gode lac on þam weofode. ²¹ God þa underfeng his lac and þære wynsumnysse bræþ and cwæð him to: 'Nelle ic nateshwon awirgean ða eorðan heononforð for mannum; andgit and geþoht menniscre heortan syndon forþhealde to yfele fram iugoþe. Eornostlice ne ofslea ic heononforð mid wætere ælc þing cuces, swa swa ic dyde. ²² Eallum dagum þære eorðan, sæd and gerip, cile and hæte, sumor and winter, dæg and niht ne geswicað.'

⁹:¹ God bletsode þa Noe and his suna and cwæð him to: 'Weahxað and beoþ gemenigfilde and afyllaþ þa eorðan. ² And beo eower ege and oga ofer ealle nitenu and fugelas and ofer ealle þa þing þe on eorðan stiriað. Ealle sæfixas sindon eowrum handum betæhte, ³ and eall þæt þe styrað and leofað beo eow to mete; swa swa growende wyrta, ic betæhte ealle eow, ⁴ buton þam anum, þæt ge flæsc mid blode ne eton. ⁵ Eower blod ic ofgange æt eallum wilddeorum and eac æt þam men. Of þæs weres handa and his broþor handa ic ofgange þæs mannes lif. ⁶ Swa hwa swa agit mannes blod, his blod byð

8:11 on æfnunge] om. C   to Noe] om. C   anum] anu C   leafum] lyeuum C   wæron adruwode] wærun adrowode C   8:12 seofon] seofan B   seo] swa heo B   gecirde] cyrde C   him] to him BC   8:13 geopenode] geopono`de´ C    þæs] þes C    hrof] rof C    and geseah] `and geseah´ C   þære] þæra B, þare C   wæs] was C   8:15 spræc] sprec C   þus] þu`s´ C    8:16 ðu] BC, om. L    þine] and ðine BC    suna] sunu C    hira] heora B, hera C    8:17 eall] eal B    ys] his C    gemenigfilde] gemænifylde B, gemanifylde C    8:18 hig] hi B    ealle] gealle C    8:20 arærde] arerde C    clænan] clænum BC    Gode²] god`e´ C   8:21 underfeng] undærfeng C; C f. 11ᵛ   þære] þare C   awirgean] awirgan C   andgit] andgyte B, angit C   heortan] heorte C   þing] ðingc B   8:22 þære] þare C   9:1 suna] sunus C   Weahxað] weaxað BC   beoþ] byð C   gemenigfilde] gemenifylde B, gemanifylde C   9:2 nitenu] nytena C   þing] ðingc B   eorðan] eorðe C   stiriað] styrað C   handum betæhte] handa betæht C   9:3 eall] eal B   beo] beoþ C   ic] hi add. BC   betæhte] betæce B   9:4 buton] butan BC   anum] ane C   flæsc] flæcs C   9:5 wilddeorum] wildeorum BC   ofgange] forgange C   9:6 mannes] ðæs mannes B

agoten. Witodlice to Godes anli`c´nisse ys se man geworht. ⁷Weaxe ge nu and beoð gemenigfilde and gaþ ofer eorðan and gefyllaþ hig.' ⁸God cwæð eft to Noe and to his sunum: ⁹'Efne nu ic sette min wedd to eow and to eowrum ofspringe, ¹⁰and to eallum þam libbendum nytenum þe of ðam arce eodon, ¹¹þæt ic nateshwon nelle heononforð eall flæsc adydan mid flodes wæterum, ne heononforð ne biþ flod tosencende þa eorðan. ¹²Ðis biþ þæt tacn mines weddes þæt ic do betwux me | and eow and eallum libbendum nytenum on ecum mægþum: ¹³ðæt ys, þæt ic sette minne renbogan on wolcnum, and he biþ tacn mines weddes betwux me and þære eorðan. ¹⁴Ðonne ic oferteo heofenan mid wolcnum, þonne æteowð min boga on þam wolcnum ¹⁵and ic beo gemindig mines weddes wið eow, þæt heononforð ne biþ flod to adiligenne eall flæsc. ¹⁶Bið þonne se min renboga on þam wolcnum, and ic hine geseo and beo gemindig þæs ecan weddes þe gesett ys betwux Gode and eallum libbendum flæsce þe ofer eorþan ys. ¹⁷Ðis biþ þæt tacn mines weddes þæt ic gesette betwux me and eallum flæsce ofer eorþan.'

f. 8ᵛ

9:18 Wæron þa Noes suna, þe of þam arce eodon, Sem and Cham and Iafeth, and Cham witodlice ys fæder þære Chananeiscre þeode. ¹⁹And of þisum þrim Noes sunum ys tosawen eall mancynn ofer eorþan. ²⁰Noe ða, yrþling, began to wircenne þæt land and gesette him wineard. ²¹And þa þa he dranc of þam wine, þa wearð he druncen and læg on his getelde unbehelod. ²²His sunu þa, Cham, geseah his gesceapu unbehelod and cidde hit his twam gebroþrum ute on felda. ²³Hwæt þa Sem and Iafeth dydon anne hwitel on hira sculdra and eodon underbæc and beheledon heora fæderes gecynd,

   9:6 anlicnisse] anlicnesse C   se] þe C   geworht] geworuht C   9:7 Weaxe ge] weaxað C   beoð] byoð C   gemenigfilde] gemænifylde B   hig] hi BC   9:9 wedd] wed B   9:10 þam] om. B   9:11 eall] eal B   flæsc] om. B, flæcs C   adydan] adydon B adidon C   wæterum] wæteru C   tosencende] tosæncende C   9:12 tacn] tacne C   mægþum] megþum C   9:13 renbogan] renboga C   tacn] tacne C   9:14 Ðonne] þone C   heofenan] heofonan BC   æteowð] æteowað B   boga] renboga C   9:15 beo] by C   flod] flote C   to] om. C   adiligenne] adylgienne B, adihlienne C; C f. 12ʳ   flæsc] flæcs C   9:16 þæs] þas C   ecan] ecean B   gesett] geset C   libbendum] libendum C   9:17 betwux] beotwux C   9:18 eodon] eodan BC   Cham] Cam C   Iafeth] iaphet B, Iaphæ C   and] om. C   Cham] Cam C   þære Chananeiscre] þare Cananyscre C   9:19 þisum] þissum C   Noes] Noe C   sunum] sune`s´ C   tosawen] tosawon C   mancynn] mancyn BC   9:20 yrþling] yrdlingc B   wineard] wingeard B   9:21 getelde] geteldum C   unbeheld] uneheled BC (alt. to -od in B)   9:22 sunu] -u corr. fr. -a, prob. by scribe B   Cham] Cam C   unbehelod] unbeheled B, unbehelede C   ute] ut BC   felda] felde C   9:23 Iafeth] iapheth B, iafæð C   dydon anne] dido ænne C   on hira sculdra] on heora sculdrum B, ofer him and ofer his sculdra C   eodon underbæc] eoden underbæcc C   beheledon] beheleden C

GENESIS

swa þæt hig ne gesawon heora fæder nacednisse. ²⁴ Noe soþlice, þa þa he awoc of þam slæpe and he ofaxode hwæt his suna him didon, ²⁵ þa cwæð he: 'Awirged ys Cham and he biþ þeowena þeowa his gebroþrum.' ²⁶ And he cwæð: 'Gebletsod ys Drihten, Semes God; beo Chanaan his þeowa. ²⁷ Gemenigfilde God Iafeth, and he wunie on Semes geteldum and beo Chanaan his þeowa.' ²⁸ Noe þa lyfode þreo hund geara and fiftig geara æfter þam flode, ²⁹ and wæron þa gefillede ealle his dagas nigon hund geara and fiftig geara, and he forðferde.

9:23 hig] hi B   heora fæder] his BC   nacednisse] næcednysse B   9:24 he¹] om. C
of þam slæpe] on þam wine C   and] om. C   didon] diden C   9:25 Cham] chanaan BC
9:26 ys] his C   Semes] Semen C   9:27 Gemenigfilde] gemænifylde B, Tobrede C
Iafeth] iapheð B, iafeð C   9:28 þa lyfode] ða leofode B, leofode þa C   þreo hund geara]
.iii. `und' geare C   geara²] geare C   9:29 gefillede] gefyllode C   geara¹] gearæ C
geara²] om. C

MSS L, B

10:1 Ðis synd Noes suna naman: Sem and Cham and Iafeth. ² Iafethes suna: Gomer and Magog and Madai, Iuan and Tubal and Mosoch and Thiras.

10:32 Ðis wæs Noes hiwræden and his mægþa, þurh þas wæron
f. 9ʳ þeoda todælede on eorðan æfter | þam [flode.]
11:1 Soðlice ealle men spræcon ane spræce. ² Ða þa hig ferdon fram eastdæle, hig fundon anne feld on Sennaar lande and wunedon

MSS L, B   10:1 Iafeth] iapheth B   10:2 Iafethes] iafeðes B   Mosoch] mosoh B   Thiras] ðiras B   10:32 flode] *om.* LB (*supplied fr.* C)   11:1 men] menn B   spræcon] ða *add.* B   11:2 hig¹] hi B   hig²] hi B   anne] ænne B   Sennaar] senaar B   wunedon] wunodon B

GENESIS [C]

MS C

¹⁰:¹ Þis is seo mægracu Noe sune`s´, Sem and Cham and Iafeðes. ² Iafeðes sunas wæron þas: Gomer and Magog, Mada and Iaban, Tubal and Moshoh and Thyras. ³⁻⁴ Gomer and Iaban, his twegen sunæ, gestrynde oþre .vii. sunes, ⁵ and fram þisum synd todælede þeoda hilænd on heora ricum, angehwilc æfter his gereorde and æfter his hiwrædene on his cynne. ⁶ Cames suna wæron þas: Chus. | and f. 12ᵛ Mesraim, Futh and Canaan. ⁷ Se Chus gestrunde .vi. sunas; ⁸ an þære wæs Nenroth. Þe Nemroth wæs mihtig on eorþan ⁹ and strang hunta ætforan Gode. Be þam `wæs´ gecweden bigword: 'swa swa Nemroth, strang hunta ætforan Gode'. ¹⁰ His rices angin wæs Babilon and Arah and Archat and Cahanne, on þam lande Sennar. ¹¹ Of þam [l]ande ferde Asur and getimbrode þa buruh Niniuen and þ`æ´re burhga streta. Oþre burh he getimbrode eac, þe hatte Chale. ¹² Þa þriddan burh þe he arærde het Reson, betwux Niniuen and Cale; þeos is micel burh. ⁷ Chuses suna Remgma gestrynde .ii. sunu, Sabba and Dadan. ¹³⁻¹⁴ Mesraim, Cames oþer sunu, gestrynde six suna. Of þam comon þa Philistei and seo mægð Capturym. ¹⁵⁻¹⁸ Canaan, Cames sunu, gestrynde .xi. suna. Of þan is tosawon þæt folc Cananeysra þeoda, ¹⁹ and heora landgemære wæron fram Sidon`i´e oð ða burh Gaza, and to þam bur`h´gum Sodoma and Gomorra, and swa forð to Bethaman and Seboim oð Lesa. ²⁰ Þa sind Cames sunu on heora yerdum and gereordum, mæ[g]þum and landum and þeodum. ²¹ Sem, Noes ylsta suna, gestrynde fif sunu: ²² Elam, Asur, Arfaxad and Ludim and Aram. ²³ Aram gestrynde .iiii. sunu`s´. ²⁴ Arfaxað gestrynde Salem; of þam asprang Heber. ²⁵ Ðam Heber wæron acenned .ii. sunu; þe an hatte Faleh, for þam þe on his dagum wæs se eorþe todæled, and his broðor hatte Iectan. ²⁶⁻⁹ Þe Iectan gestrynde .xiii. sune ³⁰ and he wæs on eastdæle, wið þone munt Sefar. ³¹ Þis sunde Semes sunus æfter heora mægþum and gereordum and hieardum on heora þeodum.

¹⁰:³² Þis is Noes hiwredæne æfter heora folcum and þeodum. Fram þissum is todælede þeoda on eorþan æfter þam flode. |

¹¹:¹ Wæs þa an gereord on eorþan and heora ealre an spræc. ² Hi f. 13ʳ ferden fram eastdele oð þæt hi comon to anum felde on þam lande

---

10:11 lande] þande   þære] *corr. from* þare   10:7 Chuses suna remgma ... dadan]
On the placing of this sentence, see p. lxxvii.   10:20 mægþum] mætþum

þæron. ³ Þa cwædon hig him betwynan: 'Uton wircean us tigelan and ælan hig on fyre.' Witodlice hig hæfdon tygelan for stan and tyrwan for weall[i]m. ⁴ And hig cwædon: 'Uton timbrian us ceastre and stypel o[þ] heofon heahne. Uton wurðian urne naman ær þam þe we sin todælede geond ealle eorðan.' ⁵ Witodlice Drihten astah nyþer, to þam þæt he gesawe þa burh and þone stipel þe Adames bearn getimbrodon. ⁶ And he cwæð: 'Ðis ys an folc and ealle hig sprecaþ an lyden, and hig begunnon þis to wircanne. Ne geswicað hig ær þan þe hit gearu sig. ⁷ Soþlice uton cuman and todælan þær heora spræce.' ⁸ Swa Drihten hig todælde of þære stowe geond ealle eorðan, ⁹ and for þam man nemde þa stowe Babel, for þam þær wæron todælede ealle spræca.

11:27 Ðis ys Thares cynryn. Thare gestrynde Abram and Nachor and Aran. Witodlice Aran gestrinde Loth. ²⁸ Aran forðferde ær þon [þe] Thare his fæder on Ur Chaldea. ²⁹ Soðlice Abram and Nachor wifudun. Abrames wif hatte Sarai and Nachores wif Melcha. ³⁰ Sarai

11:3 hig¹] hi B   hig²] hi B   hig³] hi B   weallim] weall lim B, weallum L   11:4 hig] om. B   oþ] of L   Uton] and uton B   sin] synd B   11:6 hig¹] hi B   lyden] leden B   hig²] hi B   wircanne] wyrcenne B   hig³] hi B   sig] sy B   11:7 spræce] spæce B   11:8 hig] hi B   11:9 þær] ðar B   spræca] spæce B   11:27 Ðis] *no break in* L   Thare] Ðare B   11:28 þon þe] ðan ðe B, þonne L   11:29 wifudun] wifodon B

Sennar, and þer wunedon. ³ Þa cwæð gehwa to his nyxtan: ⁴ 'Cumað and utan wircan us ane burh and ænne stypel swa heahne þæt his rof atille þa heofonan, and uton mærsian urne namon, ær þan we beon todæled[e] to eallum landum.' ⁵ God þa nyþer astah þæt he gesega þa burh and þone stypel þe Adames sunus getimbroden. ⁶ God cwæð þa: 'Efne þis his an folc and [an] gereord him ealum and hi ongunnon þis to wircenne. Ne hi ne geswicað heora geþohta ær þan þe hi mid weorce hi gefyllan. ⁷ Cumað nu eornostlice and uton niþer astigan and heora gereord þer towendon, þæt heora nan ne tocnawe his nextan stemne.' ⁸ And God þa hi todælde swa of þare stowe to eallum landum and hi geswicon to wyrcenne þa buruh. ⁹ And for þi wæs seo burh gehaten Babel, for þan þe ðær wæs todæled þæt gereord ealre eorþan. God þa hi sende þanon ofer bra[d]nesse ealra eorðan.

¹¹:¹⁰ Þas synd Semes mægþa. Sem, þa þa he wæs anhund geare, þa gestrynde he Arfaxat, twam gearum æfter þam flode. ¹¹ And he lyfode syððon .v. hund geare and gestrynde sunu and dohtra. ¹² Arfaxað þa lyfode .vxxx. geare and gestrunde Sale. ¹³ He leofode siðan he strynd`e´ Sale .iiii. `hund´ geare. and .iiii. geare. and gestrynde sunu and dohtra. ¹⁴ Sale eac leofode .xxx. geare and gestrunde Heber. ¹⁵ He leofode siððan he gestrunde Heber .iiiic. and .iiii. gear and gestrinde sunu`s´ and dohtra. ¹⁶ Heber leofode .iiii. and .xxx. geara and gestrinde Faleh. ¹⁷ He leofode siððan he | gestrinde Faleg .iiii. hund geare and .xxx. geare and gestrinde sunu f. 13ᵛ and dochtra. ¹⁸ Faleh gestrunde Reu. ¹⁹ He leofoda siððan he gestrinde Reu .ii. hund geare and .ix. geare. ²⁰ Reu soðlice lifode .ii. and .xxx. geare and gestrinde Saruh. ²¹ He lifode siððan he gestrinde Saruh .iic. geare and .vii. gear and gestrunde sunu and dohtra. ²² Saruh soðlice leofode .xxx. geare and gestrinde Nachor. ²³ He leofode siððan he gest`r´inde Nachor .iic. geare and gestrinde sunu and dohtra. ²⁴ Nachor þa leofode .xxx. geare and he gestrinde Thare. ²⁵ He leofode siððan he gestrinde Thare, .ic. geare and .ix. .x. geare and gestrinde sunu and dohtra. ²⁶ Thare leofode hundseofontig geare and gestrinde Abram and Nachor and Aran. ²⁷ Se Aran gestrinde Lot, ²⁸ and he wæs dead ær hi`s´ fæder fære on þam lande his acennednyss, on þære Chaldeiscre Hur. ²⁹ Abram þa, and Nachor, wifedon. Abrames wif hatte Sarai and Nachores wif hatte Melcha, Aranes dohter, and hire swister hatte Iesah. ³⁰ Abrame`s´

11:4 todælede] todæledū   11:6 an²] om.   11:9 bradnesse] branesse
11:28 þære] corr. from þare

wæs untymende, næfde heo nan bearn. ³¹ Witodlice Thare nam Abram his sunu and Loth his suna sunu and gelædde hig [of] Ur Chaldea, þæt hig ferdon to Chanaan lande. Hig foron oð hig comon to Aran and hig wunedon þær. ³² Thare leofode twa hund geara and fif gear and he forþferde on Aran.

Her swutelað þas ælmihtigan Godes mildheortnysse and his wundru, hu he Abraham geceas and his bletsunga him sealde and his ofspringe.

MSS L, B, C

¹²:¹ GOD CWÆÐ ÐA TO ABRAME: 'FAR OF ÐINUM LANDE AND OF ÐINRE mægðe and of þines fæder huse, and cum to þam lande þe ic þe geswutelige. ² And ic macige þe mycelre mægþe and þe ge|bletsige and þinne naman ic gemærsige and þu byst gebletsod. ³ Ic gebletsige þa þe þe bletsiað and ic awirige þa þe þe wiriað, and on þe beoð gebletsode ealre eorþan mægða.' ⁴ Abram þa ferde of Aran swa swa God him bebead and Loth ferde mid him, ⁵ mid ealre fare and mid eallum æhtum, oþ þæt hi comon to þam lande Chanaan. ⁶ And Abram sceawode þæt land and þa gemæru. Chananeus wæs þa on lande. ⁷ God þa geswutelode hine silfne Abrahame and cwæð him to: 'Ðinum ofspringe ic forgife þis land.' Hwæt þa Abram arærde þær an weofod Gode, þe him æteowde, ⁸ and ferde syþþan to þam munte be eastan Bethel, be westan Hai, and þær gesloh his geteld and arærde þær an weofod Gode and his naman þær clipode. ⁹ Ðanon he ferde eft to þam suþdæle þæs landes, ¹⁰ and hit wearþ þa micel hungergear on þam lande. Abram þa ferde to Egipta lande, wolde þær on ælþeodinisse anbidian, for þam þe se hunger þearle swiþrode. ¹¹ Mid þam þe hig wæron gehende Egipta lande, þa cwæð Abram to his wife: 'Ic wat þæt þu eart wlitig on hiwe,

11:31 sunu¹] sunu (*corr. fr.* suna) B   hig¹] hi B   of] to LB   hig²] hi B   Hig³] hi B   hig⁴] hi B   hig wunedon] hi wunodan B   *Rubric* Her . . . ofspringe] *red rustic caps.* L, *text script* B   þas] þæs B   mildheortnysse] mildheortnyss B   wundru] wundra B
    MSS L, B, C   12:1 GOD] *3-line red initial cap.* L; *5-line black initial cap.* B; *no section division indicated in* C (*no rubric*)   ÐA] *om.* C   fæder] feder C   þam] þan C
12:2 macige] macie C   mycelre] micele C   gebletsige] gebletsie C   naman] nama C   gemærsige] gemersie C   gebletsod] geblesod C   12:3 Ic] C *f. 14ʳ*   gebletsige] bletsie C   bletsiað] bletsiad C   awirige] awyrwige B, wirgæ C   wiriað] wirhgiað C   mægða] mægþe C
12:4 bebead] bead B, bebiæd C   12:5 eallum] his *add.* C   comon] becomon C   Chanaan] Canaan C   12:6 Chananeus] Cananeus C   on] þam *add.* C   12:7 Abrahame] abrame B, to Abrame C   arærde] arerde C   12:8 naman] nama C   clipode] geclipode C
12:9 eft] *om.* C   12:10 hungergear] hungorgear B, hunger C   Egipta] egitpta C   ælþeodinisse anbidian] ælþudignysse gewunie and abydian C   þam²] ðan BC   se] *om.* C
12:11 hig] hi BC   Egipta] egipte C   wife] wiue C

wif Sarai was untumende. ³¹ Hwæt þa Thare genam his tweigen sunu mid heora twam wifum and Loth, his sune suna, and gelædde hig of þare Chaldeisre Hur to þam lande [Canaan] and hig wunedon þa on Aran. ³² þa wæron gewordene Tares dagas twa hund geare and fif gear and he forðferde on Aran.

11:31 Canaan] Aran

GENESIS

¹² and þonne þa Egiptiscan þe geseoð, þonne cweþaþ hig þæt þu min wif sig, and hig ofsleað me and þe healdaþ. ¹³ Sege nu, ic þe bidde, þæt þu min swuster sig, þæt me wel sig for þe and min sawul lybbe for þinum intingan.' ¹⁴ Hi comon þa to Egipta lande and þa Egiptiscan gesawon þæt þæt wif wæs swiþe wlitig. ¹⁵ And þæs cininges ealdormen spræcon be hire wlite to þam cininge Farao and heredon hig beforan him. þæt wif wearþ þa læht and gelæd to þam cininge, ¹⁶ and Abram underfeng fela sceatta for hire. He hæfde þa on orfe and on þe⟨o⟩wum, on olfendum and on assum, micele æhta. ¹⁷ God soþlice beswang Farao þone cining mid þam mæstum witum, and ealne his hired, for Sarai, Abrames wife. ¹⁸ Farao þa het clipian Abram and cwæð him to: 'Hwæt la, hwi dest þu wið me swa?
f. 10ʳ Hwi noldest | þu secgan þæt heo þin wif ys? ¹⁹ For hwilcum intingan sædest þu þæt heo þin swuster wære? Efne nu her ys þin wif: nim hig and far þe aweg.'

12:20 Abram þa ferde of Egipta lande mid ealre his fare and Farao se cyning him funde ladmen. ¹³:¹⁻⁵ And Loth ferde forð mid him oð þæt hig comon to suþdæle, betwux Bethel and Hai, to þære stowe þe he þæt weofod ær arærde, and gebæd hine þær to Gode, and Loth samod mid him. Abram soþlice wæs swiþe welig on golde and on seolfre and on orfe and on geteldum, ⁶ swa þæt þæt land ne mihte aberan þæt hig begen ahton, he and Loth ætgædere wunedon; heora æhta wæron menigfælde and ne mihton wunian ætgædere. ⁷ Wearð eac þurh þone intingan sacu betwux Abrames hyrdemannum and Lothes. On þære tide wunedon Chananeus and Ferezeus on þam lande. ⁸ Abram þa cwæð to Lothe: 'Ic bidde þæt nan sacu ne sig

12:12 Egiptiscan] egyptiscean B, egiptyscam C   hig¹] hi BC   sig] sy B, si C   hig²] hi BC   healdaþ] ealdað C   12:13 sig¹] sy BC   þæt] BC, and þæt L   sig²] sy B, si C   sawul] sawel B, saula C   12:14 Egiptiscan] egyptiscean B   swiþe] *om.* C   12:15 þæs cininges] þas cynges C   spræcon] spæcon B   hire] hure C   cininge] cynge C   heredon hig . . . to þam cininge] gelæddon hi beforan him C   læht] gelæht B   gelæd] gelædd B   12:16 sceatta] sceattæ C   on þeowum] *om.* C   þeowum] o *lost in hole* L   olfendum] oluendum B   assum] assun and on þeowum C   æhta] æhte C   12:17 soþlice] *om.* C   Farao] pharao C   mid] C *f. 14ᵛ*   ealne] ealle C   Sarai] Sara C   12:18 Farao] Pharao C   þa het clipian] het clypian þa C   dest] dydest BC   wið me swa] swa wið me BC   noldest þu] noldestu C   heo] hii C   ys] wære C   12:19 hwilcum] hwylcon B   intingan] þingum C   swuster] swustor B   hig] hi C   12:20 Farao] Pharao C   cyning] cyng C   13:1–5 forð] *om.* C   comon] becomon C   þære] þare C   arærde] arerde C   soþlice] *om.* C   wæs] þa *add.* C   welig] weli C   seolfre] seolure C   13:6 hig] hi BC   ahton] *om.* BC   menigfælde] menigfealde B, manigfielde C   mihton] mihte C   ætgædere] togadere C   13:7 intingan] þingan (þing *appar. on eras.*, intinga *in marg.*) C   hyrdemannum] hyrdemanum C   þære] þare C   wunedon] wære (wunedon *add. above*) C   Chananeus] Cananeus C   13:8 sig] sy BC

betwux me and þe, ne betwix minum hyrdum and þinum hyrdum; wyt sind gebroþra. ⁹Efne nu eall seo eorðe liþ ætforan þe. Ic bidde, far fram me. Gif þu færst to þære winstran h`æ´lfe, ic healde þa swiþran healfe; gif þu þonne þa swiðran healfe gecist, ic fare to þære winstran healfe.' ¹⁰Loth þa beheold geond eall and geseah þæt eall se eard wiþ þa ea Iordanen wæs mirige mid wætere gemenged, swa swa godes neorxnawang, and swa swa Egipta land becumendum to Segor, ær þan þe God towende þa burga Sodoma and Gomorran. ¹¹Loth þa geceas him þone eard wið Iordanen and ferde fram eastdæle, and hig wurdon totwæmede heora ægðer fram his breðer. ¹²Abram eardode þa on þam lande Chanaan. Loth soðlice wunode on þam fæstenum þe wæron embe Iordanen, and he eardode on þære birig Sodoma. ¹³:¹³Ða Sodomitiscan menn wæron þa forcuþostan and swiðe sinfulle ætforan Gode. ¹⁴God cwæð þa to Abrame, æfter þan | þe f. 10ᵛ Loth wæs twæmed him fram: 'Ahefe up þine eagan and beheald fram þære stowe þe þu on stynst to norðdæle and to suþdæle and to eastdæle and to westdæle. ¹⁵Eall þis land þe þu gesihst ic forgife þe and þinum ofspringe on ecnisse. ¹⁶And ic do þinne ofspring swa menigfealdne swa swa þære eorðan dust. Gyf ænig man mæg geriman þære eorðan dust, þonne mæg he eac swilce geriman þinne ofspring. ¹⁷Aris nu and far geond þis land on lenge and on bræde, for þan þe ic hit þe forgife.' ¹⁸Abram þa eornostlice astirode his geteld and com and eardode wið þone dene Mambre, þæt þe ys on Hebron, and þær arærde weofod Gode.

¹⁴:¹Hit gelamp þa on ðære tide þæt þa ciningas wunnon him

13:8 ne²] and C   betwix] betwux BC   wyt sind] we sund C   gebroþra] gebroðru B
13:9 eall] eal C   liþ] ligð C   færst] fram me *add.* C   þære] þare C   hælfe] æ *corr. fr.* a L,
healfe BC   swiþran] swiþ`r´an C   healfe²] *om.* C   healfe³] *om.* C   13:10 geond eall]
om. C   se eard wiþ þa ea] *om.* C   mirige] myrge B, myrie C   gemenged] gemencged C
neorxnawang] neorxenawange C   ær þan . . . Gomorran] *om.* C   Sodoma] sodomam B
13:11 eastdæle] eastdele C   hig] hi B   totwæmede] totwæmed C   heora] C *f. 15ʳ* his
breðer] oðer C   13:12 eardode þa] þa ierdode C   Chanaan] canaan C   soðlice] *om.* C
wunode] wunedo C   fæstenum] westenum C   embe] ymbe C   he] *om.* C   eardode²]
eardade C   þære birig] *om.* C   13:13 Sodomitiscan] sodomanisca C   menn] men BC
þa] *om.* B   forcuþostan] forcuþesta C   sinfulle] sunfulla C   13:14 æfter þan . . . him
fram] *om.* C   twæmed] totwæmed B   up] upp B   þære] þare C   stynst] stenst BC
norðdæle] norðdele C   and³] *om.* C   westdæle] westdele C   13:15 Eall] eal B
gesihst] gesyxt BC   ofspringe] ofsprincge B   ecnisse] Amen *add.* C   13:16 þinne]
þine C   ofspring] ofsprincg B, ofspringe C   menigfealdne] manifielde C   þære¹] þare C
ænig] æni C   geriman þære] ariman þare C   eac swilce] *om.* C   geriman²] ariman C
13:17 geond] ofer *add.* C   lenge] lencge B, længþe C   on²] *om.* B   for þan þe] forþon C
forgife] forgiefe C   13:18 eornostlice] soðlice C   astirode] astyrede C   and eardode]
`and´ eardede C   þone] ðere C   Mambre] manbre C   þe] *om.* C   Hebron] ebron BC
arærde] arerde C

betwinan, ²⁻⁹ feower ciningas wið fif ciningas, oð þæt hig comon to gefeohte. ¹⁰ Ða feollon þa ciningas on þam gefeohte ofslagene, of Sodomam and Gomorran, þæra manfulra ðeoda, and heora geferan flugon afirhte to muntum. ¹¹ Ða namon þa sigefæstan ciningas sona on þam burgum Sodoma and Gomorra þa god þe hig ðær fundon, ¹² and eac gelæddon aweg Loth mid his æhtum, Abrames broþor sunu, þe on þam burgum eardode. ¹³ Ða ætbærst him sum man and se hit sæde Abrame, hu man his broþer sunu on bendum aweg lædde. ¹⁴ Abram þa genam ardlice þreo hund manna and eahtatyne men of his inbyrdlingum and efste wið þæs heres, oð ðæt he hig ofrad, ¹⁵ todælde þa his geferan færlice on þære nihte and him on beræsde and on eornoste hig sloh and afligde þa laue, oð þæt hig comon to Fenicen. ¹⁶ He lædde þa ongean Loth, his broþor sunu, mid eallum his æhtum and þæt oðer folc samod mid wifum and æhtum, gewunnenum sige. ¹⁷ Ða eode Sodomitiscra cining sona him togeanes ²¹ and bæd þæt he hæfde eall þæt he of þam here genam, buton þam mannum anum. ²² Abram him cwæð to: 'Ic ahebbe mine hand to þam healican Gode, ²³ se þe ys ahniend eorðan and heofenan,

f. 11^r þæt ic ne underfo furðon | anne þwang of eallum þisum þingum þe þine ær wæron, þæt þu ne secge eft, "Ic gewel'e'gode Abram", ²⁴ buton þam anum þingum þe mine geferan æton, and þæra manna dæl þe me mid comon, Aner and Escol and Mambre, nimon þas hira dæl.' ¹⁸ Þær com eac Melchisedech, se mæra Godes man se wæs cyning and Godes sacerd, and he brohte hlaf and win ¹⁹ and bletsode

14:1 betwinan] betwuonon C   14:2-9 ciningas wið fif] *om.* B   ciningas¹] cyngas C   ciningas²] cyngas C   hig] hi BC   comon] becomon C   14:10 ciningas] cyngas C   Sodomam] Sodoma C   Gomorran] gomorra C   þæra manfulra] þare manfulla C   geferan flugon] feran flogon C   muntum] munte C   14:11 namon] naman C   sigefæstan ciningas] sygefæsten cyngas C   þam burgum] þa burhgum C   þa²] þæt C   hig] hi BC   14:12 gelæddon] læddon B, gelædde C   aweg] aweig C   Abrames broþor] abrame`s´ broðer C   þe on . . . eardode] *om.* C   14:13 ætbærst] ætberst C   and se] þe C   hu man . . . lædde] *om.* C   broþer] broðor B   14:14 ardlice] heardlice C   men] *om.* C   þæs] þas C   hig] hi BC   14:15 færlice] ferlice C; C *f. 15ᵛ*   þære] þare C   beræsde] beresde C   on eornoste] *om.* C   eornoste] eornost B   hig¹] hi BC   sloh] ofsloh C   laue] lafe B   hig²] hi BC   14:16 his] hi`s´ C    samod] *om.* C    14:17 Sodomitiscra cining] sodominisa cyng C    him] `him´ C   14:18-20 *verses placed after* 14:24 *in* LBC   14:21 he of] hee hefde þæt he of C   buton] butan C   þam²] *om.* C   14:22 Abram] and abram BC   ahebbe] hahebbe C   14:23 ahniend] agnigend B, agniend C   heofenan] heofonan B   underfo] underfoo C   furðon] *om.* C   anne] ænne BC   eallum] aellum C   gewelegode] gewelgode B, welgode C   14:24 buton] butan C   þingum] ðingon B   mine geferan æton] minum geferum æten C   þæra] þare C   Aner] anær B, andhær C   Mambre] manbre C   nimon þas] niman hi þas (hi *appar. alt. to* þi) C   hira] heora B, hyre C   14:18 Melchisedech] melchisedec C   mæra] mære C   se²] þe C   cyning] cyncg C

GENESIS

Abram and cwæð: 'Gebletsod ys Abram þam healican Gode, se þe gesceop heofenan and eorðan, [20] and gebletsod ys se healica God. þurh hys gescildnisse synd þa fynd on ðinum handum oferwunnene.' And he sealde him þa teoðunge of eallum þam þingum.

[15:1] Ða þa þis gedon wæs, þa wearð Godes spræce to Abrame þurh gesihþe, him secgende: 'Ne ondræd þu þe Abram. Ic eom þin wergend and þin med byþ swiðe micel.' [2] Ða cwæð Abram: 'Eala, þu min Drihten God, hwæt gifst þu me? Ic fare butan bearnum, [3] and efne min inbyrdling biþ min yrfenuma.' [4] Ðærrihte wearð Godes spræc to Abrame, þus cweþende: 'Ne byþ þes þin yrfenuma þe þu ymbe spræce ac þone þu hæfst to yrfenuman þe of þe sylfum cymþ.' [5] God lædde hine þa ut and het hyne locian to heofonum and cwæð: 'Telle þas steorran, gif þu mage. þus menigfeald biþ þin ofspring.' [6] Abram þa gelifde Gode and hit wæs him geteald to rihtwisnisse. [7] God cwæð eft to Abrame: 'Ic eom se God þe þe lædde of þæra Chaldeiscra Hur, þæt ic þe þis land forgeafe to agenne.' [8] Abram cwæð to Gode: 'Min Drihten God, hu mæg ic hit witan þæt ic hit agan sceal?' [9] God cwæð eft to him: 'Geoffra me to lace an þriwintre hryþer and ænne þriwintre ramm and ane þriwintre gat, and sume turtlan and sume culfran.' [10] He dide þa swa and todælde hig on twa, buton þa fugelas he na todælde. [11] Ða woldon oþre fugelas fleon to þam holde, Abram hig afligde fram þam flæsce ealle. [12] Eft ða on æfnunge befeoll | slæp on Abram, and micel oga him becom þa mid þeostrum. [13] Him wæs þa gesæd swutelice þurh God: 'Wite þu þæt þin ofspring sceal wunian ælþeodig on oðrum earde and hig hig yfele geswencaþ and on þeowete gebringaþ feower hund geara. [14] Ic deme swa þeah þa þeode þe hig on þeowette gebringað

f. 11ᵛ

14:19 healican] heahlican C   gesceop] gescop BC   14:20 se healica] þe heahlice C   gescildnisse] scyldnysse B   on] of C   oferwunnene] oferwunnenne C   teoðunge] teoðunga BC   15:1 þa¹] om. B   wearð] wiarð C   spræce] spræc B, spece C   gesihþe] gesicþe C   ondræd] ondred C   15:2 gifst þu] gifstu C   bearnum] biarnum C   15:3 inbyrdling] inbyrdlincg B   yrfenuma] yrfnuma C   15:4 Ðærrihte wearð] þarrihte wiarð C   spræc] sprece C   yrfenuma] yrfnuma C   ymbe] embe B   spræce] spæce B, sprece C   hæfst] æfst C   yrfenuman] yrfnuma C   15:5 lædde] C f. 16ʳ   þa] om. C   locian] up add. C   heofonum] hefonan C   Telle] tell B, tel C   þas] þa C   mage] mæge B   menigfeald] mænifyeld C   ofspring] ofsprincg B   15:6 Gode] om. C   wæs him geteald] him was getiald C   rihtwisnisse] rihtwisnesse C   15:7 þæra Chaldeiscra] þare chaldeyscra C   forgeafe] forgiafe C   15:8 cwæð] þa add. BC   hit] om. B   witan] witen C   15:9 hryþer] hruþer C   þriwintre²] þrywinterne B, .iii. wintre C   ramm] ram BC   15:10 hig] hi B, hii C   buton] butan C   na] ne BC   15:11 þam¹] þan C   Abram] ac abram C   hig] hi BC   15:12 æfnunge] æfnunga C   befeoll] befeol B   15:13 þurh] þuruh C   wunian ælþeodig] wunion elþeodig C   and hig hig ... hund geara] and beon yfele geswencad and on þeowe gebroht iiii.c. g̅ C   hig hig] hi hi BC   þeowete] þeowte B   15:14 þeode] þeoda B   hig¹] hi BC   þeowette] ðeowte BC

and hig cumað syþþan ongean mid swiðlicum æhtum. ⁱ⁶On þære feorðan mægþe hig gecirraþ eft hider. Ne synd na git gefyllede þises folces unrihtwisnyssa, þisra Amorreiscra, oþ þas andwerdan tid. ¹⁵Ðu soþlice forð færst on sybbe þonne se tima cymð, on godre ylde, to þinum ealdfæderum.' ¹⁷Ða þa sunne eode to setle, þa sloh þær micel mist and ferde swilce an ofen, eall smociende, and leohtberende fyr ferde ofer þa lac. ¹⁸On þam dæge sealde God him sylf his wedd Abrame and cwæþ: 'Ðinum ofspringe ic forgife þis land æfter þe, fram þære Egiptiscan ea oþ Eufraten, þe þas þeoda habbaþ: ¹⁹Cynei and Cenezei, Cetmonei ²⁰and Athei, Ferezei and Rafaim, ²¹Amorrei and Chananei, Gergessei and Iebusei.'

¹⁶:¹Abrames wif wæs þa git wuniende butan cildum. And heo hæfde ane þinene, þa Egiptiscan Agar, ²and heo cwæð to hire were: 'Ðu wast þæt ic eom untymende. Nim nu mine þinene to þinum bedde þæt ic huru underfo sum fostercild of hyre.' ⁴Abram þa dyde swa swa him dihte Sarai, and Agar þa geeacnode and eac forseah hire hlæfdian. ⁵Ða cwæð Sarai to Abrame: 'Þu dest unrihtlice wiþ me. Ic let mine wylne to þe; nu wat heo þæt heo ys eacniende and forsihð me for þig. Deme God betwux me and þe.' ⁶Abram hire andwirde: 'Efne heo ys þin wyln under þinre handa: þrea hig locahu þu wylle.' Sarai hig þa geswencte and heo sona fleah ut to þam westene, ⁷þær ðær wæs an wyllspring. Ða ofseah hig Godes engel ⁸and hi sona clipode: 'Agar, Saraies þinen, hu færst | þu oþþe hwider wylt þu?' Heo andwirde þam engle: 'Ic forfleo mine hlæfdian.' ⁹Þa cwæð se engel hyre eft to: 'Gecir to þinre hlæfdian and beo geeadmet under hire handa. ¹⁰Ic secge þæt þin sæd byð swa swiþe gemenigfild þæt

15:14 hig²] hi BC   mid swiðlicum] on swilicum C   15:15–16 verses transposed LB   15:16 þære] þare C   hig] hi BC   gefyllede] gefullede C   unrihtwisnyssa] unrihtwisnesse C   Amorreiscra] amoreiscra B   þas] ða B   andwerdan] andweardan B, andwieardan C   15:15 færst] ferst C   se] ðin B, þe C   on²] un C   15:17 sunne] sunna C   an ofen] on æfen C   eall] eal B   15:18 wedd] wed B   and] C f. 16ᵛ   ofspringe] ofsprincge B   forgife] forgafe C   þære] þere C   þas þeoda] þa þeoden C   15:19–21 and¹] om. C   Cenezei] Cynezei C   Cetmonei and Athei] and Æthei Cehmonei C   Athei] ethei B   Rafaim] raphaim B   Chananei Gergessei] Cananei Gergesei C   Iebusei] Gebusei C   16:1 git] giut C   wuniende] wunigende B   butan cildum] buton cylde C   hæfde] ʼh´æfde B   16:2 heo] om. BC   untymende] untumende C   fostercild] fostorcild B   16:4 forseah] forseach C   hlæfdian] læfdian C   16:5 to¹] ʼto´ C   Abrame] abram B   nu] no C   þig] ði BC   16:6 ys] om. B   wyln] wylna C   þrea] þreo C   hig¹] hi BC   locahu] hu C   Sarai] Sarra C   hig²] om. B, hi C   16:7 wyllspring] wylsping B, wilspring C   ofseah] ofsea B   hig] hi BC   16:8 hi] hii C   Saraies þinen] om. C   Saraies] saries B   færst] ferst C   hwider] wider C   andwirde] anwirde C   hlæfdian] læfdie C   16:9 hyre] heore C   Gecir] gecyrr C   hlæfdian] læfdian C   geeadmet] geeadmed C   16:10 gemenigfild] gemanifield C

GENESIS

man hit geriman ne mæg for þære meniu. ¹¹ Efne þu geeacnodest and þu acenst sunu and þu gecigst his naman soþlice Ysmael, for þan þe God sylf gehirde þine geswencednysse. ¹² Þes byþ reþe mann and winð wiþ ealle, and ealle wið hyne, and he gewislice arærð æfre his geteld onemn his gebroþra.' ¹³ Agar þa clipode Godes naman, þe hire to spræc: 'Þu God þe me gesawe.' Heo cwæð: 'Soþlice ic geseah her þone bæftan þe me geseah.' ¹⁴ And for þig heo het þone wæterpytt 'libbendes and geseondes me'. Se pytt ys betwux Cades and Barath. ¹⁵ Agar þa acende sunu Abrame and he het hys naman Ysmahel. ¹⁶ Hundeahtatigwintre and sixwintre wæs Abram, þa þa Agar him acende Ysmahel.

¹⁷:¹ Eft þa þa he wæs nigon and hundnigontigwintre, þa ætywde God hine sylfne him and cwæð him to: 'Ic eom ælmihtig God. Gang þu ætforan me and beo fulfremed, ² and ic sette min wedd betwux me and þe and ic þe gemenigfilde swiþe þearle.' ³ Þa feoll Abram astreht to eorðan and God him cwæð to: ⁴ 'Ic eom, and min wedd mid þe, and þu bist manegra þeoda fæder. ⁵ Ne þin nama ne biþ gecyðed Abram heononforþ ac þu byst gehaten Abraham, for þan þe ic þe gesette manegra þeoda fæder ⁶ and ic gedo þæt þu wixt and ic þe gesette on þeodum, and cyningas cumaþ of þe. ⁷ And ic sette min wedd betwux me and þe, and betwux þinum ofspringe æfter þe on þinum mægþum, ecum wedde, þæt ic beo þin God and þines ofspringes æfter þe. ⁸ And ic forgife þe and þinum ofspringe þæt land ðinre ælþeodignisse, eall Chananeisc land on ece æht, and ic beo heora God.' ⁹ Eft cwæð God to Abrahame: 'And þu healtst | min   f. 12ᵛ wedd, and þin ofspring æfter þe on heora mægþum. ¹⁰ Ðis ys þæt wedd þe ge healdan sceolon, betwux me and eow and þin ofspring

---

16:10 þære meniu] ðare mænigu C   16:11 geeacnodest] ea`c´nost C   gecigst] gecyst C   naman] namam C   soþlice] *om.* C   Ysmael] ismahel BC   16:12 mann] man C   arærð] arerð C   onemn] onnemn B, onem C   16:13 hire] hiræ C   Heo] C *f. 17ʳ*   Soþlice ic] ic soðlice C   bæftan] *om.* C   16:14 þig] þi BC   geseondes] seondes B   Se] þe C   Barath] barah C   16:15 Abrame] *om.* C   he] *om.* C   Ysmahel] ismael C   16:16 Hundeahtatigwintre] hundeahtanti wintra C   þa²] *om.* C   17:1 þa²] *om.* C   nigon] nygan B   hundnigontigwintre] hundnygantigwintre B, hundnygon.w̄ C   ætywde] æteowde C   him¹] *om.* C   ælmihtig] ælmihti C   Gang] ga C   17:2 wedd] wed BC   gemenigfilde] gemanifielde C   17:3 feoll] feol B, ful C   cwæð to] to cwæð B   17:4 wedd] wed B   manegra þeoda] manigra þeode C   17:5 gecyðed Abram heononforþ] geciged heononforð (heonanforð C) abram BC   þu byst gehaten] *om.* C   þan] þam B   þe¹] *om.* C   manegra] ma`ni´gra C    17:6 wixt] weaxst C    cyningas] cinygas C    17:7 wedd] wed BC    betwux²] *om.* C    ofspringe] ofsprincge B    æfter þe²] *om.* C    17:8 forgife] gife C    ofspringe] ofspringce B    land ðinre ... eall] *om.* C    eall] eal B    Chananeisc] `cananeisc´ C   heora] hire C   17:9 Eft cwæð God] *om.* B   healtst] healdst C   wedd] wed B   ofspring] ofsprinc B   17:10 wedd] wed B   sceolon] sculon C   ofspring] ofsprincg B

æfter þe, þæt ælc hysecild betwux eow beo ymbsniden, [11] and ge emsnidað þæt flæsc eowres fylmenes, þæt beo tacn mines weddes betwux me and eow. [12] Ælc hisecild betwux eow beo ymsniden on þam eahtoþan dæge his acennednysse, and ælc werhades man on eowrum mægþum and inbyrdlingum and geboht þeowa beo ymsniden, þeah he ne beo eowres cynnes. [13] And beo min wedd on eowrum flæsce on ecum wedde. [14] Se werhades man þe ne byþ ymsniden on þam flæsce hys fylmenes, his sawul bið adilegod of his folce, for þan þe he aidlode min wedd.'

17:15 God cwæð eac to Abrahame: 'þin wif Sarai ne hat þu hig heononforþ Sarai ac hat hig Sarra. [16] Ic hig gebletsige and of hire ic þe forgife sunu, þone ic wille bletsian. He byþ on þeodum and folca cyningas cumað of him.' [17] Ða feoll Abraham on cneowum and hloh, cweþende on his heortan: 'Wen[st] þu la þæt sunu beo acenned of hundwintrum men, Sarra hundnigontigwintre nu acenne?' [18] He cwæð þa to Gode: 'Ic wisce þæt Ysmahel libbe ætforan þe.' [19] God cwæð to Abrahame: 'Ðin wif Sarra þe acenð sunu and þu gecigst his naman Isaac and ic sette min wedd to him on ecne truwan and to his ofspringe æfter him. [20] Ofer Ysmahel eac swilce ic gehirde þe; efne ic hine bletsige and geeacnige and swiþe ic hine gemenigfilde. Twelf heretogan he gestrinþ and ic hine do mycelre mægþe. [21] Min wedd soðlice ic sette to Isaace, þone þe Sarra þe acenð on þisre tide, nu ymbe twelf monð.' [22] God þa astah upp fram Abrahame, siþþan he þas spræce geendod hæfde. [23] Abraham soþlice ymbsnað his sunu Ysmahel on þone ylcan dæg swa swa God him bebead. [24] And he sylf wearþ ymbsniden þa he wæs nigon and hundnigontig geara. [27] And

17:10 æfter þe] *om.* B   ælc] ealle C   ymbsniden] emsniden B, ymbesniþen C   17:11 ge] *om.* B   emsnidað] emsniðað B, him sniþað C   fylmenes] fylmennes C   tacn] tacne C   17:12 betwux eow] *om.* C   ymsniden] ymbesniþan C   eahtoþan] eahteoðan B, viii.þan C   acennednysse] acennednusse C   and²] C *f. 17^v*   inbyrdlingum] inbyrdlincg B, inbyrdling C   ymsniden] ymbsniþan C   þeah] þeach C   17:13 wedd] wed B   wedde] wede C   17:14 ymsniden] emsniden B, ymbsniþen C   fylmenes] fylmennes C   sawul] saulwa C   aidlode] adilode C   wedd] wed B   17:15 Sarai¹] sarrai C   hig¹] hi BC   hig²] hi B   17:16 hig] hi BC   gebletsige] gebletsie C   cyningas] cynningas C   17:17 feoll] feol BC   Wenst] BC, wents L   of] *om.* BC   men] and *add.* C   hundnigontigwintre nu acenne] hundnygontigeare accenne C   17:18 He] Hee C   17:19 cwæð] þa *add.* C   truwan] ?treiwan (*orig. and alt. forms unclear*) C   ofspringe] ofsprinc B, ofsprincge C   him²] *om.* B   17:20 gehirde] gehealde B   bletsige] bletsie C   geeacnige] gearnige (*appar. alt. fr.* geacnige) C   gemenigfilde] gemanyfilde C   mægþe] myigeþe C   17:21 soðlice] soðli`ce´ C   Sarra þe] *om.* B   þisre] þissere C   ymbe] embe B   monð] monoð B, monað C   17:22 upp] up BC   spræce] word (*with* sprece *in marg. by contemp. hand*) C   17:23 Abraham] þa *add.* C   his sunu Ysmahel] ismahel is sunu C   þone ylcan dæg] þam ilcan dæge C   swa²] *om.* C   bebead] bebiad C   17:24 ymbsniden] ymbsniþan C   þa] þa ða BC   nigon] nygan B   hundnigontig] hundnygantig B, hundnygonti C

ealle werhades men hys | inhiredes, ægþer ge imbyrdlingas ge f. 13ʳ
gebohte þeowan, and ælþeodige menn þe him mid wæron, ealle
wurdon þæs dæges ymsnidene. (Nu secge we betwux þisum þæt nan
cristen man ne mot nu swa don.)
 ¹⁸:¹ God þa æteowde eft Abrahame on þam dene Mambre, þær þær
he sæt on his geteldes ingange on þære hætan þæs dæges. ² And
Abraham beseah upp and geseah þri weras standende him gehende.
Mid þam þe he hig geseah, þa efste he of þam getelde him togeanes
and astrehte hine to eorþan ³ and cwæð: 'Min drihten, gif þu me
æniges þinges tiþian wylle, ne far þu fram þinum þeowan ⁴ ær þan þe
ic fecce wæter and eowre fet aþwea, and gerestaþ eow under þisum
treowe ⁵ oþ þæt ic eow lecge hlaf ætforan, þæt ge eow gereordian,
and ge faraþ syþþan, for þig ge gecirdon to eowrum þeowan.' Hig
cwædon: 'Do swa þu spræce.' ⁶ Abraham þa efste into þam getelde to
Sarran and cwæð hire to: 'Gecned nu hrædlice þri sestras smedeman
and wirc focan.' ⁷ And he arn him sylf to his hryðera falde and genam
an fætt cealf and betæhte hys cnapan, and se cnapa hit mid ofste
ofsloh and gegearcode. ⁸ Abraham þa nam buteran and meoloc and
þæt flæsc mid þam heorðbacenum hlafum and lede him ætforan and
stod him under þam treowe wið hig. ⁹ Mid þam þe hig æton, þa
cwædon hig him to: 'Hwær ys Sarra þin wif?' He andwirde: 'On þam
telde heo ys.' ¹⁰ He cwæð him to: 'Ic cume eft to þe on þisne timan
and þin wif Sarra sceal habban sunu.' Sarra þa gehirde þas word
binnan þam getelde ¹² and hloh digellice, þus cweþende: 'Syþþan ic
ealdode and min hlaford geripod ys, sceal ic nu æniges lustes giman?'
¹³ Ða cwæð God to Abrahame: 'Hwi hloh Sarra þin wif and cwæð

17:27 inhiredes] hiredes B   imbyrdlingas] inbyrdlingas BC   ge²] C f. 18ˢ   gebohte] gebohta C   ælþeodige] eallþeodige C   menn] men BC   þæs dæges ymsnidene] þas deges ymbsniþe C   Nu secge ... don] *Interpolation; no separation in the MS*   18:1 æteowde eft] eft æteowde C   þær þær] þer þer C   geteldes] teldes C   þære hætan þæs dæges] þare hæton þas dagas (þare *alt. to* þære) C   18:2 upp] up C   geseah] þær *add.* BC   hig] hi BC   getelde] telde C   astrehte] astrechte C   18:3 æniges] aniges (*alt. to* æniges) C   tiþian] tiþien C   þinum þeowan] þinan þ`e´uwan C   18:4 þisum treowe] þissum treowum C   18:5 eow lecge hlaf] lecge eow hlaf B, lecge hlaf eow C   gereordian] gereordion B   ge²] *om.* C   þig] þi BC   Hig] hi BC   18:6 Sarran] Sarra C   hrædlice] rædlice C   sestras smedeman] systeras smedman C   18:7 fætt cealf] fæt cealf B, fæt cyealf C   gegearcode] gearcode C   18:8 nam] genam C   meoloc] meolc BC   þam¹] *om.* C   heorðbacenum] eorðbacenum C   lede] ledde C   hig] hi BC   18:9 hig¹¹] hi BC   hig²] hi BC   Hwær] hwar C   Sarra þin wif] þin wif sarra BC   andwirde] anwirde C   telde] getelde BC   18:10 habban sunu] habba suna C; C f. 18ᵛ   binnan] binn`a´n B    18:12 hloh] loh C    digellice] digollice B, digelice C    ealdode] aldode (a *alt. to* æ) C    geripod] geriped C    æniges lustes] anies lustas C    18:13 Abrahame] habra`ha´me C   hloh] loh C

GENESIS

"sceal ic nu eald wif cennan"? ¹⁴ Cwist þu la, ys ænig þing Gode earfoþe? Be þam gecwedenan andagan ic cume to þe and Sarra hæfð sunu.' ¹⁵ þa ætsoc Sarra: 'Ne hloh ic na, ac ic wæs afirht.' God cwæð þa: 'Nis hit na swa, ac þu hloge.' ¹⁶ Ða arison þa þri weras and þanon eodon swilce | hig woldon to þære byrig Sodoma, and Abraham eode forð mid and lædde hig.

¹⁸:¹⁷ God cwæð þa: 'Hu mæg ic forhelan Abrahame þæt ic don wille, ¹⁸ þonne he ys toweard o[n] micelre mægþe and þa strengstan mægþe? Nu ealre eorþan mægþa beoþ on him gebletsode. ¹⁹ Ic wat soþlice þæt he wile bebeodan hys bearnum and his hirede æfter him, þæt hig healdon Godes weg and þæt hig don rihtwisnysse and rihtne dom, þæt God gelæste for Abrahame ealle þa þing þe he hym to spræc.' ²⁰ God þa geopenude Abrahame hwæt he mid þære spræce mænde and cwæð him to: 'Ðæra Sodomitiscra hream, and ðære burhware of Gomorra, ys gemenigfyld and heora synn ys swiðe gehefegod. ²¹ Ic wylle nu faran to and geseon hwæðer hig gefyllaþ mid weorce þone hream þe me to com, oððe hit swa nys þæt ic wite.' ²² Hig gewendon þa þanon and eodon to Sodoman weard. Abraham soþlice stod þa git ætforan Gode ²³ and him to genealeahte and cwæð: 'La leof, nelt þu fordon þa rihtwisan mid þam arleasan? ²⁴ Gif on þære byrig beoþ fiftig rihtwisra manna, sceolon hig ealle samod forweorðan and þu nelt arian þære stowe for þam fiftigum rihtwisum, gyf hig þær swa fela beoð? ²⁵ Ne gewurþe hyt, la leof, þæt þu yfelne dom gesette.' ²⁶ God cwæð þa to him: 'Gif ic gemete on þære birig Sodoman fiftig rihtwisra wera, eallum ic gemiltsige for him.' ²⁷ Abraham þa andwirde and cwæð: 'Nu ic æne begann to sprecanne

18:14 Cwist þu] cwest ðu B, cweðstu C   earfoþe] earfaþe C   andagan] anddagan B, andaga C   cume] cuma C   18:15 Nis] næs C   18:16 arison] arisan C   and¹] ða add. B   eodon] eode C   hig¹] hi BC   woldon to þære byrig] to þare byri woldon C   hig²] hi BC   18:17 mæg] mæi C   18:18 toweard] towierd C   on micelre] BC, omicelre L   þa] ðære B   strengstan] strengostan B, strangsta C   mægþe²] mægþa C   ealre eorþan mægþa] eallne eorþen mægþe C   18:19 bearnum] biarnum C   hirede] hiredæ C   hig¹] hi BC   healdon] healdan C   hig²] hi BC   don rihtwisnysse] healdan rihtwisnesse C   18:20 þa] om. C   geopenude] geopenode BC   hwæt] hwæt add. B (del. by later hand) spræce mænde] sprece mende C   Ðæra Sodomitiscra] þare sodomeyscra C   ðære burhware] þare burchware C   gemenigfyld] gemenifyld B, gemanifyld C   synn] sin C   ys²] his C   gehefegod] gehefogod C   18:21 and geseon] geseon and C   hig] hi BC   gefyllaþ mid weorce þone] mid weorce gefyllaþ þane C   18:22 Hig] hi BC   gewendon] gewendan C   18:23 genealeahte] genealæhte B, genie'h'læhte C   fordon] C f. 19ʳ   þa] þone BC   arleasan] arliasan C   18:24 þære] ðare C   sceolon] scolan C   hig¹] hi B   forweorðan] forwurþan B, forspillan and forweorþan C   þære] þare C   fiftigum] .l.gum C   hig²] hi B   beoð] byð C   18:26 gemete] gemette C   þære] þare C   wera] manna C   gemiltsige] hi gemildsie C   18:27 andwirde] anwerde C   æne] ane C   begann] began BC   sprecanne] sprecenne B, sprecene C

GENESIS

to minum Drihtene, þonne ic eom dust and axe:²⁸ La leof, hwæt dest þu gif þær beoð fif and feowertig rihtwisra? Wylt þu adilegian ealle þa burh?' God cwæð þa: 'Gif ic þær gemete fif and feowertig rihtwisra, ne adilege ic þa burh.' ²⁹ Abraham cwæð þa git: 'La leof, gif þær beoð gemette feowertig rihtwisra, | hwæt dest þu þonne?' God cwæð: 'Ne ofslea ic hig, gif þær beoþ .xl.' ³⁰ Abraham cwæð þa: 'La leof, ic bidde þæt þu þe ne belge wið me gif ic spræce: Hwæt gif þær beoð þritig?' God cwæð: 'Ne do ic him na laþ, gif þær beoð þritig rihtwisra.' ³¹ Abraham cwæð þa git: 'Nu ic æne begann to sprecanne to minum Drihtne, ic wylle sprecan git: La leof, hu byþ hit gif þær beoð twentig rihtwisra?' God cwæð: 'Ne fordo ic hig, gif þær beoð twentig.' ³² Abraham cwæð þa git: 'La leof, Drihten, ic bidde þæt þu ne yrsie gif ic spræce git æne: Hu byþ hit gif þær beoð tyn rihtwisra?' God cwæþ: 'Ne adilegie ic hig, gif þær beoð tyn.' ³³ God ferde þa forð swa he gemynt hæfde and Abraham gecirde to his wununge.

¹⁹:¹ Comon þa on æfnunge twegen englas fram Gode asende to þære birig Sodoma. And Loth, Abrahames broðer sunu, sæt on ðære stræt and geseah hig. He aras þa sona and eode him togeanes and astrehte hyne ætforan þam englum ² and cwæð: 'Ic bidde eow, leof, þæt ge gecirron to minum huse and þær wunion nihtlanges, and þweað eowre fet þæt ge magon faran tomergen on eowerne weg.' Hig cwædon: 'Nateshwon, ac we wyllaþ wunian on þære stræt.' ³ Loth þa hig laþode geornlice oð þæt hig gecyrdon to his huse. He þa gearcode him gereord and hig æton.

18:27 Drihtene] drihtne B   þonne] þonnon C   axe] ahse B   18:28 þær beoð] þer byð C   rihtwisra¹] rihtwisa C   adilegian ealle] adiligian eall C   feowertig rihtwisra] feower'tig' rihtwis'r'a 'manna' C   adilege] adylegie B, adiligie C   18:29 þa git] þa B   gemette feowertig] gemet feowertig B, .xl. gemette C   rihtwisra] manna add. C   dest þu] destu C   hig] hi BC   beoþ²] bioð C   .xl.] feowertig B   18:30 þa] om. C   þe] om. C   belge] bellige C   spræce] sprece BC   beoð¹] bið C   þritig¹] þrittig B, xxx. C   him] heom C   na] om. B   gif . . . rihtwista] om. C   18:31 Nu ic æne . . . sprecan git] sentence misplaced after cwæð þa git (in 18:32) B   æne] ane C   begann] began BC   sprecanne] sprecenne B, sprecænne C   Drihtne] drihtene C   sprecan] specan B   beoð¹] bið C   rihtwisra] manna add. C (abbrev. to f̄.w̄.m̄.)   hig] hi B   gif þær beoð twentig] om. C   18:32 yrsie] yrsige BC, wið me add. C   spræce] spece BC   æne] ane (alt. to æne) C   rihtwisra] manna add. (as m̄) C   adilegie] adilgie B, adiligie C   hig] hi B   gif þær beoð tyn] om. C   18:33 ferde þa] þa ferde B   19:1 æfnunge] æfnuncga C   birig] byri B   Loth] loð B   broðer] broðor BC   ðære] þare C   and²] C f. 19ᵛ   geseah] gesieah C   hig] hi B   19:2 gecirron] cyrron B   minum] mine C   wunion] wunien C   þweað] þwæað C   magon] magan C   tomergen] tomorgen C   eowerne] eowre C   Hig] hi BC   cwædon] nelle we add. B, c`w'æden C   wunian] ut add. BC   þære] þare C   19:3 Loth] Loð B   hig¹] hi BC   hig²] hi BC   gecyrdon] cyrdon C   him] þa add. C   hig³] hi BC

GENESIS

Se leodscipe wæs swa bysmorfull þæt hig woldon fullice ongean gecynd heora galnysse gefyllan, na mid wimmannum ac swa fullice þæt us sceamað hyt openlice to secgenne, and þæt wæs heora hream þæt hig openlice heora fylþe gefremedon. [19:12] Ða cwædon þa englas to Lothe, se þe rihtlice leofode: 'Hæfst þu suna oððe dohtra on þisre byrig, oþþe aþum oþþe ænigne sibling? Gif þu hæbbe, læd hig e⟨al⟩le of ðissere byrig. [13] We sceolon soþlice adiligan ealle þas stowe, for þam þe heora hream weox to swyþe ætforan Gode and God us sende | þæt we hig fordon.' [14] Loth þa eode to his twam aþumum, þe woldon wifian on his twam dohtron, and cwæð him to: 'Arisað and faraþ of þisre stowe, for þan þe God wyle adilegian þas burh.' Ða wæs him geþuht swilce he gamnigende spræce. [15] Ða englas þa on ærne mergen cwædon to Lothe: 'Aris and nym þin wif and þine dohtra and far þe heonon, þy læs þe þu losige samod mid þisre scildigan burhware.' [16] He wandode þa git ac hig gelæhton hys hand and his wifes hand and his dohtra [17] and gelæddon hig ut of þære byrig, for þan þe God him arode. Ða englas cwædon him to: 'Beorh þinum feore. Ne beseoh þu underbæc, ne þu ne ætstand nahwar on þisum earde, ac gebeorh þe on þam munte, þæt þu samod ne losige.' [18] Ða cwæð Loth: 'Ic bidde þe min drihten, [19] nu þu þine mildheortnysse me cyddest, for þan þe ic ne mæg on þam munte me gebeorgan, þe læs þe me þær gefo sum færlic yfel. [20] Nu ys her gehende an gehwæde burh, to þære ic mæg fleon and minum feore gebeorgan.' [21] Him wæs þa geandwyrd þus: 'Ic underfeng þine bene þæt ic þa burh ne towende, nu ðu wylt þyder

f. 14ᵛ

19:3 Se leodscipe ... gefremedon] *Interpolation; no separation in the MSS* Se] seo C swa¹] swiþe C bysmorfull] bysmorful B hig¹] hi BC woldon] wolden C heora¹] hyra C galnysse] galnyssæ B, galnyssa C gefyllan] gefyllon C wimmannum] wifmannum C secgenne] seggenne C heora hream] hura ream C hig²] hi BC heora³] hyre C 19:12 cwædon] cwedon C englas] ænglas C leofode] lifode C Hæfst] hæfæst C suna] sunu B oððe] ðða C þisre byrig] þisere byri C hæbbe] habbe C hig] hi BC ealle] al *lost in hole* L ðissere] þisre B 19:13 adiligan] adylgian B, adilegian C þam] þan B sende] send`e´ C hig] hi BC 19:14 Loth] loð B, Lot C aþumum] aþume C woldon wifian] woldan wiuian C dohtron] dohtrum B, dohtran C Arisað] nu *add.* C þisre] þissere BC gamnigende] gamenigende B, gamiende C spræce] spæce C 19:15 mergen cwædon] morgen cwedon C Lothe] loðe B, lote C þine] twa *add.* C þy læs] þe les C losige] losia C þisre] þissere B scildigan] forscyldigan B, scildian C 19:16 hig] hi BC wifes] wiues C hand] *om.* C 19:17 hig] hi BC þære] þere C for þan ... arode] *om.* C englas] ænglas C him¹] heom B cwædon him] hym cwedon C þinum] þine C beseoh] beoseoh C ne¹] C *f. 20ʳ* nahwar] nahwær C earde] eardum C losige] losie C 19:18 Loth] loð B mildheortnysse] mildeortnysse C ne] *om.* C mæg on] meig of C munte] munta C þe læs] þi les C færlic] ferlic C 19:20 minum] mine C 19:21 geandwyrd] geandswarod B, ge`and´wird C

bugan. ²² Efst ardlice þyder, for þan þe ic nan þing ne do ær þan þe þu þyder cume.' And seo burh wæs gehaten for þig Segor. ²³ Loth com þa to Segor, þa þa sunne upp eode. ²⁴ And God sende to þam burgum eallbyrnende renscur mid swefle gemencged and þa sceamleasan fordyde. ²⁵ God towearp þa swa mid graman þa burga and ealne þone eard endemes towende and ealle þa burhwara forbærnde ætgædere, and eall þæt growende wæs wearð adilegod. ²⁶ Ða beseah Lothes wif unwislice underbæc and wearð sona awend to anum sealtstane, na for wiglunge ac for gewisre getacnunge. ²⁷ Ða beheold Abraham on ærne mergen þyderweard ²⁸ and geseah hu þa ysla up flugon mid þam smice. ²⁹ And God þa alysde Loth | for Abrahame. f. 15ʳ
¹⁹:³⁰ Loth þa ne dorste leng wunian on Segor ac ferde mid hys twam dohtrum afirht to þam munte, and þar on anum scræfe ealle þreo wunedon. ³¹ Ða cwæð seo yldre dohtor to hyre gingran swuster: 'Ure fæder ys eald mann and nan oþer wer ne belaf on ealre eorþan þe unc mage habban. ³² Uton fordrencean urne fæder færlice mid wine and uton licgan mid him þæt sum laf beo hys cynnes.' ³³ Hi didon þa swa and fordrencton heora fæder and eode seo yldre swyster ærost to his bedde, and se fæder nyste hu he befeng on hig for þære druncenysse, ne hu heo dearnunga aras. ³⁵ Eft hig fordrencton þone unwæran Loth and seo gingre dohtor eode to his bedde, and se fæder niste hu he befeng on hig, ne hwenne heo aras, for his druncenysse. ³⁶ Hig wæron þa eacnigende. ³⁷ And seo yldre acende sunu, þone heo het Moab, se ys Moabytiscra fæder oð þisne andweardan dæg. ³⁸ Seo oþer acende sunu, þone heo het Amon, þæt is mines folces sunu. He is þara [A]monitiscra fæder oþ þisne andweardan dæg.

19:21 bugan] bugon C   19:22 ardlice] hardlice C   þing] þinc C   þig] ði BC
19:23 Loth] Loð B   upp] up C   19:24 eallbyrnende] ealbyrnendne B   swefle gemencged] swefele gemenged C   sceamleasan] sceamlyasan C   19:25 burga] burhga C   ealne] eallne C   burhwara ... ætgædere] burhware forbernde ætgadere C   wearð] wiearð C   19:26 underbæc] underbecc C   wearð sona] sona wierð C   sealtstane] sieltstane C   wiglunge] wigluncge C   gewisre] gewissre C   19:27 mergen] merigen B, morgen C   þyderweard] þiderwiard C
19:28 up] upp B   19:29 Loth] loð B   19:30 wunian] wunion C   afirht] afyriht C   þar] ðær BC   scræfe] sʼcʼrefe C   ealle þreo wunedon] wonedun ealle þreo C   19:31 dohtor] dohter C   hyre] hure C   gingran] om. C   swuster] swyster B, swustor C   mann] man BC
oþer wer ne belaf] oðer ne laf C   habban] habbe C   19:32 Uton fordrencean] uten fordrencan C   uton licgan] utan licge C; C f. 20ᵛ   19:33 fordrencton heora] fordrenctan hyre C   swyster] swustor B, swister C   ærost] ærest B, to ærest C   hig] hi BC, ne hwænne heo aras add. B   druncenysse] druncennysse B, drucennysse C   dearnunga] dearnunge C
19:35 hig] hi B   fordrencton] ofrerdrencton C   unwæran] unwaran BC   Loth] loð B   and] ʼandʼ C   dohtor] dohter C   hig] hi BC   hwenne] hwænne B, hwanne C
druncenysse] druncennysse B   19:36 Hig] hi BC   eacnigende] giacniende C
19:37 ys] is þare C   oð] on C   andweardan] anwierden C   19:38 Seo] and seo BC   is¹] his L   is²] his L   þara] þæra B   Amonitiscra] monitiscra L   andweardan] andwierdan C

²⁰:¹ Abraham þa ferde eft to suþdæle and wunode ælþeodig on þam earde Gearara, ² and cwæð be his wife þæt heo wære his swuster. Ða sende Abimeleh þære leode cyning to and het niman þæt wif for hire wlite to him. ³ Ac God sylf him com to on swefne and cwæð to him: 'Efne þu scealt sweltan nu, Abimeleh, for þam wife ðe þu name; heo hæfþ oþerne wer.' ⁴ Abimeleh andwirde earhlice and cwæð: 'Ne ofsleh þu, Drihten, unscildine mannan. ⁵ He cwæð sylf to me þæt heo hys swuster wære and þæt wif eac sæde þæt he hyre broðer wære. Ðis ic dyde mid bilewitnysse.' ⁶ And Drihten him cwæð to: 'Ic wat þæt þu swa didest and ic þe eac for þig geheold, þæt þu wið me ne syngodest þæt þu hig gescindest, and ic þe swa geheold þæt þu hig ne hrepodest. ⁷ Agif nu þam were his wif swiþe raþe, for þan þe he ys witega and for þe gebitt. Gyf þu þis don nelt, þu bist | dead forraþe and ða þe ðe to lociaþ beoþ liflease eac.' ⁸ Abimeleh þa aras and ealle his menn clypode and sæde [him] þa word þe he on swefne gehyrde and hi wurdon ealle wundorlice afirhte. ⁹ He clypode eac Abraham on þære ylcan nihte and cwæð: 'Hwi dydest þu swa wiþ us and swylce synne gebrohtest ofer me sylfne and ofer min rice? ¹⁰ Hwæt gesawe þu mid us þæt ðu swa don woldest?' ¹¹ Abraham him cwæð to: 'Ic cwæð on minum geþance, "Ic wene þæt Godes ege ne si on þissere stowe and þæt hi willaþ me ofslean for mines wifes þingon". ¹² And heo ys swa ðeah min swustor to soþon, mines fæder dohter and na minre modor. Ic genam hig ða to wife. ¹³ And unc gewearþ syþþan þæt heo sceolde secgan þæt heo min swuster wære, swa oft swa wyt ferdon to fyrlenum eardum.' ¹⁴ Ða genam Abimelech oxan and scep, wealas and wylna, and forgeaf Abrahame, and his wif

20:1 wunode ælþeodig] wunede eallþeodig] C   earde] yerde C   Gearara] gerera B, gerafa C   20:2 swuster] swustor B, swyster (e *alt. to* o) C   Abimeleh] abimelech B, Abimelec C   þære leode cyning] þare leoda cyng C   het niman] het hi nimon C   20:3 swefne] swefene C   to him] him to C   nu] *om.* C   Abimeleh] abimalech B, Abimelec C   name] nama C   hæfþ] hæfeð C   20:4 Abimeleh] Abimalech B, Abimelec C   andwirde] anwirde C   ofsleh] ofsleah C   unscildine] unscyldigne BC   mannan] man C   20:5 cwæð sylf] sylf cwæð B   swuster] swustor BC   wære¹] were C   and] *om.* C   hyre broðer wære] wære hyre broðor B, wæs heore broþor C   dyde] cydde B   bilewitnysse] bylewitnesse C   20:6 þig] ði BC   hig¹] hi BC   gescindest] ne scyndest B   hig²] hi BC   hrepodest] repodest C   20:7 raþe] hraðe B   gebitt] gebit C   don] C *f.* 21ʳ   dead] diad C   forraþe] forhraðe BC   ðe] *om.* C   liflease] lifliase C   20:8 Abimeleh] Abimelech B, Abymelec C   menn] men BC   him] BC, eom L   swefne] swefene C   wurdon] wurdrodon (dro *del.*) B   wundorlice] wunderlice C   20:9 þære ylcan] þare ylce C   20:10 gesawe] geseaga C   20:11 minum] mine C   ege] hege C   þissere] þisre B   20:12 soþon] soðan BC   dohter] dohtor B   modor] moder C   genam hig] hi genam B   hig] hi C   20:13 swuster] swustor BC   ferdon] foran C   fyrlenum] fyrlynum B   eardum] yerdum C   20:14 Abimelech] abimalech B, Abimelec C   scep] sciap C   wylna] wilnan C   forgeaf] forgiaf C

him betæhte ungewemmed, ¹⁵ and cwæð: 'Land liþ ætforan eow; wuna þær þe leofost ys.' ¹⁶ To þam wife Sarra he cwæð: 'þusend scyllinga ic forgeaf on seolfre þinum breþer, þæt beo þe to heafod gewædon, þæt þe huru ne sceamige wið þa þe þe geseoþ, and swa hwyder swa þu færst, gemun þæt þu gelæht wære.' ¹⁷ Abraham þa gebæd for Abimelech God, ¹⁸ for þan þe God gewitnode ealle his wimmen, swa þæt heora nan ne mihte habban ænig cild for Abrahames wife, ær þam þe he hyt eft abæd.

²¹:¹ God þa geneosode Sarran, swa swa he behet, and gefylde hys word, ² swa þæt heo wearð mid cilde and on hyre ylde acende sunu on þære ylcan tide þe God gecwæð. ³ Abraham þa gecigde Isaac his sunu, ⁴ and on þam eahtoþan dæge hyne eac ymbsnaþ, swa swa God him bebead, ⁵ and he sylf wæs þa hundwintre. ⁶ Sarra cwæð þa ofwundrod: 'God me worhte hlehter. Swa hwa swa hit geaxað, he hlihþ eac mid me. ⁷ Hwa wolde gelyfan þæt Sarra sceolde lecgan cild to hyre breoste to gesoce on ylde, þæt þe heo Abrahame on his ylde acende?' | ⁸ þæt cild soþlice weox and wearð gewened, and f. 16ʳ Abraham worhte, swa swa heora gewuna wæs, mycelne gebeorscipe to blisse his mannum on þone dæg þe man þæt cild fram soce Sarra ateah. ⁹ Hit gelamp eft syþþan þæt Sarra beheold hu Agares sunu wiþ Isaac plegode ¹⁰ and cwæð to Abrahame: 'Ado þas wylne heonon. Ne byð þære wylne sunu soþlice yrfenuma mid minum bearne Isaace.' ¹¹ Abraham þa undernam hefiglice þas word. ¹² Ac God sylf him cwæð to: 'Ne sig þe hefilic geþuht, þæt þæt Sarra þe sæde be þinre cyfese, ac do swa swa heo cwæð, for þan þe þe byð geciged sæd on Isace ¹³ and ic eac swilce do þære wylne sunu micelre mægðe, for þan þe he ys eac of þinum sæde.' ¹⁴ Abraham þa aras on ærne mergen sona and alædde aweig þa wylne Agar, and

20:15 ætforan] beforan B   leofost] leofest C   20:16 Sarra] Sarran C   forgeaf] forgiaf C   gewædon] gewægdon C   þe³] *om.* C   20:17 Abimelech] Abimelec C 20:18 þe God] *om.* C   his] is C   heora] hyre C   habban ænig] haban æni C   þam] þan BC   21:1 geneosode] geneosede C   21:2 wearð] wiarð C   hyre] hure C   þære] þare C.   21:3 gecigde Isaac] geclypode issaac C   21:4 eahtoþan] eahteðan B, .viii. C ymbsnaþ] ymsnað B, ymbesnað C   swa¹] C *f. 21ᵛ*   bebead] bead C   21:5 wæs] was C hundwintre] hund wintra eald C   21:6 ofwundrod] ofwundræd C   worhte] woruhte C geaxað] geax'a'ð C   hlihþ] hlið C   eac] *om.* BC   21:7 wolde] wold'e' C   sceolde lecgan cild] lecgan sceolde cild B, scolde cild C   21:8 wearð gewened] wiarð gewænod C gewuna] wuna C   gebeorscipe] gebeorscip C   þone] þane C   þe] þe *alt. fr.* þa B   soce Sarra ateah] gesoce ateah (ateaþ C) BC   21:10 þære] þare C   bearne] biarne C 21:11 hefiglice] hefilice C   21:12 sig] sy BC   hefilic] hefiglic B, hefilice C   þinre] þire C   swa²] *om.* C   sæd] sed C   Isace] isaace B, Ysaace C   21:13 þære] þare C 21:14 ærne] *om.* C   mergen] morgen C   alædde] lædde B   aweig] aweg BC   þa wylne] *om.* C

Ismahel samod, and sealde him formete, hlaf and wæter, and gewende him ham. ²¹:¹⁴ Ða þa hig comon to þam westene, þa wurdon hig on gedwolan, ¹⁵ and þæt wæter asceortode þe wæs on þam buturuce. Heo þa alede þone sunu under sumum treowe ¹⁶ and sæt hire feorran, sarlice wepende, cwæð þæt heo nolde geseon hu þæt cild swulte. ¹⁷ God þa sylf gehirde þæs cildes stemne and asende his engel, þe þis sæde Agare: 'Hwæt dest þu, Agar? Ne beo þu afyrht. God sylf gehyrde þines suna stemne. ¹⁸ Aris nu and gim hys, for þam þe he gewyrð git micelre mægþe.' And seo moder swa dide. ¹⁹ Heo geseah þa sona, swa swa hire swutelode God, sumne wæterpytt þær onemn, and heo of þam sealde þam cnapan drincan. ²⁰ And heo wunede mid him. He weox þa ²¹ and wearð on þam westene scytta, and his modor him genam wif on Egipta lande.

²¹:²² On þære tide, cwæð se cining Abimelech and his ealdorman Phihol to Abrahame þus: 'God sylf ys mid þe on eallum þinum weorcum. | ²³ Behat nu me þurh God þæt þu me ne derige, ne minum æftergengum ne minum ofspringe, ac cyþ him mildheortnisse, swa swa ic cydde þe.' ²⁵ Abraham þa þreade Abimelech mid wordum for þam waterpytte þe his wealas him ætbrudon. ²⁶ Ða cwæð se cyning him to: 'Nyste ic nan þing þises, ne þu me hit ne sædest, ne ic hit sylf ne gehirde.' ²⁷ Abraham forgeaf þa Abimeleche lac on oxan and on sceapon and hig slogon heora wedd, heora ægþer to oþrum, þæt hig æfre wurdon gefrynd. ²⁸ Abraham þa gesette seofon lamb onsundron ²⁹ and Abimelech axode Abraham and cwæð: 'Hwæt gemænað þas lamb þe þu gelogast onsundron?' ³⁰ Abraham him andwirde: 'Ic wille þæt þu underfo þas seofon lamb æt me, þæt hig to swutelunge beon

21:14 Ismahel] ysmael C   hig¹] hi BC   hig²] hi BC   gedwolan] gedwolon C
21:15 asceortode] asceorttede C   buturuce] buteruce BC   Heo] Hu C   alede þone sunu] lædde hure sune C   sumum] sume C   21:16 hire feorran] hure furen C   sarlice] om. B   heo] hu C   21:17 þa] om. BC   þæs] þas C   asende] sende B   engel] 'ængel' C   þu²] om. C   suna] sune C   21:18 gim] geom C   þam] þan B   gewyrð] wyrð B, wirð C   moder] modor BC   21:19 (ge)seah] C f. 22ʳ   swutelode] geswutelode BC   sealde] sialde C   drincan] drincen C   21:20 wunede] wunode B, wunedon C
21:21 wearð] wiarð C   21:22 þære] þare C   se] seo C   Abimelech] abimelec C
ealdorman] aldorman C   Phihol] pichol B, fichol C   21:23 nu me] me nu BC   derige] derie C   æftergengum] ftergengum B   21:25 þreade] þriede C   Abimelech] abimelec C   21:26 him to] to him B   hit sylf] sylf hyt B   21:27 Abimeleche] abimelec C   oxan] oxum BC   sceapon] sceapum B, sciapum C   hig¹] hi BC   heora¹] hera C   wedd] wed B   heora²] om. B, hera C   hig²] hi BC   æfre] om. B   gefrynd] gefreond C   21:28 seofon] seofan B, .vii. C   21:29 Abimelech] abimalech B, abimelec C   axode] axsode C   Hwæt gemænað] whæt gemæneð C   gelogast onsundron] gelogodest onsundre C   21:30 andwirde] anwirde C   seofon] seofan B, .vii. C   hig] hi B

GENESIS

þæt ic dealf þisne pytt.' And he dyde þa swa. ³¹ For þig wæs gehaten seo stow Bersabeae, for þan þe heora ægþer sealde oðrum his wedd þær and sworon him betweonan þæt hig sibbe heoldon. ³³ Ða gewende Abimelech mid his ealdormen Phichol to Palestina lande, and Abraham belaf þær. Abraham þa plantode ænne holt on Bersabeae and þær gecigde þa mid soþum geleafan þæs ecan Godes naman, ³⁴ and he þæt land b[og]ode Philisteiscre þeode fela daga syþþan.

²²:¹ God wolde þa fandian Abrahames gehyrsumnysse and clypode his naman ² and cwæð him þus to: 'Nim þinne ancennedan sunu Isaac, þe þu lufast, and far to þam lande Visionis raþe, and geoffra hyne þær uppon anre dune.' ³ Abraham þa aras on þære ylcan nihte and ferde mid twam cnapum to þam fyrlenum lande, and Isaac samod, on assum ridende. ⁴ Ða on þone þriddan ⟨dæg⟩, þa hig þa dune gesawon, þær þær hig to sceoldon to ofsleanne Isaac, ⁵ þa cwæð Abraham to þam .ii. cnapum þus: 'Anbidiaþ eow her mid þam assum sume hwile. Ic and þæt | cild gað unc to gebiddenne and we siþþan f. 17ʳ
cumaþ sona eft to eow.' ⁶ Abraham þa het Isaac beran þone wudu to þære stowe and he sylf bær his swurd and fyr. ⁷ Isaac þa axode Abraham his fæder: 'Fæder min, ic axige hwær seo offrung sig; her ys wuda and fyr.' ⁸ Him andwyrde se fæder: 'God foresceawaþ, min sunu, him sylf þa offrunge.' ⁹ Hig comon þa to þære stowe þe him geswutelode god, and he þær weofod arærde on þa ealdan wisan and þone wudu gelogode, swa swa he hyt wolde habban to his suna bærnytte, syþþan he ofslagen wurde. He geband þa his sunu ¹⁰ and his swurd ateah, þæt he hyne geoffrode on ða ealdan wisan. ¹¹ Mid ðam þe he wolde þæt weorc begynnan, þa clipode Godes engel ardlice of heofenum: 'Abraham.' He andwyrde sona. ¹² Se engel him

21:30 pytt] wæterpytt C   21:31 þig] ði BC   seo] þeo C   Bersabeae] bersabee BC   sealde oðrum] syelde oþere C   wedd] wed B   betweonan] betwynan B, beotweonan C   hig] hi BC   heoldon] heolden C   21:33 Abimelech] abimelec C   Palestina] palestiane C   plantode] geplantode C   ænne] anne BC   Bersabeae] bersabee C   gecigde] gecyðde C   þa²] *om.* B   soþum geleafan þæs] soðan geliefen þas C   ecan] ecean B   21:34 bogode] B, bletsode L, logode C   Philisteiscre þeode] phi`li´steysra þeoda C   daga] dagas C   22:1 his] C *f. 22ᵛ*   naman] name C   22:2 þinne ancennedan] þine acennedan C   Isaac] ysaac C   raþe] hraðe B   geoffra] geofra BC   uppon] uppan BC   22:3 þære] þare C   cnapum] cnapan C   fyrlenum] furlenum C   22:4 þone] þæne C   dæg] *lost in hole* L   hig¹] hi BC   hig²] hi B   sceoldon] sceolden C   ofsleanne] ofsleane B   22:5 þam .ii. cnapum] þā mcnapum B, þam cnapum C   hwile] þæt *add.* C   gebiddenne] gebiddende C   22:6 wudu] wyde C   þære] þare C   22:7 axode] acsode þa C   axige hwær] axie ðe hwæs C   sig] sy B, seo C   22:8 fæder] feæder C   foresceawaþ] foresciawað C   sunu] sune C   22:9 Hig] hi BC   þære] þare C   wisan] wisen C   þone] *om.* C   wudu] wude C   suna] sunu C   bærnytte] bærnette B, bærnæte C   ofslagen] ofslagan C   sunu] ysaac *add.* C   22:10 geoffrode] geofrode C   wisan] wise C   22:11 ardlice] heardlice C   heofenum] heofonum B   Abraham] Abraham *add.* C   andwyrde] anwirde C   22:12 Se] þe C

cwæð ða to: 'Ne acwell þu þæt cild, ne ðine hand ne astrece ofer hys swuran. Nu ic oncneow soðlice þæt ðu ondrætst swyðe God, nu þu ðinne ancennedan sunu woldest ofslean for him.' ¹³ Ða beseah Abraham sona underbæc and geseah þær anne ramm betwyx þam bremelum, be ðam hornum gehæft. And he ahefde þone ramm to þære offrunge and hyne þær ofsnað, Gode to lace, for hys sunu Isaac. ¹⁴ He het ða þa stowe 'Dominus uidit', þæt is, 'God gesyhþ', and gyt ys gesæd swa, 'In monte Dominus uidebit', þæt ys, 'God gesyhþ on dune'. ¹⁵ Eft clipode se engel Abraham and cwæþ: ¹⁶ 'Ic swerige ðurh me sylfne, sæde se ælmihtiga, nu þu noldest arian þinum ancennedan suna, ac þe wæs min ege mare þonne his lif, ¹⁷ ic þe nu bletsige and þinne ofspring gemenigfylde swa swa steorran on heofenum and swa swa sandceosol on sæ. Þin ofspring sceal agan heora feonda gata ¹⁸ and on þinum sæde beoð ealle þeoda gebletsode, for þan þe þu gehirsumnodest minre hæse þus.' ¹⁹ Abraham þa gecyrde sona to hys
f. 17ᵛ cnapum and ferdon him ham | swa mid heofenlicre bletsunge.

MSS L, B

²³:¹ SARRA LEOFODE HUNDTEONTIG GEARA and seofon and twentig geara ² and heo syþþan forþferde, and Abraham hig bestod on þa ealdan wisan, ³ and wolde bicgan hire birgene æt þam mannum þe he mid wunude, þæt wæron Hethes suna. ⁵ Þa noldon hig nanes wurþes onfon ac forgeafon him þa birgene hys gemæccan on to birgenne. ⁷ Abraham hig þa eadmodlice bæd þæt hig bædon Effron, Soares sunu, ⁹ þæt he him sealde wiþ feo þæt twyfælde scræf þe he hæfde on his lande, on hyra gewitnysse, him sylfon to birgelse. ¹⁰ Ða cwæð Effron ¹¹ þæt he him wolde lustlice þone æcer forgifan

22:12 ða] *om.* BC   acwell] acwel BC   ofer] of C   ondrætst swyðe] swyðe ondrætst B, swiðe ondrætst C   ancennedan] accennedan C   woldest ofslean] ofslean woldest BC
22:13 underbæc] underbecc C   anne ramm betwyx] ænne ram betwux BC   bremelum] bræmelum C   hornum] hornu C   ramm] ram BC   þære offrunge] þare ofrunge C; C *f. 23ʳ* lace] ansægednysse C   Isaac] ysaace C   22:14 God¹] godes B   monte] montem C   uidebit] uidit B   God²] godes B   22:15 se] þe C   22:16 swerige] answerie C   se] þe C   arian] gearian C   ancennedan suna] acennedan sunum C   þonne] þanne C
22:17 bletsige] bletsie C   þinne] þine C   ofspring] ofspringe BC, ic *add.* C gemenigfylde] gemanifielde C   heofenum] heofonum B, hefanum C   sandceosol] sandceosel B, stancysel C   ofspring] ofsprincg B   feonda gata] freonda gatu C
22:18 beoð ealle þeoda] byoð ealla þeode C   gehirsumnodest] gehyrsumodest B, gehyrsumedest C   minre] mine C   22:19 ferdon] ferde BC   heofenlicre] heofonlicre B, hefanlicre C
MSS L, B   23:1 SARRA] *3-line red initial cap.* L   seofon] seofan B   23:2 hig] hi B   23:3 wunude] wunode B   Hethes] Ethes B   23:5 hig] hi B   gemæccan on to birgenne] gemæccean to bebyrgenne B   23:7 hig¹] hi B   hig²] hi B   Effron] efron B
23:9 twyfælde] twyfealde B   hyra] heora B   sylfon] sylfum B

MS C

²²:²⁰⁻⁴ Him wiarð siððan gesæd þat .xii. sunu wæron acennodon his breðer Nachor, þære naman sind awritene on þære ledenrace. Ræde þær se ðe willan.

²³:¹ Sarra soðlice lifede hundtweontig geara and .vii. xx gear ² and heo siððan forðferde. Abraham bestod hi þa on ða ealdan wisan ³ and siððan wolde bicgan heore byrgene. þa spæc he to þam mannum þe he mid wunedun, þæt wæron Hethes sunu, and hi þises bæd and cwæð: ⁴ 'Ic heom eallþeodig mid eow wuniende. Forgifað me, ic bidde, byriels mid eow, þæt ic minne dieadan mage bebyrigan.' ⁵ þa anwirde Hethes sunus Abrahame an[d] cwædon: ⁶ 'Gehyr us nu, lyf. þu eart mid us wuniende swa swa Godes heretoga and þu swiðe wel most on urum gecorenum birgenum bebyrige þine diadan.' ⁷ Abraham þa aras | and eadmodlice him abieah ⁸ and bæd þæt hig sprecon f. 23ᵛ his spræce to Effron, Sores sunu, ⁹ þæt he him sialde wið feo þæt twifialde scræf þe he hæfde on his lande on heora gewitnesse, him to birielse. ¹⁰ Effron þa anwirde Abrahame and cwæð: ¹¹ 'Ne byo hit na swa, lyof, ac hlyst minre spræce. þæne æcer ic þe forgife mid eallum þam scræfe ætforan þissum folce, þæt þu freolice bebirgen þær þinne diadan, gif þe swa gelicað.' ¹³ Abraham þa eft biad Effrone þæt wurð wið þam æcere. ¹⁴ Him anwirde Effron eadmodlice and cwæð: ¹⁵ 'þæt land þe þu gewilnast, ic wat þæt hit is swa god swa .iiii. hund scillinga. þis wurð is betwux ung, ac swa micel swa hit is, þu most swa þeah bebirgan þinne deadan þær, nu þu swa don wilt.'

23:5 and] an

mid þam scræfe. ¹⁶Abraham þa awæh feower hund scillinga seolfres be fullon gewihte and sealde Effrone ¹⁷wið þam æcere and wiþ þam scræfe þe læg to Mambre, ¹⁹þæt ys Hebron, and he bebyr[igd]e þær Sarran. ²⁰And he hæfde þæt land syþþan him sylfon to licreste.

²⁴:¹Abraham wæs þa eald and God hine bletsode on eallum þingum, ²and he clipode him to his yldestan gerefan þe ealle his þing bewiste and cwæð to him: 'Sete þine hand under min þeoh ³and swera me aðas, þurh þone heofenlican God, þæt þu næfre ne nyme wif Isaace minum suna of þisum menisce þe ic mid wunie, ⁴ac far to þam lande þe ic of com and nim him þær wif.' ⁵Ða cwæð se wicnere: 'Hu gif þæt wif nele hider to lande mid me? Sceal ic lædan þinne sunu eft to þam lande þe þu of ferdest?' ⁶Þa cwæð Abraham: 'Beo wær æt þam þæt ð⟨u⟩ næfre minne sunu þyder ne læde. ⁷Se heofenlica God sent his engel beforan þe and he þe wissað. ⁸Gyf þæt wif þonne hider mid þe nele faran, | ne byst þu na forsworen.' ⁹Se gerefa þa asette his swiþran hand under Abrahames þeoh and þone að him swor þa, swa he hyne sylf stafode be his suna wifunge. ¹⁰Se wicnere nam þa tyn olfendas, and of his hlafordes godum þone dæl þe he wolde, and lædde forð mid him and ferde to þam lande, be his hlafordes hæse, oþ þæt he com to Nachores byrig. ¹⁵⁻⁶⁰And he þær Isaace wif gefette, swa hyne hys hlaford het and him God wisode, swa hit on þære Ledenbec awriten ys: ræde þær se þe wylle. Ðæs wifes nama wæs Rebecca, Bathueles dohtor.

23:16 seolfres be fullon gewihte] be fullan gewihte seoflres B   23:19 Hebron] ebron B   bebyrigde] B, bebyrge L   23:20 sylfon] sylfum B   24:3 heofenlican] heofon B   menisce] mennisce B   wunie] wunige B   24:6 ðu] u *lost in hole* L   24:7 heofenlica] heofonlica B   wissað] wisað B   24:9 asette] ða *add.* B   þa²] *om.* B   suna] sunu B   24:15–60 swa¹] swa swa B   wisode] wissode B   þær] *om.* B

¹⁶ Abraham þa sona þæt seolfer him awæh, .iiii. hund scyllingan be fullan gewihte, and sealde Effrone wið þam foresædon lande on þæs folces gewitnesse. ¹⁷⁻¹⁸ And he feng to þam lande mid eallum þam treowum þe þæron ymbe stodan and mid þam twyfialdan scræfe þe lahge to Manbre, ¹⁹ þæt is soðlice Ebron, and he birigde þær Sarran. ²⁰ And he hæfde þæt land him siððan to licreste.

²⁴:¹ Abraham wæs ða eald, and God on eallum þingum hine gebletsode. ² And he þa clypode him to his yldestan gerefan, þe ealle his þing bewiste, and cwæð: 'Sete nu þine hand under min þeoh, ³ þæt ic þe halsie þurh þone hefenlican God þæt þu of þissum mennysse þe ic mid wunie wif ne geceose mine sune Ysaace. ⁵ Se wicnere him anwirde and cwæð: 'Hu gif þæt ʻwifʼ nele hider to lande mid me? Sceal ic lædan þinne sunu eft to þam lande þe þu of ferdest?' ⁶ Abraham him cwæð to: 'Beo þu | þes gewær, þæt þu f. 24ʳ
minne sunu næfre þyder ne læde. ⁷ Se hefanlica God þe me het faron þanon, and minum ofspringe, behet me þisne eard to agenne. He asent his engel ætforan þe and þu swa genimst minum sunu wif. ⁸ And gif þæt wif nele gewendan mid þe, ne bist þu forsworen, and þu huru minne sunu þider ne læde to þare lyde næfre.' ⁹ Se wicnere þa asette sona his swiðran hand under Abrahames þeoh and þone að him swor, swa swa he hine sylf stafode, be his sunu wifunga. ¹⁰ Se wicnere þa genam .x. olfendas to lade, and of his hlafordes goldum, and lædde forð mid him and ferde to þam lande be his hlafordes hæse, oð ðæt he becom to Nachores birig, ¹¹ swa on æfnunge, and anbidode him þær wiðutan þære birig wið ænne wæterpytt, on þare tide þe wimmen woldan wæter feccan. He clypode þa to Gode and cwæð mid gelyafan: ¹² 'Drihten, mines lafordes God, do mildheortnysse todæg wið me and wið minne hlaford and gewissa me nu. ¹³ Ic stande wið þisne wæterpytt and þas wimmen hider cumað wæter to feccenne, swa hyre gewune is. ¹⁴ Nu þam wimmen þe ic secge, "sete hwon þin æscen, þæt ic mahge drincen", and heo me anwirdan þus, "eac ic sylle drincan þinum olfendum", nu seo his þe þu geearcodest Ysaace þinum þeowan. And þurh þæt ic tocnawe þæt þu ciðdest mildheortnysse minum hlaforde.' ¹⁵ Þa mid þam þe he þus spræc, þa com Rebecca, Bathueles dohter, and hæfde hyre æscen uppan hure sculdrum, ¹⁶ swiðe wlitig | mæden, wolde wæter feccan. ¹⁷ Mid þam f. 24ᵛ
þe heo þæt wæter bær, þa cwæð se wer hyre to: 'Sele me hwon drincen.' ¹⁸ And heo sona him cwæð to: 'Drinc þu, leofa man, ¹⁹ and ic hlade siððan þinum olfendum wæter oð ðæt hig ealle drincan.'

24:5 wif] *in margin*   24:15 Rebecca] rebeccA

GENESIS [L]

^{24:61} On þære tide þe se esne hig hamweard lædde to his hlaforde, ⁶² eode Isaac on þam wege þe scytt to þam pytte þe ys genemned 'Puteus uiuentis æt uidentis', þæt ys 'lybbendes pytt and geseondes'. He eardode soþlice on þam suþlandum. ⁶³ He eode ut on þæt land, þencende. þa he hine beseah, þa geseah he olfendas þyderweard. ⁶⁴ Rebecca lihte of þam olfende, þa heo Isaac geseah, ⁶⁵ and cwæð to þam cnihte: 'Hwæt ys se man þe ongean us gæð?' þa cwæð he þæt hit wære his hlaford and heo nam raðe hyre wæfels and bewæfde hig. ⁶⁶ Se esne rehte þa Isaace eall hys færeld. ⁶⁷ Isaac gelædde Rebeccan into Sarran getelde, his modor, and underfeng hig to wife and lufode hig swa swiþe þæt he þæt sar forgeat þe him on his modor deaþe gelamp.

^{25:5} Abraham sealde Isace eall þæt he ahte. ⁷ Soþlice Abraham leofode anhundwintre and fif and hundseofontigwintre, ⁸ and he forðferde on godre ylde, ⁹ and Isaac and Ismael his suna hine bebirgdon on þam twifealdan scræfe þe stynt on Effrones lande, Soares suna, þæs Etheiscan, ongen Mambre, ¹⁰ þæt he bohte æt Ethes sunum. þær he ys bebirged and Sarra his wif. |

f. 18^v   ^{25:12} Ismahele wæron acenned .xii. suna. ¹³ þæs yldestan nama wæs Nabaoth; and Cedar and Abdeel and Mabsam, ¹⁴ and Mamsa and Duma and Massa, ¹⁵ and Adad and Thema and Ithur and Naphis. ¹⁷ Ismahel forðferde þa he wæs hundteontigwintre and seofon and þritigwintre. ²⁰ Isaac wæs .xl.wintre þa he nam Rebeccan to wife, Bathueles dohtor, þæs Syriscean of Mesopotamia, Labanes swuster. ²¹ And Isaac bæd Drihten for his wife, for þan þe heo wæs untymende, and he hyne gehyrde and dyde þæt Rebecca wearð geeacnod. ²² Ac þa þa litlingas fuhton on hire innoþe, þa cwæð he: 'Gif hit swa mihte beon, hwæs wære me mare þearf þonne ic mid cilde wære?' þa eode Rebecca to þam þæt heo Drihten ymbe þæt

---

24:61 hig] hi B   24:62 scytt] scyt B   æt] et B   24:65 raðe] hraþe B   hig] hi B   24:67 hig¹] hi B   hig²] hi B   25:5 Isace eall] isaace eal B   25:7 anhundwintre] anhund wintra B   hundseofontigwintre] hundseofontig wintra B   25:9 Ismael] ismahel B   hine bebirgdon] hi bebyrigdon B   twifealdan] twyfealdum B   þæs] *om*. B   Etheiscan ongen] etheiscean ongean B   25:12 acenned .xii.] acennede twelf B   25:15 Naphis] and cedma *add*. *above by a late hand* L   25:17 seofon] seofan B   þritigwintre] ðrittigwintre B   25:20 swuster] swustor B

GENESIS [C]

[20] Heo þa ageat of þam ascenne ardlice his laue, and arn to þam pytte and þa olfendas wæterede. [21] þa beheold se ærndrace þa gebicnunge swiglice, wolde witan þurh þæt hu him gewisode God, [22] and sealde hyre earpreonas eallgildene sona and gildene biagas, [26] God heriende.

24:26 heriende] herieNDE; end of C (*the caps. fill out most of the line and a homily starts on the next line with a large initial cap.*)

axode. ²³ And he cwæð: 'Twa þeoda synd on þinum innoþe and twa folc beoþ todæled on þe, and þæt [an] folc oferswið þæt oþer folc and se mara þeowað þam læssan.' ²⁴ Þa com þære cenninge tima and heo cende twegen suna. ²⁵ Se þe æror com, se wæs reod and eall ruh, and his nama wæs genemned Esau. And se oþer com swa raþe æfter þam oþrum þæt he hæfde þæs broþer fotwolman on handa, and hine man nemde Iacob. ²⁶ Isaac wæs .lx.wintre þa him wæron þas litlingas acennede. ²⁷ Ða hig afedde wæron, þa wæs Esau glæw hunta and eorþtilia. Iacob wæs bilewitte man and wunude on geteldum. ²⁸ Isaac lufode Esau for his huntnoðe and Rebecca lufode Iacob. ²⁶:³⁴ Ða Esau wæs .xl.wintre, þa nam he twa wif, Iudith, Beryþes dohtor, þæs Etheiscan, and Basemat, Helones dohtor, on þære ylcan stowe. ³⁵ Þa butu abulgon Isaace and Rebeccan.

²⁷:¹ Ða Isaac ealdode and his eagan þystrodon, þæt ne he mihte nan þing geseon. Þa clypode he Esau his yldran sunu ² and cwæð to him: 'Þu gesihst þæt ic ealdige | and ic nat hwænne mine dagas agane beoþ. ³ Nim þin gesceot, þinne cocur and þinne bogan, and gang ut and þonne þu ænig þing begite, þæs þe þu wene þæt me lycige, ⁴ bring me þæt ic ete, and ic þe bletsige ær þam þe ic swelte.' ⁵ Ða Rebecca þæt gehirde and Esau ut agan wæs, ⁶ þa cwæð heo to Iacobe hire suna: 'Ic gehirde þæt þin fæder cwæð to Esauwe þinum breþer, ⁷ "Bring me of þinum huntoþe þæt ic bletsige þe beforan Drihtne, ær ic swelte". ⁸ Sunu min, hlyst minre lare. ⁹ Far to ðære heorde and bring me twa þa betstan tyccenu, þæt ic macige mete þinum fæder þærof and he ytt lustlice. ¹⁰ Þonne þu þa in bringst, he ytt and bletsaþ þe ær he swelte.' ¹¹ Ða cwæð he to hire: 'Þu wast þæt Esau min broður ys ruh and ic eom smeþe. ¹² Gif min fæder me handlaþ and me gecnæwð, ic ondræde þæt he wene þæt ic hine wylle beswican and þæt he wirige me, næs na ne bletsige.' ¹³ Ða cwæð seo modor to him: 'Sunu min, sig seo wirignys ofer me. Do swa ic þe secge: far and bring þa þing þe ic þe bead.' ¹⁴ He ferde þa and brohte and sealde hit hys meder, and heo hit gearwode swa heo wiste þæt his fæder licode. ¹⁵ And heo scrydde Iacob mid þam deorwurþustan reafe þe heo æt ham mid hire hæfde ¹⁶ and befeold his handa mid

MSS L, B   25:23 todæled] todælede B   an] om. LB   25:24 cenninge] cennincge B   cende] acende B   25:25 æror] ær B   se²] om. B   raþe] hraðe B   broþer] broðor B   25:27 hig] hi B   glæw] gleaw B   bilewitte] bylewite B   wunude] wunode B   26:34 Beryþes] berithes B   Etheiscan] etheiscean B   26:35 butu] buta B   27:3 lycige] licie B   27:7 huntoþe] huntnoðe B   27:8 min] om. B   27:10 ytt] ett B   27:11 broður] broðor B   27:12 handlaþ] hanlað B   and²] om. B   wirige] wyrge B   27:13 sig] sy B

GENESIS

þæra tyccena fellum, and his swuran þær he nacod wæs heo befeold. [17] And heo sealde him þone mete þe heo seaþ, and hlaf, and he brohte þæt his fæder [18] and cwæð: 'Fæder min.' He andswarode and cwæð: 'Hwæt eart þu, sunu min?' [19] And Iacob cwæð: 'Ic eom Esau, þin frumcennedan sunu. Ic dyde swa þu me bebude. Aris upp and site and et of minum huntoðe, þæt þu me bletsige.' [20] Eft Isaac cwæð to his suna: 'Sunu min, hu mihtest þu hit swa hrædlice findan?' þa andswarode he and cwæð: 'Hit wæs Godes willa þæt me hræd|lice f. 19ᵛ ongean com þæt ic wolde.' [21] And Isaac cwæð: 'Ga hider near, þæt ic æthrine þin, sunu min, and fandige hwæðer þu sig min sunu Esau þe ne sig.' [22] He eode to þam fæder and Isaac cwæð, þa þa he hyne gegrapod hæfde: 'Witodlice seo stemn ys Iacobes stefn and þa handa synd Esauwes handa.' [23] And he ne gecneow hine, for þam þa ruwan handa wæron swilce þæs yldran broþur. He hyne bletsode þa [24] and cwæð: 'Eart þu Esau min sunu?' And he cwæð: 'Ia leof, ic hit eom.' [25] þa cwæð he: 'Bring me mete of þinum huntoðe, þæt ic þe bletsige.' þa he þone mete brohte, he brohte him eac win. þa he hæfde gedruncen, [26] þa cwæð he to him: 'Sunu min, gang hider and cysse me.' [27] He nealeahte and cyste hine. Sona swa he hyne onget, he bletsode hine and cwæð: 'Nu ys mines suna stenc swilce þæs landes stenc, þe Drihten bletsode. [28] Sylle þe God of heofenes deawe and of eorðan fætnisse and micelnysse hwætes and wines, [29] and þeowion þe eall folc and geeadmedun þe ealle mægða. Beo þu þinra broþra hlaford and sin þinre modur suna gebiged beforan þe. Se þe þe wirige, si he awiriged, and se þe þe bletsige, si he mid bletsunge gefylled.' [30] Uneaþe Isaac geendode þas spræce, ða Iacob ut eode, þa com Esau of huntoþe [31] and brohte in gesodenne mete and cwæð to his fæder: 'Aris, fæder min, and et of þines suna huntoþe, þæt þu me bletsige.' [32] Ða cwæþ Isaac: 'Hwæt eart þu?' He andwirde and cwæð: 'Ic eom Esau.' [33] þa aforhtode Isaac micelre forhtnisse and wundrode ungemetlice swiþe and cwæð: 'Hwæt wæs se þe me ær brohte of huntoþe and ic æt þærof, ær þu come, and ic hine bletsode and he byþ gebletsod?' [34] Ða Esau his fæder spreca gehirde, þa wearð he swiþe sarig and geomormod cwæð: 'Fæder min, | bletsa eac me.' f. 20ʳ

27:16 heo befeold] *om.* B   27:19 frumcennedan] frumcenneda B   et] ett B
27:20 þæt me] þæt hyt me swa B   27:21 sig¹] sy B   sig²] sy B   27:22 stefn]
stemn B   Esauwes] esaues B   27:23 broþur] broðor B   27:25 gedruncen]
gedrucen B   27:27 nealeahte] nealæhte B   hyne onget] him to onleat B
27:28 heofenes] heofones B   fætnisse] fæstnysse B   27:29 eall] eal B   geeadmedun]
geeaðmedun B   modur] modor B   awiriged] awyrged B   27:31 gesodenne] gesodene
B   et] ett B   27:34 spreca] spræca B

³⁵ Þa cwæð he: 'þin br[o]ðor com facenlice and nam þine bletsunga.'
³⁶ And he cwæð: 'Eac rihte ys he genemned Iacob, nu he beswac me; ær he ætbræd me mine frumcennedan and nu oþre siþe he forstæl mine bletsunga.' Eft he cwæð to þam fæder: 'Cwist þu, ne heolde þu me nane bletsunge?' ³⁷ Ða andswarode Isaac and cwæð: 'Ic gesette hine þe to hlaforde and ealle þine gebroþru beoð under his þeowdome. Ic sealde him micelnisse hwætes and wines. Hwæt mæg ic leng don?' ³⁸ Ða cwæð Esau to him: 'La fæder, hæfdest þu git ane bletsunga? Ic bidde þe þæt þu me bletsige.' Ða he swiþe weop. ³⁹ Þa wearð Isaac sarig and cwæð to him: 'Bletsige þe God on eorþan fætnysse and of heofenes deawe.'

²⁷:⁴¹ Soþlice Esau ascunode Iacob for þære bletsunge þe his fæder hine bletsode, and þohte to ofsleanne Iacob his broþur. ⁴² Ða cydde man þæt Rebeccan heora meder, þa het heo feccan hire sunu and cwæð to him: 'Esau þin broþur ðe þencþ to ofsleanne. ⁴³ Sunu min, hlyste minra worda. Aris and far to Labane minum breðer on Aram ⁴⁴ and wuna mid him sume hwile, oþ þines broþur yrre geswice, ⁴⁵ and oþ þæt he forgite þa þing þe þu him dydest, and ic sende syþþan æfter þe and hate þe feccan hider. Hwi sceal ic beon bedæled ægðer minra sunena on anum dæge?' ⁴⁶ And Rebecca cwæð to Isaace: 'Ic eom sarig for Ethes dohtrum. Gif Iacob nymð wif of þises landes mannum, nelle ic lybban.' ²⁸:¹ Isaac clipode þa Iacob and bletsode hine, and cwæð to him: 'Ne nym þu þe gemæccan of Chanaan cynne, ² ac far to Mesopotamia on Siria to Bathueles hiwrædene, þinre modor fæder, and nim þe wif of Labanes dohtrum, þines eames.'

f. 20ᵛ ²⁸:¹⁰ Iacob ferde þa of Bersabe to Aram. ¹¹ Þa he com | to sumre stowe and wolde hine þær restan æft[er] sunnan setlgange, he nam stanas and lede under his heafod and slep on þære stowe. ¹² Þa geseah he on swefne standan ane hlædre fram eorðan to heofenan, and Godes englas up stigende and nyþer stigende on þære hlædre, ¹³ and he geseah Drihten on ufeweardre þære hlædre and Drihten cwæð to him: 'Ic eom Drihten God Abrahames þines fæder, and Isaaces God. Þæt land þe þu on slæpst, ic sylle þe and þinum ofspringe. ¹⁴ And þin

---

27:35 broðor] B, bróor L   27:36 genemned] genemd B   27:39 fætnysse] fæstnysse B   heofenes] heofones B   27:41 ofsleanne] ofsleane B   broþur] broðor B   27:42 broþur] broðor B   ofsleanne] ofsleane B   27:44 broþur] broðor B   27:45 feccan hider] hider feccean B   28:1 gemæccan] gemæccean B   Chanaan] chanan B   28:11 sumre] sume`re´ B   æfter] B, æft L   setlgange] setlunge B   þære] ðere B   28:12 hlædre fram] hlæddre fra B   heofenan] heofonan B   englas up] engas upp B   hlædre²] om. B   28:13 hlædre] hlæddre B   ofspringe] ofsprincge B

GENESIS

ofspring byþ fram eastdæle oð westdæle and fram suþdæle oþ
norðdæle, and ealle eorðan mægþa beoð gebletsode þurh þe and
þurh þinne ofspring. ¹⁵ And ic healde þe swa hwær swa þu færst and
ic þe læde ongean to þison lande and gefylle ealle þa þing þe ic
spræc.' ¹⁶ Ða Iacob awoc, þa cwæð he witodlice: 'Drihten is on
þissere stowe and ic hit nyste.' ¹⁷ And he cwæð eft: 'Ealla, hu egeslic
þeos stow ys. Nys her nan þin[g] buton Godes hus and heofenes
geat.' ¹⁸ On morgen þa he aras, he nam þone stan þe he under his
heafod lede and arærde hine to mearce and get ele þær onuppan
¹⁹ and nemde þa burh Bethel, seo hatte ær Luza. ²⁰ Eac he behet behat
and cwæð: 'Gif Drihten biþ mid me and gehealt me on þam wege þe
ic fare and sylþ me hlaf to etenne and reaf to werigenne, ²¹ and gif ic
gesund gecyrre to mines fæder huse, Drihten [. . .] ²² And þes stan þe
ic arærde to mearce biþ genemned Godes hus, and of eallum þam
þingum þe þu me sylst, ic bringe þe teoþunge.'
²⁹:¹ Witodlice þa he com to þam eastlande, ² þa geseah he þær anne
pytt on þam land and þreo heorda sceapa sittende wið þone pytt, and
se pytt wæs beheled mid anum stane. ³ Ðæra hyrda gewuna wæs,
þonne hig heora heorda gegaderodon, þæt hig awylton þone stan of
þam pytte and hi | heora orf þær wæterodon and þone pytt eft f. 21ʳ
behlidon. ⁴ And he cwæð to þam hirdum: 'Broþru, hwanon synd ge?'
Hig andswaredon and cwædon: 'Of Aran.' ⁵ Þa cwæð he: 'Cunne ge
Laban, Nachores sunu?' Hig cwædon þæt hig hine cuðon. ⁶ Þa cwæð
he: 'Hu mæg he?' Hig cwædon þæt he wel mihte. Þa hig þus
spræcon, þa com Rachel his dohtor mid his heorde. ¹⁰ Þa Iacob hig
geseah and wiste þæt hit wæs his mage, and Labanes sceap his eames,
he fylste hire ¹¹ and wætorode hire heorde. ¹³ Ða Laban gehirde þæt
Iacob wæs cumen, his swustor sunu, þa arn he togeanes and clypte
hine and cyste and lædde hine into his huse, ¹⁴ and cwæð to him: 'Þu
eart min ban and min flæsc.' And þa an monuþ agan wæs, ¹⁵ þa cwæð
he to him: 'Nelle ic þæt þu me to gife hirsumige. Hwæt wylt þu to
medes habban?' ¹⁶ Laban hæfde twa dohtra; seo yldre hatte Lia and

28:14 ofspring¹] ofsprinc B   oð westdæle] *om.* B   norðdæle] norðdæl B   ofspring²]
ofsprinc B   28:15 þing] ðincg B   28:16 þissere] þisse B   28:17 Ealla] eala B
þing] ðing B, þin L   heofenes] heofones B   28:20 etenne] etene B   28:21 gecyrre]
cyrre B   Drihten] Grein adds me bið god, Crawford adds biþ God min *(following L'Isle's
addition in B) to translate Vulg.* erit mihi Dominus in Deum   29:3 hig¹] hi B   hig²] hi B
hi] *om.* B   29:4 Hig andswaredon] hi andswarodon B   29:5 Hig¹] hi B   hig²] hi B
29:6 Hig¹] hi B   hig²] hi B   29:10 hig] hi B   sceap] scep B   29:11 wætorode]
wæterode B   29:13 swustor] swuster B   29:14 monuþ] monoþ B
29:15 hirsumige] hyrsumie B

seo gingre Rachel. ⁱ⁸ Iacob lufode Rachel and cwæð: 'Ic hyrsumige þe seofon gear wiþ þinre gin[g]ran dehter.' ¹⁹ Ða cwæð Laban: 'Leofre me ys þæt ic hig sylle þe þonne oþrum men; wuna mid me.' ²⁹:²⁰ Iacob him hyrsumode þa seofon gear for Rachele and hit þuhte him feawa daga, for þære lufe þe he to hire hæfde. ²¹ Ða seofon gear agane wæron ²² and man hig sceolde him gifan, ²³ þa lædde Laban Lian his dohtor to him, ²⁴ and sealde hire ane þinene seo hatte Zelpha, and he underfeng Lian to wife. ²⁵ On mergen þa he Lian geseah, he cwæð to his sweore: 'Hwi dydest þu þus? Hu, ne þeowode ic þe seofon gear for Rachele?' ²⁶ Ða andswarode Laban and cwæð: 'Hit nis þeaw mid us þæt man þa gingran ær gife þonne þa yldran. ²⁷ Ac hafa þas ane wucan to gemæccan and ic gife þe þa oþre, wið þam þu hyrsumige me oþre seofen gear.' ²⁸ He cwæð þæt he [swa] don | wolde, and þa seo ucu agan wæs, ða nam he Rachel to wife. ²⁹ And se fæder hire sealde ane þeowene, Bala hatte. ³² Iacob gestrynde þa, be Lian, Ruben and Simeon and Levi and Iuda.

³⁰:¹ Rachel wæs untymende, ⁴ ac heo nam Balan hire þeowene and sealde Iacobe to gerestan, ⁵⁻⁸ and he gestrinde be hire Dan and Neptalim. ⁹ Ða Lia underget þæt heo leng ne tymde, þa sealde heo Zelfan, hire þinene, Iacobe to wife, ¹⁰⁻¹³ and he gestrynde be hire Gad and Aser. ¹⁷⁻²⁰ Eft he gestrynde fiftan sunu and sixtan, Isachar and Zabulon, ²¹ and ane dohtor, Dina hatte. ²² Witodlice God gehirde Racheles bene, and he gestrinde be hire Ioseph. ²⁵ Ða Iosep wæs geboren, þa bæd Iacob his sweor þæt he lete hine faran to his lande, ²⁶ mid his wifum and mid his bearnum, þe he him fore hirsumode. ⁴³ Iacob wæs þa swiþe welig and hæfde manega heorda and þeowas and þeowena, olfendas and assan. ³¹:¹ Ða cwædon Labanes bearn: 'Iacob hæfþ genumen ealle ures fæder æhta and he ys welig and mære þurh ures fæder speda.' ⁴ He sende þa and clypode Rachel and Lian ⁵ and cwæð him to: 'Ic geseo on eowres fæder þeawum þæt he nys swa wel wið me geworht swa he wæs gyrstandæg and þis æran dæg. ¹¹ Mines fæder God cwæð to me, ¹³ "Far of þis lande and cum to þam lande þe þu on wære geboren".' ¹⁴ Ða andswarode Lia and Rachel and cwædon: 'Hwæþer wit ænig þing agon of uncres fæder

---

29:16 gingre] gynre B   29:18 gingran] B, ginran L   29:19 hig] hi B
29:20 hyrsumode] -ode *alt. from* -ede B   seofon] seofan B   þuhte him] him þuhte B
29:21 Ða seofon] Ða ða seofan B   agane] agan B   29:22 hig sceolde] sceolde hi B
29:23 Lian] *om*. B   29:25 seofon] seofan B   29:26 gife] forgyfe B   29:27 hafa] ðe *add*. B   wucan] ucan B   29:28 swa] B, *om*. L   and] *om*. B   30:9 underget] undergeat B   30:10–13 gestrynde] strynde B   30:22 Ioseph] iosep B   31:5 him to] to him B   gyrstandæg] gyrsandæg B

GENESIS

æhton? [15] He sealde us swa fremde and fræt uncer wurð. [16] Ac God nam uncres fæder æhta and sealde hig unc and uncrum bearnum. Do for þam þa þing þe Drihten þe bebead.'

[31:17] Iacob aras and sette his gemæccan uppan his olfendas, and his bearn, [18] and nam ealle þa þing þe he on Mesopotamia beget forþ mid him and ferde to Isaace his fæder to Chanaan | lande. [19] On f. 22ʳ þære tide ferde Laban to his sceapa sceare, and Rachel forstæl hire fæder hæþenan godas. [20] Nolde na Iacob cyþan his sæcdom his sweore. [21] Þa he ferde, mid þam þingum þe his on riht wæron, [22] ða cydde man Labane on þam þriddan dæge þæt Iacob wæs asceacen. [23] Þa ferde Laban and his gebroþru æfter Iacobe seofon dagas and gemetton hine on Galaad. [24] Ða ætywde God Labane on swefne and cwæð to him: 'Warna þe þæt þu nan þin[g] wiþerwerdlices ne sprece ongen Iacob.' [25] And Iacob sloh his geteld on þære dune. [26] Ða cwæð Laban to Iacobe: 'Hwi dydest þu swa, þæt þu ætlæddest me mine dohtra swilce hit gehergode hæftlingas wæron? [27] Hwi woldest þu sceacan butan minre gewitnisse? Hwi noldest þu hit secgan me, þæt ic filigde þe mid blisse and mid lofsangum and mid timpanum and mid hearpum. [28] Ne þu ne bæde þæt ic mine suna cyste and mine dohtra; dyslice þu dydest. [29] Nu ic wolde þe þone unþanc mid yfele leanian, ac þines fæder God cwæð to me girstandæg, "Warna þæt þu nan þing styrnlices ne sprece ongen Iacob". [30] Be þinum agenum wille, þu ferdest to þines fæder hiwrædene. Hwi forstæle þu me mine godas?' [31] Ða cwæð Iacob: 'Ic for fram þe butan þinre gewitnysse, for þam ic ondred þæt þu me bereafodest þinra dohtra. [32] Nu þu me stale tyhst, sig se man ofslagen beforan us eallum þe þu þine hæþenan godas mid finde. Sece þine þing and nim swa hwæt swa þu þines finde.' Iacob niste þæt Rachel hæfde þa andlicnyssa forstolen.

[31:33] Eft Laban eode þa into Iacobes geteldum and s⟨o⟩hte his hæþenan godas and hig nahwær ne funde. [34] Rachel hig hæfde gehydd under anes olfendes seame. | [36] Ða wearð Iacob yrre and f. 22ᵛ cwæð to him: 'For hwilcum gylte ferdest þu þus æfter me [37] and towurpe eall min inorf? Hwæt fundest þu þinra æhta þæron, lege hit

---

31:16 hig] hi B   þing] ðingc B   31:18 beget] begeat B   31:19 sceapa sceare] scepscere B   31:20 Nolde na] þa nolde B   sæcdom] scæcdom B   31:23 seofon] seofan B   31:24 þing] B, þin L   wiþerwerdlices] wiðerweardlices B   sprece ongen] spece ongean B   31:27 hearpum] hearpan B   31:28 bæde] bide B   dyslice] and dyselice B   31:29 girstandæg] gyrsandæg B   ongen] on B   31:30 hiwrædene] hiwrædenne B   me] *om.* B   31:32 sig] sy B   andlicnyssa] anlicnyssa B   31:33 sohte] o *in hole* L   hig nahwær] hi nahwar þær B   31:34 hig] hi B   31:37 inorf] innorf B

her beforan þinum freondum and beforan minum freondum and demon hig betwux me and þe. ³⁸ Wæs ic for þam mid þe nu twentig wintra? Næron þine heorda stedige, ne ic þærof ne æt. ³⁹ Swa hwæt swa man þærof forstæl oþþe wilddeor abiton, ic hit forgeald. ⁴⁰ Dæges and nihtes ic swanc, on hætan and on cyle and on wæccan. ⁴¹ Ðus ic þeowode þe twentig wintra, feowertyne for þinum dohtrum and six for þinum heordum. ⁴² Nu þu me woldest forlætan nacodne, gif Abrahames God nære mid me, and Isaaces ege. God geseah min geswinc and þreatode þe girstandæg.' ⁴³ Þa cwæð Laban: 'Mine doh[t]ra and þine suna and þine heorda and ealle þa þing þe þu gesihst synd mine. Hwæt mæg ic þeah don minum sunon and minum magon? ⁴⁴ Ga hider near and uton syllan wedd þæt freondscipe sig betwux unc, me and þe. ⁵³ Abrahames God and Nachores God and hira fæder God deme betwix unc.' And Iacob swor þurh his fæder ege, Isaaces, ⁵⁴ and geoffrude lac on þære dune and clipode his gebroþru þæt hig æton. Þa hig geeten hæfdon, hig wunedon þær. ⁵⁵ And Laban aras on niht and cyste his suna and his dohtra and bletsode hig and cirde to his agenum hame.

³²:¹ Witodlice þa Iacob ferde, he geseah Godes englas beforan him, ² and he cwæð: 'Þis ys Godes fyrdwic.' And he nemde þære stowe naman Manaim, þæt ys 'wicstow'. ³ Soþlice he sende bodan beforan him to Esawe his breðer on Seir lande, ⁴ and cwæð to him: 'Secgaþ Esawe minum hlaforde þæt ic wracnode mid Labane and fleah hine oþ þisne dæg. ⁵ Nu ic hæbbe oxan and assan and sceap, þeowas and

f. 23ʳ þeowena, and ic sende | ærendracan to minum hlaforde þæt he min freond sig.' ⁶ Ða þa bodan ongean comon to Iacobe, þa cwædon hig: 'We comon to Esawe þinum breþer and he efst nu ongen þe mid feower hund mannum.' ⁷ And Iacob ondred him swiþe and todælde þæt folc on twa, and þa heorda and þa olfendas, ⁸ and cwæð: 'Gif Esau cymþ to anum flocce and þone ofslihþ, se oþer flocc byð gehealden.' ⁹ And eft he cwæð: 'Abrahames God, mines fæder, and Isaaces God, Drihten, þu þe me bude þæt ic ferde to þam lande þe ic wæs on geboren and bletsodest me, ¹⁰ ic eom læssa þonne ealle þine miltsunga and þonne þin soþfæstnys þe þu þinum þeowe sealdest.

31:37 hig] hi B   31:38 mid . . . wintra] me nu twentig wintra mid ðe B
31:39 wilddeor] wildeor B   31:41 wintra] wintre B   31:42 girstandæg] gyrsandæg B
31:43 dohtra] B, dohra L   31:44 sig] sy B   unc] *om.* B   31:53 hira] heora B   betwix] betwux B   31:54 geoffrude] geofrode B   gebroþru] gebroðra B   hig¹] hi B   hig geeten] hi eten B   hig³] hi B   31:55 hig] hi B   32:2 Manaim] maim B   32:3 Esawe] esau B
32:4 Esawe] esauwe B   32:5 sig] sy B   32:6 hig] hi B   Esawe] esauwe B   ongen] ongean B   32:8 flocc] floc B   32:9 eft] heft B   bletsodest] bletsode B

Mid minum stafe ic oferferde Iordane and ic hig eft ongean oferfare mid twam floccon. ⁽¹¹⁾ Alyse me of Esawes handa mines broþur, for þam þe ic hine swiþe ondræde, þe læs þe he cume and ofslea þas modra mid hira cildum. ⁽¹²⁾ Þu cwæde þæt þu me woldest wel don and þæt þu woldest minne ofspring gemenigfyldan swa sæceosol, þe nan man atellan ne mæg.' ⁽¹³⁾ He asyndrode þa lac of þam þe he hæfde Esawe his breþer: ⁽¹⁴⁾ twa hund gata and twentig buccena and twa hund eowena and twentig rammena, ⁽¹⁵⁾ þritig gefolra olfendmyrena, mid heora coltun, and feowertig cuna and twentig fearra and .xx. assmyrena, mid heora tyn coltum. ⁽¹⁶⁾ And he asende his þeowas, and ælc þæra heorda onsundrum, beforan him and cwæð to him: ⁽¹⁷⁾ 'Gif ge gemitton Esau minne broþur and he eow axie hwæs ge sin oððe hwæder ge willon oþþe hwa þa þing age þe ge mid faraþ, ⁽¹⁸⁾ ðonne cweþe ge þæt hit synd Iacobes and he hig sent Esauwe his hlaforde to lace and he cymþ him sylf æfter, ⁽²⁰⁾ þæt he þe mid his lacum gegladige and hæbbe þine miltse.' | ⁽²¹⁾ Ða lac ferdon þa beforan f. 23ᵛ him and he wunude on þære nihte on wicstowe.

³²:²² He aras þa on dægred and nam his wif mid hira endlufon sunum and oferfor þone ford þe man Iacob nemþ. ⁽²³⁾ Þa he ealle þa þing ofergebroht hæfde, þe hys wæron, ⁽²⁴⁾ he ana belaf þær bæfta. Ða wraxlode an engel wiþ hine oþ morgen. ⁽²⁵⁾ Þa geseah he þæt he hine oferswiðan ne mihte, þa æthran he his sine on his þeo and heo þærrihte forscranc. ⁽²⁶⁾ Þa cwæð se engel to Iacobe: 'Forlæt me, nu gæþ dægsteorra upp.' He andswarode and cwæð: 'Ne forlæte ic þe, ær þu bletsige me.' ⁽²⁷⁾ Þa cwæð se engel: 'Hwæt ys þin nama?' 'Iacob', cwæð he. ⁽²⁸⁾ Þa cwæð he: 'Ne byþ þin nama nateshwon Iacob genemned ac Israhel, for þam þe þu wære strang ongean God and þu bist strengra ongen menn.' ⁽²⁹⁾ Þa axode Iacob hine hwæt his nama wære. Ða cwæð he: 'Hwi axast þu minne naman?' And he bletsode hine on þære ylcan stowe. ⁽³⁰⁾ And Iacob nemde þære stowe naman Phanuel and cwæð: 'Ic geseah Drihten of ansine to ansine and ic wæs hal', ⁽³¹⁾ and sona eode sunne upp. Ða he hæfde oferfaren Phanuel, he

32:10 hig] hi B   floccon] floccum B   32:11 Esawes] esaues B   broþur] broðor B cume and ofslea] me ofslea and B   hira] heora B   32:12 man] *om.* B   32:13 Esawe] esauwe B   32:14 eowena] ewena B   32:15 þritig] þrittig B   coltun] coltum B   .xx. assmyrena] twentig asmyrena B   heora²] hyra B   32:16 and²] *om.* B 32:17 broþur] broðor B   axie] axige B   sin] synd B   hwæder] hwyder B 32:18 hig] hi B   Esauwe his hlaforde] hys hlaforde esauwe B   32:21 wunude] wunode B   32:22 hira endlufon] heora endleofan B   32:24 bæfta] bæftan B   oþ morgen] on merigen B   32:25 geseah he] he geseah B   32:28 ongen menn] ongean men B   32:30 ic²] *om.* B

wæs healt. ³² For þam, nellaþ Israhela folc etan sine git oð þisne dæg, for þam þe heo forscranc on Iacobes þeo and astifode.

³³:¹ Soþlice þa Iacob hine beseah, þa geseah he Esauw him towerd, mid feower hund mannum. Iacob todælde þa Lian bearn and Rachele and begra þæra þinena ² and sette þa þinena and hira bearn on foreweardum, and Lian mid hire bearnum on þære æfteran stowe, and Rachel and Iosep on æftewerd. ³ And he eode forð and feoll niwel on þa eorðan seofon siþon oð his broþur com. ⁴ Esau arn ongen his broþur and clipte hine and cyste hine. ⁵ Ða he hine beseah, þa ge|seah he þa wif and hira litlingas and cwæð: 'Hwæt synd þas? Gebyrað him aht to þe?' He andswarode and cwæð: 'Hit synd þa litlingas þe Drihten me forgeaf, þinum þeowe.' ⁸ Ða Esau þa lac geseah, þa cwæð he: 'Hwæt sind þas floccas þe ongen me comon?' He him andswarode and cwæð: 'Hit synd þa þing þe ic sylle þe, hlaford min, wið þinum freondscipe.' ⁹ And he cwæð: 'Broþur min, hafa þe þin. Ic hæbbe genoh.' ¹⁰⁻¹¹ Þa cwæð he: 'Ic bidde þe þæt þu onfo þissa laca þe ic þe brohte and me God sealde.' Ða underfeng he hig uneaþe ¹² and cwæð to him: 'Uton faran togædere.' ¹³ Þa cwæð Iacob: 'Þu wast þæt ic hæbbe hnesce litlingas and geeane eowa and gecelfe cy mid me. Gif ic hig to swiþe ealle drife, hig forwurþaþ. ¹⁴ Ac fare min hlaford beforan his þeowe and ic fare æfter, swa ic geseo þæt mine litlingas magon, oþ ic cume to minum hlaforde on Seir.' ¹⁵ Ða cwæð Esau: 'Ic bidde þe þæt þu nyme þe ladmenn of minum geferum þæt þe wegas wissigeon.' Ða cwæð he: 'Nys me þæs nan þearf. þæs anes ic ah þearfe þæt þu min freond sig and ic þine miltse hæbbe.' ¹⁶ Esau ferde þa to Seir ¹⁷ and Iacob com to Sochot and arærde þær his geteld and nemde þære stowe naman Sochot, þæt ys 'geteld'.

³⁵:¹ God spræc to Iacobe and cwæð to him: 'Aris and far to Bethel and earda þær and arære weofod on þære stowe Drihtne, þe he þe ætywde þa þu fluge Esau þinne broðor.' ²⁻³ Iacob ferde þa mid ealre his hiwrædene, swa him God wisode. ⁹ Eft God ætywde Iacobe and

33:1 Esauw] esau B   towerd] toweard B   33:2 foreweardum] forewerdum B   æfteran] æftran B   æftewerd] æfteweardan B   33:3 feoll] feol B   seofon] seofan B   oð] ðæt *add.* B   broþur] broðor B   33:4 ongen] ongean B   broþur] broðor B   33:5 hira] heora B   33:8 ongen] ongean B   freondscipe] gyfan *add.* B   33:9 Broþur] broðor B   33:10-11 hig] hi B   33:12 togædere] ætgædere B   33:13 eowa] eawa B   gecelfe] gecealfe B   hig¹] hi B   ealle drife hig] drife ealle hi B   33:14 oþ] ðæt *add.* B   33:15 wissigeon] wission B   sig] sy B   35:1 ætywde þa] æteowde 'þa' B   35:2-3 wisode] *At this point, a late annotator of L puts an omission mark and begins writing an addition above the line, but after five words breaks off and starts again at the bottom of the page and continues at the top of f. 24ᵛ. The addition is a summary of 33:18-20, 34, and 35:8, and was copied from B, where it was inserted by that manuscript's later twelfth-century annotator, starting at the bottom of f. 51ʳ. See p. xlix.*   35:9 ætywde] æteowde B

bletsode hine ¹⁰ and cwæð: 'Ne byð þin nama leng Iacob genemned,
ac Israhel.' ¹¹ Eac he cwæð: 'Ic eom ælmihtig God. Wex and beo
gemænigfyld on þeoda and mægða. Folc cumað of þe, and cyningas
cumaþ of þe. ¹² Þæt land þæt ic sealde Abrahame and Isaace, ic sille
þe and þinum ofspringe æfter þe.' ¹³ And he ferde fram him.

³⁵:¹⁹ Soþlice Rachel forþferde, þa heo gebær | hire sunu Beniamin, f. 24ᵛ
and Iacob hig bebyrigde on þam wege þe liþ to Euphfrate, þæt ys
Bethel. ²² Iacob hæfde twelf suna. ²³ Lian sunu: se frumcenneda,
Ruben, and Simeon and Leui and Iudas and Isachar and Zabulon.
²⁴ Rachele suna: Iosep and Beniamin. ²⁵ Balan suna, Rachele þinene:
Dan and Neptalim. ²⁶ Zelphan suna, Lian þinene: Gad and Aser. Ðis
sind Iacobes suna þe him wæron acennede on Mesopo[to]mie, Sirie.
²⁷ He com þa to Isaace his fæder on Mambre, Arbea cæstre, þæt ys
Ephron, þær wracnode Abraham and Isaac. ²⁸ [. . .] hundteontig
wintra and hundeahtatig wintra. ²⁹ And Isaac forþferde on godre ylde
and his suna hine bebirigdon, Esau and Iacob, on Ephron. ³⁶:⁶ Esau
nam his wif and his suna and his dohtra and ealle his æhta and his
men and his heorda and eall þæt he ahte on Chanaan lande and for to
oþrum rice and gewat fram Iacobe his breþer. ⁷ Soþlice hig wæron
swiþe welige and ne mihton ætgædere wunian, ne þæt land hig ne
mihte acuman, for þam þe hig hæfdon manega heorda. ⁸ And Esau
eardude on Seir dune, þæt ys Edom. ³⁷:¹ Iacob eardude on Chanaan
lande, þær his fæder wracnode.

Her cydde God ælmihtig his mildheortnysse þe he Abrahame
behet on Iosepe, Abrahames ofspringe.

³⁷:² Ða Iosep wæs sixtynewintre, he heold 'his' fæder heorde mid
his broðrum and he wæs mid Balan sunum and Zelphan, his fæder
wifa. He gewregde his broþru to hira fæder þære mæstan wrohte.

35:11 ælmihtig] ælmihti B   Wex] weax B   gemænigfyld] gemenigfyld B
35:19 hig] hi B   Euphfrate] eufrate B   35:25 Balan] bolan B
35:26 Mesopotomie] mesopomie L, mesopotamia B   35:27 cæstre] cæste B
wracnode] wræcnode B   35:28 hundteontig] *a translation of preceding Vulg. et
completi sunt dies Isaac is absent; Crawford uses L'Isle's addition to B:* and gefyllede synd
dagas Isaac   36:6 Chanaan] chanan B   36:7 hig¹] hi B   hig²] hi B   hig³] hi B
36:8 eardude] eardode B   Seir] segir B   37:1 eardude] eardode B

MSS L, B, Co, Oᵂ *(to 37:2 only)*   Rubric Her cydde . . . ofspringe] *in red rustic caps.*
LB   Her cydde] Co *starts (p. 151; no rubrication);* Oᵂ *has rubric and part of 37:2 only*
cydde] cyððe Oᵂ   on Iosepe] and iosepe and Co, and iosepe Oᵂ   ofspringe] ofsprincge
BCo   37:2 Ða] *3-line green initial cap.* L, *6-line red initial cap.* B; þa þa CoOᵂ
sixtynewintre] .xvi. wintra Co, sixtene wintra Oᵂ   broðrum] gebroðrum CoOᵂ   Balan]
bolan B, belan Co   Zelphan] zeluan Co   wifa] wiua Co   He gewregde] ac hine
gewregdon Co   hira] heora BCo   wrohte] wrohtæ Co

³ Soþlice Israhel lufode Iosep ofer [ealle] his suna, for þan þe he hine gestrynde on his ylde, and het wircean him hringfage tunecan. ⁴ Ða his broþru þæt gesawon, þæt his fæder hine swiþor lufode þonne his oþre suna, þa ascunodon hig hine and ne mihton nane freondrædene wið hine habban. ⁵ Witodlice hit gelamp þæt hine mætte and he rehte þæt his broþrum. þurh þæt hig | hine hatedon þe swiþor. ⁶ And he cwæð to him: 'Gehirað min swefen þe me mætte. ⁷ Me þuhte þæt we bundon sceafas on æcere and þæt min sceaf arise and stode uprihte omiddan eowrum sceafum, and eowre gilmas stodon ymbutan and abugon to minum sceafe.' ⁸ Þ'a' cwædon his gebroþru: 'Cwist þu, bist þu ure cyning oþþe beoþ we þine hyrmen?' Witodlice þurh þis swefn and þurh þas spræca, hig hine hatedon and hæfdon andan to him. ⁹ Oþer swefen hine mætte and he rehte þæt his broðrum and cwæð: 'Ic geseah on swefne swilce sunne and mona and endleofun steorran, and ealle abugon me.' ¹⁰ Ða he þæt his fæder and his broþrum rehte, þa þreatode se fæder hine and cwæð: 'Hwæt sceal þis swefen beon þe þu gesawe? Sceolon we abugan þe, ic and þin modur and þine gebroþru?' ¹¹ Witodlice his gebroþru yrsodon swiþe wið hine; se fæder hit gemænde stille.

37:12 Ða his gebroþru wæron to lange on Sichem mid heora fæder heordum on læsum, ¹³ ða cwæð Israhel to him: 'þine gebroþru healdaþ scep on Sichima. ¹⁴ Far to him and loca hwæþer hit wel si mid him and mid heora heordum, and cum to me and cyð me hu hit si.' He com þa to Sichem fram Ebron dene, ¹⁵ and hine gemitte þær an man, þa he eode on gedwolan, and axode hine hwæt he sohte.

MSS L, B, Co   37:3 Israhel] israel B   lufode] luuode Co   ofer] ouer Co   ealle] BCo, *om.* L   þan] þam B   wircean him] him wyrcean B, him weorcan Co   hringfage] ringfage Co   37:4 broþru] gebroðru B, gebroðra Co   swiþor] swyðe B   ascunodon hig] onscunodon hi B, onscunedon hi Co   mihton] mihte Co   37:5 hine] hyne *alt. to* hym *by eras.* B, him Co   mætte] gemætte an sweuen Co   broþrum] gebroðrum BCo   þurh] þuruh Co   hig] hi B   37:6 him] heom Co   Gehirað] gehyrat B   swefen] swefn B, sweuen Co   mætte] gemætte Co   37:7 sceafas] sceauas Co   þæt] *om.* Co   sceaf] scef B   uprihte] upprihte B   omiddan] on middan BCo   ymbutan] abuton Co   sceafe] sceaue Co   37:8 gebroþru] gebroðra Co   þu'] la *add.* B   cyning] kininc Co   beoþ] beo Co   swefn] swefen B, sweuen Co   spræca] spræce Co   hig] hi BCo   37:9 swefen] sweuen Co   hine mætte] him gemætte Co   endleofun] endleofan B, endleouan Co   ealle] hig *add.* Co   abugon] onbugon BCo   me] ongean me Co   37:10 broþrum] gebroþrum Co   þreatode] aðreatode B   se] his Co   swefen] *om.* Co   Sceolon] sculon Co   modur] modor BCo   gebroþru] gebroðra Co   37:11 gebroþru] gebroðra BCo   gemænde stille] mænde stillice Co   37:12 Ða] þa *add.* Co   gebroþru] gebroðra Co   fæder] uæder Co   læsum] læswum BCo   37:13 Israhel] isrl B   him] iosepe Co   gebroþru] gebroðra Co   scep] sceap Co   Sichima] sihhima Co   37:14 him¹] heom Co   wel si] si wel Co   him²] heom Co   37:15 gemitte] gemette Co   and axode] þa axode he Co

GENESIS 65

¹⁶ He andswarode and cwæð: 'Ic sece mine gebroþru, hwar hig healdon hyra heorda.' ¹⁷ Ða cwæð se man to him: 'Hig ferdon of þisse stowe. Ic gehirde þæt hig cwædon þæt hig woldon to Dothaim.' Iosep ferde to Dothaim æfter his gebroþrum. ¹⁸ Þa hig hine feorran gesawon, ær þam þe he him to come, hig þohton hine to ofsleanne, ¹⁹ and cwædon him betwynan: 'Her gæþ se swefnigend. ²⁰ Uton hine ofslean and don hine on þone ealdan pytt and secgan þæt wilddeor hine fræton. þonne biþ gesyne hwæt him his swefn fremion.' ²¹ Soþlice þa Ruben þis gehirde, | he þohte hine to generianne of f. 25ᵛ hira handum and cwæð: ²² 'Ne ofslea we hine, ne we his blod ne ageoton, ac wurpaþ hine on þone pytt and healdað eowre handa unbesmitene.' Þæt he sæde, for þam þe he wolde hine generian of hira handum, and his fæder agifan. ²³ Sona swa he to his gebroþrum com, swa bereafodon hig hine his tunecan ²⁴ and dydon hine on þone wæterleasan pytt. ²⁵ And þa hig woldon etan, hig gesawon twegen Ysmahelitisce wegfarende men, cuman of Galaad and læddon wyrtgemang on hira olfendum, and tyrwan and stacten, on Egipta land. ²⁶ Ða cwæð Iudas to his gebroþrum: 'Hwæt fremaþ us, þeah we urne broðor ofslean? ²⁷ Selre ys þæt we hine syllon to ceape Ysmahelitum, þæt ure handa beon unbesmitene. He ys ure broþor and ure flæsc.' Ða cwædon his gebroþru þæt hit swa mihte beon. ²⁸ And þa þær foron Madianisce cypan, hig tugon hine upp of þam pytte and sealdon hine Ysmahelitum wiþ þritigum penegum. Ða hig hine læddon on Egipta land. ²⁹ Þa Ruben eft com to þam pytte and þone cnapan þar ne funde, þa tær he his claþas ³⁰ and cwæð to his

37:16 andswarode] iosep add. Co   gebroþru] gebroðra Co   healdon hyra heorda] hyre heorde healdan Co   hyra] heora B   37:17 Hig¹] hi BCo   ferdon] uerdon Co   þisse] ðissere Co   hig²] hi BCo   ferde] þa add. Co   37:18 hig¹] hi BCo   þam] þan Co   him to] to heom Co   hig²] hi B   ofsleanne] ofsleane B   37:19 betwynan] betweonan Co   swefnigend] swefniend B   37:20 secgan] urum uæder add. Co   wilddeor] wildeor B, wilde deor Co   gesyne] gesene Co   swefn] swefen B, sweuen Co   fremion] fremige Co   37:21 generianne] generienne B, genergienne Co   hira] heora BCo   37:22 we¹] ge Co   wurpaþ] wyrpað Co   þam] þon Co   hira] heora BCo   agifan] agiuan Co   37:23 gebroþrum] broðrum B   bereafodon] bereauodon Co   hig] hi B   37:24 wæterleasan] ealdan Co   37:25 And þa] Co p. 152   hig¹] hi B   woldon] woldan Co   hig²] hi BCo   Ysmahelitisce wegfarende] ismaelitisce weguerende Co   cuman] comon Co   hira] heora BCo   olfendum] olfendon B, oluendum Co   37:27 Ysmahelitum] ismaelitum BCo, and add. Co   ys²] his Co   gebroþru] gebroðra Co   37:28 þær] þar Co   foron] forun B, uoran Co   cypan] cypmen Co   hig¹] hi BCo   hig tugon hine] þa tugon hi hine Co   upp] up BCo   sealdon] sealdan Co   Ysmahelitum] ismaelitum BCo   þritigum] ðrittigum B, .iii. Co   penegum] penegan Co   Ða] and BCo   hig²] hi B   læddon on] læddan to Co   land] lande Co   37:29 Ruben eft com] com ruben eft Co   þar] ðær B   funde] uunde Co   tær] tær with 2nd r appar. add. later B, totær Co

broþrum: 'Nys se cnapa her; hwæder ga ic?' ³¹ Þa namon hig an ticcen and ofsnidon hit and bedypton his tunecan on þam blode, ³² and brohton to hira fæder and cwædon: 'þas tunecan we fundon; sceawa hwæþer hit sig þines suna þe ne sig.' ³³ Þa cwæð se fæder, þa þa he hig gecneow: 'Hit ys mines suna tunece. Wilddeor fræton Iosep.' ³⁴ He tær his reaf and scridde hine mid hæran and weop his sunu lange tide. ³⁵ Soþlice his bearn hig gesa⟨m⟩nedon to þam þæt hig hira fæder gefrefredon. He nolde nane frefrunge undorfon ac cwæð, wepende, 'Ic fare to minum suna to helle.' ³⁶ Ða Madianiscean sealdon | Iosep on Egipta land Putifare, þam afyrydan Faraones cempena ealdre.

³⁸:¹ On þa tid ferde Iuda[s] fram his gebroþrum to anum Adolamityscum men, ² and nam þær an Chananeisc wif, seo wæs genemned Sue. ³ Be þære he gestrynde þri suna, Her and Onam and Sela. ⁶ Soþlice Iudas sealde Here his suna wif, seo wæs genemned Thamar. ⁷ Her forðferde butan bearnum. ¹¹ Ða cwæð Iudas to Thamare his snore: 'Beo weodewe oð þæt Sela min sunu geweaxe.' Ða for heo and wunude on hire fæder huse. ¹² Æfter manegum dagum, forðferde Iudas wif. þa for he to his scepscere, he and Hiras his scephirde se Odolamitiscea, on þamnatha. ¹³ Ða cydde man Thamare þæt hire sweor for to Thamnaþa, scep to sciranne, ¹⁴ ða dide heo of hire wydewan reaf and nam hire walcan and scrydde hig mid oþrum reafe and sæt on þam wege þe læg to þamnatha, for þam þe Sela, for his geoguðe, hig ne nam to gemæccan. ¹⁵ Ða Iudas

37:30 broþrum] gebroðrum Co   cnapa] na *add*. Co   hwæder] hwyder BCo   ic] nu *add*. Co   37:31 hig] hi B   ofsnidon] ofsniðon BCo   37:32 hira] heora BCo   fæder] uæder Co   fundon] uundon Co   sceawa] nu *add*. Co   sig¹] sy B, si Co   þe] hyt *add*. Co   sig²] sy BCo   37:33 fæder] uæder Co   hig] hi B   tunece] þa cwædon hi *add*. B, hig cwædon þa *add*. Co   Wilddeor] wildeor B, wilde deor Co   Iosep] þinne suna *add*. Co   37:34 tær] totær B, tær ða Co   his sunu] hyne Co   37:35 hig¹] hi BCo   gesamnedon] m *lost in hole* L, gesamnodon B, gesamnode Co   hig hira] hi heora BCo   gefrefredon] gefrefrodon BCo   He] ac he Co   undorfon] underfon BCo   suna] sunu Co   37:36 Madianiscean sealdon] madianiscan sealdan Co   on] to Co   Putifare] putiphare Co   afyrydan] afyredan BCo   cempena] kempena Co   38:1 þa tid] þare ylcan tyde Co   ferde] for BCo   Iudas] BCo, iuda L   gebroþrum] broðrum B   Adolamityscum] odolamitiscum Co   38:2 þær] þar Co   38:6 suna] sunu Co   38:7 Her] Here LBCo   butan] buton Co   38:11 snore] snoru Co   Beo] þu *add*. Co   weodewe] wydewe B, wuduwe Co   and] *om*. Co   wunude] wunode B, wuduwe Co   38:12 Æfter] þa æfter Co   dagum] gearum Co   for he] sume dæge for iudas Co   scepscere] sceapscære Co   he²] *om*. Co   scephirde se Odolamitiscea on þamnatha (thamnaða B)] sceaphyrda and se idolamitisce for to thamnatha Co   38:13 Thamare] þamare B   sweor] swegre Co   Thamnaþa] ðamnatha BCo   scep to sciranne] hys scep to scyrene B, his sceapscære Co   38:14 wydewan] wuduwan Co   hig¹] hi BCo   reafe] reaue and eode Co   þamnatha] þamnaða B   geoguðe] geogoðe B   hig²] hi BCo   ne nam] genam Co   gemæccan] gemacan B   38:15 Iudas hig geseah] geseah iudas hig Co

GENESIS

hig geseah, þa wende he þæt hit wære sum myltystre; heo helode hire nebb, þæt he hig ne mihte gecnawan. [16] And he cwæð to hire: 'Læt me habban þe.' He nyste þæt heo wæs his snoru. Ða cwæð heo: 'Hwæt sylst þu me, wiþ þam þe þu mines gemana bruce?' [17] Þa cwæð he: 'Ic sende þe an ticcen of minre heorde.' And heo cwæð eft: 'Ic þolige loca hwæt þu wylle, gif þu me sylst underwedd, oþ þæt þu me sende þæt þu me behætst.' [18] Þa cwæð Iudas: 'Hwæt wilt þu to underwedde nyman?' Þa cwæð heo: 'Þinne hring and þinne beah and þinne stæf, þe þu on handa hæfst.' Witodlice æt þam cyrre heo wearð mid cilde, [19] and heo eode þanon. [20] Iudas sende an tyccen wið his Odolamitiscean hirde, þæt he fette þæt underwedd þe he þam wife sealde. [21] Þa he hig findan ne mihte, þa axode he þæs landes men hwar þæt wif wære þe æt þæra wega gelæte | sæt. Þa cwædon   f. 26ᵛ hig þæt þær nan myltystre on lande nære. [22] Þa cirde he to Iudan and cwæð to him: 'Ne mihte ic hig findan and þa landes men me sædon þæt þær nan myltystre ne sæte.' [23] Þa cwæð iudas: 'Hæbbe hire þæt heo hafað. Ne mæg heo us lease tellan. Ic hire sende þæt ic hire behet and þu hig ne fundest.' [24] Ða æfter þrim monþum, hig cwædon to Iudan: 'Thamar þin snoru ys forlegen and hire innoð ys weaxende.' Þa cwæð Iudas: 'Lædað hig forþ and forbærnað hig.' [25] Þa heo wæs to þam witum gelædd, þa sende heo to hire sweore and cwæð: 'Be þam men ic eom mid cilde þe þisne hring ah and þisne beah and þisne stæf. Sceawa hwa hig age.' [26] Þa he þa lac gecneow, þa cwæð he: 'Heo ys rihtwisre þonne ic, for þam ic hig ne sealde Sela minum suna, and þeah næfde he hig syþþan.' [27] On þære cenningtide, ætywde twegen getwisan on hire innoþe and on þæra cilda forðcyme,

38:15 hig¹] hi B   sum] *om.* Co   myltystre] myltresse Co   heo] ac heo Co   helode] helede B   nebb] neb BCo   hig²] hi B   38:16 And he cwæð] ða cwæð he Co   þe] and *add.* Co   heo¹] hit Co   sylst þu] sylstu B   mines] mine Co   gemana] gemanan B, gemacan Co   38:17 sende þe] ðe sænde Co   þolige] ðolie Co   underwedd] underwed Co   sende²] sænde Co   38:18 hring] ringc Co   hæfst] hauast Co   þam] ylcan *add.* BCo   38:19 eode] ða *add.* B   38:20 Iudas sende] and iudas hyre sænde Co   Odolamitiscean] odalamitiscan Co   þæt he fette] and he scolde feccan Co   underwedd] underwed Co   þe he] Co *p. 153*   wife] wiue Co   38:21 he hig findan ne mihte] ne mihte he hig findan nahwar Co   hig¹] hi B   þæs] ða BCo   gelæte] gelæta B   sæt] sæte Co   hig²] hi B   þær] þar Co   myltystre] myltresse Co   38:22 Ne mihte ic hig] þæt he hig ne mihte nahwar Co   hig] hy B   and] eac *add.* Co   me] *om.* B   sædon] cwædon B   þær] þar Co   myltystre] myltresse Co   38:23 Hæbbe] habbe Co   þæt heo hafað] *om.* B, þæt þæt heo hauað Co   sende] sænde Co   hig] hy B   fundest] mihtest findan Co   38:24 hig¹] hi BCo   hig²] hi B   hig³] hi B   38:25 gelædd] gelæd BCo   sende] sænde Co   sweore] swegre Co   hring] ringc Co   Sceawa] nu *add.* Co   hig] hi B, þis Co   38:26 þa lac] þæt eal Co   rihtwisre] rihtwisra Co   for þam] þæt is for ðan þe Co   hig¹] hi B   Sela] selan Co   suna] sunu Co   þeah] þeahhwæðere Co   hig²] hi B   38:27 þære cenningtide] þare kennigctide Co   ætywde] æteowdon B, ætywdon Co   þæra] *om.* Co

se oþer ræhte forþ his hand and seo broþorþinenu wrað wurmreadne þræd þæron and cwæð: 'þes cymð raþor.' ²⁹ And he teh þa hand ongen and se oþer com. þa cwæð þæt wif: 'Hwi ys weall todæled for þe?' And for þam heo nemde his naman Phares. ³⁰ Siþþan com se oðer, on þæs handa wæs se þræd; þone heo nemde Zara.

³⁹:¹ Witodlice man lædde Iosep on Egipta land and hine gebohte Putifar se afyrida, Pharaones heres ealdor, Egiptisc man, æt þam Ismahelitiscum mannum þe hine þider læddon. ² And Drihten wæs mid him. Se man wæs weldonde on eallum þingum and wunode on his hlafordes huse. ³ He wiste ful georne þæt God hine lufode and ealle þa þing þe he dyde, he dyde be his dihte. ⁴ Iosep hæfde mycele gife æt his hlaforde and þenode him and betæhte him eall þæt he f. 27ʳ ahte to bewitanne. ⁵ And Drihten bletsode þæs Egiptiscan | æhta for Iosepes þingon and gemenigfylde his speda, ægþer ge on tunum ge on landum. ⁶ Iosep wæs fæger and wlitig on ansyne. ⁷ Witodlice his hlæfdige lufode hine and cwæð to him: 'Slap mid me.' ⁸ And he nateshwon hire þæs tiþian nolde ac he cwæð: 'Min hlaford me hæfþ betæht ealle his þing and he nat hwæt he ealles hæfð. ⁹ Næfþ he nan þing þæt ne sig on minum anwealde, buton þu þe his wif eart. Hu mæg ic swa yfele wiþ hine don and wið God singian?' ¹⁰ Þilcum wordum heo him befelh ælce dæg and þæt wif wearð wraþ þam geongan cnapan, and he onscunede unrihthæmed. ¹¹ Hit gelamp sume dæg þæt Iosep wæs ana innan his hlafordes huse ¹² and heo teh hine be his claþum and cwæð to him: 'Slap mid me.' þa ætarn he ut and forlet his wæfels on hire handan. ¹⁴ Ða hrymde heo to hire hiwun and cwæð: 'Nu he lædde inn þisne Ebreiscan man þæt he

38:27 his] his his L   broþorþinenu] byrþerþinenu B, byðerþinenu Co   wurmreadne] wyrmreadne BCo   þæron] þaron Co   raþor] hraþor B   38:29 teh] teah B, teah eft Co   ongen] ongean BCo   com] þa *add.* B   hwi] wig Co   weall] weal Co   þe] þi Co   þam] þan Co   Phares] fares Co   38:30 þræd] wyrmreada þræd Co   39:1 hine] þar *add.* Co   Putifar] putiphar B   afyrida] afyredea B, afyreda Co   Pharaones] faraones Co   Ismahelitiscum] ismaelitiscum BCo   39:2 weldonde] ʻwelʼdonde Co   þingum] þinge Co   39:3 þing] þinge Co   he dyde²] *om.* B   39:4 mycele] micle B   gife æt] gyuu to Co   eall] eal B bewitanne] bewitenne B   39:5 Egiptiscan] egiptiscean B   þingon] þingum Co gemenigfylde] gemænifylde B, gemænigfylde Co   39:7 lufode hine] hine luuode Co 39:8 And he … tiþian nolde] ac he nolde nateshwon hyre þæs tiðian Co   hlaford] hlauord Co þing] þinge Co   hwæt he ealles hæfð] ealles hwæt he ah Co   39:9 Næfþ] nafað Co   þing] ðinge Co   sig] sy B, si Co   þu] þe Co   wiþ hine don] don wið hine Co   39:10 þilcum] þillicum Co   heo him] hy hine Co   befelh] befealh BCo   and þæt wif wearð] þa wearð þæt wif Co   þam] þan Co   geongan] geongum B   and²] for ðan þe Co   onscunede] ascunode B 39:11 gelamp] gelampt þa Co   dæg] dæge Co   innan] on Co   39:12 and heo teh] þa teah hy Co   teh] teah B   wæfels] wæfel B, wauels Co   handan] handum B, handa Co 39:14 hrymde] rymde Co   hiwun] hywum BCo   he lædde … bysmorode us] com þes ebreisca cnapa in to me þæt he me gebismrode Co   Ebreiscan] ebreiscean B

GENESIS

bysmorode us. He eode into me to þam þæt he me ofername, [15] and þa he gehirde þæt ic hrimde, þa forlet he his wæfels and fleah ut.' [16] þisne unwrenc heo geþohte and þa hire hlaford ham com, [17] þa cwæð heo: 'Se Ebreisca weal þe þu hider brohtest eode in to me þæt he me bysmrode, [18] and þa ic hrymde, þa forlet he his wæfels and arn ut.' [19] Ða se hlaford þæt gehirde, þa wearð he swiþe yrre and gelyfde hire wordum wel [20] and wearp Iosep on cweartern, þær man þæs cyningæs ræplingas heold, and he wæs þær belocen. [21] And Drihten wæs mid him and gemiltsode him and gedyde þæt þæs cwearternes ealdor him wærþ swiþe hold. [22] Se him betæhte ealle þa gebundenan men þe þar gehæfte wæron. [23] And he ne cuþe nan þing þaron, þa hig him betæhte wæron, ac Drihten wæs mid him and dihte him hwæt he don sc`e´olde.

[40:1] Ða þis wæs þus gedon, þa gelamp hit þæt twegen afyryde men agylton wiþ heora hlaford, Egipta cynges byrle | and his bæcistre, f. 27ᵛ [2] and Farao wearþ swiþe yrre. Ðara oþer bewiste his byrlas, oþer his bæcestran. [3] þa dyde hig man on cweartern, on þam wæs eac Iosep gebunden, [4] and þæs cwearternes hirde hig betæhte Iosepe and he þenode him. [5] Binnan firste hig gesawon begen swefen on anre nihte. [6] þa wæron hig swiþe unrote on morgen [8] and cwædon to Iosepe: 'Wit gesawon swefen ac wyt nyton hwa hyt unc atelle hwæt hit behealde.' Ða cwæð Iosep: 'Secgaþ me hwæt git gesawon.' [9] þa rehte þæra byrla ealdor him his swefn and cwæð: 'Ic geseah wineard, [10] on þam wæron þreo clystru, and ic geseah þæron weaxende blosman, litlum and litlum, and æfter þam blosmum, winberigean, [11] and

39:14 bysmorode] bysmrode B   to þam] for ðan Co   39:15 and] ac Co   hrimde] rymde Co   wæfels] wæuels Co   39:16 unwrenc] wrenc Co   geþohte] beþohte hyre sylf Co   39:17 Ebreisca] ebreiscea B, ebreisce Co; Co *p. 154*   weal] wealh B   þu] me *add.* Co   bysmrode] bysmrude B, gebysmrode Co   39:18 and þa] ac sona swa Co   þa forlet he] he forlet me and Co   39:19 hlaford] hlauord Co   hire wordum wel] swiðe wel hyre wordum B, wel heora wordum Co   39:20 wearp] ða *add.* Co   cweartern] cwearterne Co   man] mon Co   cyningæs] cyninges B, kyninges Co   ræplingas] ræplinges Co   39:21 gemiltsode] miltsode B   wærþ] wearþ BCo   39:22 gebundenan] gebundnen Co   þar] þær B   39:23 þing] þingc Co   þaron] þæron B   þa] þa þa Co   hig] hi BCo   sceolde] e *above* L, scold.e Co   40:1 afyryde men agylton] men agylten of hirede Co   afyryde] afyrede B   hlaford] hlauord Co   cynges] kyninges Co   bæcistre] bæcestre BCo   40:2 Farao] pharao B, faraon Co   wearþ] wear B, wæs Co   yrre] wið hi *add.* Co   Ðara] se Co   byrlas] and se *add.* Co   40:3 hig] hi B   hig man] man hig Co   cweartern] cwearten B, cwearterne Co   eac] `eac´ Co   40:4 hig] hi B   him] heom Co   40:5 Binnan firste] þa binnan þam fyrste Co   hig] hi B   gesawon begen] beggen gesawon Co   swefen] swefn B, sweuen Co   40:6 hig] hi B   morgen] merigen B, mergen Co   40:8 swefen] swefn B, sweuen Co   Secgaþ] seccað Co   40:9 þæra] ðare Co   swefn] sweuen Co   wineard] wingeard BCo   40:10 blosman] blostman B   blosmum winberigean] blostmum winberian B, blosman winbergan Co

GENESIS

Pharaones drincefæt o[n] minre handa; and ic nam þa winberian and wrang on þæt fæt and sealde Faraone.' [12] Þa cwæð Iosep: 'þis ys þin swefen. þa þreo clystru þæt sind git þri dagas, [13] æfter þam Pharao geþencþ þine þenunga and he geset þe to þære ylcan note þe þu ær hæfdest and þu silst him his drincefæt swa þu ær dydest. [14] Geþence me, þonne þe þin wise licie, and lære Pharao þæt he me ut alæde of þisum cwearterne, [15] for þam þe ic wæs dearnunga forstolen of Ebrea lande and her unscildig on pytt beworpen.' [16] Ða þæra bæcistra ealdor gehirde hu glæwlice he þæt swefen rehte, þa cwæð he: 'Ic geseah swefen, þæt ys þæt ic hæfde þri windlas mid meluwe ofer min heafod, [17] and on þam ufemystan windle wære manegra cynna gebæc and fugelas æton of þam.' [18] Ða andswarode Iosep and cwæð: 'þis ys þin swefen. þa þri windlas, þæt sind þri dagas nu git, [19] and æfter þam hæt Pharao þe ahon on rode and fugelas fretaþ þin flæsc.' [20] Siþþan wæs se þridda dæg Pharaones gebyrdtide, þa worhte he micelne gebeorscipe his cnihtum. Gemang þam, þa geþohte he | þæra byrla ealdor and þæra bæcistra, [21] and he gesette þæra byrla magister to þære note þe he ær hæfde. [22] þone oþerne he het hon on gealgan. Ða wæs Iosepes soþfæstnys afandod [23] and þeahhwæþere þæra byrla ealdor forgeat Iosepes ærynde.

[41:1] Æfter twam gearum, Pharao mætte þæt he stode be anre ea, [2] and him þuhte þæt he gesawe gan upp of þam flode seofan fægre oxan, and swiðe fætte, and hig man læswode on Morium lande. [3] Him þuhte eac þæt he gesawe cuman oðre seofon oxan upp of þære

40:11 Pharaones drincefæt] faraones drenceuætt Co   on minre] B, ominre L, on minra Co   winberian] winbergan Co   fæt] fætt Co   Faraone] pharaone B   40:12 ys] his Co   swefen] swefn B, sweuen Co   git þri dagas] .iii. dagas nu git and Co   40:13 Pharao geþencþ] faraon geðen`c´gð Co   þære] þare Co   drincefæt swa] drenceuætt eal swa Co   40:14 Geþence] and geðenc B   wise] wel add. Co   lære Pharao] lær faraon Co   þisum] þison B   40:15 þam] ðon Co   of] on Co   pytt] pit B   40:16 Ða þæra] and þa ðara Co   bæcistra] bæcestra BCo   glæwlice] gleawlice BCo   swefen[1]] swefn B, sweuen Co   Ic geseah] la leof ic geseh Co   swefen[2]] swefn B, sweuen Co   þæt ys] me þuhte Co   meluwe] melewe B   40:17 and[1]] þæt add. Co   ufemystan] yfemestan B, uuemestan Co   manegra] manega Co   fugelas] fugelos Co   æton] ætan B

MSS L, B, Co, O (intermittently)   40:18 andswarode] andwyrde Co   swefen] swefn B, sweuen Co   40:19 Pharao] farao B, faraon Co   40:20 þridda] iii[da] Co   Pharaones] faraones Co   gebyrdtide] gebyrdtid B, gebyrtyd Co   gebeorscipe] beorscipe B, gebyrscipe Co   cnihtum] þa add. Co   Gemang] amang CoO   bæcistra] bæcestra BCoO   40:21 magister] ealdor Co   þære] ilcan add. Co   40:22 þone] and þone Co   soþfæstnys] soðfæstnes O   afandod] auandod Co   40:23 ærynde] ærende BCo   41:1 Pharao] faraone Co   41:2 upp] up BCo   seofan] seofon B, .vii. Co   fægre] fægere Co   fætte] uætte Co; break in Co: leaf lost between pp. 154 and 155

MSS L, B, O   hig] hi B   læswode] læsude B   Morium] morigum B, moregum O   41:3 upp] up B

GENESIS

ea, þa wæron fule and swiþe hlæne, and hi eodon be þære ea ofrun on grenum stowum ⁴and abiton þa fættan oxan and fræton hig. Þa awoc Pharao ⁵and slep eft, and hine mætte oþer swefen. Him þuhte þæt he gesawe seofon ear wexan on anum healme, fulle and fægre. ⁶And he geseah oðre seofon, lyþre and forscruncene, ⁷þa fræton ealle þa fægran. Þa awoc Pharao of slæpe. ⁸On morgen he wearð swiþe forht and sende to Egipta wisustan witan and rehte him his swefen and bæd þæt hig him sædon hwæt þæt swefen beheolde. ⁹Þa geþohte þæra byrla ealdor hu he rehte his swefen Iosepe, and cwæð: ¹⁰'Se cyning wæs yrre wiþ me and het sceofan me and þæra bæcistra ealdor on cweartern. ¹¹Þa mætte unc begen swefen anre nihte. ¹²Þa wæs þær an Ebreisc cnapa inne mid unc. Þam wit rehton uncer swefen ¹³ and he sæde unc eall swa hit siþþan aeode. Ic wæs eft gesett to minre þenunge and hine man heng, eal swa he unc ær sæde.' ¹⁴Hyne man dyde upp be þæs cyninges bebode and hine man efosode and scrydde hine and brohte hine to þam cynge.

⁴¹:¹⁵PHARAO CWÆÐ: 'IC GESEAH SWEFEN and ic ne mæg nanne mann findan þe me secge hwæt hit behealde. Ic gehirde | secgan þæt þu wære gleaw þæron.' ¹⁶Ða cwæð Iosep: 'Hwæt mæg ic f. 28ᵛ
don buton me God wisige?' ¹⁷Witodlice Pharao rehte Iosepe þa swefen þe hine mætte, eal swa hit her bufan awriten ys, be þam oxum and be þam earum, ²⁴and cwæð: 'Ic hit rehte þam yldostan Egiptan witun and næs heora nan þe þar ænig þing on cuþe.' ²⁵Ða andswarode Iosep and cwæð: 'Þis swefen ys anræde. God ætywde Pharaone hwæt he don wyle. ²⁶'Þa´ seofon fægran oxan and þa seofon fægran ear getacniaþ seofon wæstmbære gear and welige. ²⁷Þa seofon hlænan oxan and þa seofon lyþran ear geta[c]niað seofon hungergear. ²⁹Nu her cumað seofen swiðe wæstmbære gear and swiþe welige ofer eall Egipta land. ³⁰And þæræfter cumaþ oþre seofene, mid swa micelre wædle and hun[g]re þæt man forgitt þa ærran gear, and hunger fordeþ ealle eorðan. ³²Soþlice hit ys Godes

41:4 fættan] fætte B   hig] hi B   Pharao] farao B   41:5 swefen] swefn B   wexan] weaxan B   fægre] fægere B   41:6 seofon] seofan B   41:7 fægran] fægeran B
41:8 wisustan] wisoste B   hig] hi B   swefen²] swefn B   41:9 swefen] swefn B
41:10 sceofan] sceofan (*with* u *above* eo *in contemp. hand*) B   41:11 swefen] *add.* on B
41:12 swefen] swefn B   41:13 eall] eal B   gesett] geset BO   41:14 upp] up B   cyninges] cynges B   efosode] efesode BO   41:15 PHARAO] *4-line purple initial cap.* L, Farao B   SWEFEN] swefn B   nanne] næn⟨ne⟩O   mann] man B   41:16 buton] butan B; *break in* O
MSS L, B   41:17 swefen] swefn B   41:24 yldostan Egiptan witun] yldostan egypta witan B   þar] þær B   41:25 swefen] swefn B   41:26 fægran¹] fægeran B
fægran²] fægeran B   ear] ða *add.* B   41:27 getacniað] B, getaniað L   41:29 seofen] seofon B   41:30 seofene] seofone B   hungre] B, hunre L   forgitt] forgyt B

spræc and his warnung, and seo tid cymþ hrædlice. ³³ Nu ys hit ful wærlic þæt se cyning him ceose sumne wisne man, and glæwne, and gesette hine ofer Egipta land. ³⁴ And se sette gerefan geond eall þæt rice, þæt hig gegaderion togædere þæne fiftan dæl ealra wæstma þas seofon wæstmberan gear, ³⁵ þæt ælc hwæte þe on Pharaones anwealde sig, sig belocen and on burgum gehealden, ³⁶ to hylpe on þam seofon toweardum hungorgearum, þæt egipte ne forwurðon.' ³⁷ Ða licode Pharaone and eallum his þegnum his ræd. ³⁸ And he cwæð to him: 'Hwar magon we findan swilcne man þe mid Godes gife sig swa afylled?' ³⁹ Witodlice he cwæð to Iosepe: 'God þe ætywde ealle þa þing þe þu spræce. Hwar mæg ic wisran findan þonne þu eart oððe furþon þinne gelican? ⁴¹ Ic gesette þe ofer eall Egipta land to gerefan and eall folc hyrð þe.' ⁴² And he nam his hring on his agenre handa and dyde on his hand, and scrydde hine mid linenum reafe | and dyde gyldene healsmyne ymbe his swuran, ⁴³ and sette hine on his oþer cræt. And se bydel bead þæt eall folc bigdon heora cneow beforan him and wiston þæt he wære gerefa ofer eall Egipta land. ⁴⁴ Eft se cyning cwæð to Iosepe: 'Ne færð nan man butan þinum bebode, ne hider ne þider on eallum Egipta lande.' ⁴⁵ And he awende his naman and nemde hine on Egiptisc 'middaneardes hælend' and sealde him Aseneth to wife, Putifares dohtor þæs sacerdes, of þære byrig þe ys genemned Eliopoleas, þæt ys on Englisc 'sunnan burh'.

⁴¹:⁴⁶ Witodlice Iosep wæs þritigwintre, þa he ymbefor ealle Egipta ricu, ⁴⁷⁻⁹ and gegaderode on þam seofon wæstmbæron gearum swa micel hwætes þæt hys ne mihte nan man witan nan gemet, and beleac hine on burgum. ⁵⁰⁻² Iosep gestrynde twegen suna ær þa hungorgearas comon, Mannases and Ephraim. ⁵³ Witodlice þa þa seofon godan gear agane wæron, ⁵⁴ ða comon þa seofan hungorgear þe Iosep foresæde, and þær weox hungor. ⁵⁵ Ða þæt folc hingrode, þa clypodon hig to Pharao and bædon him metes. He andswarode and cwæð: 'Gað to Iosepe and doð swa hwæt swa he cow secge.'

41:33 glæwne] gleawne B   hine] om. B   41:34 eall] eal B   hig] hi B   þæne] þone B   wæstmberan] wæstmbæran B   41:35 þæt] and þæt B   sig sig] sy sy B   41:36 hylpe] helpe B   seofon] seofan B   41:38 sig] sy B   41:39 þing] þingc B   Hwar] hwær B   41:41 gesette] sette B   eall¹] eal B   eall²] eal B   41:42 agenre] agenra B   41:43 eall¹] eal B   cneow] cneowa B   eall²] eal B   41:44 bebode] gebode B   41:45 Putifares] putiphares B   Eliopoleas] eliopoleos B   burh] buruh B   41:46 þritigwintre] þrittigwintre B   ymbefor] embefor B   41:47–9 wæstmbæron] wæstmbærum B   41:50–2 hungorgearas] hungergearas B   Ephraim] effraim B   41:54 seofan hungorgear] seofon hungergear B   hungor] hunger B   41:55 hig] hi B   Pharao] pharaone B

⁵⁶ Dæghwamlice hungor weox and Iosep untynde ealle þa bernu and sealde hwæte þam Egiptiscan mannum to ceape.
⁴²:¹ Ða gehirde Iacob secgan þæt man sealde hwæte on Egipta lande, þa cwæð he to his sunum: ² 'Ic gehirde secgan þæt hwæte wære on Egipta lande to ceape. Faraþ and bicgað us mete, þæt we ne forwurþon.' ³ Þa foron Iosepes tyn gebroþru to Egiptum and woldon bicgan hwæte, ⁴ and Iacob hæfde Beniamin æt ham. ⁵ Hig foron mid oþrum cepmannum. Witudlice hungor wæs on Chanaan, ⁶ and Iosep wæs Egipta ealdor and on his anwealde man sealde þone hwæte. Ða hys gebroþru to him comon, ⁷⁻⁸ he gecneow hig eall, and hira nan ne gecneow | hine, and spræc heardlicor wið hig þonne wiþ fremde men and cwæð to him: 'Hwanon comon ge?' Þa cwædon hig: 'Of Chanaan lande, þæt we us mete bohton.' ⁹ Ða gemunde Iosep þa swefen þe hine æt sumon cyrre ær mætte and cwæð to him: 'Ge synd sceaweras.' ¹⁰ Þa cwædon hig: 'Nys hit swa, hlaford, ac we synd þine þeowas and we comon to þam þæt we bohton þa þing þe we mihton big libban. ¹¹ Ealle we synd anes esnes suna. Mid sibbe we comon hider, næs mid searwum.' ¹² Ða cwæð he: 'On oðre wisan hit ys. Ge comon þis land to sceawienne.' ¹³ Þa cwædon hig: 'Ða twelf þine þeowas sind gebroðru, synd anes esnes suna on Chanaan lande, and se gin[g]sta ys mid urum fæder and [oþer] na ma.' ¹⁴ 'Þæt ys þæt ic eow ær sæde,' cwæð he, 'ge synd sceaweras. ¹⁵ Swa ic age Pharaones helde, ne faraþ ge ealle heonon ær þam þe eower læssa broþor cume hider. ¹⁶ Ac fare eower an and bringe hine hider, þæt ic wite hwæþer hit sig þe soþ þe leas þæt ge secgað.' ¹⁷ He betæhte hig þa þri dagas to hirdnysse. ¹⁸ Þan þriddan dæge hig man lædde [of] þam cwearterne and he cwæð: 'Faroð swa ic eow bebead, þæt ge magon lybban. Ic ondræde me God, gif ic riht næbbe. ¹⁹ Beo eower an broþor her on cwearterne and fare ge mid þam hwæte þe ge bohton on eowrum huse, ²⁰ and lædað eowerne gingstan broðor to me.' Hig dydon swa he him bebead, ²¹ and cwædon him betwynan:

f. 29ᵛ

41:56 hungor] hunger B   untynde] ontinde B   Egiptiscan] egyptiscum B   42:3 foron] LB; ferdon *add. above, perhaps by copyist* L   gebroþru] gebroþro B   42:5 Hig] hy B   cepmannum] cypmannum B   Witudlice] witodlice B   42:7-8 hig¹] hi B   hira] heora B   hig²] hi B   hig³] hi B   42:9 sumon] sumum B   mætte] gemætte B   synd] syndon B   42:10 hig] hi B   42:12 sceawienne] sceawianne B   42:13 hig] hi B   synd] hi sind B   gingsta] gyngsta B, ginsta L   oþer] *om.* LB   42:15 eower læssa] eowwer læsta B   42:16 hwæþer] hwæð B   sig] sy B   42:17 hig] hi B   42:18 þan] on þam B   hig] hi B   of] to LB   næbbe] nabbe B   42:19 on eowrum huse] to eowrum husum B
   MSS L, B, Co   42:20 gingstan] geongestan B   Co *restarts, p. 155, at* hider   to me] hider to me Co   Hig] hi BCo   swa] swa swa Co   him] heom Co   42:21 him betwynan] heom betweonan Co

'Be gewirhtum we þoliað þas þing. We singodon on urum breþer and we gesawon hys angsumnisse, þa he us georne friþes bæd, and we him nanes ne tiþedon. For þam com þis geswinc ofer us.' ^{22} Ða cwæð Ruben: 'Cweþe ge, ne sæde ic eow, "ne singie ge on þam cnapan", and ge me ne gehirdun? Nu hine man wricð.' ^{23} Hig nyston þæt Iosep hig gecneow. ^{24} And he wende hine lithwon fram him and weop, and wende eft to him ^{25} and nam Simeon and band hine

f. 30^r beforan him, and bead his þegnum þæt hig fyldon hira saccas | mid hwæte and ledon dearnunga hira ælces feoh on hys sacc, and formete to eacan, and hig dydon swa. ^{26} And hig foron and læddon heora hwæte on heora assan.

42:27-8 Þa hig be wege wæron, þa undyde hira an his sacc and wolde syllan his assan foddur. Þa cwæð he to his gebroþrum, þa he þæt feoh geseah on þæs sacces muðe: 'Her ic hæbbe funden min feoh on þis sacces muþe.' Þa wurdon hig afyrhte and cwædon him betwynan: 'Hwæt ys þis þæt God us dyde?' ^{29} Þa comon hig to Iacobe hira fæder on Chanaan lande and rehton him ealle þa þing þe him on siþe gelumpon ^{30} and hu stiþe se landhlaford spræc wið hig, and hig cwædon: 'Se landhlaford wende þæt we wæron sceaweras, ^{31} and we cwædon, "We synd full getreowe. Ne þence we nanes yfeles. ^{32} We twelf gebroður wæron anes esnes suna. Se an ys dead and se gingsta ys mid urum fæder." ^{33} Ða cwæð he to us, "Ic wylle fandian hwæþer ge getreowe synd. Lætað eowerne anne broþur mid me and nimað þa þing þe eowre hiwenu beþurfon and faraþ ^{34} and lædað eowerne

42:21 þing] þingc Co   singodon] syngedon Co   breþer] broðer Co   gesawon] sawon Co   angsumnisse þa] angsumnisse and Co   and^3] ac Co   tiþedon] tiðodon BCo   ofer] ouer Co   42:22 eow ne singie ge] ær þæt ge syngodon Co   gehirdun] gehyrdon B, gelyfdon Co   Nu hine man] ac nu man hine Co   wricð] wrihð B, wrecð Co   42:23 Hig^1] hy B   hig^2] hy B   42:24 wende^1] wænde Co   hine] þa add. Co   him^1] heom Co   wende^2] wænde Co   him^2] heom Co   42:25 beforan him] beuoran heom Co   hig fyldon hira] hi gefyldon heora BCo   ledon] legdon Co   dearnunga] dearninga B   hira^2] heora BCo   feoh] seoluor Co   hys sacc] heora saccan Co   hig^2] hi BCo   42:26 And hig foron] hi uoron þa Co   hig] hi B   assan] assum Co   42:27-8 hig^1] hi BCo   hira] heora BCo   foddur] foddor B, fodder Co   Her ic hæbbe . . . muþe] þis feoh is eal her on urum saccum þe we mid ceapodon Co   þa wurdon hig] hi wurdon þa ealle Co   hig^2] hi B   him] heom Co   betwynan] betweonan BCo   þis þæt God] he þe þis god Co   dyde] gedyde Co   42:29 hig] hi B   hira] heora BCo   þing] þingc Co   him] heom Co   42:30 landhlaford] landhlauord Co   hig^1] hi BCo   hig^2] om. BCo   landhlaford] landhlauord Co   wæron sceaweras] sceaweras wæron Co   42:31 full getreowe] ful getriwe BCo   we^2] om. B   yfeles] yueles Co   42:32 gebroður] gebroðra BCo   suna] and we him sædon add. Co   gingsta] gyngesta B, gingesta Co   fæder] uæder Co   42:33 fandian] geuandian Co   getreowe] getriwe BCo   eowerne] eowwerne Co   anne broþur] ænne broþor BCo   þing] þinc Co   hiwenu] hywan B, hiwon Co

gingstan broþur to me, þæt ic wite þæt ge sceaweras ne sin, and þæt ge þisne eowerne broþur feccon þe her on bende sitt and þæt ge syþþan leafe habbon to bicg`e´anne þæt þæt ge wyllað".' ³⁵ Đa hig þus spræcon, þa guton hig hira hwæte of hira saccon and fundon þæron eall hyra feoh, and hig wurdon ealle afærede. ⁴²:³⁶ ĐA CWÆÐ IACOB HIRA FÆDER: 'Bearnleasne ge habbað me gedonne. Næbbe ic Iosep and Simeon ys on bendum; nu ge nymaþ Beniamin æt me.' ³⁷ Đa andswarode Ruben and cwæð: 'Ic hæbbe twegen suna. Ofsleh þa begen, gif ic hine þe ongen ne bringe. Syle hine me on hand and ic hyne agife eft þinre handa.' ³⁸ þa cwæð Iacob: 'Ne færð mid eow Beniamin. Iosep his broþur ys dead and he ys ana to lafe. Gif him | hwilc yfel on þam lande gelimpð, æfre ic f. 30ᵛ wurðe syþþan geomriende.' ⁴³:¹⁻² Gemang þam hungre, þa se mete geteorude þe hig of Egipta lande brohton, Iacob cwæð to his sunum: 'Farað and bicgað us sumne dæl metes.' ³ Đa cwæð Iudas: 'þæs landes ealdor swor aþas beforan us þæt we ne moston cuman beforan him, buton we bringon urne gingstan broþur mid us. ⁴ Witodlice gif þu wylt hine mid us sendan, we farað ætgædere and bicgað þa þingc þe we beþurfon. ⁵ Gif þu þonne nelt, ne cume we þær.' ⁶ Đa cwæð Israhel to him: 'Earmlice dydon ge wiþ me, þa ge him sædon þæt ge a ma gebroþra hæfdon.' ⁷ þa cwædon hig: 'Se man us axode eall be endebyrdnysse ymbe ure cynn and hwæþer ure fæder leofode and hwæðer we broþur hæfdon, and we him andswaredon þæs þe he us axode. We nyston þæt he þæs girnan wolde þæt we urne broþur

42:34 gingstan] gingestan Co   broþur] broðor BCo   sin] sind B, beon Co   broþur] broþor BCo   feccon] geueccan Co   bende] bendum BCo   habbon] habban BCo bicgeanne] bigcanne Co   þæt þæt] loca hwæt Co   wyllað] willan Co   42:35 hig¹] hi B spræcon] spæcon B   guton hig hira] tugon hi heora BCo   hira saccon] heora saccum BCo þæron] þar Co   hyra] heora B   hig³] hi BCo   42:36 ÐA] *3-line red initial cap.* L HIRA] heora BCo   FÆDER] uæder Co   Bearnleasne] bearnlease Co   gedonne] gedon Co   ic] nu *add.* Co   on bendum] gebunden and Co   nymaþ] willað niman Co 42:37 andswarode] andswerode Co   Ofsleh] ofsleah B   begen] beggen Co   ongen] ongean BCo   agife eft] giue ðe on Co   42:38 færð] cymð Co   mid eow Beniamin] beniamin mid eow BCo   Iosep] for ðon iosep Co   his broþur] *om.* B, his broðor Co   ys²] his B   lafe] laue Co   Gif] and hu þonne gif Co   43:1-2 Gemang] ða amang Co geteorude] geteorode B, ateorode Co   hig] hi BCo   Iacob cwæð] þa cwæð iacob Co Farað] to egipta lande *add.* Co   43:3 beforan¹] beuoran Co   cuman beforan] cumon beuoran Co   buton] butan B   bringon] brohton Co   gingstan broþur] gyngestan broþor BCo   43:4 Witodlice] nu witodlice Co   wylt hine] hine wilt Co   sendan] sændon Co farað] uarað Co   þingc] þing B   beþurfon] beþuruon Co   43:5 Gif] Co *p. 156*   ne cume we þær] ne durre we þar cumon Co   we] þonne *add.* B   43:6 him¹] heom Co 43:7 hig] hi BCo   eall] eal BCo   endebyrdnysse ymbe] endebyrdnesse ymbon Co   cynn] cyn BCo   fæder leofode] uæder leouode Co   broþur¹] broþor B, gebroðra Co andswaredon] andswarodon B, andwerdon Co   We] and we Co   broþur²] broþor BCo

þyder læddon.' ⁸ Iudas cwæð eft to his fæder: 'Send þone cnapan mid me, þæt we magon bicgan þa þing þe we beþurfon, þæt we ne forwurþon. ⁹ Ic underfo þone cnapan: bide his me eft. And buton ic hine bringe eft ham and þe sylle, beo ic scildig. ¹⁰ Gif þeos ylding nære, nu we wæron cumene oþre siþe.' ¹¹ Ða cwæð Israhel: 'Gif ge neade swa don sceolon, doþ swa ge wyllon. Nymað of eowrum selustan wæstmum on fatum and bringað þam men lac, sumne dæl tyrwan and hunig and stor and æcirnu and hnite, ¹² and twa swa micel feos swa ge ær hæfdon, þe læs þe ge sin gedwealde, ¹³ and nimaþ eowerne broþor and farað to þam menn. ¹⁴ Min Drihten hine gedo glædne wið eow, þæt he agife eow eowerne broþor þe he mid him hæfþ, and eac Beniamin. Ic eom nu bereafod minra bearna.'

⁴³:¹⁵ Þa namon hig þa lac and twigfeald feoh and Beniamin and foron to Egipta lande to Iosepe. ¹⁶ Ða he hig geseah, and Beniamin mid him, þa cwæð he to his geferan: 'Læde in þas menn and gearwa ure | þenunga, þæt hig magon etan mid me to middes dæges.' ¹⁷ And he dyde swa him beboden wæs. ¹⁸ Ða hig þarinne wæron, þa wurdon hig swiþe afirhte and cwædon him betwynan: 'For þam feo þe we on urum saccon fundon we synd hider inn gelædde, þæt he us æt urum asson bereafige and æt urum þingon, and us sylfe þeowige.' ¹⁹⁻²⁰ Þa cwædon hig to þam wicnere: 'We biddað þe, leof, þæt þu hlyste ure spræce. Hwilon ær we wæron her and bohton us hwæte. ²¹ Þa we geceapod heafodon and we hamweard wæron, þa undydon we ure

  43:7 læddon] læddan B, lædan scolde Co 43:8 bicgan] bicgean B þing] þinc Co forwurþon] forwyrðon Co 43:9 underfo] underuo Co cnapan] and add. Co me eft] eˈfˈt æt me Co sylle] betæce Co ic³] deaðes add. Co 43:10 þeos ylding] þys yldingc Co siþe] syðan Co
  MSS L, B, Co, O (intermittently) 43:11 ge¹] þonne add. Co neade] nyde BCo swa¹] om. Co sceolon] sculon Co wyllon] willan Co of eowrum] eac of eowrum Co, eac eower O selustan] selostan B, selestum CoO wæstmum] westmum and O fatum] uatum Co bringað] brincgað Co, bryngað O lac] to lake and Co, lac and O stor] and recels add. Co æcirnu] æcerenu CoO hnite] hnytu B 43:12 feos] seolfres Co þe¹] þi Co sin] sind B, beon CoO gedwealde] gedwelode B, gedwealdon O 43:13 menn] men BCoO 43:14 gedo] do Co þæt] and þæt CoO agife] gyue Co he²] þær add. CoO hæfþ] hafað CoO eac] min cyld add. Co bereafod] bereauod Co 43:15 namon] naman Co hig] hi BCo twigfeald] twifeald B, twiueald Co, twyfeald O 43:16 hig¹] hi BCo, hy O him] heom Co his geferan] þan gereuan Co Læde] læd CoO menn] men BCoO hig²] hi BCo middes dæges] middæges BCoO 43:17 him beboden wæs] he him beboden hæfde Co 43:18 hig¹] hy BCo þarinne] þærinne B, þerinne Co wurdon] wurþon B, wyrdon Co him betwynan] heom betweonan CoO feo] feohe Co saccon] saccum B, sacce Co inn] in B he us] he wile ˋusˊ Co asson] assum BCo bereafige] bereauian Co æt] om. Co þingon] þingum BCo, þyngum O 43:19–20 hig] hi BCo spræce] spæce BO Hwilon] hwilum B, whilon Co 43:21 þa¹] and þa Co heafodon] hæfdon BCoO hamweard] hamwerd CoO undydon] undydan Co

saccas. Þa fundon we þæt feoh þæron þe we ær sældon. Nu hæbbe we hit broht ongen be þam ylcan gewihte [22] and eac oðer sylfor mid to ceapienne. Nyte we hwa hit on ure saccas dyde.' [23] Ða cwæð se gerefa: 'Sib si mid eow. Ne ondræde ge eow; eower God and eowres fæder God eow sealde goldhord on eowre saccas. Witudlice þæt feoh þæt ge me sealdon ic hæbbe afandud.' And he lædde Simeon ut to him. [24] And hig þwogon hira fet and he sealde hira assan foddur. [25] Soþlice hig ledon forþ hira lac, ongen þætte Iosep in eode, [26] and feollon on þa eorðan and geeaðmeddon wið hine. [27] Iosep hig oncneow þa arfullice and axode hig hwæþer hira fæder wære hal, þe hig him foresædon, oððe hwæþer he lyfode. [28] Þa cwædon hig: 'Gesund ys þin þeow ure fæder; git he leofað.' [29] Ða Iosep geseah hys gemedrydan broþor Beniamin, þa cwæð he: 'Ys þis se cnapa þe ge me foresædon?' And eft he cwæð: 'God gemiltsige þe, sunu min.' [30] And he wearþ swa swiþe astirod, þæt him feollon tearas for his broþor þingon and he eode into his beddclyfan and weop. [31] And þa he þæs geswac, þa eode he eft ut to him [32] and hig æton, onsundron þa Egyptiscean, onsundron þa Ebreiscan. Hit næs na alyfed þæt hig ætgædere æton. [34] And hig man oferdrencte.

[44:1] Ða bead Iosep his gerefan and cwæð: 'Fylle hira | saccas mid f. 31ᵛ
hwæte and lege hira ælces feoh on his agenne sacc. [2] And nym minne sylfrenan læfyl and þæs hwætes wurð þe he þe sealde and do on þæs gingstan sacc.' And he dyde swa. [3] On morgen þa hig ferdon, [4] and

43:21 þæron] þaron O sældon] sealdon BCoO hæbbe] habbe Co broht] gebroht Co ongen] ongean BCoO 43:22 sylfor] seolfor BO, seoluor Co ceapienne] ceapianne B Nyte] nyton Co ure] urum CoO 43:23 gerefa] reua Co Sib si] sy sib Co eow eower God and eowres fæder God] eowerne god forðon eower god Co, eow eower`ne´ god and eower.. god O God] godd B God] godd B eowre] eower Co Witudlice] witodlice BCoO þæt²] þe BCoO hæbbe] habbe Co afandud] afandod BO, auandod Co Simeon ut] þa ut symeon Co to him] mid hym B 43:24 hig] om. B, hi Co, hy O hira¹] heora BCoO hira²] heora BCoO foddur] foddor BCoO 43:25 hig] hi BCo, hyg O ledon] legdon Co hira] heora BCoO ongen þætte] ongean þæt BCoO 43:26 on þa eorðan and geeaðmeddon wið hine] ealle to his fotum Co and geaðmeddon wið hine] om. O 43:27 hig¹] hi BCo, hyg O þa] om. Co arfullice] arwyrðlice Co hig²] hi BCo, om. O hwæþer¹] hwaðer CoO hira] heora BCoO wære hal] hal wære CoO hig³] hi BCo hwæþer²] om. Co lyfode] leofode BCoO 43:28 hig] hi B ys] he is Co 43:29 geseah] geseh Co gemedrydan] gemeddredan BCoO gemiltsige] miltsige Co 43:30 wearþ] þa add. Co astirod] astyred Co tearas] of his eagan add. CoO; Co p. 157 þingon] þingum Co beddclyfan] bedcleofan B, beorclyfan Co weop] swiðe sare add. CoO 43:31 geswac] wopes geswican hæfde CoO eft] om. BCo ut to him] into heom Co 43:32 hig¹] hi BCo æton] ætsomne add. CoO Egiptiscean] egyptiscan and Co onsundron þa ebreiscan] om. B Ebreiscan] ebreiscon O alyfed] alyued Co hig²] hi BCo 43:34 hig] hi BCo 44:1 gerefan] gereuan Co Fylle] fyllað Co, fyl O hira¹] heora BCO hira²] heora BCoO sacc] sac B 44:2 sylfrenan] seolfrena Co, seolfrenan O læfyl] læfel B, læuel Co wurð] weorð CoO þe²] om. BCoO gingstan] gyngestan B, gingestan CoO 44:3 morgen] merigen B, mergen Co hig] hy B, hi Co ferdon] uerdon Co

hig wæron butan birig and hæfdon sumne dæl weges gefaren, þa cwæð Iosep to his gerefan: 'Aris and far æfter þisum mannum and þonne þu hig gefangen hæbbe, þonne axa þu hig hwi hig woldon gildan god mid yfele, ⁵and se læfel þe ge forstælon wæs minum hlaforde swiþe dyre: yfele ge dydon.' ⁶He dyde swa him beboden wæs. And þa hig gefangene wæron, ⁷hig cwædon: 'Hwi tihþ ure hlaford us swa micles falses? ⁸þæt feoh þe we fundon on ure saccon we læddon to þe o[f] Chanaan lande. Wenst þu þæt we þines hlafordes gold oþþe his seolfor stælon? ⁹Sece hyt and sig he ofslagen, se þe þu hit mid finde.' ¹⁰Ða cwæð he: 'Sig hit swa ge cweden. Mid swa hwam swa ic hit mid finde, beo he min þeow and beon þa oþre clæne.' ¹¹Hig efston þa and dydon hira saccas nyþer, ¹²and he sohte fram þam yldestan oð þone gingestan oþ he funde þone læfyl on Beniamines sacce. ¹³And hig wurdon swiþe dreorige and symdon hira assan and cyrdon eft to þære birig. ¹⁴Ða eode Iudas firmest in mid his broðrum to Iosepe and hig feollon ealle ætgædere beforan Iosepe. ¹⁵And he cwæð to him: 'Hwi woldon ge swa don? Wendon ge þæt ge mihton bedidrian minne gelican?' ¹⁶Ða cwæð Iudas to him: 'Hwæt magon we cweþan ongen urne hlaford? Nabbe we nane tale ongen þe. God hæfþ arasod ure unrihtwi⟨s⟩nissa. Nu we synd ealle þine þeowas, ægðer ge we ge se þe se læfel mid funden ys.' ¹⁷Ða cwæð Iosep: 'Nelle Godd þæt ic swa do, ac sig se min þeowa þe þone
f. 32ʳ læfyl | forstæl, and fare ge frige to eowrum fæder.' ¹⁸Ða eode Iudas him near and spræc þristlicor wið hine: 'Ic bidde þe, hlaford, þæt ic mote butan yrre wið þe sprecan. þu eart min hlaford under

44:4 hig¹] hi B   butan] buton O, þara *add.* Co   hæfdon] eac *add.* Co   gefaren] geuaran Co   hig²] hi B   hig³] hi BCo   hig⁴] hi BCo   gildan god mid yfele] god mid yfele forgildan Co   O *lost until 45:2*   44:5 and] sege heom þæt *add.* Co   læfel] læuel Co   ge forstælon] hi forstolen habbað Co   hlaforde] hlauorde Co   yfele ge dydon] yuele habbe ge gedon Co   44:6 dyde] þa *add.* Co   hig] hi B   44:7 hig] hi BCo   hlaford] hlauord Co   micles] miceles BCo   44:8 fundon] uundon Co   ure saccon] urum saccum BCo   we²] þæt we Co   of] BCo, on L   Wenst þu] wenstu B   þines hlafordes gold oþþe his seolfor stælon] þines hlafordes (hlauordes Co) gold oþþe hys seolfor BCo   44:9 Sece] sec Co   sig] si B, sy Co   ofslagen] ofslegen B, ofslagan Co   hit] hine Co   44:10 Sig] sy BCo   cweden] cwædon BCo   hwam] hwan Co   min] mines hlauordes Co   44:11 Hig] hy B, and hi Co   hira] heora BCo   44:12 gingestan] gynstan B   oþ] þæt *add.* Co   læfyl] læfel B, læuel Co   44:13 hig] hy B, hi ealle Co   wurdon] wyrdon Co   dreorige] dreorie B   symdon hira] semdon heora BCo   44:14 broðrum] gebroðrum Co   hig] hi BCo   beforan] beuoran Co   44:15 to him] *om.* Co   bedidrian] diddrian B, bedydryan Co   44:16 ongen] ongean BCo   urne] þe Co   Nabbe] næbbe B   tale] tala Co   ongen] ongean BCo   arasod] afandod B   unrihtwisnissa] *first* s *lost in hole* L, unrihtwisnesse Co   læfel] læuel Co   44:17 Godd] god BCo   sig] si BCo   se] he Co   læfyl] læfel B, læuel Co   frige] *om.* Co   44:18 þristlicor] þristelicor Co   hlaford¹] hlauord Co   butan] buton Co   sprecan] specan B, sprece Co   hlaford²] hlauord Co

Pharaone. ⁱ⁹ þu axodest us ær hwæþer we hæfdon fæder oþþe broþur ²⁰ and we cwædon we habbaþ ealdne fæder and he hæfð mid him urne gingstan broþur, þone he gestrinde on his ylde, and his gemedrydan broþur wæs dead, and he lufað hine anne ofer us ealle. ²¹⁻³¹ And þu bude us þæt we hyne læddon to þe, þæt þu hine gesawe and wistest be þam þæt we næron sceaweras. Nu we habbaþ hine earfoþlice begiten æt urum fæder and hine hider broht. ³² And ic swor aþas minum fæder þæt ic hine ham ongen to him brohte, and ic hine nam on minne truwan and cwæð to him, "Buton ic hine ongen bringe eft to þe, ic beo æfre scildig wið þe". ³³ Hlaford min, læt þone cnapan faran ham mid his broðrum and ic beo þin þeowa for hine. ³⁴ Ne dear ic ham faran butan þam cnapan, þy læs þe ic geseo mines fæder sarnisse.'

⁴⁵:¹ Ða ne mihte Iosep hyne leng dyrnan ac he draf ealle þa Egiptiscan ut þæt nan fremde man betwyx him nære. ² And he weop and clypode hludre stefne, þæt þa Egiptiscan gehyrdon and eall Pharones hired. ³ And he cwæð to his gebroþrum: 'Ic eom Iosep. Lyfaþ ure fæder nu git?' Ða ne mihton his gebroþru him for ege geandwyrdan. ⁴ Þa grete [he] hig arwurðlice and cwæð: 'Ic eom Iosep eower broþur, þe ge sealdon on Egipta land. ⁵ Ne ondræde ge eow nan þing, ne eow ne ofþince þæt ge me sealdon on þis rice. Soþlice for eowre þearfe me sende God on Egipta land. ⁶ Nu twa gear wæs hungor ofer ealle eorðan and git sceolon fife, on þam man ne mæg naþer ne erian ne ripan. ⁷ And God | me sende to þam þæt ge beon f. 32ᵛ gehealdene and þæt ge habbon þæt ge magon big lybban. ⁸ Þæt næs na eowres þances ac þurh God þe ic þurh his willan hider asend wæs. Se dyde me swilce ic Pharaones fæder wære and hys hiredes hlaford

44:18 Pharaone] faraone Co   44:19 broþur] modor BCo   44:20 fæder] uæder Co   gingstan broþur] gynstan broþor B, gingestan broðor Co   gemedrydan broþur] gemedreda broþor B, gemeddredan broðor Co   lufað] luuað Co   anne] ænne BCo   ofer] ouer Co   44:21–31 læddon] læddan B   wistest] woldest witan Co   be þam] *om.* B   næron sceaweras] sceaweras næron B   næron] næran Co   begiten] begitan Co   fæder] uæder Co   broht] gebroht Co   44:32 ongen¹] ongean BCo   minne] minan B   Buton] butan B   ongen²] ongean BCo   44:33 Hlaford] hlauord Co   þone cnapan faran] faran þone cnapan Co   broðrum] gebroþrum B   hine] him Co   44:34 ham] *om.* Co   þy] þe B, þi Co   45:1 leng dyrnan] na lenge bedyrnan Co   betwyx him nære] nære betweox him Co; Co *p. 158*   betwyx] betwuh B   45:2 weop] ða *add.* Co   hludre stefne] hluddre stemne BCo   Egiptiscan] hit *add.* Co   eall] eal B   Pharones] pharaones B, faraones Co   45:3 Lyfaþ] leofaþ BCo   gebroþru] gebroðra Co   geandwyrdan] geandwerdan CoO   45:4 grete] grette BCoO   he] BCoO, *om.* L   broþur] broðor BCoO   on] to CoO   land] lande CoO   45:5 þing] þinc Co, ðyngc O   þearfe] þearue Co   sende] sænde CoO   on] to CoO   land] lande CoO   45:6 hungor] hunger B   sceolon] sculon CoO   naþer] *om.* B   45:7 sende] sænde CoO   and²] ac CoO   habbon] habban Co   45:8 ac] wæs *add.* CoO   þe] þæt Co   asend] asænd Co   wæs] and *add.* Co   Pharaones] faraones CoO   Pharaones fæder wære] wære faraones fæder Co   hlaford] hlauord Co

and he sette me to ealdre ofer Egipta land. ⁹Faraþ hrædlice to minum fæder and secgaþ him þæt God me sette to hlaforde eallum Egiptum. Beodað him þæt he fare to me ¹⁰ and wunige on Gessen lande and beo me gehende, he and his suna and his bearna bearn and eowre sceap and eower hryþerheorda and eall þæt ge agon, ¹¹ and ic eow fede. Git synd fif hungorger bæftan. Doþ þus, þæt ge ne forwurþon. ¹² Nu ge geseoþ hu hit mid me ys and ge gehiraþ hwæt ic to eow sprece. ¹³ Cyþað minum fæder eall min wuldor and ealle þa þing þe ge gesawon on Egipta lande. Efstaþ and lædað hine to me.' ¹⁵ And he clypte hira ælcne and cyste hig and weop. Æfter þison hig dorston sprecan wiþ hine. ¹⁶ Ða spræc man ofer eall and widmærsude þæt Iosepes broðru comon to Pharaone. And Pharao wæs glæd, and eall his hired. ¹⁷ And he bead Iosepe þæt he bude his broþrum and þus cwæde: 'Symað eowre assan and faraþ to Chanaan lande ¹⁸ and nymað þær eowerne fæder and eowere mægþe and cumaþ to me and ic eow sylle ealle Egipta god. ¹⁹ Beod him eac þæt hig nymon wænas to hira cildfare and to hira gemæccena, and beod him eac þæt hig nymon hira fæder and efston hider swa hig raþost magon. ²⁰ And ne forlæte ge nan þing of eowrum yddisce, for þam ealle Egipta speda beoð eowre.'

⁴⁵:²¹ Israheles suna dydon swa him beboden wæs. And iosep him sealde wænas, eall swa Pharao him bead, and formete, ²² ⟨and⟩ sealde hira ælcum twa scrud, and he sealde Beniamine fif scrud and þreo hundred sylfringa. ²³ And he sende his fæder tyn assan, þa wæron

45:8 sette] gesette CoO   to] hiredes *add.* CoO   land] lande Co   45:9 hrædlice] rædlice O   hlaforde] hlauorde Co   45:10 gehende] gehænde CoO   eowre sceap and eowre hryþerheorda] eowre sceaphyrdas and eowre hryðerhyrdas Co, eower sceapheordas and eowere riðerhyrdas O   eowre sceap] eower scep B   eall] eal BCoO   ge] 'ge' Co   45:11 hungorger] hungergear B, hungorgear Co, hungerger O   bæftan] bæfton BCo   forwurþon] forwyrðon Co, forwurþan O   45:12 to eow] eow B, eow to Co   45:13 Cyþað] kyðað Co   eall] eal BCo   þing] þingc BO, þinc Co   Efstaþ] nu *add.* CoO   45:15 hira] heora BCoO   hig¹] hi Co, hyg O   weop] þa *add.* CoO   þison] þisum Co   hig²] hi BCo   dorston] BCoO, ne dorston L   45:16 eall¹] eal BCoO   widmærsude] widmærsode BCoO   broðru] gebroðra Co   Pharaone] faraone CoO   Pharao] farao CoO   eall²] eal BCo   45:17 broþrum] gebroðrum CoO   cwæde] cwæþ BCo   Symað] semað Co   eowre] eower O   45:18 þær] *om.* Co   eowerne] eowera Co   eowere] eowre B, eower Co   45:19 him¹] heom Co, hym O   hig¹] hi BCo   nymon] niman CoO   wænas to . . . nymon] *om.* CoO   hira cildfare] heora fære B   hira²] heora B   him²] heom B   hig²] hy B, hi Co   nymon] niman B   hira³] heora BCoO   hig³] hi Co   45:20 forlæte ge . . . yddisce] forlæton ge eowres ydysces nan ðinc Co, forlæte ge eowerer yddisces nan ðyngc O   þing] þingc BCo   45:21 him] heom BCo   sealde] sænde Co   eall] eal BCoO   Pharao] farao CoO   bead] bebead Co   45:22 and¹] *lost in hole* L   hira] heora BCoO   and he sealde Beniamine fif scrud] *om.* Co   þreo hundred] þreo hundryd B, .ccc. Co   45:23 sende] sænde Co   tyn] .x. Co, ten O

gesymed mid feo | and mid hrægle and mid Egipta welun, and tyn þe bæron hwæte and hlaf. ²⁴ Witudlice he let þa his gebroþru faran and cwæð to him: 'Ne forlæte ge nan þing be wege ac beoþ swyþe gesome.' ²⁵ Hig foron of Egipta lande and comon to Chanaan lande to Iacobe hira fæder, ²⁶ and cwædon to him: 'Iosep lyfað, þin sunu, and wealt ealles Egipta landes.' Ða Iacob þæt gehirde, þa þuhte him swilce he of hefegum slæpe awacode and þeah he him ne gelyfde. ²⁷ Hig rehton him hira færeld be endebyrdnysse, and þa he geseah þa wænas and ealle þa þing þe him gesende wæron, his gast wearð geedcwicod. ²⁸ And he cwæð: 'Genoh ic hæbbe gif Iosep min sunu git leofað. Ic fare and geseo hine, ær þam þe ic swelte.' ⁴⁶:¹ Israhel ferde þa mid eallum þam þe he hæfde oþ þæt he com to aðsware pytte and þær offrude lac Isaaces Gode, his fæder. ² And God hine gehirde and clypode hine and cwæð to him: 'Iacob, Iacob.' And he him andswarode and cwæð: 'Her ic eom.' ³ And God cwæð to him: 'Ic eom se strengsta God þines fæder. Ne ondræd þu þe ac far on Egipta land, for þam þe ic gedo þe þær weligne. ⁴ Ic fare þider mid þe and þanon ic þe læde.' ⁵ Iacob aras þa fram þam pytte and hys suna hine namon, mid litlingum and mid hira wifum and mid þam wænum þe Pharao þider sende þone ealdan man on to ferianne, ⁶ and ealle þa þing þe he ahte on Chanaan lande, and he com on Egipta land mid eallum his cynne.

⁴⁶:⁸ Soðlice þis synd Israhela naman þe in foron on Egipta land, he mid his sunum. Se frumcenneda, Ruben. ⁹ Rubenes suna: Enoch and

45:23 gesymed] gesemede Co, gesemed O   hrægle] rægle Co, ragl O   Egipta] egyptum Co   welun] welum BCoO   þe] þa Co   hwæte and hlaf] hlaf and hwæte CoO   45:24 Witudlice] witodlice BCoO   gebroþru] gebroðra CoO, þa *add.* Co   and] he *add.* O   him] heom Co   þing] þingc CoO   ac] and CoO   45:25 Hig] hy B, hi CoO   foron] þa *add.* CoO   comon] þa *add.* Co   hira] heora BCoO; Co *p. 159*   45:26 him¹] la leof fæder *add.* Co   lyfað] leofaþ BCoO   sunu] suna Co   hefegum] hᵉrᵉefegum B, heuegum Co   awacode] awæcnode B, awacnode CoO   þeah he him] þeah hym B, þeahhwæðere him Co, þeahhwæðre hym O   45:27 Hig] hy B, hi Co   him¹] þa eall of Co, þa O   hira] heora BCoO   færeld] færelde eall Co   endebyrdnysse] endebyrdnesse Co   þa¹] þa þa CoO   þing] ðyngc BO   gesende wæron] gesænd wæren Co, gesæd wæron O   geedcwicod] geedcucod CoO   45:28 sunu] suna Co   fare] nu *add.* Co   þam þe] 'þā ðe' *(contemp.)* O   þe] *om.* B   swelte] swylte Co, swilte O   46:1 aðsware] aðswara Co   offrude] offrode BCo   46:2 clypode] cleopode Co, cliopode O   hine and cwæð to him] to him and cwæð Co   eom] hlaford *add.* Co   46:3 strengsta] strensta B, stranga CoO   on] to CoO   land] lande CoO   gedo] do B   þær] *om.* CoO   46:4 fare] nu *add.* CoO   46:5 namon] naman Co   hira] heora BCo   Pharao] farao BCo   sende þone ealdan] sænde þonne ealda Co   ferianne] ferienne Co, ferigenne O   46:6 þing] þingc B, þyncg O   on¹] to O   on²] þa to CoO   land] lande CoO   cynne] kynne Co   46:8 Soðlice] *3-line green initial cap.* L   Israhela] ysraela O   in] *om.* CoO   foron] uoran Co   on] in to CoO   land] lande CoO   frumcenneda] phrumcennedaB, frumcænneda O   46:9 Rubenes] and rubenes CoO   Enoch] enoh BCo

82   GENESIS

Phallu and Charm. ¹⁰ Simeones suna: Gamuel and Diamin and
Achod and Iachim and Saher and Saul, Chananides sunu. ¹¹ And
Leuies suna: Ierson and Caath and Merari. ¹² Iudas suna: Her and
f. 33ᵛ Onam and Sela and Phares and Zaram. Her and | Onam forþferdon
on Chanaan lande, and Pharese wæron suna acennede, Esrom and
Amul. ¹³ Isachares suna: Thola and Phua and Iob and Semrom.
¹⁴ Zabulones suna: Sared and Elon and Iaelel. ¹⁵ þis synd Lian suna,
þe heo cende on Mesopotamia, Sirie, mid Dina hire dehter. þæt
wæron ealra þreo and þritig, mid sunum and mid dohtrum. ¹⁶ Gades
suna: Sephio and Thagis, Suni and Esebon, Her and Arodi and
Areli. ¹⁷ Asseres suna: Gamne and Gessui and Iesua and Beria, and
Sara heora swustor. Berian suna: Hebel and Melchiel.

⁴⁶:¹⁹ Rachele suna, Iacobes wifes: Iosep and Beniamin. ²⁰ And Iosep
gestrynde suna on Egipta lande be Aseneð, Putifares dehter, þæs
sacerdes of Eliopoleus: Manneses and Ephraim. ²¹ Beniamines suna:
Bela and Bechor and Asbel, Gera and Naam and Hehi and Ros,
Moim and Oppham and Ared. ²² Rachel acende Iacobe feowertyne
suna. ²³ Danis suna: [Husim]. ²⁴ [Neptalines suna]: Hasiel and Guni
and Iesser and Salem.

⁴⁶:²⁷ Witudlice Iacob ferde hundseofontigra sum on Egipta land.
²⁸ He sende Iudas beforan him to Iosepe, þæt he cydde him þæt he
come ongen hyne to Iesen. ²⁹ þa he þyder com, Iosep gegearwude

    46:9 Phallu] fallu Co   46:10 Saul] sauw Co   Chananides] chana..nytedes Co,
chananitides O   sunu] suna BCoO   46:11 Leuies suna] CoO, leuies sues suna LB
Caath] chaath B, caað Co   46:12 Onam] onham Co   Phares] fares CoO   Zaram] saram
Co   Onam] oman B, onham Co   Pharese] farase BO, fares Co   wæron suna] suna wæron Co
acennede] akennede Co, acænnede O   Amul] amuel CoO   46:13 Isachares] þis wæron
isacheres (issacheres O) CoO   Phua] fua B   46:14 Zabulones] and ðis wæron zabules
CoO   46:15 cende] akende Co, acænde O   Mesopotamia] mesopotamie B,
mesopotamiga O   Dina] dian Co, dinan O   hire dehter] hired hter O   þritig] .xxx. BCo,
ðrittig O   46:16 Gades suna] ðis wæron gaades suna CoO   Esebon] essebon BCoO
46:17 Asseres suna] ðis wæron asseras (asseres O) suna CoO   Gessui] iessui Co   Iesua]
gessua B, gesua O   Beria] bæria Co   swustor] sweostor Co   Berian suna Hebel and
Melchiel] *om.* Co   Berian] þis wæron berian O   46:19 Rachele] ðis wæron racheles CoO
wifes] wiues Co   46:20 Aseneð] aseneth BO, asenehte Co   Putifares] putiphares BCo
dehter] dohter Co   Eliopoleus] elipoleus B   Manneses] manases B, and hi (hyg O) hatton
manases CoO   Ephraim] efraim B, effraim CoO   46:21 Beniamines] ðis wæron
beniamines CoO   Bechor] bethor Co   Asbel] *add.* B, arbel Co   Gera] iera Co   and⁴]
om. BCoO   Hehi] rehi CoO   Oppham O] opfam Co   46:22 acende] akende be Co,
acænde O   feowertyne] .xiii. Co   46:23 Danis] þus hatte danis CoO   Husim] BO, vsim
Co, *om.* L   Neptalines suna] B, *om.* L, þis wæron neptalimes suna CoO   Guni] gum Co
46:27 Witudlice] witodlice BCoO   hundseofontigra] lxxʳᵃ Co   on] to CoO   land] lande Co,
'lande' O   46:28 He sende] þa sænde he CoO   beforan] beuoran Co   þæt he cydde] and
he cydde B, þæt he sceolde (scolde O) cyðan CoO; Co *p. 160* ongen] ongean BCo   Iesen]
iessen B, iessen lande Co, gessen lande O   46:29 þa] þonne CoO   com] come CoO
Iosep] þa *add.* CoO   gegearwude] gegearwode BO, gearwode Co

hys cræt and for ongen hys fæder. And þa he hyne geseah, he clypte hyne and weop. ³⁰ And Iacob cwæð: 'Nu ic mæg sweltan bliþelice, nu ic þe geseo, and þe mine æhta betæcan.' ³¹ And Iosep cwæð to his broþrum and to ealre hys hiwrædene: 'Ic fare and cyþe Phar`a´one þæt ge comun to me, ³² and ic secge him þæt ge synd hyrdas and habbaþ broht hider mid eow eall þæt ge ahton. ³³ And þonne he eow clypað and axaþ hwæt ge don cunnon, ³⁴ ðonne secge ge him þæt ge synd scephirdas fram cildhade, ge we ge ure fæderas, oþ þisne andweardan dæg. Secgað þuss þæt ge magon eardian on Ges`s´en lande, for þan þe | ealle Egiptisce onscuniaþ scephyrdas.' ⁴⁷:¹ Ða f. 34ʳ
eode Iosep into Pharaone and cwæð to him: 'Min fæder and mine gebroþu and heora scepheorda and heora hryðerheorda and ealle þa þing þe hig agon comon of Chanaan lande and nu hig synd on Gessen lande.' ² Witudlice he lædde his fif gincstan broþru beforan þone cyng. ³ Þa he axode hwæt hig wyrcean cuþon, hig andswaredon and cwædon: 'We synd scephyrdas þine þeowas, we and ure fæderas. ⁴ We comun to þam þæt we wunedon on þinum lande, for þam þe we nabbað nan gærs urum heordum and hungor wyxþ on Chanaan, and we biddað þæt we þine þeowas beon moton on Gessen lande.' ⁵ Ða cwæð se cyng to Iosepe: 'Þin fæder and þine gebroþru comon. ⁶ Þu canst Egipta land; geloga hig on þære selostan stowe and syle him Gessen land, and gif þu wite þæt hig glæwe sin, sete hig to ealdrum ofer mine heorda.' ⁷ Æfter þisum lædde Iosep his fæder into þam

46:29 cræt] carm Co   ongen] ongean BCoO   clypte] clypode B, cleopodo Co, clipte O   46:30 sweltan] swyltan CoO   betæcan] betæcean B, betæce Co   46:31 cwæð] þa add. CoO   broþrum] gebroðrum CoO   ealre] ealle Co   hiwrædene] ræddene B   fare] fara nu Co, fare nu O   Pharaone] faraone BCo   comun] comon BCoO   46:32 broht] gebroht CoO   hider] om. Co   eall] eal BCo   46:33 axaþ] eow add. CoO   46:34 ge¹] om. BO   scephirdas] sceaphyrdas CoO   ure] eowre Co   andweardan] andwerdan Co   þuss] ðus BCoO   eardian] eardigæan O   Gesen] iessen Co   þan] þam B   Egiptisce] egyptiscan CoO   onscuniaþ] onscunian Co   scephyrdas] sceaphyrdas CoO   47:1 Pharaone] faraone CoO   gebroþu] gebroþra CoO   heora¹] hyra Co   scepheorda] sceaphirdas CoO   heora²] hyra Co   hryðerheorda] hryðerhyrdas CoO   þing] þingc CoO   hig¹] hi Co   and nu ... lande] om. Co   hig²] hi B   47:2 Witudlice] witodlice BCoO   he lædde] om. Co   his] þa his CoO   gincstan] gingstan BO, gingestan Co   broþru] gebroðra CoO   beforan] beuoran Co, beforon O   cyng] cyngc B, kyninge Co, cynyngc O   47:3 he axode] axode he hi (hyg O) CoO   hig¹] hy B, hi Co   wyrcean] wyrcan CoO   cuþon] cuðe Co   hig²] hi BCo   andswaredon] andswarodon B, andswerodon him Co, andsweredon hym O   scephyrdas] sceaphyrdas CoO   47:4 comun] comon BCoO   to þam] hider add. Co, þyder add. O   wunedon] wunodon B   hungor] hunger O   wyxþ] wyxt B, is CoO   Chanaan] chanaan (cha`na´an Co) lande CoO    biddað] þe nu add. CoO    Gessen] iessen B    47:5 cyng] cining B, cyningc CoO    gebroþru] gebroðra Co    comon] syndon cumene hyder Co, synd cymene hyder O    47:6 hig¹] hi B    þære] þam Co, þæ`re´ O   selostan] selestan BCo   stowe] healf Co   him] heom Co   Gessen] iessen B   and²] om. CoO   glæwe sin] gleawe synd BCo   hig³] hi BCo   heorda] heorde CoO   47:7 Æfter] decorative black initial cap. L

cynge and sette hine beforan him. Þa bletsode he hyne and axode hyne hu eald he wære. ⁹ Þa andswarode he and cwæð: 'Anhundwintre and þritigwintre.' ¹⁰ And se cyning hyne bletsude and he eode ut. ⁴⁷:¹¹ Iosep sealde his gebroþrum tun on Egipta lande on þam selustan ende Ramases, eall swa Pharao him bead, ¹² and fedde hig and ealle his fæder hiwrædene. ¹³ Soþlice hlafes wæs wana on eallum ymbhwyrftum and hunger fornam swiþust Egipte and Chanaan land, ¹⁴ and Iosep hæfde gegaderod eall þæt feoh þe hig ahton and gebroht on þæs cynges maðmhuse. ¹⁵ Þa hyra | feoh geteorode, þa com eall Egipta folc to Iosepe and cwædon to him: 'Syle us mete; hwi swelte we beforan þe, nu we nabbaþ feoh?' ¹⁶ He andswarode him and cwæð: 'Drifaþ hider eowre orf, gif ge feoh nabbaþ, and ic sylle eow þær wiþ mete.' ¹⁷ And hig dydon swa and he sealde him andlyfene, wiþ horsum and wið hryþerum and wiþ sceapon and wiþ asson, and fedde hig þæt gear, wiþ heora orfe. ¹⁸ Þa comon hig eft to him on þam æfteran geare and cwædon: 'Ne hele we þe, hlaford, þæt we nabbað naþer ne feoh ne orf, and þu sylf wast þæt we nan þing nabbaþ, buton land and lichaman. ¹⁹ Hwi swelte we beforan þe? We and ure land beoð þine; bige us to þæs cynges þeowette and sile us sæd, þæt þæt land ne licge weste and we forwurþon.' ²⁰ Witudlice Iosep bohte eall Egipta land, þa hig ciptun ealle hira hamas for þæs hungres micelnyssa, and he betæhte hig Pharaone, ²¹ and eall hira folc fram ende oþ oþerne Egipta

47:7 cynge] cyninge B, kyninge Co, cynincge O   beforan] beuoran Co   him] *om.* B   he¹] se kining CoO   47:9 andswarode] andswerode Co   he] him *add.* BCo   Anhundwintre] anhund wintra CoO   and þritigwintre] *om.* CoO   47:10 cyning] cyningc Co   bletsode] bletsode B   47:11 selustan] selistan B, selestan CoO   eall] eal BCoO   Pharao] farao BCoO   bead] bebead CoO   47:12 hig] hi BCo, hyg O   47:13 hlafes] hlaf B, hlaues Co   ymbhwyrftum] 'middangeorde' *gloss add. above* O   hunger] hungor BCoO   swiþust] swyþost BCoO   47:14 eall] eal BCoO   hig] hi BCo, hyg O   cynges] cyninges B, kynges Co, cynincges O   maðmhuse] madmhuse CoO   47:15 þa] þa þa Co   hyra] heora BCoO   geteorode] ateorade CoO   eall] eal O   mete] hlauord *add.* Co   hwi swelte we] elles we sculon swyltan Co, elles we swylton O   nabbaþ feoh] feoh nabbaþ BCoO   47:16 andswarode] andswerade Co, andswerode O   him] heom Co   and¹] þa and CoO   Drifaþ] driuað Co   eowre] eower CoO   nabbaþ] nabban Co, nabbon O   sylle eow] eow sille BCoO   þær wiþ mete] mete þar wið Co   47:17 hig¹] hi BCo   him] heom Co   hryþerum] riðerum O   sceapon] sceapum BCoO   asson] assan B, assum Co   fedde he hig þæt gear] he uedde hi Co, he fedde þæt gear hyg O   hig²] hi B   47:18 hig] hi BCo   æfteran] æftran BCo   þe] nu *add.* O   hlaford] hlauord Co   naþer] naþor B   wast] *End of* Co
MSS L, B, O   47:19 swelte we] we ðuus swyltan O   cynges þeowette] cyncges þeowote B, cynincges ðeowte O   47:20 Witudlice] witodlice BO   eall] eal BO   þa hig] þa hy B, and hyg O   ciptun] cypton B, becypton ða O   hira] heora BO   micelnyssa] micelnysse B, micelnesse O   hig²] hi B   Pharaone] þa faraone O   47:21 eall] eal B   hira] heora BO

landes, ²² buton þara sacerda land þe se cyng him sealde; þa man fedde of þæs cynges berne, for þam hig ne sealdon hira land. ²³ Ða cwæð Iosep to þam folce: 'Nu ge sylfe witun þæt Pharao ah ægþer ge eow ge eower land. Nimaþ sæd and sawaþ þæt land, ²⁴ þæt ge habbon wæstmas, and syllaþ þam cynge þone fiftan dæl. Þa feower ic eow lyfe to sæde and to mete eow and eowrum hiwenum and eowrum bearnum.' ²⁵ Hig andswaredon and cwædon: 'Æt þe ys ure lif gelang. Beseoh to us and we þeowiaþ bliþelice þam cynge.' ²⁶ Of þam dæge oþ þisne andweardan dæg, man gilt þam cynge þone fiftan dæl ofer ealle Egipta land to geseted|nysse, butan þam sacerdlande þe wæs æfre frig.   f. 35ʳ

⁴⁷:²⁷ Witudlice Israhel wunode on Egipto, þæt ys on Gessen lande, and ahte þæt and wæs gemenigfyld swiþe ²⁸ and lyfode þær on seofentyne ger. Ealle his lifes dagas wæron hundteontig wintra and seofon and .xl. wintra. ²⁹ And þa he geseah þæt his endedæg him genealæhte, he clypode Iosep his sunu and cwæð to him: 'Sete þine hand under min þeoh and cyð me þine soþfæstnysse and swera me þæt þu me næfre ne bebirge on Egipta lande, ³⁰ ac do þæt ic reste mid minum fæderum. Læde me of þison lande and bebirge me mid minum yldrum.' And Iosep swor þæt he swa don wolde.

⁴⁸:¹ Þa þis wæs þus gedon, þa cydde man Iosepe þæt his fæder wære gesiclod, and he nam his twegen suna, Mannases and Effraim, and com þider. ² Þa cydde man Israhele þæt Iosep his sunu wære cumen, þa elnode he hine and sæt upp, ³ and cwæð, þa he in eode: 'Ælmihtig God me ætywde on Luza, þæt ys on Chanaan lande, and bletsode me ⁴ and cwæð, "Ic þe gemenigfylde and ic sylle þe þis land and þinum cynne æfter þe to ecere æhte". ⁵ Witudlice þine twegen suna, þe acennede wæron on Egipta lande ær þam þe ic hider come, hig beoþ mine: Ephraim and Mannases, swa Ruben and Simeon, beoþ mid me getealde and faraðˇ mid me. ⁶ Staþola þu þa oðra on hira hamon. ⁷ Me wæs Rachel dead be wege, þa ic for of Mesopotamie on

47:22 þara] þæra B   cyng] cyning B, cynincg O   cynges] cyninges B, cynincges O   berne] berene B   hig] hi B   sealdon] na *add.* O   hira] heora BO   47:23 witun] witon BO   Pharao] farao BO   eower] eowwer B   Nimaþ] nu *add.* O   47:24 cynge] cyninge B   feower] O *ends at* feow   hiwenum] hiwum B
    MSS L, B   47:25 Hig] hi B   cynge] cyninge B   47:26 dæg] *om.* B   cynge] cynincge B   ealle] eal B   gesetednysse] gesetnysse B   butan] buton B   47:27 Witudlice] witodlice B   Egipto] egipta B   gemenigfyld] gemænifyld B   47:28 lyfode] leofode B   ger] gear B   47:29 his¹] is B   sunu] suna B   bebirge] bebirige B   47:30 þison] þisum B   bebirge] bebirig B   48:1 gesiclod] gesycled B   Effraim] efraim B   48:2 sunu wære] suna wær B   upp] up B   48:3 Chanaan] chanaa B   me²] *om.* B   48:4 þe¹] *om.* B   gemenigfylde] gemænigfylde B   ecere] ecre B   48:5 Witudlice] witodlice B   suna] ða *add.* B   þe²] *om.* B   hig] hi B   48:6 Staþola] staþala B   oðra] oþre B   hira] heora B

Chanaan lande. Hit wæs lencten tid and ic for to E'u'phrata and bebirigde hig wið þone weg þe ys on Euphrata. Seo ys oþre | naman genemned Bethleem.' ⁸ Þa he his suna geseah, þa cwæð he: 'Hwæt synd þas?' ⁹ He andswarode and cwæð: 'Mine suna þe me God sealde on þisse stowe.' Þa cwæð he: 'Læde hig to me, þæt ic hig bletsige.' ¹⁰ Israheles eagan þystrodon for þære micclan ylde, þæt he ne mihte beorhte geseon. Þa fette hig man to him and he cyste hig ¹¹ and cwæð to his suna: 'Gode þanc þæt ic þe hæbbe and þæt ic þine suna geseah.' ¹² And Iosep hi nam of þæs fæder bearme and he abeah to þære eorþan and geeaþmedde hine, ¹³ and sette Ephraim on his swiþran hand, þæt wæs on Israheles wynstran hand, and Mannases on his winstran hand, þæt wæs on Israheles swiþran healfe, and dyde begen to him. ¹⁴ He hefde þa his swiþran hand ofer Effraimes heafod, þæs gingran broþur, and his wynstran ofer Mannases heafod, þe yldra wæs, ¹⁵ and he bletsode Iosep his sunu and cwæð: 'Drihten, þu þe mine fæderas on þinre gesihþe eodon, Abraham and Isaac; God, þu þe me feddest fram cildhade oþ þisne dæg. ¹⁶ Se engel þe me nerode of eallum yfelum bletsige þas cnapan, and si min nama genemned ofer hig, and minra fædera Abrahames and Isaaces, and weaxen hig manifældlice on eorðan.' ¹⁷ Ða Iosep geseah þæt his fæder sette his swiþran hand ofer Effraimes heafod, he wearð swiþe sari and nam þæs fæder hand, þohte hi to ahebbanne of Effraimes heafde and gesettan ofer Mannases heafod, ¹⁸ and cwæð to his fæder: 'Ne gebyraþ hit swa, fæder, | for þam þes ys frumcenned. Sete þine swiþran hand ofer his heafod.' ¹⁹ Þa onscunode he þæt and cwæð: 'Ic wat, sunu, ic wat. Þes byð gemenigfild on folce and his gingra broþur biþ his ealdor, and his cynn wyxþ on þeoda.' ²⁰ And he bletsode hig and cwæð: 'On þe biþ gebletsud Israhela God and be eow man cwið þus, "Si God mid þe swa he wæs mid Effraime and Mannases".' ²¹ And he gesette Efraim beforan Mannases and cwæð to Iosepe his suna: 'Nu ic swelte and God byþ mid eow and eow eft gelæt to eowre

---

48:7 Euphrata¹] eufrata B   hig] hy B   Euphrata²] eufrata B   ys] on add. B
48:9 andswarode] andwyrde B   þisse] þysre B   hig¹] hi B   þæt] and B   hig²] hi B
48:10 Israheles eagan] israeles eagon B   micclan] miclan B   hig¹] hi B   hig²] hi B
48:13 Ephraim] efraim B   48:14 Effraimes] efraimes B   broþur] broðor B
48:15 gesihþe] sihðe B   48:16 engel] encgel B   me] þe (scored through, with me add. by late hand) B   nerode] nerede B   hig¹] hi B   hig manifældlice] hi manifealdlice B
48:17 Effraimes] efraimes B   sari] sarig B   hand] and add. B (prob. 12-c.)   ahebbanne] ahebbenne B   Effraimes] efraimes B   48:18 gebyraþ] gebireþ B   þes] þe he B
48:19 gemenigfild] gemænigfild B   broþur] broþor B   cynn wyxþ] cyn wyxt B
48:20 hig] hi B   gebletsud] gebletsod B   Effraime] efraime B   48:21 And he . . . Mannases] om. B   eowre] eowra B

fædera lande. ²² Ic sylle þe anne dæl toforan þinum broþrum, þone ic nam of Amorreus handan mid gefeohte.'

⁴⁹:¹ Soþlice Iacob clypode his suna and cwæð to him: 'Beoð ætgædere, þæt ic eow cyþe þa þing þe eow towearde synd and hu eower ælcon gebyreð ær his ende.' ³⁻²⁷ He him sæde þa swa hit on þære Lydenbec awriten ys, ræde þar se þe wylle. ²⁸ Þa he hit him eall asæd hæfde, þa bletsode he ælcne onsundrum, ²⁹ and cwæð to him: 'Bebirigað me mid minum fæderum on þam twyfældan scræfe, þe ys on Ephrones lande, þæs Etheiscan, ³⁰ þæt bohte Abraham æt Ephrone þam Etheiscan, him to birgenne. ³¹ Þær hine man birgde and Sarran his wif; þær wæs Isaac bebirged mid Rebeccan and þær liþ eac Lia bebirged.' ³² And þa he þus gesprecen hæfde, he feold his fet uppan his bedd and geendude and wæs to his folce gelædd.

⁵⁰:¹ Þa Iosep þæt geseah, þa feoll he uppan hine and weop, ² and bead his þeowan, læcon, þæt hig mid wyrtgemangum hyne be[h]-wur[f]on. Hig dydon swa. | ³ Feowertig daga hit wæs þeaw þæt man f. 36ᵛ sceolde wepan ælcne deadne mann and eall þæt folc hyne weop hundseofontig daga. ⁴ Þa þæs wopes dagas agane wæron, Iosep cwæð to Pharaones hirede: 'Secgað Pharaone ⁵ þæt min fæder me bæd þæt ic hine bebirgde on þære birgenne þe he sylf dealf on Chanaan lande. Biddað hine þæt he me sylle leafe.' ⁶ And Pharao cwæð: 'Far and bebirge þinne fæder, swa he þe bæd.' ⁷ He for þa, and Pharaones yldestan hiredmen foron mid him, and ealle þa betstborenan on Egipta lande mid him forun. ⁸ And eac his gebroðru mid and eall hira hiwræden, butun geongum litlingum and heordum, þa hig forleton on Gessen lande. ⁹ He hæfde on his geferrædene cratu and ridende men, and þær wæs micel folc. ¹⁰ Þa foron hig oþ hig comon to þære þirsceflore þe ys begeondan Iordanem. Þar hig wæron seofon dagas fulle and þær mærlice þæt lic behwurfon mid miclum wope. ¹¹ Ða þæt gesawon þa Chananeiscan, þa cwædon hig: 'Þis ys micel wop

48:22 Amorreus handan] amoreus handum B   49:1 Soþlice] *3-line red initial cap*. L
49:3–27 Lydenbec] ledenbec B   þar] þær B   49:28 eall] eal B   onsundrum]
onsundron B   49:29 Bebirigað] bebyriaþ B   twyfældan] twifealdan B   49:30 bohte
Abraham] he bohte B   Etheiscan] etheiscean B   49:31 birgde] birigde B   bebirged¹]
bebiriged B   eac] *om*. B   bebirged²] bebiriged B   49:32 bedd] bed B   geendude]
geendode B   gelædd] gelæd B   50:1 feoll] feol B   50:2 læcon] læcean B   hig¹] hi B
behwurfon] B, bewurpon L   Hig²] hi B   50:3 mann] mannan B   eall] eal B
50:4 Pharaone] faraone B   50:5 bebirgde] bebyrigde B   birgenne] byrgene B
50:7 yldestan] ildstan B   forun] foron B   50:8 eall hira] eal heora B   butun] buton B
heordum] hyrdum B   hig] hi B   50:9 geferrædene] geferræddene B   50:10 hig¹]
hi B   hig²] hi B   Iordanem] iordanen B   hig³] hi B   50:11 Chananeiscan]
chananeiscean B   hig¹] hi B

þisra Egiptiscra manna.' And for þam hig nemdon þa stowe 'Egipta wopstow'. ¹² Witudlice Iacobes suna dydon eall swa he him bebead ¹³ and feredon hine to Chanaan lande and hine þær bebirgdon on þam twyfealdan scræfe þe Abraham bohte, mid lande mid ealle, to licreste æt Ephrone þam Etheiscan, ongen Mambre.

⁵⁰:¹⁴ And Iosep gewende on Egipta land mid his gebroðrum and eallum his geferum, syþþan his fæder bebirged wæs. ¹⁵ Æfter þison his gebroþru him ondredon and spræcon him betwynan: 'Wenan we magon þæt he geþence | þone teonan þe we him dydon and þæt he us mid yfele lænie.' ¹⁶ And hig cwædon to him: 'Ure fæder bead us, ær þam þe he forð ferde, ¹⁷ þæt we sædun þe þas word, "Ic bidde þe, sunu min, þæt þu forgife þone gylt and þa unrihtwisnisse þe hig wið þe worhton". We biddað þe eac þæt þu hit us, þæs Godes þeowes þances þines fæder, forgife.' Þa Iosep þæt gehirde, þa weop he, ¹⁸ and his gebroþru onbugon to him and cwædon: 'We synd þine þeowas.' ¹⁹ Þa andswarode he him and cwæð: 'Ne ondræde ge eow. Cweðe ge, magon we Godes willan onscunian? ²⁰ Ge þohton yfele be me and God gewende þæt yfel to gode, þæt he me upp ahofe, swa ge nu geseoþ, and he gehælde manega folc. ²¹ Ne ondrædaþ eow. Ic eow fede, and eower litlingas.' And he frefrode hig and spræc glædlice, ²² and wunude on Egipta lande mid eallre his fæder hiwrædenne. And he leofode an hund wintra and tyn gear and he geseah Effraimes suna oð þa þriddan cneorysse. Machires suna, Mannases suna, wæron acennede on Iosepes anwealde. ²³ Þa þis wæs þus gedon, he cwæð to his broþrum: 'Æfter minum deaþe, God cymð to eow and deþ þæt ge farað of þison lande to þam lande þe he swor Abrahame and Isaace and Iacobe.' ²⁴ And he cwæð: 'Lædað mine ban of þison lande.' ²⁵ Iosep forðferde þa he wæs anhundwintre and tynwintre, and hine man bebirgde mid wyrtgemange. He wæs gelædd on his stowe of Egipta lande.

50:11 þisra] þissa B   hig] hi B   50:12 Witudlice] witodlice B   eall] eal B
50:13 bebirgdon] bebyrigdon B   ongen] ongean B   50:14 on Egipta land] to egypta lande B   bebirged] bebyriged B   50:15 þison] þisum B   spræcon] spæcon B   betwynan] betweonan B   dydon] ær didon B   lænie] leanige B   50:16 hig] hi B   50:17 sædun] sædon B   unrihtwisnisse] unrihtwisnesse B   hig] hi B   þeowes] om. B   50:18 onbugon] bugon B   synd] sindon B   50:20 upp] up B   50:21 eower] eowwer B   hig] hi B
50:22 wunude] wunode B   eallre] ealre B   hiwrædenne] hiwrædene B   Effraimes] efraimes B   cneorysse] cneorissae B   Machires] macharies B   Mannases] manases B
50:23 broþrum] gebroþrum B   he²] ic B   50:24 þison] þisum B
    MSS L, B, Oʷ   50:25 anhundwintre] anhund wintra BOʷ   tynwintre] tinwintre B, ten wintra Oʷ   bebirgde] bebyrigde BOʷ   gelædd on his stowe] gelæd of his stowe B, gelæd to his earde Oʷ   of Egipta lande] to his agenum gecynde. and wearþ bebirged on middan his agenum cynne þær his lichama hine gerestað oð þisne andweardan dæg. Sy lof and wuldor þam wellwillendan hælend aa on ecnysse. Amen. add. Oʷ

[EXODUS]

'Ellesmoth' on Hebreisc, 'Exodus' on Grecisc, 'Exitus' on Lyden, f. 37ʳ
'Utfæreld' on Englisc.

¹:¹ ÞYS SYND ISRAELA BEARNA NAMAN ÐE MID IACOBE |
foron on Egipta land. Hig foron ealle mid hira hiwun: ² Ruben and f. 37ᵛ
Simeon, Leui and Iuda, ³ Isachar and Zabulon, Beniamin, ⁴ Dan and
Neptalim, Gad and Aser. ⁵ Witodlice ealra þæra manna þe foron on
Egipta lande and of Iacobes ofspringe comon wæron fif and
hundseofontig. Soðlice Iosep wæs on Egipta lande. ⁶ And þa he
dead wæs, and ealle his gebroðru and his neamagas, ⁷ Israela folc
weox swilce hig of eorþan spryttende wæron, gemenigfylde and
swyþe gestrangode, þæt land gefyldon. ⁸ Gemang þam aras niwe cing
ofer Egipta land þe nyste hwæt Iosep wæs ⁹ and cwæð to hys folce:
'Nu ys Israela folc micel and strengre þonne we. ¹⁰ Gegaderiað eow
wislice and uton gehynan hyt, þæt hyt to menigfeald ne wurþe, and
gif ure fynd us mid gefeohte gesecað and us oferwinnaþ, þonne farað
hig of lande.' ¹¹ Witudlice he sette him weorca mægestras, þæt hig
gehyndon hig mid hefegum byrþenum, and hig getimbrodun Pharaones
eardungburga Phiton and Rameses. ¹² Swa hig swiþor wæron
geswencte, swa wæron hig swiþor gemenigfilde and weoxon. ¹³ And
þa Egiptiscean hatedon þa Israeliscean and swencton hig ¹⁴ and to
yrmðe hyra lif gelæddon, mid heardum weorcum clames and tigelan
and mid ælcon þeowdome þe hig on eorþweorcum gehynede wæron.

¹:¹⁵ Soþlice Egipta cyning cwæð to þam þinenum þe þam Ebreiscean
wifun þenodon, þonne hig bearn cendon, þæra oþer wæs
genemned Sephora and oðer Phua, ¹⁶ and bead him þus: 'þonne
git þeniaþ þam Ebreiscean wifum | and hira cenningtid cymð, gif hit f. 38ʳ

MSS L, B   *Rubric on 2 lines in red in* L. *In* B, f. 72ᵛ, *there is no break and no indication
of the start of a new book.*   *Rubric* Ellesmoth ... englisc] *om.* B   1:1 ÞYS] 6-line
green initial cap. on last line of page extends into lower margin   ISRAELA] israhela B   Hig]
hi B   hira hiwun] heora hiwum B   1:2 and¹] *om.* B   1:5 þæra] þara B   lande¹]
land B   comon] *om.* B   hundseofontig] hundseofonti B   1:7 Israela] israhela B   hig]
hi B   1:8 cing] cyning B   1:9 Israela] israhela B   1:10 hig] hi B
1:11 Witudlice] witodlice B   mægestras] mægstras B   hig¹] hy B   hig²] hi B   hefegum]
hefigum B   hig getimbrodun] hi getymbrodon B   1:12 hig¹] hi B   hig²] hi B
gemenigfilde] gemenifylde B   1:13 Egiptiscean] egyptiscan B   Israeliscean]
ysrahelyscan B   hig] hi B   1:14 hyra] heora B   hig] hi B   1:15 cyning] cyningc B
Ebreiscean wifun] ebreiscum wifum B   1:16 Ebreiscean] ebreiscum B   hira] heora B

hysecild byþ, ofsleað þæt. Gif hit si mædencild, healdaþ þæt.' [17] Soþlice þa þinena him ondredon God and ne dydon swa se Egyptiscea cyng him bebead ac heoldon þa wæpnedcild. [18] Þa clypode se cyng hig to him and cwæð to him: 'Hwi woldon git þæt don, þæt git þa wæpnedcild heoldon?' [19] Þa andswarodon hig and cwædon: 'Ne synd þa Ebreiscean wif swilce þa Egiptiscean. Hig sint wære and cunnon þenunga and hig cennað ær þam þe wyt cumon to him.' [20] Witodlice God dyde wel þam þinenum and þæt folc weox and wæs swiþe gestrangod, [21] and for þam þe þa þinena him God ondredon, he getimbrode him hus. [22] Soðlice Pharao bebead eallum his folce and cwæð: 'Swa hwæt swa wæpnedhades beo acenned, wurpað hit ut on þæt wæter and healdaþ þa mædencild.'

[2:1] Æfter þison, for an esne of Leuies hiwrædene and nam wif on his agenum cynne, [2] seo geeacnude and cende sunu. And þa heo geseah þæt he fæger wæs, þa hydde heo hine þri monþas. [3] Þa heo þa hine bediglian ne mihte, þa nam heo anne riscenne windel on scipwisan gesceapenne and smirode hine mid tyrwan and mid pice and lede þæt cild þæron and asette hyne on anum hreodbedde be þæs flodes ofre. [4] And his swustor stod feorran and beheold hu þæt þing gewurde. [5] Þa eode Pharaones dohtor and wolde hig þwean æt þam wætere and hyre mædenu eodon be þæs wæteres ofre. Þa heo geseah þone windel on þam rixum, þa sende heo ane hire þinena þider and het hyne feccan. [6] Þa heo þone windel | undyde and þæt cild þæron geseah wepende, þa gemiltsode heo him and cwæð: 'Þis ys of þæra Ebrea cildum.' [7] Þa cwæð þæs cildes swustor: 'Wilt þu þæt ic ga and clipie þe an Ebreisc wif, þæt þis cild fedan mæge?' [8] Þa andswarode heo and cwæð: 'Ga.' Þa eode þæt mæden and clypode þæs cildes modor, [9] and Pharaones dohtor cwæð to hire: 'Underfoh þis cild and fed hit me and ic þe sylle þine mede.' Þæt wif underfeng þone cnapan and hine fedde and sealde Pharaones dehter. [10] And heo hine lufode and hæfde for sunu hyre, and nemde his naman Moisi and cwæð: 'For þam þe ic hine of wætere genam.' [11] On þam dagum syþþan Moises geweox, þa for he to his broþrum and geseah hira geswencednyssa and hu sum Egiptisc man sloh sumne Ebreiscne of

---

1:16 si mædencild] mædencyld sy B   1:17 Egyptiscea cyng] egyptisca cync B
18 hig] hi B   1:19 hig] hi B   Ebreiscean] ebreiscan B   Egiptiscean] egyptiscan B   Hig sint] hi synd B   hig³] hi B   cumon] cumaþ B   2:2 geeacnude] geeacnode B   2:3 anne riscenne] ænne risscenne B   gesceapenne] gesceapene B   2:4 þing] þingc B   2:5 hig] hi B   mædenu] mædene B   þinena] þinene B   2:9 Pharaones] faraones B   2:10 for sunu hyre] hire for suna B   naman] nama B   2:11 hira] heora B

his broþrum. ¹² Þa beseah he hyne ymbutan hider and þider and geseah þæt þær nan man gehende næs, þa ofsloh he þone Egiptiscean and behidde hyne on þam sande. ¹³ And eft oðre dæg, þa he ut eode, he geseh twegen Ebreisce him betwynan sacan. Ða cwæð he to þam oþrum: 'Hwi flitst þu wiþ þinne nextan?' ¹⁴ Ða andswarode he and cwæð: 'Hwa gesette þe to ealdre and to deman ofer us? Wilt þu ofslean me, swa þu girstandæg þone Egiptiscan ofsloge?' Ða ondred Moises him and cwæð: 'Hwanon ys þis word open geworden?' ¹⁵ Þa Pharao gehyrde þas spræce and sohte Moises to ofsleanne, þa fleah he of his gesihþe and wunude on Madian lande, and sæt wið anne pytt. ¹⁶ Þa hæfde se sacerd on Madian seofon dohtra, þa comon hig wæter to hladanne. And þa hira wæterfatu ful|le wæron, ða woldon f. 39ʳ
hig heora fæder orf wæterian. ¹⁷ Þa comon þa hirdas þarto and adrifon hig aweg, þa aras Moises and bewerode þa mædenu and gewæterode hira sceap. ¹⁸ Þa hig ham comon to Raguele hira fæder, þa cwæð he to him: 'Hwi comon ge raþur þonne eower gewuna wæs?' ¹⁹ Þa andswaredon hig and cwædon: 'An Egiptisc esne us generede of þara hyrda handum and eac hlod wæter mid us and sealde þam sceapum drincan.' ²⁰ Þa cwæð he: 'Hwar ys he? Hwi forleton ge þone man? Clipiað hyne þæt he mid us ete.' ²¹ Soþlice Moises swor þæt he wolde mid him eardian and nam Sephoram his dohtor to wife. ²² Seo cende sunu, þone he genemde Gerson and þus cwæð: 'Ic wæs utacimen on ælþeodig land.' ²³ Æfter langre tide Egipta cyning forðferde and Israela bearn clypod[on] geomr`i´ende for þam weorcum. And hira clypung com to Gode fram þam weorcum ²⁴ and he gehirde heora geomrungæ and gemunde þara getreowþa þe he behet Abrahame and Isaace and Iacobe, ²⁵ and beseah to Israhela bearnum and alysde hig.
³:¹ Soþlice Moises heold his mæges sceap, þæs sacerdes on Madian, þæs nama wæs Iethro. And þa he draf his heorde to inneweardum þam westene, he com to Godes dune þe man Oreb nemþ. ² And Drihten him æteowde on fires lige, on middan anre

2:12 Egiptiscean] egyptiscan B 2:13 geseh] geseah B Hwi flitst þu] hwig tlitsðu B nextan] nehstan B 2:14 girstandæg] gyrsandæg B Egiptiscan] egyptiscean B 2:15 Pharao] farao B wunude] wunode B anne] ænne B 2:16 seofon] seofan B hladanne] hladene B hira] heora B 2:17 bewerode] bewerede B hira] heora B 2:18 hig] hi B hira] heora B raþur] hraþor B 2:19 andswaredon hig] andswarodon hi B þara] þæra B hlod] ure add. B 2:20 Hwar] hwær B forleton] forlete B 2:22 cende] him add. B utacimen] utacymen B ælþeodig] elðeodig B 2:23 Israela] israhela B clypodon] clypode L, clypedon B hira] heora B 2:24 geomrungæ] geomrunge B þara] þa B 2:25 Israhela] Israela B hig] hi B 3:1 nama] B, naman L Oreb nemþ] oreph nemneþ B

92   EXODUS

bremelþyrnan, and he geseah þæt seo þyrne barn and næs forburnen. ³þa cwæð Moises: 'Ic ga and geseo þas miclan gesihþe, hwi þeos
f. 39ᵛ þyrne ne si forbærned.' ⁴ Soþlice þa Drihten geseah þæt he | ferde to geseonne, he clypode hine of midre þære bremelþyrnan and cwæþ: 'Moises, Moises.' And he andswarode and cwæð: 'Her ic eom.' ⁵ And he cwæð: 'Ne genealæce þu hider. Do þin gescy of þinum fotum. Soþlice seo stow þe þu on stynst ys halig eorðe.' ⁶ And he cwæð: 'Ic eom þines fæder Abrahames God and Isaaces God and Iacobes God.' Moises hydde his nebb; he ne dorste beseon ongen God. ⁷ Ða cwæð God to him: 'Ic geseah mines folces geswencednysse on Egipta lande and ic gehirde hira clypunge for þære heardnysse þe þa weorc bewiton, ⁸ and ic wiste hira sar and ic astah nyþer, þæt ic hig alysde of Egipta handum and þæt ic hig ut alædde of þam lande to godum lande and widgillum, on þæt land þe þe flewð meolece and hunie, to þam stow[um] þær Chananeus ys, and Etheus, Amoreus and Pherezeus, Eueus and Gebuseus. ⁹ Witodlice Israela bearna clypung com to me and ic geseah hira geswencednysse þe hig fram Egipton þolodon. ¹⁰ Ac cum, ic sende þe to Pharaone, þæt þu ut alæde min folc, Israela bearn, of Egipta lande.' ¹¹ And þa cwæð Moises to Gode: 'Hwæt eom ic þæt ic ga to Pharaone and ut alæd[e] Israela bearn of Egipta lande?' ¹² þa cwæð he to him: 'Ic beo mid þe. þæt þu hæfst to tacne þæt ic þe sende: þonne þu ut alætst min folc of Egipta lande, þu offrast Gode uppan þisse dune.' ¹³ þa cwæð Moises to him: 'Nu ic ga to Israela bearnum and secge him, "Eower fædera God me sende to eow". Gif hig cweþaþ to me, "Hwæt ys hys
f. 40ʳ nama?", hwæt | secge ic him?' ¹⁴ þa cwæð God to Moise: 'Ic eom se þe eom.' Cwæð he: 'Sege þus Israela bearnum: "Se þe ys me sende to eow."' ¹⁵ And eft cwæð God to Moise. 'Sege þas þing Israela bearnum: "Drihten ura fædera God, Abrahames God and Isaaces [God] and Iacobes God, me sende to eow. þæt ys min nama on ecnisse and þæt ys min gemynd on cneoresse and on cneoresse." ¹⁶ Ga and gegadera Israela bearna ealdras and cweþ to him, "Drihten

3:2 forburnen] forburnan B   3:3 þas] þa B   3:4 þa] om. B   hine] om. B   midre] middre B   andswarode] andwyrde B   3:5 stynst] stentst B   3:6 he¹] om. B   Abrahames God and Isaaces] om. B   ongen] ongean B   3:7 hira clypunge] heora cleopunge B   bewiton] bewitan B   3:8 hira] heora B   hig¹] hy B   hig²] hy B   meolece] meolce B   stowum] stowe L, swotum B   Gebuseus] iebuseus B   3:9 Israela] ysrahela B   me] gode B   hira] heora B   hig] hy B   þolodon] þoledon B   3:10 Pharaone] faraone B   ut] om. B   Israela] israhela B   3:11 alæde] alædynde L, alædende B   Israela] israhela B   3:13 Israela] israhela B   secge] ic secge B   Eower] eowera B   hig] hi B   3:14 Israela] israhela B   3:15 Israela] israhela B   ura] ure B   God⁴] om. L   and þæt] þæt B   cneoresse²] cneresse B   3:16 ealdras] ealdros B

eowre fædera God me ætywde, Abrahames God and Isaaces God and Iacobes God, þus cweþende: Cumende ic com to eow and ic geseah ealle þa þing þe eow belumpon on Egipta lande." [17] And ic cwæð þæt ic eow ut alæde of Egipta geswencednysse on þæt land þe Chananeus on ys, and Etheus, Amoreus and Pherezeus, Eueus and Iebuseus, on þam lande fleowð meoloc and hunig, [18] and hig gehiraþ þine stemne. Þu gæst inn, and þa yldestan of Israela folce, to Egipta cynge and cwyst to him, "Ebrea God us clypode and het us faran þreora daga færeld þurh þæt westen, þæt we offrion urum Drihtne Gode". [19] Ac ic wat þæt Egipta cyng eow ne forlæt þæt ge faron, buton þurh strange hand. [20] Soþlice ic astrecce mine hand and slea Egipta land on eallum minum wundrum þe ic wirce on heora lande; æfter þison, he eow forlæt. [21] And ic sylle þison folce gife beforan þam Egiptiscean folce, and þonne git ut faraþ, ne fare ge idelhende, [22] ac þa Israeliscan wif biddaþ æt þam Egiptiscean wifon, æt hira nehgeburum and æt hira husbondum, sylfrene | fatu and gyldene, and reaf, and gedoð þa on eowre suna and eowre dohtra, and reafiaþ Egipte.' f. 40ᵛ

[4:1] Ða andswarude Moises and cwæð: 'Hig ne gelyfaþ me, ne mine stemne ne gehiraþ, ac hig secgaþ, "ne ætywde þe God".' [2] Witodlice he cwæð to him: 'Hwæt ys þæt þu hæfst on þinre handa?' Ða andswarode he and cwæð: 'Hit ys gird.' [3] And Drihten cwæð: 'Wurp hig on þa eorðan.' And he wearp, and heo wæs gewend to næddran, swa þæt Moises fleah. [4] And Drihten cwæð: 'Astrece þine hand and nym hyre steort.' And he astrehte his hand and nam hig, and heo wæs gewend eft to girde. [5] 'Þæt hig gelyfon þæt Drihten þinra fædera God þe ætywde, Abrahames God and Isaaces God and Iacobes God.' [6] And Drihten cwæð: 'Do þine hand on þinne bosum.' Ða he hig dyde on his bosum, þa brohte he hig forð hreofle, swa hwit swa snaw. [7] Ða cwæð he: 'Teoh eft þine hand on þinne bosum.' Þa teah he hig ongean and brohte hi eft ut, and heo wæs gelic þam oþrum flæsce. [8] And he cwæð: 'Gif hig ne gelyfað þe, ne ne gehiraþ þæs æran tacnes spræce, hig gelyfaþ þam worde þæs æfterfiliendan tacnes. [9] Witodlice

3:16 ætywde] æteowde B   com] eom B   þing] þingc B   3:17 Iebuseus] ıebusseus B   fleowð meoloc] flewð meolc B   3:18 hig] hi B   Israela] israhela B   cynge] cyninge B   offrion] offrian B   3:19 cyng] cyngc B   3:20 slea] on add. B (later eras.)   þison] þysum B   3:21 Egiptiscean] egyptyscan   idelhende] ydelhynde B   3:22 Israeliscan] israhelyscan B   Egiptiscean wifon] egyptyscan wifum B   hira nehgeburum] heora neahgeburum B   hira²] heora B   and eowre] and on eowræ B   4:1 andswarude] andswarode B   Hig¹] hi B   hig²] hi B   ætywde] æteowde B   4:3 hig] hy B   4:5 hig] hy B   4:6 hig¹] hi B   hig²] hi B   hreofle] hreofe B   4:7 bosum] bosm B   4:8 hig¹] hy B   æran] ærran B   hig²] hi B   æfterfiliendan] æfterfyligendan B

gif hi þison twam tacnum ne gelyfað, ne ne gehyraþ þine stefne, nym
þæt wæter on þam flode and geot hit uppan drie eorþan and swa
hwæt swa þu hlætst of þam flode, hit biþ geworden to blode.' [10] þa
cwæð Moises: 'Drihten, þu wast næs ic næfre gespræce and syþþan
þu spræce to þinum þeowe ic hæfde þe lætran tungan.' [11] þa cwæð
Drihten to him: 'Hwa geworhte mannes muð oþþe hwa geworhte
f. 41[r] dumne oþþe deaf|ne, and blinde oþþe geseondne? Hu næs ic hyt?
[12] Far nu, and ic beo on þinu[m] muþe and lære þe hwæt þu sprecan
scealt.' [13] And he cwæð: 'Ic bidde þe, Drihten, send þone þe þu to
sendenne eart.' [14] þa wæs Drihten yrre wið Moises and cwæð: 'Aaron
þin broþur, deacon, he hæfþ gode spræce. Nu he cymð ongen þe and
he geblissaþ on his heortan, þonne he þe gesihþ. [15] Sprec to him and
sete min word on his muð, and ic beo on þinum muþe and on his
muþe, þæt ic ætywe inc hwæt git don sceolon. [16] He spricð for þe to
þam folce and biþ þin muþ. þu gewissast him þa þing þe Gode
belimpað. [17] Nym witodlice þas girde on þine hand mid þære þu
scealt wundru and tacnu wircan.'

[4:18] þa for Moises and gecirde to his mæge, þam wæs Iethro nama,
and cwæð to him: 'Ic wille faran to minum magon on Egipta land,
þæt ic geseo hwæþer hi þa git libbon. And Iethro cwæð: 'Ga on
sybbe.' [19] Witodlice Drihten cwæð to Moise on Madian: 'Far on
Egipta land. Soþlice ealle þa synd deade, þe þe ofslean woldon.'
[20] Moises nam his wif and his cild and sette hig uppan assan and for
on Egipta land and bær Godes girde on his handa. [21] And Drihten
cwæð to him, þa he for on Egipta land: 'Wite þu georne þæt þu do
ealle þa tacn þe ic þe bebead beforan Faraone. Ic ahyrde Pharaones
heortan, þæt he nele þin word gehiran ne min folc forlætan. [22] þonne
cweþ þu to him, "Drihten het þe secgan þas þing: Israel ys min
frumcenneda sunu. [23] Ic cweþe, forlæt minne sunu, þæt he þeowie
f. 41[v] me, and þu noldest hyne forlætan. Witodlice ic ofslea | þinne
frumcennedan sunu".' [27] Drihten cwæð to Aarone: 'Ga ongean
Moises on þæt westen.' And he for ongean hine to Godes dune and
cyste hine, [28] and Moises rehte Aarone ealle Drihtnes word, þe he hine
fore sende, and þa tacn þe he him bebead. [29] And hig forun ætgædere
and gegaderodon ealle þa yldestan of Israela mægþe, [30] and Aaron spræc

4:9 stefne] stemne B   drie] drige B   4:11 dumne] dumbne B   blinde] blindne B
geseondne] geseonde B   4:13 sendenne] sendene B   4:14 broþur deacon] broþor
diacon B   ongen] ongean B   4:15 Sprec] spec B   and on his muþe] om. B   ætywe] B,
ætywde L   sceolon] scylon B   4:17 tacnu] tacna B   4:18 magon] magum B   þa²]
om. B   4:20 hig] hi B   4:22 Israel] israhel B   4:23 þeowie] ðeowige B
4:29 hig forun] hi foron B   Israela] israhela B   4:30 spræc] spæc B

ealle þa word þe God spræc to Moise and worhte tacn beforan eallum þam folce. ³¹ And þæt folc gelyfde and hig gehirdon þæt Drihten gemiltsode Israela mægþa and þæt he geseah hira geswencednysse, and hig gebædon hig to Gode nywel astrehte on eorðan.

⁵:¹ Æfter þison Moises and Aaron eodon inn and cwædon to Pharaone: 'Ebrea God het secgan þe þas þing: "Forlæt min folc þæt hit mæge offrian me on þam westene." ' ² And he andswarode and cwæð: 'Hwæt ys se Drihten þæt ic hym hiran scile and Israela folc forlætan? Ne cann ic Drihten, ne ic nelle forlætan Israela folc.' ³ þa cwædon hig: 'Ebrea God us bebead þæt we foron þreora daga færeld on þæt westen, þæt we offrion urum Drihtne Gode, þæt us cwealm on ne becume, ne swurdes ecg.' ⁴ Ða cwæð Pharao, Egipta cyng, to Moise and to Aarone: 'Hwi mirrað git þis folc fram heora weorcum? Gaþ to eowrum weorcum.' ⁵ And Pharao cwæð to his folce: 'Ge geseoþ þæt þis Ebreisce folc ys micel and wixst swiþe, and swiþor wyle, gif we him reste syllaþ fram heora weorcum.' ⁶ Witodlice Pharao bebead on þam dæge þam weorcgerefum and þæs folces | þenum, þus cweþende: ⁷ 'Ne sylle ge lengnan cef þis f.42ʳ Ebreiscan folce to tigelgeweorce, swa ge ær didon, ac gan and gadrion him sylfe þæt healm. ⁸ And asettaþ him þæt ilce tigolgeweorc þe hig ær worhton, ne ge nan þing ne gewanion. Soþlice hig synd æmtige and for þam hig hrymað and cweþaþ, "uton faran and offrian urum Gode". ⁹ Beon hig gehinede and gefyllon þa weorc, þæt hig ne hlyston leasum wordum.' ¹⁰ Witodlice þa weorcgerefan and þa þenas eodon ut and cwædon to þam folce: 'Pharao byt þæt eow mann ne sylle leng nan cef,¹¹ ac gaþ and gadriaþ swa hwar swa ge hit findan magon, and nan ðing ne byþ gewanod of eowrum geweorce.' ¹² And þæt folc wæs todrifen ofer eall Egipta land, cef to gadrienne. ¹³ Witodlice þa weorcgerefan stodon mid him and cwædon: 'Gefyllað eower geweorc dæghwamlice swa ge ær didon, þa eow man cef sealde.' ¹⁴ And Pharaones þenas swungon þa þe bewiston Israela folces weorc and þus cwædon: 'Hwi ne gefylle ge þara tigelena gemet

4:31 hig¹] hi B   Israela mægþa] israhela mægþe B   hira] heora B   hig²] hi B   hig³] hi B   5:1 inn] in B   5:2 andswarode] andwyrde B   scile] scule B   Israela¹] israhela B   cann] can B   Israela²] israhela B   5:3 hig] hi B   offrion] offrian B   5:4 Pharao] farao B   5:5 Pharao] farao B   wixst] wyxt B   him] heom B   5:7 cef] ceaf B   tigelgeweorce] tigolgeweorce B   swa] s`w´a B   gadrion] gaderian B   sylfe] sylf B   þæt] om. B   5:8 ilce] illce B   hig¹] hi B   hig²] hi B   hig³] hy B   5:9 hig¹] hi B   hig²] hi B   5:10 eow mann] man eow B   cef] ceaf B   5:11 gadriaþ] gaderiaþ B   5:12 cef] ceaf B   gadrienne] gaderienne B   5:13 him] heom B   eower geweorc] eowwer weorc B   eow man cef] man eow ceaf B   5:14 Pharaones] faraones B   Israela] israhela B   þara] þæra B

96   EXODUS

swa ge ær dydon, ne girstandæg ne todæg?' ⁱ⁵þa comun Israhela folces prafostas and clypodon to Pharaone and þus cwædon: 'Hwi dest þu þus wið þine þeowas? ¹⁶Us man ne sylþ nan cef and byt us þæt ilce tigulgeweorc. Nu we þine þeowas synd beswungene and unrihtlice hit is gedon wið þin folc.' ¹⁷þa cwæð he: 'Ge synd æmtige and idele and for þam gebiddaþ, "lætaþ us faran and offrian urum Gode". ¹⁸Gaþ witodlice and wircað. Ne sylþ eow nan man cef and ge
f. 42ᵛ sceolon | agifan þæt ilce tigolgetel þe ge ær gewuna wæron.' ¹⁹And Israhela folces prafostas gesawon þæt hig wæron geswencte, for þam þe him wæs gesæd þæt him nære nan þing þæs tigolgeweorces forgifen, buton on þam ylcan gemete þe hig ær gewuna wæron.

⁵:²⁰þa urnon þa Israheliscan ongen Moises and Aaron, þa hig ut eodon fram Pharaone, ²¹and cwædon to him: 'Geseo Drihten and deme hwæt git us gelæred habbað. Ge habbaþ us gedon laþe Pharaone and eallum his folce and gemacod þæt hig wyllað us mid hyra swurdum ofslean.' ²²Đa cwæð Moises to Drihtne: 'Drihten, hwi swencst þu þis folc? Hwi sentst þu me to Pharaone, ²³þæt ic sprece on þinum naman? He swencð þin folc and þu hit nelt alysan.' ⁶:¹Đa cwæð Drihten to Moise: 'þu scealt geseon þa þing þe ic don wylle Pharaone. Soþlice þurh strange miht he hi sceal forlætan and þurh menige hand he hig ut forlæt of his lande.' ²Đa cwæð Drihten to Moise: 'Ic eom Drihten, ³þe ætyde Abrahame and Isace and Iacobe, ælmihtig God, and min nama ys Adonai' (þæt ys 'wundorlic' on ure geþeode), ⁴'and ic behet minne truwan, þæt ic sealde him Chanaan land, þe hig on wracnodon and utancymene wæron. ⁵Ic gehyrde Israhela bearna geomrunga and þa yrmða þe þa Egiptis[ce]an him dydon, and ic gemunde minra treowða þe ic Abrahame behet. ⁶Sege for þam Israhela bearnum, "Ic eom Drihten þe eow ut alæde of Egipta cwearterne and of hira þeowete, and alyse on hean |
f. 43ʳ earme and on mihtigum dome, ⁷and genyme eow me to folce and beo eower God, and ge witon þæt ic eom eower God þe eow ut alæde of Egipta cwearterne ⁸and in gelæde on þæt land þe ic Abrahame and

5:14 girstandæg] gyrsandæg B   5:15 comun] comon B   prafostas] prafastas B
dest þu] destu B   5:16 sylþ] sylleð B   cef] ceaf B   tigulgeweorc] tygelgeweorc B
5:18 wircað] wyrceað B   nan man cef] man nan ceaf B   tigolgetel] tigelgetæl B
5:19 prafostas] prafastas B   hig¹] hy B   hig²] hi B   5:20 ongen] ongean B
Pharaone] faraone B   5:21 Geseo] gescoh B   hig] hy B   hyra] heora B
5:22 swencst þu] swincð B   6:1 þing] þingc B   þurh] þurþ B   hig] hi B
6:3 ætyde] æteowde B   Isace] isaace B   and³] om. B   6:4 hig] hi B   utancymene]
utoncymene B   6:5 Egiptiscean] B, egiptisan L   Abrahame] abrame B
6:6 Israhela] Israela B   alæde] alædde B   hira] heora B   alyse] alysde B   earme]
hearme B   6:7 me] om. B   eower¹] eowwer B   God²] godd B

Isace and Iacobe behet, þæt ic sylle eow to agenne, ic Drihten, eower God".' ⁹Moises sæde ealle þas þing Israhela bearnum; þa ne gelyfdon hig him for hira yrmþum and for þam heardum weorcum þe him on sæt. ¹⁰þa cwæð Drihten to Moise: ¹¹'Ga into Pharaone, Egipta cynincge, and sege him þæt he læte faran Israhela bearn of Egipta lande.' ¹²Moises andswarode beforan Drihtne and cwæð: 'Nu Israhela bearn me ne gelyfað, ne ne gehiraþ. Hwanon wyle Faraon me gelyfan, and ic eom ungetinge on spræce?'
⁶:¹⁴⁻¹⁹Her telþ ymbe Moises cynren and Aarones. Hig wæron geboren of Leuies mægþe. ²⁰Amram hatte hira fæder. He nam wif, seo hatte Iochabeth. Heo wæs his fæderan dohtor and heo gebær twegen suna, Moises and Aaron. And Amram lyfode hundteontig wintra and seofon and þritig wintra. ²⁶þis ys se Moises and Aaron þam God bebead þæt hig ut alæddon Israhela folc of Egipta lande. ²⁷Hig spræcon to Pharaone Egipta cynge þæt he lete faran Israhela folc of Egipta lande. ²⁸On dæg, þa God spræc to Moise on Egipta lande, ²⁹he cwæð to him: 'Ic eom Drihten. Sprec to Pharaone, Egipta cynge, ealle þing þe ic to þe sprece.' ³⁰And Moises cwæð to Drihtne: 'Ic eom unhrædspræce; hu gelyfð Pharao me?' | ⁷:¹And Drihten f. 43ᵛ cwæð to Moise: 'Nu ic gesette þe Pharaone to Gode and Aaron þin broþor byð þin witega. ²þu spricst ealle þa þing þe ic þe bebeode, and he spricð to Faraone þæt he forlæte Israhela folc of his lande, ³and ic ahyrde his heortan þæt he hig nele forlætan, and ic gemænigfealde mine tacnu. and mine forebeacnu on Egipta lande. ⁴And he eow ne gehirð and ic asende mine hand ofer Egipta land and ut alæde minne here and min folc, Israhela bearn, of Egipta lande þurh þa mæstan wundru. ⁵And þa Egiptiscean witon þæt ic eom Drihten, þe ic astrecce mine hand ofer Egipta land and ut alæde Israhela bearn of hira midlene.' ⁶Witodlice Moises and Aaron dydon eall swa Drihten him bebead.
⁷:⁷Soþlice Moises wæs hundeahtatigwintre and Aaron þreo and hundeahtatigwintre þa hig spræcon to Pharaone. ⁸And Drihten

6:8 Isace] isaace B   6:9 hig] hi B   hira] heora B   heardum] heardan B
6:11 cynincge] cynge B   6:12 Faraon] pharaon B   6:14–19 ymbe] embe B
cynren] cynryn B   Hig] hy B   6:20 hira] heora B   Iochabeth] iochabetþ B   lyfode
hundteontig] leofode hundteonti B   6:26 þam] þe B   hig] hi B   6:27 Hig spræcon]
hi spæcon B   cynge] cyninge B   6:29 Sprec] spec B   cynge] cyninge B   ealle] ða *add.*
B   sprece] spece B   6:30 unhrædspræce] unhrædspæce B   Pharao] farao B
7:2 spricst] sprecst B   Faraone] pharaone B   7:3 hig] hy B   gemænigfealde]
gemænifealde B   7:5 Egiptiscean witon] egyptyscan witan B   astrecce] strecce B
hira] heora B   7:6 eall] eal B   7:7 Soþlice] *3-line red initial cap.* L   hig spræcon] hy
spæcon B

EXODUS

cwæð to Moise and to Aarone: [9] 'þonne Pharao inc gesichþ, þonne cwið he to inc, "Wyrcaþ sum tacn beforan me, þæt ic mæge eow gelyfan". Þonne cweþ þu to Aarone þinum breþer, "Nym þine girde and weorp hig beforan Pharaone and heo wyrð to næddran".' [10] Witodlice þa Moises and Aaron eodun to Pharaone, þa dydon hig swa Drihten him bebead and Aaron nam his gyrde and wearp beforan Pharaone and his þegnum, and heo wearð to næddran. [11] Soþlice Pharaon gegaderude ealle þa dricræftegustan men and hig worhton oþer swilc þing þurh hira drycræft | and þurh Egiptisce galdru. [12] And hig wurpon ealle hira girda nyþer and hi wurdon to næddrum, ac Aarones gird forswealh ealle heora girda. [13] Þa gebealh Pharao hyne and ne let hig faran na, swa Drihten him bebead. [14] Soðlice Drihten cwæð to Moise: 'Pharaones heorte ys gehefegod; nele he min folc forlætan. [15] Ga to him tomorgen, þonne he ut gæþ to þam wætere, and stand ongean hine uppan þæs wætres ofre, and nym þe on hand þa girde þe to næddran gewearð [16] and cweþ to him: 'Ebrea God me sende to þe and cwæð, "Forlæt min folc þæt hit offrie me on þam westene", and þu hit noldest git gehiran. [17] Witodlice Drihten cwið þas þing, "Be þison þu wast þæt ic eom Drihten: nu ic slea mid þisse girde þe ys on minre handan þises flodes wæter and hyt byþ geworden to blode [18] and þa fixas þe synd on þam flode acwelað and þa wæteru forrotiað, and þa Egiptiscan beoþ geswencede, þe þæs flodes wæter drincað".' [19] Witodlice Drihten cwæð to Moise: 'Sege Aarone, "Aþene þine hand ofer ealle Egipta wætro and flodas, ge ofer burnan ge ofer meras and ofer ealle wæterpyttas, þæt hig sin gewend to blode, and sig blod ofer eall Egipta land, ge on treowenum fatum ge on stænenum".' [20] Soðlice Moises and Aaron dydon swa Drihten him bebead, and he hof upp his girde and sloh þæt wæter beforan Faraone and his þegnum, and hit wearþ to blode. [21] And þa fixas þe wæron on þam wætere wurdon deade | and þæt wæter forrotode and þa Egiptiscan ne mihton drincan þæt wæter, for þam hira wætero wæron geworden

---

7:9 gesichþ] gesyhð B   cwið] cweð B   Wyrcaþ] wyrceað B   weorp hig] wurp hi B
7:10 Moises] moyse B   eodun] eodon B   Pharaone] faraone B   hig] hy B
7:11 Pharaon gegaderude] pharao gegadorode B   hig] hy B   hira] heora B   Egiptisce] egyptyscan B   7:12 hig] hy B   hira] heora B   7:13 hig] hi B   7:15 þonne] þone B   uppan] uppon B   wætres] wæteres B   7:16 offrie] offrige B   gehiran] forlætan B
7:17 þisse] þyssere B   handan] handa B   7:19 wætro] wæteru B   hig sin] hi synd B   sig] sy B   eall] eal B   treowenum] trywenum B   7:20 Soðlice] *3-line red initial cap.* L   Drihten him] him drihten   upp] up B   Faraone] pharaone B   wearþ] weað B
7:21 forrotode] forrotede B   hira wætero] heora wætera B

to blode. ²² And Pharaones heorte wæs ahyrd and nolde hig gehiran, swa Drihtæn him bebead, ²³ ac awende hine fram him and eode into his botle and nolde nan þing Godes word underfon on his heortan. ²⁴ And witodlice ealle þa Egiptiscan dulfon wæterpyttas neah þam flode and woldon drincan, ac hi ne mihton drincan ²⁵ seofon dagum of þam wætere, siþþan God het þæt wæter to blode gewurþan.

⁸:¹ And Drihten cwæð to Moise: 'Ga into Pharaone and cweþ to him, "Drihten þe het secgan þas þing: Forlæt min folc þæt hit offrie me. ² Soþlice, gif þu hit nelt forlætan, ic sende froxas ofer ealle þine landgemæro, ³ and þæt flod awylþ eall froxum and hi astigaþ and gaþ into þinum huse and to þinum bedde and to þinum [bed]clyfan and to þinra þegna husum and on þin folc and on þine ofnas and on þine metelafa, ⁴ and to þe and to þinum folce and into eallum þinum þeowum gað þa froxas."' ⁵ And Drihten cwæð to Moise: 'Cweð to Aarone, "Hefe upp þine hand ofer eall þæt flod and ofer burna and ofer moras, and alæd upp þa froxas ofer eall Egipta land".' ⁶ And Aaron hof upp his hand ofer Egipta wætro and þa froxas astigon upp ofer eall Egipta land. ⁸ Witodlice Pharao clipode Moise and Aaron and cwæþ to him: 'Biddað eowerne Drihten þæt he adrife ealle þas froxas fram me and fram minum folc, and ic forlæte þæt Israhelisce folc, | þæt hit offrie Gode.' ⁹ Þa cwæð Moises to Pharaone: 'Gesette f. 45ʳ me anne andagan, hwænne þu wylle þæt ic for þe gebidde and for þin folc, þæt þa froxas beo adrifene fram þe and fram þinum þegnum and þæt hig faran on wætru.' ¹⁰ Þa andswarude Pharao and cwæð: 'Nu tomorgen.' Þa cwæð Moises: 'Ic do neah þam þe þu cwæde, þæt þu wite þæt nys nan oþer swilc God swilce ure God, ¹¹ and þa froxas faraþ fram þe and fram þinum þegnum.' ¹² Ða eode Moises and Aaron ut fram Pharaone and Moises clypode to Drihtne for þam wordum þe he spræc beforan Faraone be þam froxum. ¹³ And Drihten dyde eall swa Moises hine bæd and þa froxas wurdon deade on hira husum and on hira æcrum.

⁸:¹⁵ Þa Farao geseah þæt he reste hæfde, he ahyrde his heortan and ne let hig faran swa Drihten him bebead. ¹⁶ And Drihten cwæð to

---

7:22 hig] hy B   Drihtæn] drihten B   7:24 Egiptiscan] egyptyscean B   drincan²] 'drincan' B   8:2 landgemæro] landgemæru B   8:3 huse] husum B   bedclyfan] hordclyfan LB   8:4 þa] þas B   8:5 upp¹] up B   eall¹] eal B   upp²] up B
8:6 hof upp] ahof up B   ofer¹] eal add. B   wætro] wæteru B   upp²] up B   eall] eal B
8:8 offrie] offrige B   8:9 Gesette] gesete B   anne] om. B   þa] þas B   beo] beon B
þegnum] folce B   and³] om. B   hig] hi B   wætru] wæteru B   8:10 andswarude] andswarode B   8:12 Faraone] pharaone B   8:13 eall] eal B   hine] om. B   hira¹] heora B   hira æcrum] heora æcerum B   8:15 hig] hi B

Moise: 'Cweþ to Aarone, "ahefe þine girde and sleh on eorðan, þæt gnættas gewurþon ofer eall Egipta land".' [17] And Aaron ahefde upp his hand and sloh mid þære girde on þa eorðan and gnættas wæron gewordene on mannum and on yrfe, and eall þære eorðan dust wæs geworden to gnættum ofer eall Egipta land. [19] þa cwædon þa dryas to Pharaone: 'þis ys Godes miht.' And his heorte wearþ ahyrd and he hig ne gehirde, swa Drihten bebead. [20] And Drihten cwæð to Moise: 'Aris on dægred and stand beforan Pharaone. Soðlice he gæð ut to þam wætrum. þonne cwyst þu to him, "Drihten cwið þas þing:

f. 45ᵛ Forlæt min folc þæt hit offrie me, [21] and gif þu hit ne | forlætst, witodlice ic sende on þe and on þin folc and on þine hus eall fleogena cynn, and eall Egipta land bið gefylled mid mislicum fleogena cynne, [22] and ic wirce þonne on dæg micle wundra on Gesen lande, þær min folc ys, þæt þær ne beoð nane fleogan, þæt þu wite þæt ic eom Drihten, [23] and ic sette dal betwux þin folc and min folc: tomorgen biþ þæt tacn".' [24] And Drihten dyde swa, and þæt mæste fleogena cynn comon on Faraones hofun and on eall Egipta land, and eorðe wæs amyrred þurh þa fleogan. [25] Pharao clypode Moises and Aaron and cwæð to him: 'Gaþ and offriað eowrum Gode on þison lande.' [26] And Moises cwæð: 'Hit ne mæg swa beon. Sceolon we offrian urum Drihtne þa þing þe Egiptisce onscuniað to offrianne? Gif we cwellað beforan Egiptum þa þing þe hig wurðiaþ, hi us oftorfiað mid stanum. [27] þreora daga færeld we sceolon faran on þæt westen and offrian urum Drihtene swa he us bebead.' [28] Ða cwæð Pharao: 'Ic eow forlæte þæt ge offrian Drihtne eowrum Gode on westene and þeahhwæðere, ne fare ge to feorr. Gebiddað for me.' [29] And Moises cwæð, þa he ut eode: 'For þe ic gebidde and þeos fleoge færð fram þe and fram þinum folce nu tomorgen. þeahhwæþre ne leoh þu leng, þæt þu ne forlæte þæt folc þæt hit offrie Gode lac.' [30] Ða Moises ut eode fram Pharaone, he hyne gebæd to Drihtne. [31] And Drihten dyde

f. 46ʳ swa he hyne bæd and adraf þa fleogan fram Pharaone | and fram his

8:16 sleh] sleah B   eall] eal B   8:17 upp] up B   yrfe] orfe B   eall þære] eal þæræ B   8:19 hig] hi B   Drihten] him *add.* B   8:20 beforan] bephoran B   wætrum] wæterum B   cwyst] cwest B   offrie] offrige B   8:21 eall¹] ealle B   cynn] full B   mislicum] mistlicum B   8:22 micle] micele B   Gesen] gessen B   þær²] ðar B   8:23 betwux] betwyx B   tomorgen] tomerigen B   8:24 cynn] cyn B   hofun] hofon B   8:25 clypode] cleopode B   8:26 offrian] ofrian B   Egiptisce] egipte B   offrianne] offrian`n´e B   hig] hi B   8:27 offrian] ofrian B   Drihtene] drihtne B   bebead] *followed by decorative colon* L   8:28 Ða] *3-line red initial cap.* L   Pharao] farao B   offrian] ofrian B   feorr] feor B   8:29 tomorgen] tomergen and B   þeahhwæþre] þeahhwæðere B   offrie] offrige B   lac] *om.* B   8:30 Pharaone] faraone B   8:31 Pharaone] faraone B

folce, þæt þær ne wearð nan to lafe. ³² Þa wearð Faraones heorte gehefegod, swa þæt he witodlice æt þam cirre nolde þæt folc forlætan.

⁹:¹ Soþlice Drihten cwæð to Moise: 'Ga in to Faraone and cweð to him: 'Drihten, Ebrea God, segð þas þing, "Forlæt min folc, þæt hit offrie me on westene. ² Gif þu þæt git don nelt and þæt folc ofhæfst, ³ witodlice min hand byð ofer þine æceras and ofslihþ þine hors and þine assan and olfendas and oxan and scep mid hefegum cwealme, ⁴ and Drihten wircð wundor betwux Israhela æhtum and Egipta æhtum, þæt nan þing ne forwyrð of þam þingum þe belimpað to Israhela bearnum."' ⁵ And Drihten gesette andagan and cwæð: 'Nu tomorgen deþ Drihten þas þing on eorðan.' ⁶ Witodlice Drihten dyde þas þing. On oþrum dæge wurdon ealle Egipta nytenu deade. Soðlice Israhela bearna nyten[a] ne forwearð nan þing. ⁷ And Pharao sende and het hit sceawian; þa næs þær nan þing dead of þam þe Israhela folc ahton. þa wearð Faraones heorte gehefegod, þæt he ne forlet þæt folc. ⁸ And Drihten cwæð to Moise and to Aarone: 'Nymað handfulle axan of þam ofene and wurpe Moises þa axan upp beforan Pharaone, ⁹ þæt dust gewyrð ofer eall Egipta lande. Soðlice on mannum and on nytenum beoð wunda and swellende blæddran ofer eall Egipta land.' ¹⁰ And hi namun þa axan beforan Pharaone | and Moises wearp þa hi   f. 46ᵛ
upp and swellende blæddran and wunda wurdon on ðam mannum and on þam nytenum, ¹¹ swa þæt þa dryas ne mihton standan beforan Moise for þam wundum þe him on wæron and on eallum Egipta lande. ¹² And Drihten ahyrde Pharaones heortan, þæt he hig ne gehirde, swa Drihten bebead Moise.

⁹:¹³ Witodlice Drihten cwæð to Moise: 'Aris tomorgen and stand beforan Faraone and cweþ to him, "Drihten, Ebrea God, cwið þas þing: Forlæt myn folc þæt hit offrie me, ¹⁴ for þam æt þison cirre ic sende eall min wito ofer þe and ofer þin folc, þæt þu wite þæt ne si min gelica on ealre eorðan. ¹⁵ Nu ic ahebbe up mine hand and ic ofslea þe and þin folc mid cwealme, and þu forwyrst. ¹⁶ For þam ic þe gesette, þæt ic mine strengþe on þe gecyðe and þæt min nama sig

9:1 Soþlice] *3-line green initial cap.* L   Faraone] pharaone B   offrie] ofrie B
9:2 þæt git don nelt] ðæt onscunast B   ofhæfst] hæfst B   9:3 scep] sceap B   9:4 of] on B   belimpað] belympð B   to] 'to' B   9:5 tomorgen] tomerigen B   9:6 nytena] nytenu LB   9:7 Pharao] farao B   þær] þar B   Faraones] pharaones B   forlet] forlæt B
9:8 ofene] ofne B   upp] up B   Pharaone] faraone B   9:9 eall¹] eal B   lande] land B
eall²] eal B   9:10 namun] namon B   Pharaone] faraone B   þa²] *om.* B   swellende blæddran] swellendae blædran B   9:13 Witodlice] *5-line red initial cap.* L   tomergen] tomerigen B   Faraone] pharaone B   offrie] offrige B   9:14 þison] þysum B   eall] eal B
ofer²] eal *add.* B   9:16 þe¹] *om.* B   strengþe] strengðo B   sig] si B

gecyþed ofer ealle eorðan. [17] Gyt þu hæfst min folc and nelt hyt forlætan. [18] Witodlice nu tomorgen on þisse ylcan tide ic sende micelne hagol, swilce on Egipta lande næs fram þam dæge þe hit gestaðelod wæs oþ þas dagas. [19] Soðlice send nu rihte and gegadera ealle þine nytenu and ealle þine þing þe þu on æcere hæfst. Witodlice men and nytenu sweltað and ealle þa þing þe ute beoð, and se hagol him onufan fealð." ' [20] Se þe Drihtnes word ondred of Faraones folce, se fleah mid his mannum and nytenum into husum, [21] and se þe Drihtnes word forgimde, he forlet his men and his ny|tenu ute. [22] And Drihten cwæð to Moise: 'Ahefe up þine hand, þæt hagol gewurðe ofer eall Egipta land [and ofer menn and ofer nytenu and ofer eall Egypta land].' [23] And Moises aðenod[e] his girde upp and Drihten sende þunorrada and hagul and byrnende ligetta ofer eall Egipta land, and Drihten let rinan [24] hagol wið fyr gemenged, and hig ferdon ætgædere, and swa mycel he wæs swa næfre ær ne ætywde on eallum Egipta lande syððan seo þeod gesceapen wæs. [25] And se hagol sloh on eallum Egipta lande ealle þa þing þe ute wæron, ægðer ge men ge nytenu, and eall Egipta gærs se hagol fordyde and ælc treow þe wæs on þam rice he tobræc. [26] And on Gesen lande, þar Israhela bearn on wæron, ne com nan dæl þæs hagoles. [27] Þa sende Farao to Moise and to Aarone and cwæð to him: 'Ic winne ongen Drihten. Ic wat þæt ic and min folc synd arlease. [28] Biddað Drihten þæt his þunorrada and þes hagol geswicon and ic wille eow forlætan and ge ne þurfon her leng wunian.' [29] Moises cwæð: 'Þonne ic ga ut of þisse birig, ic ahebbe up mine hand to Drihtne and þa þunorrada and se hagol geswicað, þæt þu wite þæt eorðe ys Drihtnes. [30] Ic wat soþlice þæt þu and þin folc nu git eow Drihten ne ondrædað.' [31] Witodlice eall hira flex and hira beras wæron fordone, for þam þe hig wæron on þa tid grene. [33] Þa Moises eode ut of þære birig fram Faraone, he ahof upp his hand to Drihtne and se hagol and þa þunorrada geswicon and hit wearð eall | smylte

9:17 Gyt] Gyf B   9:18 gestaðelod] gestaþolod B   9:19 men] menn B
MSS L, B, N (*some readings now available*)   9:20 Drihtnes word ondred] drihtnes wordes ondred B, drihten ondræd N   9:21 men] menn B   nytenu] nyteneu (*2nd* e *marked for deletion*) B   9:22 up] upp B   and ofer menn and ofer nytenu and ofer eall Egypta land] BN, *om.* L   menn] men N   eall²] eal N   9:23 aðenode] BN, aðenod (*space for letter follows; no appar. eras.*) L   upp] up N   hagul] hagol BN   ligetta] ligeta B   eall] eal B   9:24 gemenged] gemengod N   hig] hi BN   9:25 eall] eal B   tobræc] tobrec N   9:26 Gesen] gessen BN   þar] þær BN   on²] *om.* B   9:27 Farao] pharao B   ongen] ongean BN   9:28 þes] þæs N   9:29 ga ut] ut ga BN   þisse] ðissere B   9:31 eall] eal B   hira¹] heora BN   flex] fleax B   hira²] heora BN   beras] BN, bernas L   hig] hi BN   9:33 Faraone] pharaone B   upp] up B

ofer þa þeode. ³⁴ Soþlice þa Farao geseah þæt se hagol and þa
þunorrada geswicon, þa ihte he eft his synna ³⁵ and his heorte and his
folces wæs ahyrd and he nolde forlætan þæt Israhelisce folc, swa God
him bebead þurh Moisen.

¹⁰:¹ And Drihten cwæð to Moise: 'Ga into Pharaone. Ic ahyrde his
heortan, and his folces, þæt hig nellað þe gehiran. ² And telle þinum
suna and þinum magum hu oft ic hæbbe fordon þa Egiptiscan and
worhte mine wundru on him.' ³ Moises and Aaron eodon into
Pharaone and cwædon to him: 'Forlæt Godes folc þæt hit offrie
him þas þing þe Ebrea God byt. Hu lange wylt þu beon me
ungehirsum? ⁴ Soðlice gif þu min folc forlætan nelt, nu tomorgen
ic sende gærstapan ofer eall þin rice ⁵ and ofer ealle þine eorðan, and
hig fretað eall þæt þe growende ys, þæt þam hagole to lafe wæs, ge
[on] treowe ge on æcron, ge on eallum growendum þingon hig
forgnagað. ⁶ And hig gefyllað þine hus, and þinra þegena and ealles
þines folces, ofer eall Egipta land, and swa fela hira byð swa ge ne
eowre yldran ne gesawon syþþan hig geborene wæron.' And Moises
eode ut fram Pharaone. ⁷ Witodlice Faraones þegnas cwædon to him:
'Hu lange sceolon we þolian þas yrmðe? Forlæt þas men þæt hig
offrion hira Gode. Hu ne gesihst þu þæt eall Egipta land mot
forwurðan?' ⁸ And hig clipodon ongen Moises and Aaron and
cwædon: 'Hu fela manna wille ge on eowrum cynne þæt faron and
eowrum Gode offrion?' | ⁹ Moises him andwirde and cwæð: 'We   f. 48ʳ
wyllað faran mid wifum and mid cildum, mid ealdum and mid
geongum and mid eallum urum cynne and mid eallum urum yrfe,
and offrian wurðlice urum Drihtne, for þam þe hit ys halig tid.' ¹⁰ þa
andswarude Farao and cwæð: 'Hu mage ge þ[æ]s frimdie beon, ge þe
mine þeowas syndon, þæt ge sceolon faran fram me mid eallum
eowrum cynne and eowrum Gode offrian? ¹¹ Hit ne mæg na swa
beon, ac ceosað swa fela manna of eowrum cynne swa ge wyllon þæt
eowrum Gode offrian, swa ge sylfe ær bædon.' And hig wurdon
þærrihte ut adrifene fram Pharaone.

9:34 þa¹] `þa´ B   Farao] pharao B   ihte] icte N   9:35 Moisen] moysen B, moyses N
10:1 Ic] and ic B   hig] hi BN   þe] *om.* N   10:2 telle] tele N   Egiptiscan] egyptiscean
N   wundru] wundra N   10:3 Pharaone] faraone N   Forlæt] forlet N   offrie] offrige
BN   þing] ðingc B   10:5 hig¹] hi BN   eall] eal N   þe] *om.* BN   on] BN, *eras.* L
treowe] treowum B   æcron] æcerum B, æcoron N   þingon hig] ðingum hi BN
10:6 hig¹] hi BN   þinra þegena] þinre ðegna B, ðinra ðegna N   hira] heora BN   eowre]
eower BN   hig²] hi BN   10:7 Faraones] pharaones B   yrmðe] yrmðu B   hig] hi BN
offrion] offrian B   hira] heora BN   gesihst þu] gesihstu B   10:8 hig] hi BN   ongen]
ongean B   faron] faran B   offrion] offrian B   N *absent to 13:20*   10:10 andswarude]
andswarode B   þæs] þas L   frimdie] frymdige B   sceolon] sceolan B

^{10:12} Witodlice Drihten cwæð to Moise: 'Ahefe þine hand ofer Egipta land, þæt gærstapan cumon and freton eall þæt gærs þe þam hagole to lafe wæs.' ¹³ And Moises ahof up his girde ofer Egipta land and Drihten dyde þæt þær bleow byrnende wind ealne þone dæg and ealle þa niht, and on mergen se byrnenda wind brohte gærstapan, ¹⁴ þa foron ofer eall Egipta land, swilce næfre ær þære tide næron, ne æfter towearde ne sint. ¹⁵ Witodlice hig fræton eall þæt se hagol ær læfde, þæt nan þing næs grenes læfed, ne on gærse ne on treowum, on eallum Egipta lande. ¹⁶ For þam þingum, clipode Pharao hrædlice Moises and Aaron and cwæð to him: 'Ic agilte wið eowerne Drihten and wiþ eow, ¹⁷ ac forgifað me minne gylt, nu æt þison cyrre, and biddaþ incerne God þæt he adrife þisne deað fram me.' ¹⁸ And he eode ut fram Pharaone | and gebæd hine to Drihtne. ¹⁹ Þa sende God wind fram westdæle and awearp þa gærstapan on þa Readan Sæ, þæt þær ne wearð furþon an to lafe on eallum Egipta lande. ²⁰ And Drihten ahyrde Faraones heortan and he ne forlet Israhela bearn.

^{10:21} Soðlice Drihten cwæð to Moise: 'Aahefe upp þine hand, þæt þystro cumon ofer eall Egipta land, swa þicce þæt hig grapion.' ²² And Moises ahof upp his hand, and egeslice þystra wæron gewordene on eallum Egipta lande, ²³ þæt nan man ne geseah oðerne þrim dagum, ne he hyne ne astyrede of þære stowe þe he on wæs. Soðlice swa hwar swa Israhela bearn wæron, þær wæs leoht. ²⁴ Þa clipode [Pharao] Moises and Aaron and cwæð to him: 'Gað and offriaþ eowrum Gode. Foran eowre yrfe sceal beon her.' ²⁵ Þa cwæð Moises: 'Wilt þu us syllan offrunge þæt we bringon urum Gode? ²⁶ Eall ure yrfe færð mid us. Ne wyrð her nan to lafe, for þam þe we hira beþurfon to Drihtnes offrunge, ures Godes, and we nyton furþon git hwæt seo offrung beon sceal, ær we to þære stowe cumon.' ²⁷ Soðlice Drihten ahyrde Pharaones heortan and he nolde hig forlætan. ²⁸ Þa cwæð Pharao to Moise: 'Far fram me and warna þæt ic þe leng ne geseo. Swa hwilce dæg swa ic þe geseo, þu scealt sweltan.' ²⁹ Moises him andswarude and cwæð: 'Si hit swa þu cwæde; ne geseo ic þe næfre leng.'

MSS L, B   10:12 eall] eal B   10:13 byrnenda] byrnende B   10:14 sint] synd B   10:15 hig] hi B   eall] eal B   10:16 þingum] ðingon B   10:17 þison] ðisum B   incerne] eowerne B   10:18 Pharaone] faraone B   10:19 sende] asende B   10:20 bearn] *followed by decorative colon* L   10:21 Soðlice] *3-line red initial cap.* L   upp] up B   þystro cumon] ðystru cuman B   eall] eal B   hig grapion] hi grapian B   10:22 upp] up B   þystra] ðystru B   10:23 astyrede] astyrode B   þær] þar B   10:24 Pharao] B, *om.* L   10:25 offrunge] ofrunge B   10:26 hira] heora B   offrunge] ofrunge B   offrung] ofrung B   10:27 Pharaones] faraones B   hig] hy B   10:28 Pharao] farao B   10:29 andswarude] andwyrde B

EXODUS

^{11:1} And Drihten cwæð to Moise: 'Nu git ic hreppe Pharao mid anum wite, and Egipta land, and æfter þison | he eow forlæt and nyt eow þæt ge faron ut. ² Witodlice þu scealt beodan Israhela folce þæt esne bidde æt hys frynd, and wif æt hire nehgeburan, gyldene fatu and sylfrene. Soðlice Drihten sylþ gife his folce beforan þam Egiptiscum.' And Moises wæs swiðe mære man on Egipta lande beforan eallum Pharaones folce. ⁴ And he cwæð: 'Drihten cwið þas þing, "To middre nihte ic gange ut on Egipta land ⁵ and ofslea ælc frumcenned cild on Egipta lande, fram Pharaones frumcennedan suna þe sit on his cynesetle oð þære wylne frumcennedan sunu þe sitt æt þære cweornan, and ealle þara nytena frumcennedan. ⁶ And micel hream byþ ofer eall Egipta land, swilce ær nas, ne æfter ne cymð. ⁷ Soðlice of Israhela folce ne forwyrð ne mann ne nyten, þæt ge witon hu wundorlice Drihten todælde þæt Egiptisce folc and þæt Israhelisce folc. ⁸ And eall þin folc færð to me and me geeaðmet and cwið: Far ut, and eall þæt folc, þe þe hiran sceal." Æfter þison we farað ut.' ⁹ And he eode fram Faraone and wæs swiðe yrre. Soðlice Drihten cwæð to Moise: 'Ne hyrð Pharao inc, þeah þe fela tacnu synd gewordene on Egipta lande.' ¹⁰ Witodlice Moises and Aaron worhton ealle þa wundru and þa foretacnu þe her awritene synd beforan Pharaone, and Drihten ahyrde Pharaones heortan þæt he ne forlet Israhela folc of hys lande. |

^{12:1} Witodlice Drihten cwæð to Moise and to Aarone on Egipta lande: ² 'þes monð biþ eowre ærestan monð on gere. ³ Sprecað to eallum Israhela folce and secgað him, "On þam teoðan dæge þises monðes, nyme ælc mann an lamb to his hiwrædene, ⁴ and gif þær læs manna beo þonne þæt lamb etan mæge, nyme his neahgebur þe him next byð, swa fela swa þæt lamb etan magon. ⁵ Witodlice þæt lamb sceal beon anwintre purlamb, clæne and unwemme. On þa ylcan wisan nymað ticcenu ⁶ and healdað þæt oþ þone feowerteoðan dæg þæs monðes and offrian eall Israhela folc þæt on æfen. ⁷ And nymon of his blode and smiton on ægðer gedyre and on þa ofergedyru on þam husum þær hig hit inne etað. ⁸ And eton ealle þæt flæsc on fyre

---

11:1 hreppe] reppe B   faron] faran B   11:2 nehgeburan] neahgeburum B
11:3 Pharaones] faraones B   11:4 middre] midre B   11:5 sitt] sit B   ealle þara]
ealre ðære B   11:6 eall] eal B   nas] nes B   11:7 mann] man B   11:8 eall¹] eal
þis B   eall²] eal B   11:9 hyrð Pharao] gehyrð farao B   tacnu] tacna B
11:10 foretacnu] forebeacnu B   lande] *followed by decorative colon* L   12:1 Witodlice]
5-line green initial cap. L   12:2 eowre ærestan] eower æresta B   gere] geare B
12:3 mann] man B   12:4 beo] beon B   next] nyxt B   12:6 offrian] ofrian B
12:7 gedyre] gedyrne B   and on þa ofergedyru] *om.* B   hig] hi B   12:8 ealle] eal B

gebrædd on ðære nihte, and þeorfe hlafas mid þære lactucan þe on felda wixð. ⁹ Ne ne eton ge of þam nan þing hreowes ne mid wætere gesoden, ac sig hit eall on fyre gebrædd. Etað his heafod and his fet and his innewærde, ¹⁰ [and ne brece ge nan ban,] ne ðær ne beo nan þing to laue on morgen. Gif þær hwæt to lafe beo, forbærnað hit eall on fyre. ¹¹ Begyrdað eower lendenu and habbaþ gescy on eowrum fotum and stafas on handum, and etað hrædlice; witodlice hit ys Godes faru. ¹² And ic fare on ðære nihte ofer eall Egipta land and ofslea ælc frumcenned, ge on mannum ge on nytenum, on Egipta lande and ic Drihten wirce wundru on Egipta [godum]. | ¹³ Soðlice þæt blod eow byð to tacne on þam husum þe ge on beoð. þonne ic þæt blod geseo, þonne forbuge ic eow and eower nan ne byð forspilled þonne ic slea Egipta land. ¹⁴ Gemunað þisne dæg and wurðiaþ hine, Drihtne to freolse, on eowrum cynrene. ¹⁵ And etað þeorf seofon dagas and ne beo nan beorma on ðam forman dæge on eowrum husum. Swa hwilc man swa ytt gebyrmed on þam forman dæge oð þone seofoðan, se man forwyrð of Israhela folce. ¹⁶ Se forma dæg biþ halig, and se seofoða byð eall swa. Ne wirce ge nan þing on þam dagum, buton þa þing þe ge etan scylon. ¹⁷ And healdað 'þeorfe mettas'; soðlice on þam forman dæge ic alæde ut eowerne here of Egipta lande. And wurðiað þisne dæg on ecnysse on eowre cynrene. ¹⁸ On þam forman monþe, þæs monðes feowerteoðan dæges, ge sceolon etan on æfen þeorf, oð þone an and twentogoðan dæg þæs ylcan monðes on æfen. ¹⁹⁻²⁰ Ne beo nan gebyrmed mete seofon dagum on eowrum husum. Se þe ytt gebyrmed, se man forwyrð of Israhela folce. Ne ete ge nan þing onhafenes, ne utancymene ne innan lande geborene, on eallum eowrum eardungstowum."'

¹²:²¹ Soðlice Moises clypode ealle Israhela folces ealdras and cwæð to him: 'Gað and nymað nyten þurh eower hi[w]rædene and offriað pase' (þæt ys færeld) ²² 'and dyppað ysopan sceaft on þam blode þe is on þam þerxolde and sprengað on þæt oferslege and on ægþer |

12:8 gebrædd] gebræd B   wixð] wyxt B   12:9 hreowes] hreawes B   sig] si B gebrædd] gebræd B   innewærde] innewearde B   12:10 and ne brece ge nan ban] B, *restored by L'Isle on eras.* L *(see p. cxv)*   laue] lafe B   12:11 eower] eowre B 12:12 wundru] wundra B   godum] B, lande L   12:14 freolse] lofe B   cynrene] cynryne B   12:15 ytt] et B   oð þone] oððe on þone B   12:16 eall] eal B scylon] sceolan B   12:17 eowerne] eowwerne B   eowre cynrene] eowrum cynryne B 12:18 monðes] B, þæs *add.* L   twentogoðan] twentigan B   12:19–20 innan] in B 12:21 Israhela] ysraheles B   hiwrædene] B, higrædene L   pase] h *add. above* pa *(apparently by 11th/12th-c. Latin glossator)* L, pa.e (s *add. by a late hand on eras.*) B færeld] færed B   12:22 sceaft] sceaf B   þerxolde] ðrexwolde B   sprengað] spreng B

gedyre. Ne ga eower nan ut of his huse ær on morgen. ²³ Soðlice f. 50ᵛ
Drihten færð and ofslihð þa Egiptiscan, and þonne he gesihð þæt
blod on þam oferslege and on ægðrum gedyre, he forgæð þæs huses
duru and ne læt slean nanne mann on eowrum husum. ²⁴ Gehealdað
þis geb[o]d on ecnysse. ²⁵ And þonne ge in gað on þæt land þe
Drihten eow syllan wyle, swa he eow behet, begimað þissa geset-
ednysse. ²⁶ And þonne þæt folc cwið, "Hwæt ys þeos gesetednys?",
²⁷ [. . .] hit ys Godes færeldes offrung, þa he for ofer Israhela bearna
hus and sloh þa Egiptiscan and eower cynn ahredde.' And þæt folc
hit eadmodlice to Gode gebæd ²⁸ and foron ut of þam lande, swa
Drihten bebead Moise and Aarone.

12:29 Witodlice hit gewearð to middre nihte þæt Drihten acwealde
ælc frumcenned cild on Egipta lande, [fram] Faraones yltsan sunu,
þe sitt on his cynesetle, oð þære gehæftan wylne frumcennedan cild,
þe sæt on þam cwerterne, and eall hira nytena frumcenned. ³⁰ And
Pharao aras on niht, and his þegnas and eall Egipta folc, and micel
hream wearð up asprungen on Egipta lande and næs nan hus on
eallum Egipta lande þe lic inne ne læge. ³¹ Þa het Pharao clypian
Moises and Aaron and cwæð to him: 'Arisað and farað ut of minum
lande mid eallum Israela cynne and offriað eowrum Gode, swa ge
frimdie wæron. ³² And nimað eowre hryðerheorda and eower sceap-
heorda and eall eower orf, and farað of minum lande and gebiddað
for me and for min | folc.' ³³ And þa Egiptiscan nyddon þæt f. 51ʳ
Israhelisce folc ut of hira lande and þus cwædon: 'Ealle we moton
sweltan.' ³⁴ Witodlice þæt Israhelisce folc nam gesyft melu, ær þam
þe hit gebyrmed wære, and bundon on hira claþum. ³⁵ And Israhela
bearn dydon eal swa Drihten him bebead and abædon æt þam
Egitpiscon hira gyldenan fatu and hyra sylfrenan and ealle hira
bets[t]an reaf. ³⁶ And Drihten his folc wurðode, Israhela bearn,
mid þara Egiptiscan gestreone. ³⁷ And Israhela bearn foron of
Rammessæ to Sochoð, neh six hundred [þusend] wæpmanna,

12:22 morgen] mergen B   12:23 mann] man B   12:24 gebod] B, gebed L
12:25 begimað] gymað B   gesetednysse] gesetnyssa B   12:26 gesetednys] gesetnys B
12:27 hit ys] *Grein and Crawford supply* þonne *before*   offrung] ofrung B   cynn ahredde]
cyn aredde B   12:29 middre] midre B   fram] and LB   yltsan] yldestan B   sitt] sit B
cwerterne] cwearterne B   eall hira nytena] eal heora nytenu B   12:30 Pharao] farao B
eall] eal B   þe] þæt B   12:31 Pharao] farao B   and cwæð] *om.* B   Israela] israhela B
frimdie] frymdige B   12:32 eowre hryðerheorda] eower hriðerhyrda B   sceapheorda]
sceaphyrda B   eall] eal B   and⁵] *om.* B   12:33 hira] heora B   cwædon] cwædan B
12:34 hira] heora B   12:35 Egitpiscon hira gyldenan] egyptiscan heora gyldene B
hyra] heora B   hira] heora B   betstan] B, betsan L   12:37 neh] neah B   þusend] *om.*
LB

butan wifum and cildum, ³⁸ mid eallum hira yrfe, sceapa and hryðera, and ælces cynnes orfe þe hig ahton. ³⁹ And hi bocon þæt melu þe hig of Egipta lande bæron and worhton þeorfe heorðbacene hlafas, and hig ne moston rum habban þæt hig hit on riht gebocon, for þam Egiptiscan þe hig ut nyddon of hira lande. ⁴⁰ Witodlice Israhela bearn wæron on Egipta lande feower hund wintra and þritig wintra ⁴¹ and syþþan foron Israhela bearn of Egipta lande. ⁴² Þas niht sceolon ealle Israhela bearn begiman, þe hig God ut ælædde of Egipta lande.

^{13:19} Witodlice Moises nam Iosepes ban mid him, for þam þe he halsode Israhela bearn, and cwæð: 'Drihten wyle eow git gemiltsian; alædað mine ban forð mid eow'. ²⁰ And hig foron fram Socho and wicodon æt Etham, on þam itemystan ende þæs westenes. ²¹ And

f. 51^v Drihten for beforan him and swutelode him þone weg on | dæg þurh swert tacn, on sweres gelicnysse, and on niht swilce an byrnende swer him for beforan, ²² and symle him gelæste þæt sweorte tacn on dæg and þæt fyrene on niht. ^{14:1} Drihten spræc to Moise and cwæð: ² 'Sege Israhela bearnum þæt hig gecirron ongen Phiaroth. Seo stow ys betwynan Magdalum and þære Readan Sæ, ongen Behelsefon, and ceosað eow wicstowe be þære sæ on minre gesihþe. ⁴ And Farao hæfð gegaderode ealne his here and wyle eow ofslean, and ic gecyþe on Pharaone and on eallum his here þæt ic eom eower God.' ⁵ Þa cyðde man Faraone hwar þæt Israhelisce folc gewicod hæfde, wið þa Readan Sæ, þa wearð Pharaones heorte awend, and ealles his folces, fram þam þe hig ær Drihtne beheton. Þa het Pharao gegadrian eall his folc togædere. Þa hig gegaderode wæron, þa cwæð he to him: 'Hu wylle we don ymbe þis Israhelisce folc, þe ure wealas syndon and ure unðances of þis lande faran wyllað?' Þa cwæð Farao and eall þæt folc: 'Uton him faran on and ofslean hig and ne lætan nanne lybban on eallum hira cynne.' ⁶ Þa gegaderode Pharao ealle his ealdormen and ealne his here, ⁷ and gegaderode six

12:38 hira] heora B   ælces] B, on ælces (on *partly erased*) L   hig] hi B   12:39 hig¹] hi B   hig²] hi B   rum] hrum B   hig³] hi B   gebocon] bocon B   hig⁴] hi B   hira] heora B   12:40 Witodlice] *enlarged black initial cap.* L   12:42 hig god] god hi B   ælædde] alædde B   13:19 Witodlice] *enlarged black initial cap.* L
MSS L, B, N   13:20 hig] hi BN   itemystan] ytemestan BN   13:21 him¹] heom BN   weg] wæg N   swert] sweart BN   13:22 sweorte] swearte BN   14:1 Drihten] *enlarged black initial cap., no line break* L   14:2 hig] hi BN   ongen¹] ongean B   Phiaroth] phearoth N   betwynan] betweonan B   Magdalum] magdalem BN   ongen²] ongean B   Behelsefon] behelsephon B, behesephon N   14:4 gegaderode] gegaderod B   gecyþe] cyðe B   14:5 cyðde] cydde BN   Faraone] pharaone B, *om*. N (*appar.*)   hwar] hwær BN   Pharaones] faraones B   hig¹] hi BN   Pharao gegadrian] farao gegaderian BN   hig²] hi BN   gegaderode] gegaderod N   faran¹] *om*. BN   hig³] hi BN   nanne] nænne B   hira] heora BN   14:6 Pharao] farao BN   ealdormen] ealdormenn B

hundred godra crata, þe man [of] feohtan sceal on þam lande, and ealle þa cratu butan þam þe on Egipta lande wæron and ealne þone fultum þe he on Egipta lande begitan mihte, ⁹and beferde þæt Israhelisce folc þær | hig gewicode wæron, be þære Readan Sæ. ¹⁰þa f. 52ʳ
þæt Israhelisce folc beseah on Faraones here, ¹¹þa clypodon hig to Moise and cwædon: 'Earme hæfst þu us forlæred. Hwi ne moston we þeowian Faraone urum hlaforde on Egipta lande? Hwi woldest þu us ut alædan, ¹²nu we moton beon ofslagene on þis westene? Betere us wære þæt we hyrdon Pharaone urum hlaforde þonne we sceoldon beon on þis westene ofslagene.' ¹³þa cwæð Moises to þam folce: 'Ne ondrædað eow. Standað and geseoð Drihtnes mærða, þe he todæg wircan wyle. Soðlice þa Egiptiscan þe ge nu geseoð and eow fore ondrædað, ne geseo ge hig næfre ma. ¹⁴Beoð eow stille and Drihten fiht for eow.' ¹⁵Ða cwæð Drihten to Moise: 'Sege Israhela folce þæt hig faron to þære Readan Sæ, ¹⁶and aðene þine girde ofer þa sæ and todæl hig, þæt Israhelisce folc ga drium fotum innan þa sæ. ¹⁷And ic ahyrde Pharaones heortan and his folces þæt hig farað æfter eow innan þa sæ, þæt ic beo gemærsod on Pharaone and on eallum his here and on eallum his cratum ¹⁸and þa Egiptiscan witon þæt ic eom Drihten eower God.' ²¹þa Moises aþenode his hand ofer þa sæ, þa sende Drihten micelne wind ealle þa niht and gewende þa sæ to drium, and þæt wæter wearð on twa todæled and læg an drie stræt þurh þa sæ, ²²and þæt wæter stod on twa healfa þære stræte, swilce twegen hege weallas. þa for eall Israhela folc þurh þa sæ on þone weg þe Drihten him | geworhte and comon hale and gesunde þurh þa sæ, f. 52ᵛ
swa Drihten him behet. ²³Ða Pharao com to þære sæ, and eall his here, þa for he on þone ylcan weg æfter Israhela folce on dægred, mid eallum his folce and mid eallum his wæpnum. ²⁶þa cwæð Drihten to Moise: 'Aþena þine hand ofer þa sæ and ofer Pharaon and ofer ealne his here.' ²⁷And he ahefde up his hand and seo sæ sloh togædere and ahwylfde Pharaones cratu ²⁸and adrencte hine sylfne and eall his folc, þæt þar ne wearð furðon to laue an þe lif gebyrode.

14:7 of] BN, *om.* L   sceal] mihte BN   on³] BN, ongen L (gen *later eras.*)   begitan] begyten N   14:9 hig] hi B   14:10 Faraones] pharaones B   14:11 hig] hi B   ut] *om.* N   14:12 Pharaone] faraone N   14:13 wircan] wyrcean B   Egiptiscan] egyptiscean N   hig] hi BN   14:15 hig] hi BN   faron] faran B   14:16 hig] hi B   Israhelisce] israhela B, isrłæ N   14:17 Pharaones] faraones N   hig] hi B   Pharaone] faraone N   cratum] crætum BN   14:18 Egiptiscan] egyptiscean B   eower] eowwer B   14:21 aþenode] aþeonode N   drie] drige BN   14:22 hege] heage BN   and²] and ða BN   14:23 Pharao] farao N   eall] eal BN; *end of readings from* N   14:26 Aþena] aðene B   Pharaon] faraon B   14:27 And he ahefde up his hand] *om.* B   14:28 eall] eal B   þar] ðær B   to laue an] an to lafe B   gebyrode] gebyrede B

²⁹ Soðlice Moises and Israhela folc foron þurh þa sæ drium fotum. ³⁰ And Drihten alysde on þam dæge Israhela folc of þara Egiptiscan handum ³¹ and hig gesawon þa Egiptiscan deade, upp to lande aworpene, þe hira ær ehton on ðam lande þe hig þa to cumene wæron, and þæt Israhelisce folc ondredon him Drihten and hyrdon Gode and Moise his þeowe.

¹⁵:¹ Ða Moises hæfde gefaren ofer þa Readan Sæ, þa gegaderode he eall Israhela folc togædere and sang Gode lofsang mid eallum þam folce and þancode Gode ealra þara miltsa and þæra mærða and ealra þara wundra þe God on him gedon hæfde and on his cynne. ²⁰ Maria wæs gehaten Moises swustur. Heo gesamnode ealle þa wifmenn togædere on Israhela cynne and namon hira hearpan him on hand ²¹ and heredon God and wuldrodon, ægðer ge mid hearpan ge mid lofsange. ²² Witodlice Moises lædde Israhela folc | fram þære Readan Sæ and hig foron on an westen þe ys Sur genemned. And hig foron þri dagas þurh þæt westen þæt hig nan wæter ne gemetton, ²³ oð þæt hig comon to ðære stowe þe ys Mara genemned (þæt ys on ure lyden 'biternys'). Þa ne mihton hig drincan þæt wæter, for þam þe hit wæs biter. Þa heton hig ealle his naman Mara (þæt ys on ure lyden 'biternys'). ²⁴ Þa gegaderode eall þæt Israhelisce folc ongean Moises and Aaron and cwædon: 'Hwæt sceolon we drincan? We ne magon drincan þis wæter for his biternysse.' ²⁵ Þa clypode Moises to Drihtne and sæde him þæs folces neode, þa ætywde Drihten Moise an treowcyn and het don þæt treow on þæt wæter, and hit wearð syþþan wered to drincanne. ²⁷ Þa comon hig to Helim, and þær wæron twelf wyllas and hundseofontig palmtreowa, and wicodon þær be þam wætrum.

¹⁶:¹ Þa ferdon hig þanon þi fiftigoðan dæge þæs æfteran monþes þæs þe hig ut ferdon of Egipta lande, ² þa gegaderode eft eall þæt Israhelisce folc togædere ongen Moises and Aaron and cwædon: ³ 'We hæfdon hlaf and flæsc genoh on Egipta lande. Hwi woldon git lædan us ut of Egipta lande innan þis westen, þæt we her hungre acwelon?' ¹¹⁻¹² Þa gehyrde Drihten Israhela folces murcnunge, þa

MSS L, B   14:30 þara Egiptiscan] ðæra egyptiscra B   14: 31 hig¹] hi B   upp] up B   hira] heora B   hig²] hi B   to²] 'to' B   15:1 eall] eal B   þara¹] ðæra B   þara²] þæra B   15:20 swustur] swustor B   wifmenn] wifmen B   hira] heora B   15:22 hig¹] hi B   hig²] hi B   hig³] hi B   gemetton] gemytton B   15:23 hig¹] hi B   lyden] leden B   hig²] hi B   for þam] for þan B   hig³] hi B   lyden] leden B   15:25 ætywde] æteowde B   drincanne] drincenne B   15:27 hig] hi B   hundseofontig] hundseofonti B   wætrum] wæterum B   16:1 hig¹] hi B   þi] on ðam B   æfteran] æftran B   hig²] hi B   16:2 ongen] ongean B   16:11-12 Israhela] israheles B

cwæð Drihten to Moise: 'To æfen ic sende þisum folce flæsc to etanne and tomorgen ic gedo þæt hig beoð mid hlafe gefylled, þæt ge witon þæt ic eom Drihten eower God.' [13] Hit gewearð þa on æfen þæt Drihten | gesende swa micel fugolcyn on hira wicstowe swilce f. 53ᵛ
erschenna (þæt ys on Lyden 'coturnix'), and hig namon on þam fugelcynne and slogon swa fela swa hig woldon, þæt hig genoh hæfdon and æton. Witodlice on morgen wæs þæt deaw abutan þa fyrdwic [14] swilce hit hagoles eorðhele wære and swilce hit on pilan gepilod wære. [15] Ða hig þæt gesawon, þa cwædon hig betwynan him, 'Manhu?', þæt ys, 'hwæt ys þis?', for þam hig niston hwæt hit wæs. Þa cwæð Moises: 'Þis ys se hlaf þe Drihten eow sealde to etanne [16] and bebead þæt ælc man gadrie swa micel þæt he genoh hæbbe to etanne,' þæt ys an gemetfæt full, þe hig 'gomor' heton. [17] And Israhela bearn dydon swa and gaderodon, sum mare sum læsse. [18] Se þe mare gaderude næfde na mare, ne se þe læsse gegearwode næfde na læsse, ac ælc þæt he genoh hæfde. [19] Þa bead Moises him þæt hig his nan þing ne læfdon ofer niht. [20] Þa læfdon hig hit sume oð hit morgen wæs, and hit wearð wyrmum acreowed and hit forrotode. Þa wæs Moises yrre. [21] And hig gaderodon on morgen þæt hig genoh hæfdon, and þa seo sunne scan, þa formeolt hit. [22] On þam sixtan dæge hig gaderodon twyfealdlice. Þa comon þa ealdras and rehton hit Moise, [23] þa cwæð he to him: 'Sæterndæges rest ys Drihtne gehalgod. Gearwiað tomorgen þæt ge to gearwienne habbon and healdað oþ morgen þæt þær to lafe beo.' [24] Þa dydon hig swa and hit ne rotode, ne hig ne fundon nan þing fules þæron. [25] And Moises cwæð: | 'Etað hit todæg, for þam þe hit ys Drihtnes restedæg, for f. 54ʳ
þam ge hit ne findað todæg on eorðan. [26] Gadriaþ hit six dagas; ne finde ge hit on þam seofoðan.' [27] Hig eodon ut on 'þam' seofoðan dæge and ne fundon nan þing. [28] Þa cwæð Drihten to Moise: 'Hu

16:11–12 þisum] þison B   etanne] etene B   tomorgen] tomerigen B   hig] hi B
16:13 fugolcyn] fugelcyn B   hira] heora B   erschenna] edischenna B   Lyden] leden B   coturnix] cuturnix B   hig¹] hi B   hig²] hi B   hig³] hi B   morgen] merigen B
16:15 hig¹] hi B   hig²] hi B   hig³] hi B   etanne] etenne B   16:16 gadrie] gaderie B   etanne] etenne B   ⟨gemet⟩fæt full] *Start of* P
    MSS L, B, P (*intermittent*)   full] ful BP   hig] hi BP   16:17 gaderodon] gadrodon BP
16:18 gaderude] gegaderode B, gaderode P   læsse] lesse P   gegearwode næfde] gaderode næfre BP   he] *om.* BP   16:19 hig] hi BP   þing] þingc P   16:20 hig] hi BP   acreowed] acreowyd B, creowyd P   16:21 hig¹] hi BP   hig²] hi BP   genoh] ge P   scan] scean BP
16:22 hig gaderodon] hi gegæderodon BP   16:23 Sæterndæges] sæternesdæges BP   tomorgen] tomergen B, tomerigen P   gearwienne] gearwiænne B   morgen] merigen BP
þær] ðar BP   16:24 hig¹] hi BP   hig²] hi BP   þing] ðingc BP   16:25 þam¹] ðan BP   hit ys Drihtnes restedæg] his drihṅ ristendæg P   16:26 Gadriaþ] gaderiað BP   seofoðan] on þam seofoþan *add.* L (*later scored through*)   16:27 Hig] hi BP   þing] ðingc BP

lange nelle ge healdan mine bebodu?' ²⁹ On þam sixtan dæge he him sylð twifealdne mete. Beo ælc æt ham and ne ga nan ut on þam seofoðan dæge.' ³⁰ And reste þæt folc hit on þam seofoðan dæge ³¹ and nemdon þone mete 'manna', þæs swæc wæs swilce smedema mid hunige. ^{33–4} And Moises het nyman þæt gemetfæt full and setton beforan Drihtne on þam getelde to healdanne. ³⁵ Israhela bearn æton heofonlicne mete feowertig wintra oð hig comon to Chanaan lande.

^{17:1} Hig foron of Sin þam westene and wicodon on Rafadim, þær næs nan wæter. ² Þa murcnudon hig ongen Moises and cwædon: 'Hwi læddest þu us ut of Egipta lande, þæt þu woldest us ofslean, and ure bearn, mid þurste?' ⁴ Þa clypode Moises to Drihtne and þus cwæð: 'Hu sceal ic don ymbe þis folc? Nu binnan litlon fyrste hig wyllað me oftorfian.' ⁵ Þa cwæð Drihten to Moise: 'Clypa to þe þa yltsan of Israhela folce and nim þa girde on þine hand, þe þu þæt wæter mid sloge. ⁶ And ic stande beforan þe uppan Oreb stane. And sleh þone stan and þæt wæter gæð ut of him, þæt þæt folc hæfð genoh to drincanne.' Þa dyde Moises swa, ⁷ and genemde þa stowe 'costung' for Israhela bearna sace, for þam þe hig cwædon, 'Ys Drihten | mid us þe nys?'

f. 54ᵛ

^{17:8} Witodlice Amalech com and feaht ongean Israhela folc on Rafidim. ⁹ Þa cwæð Moises to Iosue: 'Ceos þe geferan and feoht ongen Amalech. Ic stande tomorgen uppon þis beorge and hæbbe Drihtnes girde on minre handa.' ¹⁰ And Iosue dyde eal swa Moises him bebead and feht ongen Amalech. Witodlice Moises and Aaron and Ur stigon uppan þone beorh. ¹¹ Þonne Moises his handa up ahof, þonne hæfde Israhela folc sie. Gif he þonne lithwon slacode, þonne hæfde Amalech sie. ¹² Þa Moises handa wæron werie, þa namon hig anne stan and ledon under hine and he sæt uppan þam stane. Witodlice Aaron and Ur underwriðedon Moises handa on ægðre healfe and hig ne slacedon nan þing syþþan, ær sunne to setle eode.

 16:28 bebodu] beboda BP 16:29 sixtan] .vi.tan P 16:31 manna] man B
smedema] smedma BP 16:33–4 full] ful BP setton] settan BP healdanne] healdene BP 16:35 heofonlicne] hefonlice B hig] hi BP 17:1 Hig] hi BP Rafadim] rafidim B 17:2 murcnudon hig] murcnodon hi BP ongen] ongean B læddest þu] læddesðu B 17:4 Hu] *alt. to* hw̄, *appar. by 11/12th-c. glossator (for Lat.* quid*)* L ymbe] embe P litlon] lytlan BP hig] hi BP 17:5 yltsan] yldestan B of] on BP 17:6 uppan] uppon B, oppon P sleh] sleah B drincanne] drincenne BP 17:7 costung] costnung BP þam] ðan BP hig] hi BP 17:8 Amalech] amaleh B ongean] on P Rafidim] raphidim BP 17:9 ongen] ongean BP Amalech] *corr. fr.* ahimelech *(prob. contemp.)* L minre] *om.* B 17:10 eal] eall P feht ongen] feaht ongean BP stigon] stigon sti P uppan] uppon BP 17:11 sie¹] sige BP lithwon] lytwhon B sie²] sige BP 17:12 werie] werige BP hig¹] hi BP anne] ænne B under] undor B uppan] uppon BP hig²] hi BP slacedon] slacodon BP

¹³ And Iosue aflymde Amalech and his folc mid swurdes ecge. ¹⁴ Þa cwæð Drihten to Moise: 'Writ þis on bec to gemynde, and syle Iosue. Witodlice ic adilige Amaleches gemynd under heofone.' ¹⁵ Þa worhte Moises an weofod and genemde his naman 'Drihten ys min upahafenys', ¹⁶ for þam þe Drihtnes cynesetles mægen, and Godes gefeoht, byð ongen Amelech of cneoresse on cneoresse.

¹⁸:¹ Iethro se sacerd on Madian gehirde hu Drihten alædde Israhela folc of Egipta lande. ² Þa lædde he mid him Sefforam, Moises wif, ongen hine, and his twegen suna; oðer hatte Gerson, oþer Eliezer. ⁷ He eode ut ongen Iethro and cyste hyne, and hig gretton hig gesybsumum wordum. Þa Moises in eode to his getelde, ⁸ þa rehte he Iehtro his mæge | ealle þa þing þe God dyde Pharaone and Egipta f. 55ʳ folce and hu he alysde Israhela folc of Egipta lande. ⁹ Þa wæs Iethro bliþe for eallum þam godum þe Drihten dyde Israhela folce, for þig þe he hig generode of Egipta lande, ¹⁰ and cwæð: 'Si Drihten gebletsod þe eow alysde of Egipta lande and of Pharaones handa. ¹¹ Nu ic wat þæt Drihten ys mære ofer ealle godas, for þam þe hig wæron ofermode ongen hig.' ¹² Iethro brohte Gode offrunga, and Aaron and ealle þa yldestan comon and æton mid him beforan Drihtne. ¹³ Þig oðre dæge sæt Moises, þæt he wolde deman þam folce þe him beforan stod. ¹⁴ Þa Iethro þæt geseah, þa cwæð he: 'Hwæt dest þu on þis folce? Hwi swingst þu ana, and eall folc anbidað fram mergene oð æfen?' ¹⁵⁻¹⁶ Þa Moises him andwyrde and cwæð: 'Þæt folc cymð to me and bitt me þæt ic him deme and cyþe him Godes bebodu and his æ.' ¹⁷ And he cwæð: 'Ne dest þu na wel. ¹⁸ Þu eart mid dysigum geswince geswenced, ægðer ge þu ge þis folc þe mid þe ys. Ne miht þu ana hit acuman. ¹⁹ Ac gehyr min`e´ word and minne ræd and Drihten byð mid þe. Beo[ð] þis folce on ðam ðingon þe to Gode belimpað, þæt þu recce him þa þing þe God bebyt ²⁰ and atywe him hys æ and hu hine man wurðian scyle and þone weg þe hig onfaran sceolon and þæt weorc þe hig wircan sceolon. ²¹ Geceos of eallum

17:13 ecge] eccge P 17:14 adilige] adylgye B, adilgige P; P *breaks off* 17:15 upahafenys] upahafennys B 17:16 ongen Amelech] ongean amaleh B on cneoresse] *om.* B 18:1 Iethro] *enlarged black initial cap. but no line break* L 18:2 ongen] ongean B 18:7 ongen] ongean B hig gretton hig] hi gegretton hi B 18:8 þing] ðingc B Pharaone] faraone B 18:9 Iethro] gethro B þig] ði B hig] hi B of] on B 18:10 lande] *om.* L 18:11 hig¹] hi B ongen hig] ongean hi B 18:13 þig oðre] Ða on oðrum B þæt] and þæt L, and B 18:14 swingst] swincst B eall] eal B mergene] merigene B 18:15-16 bitt] bit B bebodu] beboda B 18:18 dysigum] dysegum B þis] þin B ana hit] hit ana B 18:19 mine] e *squeezed in, possibly by copyist* L, min B Beoð] beod L, beo B folce] folc B bebyt] bebytt B 18:20 atywe] ætywe B scyle] sceole B hig¹] hi B hig wircan sceolon] hi weorcan sceolan B

þison folce wise men and soðfæste and þa þe him God ondrædon and gitsunge hation, and gesete of him þusendmen and [h]undrydmen and fiftiesmen and teoðingmen, ²²þe deman þam folce on ealle tid. þæt þær mæst si, reccon | hig hit þe, and demon hig þa læssan þing, and hit byð þe leohtre, gif þu þa byrþene todælst. ²³ Gif þu þæt dest, þu gefylst Godes hæse and his bebodu and cyrre eall þis folc ham on sibbe.' ²⁴ Moises dyde ealle þa þing þe he lærde, þa he þis gehirde, ²⁵ and geceas arwurðe weras of eallum Israhela folce, and gesette hig þam folce to ealdron þusendmenn and hundredmenn and fiftigesmenn and teoþingmenn, ²⁶ þe demd[on] þam folce on ealle tid. þæt þar hefegost wæs, hig rehton him, and demdon þa leohtran þing. ²⁷ þa forlet he Iethro and for ham to his lande.

¹⁹:¹ On þam þriddan monðe þe Israela folc ferde of Egipta lande, hig ferdon to Sinai westene. ² þa hig foron of Rafidim, hig wicodon on þære sylfan stowe and Israela folc slogon hira geteld feorr fram þam munte. ³ Moises astah to Gode and Drihten hine clypode of þam munte and cwæð: 'Sege þas þing Iacubus cynne and cyþ Israhela folce, and þus cweþ, ⁴ "Ge sylfe gesawon þa þing þe ic dyde þam Egiptiscan and hu ic gefriðode eow. ⁵ Gif ge min word gehirað and mine treowða gehealdaþ, ge beoð me gecorene of eallum folcum. Eall eorðe ys min, ⁶ and ge beoð mine sacerdas and halig þeod." Ðis synd þa word þe þu scealt sprecan to Israhela folce.' ⁷ þa com Moises and rehte þæs folces ealdrum ealle þa spræca þe Drihten bebead, ⁸ and þæt folc cwæð þæt hig woldon þæt don. þa brohte Moises þæs folces word to Drihtne ⁹ and Drihten cwæð to him: 'Nu ic cume to þe on sweartum wolcne, þæt þis folc gehire þæt ic sprece | to þe and gelyfe þe on ecnysse.' Witodlice Moises cydde Drihtne þæs folces word, ¹⁰ and he cwæð to him: 'Gehalga hig todæg and wacxon hig tomergen hira reaf, ¹¹ and sin gearwe to þam þryddan dæge. On þam dæge, Drihten cymð beforan eallum folce uppan Sinai munt,

18:21 þison] ðysum B   ondrædon] ondrædan B   hundrydmen] hundredmen B, undrydmen L   fiftiesmen] fiftigesmen B   18:22 ealle tid] eallum tidum B   hig¹] hi B   hig²] hi B   læssan] læsse B   þe³] ðe þe B   18:24 þing] ðingc B   18:25 geceas arwurðe] geces arode B   hig] hi B   þusendmenn] þusendmen B   hundredmenn] hundredmen B   fiftigesmenn] fiftigesmen B   teoþingmenn] teoðingcmen B   18:26 demdon] B, demde L   ealle tid] eallum tidum B   þar] ðær B   hig] hi B   leohtran þing] leohtra ðingc B   19:1 Israela] israhela B   hig] hi B   19:2 hig¹] hi B   Rafidim hig] raphidim hi B   Israela] israhela B   hira] heora B   feorr] feor B   19:3 Iacubus] iacobes B   19:4 þing] ðingc B   Egiptiscan] egyptyscum B   gefriðode] gefyrðrode B   19:5 Eall] eal B   19:6 þeod] ðeow B   Ðis synd] P *restarts fragmentarily*   sprecan] specan B   19:7 spræca] spæca B   19:8 hig] hi B   19:10 hig] hi B   wacxon hig tomergen hira reaf] waxan hi tomerigen heora hreaf B   19:11 sin] beon BP   gearwe] gearuwe B   munt] munte B

¹² and þu tæcst Israhela folce gemæro abutan þone munt and cwist, "Warniað þæt ge ne cumon to neh þison munte; ælc þære þe his æthrinð, swelte se deaðe". ¹³ And ne ofslea hine nan man mid his handa ac si he mid stanum oftorfod oððe mid flanum ofscotod. Si hit man si hit nyten, ne mot hit lybban. Þonne ge gehiron mid þam byman blawan, þonne faron ge on þone munt.' ¹⁴ And Moises eode nyðer of þam munte to þam folce and gehalgode hit. And þa hig hira reaf woxon, ¹⁵ þa cwæð he to him: 'Beoð gearwe to þam þriddan dæge and ne cume eower nan neh his wife.' ¹⁶ Þa com se þrydda dæg and ligetta and þunor and þicce genip oferwreh þone munt and byman sweg wæs gehired and eall þæt folc him ondred þe wæs on þam fyrdwicon. ¹⁷ Þa Moises hig ut alædde ongen Drihten. Hig stodon on niðewerdon þam munte. ¹⁸ And eall Sinai munt smeac, for þam þe Drihten wæs uppan him on fyre, and se smic aras of him and eall se munt wæs egeslic. ¹⁹ And þære byman sweg weox swa leng swa swiðor. Moises spræc and Drihten him andwyrde. ²⁰ And Drihten eode uppan þæs muntes cnæp and clypode Moises to him and cwæð to him: ²¹ 'Ga nyðer and cyð þis folce þæt hig ne gan ofer þa gemæro, þe læs hig swelton. ²² Sin þa sacerdas ge|halgode þe beforan Drihten gað, þæt ic hig ne slea.' ²³ And Moises cwæð to Drihtne: 'Ne mæg þis folc astigan on Sinai munt; þu hete settan gemæro abutan and hine gehalgian.' ²⁴ Drihten cwæð to him: 'Ga nyðer to þis folce, and Aaron mid þe; ne cumon þa sacerdas neh Drihtne, þe læs hig swelton.' ²⁵ Moises eode niðer to þam folce and rehte hit eall him. f. 56ᵛ

²⁰:¹ God spræc þus: ² 'Ic eom Drihten þin God. ⁴ Ne wirc þu þe agrafene godas, ⁵ ne ne wurða. Ic wrece fædera unrihtwisnysse on bearnum, ⁶ and ic do mildheortnysse þam þe me lufiað and mine bebodu healdað. ⁷ Ne nem þu Drihtnes naman on ydel; ne byð unscyldig, se ðe his naman on ydel nemð. ⁸ Gehalga þone restedæg. ⁹ Wirc six dagas ealle þine weorc. ¹⁰ Se seofoða ys Drihtnes restedæg,

19:12 neh þison] neah ðisum B   þære] ðara B   19:13 ge gehiron ... þonne] *om.* BP   faron] fare B   19:14 And¹] *enlarged black* 7 L   hig] hi BP   hira] heora B   19:15 gearwe] gearuwe B   eower] eowwer B   neh] neah B   19:16 þrydda] þriddan P   ligetta] ligeta B   oferwreh] oferwreah B   eall] eal B   19:17 hig¹] hi B   alædde ongen] lædde ongean B   Hig²] hi BP   niðewerdon] nyðeweardon B   19:18 eall¹] eal B   eall²] eal BP   19:19 leng] lenge P   19:20 uppan] uppon B   19:21 hig¹] hi B   þa] ðis B   hig swelton] hi swylton B   19:22 sacerdas] sæcerdas B   Drihten] drihtne B   hig] hi B   19:24 neh] neah B   hig] hi BP   20:1 God] *2-line black initial cap.* L, And god B   20:5 unrihtwisnysse] unrihtwisnesse B   20:6 mildheortnysse] mildheortnesse B   bebodu] bebeodu P   20:7 nem] nemne B   naman¹] nama B   byð] he *add.* B   naman²] nama B   20:8 restedæg] restendæg B

þines Godes. Ne wirc þu nan weorc on þam dæge, ne nan þara þe mid þe beo. ⁱⁱOn six dagon God geworhte heofenan and eorðan and sæ and ealle þa þing þe on him synd, and reste þy seofoðan dæge and gehalgode hyne. ¹²Arwurða fæder and modor. ¹³Ne sleh þu. ¹⁴Ne synga þu. ¹⁵Ne stel þu. ¹⁶Ne beo þu on liesre gewitnysse ongen þinne nehstan. ¹⁷Ne wilna þu þines nehstan huses, ne þu his wifes, ne his wyeles, ne his wylne, ne his oxan, ne his assan, ne nan þara þinga þe his synd.' ¹⁸Witodlice eall folc gehirdon stefna and byman sweg and gesawon leohtfato and þone munt smeocan. þa wæron hig afærede ¹⁹and cwædon to Moise: 'Spec to us and we hlystað. Ne sprece Drihten to us, þe læs we swelton.' ²⁰Moises cwæð to him: | 'Ne ondrædað eow. God com þæt he wolde fandian eower.' ²¹þæt folc wæs afæred and Moises eode to þam genipe þe God on wæs. ²²Gemang þam, Drihten spræc to Moise and cwæð: 'Ge gesawon þæt ic spræc of heofene. ²³Ne wyrce ge sylfrene godas and gyldene. ²⁴Wyrcað weofod of eorðan and offriað uppan þam onsægednyssa, scep and oxan, on ælcere stowe þe mines naman gemynd on si. Ic cume to þe and gebletsie þe. ²⁵Gif þu stænen weofod me wyrce, ne timbra þu þæt of gesnidenum stanum. Gif þu þin tol ahefst ofer hyt, hit bið besmiten. ²⁶Ne ga þu on stapun to minum weofode, þe læs man geseo þine sceame.

²¹:¹'Ðis synd þa domas þe ðu him tæcan scealt. ²Gif þu Ebreiscne þeow bigst, þeowie þe six ger and beo him freoh on þam seofoðan. ³Ga he ut mid swilcum reafe swilce he in com; gif he wif hæbbe, ga heo ut mid him. ⁴Gif he næbbe, and his hlaford him wif sylle and hig suna hæbbon and dohtra, þæt wif and hire winclo beoð þæs hlafordes. Ga he ut mid his hætron swylcon he in com. ⁵Gif se wiel cwið, "Me ys min hlaford leof, and min wif and mine winclo: nelle ic gan ut, ne beon frig", ⁶bringe his hlaford hine to þæs haligdomes dura and þyrlie his eare mid anum æle and be he his þeow a world. ⁷Gif hwa becypð his dohtor to þeowienne, ne gæð heo ut swa

20:10 þara] ðæra B   20:11 heofenan] heofonan B   þing] ðinc B   gehalgode] he halgode B   20:16 liesre gewitnysse ongen] leasre gewitnesse ne ongean B   nehstan] nextan BP   20:17 nehstan] nextan B   wyeles] weales B, wealas P   þara] ðæra B   20:18 eall] eal B   leohtfato] leohtfatu B   hig] hi P   20:19 Spec] sprec B   sprece] spece B, spæce P   læs] ðe *add.* B   20:20 eower] eowwer B   20:21 wæs afæ⟨red⟩] P *breaks off*   20:22 heofene] heofone B   20:23 and] ne B   20:24 Wyrcað] ac weorcað B   gebletsie] gebletsige B   20:25 ne timbra] getimbra B   20:26 stapun] stapum B   sceame] sceama B   21:2 þeowie] þeowige B   ger] gear B   21:4 hig] hi B   hæbbon] habbon B   winclo beoð] wenclo beo B   hætron] hæteron B   21:5 wiel] weal B   winclo] wenclo B   21:6 haligdomes] halidomes B   þyrlie] ðyrlige B   be] beo B   he] *om.* B   world] woruld B   21:7 to þeowienne] on ðeowene B

þeowena gewuna ys. ⁸ Gif heo mislicað þam hlaforde, forlæte hig; ne mot he hig fremdum folce syllan, gyf he hig forhogie. ⁹ Gif he hig his suna beweddað, do hire æfter dohtra gewuna. ¹⁰ Gif he oðre him | nymð, he sceal foresceawian þa mædene [gyfta and] reaf and hire   f. 57ᵛ mægdhades wurð, þæt synd twelf scillingas be twelf penigon. ¹¹ Gif he þas þreo þing ne deð, ga hire ut to gife, butan feo. ¹² Se þe mann wundað and wyle hine ofslean, swelte he deaþe. ¹³ Se þe nan þing ne syrwde, ac hyne God sealde on his hand, ic gesette him hwæder he bugan sceal. ¹⁴ Gif hwa ofslihð his nehstan, do hine fram minum weofode, þæt he swelte. ¹⁵ Se þe slea his fæder oððe his modor, swelte he deaðe. ¹⁶ Se þe man forstele and hine gesylle, swelte he deaþe. ¹⁷ Se þe his fæder wyrge oððe his modor, swelte he deaðe. ¹⁸ Gif men cidað and hira oðer hys nextan mid stane wyrpð oþþe mid fyste slicþ, and he dead ne bið ac lið on bedde seoc, ¹⁹ gif he arist and ut gæþ mid his stafe, he bið unscildig þe hine sloh; gilde swa þeah his weorc and þæt hine man hæle. ²⁰ Se þe his wiel slicþ mid girde, oððe his wylne, and hig deade beoð þurh his handa [. . .]. ²¹ Gif he anne dæg oþþe twegen lyfað ofer þæt, he bið unscildig, for þam hit ys his feoh. ²² Gif men sacað and hwilc slicð eacniende wif and hig bearnlease gedeð, and heo alyfað, bete swa micel swa þæs wifes wer girnð and deman tæcan. ²³ Gif hit swa ne bið, and heo æfter þam dead bið, sylle lif wið life, ²⁴ eage wið eagan, toð wið teþ, hand wið handa, fot wið fet, ²⁵ bærninge wið bærninge, wunde wið wunde, læl wið læle. ²⁶ Gif hwa slea his weales eage ut, oððe his wylne, and hig anege gedo, læte hig frige for þam eagan þe he ut adyde. | ²⁷ Gif he   f. 58ʳ toð of aslea, læte hig frie. ²⁸ Gif oxa hnite wer oððe wif, and hig deade beoþ, si he mid stanum oftorfod. Ne ete man his flæsc; his hlaford bið unscildig. ²⁹ Gif se oxa hnitel wære for dæge oþþe for twam, and hig hit his hlaforde cyddon and he hine belucan nolde, and he wer oððe wif ofhnit, oftorfie man þone oxan mid stanum and

21:7 þeowena] ðeowyna B   21:8 forlæte] and forlæte LB   hig¹] hi B   hig²] hi B   gyf] þeah B   hig³] hi B   21:9 Gif he hig his suna] gyf heo is B   gewuna] gewunan B   21:10 he sceal foresceawian þa mædene gyfta and reaf] forgyfe he ðæt mæden and sylle hyre reaf B   gyfta and] gyf *add. on eras., with* ta 7 *above (appar. by 11/12th-c. glossator)* L   mægdhades] mægþhades B   penigon] pænegon B   21:11 þing] þingc B   21:12 mann] man B   21:13 hwæder] hwider B   sceal] sceall B   21:14 nehstan] nextan B   21:16–17 *The two verses are transposed in* B   16 swelte] swylte B   21:17 wyrge] wyrige B   21:18 hira oðer hys nextan] heora aðer oþerne B   slicþ] slyhð B   lið] B, licð L (c *later del.*)   21:20 wiel] wealh B   hig] hi B   handa] *Grein and Crawford add* he bið scildig   21:21 anne] ænne B   lyfað] leofað B   21:22 sacað] i *add. above, poss. by 11/12th-c. glossator* L   slicð] slyhð B   hig] hi B   alyfað] aleofað B   tæcan] tæcon B   21:25 læl] læll B   læle] lælle B   21:26 hig¹] hi B   hig²] hi B   21:27 frie] frige B   21:28 and hig] ðæt hi B   21:29 hnitel] hnitol B   hig] hi B

ofslea þone hlaford. ³⁰ Gif he betan mote, sylle wið his life swa hwæt swa him man scrife. ³¹ Be gelicon dome, gif he ofhnit sunu oððe dohter. ³² Gif he wiel oþþe wylne amyrð, sylle þam hlaforde þritig scillinga seolfres and si se oxa mid stanum oftorfod. ³³ Gif hwa pytt adelfe and hyne ne oferhelie and þær fealle on oxa oððe assa, ³⁴ gilde þæs pyttes hlaford þæra nytena wurð, and þæt þar dead byð, byð his. ³⁵ Gif utancymene oxa oþres oxan gewundað, gesyllon þone oxan and todælon þæt wurð and þæs deadan hold him betwynan. ³⁶ Gif se oxa hnitol wæs and se hlaford hine ne heold, gilde oxan mid oxan and hæbbe him þone deadan.

²²:¹ 'Gif hwa stylþ oxan oððe sceap, and ofslihþ, sylle fif oxan for anne and feower scep for an. ² Gif man þeof gemete and he hus brece and hine man þar gewundie, se slaga bið unscildig. ³ Gif he sunnan scinendre þæt deð, he biþ scildig, and swelte he. Gif he næbbe hwæt he wið þære stale sylle, sylle hine man wið feo. ⁴ Gif man cuca finde | þæt he stæl, oxa oððe assa oððe scep, gilde be twifealdon. ⁵ Gif hwa æt æceras oþþe wingerd, gilde of his agenum be þæs demmes ehte. ⁶ Gif fyr bærne mugan oððe standenne æceras, gilde þone byrst þe þæt fyr ontende. ⁷ Gif hwa befæste his feoh to hyrdnysse, and hit man forstylþ þam þe hit underfehð, gif man þone þeof finde, gilde be twifealdon. ⁸⁻⁹ Gif se hushlaford hit nat ladie hine, and gif him man gedeme, gilde be twifealdon. ¹⁰ Gif hwa befæstð his nehstan ænig nyten and hit biþ dead oþþe gelewed oððe ætbroden, and hit nan man ne gesihþ, ¹¹ sylle him að and ne nyde hine to gilde. ¹² Gif hit forstolen beo, gilde þam hlaforde þone byrst. ¹³ Gif hit wildeor abitað, bere forð þæt abitene and ne agife. ¹⁴ Se þe æt his nehstan hwæt to læne abit, gif hit gelewed bið oððe dead, bæftan þam hlaforde, nyde hine man þæt he hit gilde. ¹⁵ [. . .] swiþust gif hit beforan þam hlaforde wæs for his weorces hire. ¹⁶ Gif hwa lið mid unbeweddudre fæmnan, nyme he hig to riht wife. ¹⁷ Gif se fæder hig

f. 58ᵛ

21:30 him man] man him B 21:31 gelicon] gelican B dohter] dohtor B
21:32 wiel] weal B wylne] wylnan B 21:33 pytt] pyt B fealle] afealle B
21:34 þæra] þara B þar] þær B 21:35 utancymene] utacymene B oxan¹] oxsan B
betwynan] betweonan B 21:36 oxan¹] oxa B 22:1 anne] ænne B scep] sceap B
an] anum B 22:2 þar] þær B 22:3 scinendre] scinende B hine man] man hine B
22:4 cuca] cucu B oxa] oxan B assa] assan B 22:5 æt] ett B wingerd] wingeard B
22:6 standenne] standende B 22:7 hyrdnysse] hyrdnesse B 22:8–9 twifealdon]
twyfealdan B 22:10 befæstð] befæste B nehstan] nyxtan B 22.13 bere] 'b'ere
(*orig.* fere?) B 22:14 nehstan] nextan B hine man] man hine B 22:15 swiþust . . .
weorces hire] *The sentence is corrupt in both L and B; some words are appar. wanting before*
swiþust; *see pp.* cvi–cvii swiþust] *partly del.* L, swiðost B 22:16 unbeweddudre]
unbeweddodre B he] *om.* B hig] hi B 22:17 hig] hi B

him syllan nelle, gilde be þære giftan mæðe. ⁱ⁸ Ne læt þu lybban þa þe geunlybban wircon. ¹⁹ Ðone þe hæme wið nyten, ne læt þu lybban. ²⁰ Se þe godun offrie buton Gode anum, slea hine man. ²¹ Ne geunret þu ælþeodige; ge wæron ælþeodie on Egipta lande. ²² Ne deriað wudewun ne steopcildum. ²³ Gif ge him deriað, hig hrymað to me and ic gehire hira hream ²⁴ and ic eow ofslea mid swurde, | and f. 59ʳ eower wif beoð wudewan and eowre bearn steopcild. ²⁶ Gif þu wed nime æt þinum nehstan, agif him his reaf ær sunnan setlegange. ²⁸ Ne tæl þu ne wirig þu þines folces ealdor. ²⁹ Ne yld þu mid teoþungum, ne mid frumsceattum. Sylle me þin forme bearn. ³⁰ Do eall swa of hruþerum and of sceapun. Seofon dagas hit bið mid his meder; syle hit me on þam ehtuþan. ³¹ Þæt flæsc þæt wildro abiton, ne ete ge, ac weorpað hit hundum.

²³:¹ 'Ne underfo ge lease gewitnysse. ² Ne filig þu þam folce þe yfel wylle don, ne beforan manegon soþes ne wanda. ³ Ne miltsa þu þearfan on gemange. ⁴ Gif þu gemete þines feondes oxan oððe assan, læde hine to him. ⁵ Gif þu geseo his assan licgan under byrþene, ne ga þu þanon ac hefe hine up mid him. ⁶ Ne þu ne wanda on ðearfan dome. ⁷ Fleoh leasunga. Unscildigne and rihtwisne ne ofsleh þu. ⁸ Ne nim þu lac; þa ablendað glæwne and awendað rihtwisra word. ⁹ Ne beo þu ælþeodegum gram, for þam ge wæron ælþeodie on Egipta lande. ¹⁰ Saw six ger þin land and gadera his wæstmas ¹¹ and læt hit restan on þam seofoðan, þæt þearfan eton þærof and wildeor. Do þu [swa] on þinum winearde and on þinum elebeamon. ¹² Wirc six dagas and geswic on þam seofoðan, þæt þin oxa and þin assa hig gereston and þæt þinre wylne sunu si gehyrt, and se utancymena. ¹³ Healdað ealle þa þing þe ic eow sæde and ne swerie ge þurh utancymena goda naman. ¹⁴ Þriwa on gere gewurðiaþ | minne freols. f. 59ᵛ

22:18 geunlybban] unlybban B   22:19 þu] hine *add.* B   22:20 godun] godum B   hine man] man hine B   22:21 ælþeodige] elðeodigne B   ælþeodie] elþeodige B   22:22 wudewun] wudewum B   22:23 hig hrymað] hi rymaþ B   hira] heora B   22:24 eower] eowwer B   22:26 nehstan] nextan B   setlegange] setlunge B   22:29 frumsceattum] sceattum *scored through and* wæstmas *add. by 11/12th-c. glossator* L   Sylle] syle B   22:30 eall] eal B   hruþerum] hryðerum B   sceapun] sceapum B   ehtuþan] eahtoþan B   22:31 wildro] wildeor B   weorpað] wurpaþ B   23:1 gewitnysse] gewitnesse B   23:4 læde] læd B   23:6 ðearfan] þerfan B   23:7 ofsleh] ofsleah B   23:8 þu lac] P *starts again, continuously*   glæwne] gleawne BP   23:9 ælþeodegum] elðeodigum BP   þam] þe *add.* BP   ælþeodie] elþeodige BP   23:10 six] .v`ï´. P    ger] gear BP    23:11 þearfan] ðearfon P    þu swa] swa *om.* LBP (*Lat.* ita), þu *alt. to* swa *in* L, *poss. by 11/12th-c. glossator, and Grein and Crawford follow*    winearde] wingearde BP    23:12 six] .v`ï´. P   seofoðan] .vii.foðan P   þæt¹] and B   assa] assan P   hig] hi BP   gereston] gerestan B   wylne] wylnan B   utancymena] utacymena B   23:13 þing] ðingc P   swerie] swerige P   23:14 gere] geare B, geara P

120   EXODUS

¹⁵ þu ytst þeorf symbel. Seofon dagas ge etað þeorf, swa ic þe
bebead, on þæs monþes tid niwra wæstma, þa þu ut fore of Egipta
lande. Ne cymst þu butan ælmyssan on mine gesihþe. ¹⁶ Heald þa
symbeltide þæs monþes frumsceatta þines weorces, þæ þu on lande
sæwst, and on geres utgange, þonne þu gegaderast þine wæstmas
togædere. ¹⁷ þriwa on gere ælc wæpnedman ætywð beforan Drihtne.
¹⁸ Ne offra þu þinre onsægednysse blod uppan beorman, ne rysel ne
belifð oþ morgen. ¹⁹ Bring þine frumsceattas to Godes huse. ²⁰ Nu ic
sende minne engel þæt þe læde into þære stowe þe ic gegearwode.
²¹ Gim his and gehir his stemne, for þam he [ne] forgifð þonne ge
singiaþ and min nama ys on him. ²² Ic beo þinra feonda feond ²³ and
þe in gelæde to Amareus lande. ²⁴ Ne geeaðmed þu hira godas ac
tobrec hira anlicnyssa. ²⁵ þeowiað Drihtne. Ic gebletsie eow and do
ælce untrumnysse fram eow, ²⁶ and geice eower dagas ²⁷ and aflyme
þine fynd beforan þe. ²⁸ And ic asende hyrnytta þe aflymað Efeum
and Chananeum, twelf monþum ær þu in fare. ³¹ Ic sette þine
gemæro fram þære Readan Sæ oþ Palastinas sæ and fram þam
westene oð flod. ³² Nafa þu nane sibbe wið hira godas, ³³ þi læs hig þe
beswicon.'

²⁴:¹ He cwæð to Moise: 'Astih to Drihtne, þu and Aaron, Nadab
and Abiu, and hundseofentig ealde of Israhela folce, and eaðmedað
f. 60ʳ feorr. ² Moises ana astihþ | to Drihtne.' ³ Moises com eft and rehte
þam folce ealle Drihtnes word and hig cwædon anre stemne: 'We
doð ealle Drihtnes word þe he spræc.' ⁴ Moyses wrat ealle Drihtnes
spræca and aras on morgen and getimbrode an weofod æt þam munte
nyþewerdon, and twelf mearca on twelf Israhela mægþum. ⁵ Moises
sende cnihtas þæt offrodon twelf cealfas, ⁶ and Moises nam healf þæt
blod and dyde on geryde orcas and get þæt oðer uppan þæt weofod,
⁷ and rædde his boc þam folce. And hig cwædon: 'We doð ealle þa
þing þe Drihten bebead and beoð hirsume.' ⁸ And he nam þæt blod

23:15 cymst þu] cymstu B   ælmyssan] ælmessan B   23:16 þæ] þe BP
23:17 þriwa] .iii. P   gere] geare BP   23:18 offra] ofra B   þinre] þine B
onsægednysse] onsægdnyssae B   rysel] rysle BP   morgen] merigen BP   23:19 Godes]
godas P   23:20 Nu] na P   engel] encgel P   23:21 þam] þe add. BP   ne] om. LBP
þonne] þone B   23:23 in] inn P   Amareus] 2nd a alt. to o L   23:24 hira¹] heora
BP   23:25 gebletsie] bletsige B, blætsige P   untrumnysse] untrumnyssae B   fram
eow] eow fram BP   23:28 hyrnytta] hyrnetta BP   aflymað] aflymeþ B   twelf] twel P
23:31 þære] þare B   oþ Palastinas sæ] om. BP   and] ʻandʼ P   23:32 hira] heora BP
23:33 hig] ðe hig BP   24:1 hundseofentig] hundseofontig BP   eaðmedað] geeadmedaþ
BP   feorr] feor B   24:3 hig] hi BP   24:4 spræca] spæca B   nyþewerdon]
nyðeweardon B, nyþeweardan P   mearca] meara P   24:5 offrodon] offrodan B
24:6 get] geat B   24:7 hig] hi BP   þing] ðingc BP   hirsume] gehyrsume BP

and sprengde þæt folc and cwæð: 'þis ys þære treowðe blod þe Drihten eow behet be eallon þison spræcon.' ⁹Moises and Aaron, Nadab and Abiu, and hundseofontig Israhela folces ealdro ast[igon], ¹⁰ and hig gesawon Israhela God. Under his fotun wæs swilce þæs stanes [. . .] þe man 'saphiros' on Leden nemð, and swilce seo heofone, þonne heo smylte byð. ¹¹ Israhela bearn gesawon Drihten and æton and druncon.

²⁹:⁹ 'Siððan þu gehalgast hira handa, ¹⁰ þu offrast an celf. Aaron and his suna settað hira handa uppan his heafod ¹¹ and þu cwelst hit on Drihtnes gesihþe, wið þære cyðnesse getelde dura. ¹² And þu smitst cealfes blod mid þinum fingre on þæs weofodes hyrnan and gitst þæt oðer undernyðan. ¹³ And þone rysel and þære lifre nett and twegen lundagan | mid gelynde þu bærnst þær uppan. ¹⁴ þæs cealfes f. 60ᵛ flæsc and fell and gor þu bærnst ute, butan fyrdwicon, for þam hit ys for synne. ¹⁵ Nym anne ramm; Aaron and his suna settað hira handa uppan his heafod. ¹⁶ þonne þu hine cwelst, þu nymst his blod and gitst abutan þæt weofod. ¹⁷ þone ramm þu snitst to sticcon; his innewerde and his fet þu legst uppan his heafod. ¹⁸ And þu offrast ealne þone ram on fyres bryne uppan þam weofode; he ys Drihtne wynsum onsægednys. ¹⁹ þu nimst oþerne ram, and Aaron and his suna settað heora handa ofer his heafod. ²⁰ And þonne þu hine offrast, þu nymst his blod and smitst ofer utewerd Aarones swyðre eare, and his suna, and ofer hira handa þuman and þæs swyðran fotes micclan tan, and þu gitst þæt blod uppan þæt weofod and ymbeutan. ²¹ And þonne þu nymst of þam blode þe ys uppan þam weofode, and of þam smiringele, þu sprenst Aaron and his reaf, and his suna and hira reaf. ²² þu nymst þone rysle of þam ramme and þone tægl and þone heorthaman and ðære lifre nett and twegen lundlagan mid gelynde and þone swyþran boh, for þam hit ys halgung ram, ²³ and anne holne hlaf mid ele gesprengendne and anne gebigendne hlaf, of

24:8 sprengde] sprengcde P be eallon] beallum B, be allon P 24:9 astigon] BP, astah L 24:10 hig] hi BP God] and add. B fotun] foton BP stanes] Grein and Crawford add. weorc 24:11 druncon] On the disruptive narrative break at this point (in all MSS), see pp. cviii–cix 29:9 Siððan] 3-line red initial cap. L hira] heora B 29:10 celf] cealf BP hira] heora BP 29:11 cyðnesse] cyðnysse BP 29:12 smitst] LBP; alt. to nymst in L appar. by 11/12th-c. glossator cealfes] þæs cealfes BP weofodes] P breaks off again 29:13 rysel] rysle B nett] net B þær] þar B 29:14 butan] þam add. B 29:15 anne ramm] ænne ram B hira] heora B 29:17 ramm] ram B snitst] snipst B innewerde] innewearde B 29:18 onsægednys] onsægdnys B 29:20 smitst] LB; alt. to settest (it appears) in L (by L'Isle?) utewerd] uteweard B micclan] miclan B 29:21 smiringele] smyringcele B sprenst] sprængst B hira] heora B 29:22 nett] net B 29:23 gesprengendne] gespregnedne B anne] ænne B gebigendne] gebigedne B

þæra þeorfra hlafa windle beforan Drihtne, ²⁴ and þu setst ealle þa uppan Aarones handa, and his suna, and gehalgast hig and upp ahefst beforan Drihtne. ²⁵ And þu nymst eall of hira handum and onælst beforan Drihtne, for þam hit ys his off|rung. ²⁶ Þu nymst þæt anribb of þam ramme þe Aaron gehalgod wæs and gehalgast hit and upp ahefst beforan Drihtne, and hit gescitt to his dæle. ²⁷ And eac þu gehalgast þæt gehalgode anribb and þone boh þe þu of þam ramme asyndrodest, ²⁸ þe Aaron of gehalgod wæs, and his suna, and hig gesceotað to Aarones dæle, and his suna, ecre lage fram Israhela bearnum. ²⁹ Þæt halie reaf þæt Aaron wereð, his suna habbað æfter him, þæt hig sin gesmirode on þam and hira handa gehalgode. ³⁰ Seofan dagas he wereð þæt, se þe to bisceope bið gesett for hine, þæt he þenie on þam halierne. ³¹ Þu nymst þære halgunge ramm and sy[þst] his flæsc on haligre stowe ³² and Aaron and his suna etað of þam. Hig etað þa hlafas on ðam windle on þæs geteldes forebirig. ³³ Ne ete nan utancymen of þam. ³⁴ Gif þær hwæt to lafe beo, bærn þæt on morgen. ³⁵ Do ealle þa þing þe ic þe bebead, ofer Aaron and ofer his suna. Seofon dagas þu gehalgast hira handa, ³⁶ and þu offrast ælce dæg an cealf for synne and þu aclænsast þæt weofod and smirest and gehalgast. ³⁷ Seofon dagas þu feormast þæt weofod and halgast, and hit bið haligre halig, and ælc þæra þe his onhrinð bið gehalgod. ³⁸ Þu dest ælce dæg on þæt weofod twa enetere lamb, ³⁹ an lamb on morgen, oðer on æfen. ⁴⁰ Teoðan dæl smedeman mid gecnucedon ele gesprengede, | and win, to offrunge. ⁴¹ Oðer lamb þu offrast on æfen, æfter þære dægred offrunge gewunan. ⁴³ Æt þæs geteldes dura beforan Drihtne, þar ic gesette þæt ic sprece to þe ⁴⁴ and þar ic halgie þæt geteld and þæt weofod and Aaron and his suna, ⁴⁵ and ic eardie onmiddan Israhela bearnum, ⁴⁶ ic Drihten þe eow ut alædde of Egipta lande.'

³¹:¹² Drihten spræc to Moise and cwæð: 'Healdað minne restedæg; he ys tacn betwux me and eow. ¹⁴ Se þe hine besmit, swelte he deaþe.

29:23 þeorfra] þeorfa B   hlafa] om. B   29:24 hig] hi B   upp] up B
29:25 And] enlarged 7 L   hira] heora B   29:26 anribb] andrib B   upp] up B   gescitt] gescyt B   29:27 gehalgast] gehalgost B   anribb] andrib B   29:29 halie] halige B   wereð] werað B   gesmirode] gesmyrede B   hira] heora B   29:30 Seofan] seofon B   wereð] weraþ B   gesett] geset B   29:31 ramm] ram B   syþst] B, systð L   29:35 þing] þingc B   29:37 onhrinð] onrinð B   29:38 enetere] enetre B   29:40 Teoðan ... offrunge] A translation of Lat. in agno uno has been lost from this sentence in LB   smedeman] smedman B   gecnucedon] gecnucedum B   gesprengede] gesprengende L, gesprengcgende B   offrunge] offrungae B   29:43 þar] þær B   sprece] spræce B   29:44 þar] þær B   29:45 eardie] eardige B   29:46 ⟨alæ⟩dde of] P restarts fragmentarily

Se þe weorc wirce, forwurðe he. ¹⁵ Six dagas þu wircst; on þam seofoðan þu rest. ¹⁷ On six dagon God geworhte heofon and eorðan and on þam seofoðan he hine reste.' ¹⁸ He sealde Moise twa stænene wexbreda, mid Godes handa agrafene, on Sinai dune. ³²:¹ þa þæt folc geseh þæt Moises wæs lange uppan þam munte and nyþer ne eode, and hig gegaderodon hig ealle togædere ongen Aaron and cwædon: 'Aris and wirce us godas þæt faron beforan us; we nyton hwæt Moises gefaren hæfð, þe us ut alædde of Egipta lande.' ² þa cwæð Aaron to him: 'Nymað gyldene earhringas of eower wifa earon and of eower dohtra and bringað to me.' ⁴ þa nam he þæt gold and get [þærof] an celf, and hig cwædon: 'Israhel, þis ys þin God þe þe ut alædde of Egipta lande.' ⁵ þa Aaron þæt geseah, þa timbrode he weofod beforan him and het bydelas beodan and þus cweðan: 'Tomorgen byð Drihtnes simbeldæg.' | ⁶ And he aras on morgen, f. 62ʳ and hi brohton offrunga and gesibsume onsægednyssa, and þæt folc sæt and æt and dranc, and arison and plegedon.

³²:⁷ Drihten spræc to Moise: 'Ga nyðer. þin folc hæfð gesingod, þe þu ut alæddest of Egipta lande. ⁸ Hig bugon raðe of þam wege þe þu him tæhtest. Hig habbað him gegoten an gylden celf and habbað him for God, and gebiddað him þærto and offriað him. þæt Israhelisce folc cweþ, "þis ys ure God þe us ut alædde of Egipta lande".' ⁹ And eft Drihten cwæð to Moise: 'Ic geseo þæt þis folc ys heardes modes. ¹⁰ Læt me þæt ic hig fordo, nu hig me abolgen habbað, and ic sette þe to ealdre ofer micle þeode and mære.' ¹¹ Moises gebæd hine to Drihtne and cwæð: '[Drihten,] ne beo þu yrre ongen þin folc, þeh hig agylt habbon, ¹² þæt þa Egiptiscan ne cweðon þæt þu hig litelice ut alæddest and syþþan acwealdest. Miltsa þinum folce, þeh hit gesyngod hæbbe, ¹³ for þam getreowðum þe þu Abrahame gehete, þæt þu woldest his cynn gemenigfealdan swa steorran beoð on heofenum.' ¹⁴ And Drihtnes yrre wearð geliþegod ongen þæt folc.

31:14 wirce] weorce B   forwurðe] forweorðe B   31:17 heofon] heofonan B
31:18 agrafene] agrauene P   32:1 geseh] geseah B   wæs] to *add*. B   hig¹] hi B   hig²]
hi BP   ongen] ongean B   faron] faran B   32:2 him] heom B   earhringas] ear`h´ringas
B   eower²] eowwer B   32:4 get] geat B   þærof] þæroff B, ⟨þær⟩of P, *om*. L   celf]
cealf B   hig] hi BP   32:5 simbeldæg] symbeltid B   32:6 sæt] set P   plegedon]
plegodon B   32:7 Drihten] *3-line red initial cap*. L   32:8 Hig¹] hi B   Hig²] hi B
celf] cealf BP   him⁴] hi B   offriað] ofriað B   him⁵] and *add*. B   Israhelisce] israhela B
32:10 hig¹] hi BP   hig²] hi B   þe] `þe´ B   micle] micele BP   32:11 Drihten] BP,
om. L   ongen] ongean B   þeh hig] þeah hi B   habbon] habban B   32:12 Egiptiscan]
egiptiscean BP   hig] hi B   þeh] þeah B   32:13 gehete] behete B   gemenigfealdan]
gemænifyldan B, gemenig⟨...⟩ P   heofenum] heofonum B   32:14 ongen] ongean B

EXODUS

^{32:15} Moises eode þa adun of þam munte and hæfde him on handa twa stænene tabulan, ¹⁶ þa wæron mid Godes agenum fingre awritene. ¹⁷ þa cwæð Iosue to Moise: 'Hwæt ys þes hream þe ic gehire on þis folce, swilc hit gefeoht si?' ¹⁸ þa cwæð Moises to him: 'Nis se hream | to gefeohte ac singende stefne ic gehire.' ¹⁹ þa Moises to þam fyrdwicon com, þa geseh he þæt gildene celf, þe hig geworht hæfdon him to gode, and þæt folc eall singende abutan þæt celf. þa werp he þa tabulan of his handa, þæt hig eall toburston, ²⁰ and nam þæt gildene celf þæt hig geworht hæfdon and forbærnde and forbrytte eall to duste. ²¹ þa cwæð Moises to Aarone: 'Hwæt hæfð þis folc gedon? Hit hæfð geworht ane þa mæstan synne and Gode þa laþustan.' ²² þa andswarude Aaron Moise and cwæð: 'Hlaford, ne belg þu ongen me. þu canst þis folc, þæt hit eall to yfele gewend ys. ²³ Hig cwædon to me, þa þu him fram wære and wið God spæce, "Niton we hwæt Moises gefaren hæfð, þe us ut alædde of Egipta lande", and þæt folc bæd me þæt hig moston him wircan godas, swa þa Egiptiscan dydon. ²⁴ þa cwæð ic to him, "Nymað eall eower gold and bringað to me, and eower wifa earhringas and eower dohtra", and hig brohton þa hira gold to me and ic hit het weorpan on fyr and wircan þærof anes celfes gelicnysse.' ²⁵ þa geseh Moises þæt Aaron hæfde bereafod þæt folc æt hira golde, for þam unrihte þe hig gedon hæfdon, and þæt Moise wel licode, þæt hig æt hira golde bereafode wæron. ²⁶ þa cwæð Moises to þam folce: 'Ælc þæra þe Godes freond si, filie me todæg, þæt we magon wrecan Godes yrre on þam mannon þe God forlæten habbað.' þa beah eall | Leuiges mægð to Moise. ²⁷ þa cwæð Moises to Leuies mægðe: 'Nymaþ eowre wæpn and gað forð mid me and wrecað Godes yrre on þam mannum þe hyne forlæten habbaþ, and ne sparige eower nan, ne broðor ne sunu ne mæg, þe þæt unriht ongen God worhton.' ²⁸ And Leuiges mægð dyde eall swa Moises him bebead and ofslogon on hira agenum cynne þreo and twentig þusendra manna. ²⁹ þa cwæð Moises to him:

32:17 hream] 'h'ream B   swilc] swilce BP   32:19 geseh] geseah B   celf¹] cealf B   hig¹] hi BP   eall¹] eal B   celf²] cealf B   werp] wearp B   hig eall] hi eal B   32:20 celf þæt] cealf þe BP   hig] hi B   32:21 ane] *om.* BP   32:22 andswarude] andswarode BP   belg] belh B   ongen] ongean B   32:23 Hig¹] hi B   hig²] hi BP   wircan] wyrcean B   Egiptiscan] egyptiscean B   32:24 ic to] P *ends*

MSS L, B   32:24 eower¹] eowwer B   eower³] eowwer B   hig] hi B   hira] heora B   weorpan] wurpan B   wircan þærof] wyrcean þæroff B   celfes] cealfes B   32:25 geseh] geseah B   hira¹] heora B   hig¹] hi B   Moise] moyses B   hig²] hi B   hira²] heora B   32:26 mannon] mannum B   eall] eal B   Leuiges] leuies B   32:27 eower] eowwer B   ongen] ongean B   32:28 Leuiges] leuies B   eall] eal B   hira] heora B   þusendra] þusenda B

'Todæg ge habbað Gode gecwemede and eowere handa gehalgode, for þi þe ge eowre agene nehstan ofslogon, þe Gode abulgon.'
³²:³⁰ Æfter oþron dæge, Moises spræc to Israhela folce and cwæð to him: 'Ge syngodon þa mæstan synne ongen God and gif ic Drihten æniges þinges biddan dear for eowre scilde, ic wille for eow gebiddan.' ³¹ Þa gebæd Moises to Drihtne and cwæð: 'Ic halsige þe Drihten, miltsa þison folce, þeah hit gesingod hæbbe. Hig worhton him gildene godas and forleton þe. ³² Forgif him þa synne, and gif þu him gemiltsian nelt, adilga me of þinre bec þe þu me on awrite.' ³³ Drihten andswarode Moise and cwæð to him: 'Se þe on me gesyngað, ic hine adilige of minre bec. ³⁴ Ga þu and læde þis folc þæder þe ic þe ær sæde, and min engel færð beforan þe and on þam itemistan dæge ic gewrece þa synne þe þis folc wið me geworht hæfð. ³⁵ And þis Israhelisce folc ys ofslagen for þam gylte þe hig | worhton f. 63ᵛ
þæt gildene celf and wurðodon hit for god and forleton me.'
³³:¹ Drihten cwæð to Moise: 'Far of þisse stowe, and þin folc, to þam lande þe ic behet Abrahame and Isaace and Iacobe, and ic hit sylle þinum cynne. ² And ic sende minne engel beforan þe and drife ut Chananeum and Amorreum and Etheum and Ferezeum and Eueum and Iebuseum, ³ and þu færst on þæt land þe ys wæstmbære, ægþer ge on hunie ge on meoluce. Ne fare ic sylf mid þe, for þam þe þis folc ys heardheort, þe læs ic þe be wege fordo.' ⁴ Þæt folc weop, þa hig þis gehirdon, and hira nan hine ne scridde swa hira gewuna wæs. ⁵ Drihten cwæð to Moise: 'Sege þam folce þæt hig sind heardheorte. "Æne ic fare to þe and adilgige þe. Alege nu þine glenga, þæt ic wite hu ic þe ymbe do."' ⁶ Þæt Israhelisce folc aledon hira glenga on Oreb dune. ⁷ Þa het Moises slean an geteld butan hira wicstowe and nemde hit 'Godes geteld', and þæt folc þe hæfde ænige spræce, eode ut to þam getelde. ⁸ Þonne Moises ut eode to þam getelde, eall þæt folc aras and stodon on hira [getelda] durum and beheoldon Moises oð he inn eode to þam getelde. ⁹ Þonne he inn eode, þonne com genip and stod æt þære dura and God spræc wið

32:29 gecwemede] gecwemed B   eowere] eowre B   þi] þam B   nehstan] nextan B
32:30 Æfter] *3-line green and red initial cap.* L   oþron] oþrum B   ongen] ongean B
32:31 halsige] halsie B   miltsa] milsa B   þison] þisum B   Hig] hi B   forleton] forletan B
32:32 him¹] heom B   adilga] adylega B   32:33 adilige] adylgie B   32:34 læde] læd B   þæder] þider B   itemistan] ytemestan B   32:35 hig] hi B   celf] cealf B
33:1 Drihten] *3-line red initial cap.* L   33:2 drife] adrife B   Ferezeum] pherezeum B
33:3 hunie] hunige B   meoluce] meolce B   fare] fere B   þam] þan B   33:4 hig] hi B
hira¹] heora B   hira²] heora B   33:5 adilgige] adylgie B   ymbe] embe B   33:6 hira
glenga] heora glencga B   33:7 spræce] spæce B   33:8 þonne] ða B   getelda] B, *om.* L

Moises, [10] and hig ealle gesawon þæt þæt genip stod æt þæs geteldes dura and hig stodun and gebædun hig æt hira getelda durum. [11] Drihten spræc wið Moises swa man spricð wiþ his freond, | and þa he cirde to þære wicstowe, þa gebad Iosue, Nunes sunu, on þam getelde. [12] Moyses cwæð to Drihtne: 'Þu bitst me þæt ic læde ut þis folc and ne gesegst me hwæne þu mid me sendan wille, and cwist, "Ic can þe be naman and þu hæfst gife beforan me". [13] Gif ic ænige gife hæbbe beforan þe, ætyw me þine annsine, þæt ic cunne þe and hæbbe gife beforan þinum eagum. Sceawa þis folc.' [14] And Drihten cwæð: 'Min ansin færþ beforan þe and ic sylle þe reste.' [15] Þa cwæð Moises: 'Gif þu silf mid us ne færst, ne læd þu us of þisse stowe. [16] Be hwam magon we witan þæt we gife habbon beforan þe, buton þu fare mid us, þæt us ealle menn wurþion þe ofer eorðan eardiaþ?' [17] Drihten cwæð to Moise: 'Ic do swa þu cwæde. Þu hæfst gife beforan me and ic cann þe be naman.' [18] And Moises cwæð: 'Ætyw me þin wuldor.' [19] Þa [a]ndswarode he and cwæð: 'Ic ætywe þe ælc god and ic beo genemned þin Drihten, and ic gemiltsige þam þe ic wille and þam þe me licað.' [20] And eft he cwæð: 'Ne miht þu me geseon. Ne gesihþ me nan lybbende mann. [22] Ic gescilde þe mid minre swyðran handan, þa hwile þe ic forþ ga, [23] and ic do mine hand aweg and þu gesihst me æftewearde. Ne miht þu mine ansine geseon.'

[34:1] And he cwæð siþþan: 'Wirc þe twa stænene tabulan, þam oðrum gelice, and ic write þæron þa word þe on þam oþrum wæron, | þe ðu bræce. [2] Beo tomorgen gearu and ga uppan Sinai dune and stand mid me uppan þære dune ufeweardre. [3] Ne cume nan mann uppan þære dune, ne nan nyten.' [4] He worhte twa stænene tabulan, swilce þa oðre wæron, and aras on niht and eode uppan Sinai dune, swa Drihten him bebead, and bær þa tabulan mid him. [5] And þa Drihten eode nyðer þurh þæt genip, þa Moises stod mid him and nemde Drihtnes naman, [6] and cwæð þa he forð eode: 'Drihten, wealdend, mildheort God, arfæst and geþildig and soþfæst, [7] þu þe gehiltst mildheortnysse and agiltst fædera unrihtwisnysse hira bearnum.' [8] And Moises cwæð: 'Gif ic gife hæbbe on

---

33:10 hig¹] hi B   hig stodun] hi stodon B   gebædun hig] gebædon hi B   hira] heora B
33:11 man] mann B   33:12 gesegst] segst B   33:13 annsine] ansyne B
33:16 hwam] hwan B   menn] men B   33:17 cann] can B   33:19 andswarode] B, ndswarode L   33:20 gesihþ] syhð B   mann] man B   33:22 handan] handa B
33:23 gesihst] gesixð B   æftewearde] æfterweardne B   34:2 uppan²] uppon B
34:3 mann] man B   34:5 þa²] a *alt. fr.* u L, and B   mid] mi B   34:6 wealdend] waldend B   34:7 hira] heora B

þinre gesihþe, ic bidde þe þæt þu fare mid us, for þam þis folc ys heardheort. Forgif us ure synna, þæt we beon þine agene.' ¹⁰ Drihten him andswarode and cwæð: 'Ic sylle mine getreowþe eallum geleafullum and ic wirce þa tacnu þe næfre nan man ne geseah ær on anum lande, þæt þis folc geseo Drihtnes egeslice weorc þe ic wirce betweohs him. ¹¹ Heald ealle þa þing þe ic þe todæg bead. Ic silf adrife ut beforan þe Amorreum and Chananeum and Etheum, Pherezeum and Eueum and Iebuseum. ¹² Warna þe þæt þu næfre freondrædene nyme wið þa landes men, ¹³ ac towurp hira weofudu and tobrec hira anlicnyssa and forceorf hira wu|das. ¹⁴ Ne geeaðmede   f. 65ʳ þu þe to hira unrihtan godum. ¹⁵ Ne nim þu nane sibbe wið þæs landes menn, þe læs þe hira ænig þe swice, ne et þu of hira offrunga þe hig ofriað hira godum and geeaðmedað hira hearga. ¹⁶ Ne nim þu wif of hira cynne þinum sunum, þe læs þe hig gedon þæt þine bearn singion on hira godas, æfter þam þe hig singiað. ¹⁷ Ne wirc þu þe gegotene godas. ¹⁸ Þeorfne hlaf þu scealt etan seofon dagas, swa ic þe bebead, on niwra monþa tide. Soðlice on lengtentide monðes þu fore of Egipta lande. ¹⁹ Ælc frumcenned þing wæpnedcynnes bið min of eallum nytenum, ge of hruþerum ge of sceapon. ²⁰ Assan frumcennede þu scealt alysan mid sceap; gif þu þonne wurð for hit ne sylst, hit sceal sweltan. Þinra bearna frumcenned þu scealt alysan. Ne cum þu to minum huse idelhende. ²¹ Wirc six dagas and freolsa þone seofoðan. ²³ Þriwa on gere, ælc wæpnedman sceal cuman to Godes huse. ²⁴ And ic adrife hæðene fram þe and geryme þine gemæro.' ²⁷ Drihten cwæð to Moise: '[. . .] þæt ic behet þe freondscipe and Israhela folce.' ²⁸ Moises wæs þa mid Drihtne .xl. daga and .xl. nihta, swa he ne æt ne dranc and wrat þa tyn word þe Drihten him bebead. ²⁹ Þa Moises nyðer eode of Sinai dune, he hæfde þa tabulan on handa and nyste þæt he wæs gehyrned, for þam þe he wið God spræc. ³⁰ Aaron and Israhela folc gesawon | þæt Moises wæs gehyrned and   f. 65ᵛ

34:10 andswarode] andwyrde B   getreowþe] tryfþe B   geleafullum] geleaffullum B   anum] nanum B   betweohs] betweox B   34:11 þing] þincg B   Pherezeum] ferezeum B   Iebuseum] iebusseum B   34:12 nyme] ne genime B   34:13 hira weofudu] heora weofodu B   hira²] heora B   hira³] heora B   34:14 geeaðmede] geeadmede B   hira unrihtan] heora unrihtum B   34:15 hira²] heora B   hig ofriað hira] hi offriaþ heora B   hira hearga] heora he`a´rga B   34:16 hira¹] heora B   hig¹] hi B   singion] singian B   hira²] heora B   hig²] hi B   34:18 lengtentide monðes] lenctenmonþes tide B   of] off B   34:19 þing] ðincg B   hruþerum] hryðerum B   sceapon] sceapum B   34:20 frumcennede] frumcennedne B   sceap] sceape B   34:23 gere] geare B   wæpnedman sceal] wæpnedmann sceall B   34:27 Drihten cwæð . . . folce] *In both L and B a few words of translation appear to have been lost in this sentence, but there is no gap in the MSS*   34:28 .xl.¹] feowertig B   .xl.²] feowertig B   æt] ætt B   ne] ne *add*. B

ne dorston him neah cuman. ³¹ Þa clipode he hig, þa cirde Aaron and þa yldestan men to him, and siþþan he wið hig spræc, ³² þa com eall Israhela folc to him and he bebead him ealle þa þing þe Drihten bebead him on Sinai dune. ³³ And þonne he wið hig gesprecen hæfde, he heng hrægl beforan his nebb.

³⁵:¹ Moises cwæð to eallum Israhela folce: 'þis synd þa þing þe Drihten bebead. ² Wirceað six dagas and freolsiað þone seofoðan Gode to wurðmynte. Se þe wircð on þam seofoþan dæge, si he ofslagen. ³ Ne onæle ge nan fyr on þam dæge.'

34:31 hig¹] hi B   hig²] hi B   34:32 þing] þinc B   bebead him] him bebead B
34:33 nebb] neb B   35:1 þing] þinc B   35:2 seofoþan] seofoþam B

[LEVITICUS]

Her onginneð seo þridde boc, þe ys genemned on Ebreisc 'Vaiecra' and 'Leuiticus' on Grecisc and 'Ministerialis' on Lyden, þæt is 'þenungboc' on Englisc, for þam þara sacerda þenunga sind þar awritene.

1:1 DRIHTEN CLIPODE TO MOISE on þære halgan wurðungstowe and þus cwæð: ² 'Sege Israhela bearnum, "Gif hwilc eower wille Gode offrunga bringan of nytenum, þæt ys of hriðerum and of sceapum, ³ and seo offrung be þam fullan beon scile, þonne bringe he of hriðerun an unwemme oxancelf to þære halgan stowe dura, Drihten mid to gladienne, ⁴ and asette his hand ofer þære offrunge heafod. þonne bið heo andfenge and fremiende to his clænsunge. ⁵ Offrige þonne þæt celf | beforan Drihtne, and Aarones suna, þæs f. 66ʳ sacerdes, offrion þæs celfes blod and geoton embutan þæt weofod þe ys beforan þære halgan stowe dura, ⁶ and hyldon þa offrunga and ceorfon to sticcon, ⁷ and don fyr innan þæt weofod ⁸ uppan þa sticceon þe þær tosnidene beoð, þæt heafod and ealle þa þing þe to þære lifre clifiað, ⁹ and waxan þæt innewerde and þa fet. And se sacerd forbærnð þa, Drihtne to leohte and to wynsumum stence. ¹⁰ Gif seo offrung þonne beo of sceapon oððe of gatun, bringe enitre offrunga and unwemme ¹¹ and offrige þa beforan Drihtne æt þæs weofudes sidan þe ys on norð healfe, and geoton Aarones suna þæt blod uppan þæt weofud embutan, ¹² and todælon þa lima, þæt heafod and ealle þa þing þe to þære lifre clifiað, and lecgeon uppan þone wudu þe man þæt fyr sceal under don. ¹³ Waxan þonne þæt innewerde, and se sacerd bærnð hit eall uppan þam weofude to wynsumum s[w]æcce. ¹⁴ Gif seo offrung þonne bið of fugelum,

MSS L, B   Rubric starts on same line as last word of Exodus, and fills four further lines, alternately metallic red and red. In B (f. 105ᵛ), the rubric is in small rustic caps., squeezed to the left of an illustration.   Rubric onginneð] ongynð B   Ebreisc] ebreis B   Lyden] leden B   þam þara] ðan ðe ðæra B   þar] ðæron B   1:1 DRIHTEN] *4-line red and green decorative initial cap.* L   1:3 scile] sceole B   hriðerun] hryþerum B   oxancelf] oxancealf B   gladienne] gegladienne B   1:4 asette] sette B   1:5 Offrige] ofrie B   celf] cealf B   offrion] offrian B   celfes] cealfes B   1:6 ceorfon] ceorfan B   1:7 sticceon] sticceom B   1:8 þing] þingc B   1:9 innewerde] innewearde B   fet] fell B   forbærnð] forbærne B   1:10 gatun] gaton B   1:11 offrige] offrie B   weofudes] weofodes B   weofud embutan] weofod ymbutan B   1:12 lima] *and add.* B   þing] þingc B   to] on B   lecgeon] lecgon B   1:13 innewerde] innewearde B   uppan] uppon B   weofude] weofode B   swæcce] spæcce LB

LEVITICUS

þonne bringe he turtlan and culfran briddas, [15] and offrige [se] sacerd æt þam weofude and bige þone swuran and læte yrnan þæt blod niþer andlang þæs weofudes, [16] and wurpe þone cropp and þa feðera wiðæftan þæt weofod on easthealfe, on ðære stowe þe man þa axan git. [17] Ætbred of þa feðeru, næs ne ceorfe, and bærne hig uppan þam
f. 66ᵛ weofude, Drihtne to offrunge and to | wynsumum s[w]æcce.
 [2:1] "Þonne man bringe offrunge Drihtne, nime smedeman and geote ele on uppan, and stor, [2] and bringe to Aarones sunun, þ[æ]s sacerdes, and nime hira [an] ane handfulle smedeman and eles and stores and lecge uppan þæt weofod, Drihtne to wurþunga. [3] And þæt þær to lafe bið, þæt bið Aarones and his bearna. [4] Bring clæne ofenbacene hlafas, mid ele gesmirede, butan beorman. [6] Tobrec hig litlum and ge'o'te ele on uppan. [11] Ne do mann nanne beorman ne hunig to nanre offrunga. [12] Bringað dæl þærof and ne cume hit uppan þam weofude. [13] Þu scealt [. . .] to ælcere offrunga.
 [3:1] "Gif he hriðeru offrian wille, bringe unwemme fear oððe heafre, [2] and setton Aarones suna hira handa uppan þære offrunga heafod and geotaþ þæt blod ymbeutan þæt weofud. [3] And bringon þone rysle, þe þa heortgesida mid beoð oferwr[ogen], to þam weofude and eall þæt þærinne fættest si, [4] and þa lundlagan mid hira [rysle], [5] and bærnon uppan þam weofode, Drihtne to lace. [6] Gif he sceap bringe, ram oððe eowe, sin hig unwemme. [7] Gif he lamb bringe, [8] geoton Aarones suna his blod imbutan þæt weofod [9] and bringon Drihtne þone rysel and tægl [10] and gelynde, [11] and bærne se sacerd hit uppan þam weofode. [12] And gif man gat offrige, do man on þa ylcan wisan. [16] Ælc rysel sceal Drihtne to leohte. [17] Ne ete ge naðer ne rysel ne
f. 67ʳ blod. [4:3] Gif se gehalgoda sacerd | syngað and deð þæt þæt folc syngie, offrige Drihtne unwemme celf [4] and læde hit to þæs temples dura. [5] Nyme þonne of ðæs celfes blode and sprenge seofon siðon on þæs temples wahryft. [13] Gif eall Israhela folc syngað þurh ungewiss, [14] bringe an celf to þam temple and læde hit to ðære dura [15] and

---

1:14 culfran] tulfran B 1:15 offrige] offrie B se sacerd] B, þam sacerde L weofude] weofode B weofudes] weofodes B 1:17 Ætbred] ætbrede B hig] hi B weofude] weofode B swæcce] spæcce LB 2:1 smedeman] smedman B 2:2 sunun] sunum B þæs] B, þas L hira] heora B an] B, *om.* L 2:6 hig] hi B geote] gete *with* o *above, prob. by orig. scribe* L 2:11 mann] man B 2:12 weofude] weofode B 2:13 scealt] *Grein and Crawford supply* bringan sealt 3:1 fear] fearr B heafre] heafare B 3:2 hira] heora B ymbeutan] ymbutan B weofud] weofod B 3:3 heortgesida] heortgesidu B oferwrogen] B, oferwrihð L weofude] weofode B fættest] fæstest B 3:4 hira] hire B rysle] B, *om.* L 3:6 ram] ramm B hig] hi B 3:10 gelynde] gelyndu B 4:3 gehalgoda] gehalgode B offrige] offrie B celf] cealf B 4:5 celfes] cealfes B sprenge] sprencge B 4:14 celf] cealf B

LEVITICUS

setton þæs folces ealdoran hira handa uppan his heafod. And þonne þæt celf geoffrod sig, [16] nime se sacerd his blod [17] and dyppe his finger þæron and sprenge seofon siðon on þæt ryft, [18] and smite of þam sylfan blode on þæs weofodes hyrnan and geote þæt þær to lafe bið æt þam weofode nyþan, [19] and bærne þone rysel uppan þam weofode. [20] And gebidde se sacerd for hig, [21] and forbærne þæt celf butan þære wicstowe. [22] Gif se ealdor syngað, bringað anne buccan to bote. [27] Gif folces man syngað þurh nytenys, [28] and his gylt undergit, bringe ane gat to bote to þam temple. [5:1] Gif man wat þæ[t] oðer man swerað, he bið scildig gif he hit forhilþ. [4] Se man þe swereð man and eft his gilt ongit, [6] bringe an cilforlamb to bote, oþþe gat, for hine and for his synne, [7] and gif he nyten næbbe, bringe twa turtlan oððe twegen culfran briddas, anne for ðære synne, oðerne to offrunga. [11] Gif he næbbe turtlan ne culfran, bringe melu."'

[6:19] Drihten spræc to Moise and þus cwæð: [20] 'Beod Aarone and his sunum þæt hig bringan Drihtne to offrunge, on þam dæge þe hig man smirað and halgað, | melues, þone teoðan dæl þæs gemetes þe f. 67ᵛ man nemð 'ephi', healf ær undern, healf ofer undern. [21] Þa sceolon beon elebacene and wearme. [23] Ne ete nan man of þæra sacerda offrunga ac forbærne hig man ealle.' [24] Drihten spræc to Moise and þus cwæð: [26, 29] 'Ne ete nan man of ðære offrunga þe man Drihtne bringð, buton þa sacerdas and hira cynn. [7:17] And gif þær hwæt to lafe bið ofer þa twegen dagas, forbærne hit man þæs þriddan dæges. [25] Gif hwa þæt smeru oððe þæt blod [ytt], þe bið Gode geoffrud, he sceal forwurðan. [31-2] Se swiðra boh and þa ribb sceal beon Aarones and his sunena of ðære offrunga þe man for gesibbsumnysse offriað.' [8:1] Drihten spræc to Moise and þus cwæð: [2] 'Nim Aaron and his suna and hira reaf and smiringele and an celf for synne and twegen rammas and þeorfe hlafas, [3] and gadera eall folc to þæs temples dura.' [4] Moises dyde swa Drihten bebead [5] and cwæð to þam folce: 'Þis Drihten bebead.' [6] He þwoh þa Aaron and his suna [7] and scridde þone bisceop mid linenum reafe and girde hine and dyde ymbe hine blæhwene tunecan and lede eaxlclað ofer hine [8] and band to þam

4:15 celf] cealf B   sig] sy B   4:17 ryft] wahrift B   4:20 hig] hi B   4:21 celf] cealf B   4:22 bringað] bringe B   4:27 nytenys] nytennysse B   4:28 to þam] 'to' ðam B   5:1 þæt] B, þær L   5:4 swereð] swerað B   5:6 cilforlamb] cylferlamb B   5:7 anne] ænne B   6:20 hig bringan] hi bringon B   hig²] hi B   nemð] nemneð B   6:21 elebacene] B, elebracene L   6:23 hig] hi B   6:26, 29 buton] butan B   hira] heora B   7:17 þa] om. B   7:25 ytt] B, hit L   geoffrud] geoffrad B   7:31-2 ribb] andrib B (with and scored through)   sceal] sceolon B   gesibbsumnysse offriað] gesibsumnysse offrað B   8:2 hira] heora B   celf] cealf B   8:4 Drihten] him add. B   8:7 blæhwene] blæhæwene B   eaxlclað] eaxclað B

LEVITICUS

rationale, on þam wæs awriten lar and soþfæstnys, [9] and band his heafod mid claþe and mid gehalgodon gildenbe[n]de, swa Drihten him bebead. [10–11] And he nam þæne smiringele and smirode þa halgan stowe and þæt weofod and ealle hira fatu, and halgode þæt arfæt. [12] And he get ele uppan Aarones heafod and smirode hine and gehalgode. [13] And he scridde his suna mid and girde hig and hufode, swa Drihten bebead, [14] and brohte an celf for synne, and Aaron and his suna setton hira handa uppan his heafod [15] and offrodon hit and smirodon þæs weofodes hyrnan mid þam blode and guton þæt þær to lafe wæs under þæt weofod, [16] and bærndon þone rysle and þa lundlagan uppan þam weofode. [17] And þæt celf hig bærndon butan þære wicstowe mid felle and mid flæsce, swa Drihten him bead. [18] Hig offrodon anne ram and guton his blod imbutan þæt weofod [20] and curfon þone ram eall to sticceon [21] and forbærndon uppan þam weofode, for þam þe he wæs Drihtnes offrung. [22–3] Ða Moises þone ramm offrude, he æthran mid þam blode Aarones swiðre eare and his swiðran þuman and þæs wynstran fotes miclan tan. [24] Þa he þus gedon hæfde, he get þæt blod uppan þæt weofod, þe þær to lafe wæs. [25] Þone tægl and eall þæt smeru and twegen lundlagan mid gelyndum [28] hig forbærndon uppan þam weofode. [31] And þa he hig þus gehalgod hæfde, þa cwæð he: 'Seoðaþ eowerne mete beforan þæs temples dura and etað þær, swa Drihten bebead and þus cwæð, "Ete Aaron and his suna", [32] and swa hwæt swa þær to lafe beo, oððe of flæsce oþþe of hlafe, forbærne man þæt. [33] Ne fare ge seofon dagum of þære stowe durum [35] ac healdaþ þær wear|de dæges and nihtes, swa Drihten bebead.' [36] Aaron and his suna dydon ealle þa þing þe Drihten him bebead þurh Moisen.

[9:1] Æfter seofon dagum Moises clipode Aaron and his suna and þa betstborenan of Israhela folce and cwæð to him: [2] 'Offriað an celf and anne ram for synne, ægþer unwemme, [3] and beodað Israhela folce þæt hig offrian for synne buccan and celf and lamb, ælc enitre and unwemme, [4] and for gesibsumnysse oxan and ramm. Todæg Drihten ætywþ.' [5] Hig namon þa ealle þa þing þe Moises him bebead and

---

8:9 gehalgodon] gehalgodan B   gildenbende] B, gildenbeade L   8:10–11 þæne smiringele] ðone smyringcele B   hira] heora B   8:12 get] geat B   8:13 mid] midd B   hig] hi B   8:14 celf] cealf B   hira] heora B   8:17 celf hig] cealf hi B   bead] bebead B   8:18 Hig] hi B   ram] ramm B   8:21 þam²] ðan B   8:22–3 offrude] offrode B   8:24 get] geat B   8:28 hig] hi B   8:31 hig] hi B   eowerne] eowwerne B   þær] þæra LB; *Crawford emends to* þær þa   8:33 dagum] dagon B   8:36 þing] þingc B   9:2 celf] cealf B   9:3 hig offrian] hi offrion B   celf] cealf B   enitre] anwintre B   9:4 gesibsumnysse] sibsumnesse B   9:5 Hig] hi B   þing] ðingc B

LEVITICUS

brohton to þæs temples dura, ⁶and Moises cwæð to þam folce: 'Wirceað þæt Drihten eow bebead and Drihten eow ætywð.' ²³ Þa Aaron geoffrud hæfde and þæt folc gebletsod, swa Moises him bead, þa eode he nyþer. Ða ætywde Godes wuldor eallum þam folce. ²⁴ And com fyr of Gode and forbærnde ealle þa offrunga þe uppan þam weofude wæron, and þa þæt folc þæt geseah, þa feollun hig niðer and heredon Drihten. ¹⁰:¹ Ða namon Aarones suna Nadab and Abiud hira storcillan and onældon þæron ungehalgod fyr, þæt him forboden wæs beforan Gode. ² And fyr com þærrihte and forbærnde hig to deaþe. ³ Þa swugode Aaron and wæs sarig. ⁴ Ða bead Moises Missabele and Elifaphan, Acsicheles sunum, Aarones fæderan, þæt hig namon hira maga lic and bæron butan wicstowe. ⁵ And hig eodon sona and bæron hig aweg and wurpon hig ut, swa him beboden wæs. ⁶ Moises cwæð to Aarone and to Eleazare | and to Ithamare, his f. 69ʳ sunum: 'Forlætað eowre hreowsunga, þe læs ge habbon Godes yrre.' ⁸ Drihten spræc to Aarone and to his sunum: ⁹ 'Ne drince ge nan þing þæs þe man mæg dr[unce]n of beon þonne ge gan into þære halgan stowe, þe læs ge sweltun.

¹¹:¹ Drihten spræc to Moise and to Aarone: ² 'Secgað Israhela bearnum ³ þæt hig eton þa nytenu þe hira clawe todælede beoð and ceowað. ⁴ "Ne ete ge þa þing þe ceowað and clawe ne todælað, swa olfend. ⁶⁻⁸ Hara and swyn synd forbodene to æthrinenne. ⁹ Ne ete ge nanne fisc, buton þa þe habbað finnas and scilla; ¹² þa oðre synd unclæne. ¹³⁻¹⁴ Ne ete ge nan þing hafoccynnes ne earncynnes, ¹⁵⁻¹⁶ ne ulan ne nan [þing] hrefncynnes.

¹⁸:⁶ "Ne hæme nan man wið his magan, ¹⁶ ne wið his mæges wif. ³⁰ Healdað mine bebodu. Ne do ge þa þing þe þa didon þe beforan eow wæron, þe læs ge beon besmitene. Ic eom Drihten eower God. ¹⁹:³ Arwurðiað eowerne fæder and eowwre modor and healdað mine fæstdagas. ¹¹ Ne stel þu. Ne leoh þu. Ne beswic þu þinne neaxtan. ¹² Ne swera þu man on minum naman. Ic eom Drihten. ¹³ Ne bysmra þu þinne mæg. Nafa þu ane niht unforgolden þæs weorc þe þe wirce.

9:23 geoffrud] geofrod B   bead] bebead B   9:24 offrunga] ofrunga B   weofude] weofode B   feollun hig] feollon hi B   10:1 hira] heora B   ungehalgod] unhalgod B 10:2 hig] hi B   10:4 Elifaphan] elifafan B   Acsicheles] aczicheles B   hig] hi B   hira] heora B   10:5 hig¹] hi B   hig²] hi B   hig³] hi B   10:6 Ithamare] iðamare B   sunum] sunon B   10:9 þing] ðingc B   druncen] B, drincan L   sweltun] swylton B 11:3 hig] hi B   hira clawe] heora clawa B   11:4 þing] ðingc B   ceowað] 'ne' ceowað B clawe] clawa B   11:6–8 æthrinenne] æthrinene B   11:13–14 þing] ðingc B 11:15–16 þing] þingc B, om. L   18:30 þa þing] nan dingc B   19:3 eowwre] eowre B fæstdagas] fæstendagas B; f alt. to r in L (poss. by 11/12th-c. glossator)   19:11 neaxtan] nextan B

LEVITICUS

¹⁴ Ne wirige þu deafe, ne scremme þu blinde. Ondræd þinne God. ¹⁵ Ne dem nan unriht. Ne forseoh þu þea[r]fan. Ne arwurða þone rican. Deme rihte þinum nextan. ¹⁶ Ne beo þu sacfull. ¹⁷ Ne hata þu þinne nextan on þinre heortan ac þrea hine openlice. | ¹⁸ Ne tyn þu þine neahgeburas. Lufa þinne freond swa þe sylfne. Ic eom Drihten. ¹⁹ Healdað mine æ. Ne do þu þæt nytenu hæmon mid oðres cynnes nitenum. Ne saw þu þinne æcyr mid gemengedum sæde. ²³ Ne ete ge þæra treowa bleda þe ge plantigeað ²⁵ ær þam fiftan geare. ²⁶ Ne eton ge blod, ne ne gimon hwata ne swefna. ²⁷ Ne ge eow ne efesion, ne beard ne sciron. ²⁹ Ne læt þu þine dohtor beon myltestre, þe læs þin land sig mid mane gefylled. ³¹ Ne gim þu drycræfta ne galdra. ³² Arwurða ealdne man and ondræd þe þinne God. ³³ Ne hyrwe ge utancymene man, ³⁴ ac si he gemang eow swa inlendisc and lufiað hine swa eow sylfe, for þam þe ge wæron utacymene on Egipta lande. ³⁶ Habbað rihtne anmittan and emne wæga and emne gemetu and sestras. Ic eom Drihten eower God þe eow alædde of Egipta lande. ³⁷ Healdað mine bebodu and mine domas. ²⁰:² Gif ænig man gelyfe on Moloches hearch, swelte he deaðe; hæne hine man mid stanum. ⁹ Gif hwa wirigð his fæder and his modur, he sceal sweltan. ²⁷ Se man þe bega wiccecræft, swelte he deaðe." '

²³:¹ Drihten spræc to Moise and þus cwæð: 'Sege Israhela folce, "Ðis sind þa dagas þe ge sceolun Drihtne halgian and wurðian. ⁵ On þam feowerteoðan dæge þæs forman monðes on æfen biþ Drihtnes færeld. ¹⁰ And þonne ge in cumað on þæt land þe ic eow sille, ²² ne ripe ge to clæne, ne ge ne gaderion þa ear þe | bæftan eow beoð, ac lætað þea`r´fan and utacymene hig lesan." '

²⁴:¹⁰ Sum egiptisc man gestrinde sunu be Israheliscum wife onmang Israhela folce. Þa flat he wið anne Israheliscne man ¹¹ and hyrwde Godes naman and wirigde hine, þa lædde hine man to Moise. His modor [hatte] Salomith, Dabrius dohtor of Danis cynne, ¹² and hig didon hine on cweartern oð hig wiston hwæt Drihten be him tæhte. ¹³ Ða cwæð Drihten to Moise: ¹⁴ 'Læd ut þone hyrwend wiðutan þa wicstowe and setton ealle þa þe his word gehirdon hira

---

19:14 wirige] wyrie B   19:15 þearfan] B, þeafan L   19:16 sacfull] sacful B
19:19 æcyr] æcer B   gemengedum] gemengdum B   19:23 plantigeað] plantiað B
19:26 eton] ete B   gimon] gyman B   19:27 sciron] sceron B   19:29 sig] sy B
19:32 Arwurða] arwurðe B   19:36 alædde] ælædde B   20:2 hearch] hearh B
20:9 modur] modor B   23:1 sceolun] sceolon B   23:5 þæs] þes B
23:22 gaderion] gaderian B   bæftan] bæfton B   þearfan] r above, appar. contemp. L
utacymene hig] utacymene hi B   24:10 Israheliscum] israheliscon B   24:11 hatte] B, om. L   Danis] danes B   24:12 hig²] hi B   24:14 hyrwend] hyruwend B   hira] heora B

LEVITICUS

handa uppan his heafod, and oftorfige eall [þæt] folc hine. [15-16] And cweþ to Israhela folce, "Se man þe wirigð Drihtnes naman, swelte he deaðe. [17] Se þe man ofslihð oþþe gewundað, he sceal sweltan. [18] Se þe orf ofslihð, gilde heafod wið heafode. [19] Gif neahgebur wið oþerne agilte, do him man þæt ylce þæt he þam oðrum dyde. [20] Gilde eage mid eagan, and toð mid teð, [22] si he landes man, si he utlendisc."' [23] Israhela bearn dydon swa Drihten Moise bebead.

[25:1] Drihten spræc to Moise on Sinai dune and cwæð: [2] 'Sprec to Israhela folce þas word: "þonne ge in cumað on þæt land þe ic eow sylle, freolsiað Drihtnes restedæg. [3] Six gear þu scealt sawan and wircean þinne wineard and gaderian hira wæstmas. [4] þæt seofoðe ger þæt land bið freoh þurh Drihtnes gife. Ne saw þu þonne, ne rip, ne þinne wineard ne wirc, [5] ne hira wæstmas ne gadera, þonne hig weaxað sylfwilles, | for þam þe hit bið restenger. [10] And þæt fifteoðe f. 70ᵛ ger bið halig and forgifenisse ger. On þam forgifenisse geare man sceal freogan ælcne þeowan, buton he fram his halforde nelle. [11] [Gyf he þonne fram his hlaforde nelle,] læde man hine to þæs temples dura and þirlige his eare mid ale and beo he æfre syððan þeow. [17] Ne swencað eowre magas. Ondrædaþ eowerne Drihten eowre God. [18] Healdað mine bebodu and mine domas, þæt ge lybbon eowre lif butan ælcre sorge. [20] Gif hwa þonne cwyð, 'Hwæt ete we on þam seofoðan geare gif we ne sawað ne ne gaderiað ure wæstmas?', [21] ic eow sylle mine bletsunga, þæt an gear bringð þreora geara wæstmas. [22] Sawað on þam eahteoðan geare and etað ealde wæstmas o[þ] þæt nigoðe gear and o[þ] niwe cumað. [23] Ne sylle ge þæt land on ece yrfe for þam þe hit ys Godes and ge synd utacymene and mine tilian. [25] Gif þin wanspediga mæg beo mid þe, ne nim þu na mare æt him to hyre þonne þu sealdest. [37] Ne syle þu þin feoh to hyre. [39] þeah þin nehxta for his yrmðe gange on þeowet, nafa þu hine for weal [40] a[c] for medgildan. [42] Hig sind mine þeowas and ic hig alædde of egipta

24:14 oftorfige] oftorfie B   þæt] B, *om.* L (*add. above at uncertain date*)
24:15–16 man] mann B   24:18 heafode] heafde B   24:20 eagan] eagum B
25:1 Drihten] *enlarged black initial cap., new line* L   25:2 Sprec] *om.* B   in] inn B
restedæg] restendæg B   25:3 wineard] wingeard B   hira] heora B   25:4 ger] gear B
ne rip] ne ne rip B   wineard] wingeard B   25:5 hira] heora B   hig] hi B   þam] þa`n´
B   restenger] restengear B   25:10 ger] gear B   forgifenisse] forgyfenesse B   ger] gear
B, gere L   sceal freogan] sceall freogean B   buton] butan B   25:11 Gyf he . . . nelle]
B, *om.* L   þirlige] þyrlige B   ale] anum æle B   25:17 swencað eowre] swenceað
eowerne B   25:18 eowre] eower B   ælcre sorge] ælcere sorhge B   25:22 eahteoðan]
eahtoðan B   oþ¹] of LB   oþ²] of LB (*late corr. in* L)   25:23 Godes] *om.* B (*Crawford supplies* min)   synd utacymene] syndon utacymene B   25:39 nehxta] nexta B   weal] wealh B   25:40 ac] B, a L   25:42 Hig¹] hi B   hig alædde] hi gelædde B

lande. ⁴⁴Nabbon ge wealas ne wylna of eowrum cynne ac of þam
þeodum þe eow ymbutan synd and of utancymenum. ⁵⁵Israhela
bearn sind mine þeowas þe ic ut alædde of egipta lande.
²⁶:¹ "Ic eom Drihten eowre God. Ne wirce ge eow hearga, ne
agrafene godas. Ic eom Drihten. ³Gif ge | healdað mine bebodu, ic
eow sylle fulle wæstmas and ge etað to fylle and ge eardiað butan ege
on eowrum lande, ⁶and ic sylle sibbe on eowrum [gemærum] and ge
beoð butan brogan. Ic afyrre yfele wilddeor and gewinn fram eow.
⁷Ge feohtað wið eowre fynd and hig feallað beforan eow. ⁸Fif eower
filiað hira hundteontig, and hundteontig eowre fleoð hira tyn
þusendu. Eowre fynd feallað beforan eow. ⁹Ic eow geseo and do
þæt ge weaxað. Ge beoþ gemenigfylde and ic fæstnige min wedd mid
eow. ¹⁰Ge etað ealde mettas o[þ] eow niwe cumon. ¹¹Ic sette mine
halgan stowe tomiddes eowre and ne awurpe ic eow, ¹²ac ic ga
betwyx eow and ic beo eower God and ge beoð min folc. ¹³Ic eom
Drihten eower God þe eow ut alædde of Egipta lande, þæt ge me
þeowudon, and ic eom se þe tobræc þa raceteagan ymbutan eowrum
swuran and alysde eow. ¹⁴Gif ge me ne gehirað and mine bebodu
forhogiað, ¹⁵and mine æ and mine domas forseoð and ne doð min
wedd for naht, ¹⁶ic gedo eow þas þing. Ic sende hrædlice fyr and
gewirce eow to wædlan. On idel ge swincað and eowre fynd his
brucað. ¹⁷Ic wiðstande ongen eow and ge feallað beforan eowrum
feondum and gehirað þam þe eow hatiað. Ge fleoð, þeah eow man ne
drife. ¹⁸Ic eow do seofonfealdne ege, ¹⁹and ic forbrece eowre
ofermodignisse heardnysse, and ic gedo þæt eow bið ægþer heard,
ge heofene ge eorðe. ²⁰And eall eower geswinc bið idel; ne bringð
eorðe eow nane wæstmas. ²²And ic sende on eow | wildeor þæt
forspillon eow and eowre nytenu. ²³Gif ge nellað onfon mine lare
and gað ongen me, ²⁴ic ga ongen eow and slea eow. ²⁵And þonne ge
fleoð fram birig to birig, ic sende cwealm on eow ²⁶and hungor, swa
þæt fif bacað on anum ofene and ge etað hlaf be gewihte and ge ne
beoð [fulle]. ²⁸And ic witnige eow seofon [witon], swa þæt ge etað

25:44 ymbutan] abuton B   25:55 þeowas] ðeowan B   26:1 eowre] eowwer B
26:3 bebodu] beboda B   26:6 gemærum] B, om. L   wilddeor] wildeor B   gewinn]
gewin B   26:7 hig feallað] hi hreosað B   26:8 eower filiað hira] eowre fliað heora B
fleoð hira] sleað heora B   þusendu] ðusenda B   26:9 weaxað] and add. B
gemenigfylde] gemænifylde B   fæstnige] fæstnie B   wedd] wed B   26:10 oþ] of L
(*late corr.*)   26:12 betwyx] betwux B   26:13 God] godd B   þeowudon] ðeowodon
B   raceteagan] racyntan B   26:14 me] 'me' B   26:16 þing] ðingc B
26:17 ongen] ongean B   26:19 heofene] heofone B   26:20 eower] eowre B   bið
idel] beoð idele B   bringð] seo add. B   26:23 onfon] B, ongen fon L (gen del.)   ongen]
ongean B   26:26 ofene] ofne B   fulle] B, om. L   26:28 witon] B, om. L

LEVITICUS

eowre suna and eowre dohtra flæsc. ³⁰ And ic towurpe eowre heagan getimbru and eowre hearga ic tobrece, and ge feallað betwix eowrum deofulgildum. ³¹ And ic onscunige eow, swa þæt ic do eowre burga weste and eowre stowe, ³² and ic fordo eow and eowre fynd wafiað eowre. ³³ Ic todrife eow ³⁵ and þæt land lið on reste, for þam þe hit ne reste þa hwile þe ge þær on wunedon. ³⁶ And þa þe þær to lafe beoð, þa beoð on swa miclum ege þæt hig fleoð leafes sweg, swilce hit swurd sig. Hig feallað þeah hig nan man ne slea, and fleoð þeah him nan man wið ne feohte ³⁹ And for eowrum agenum gylte ge beoð geswencte, ⁴⁰ oþ ge andetton eowre synna, and eowre yldrena, mid þam hig me gremedon and eodon ongen me. ⁴¹ And ic ga ongen eow and gelæde eow on feonda land, o[þ] eowre lyþre mod ablisige. þonne gebidde ge for eowrum arleasnissum, ⁴² and ic [g]yme min wedd þe ic behet Abrahame and Isaace and Iacobe. Ic gime þæs landes; ⁴³ þonne ge hit forlætað, hit licað me þeah hit weste sig. ⁴⁴ Ic eom Drihten eowre God ⁴⁵ þe eow ut alædde of Egipta lande beforan ealles folces gesihþe."' |

Đis synd þa bebodu and domas and laga þe Drihten gesette betwyx him and Israhela folce on Sinai dune.

26:30 betwix] betwux B   deofulgildum] deofolgyldum B   26:31 eowre²] eowra B
26:32 eowre²] eower B   26:35 þam] ðan B   wunedon] wunodon B   26:36 hig¹] hi
B   sig] sy B   Hig²] hi B   hig³] hi B   26:40 oþ] ðæt add. B   andetton] andettan B
eowre²] eower B   hig] hi B   26:41 ongen] ongean B   gelæde] læde B   oþ] B, of L
eowre] eower B   26:42 gyme] nyme L, nime B   26:43 sig] sy B   26:44 eowre]
eower B   26:45 betwyx] betwux B

[NUMBERS]

Her onginð seo boc þe ys genemned on Ebreisc 'Vagedaber', þæt ys on Lyden 'Numerus' and on Englisc 'getel', for þam þe Israhela bearn wæron on þære getealde.

^{1:1} DRIHTEN SPRÆC WITODLICE TO MOISE ON SINAI dune on þære halgan stowe, on þam forman dæge þæs æfteran monðes, on þam oðrum geare þe hig foron of Egipta lande: ²'Nim and telle Israhela folc swa hwæt swa si wæpnedhades, ³fram twentig wintrum and ofer, þæt ealle þa strengestan of Israhela folce telle þu and Aaron heapmælum. ⁴And þæra mægða ealdras beoð [mid] inc mid hira hiredum, ⁵þe þis sint hira naman: Of Ruben, Elisur, Sedeures sunu. ⁶Of Simeon, Salamiel, Suri[s]addais sunu. ⁷Of Iuda, Nason, Aminadabis sunu. ⁸Of Isachar, Nathanael, Suares sunu. ⁹Of Zabulon, Heliab, Elonis sunu. ¹⁰Iosepes bearna: Of Ephraim, Elisama, Amiiudes sunu. Of Mannase, Gamiliel, Phadasures sunu. ¹¹Of Beniamin, Abidan, Gedeonis sunu. ¹²Of Dan, Abiezer, Amisaddages sunu. ¹³Of Aser, Pheziel, Ochranes sunu. ¹⁴Of Gad, Eliazapha, Dueles sunu. ¹⁵Of Neptalim, Ahira, Enananis sunu.' ¹⁶Ðis sind þe wæron þa æðelostan ealdras geond þa scira and Israhela heafodmen. ¹⁷Moises and Aaron gegaderodon ealle þas ¹⁸on f. 72ᵛ þam forman dæge þæs | æftran monðes, and demdon him ¹⁹swa Drihten bebead Moise, and hig man tealde on Sinai westene. ⁴⁵Ðus fela wæs þæra manna þe Moises and Aaron and þa twelf Israhela ealdras getealdon fram twentigum wintrum and bufan, þam þæra þe to gefeohte faran mihton: six hund þusenda and þreo þusenda and fif hundred and fiftig. ⁴⁷Ða sacerdas mid hira hirede næron getealde mid him, ⁴⁸for þam þe Drihten bebead Moyse: ⁴⁹'Ne telle þu Leuies

MSS L, B   Rubric in 4 lines, alternately metallic red and red. In B (f. 111ʳ), the rubric is at the top of a page, in caps.   Rubric Vagedaber] ualedaber B   Lyden] leden B   þam] ðan B   getealde] *followed by decorative colon* L   1:1 DRIHTEN] *3-line green initial cap.* L, rihten (*unfilled space for* D) B   æfteran] æftran B   hig] hi B   1:2 si wæpnedhades] wæpnedhades sy   1:3 twentig] twentigum B   strengestan] strengeston B   1:4 mid] B, *om.* L   hira] heora B   1:5 sint hira] synd heora B   Ruben] rubene B   Elisur] lisur B   1:6 Surisaddais] B, suri raddais L   1:7 Nason] naason B   1:9 Heliab Elonis] elia belonis B   1:10 Ephraim] efraim B   Of^a] on B   Gamiliel] gamaliel B   1:12 Dan Abiezer] dana biezer (b *alt. by later hand to* h) L   Amisaddages] amisadaies B   1:16 sind] ða *add.* B   heafodmen] heafodmenn B   1:19 Drihten] drihten him L (him *del.*)   hig] hi B   1:45 bufan] butan B   1:47 hira] heora B   1:48 þam] ðan B

mægðe, ne sete þu hig mid Israhela folce, ⁵⁰ ac sete hig to þære halgan stowe and to þam þingum þe þærto belimpað.' ⁵⁴ Israhela bearn didon neah eallon þam þingum þe Drihten bebead þurh Moisen. ²:³² And ealles hira heres wæs, þa he todæled wæs, si`x´ hund þusenda and þreo þusenda and fif hundrydo and fiftig. ³⁴ Hig foron floccmælum mid hira hiredum.

³:²⁻³ Þis sint Aarones bearna naman þe to sacerdum gehalgode wæron: Nadab, his frumcenneda sunu, and Abiud and Eleazar and Ithamar. ⁴ Nadab and Abiud wurdon deade þa hig brohton þæt unhalgode fir beforan Drihtnes gesihðe on Sinai westene, butan bearnum. Eleazar and Ithamar brucon sacerdhades beforan hira fæder Aarone. ⁵ Drihten spræc to Moise and cwæð: ⁶ 'Nim Leuies mægðe and sete hig under Aarone, þæt hig þenigeon him and healdon ⁷ and begimon þæra þinga þe to þære halgan eardungstowe belimpað. ⁹⁻¹⁰ Beon hig þenas under Aarone and his sunum. | Gesete Aaron and f. 73ʳ his suna to sacerdum. Gif hwilc utacymen man beginne to þenienne, swelte he deaðe. ¹² Ic nam Leuies cynn æt Israela folce for ælc frumcenned, and hi synd mine þenas. ¹³ Min bið ælc frumcenned siððan ic sloh þa frumcennedan on Egipta lande, ægþer ge on mannum ge on nytenum.' ¹⁴ Drihten cwæð to Moise on Sinai westene: ¹⁵ 'Telle ælcne wæpnedman on Leuies mægðe fram anum monðe and bufan þam.' ¹⁶ Moises þa tealde swa Drihten him bebead. ¹⁷ [Leuies] þri suna: Gerson and Caath and Merari. ²¹⁻² Gersones hiredes wæron seofon þusenda and fif hundredu; ²³ þa heoldon þa halgan eardung-stowe on westhealfe. ²⁷⁻⁸ Caathes hiredes wæron eahta þusendo and six hundrydu; ²⁹ þa heoldon þa halgan eardungstowe on suðhealfe. ³³⁻⁴ Meraries hiredes wæron six þusendo and twa hundrydo; ³⁵ þa heoldon þa halgan stowe on norðhealfe. ³⁸ Moises and Aaron and heora bærn gimdon þæs temples onmiddan Israela folce. ³⁹ þa Moises and Aaron þa Leuite geteald heafdon, eall swa Drihten him bebead, þa wæron hira twa and twentig þusenda.

1:49 hig] hi B   1:50 hig] hi B   þingum] ðingon B   1:54 þam] om. B   þingum] ðingon B   2:32 hira] heora B   six] appar. corr. late fr. sis L, fif B   and þreo þusenda] þreo and hund þusenda (and hund del.) L, þreo and hundeahtatig ðusenda B   hundrydo] hundredo B   2:34 floccmælum] flocmælum B   hira] heora B   3:2-3 sint] synd B   Ithamar] iðamar B   3:4 hig] hi B   unhalgode] ungehalgode B   Ithamar] iðamar B   hira] heora B   3:6 hig¹] hi B   hig þenigeon] hi ðenion B   3:9-10 hig] hi B   Aaron] B, aarone L   þenienne] ðenigenne B   3:12 Israela] israhela B   for] ðam add. B   3:15 Telle] tele B   3:17 Leuies] B, om. L   3:21-2 hundredu] hundrydu B   3:27-8 þusendo] ðusenda B   3:33-4 þusendo] `þusend´ (appar. on eras.) B   hundrydo] hundrydu B   3:38 bærn] bearn B   Israela] israhela B   3:39 heafdon eall swa] hæfdon eal swa B   hira] heora B

NUMBERS

⁶:²² Drihten spræc to Moise and cwæð: ²³ 'Sprec to Aarone and to his sunum, "þonne ge bletsiað Israela folc, cweðaþ þus: ²⁴ Bletsie eow God and gehealde eow ²⁵ and ætywe eow Drihten his ansine and gemiltsie eow. ²⁶ Gewende Drihten his andwlitan to eow and sylle eow sibbe." ²⁷ Clipion mine naman and ic bletsie hig.' ⁸:²⁰ Israela

f. 73ᵛ bearn dydon neah þam þe Drihten him bebead | þurh Moisen.

¹⁰:²⁸ Ða hig ut foron of Egipta lande, swa him God wisode. ²⁹ Þa cwæð Moises to Iobabe his mæge, Ragueles suna þam Madianitiscean: 'We willað faran to þam lande þe God us syllan wyle. Far mid us þæt we þe weligne gedon, for þam þe Drihten behet God Israela folce.' ³⁰ He andswarude and cwæð: 'Ne fare ic mid eow ac ic gewende to minum earde þær ic geboren wæs.' ³¹ Þa cwæð Moises: 'Ne forlæt þu us. Þu canst wegas geond þæt westen ac beo ure ladmann, ³² and þonne þu mid us cymsð, we þe syllað swa hwæt swa þær selost bið of þam æhtum þe Drihten us sylþ.' ³³ Hig foron of Drihtnes munte þreora daga færeld and Drihtnes earc for beforan him þri dagas, sceawiende þa wicstowa. ³⁴ Drihtnes genip for ofer hig on dæg, þonne hig forun. ³⁵ Ðonne seo earc wæs upp ahafen, þonne cwæð Moyses: 'Aris, Drihten, and todrif þine fynd, þæt þa fleon fram þinre ansine þe þe hatedon.' ³⁶ And þonne heo asett wæs he cwæð: 'Gewend Drihten to Israela folce.'

¹¹:¹ Gemang þam aras micel murcnung on þam folce ongen Drihten and hig wæron sarie for hira geswince. Þa he þæt gehirde, þa wearð he yrre, and Drihtenes fyr wearð onæled and forbærnde þone ytemistan dæl þæs folces. ² Þa clipode þæt folc to Moyse and Moises gebæd to Drihtne and þæt fyr geswac. ³ And he nemde þære stowe naman 'Onal', for þam þe Drihtenes fyr wæs þær onæled

f. 74ʳ ongen þæt folc. ⁴ Þæt gemengede folc | wearð gefylled mid gifernisse and sæton and weopon mid Israhela folce and cwædon: 'Hwa sylþ us

6:23 bletsiað] bletsion B, on *add.* L   Israela] israhela B   6:24 Bletsie] gebletsie B
6:26 Gewende] and gewende B   6:27 mine] minne B   hig] hi B   8:20 Israela]
israhela B   10:28 Ða] Ln *starts (some words lost at right edge of MS, esp. in 11:14–19, 12:5–12, and 13:30–14:3)*

MSS L, B, Ln   hig] hi BLn   ut foron] þa ut foran Ln   wisode] wissode BLn
10:29 þam³] ðan BLn   Israela] israhela BLn   10:30 andswarude] andswarode BLn
10:31 westen] wæsten Ln   ladmann] ladman BLn   10:32 cymsð] cymst BLn   selost]
sælost Ln   10:33 Hig] hi BLn   sceawiende] sceawigende Ln   wicstowa] wicstowe
BLn   10:34 hig¹] hi BLn   hig²] hi BLn   forun] foron B   10:35 seo] se Ln   wæs]
wæs wæs Ln   upp] up BLn   10:36 asett] aset BLn   Israela] israhela BLn
11:1 ongen] ongean BLn   hig] hi BLn   hira] heora BLn   Drihtenes] drihtnes BLn
ytemistan] ytemestan BLn   11:3 þam] þan BLn   Drihtenes] drihtnes BLn   ongen]
ongean BLn   11:4 gemengede] gemengde Ln   weopon] wepon Ln   Israhela]
hisrahela Ln

flæsc to etanne. ⁵ We gemunon hu fela fixa wæ hæfdon to gife on Egipta lande and we hæfdon cucumeres' (þæt synd eorðæppla) 'and pepones and porleac and eneleac and manega oþre þing. ⁶ Nu we sind hlæne. Næbbe we nan þing to ettanne buton "manna".' Swa hig heton þone heofonlican mete þe hig God mid fedde, ⁷ þæt wæs swilce coryandran sæd, hwites bleos swa cristalla. ⁸ Þæt hig gadredon and grundon on cwyrne oððe briton and sudon on croccan, and worhton hlafas þærof, þa wæron swilce hig wæron elebacene. ⁹ Ðonne þæt deaw com on niht, þonne com þærmid se heofonlica mete, þe þe hig 'manna' heton. ¹⁰ Moyses gehirde þæt þæt folc weop, ælc æt his geteldes dura, and Godes yrre astah swiðe and hit þuhte Moise swiþe hefitime. ¹¹ And he cwæð to Drihtne: 'Hwi swenctest þu þinne þeow? Hwi næbbe ic nane gife beforan þe and hwi settest þu þises folces swarnysse uppan me? ¹² Cwist þu, geeacnode ic hig ealle oððe acende ic hig, þæt þu me bude þæt ic hig bære on minum bosume swa fostormodor deð cyld and þæt ic bære on þæt land þe þu hira fæderum fore swore? ¹³ Hwanon sceolde me cuman flæsc þæt ic sylle þison folce? Hig wepað ongen me and cweðaþ, "Sile us flæsc to etanne". ¹⁴ Ne mæg ic ana acuman eall þis folc; hit ys me swiðe hefig. ¹⁵ Buton þu elles wylle, ic bidde þe þæt þu me | ofslea and þæt ic f. 74ᵛ hæbbe gife beforan þe, þæt ic ne si mid swa miclum yfele geswenct.'
¹⁶ Drihten cwæð to Moise: 'Geceos me hundseofontig manna of Israhela folces ealdrum, þe þu wite þæt sin staþulfæste and lareowas, and læde hig to þære eardungstowe dura, þæt hig standon þær mid þe, ¹⁷ oþ þæt ic niðer astige and wið þe sprece. And ic nyme of þinum gaste and sille him and hig underfoð þis folc mid þe, þæt þu ne si ana gehefegod. ¹⁸ Sege þam folce, "Beoð geheorte. Tomorgen ge etað flæsc, for þam þe ge weopon beforan me and cwædon, 'Hwa silþ us flæsc? Wel us wæs on Egipta lande.' Drihten eow silþ flæsc

11:5 gemunon] gemunan Ln   wæ] we BLn   eorðæppla] eorðæpla B   eneleac] enneleac BLn   þing] þingc B   11:6 Næbbe] nabbe BLn   þing] þincg B, þingc Ln   ettanne] etene B, etanne Ln   buton manna] butan man BLn   hig¹] hi BLn   hig²] hi BLn   11:8 hig¹] hi BLn   gadredon] gaderodon B   briton] brytton BLn   sudon] sudan Ln   worhton] wrohtan Ln   hig²] hi BLn   elebacene] elebakene Ln   11:9 þe þe] þe B   hig manna] hi man BLn   11:10 weop] wep Ln   hefitime] hefigtyme Ln   11:11 swenctest] geswenctest B   næbbe] nabbe BLn   11:12 hig¹] hi BLn   hig²] hi BLn   hig³] hi BLn   bosume] bosme BLn   fostormodor] fostormoder Ln   hira] heora Ln   11:13 Hwanon] hwanan B   sceolde] scolde Ln   Hig] hi BLn   ongen] ongean BLn   11:15 Buton] butan BLn   þæt²] om. B   miclum] mycclum Ln   11:16 sin staþulfæste] synd staðolfæste B   læde hig] læd hi BLn   hig²] hi BLn   11:17 hig] hi BLn   11:18 Tomorgen] tomerigen B   þam] ðan B   weopon] weopan Ln   and] hi add. B

and ge etað, ¹⁹ næs to anum dæge, ne to twam ne to fifon ne to tynum ne to twentigum, ²⁰ ac fullne monoð, oþ hit gæð þurh eowre næsþyrlu and si gewend to wlættan, for þam þe ge gremedon Drihten and weopon beforan him and cwædon, 'Hwi foron we ut of Egipta lande?' " ' ²¹ Moises cwæð to Drihtne: 'þises folces ys six hund þusenda gangendra manna, and þu segst ic sylle him flæsc fullne monað. ²² Cwist þu, bið sceapa oððe hruðera swa fela ofslagen þæt hig genoh habbon, oððe beoþ ealle sæfixas gegaderod tosomne þæt hig gefyllon þis folc?' ²³ Drihten him andwirde and cwæð: 'Cwist þu, ys Drihtnes hand unmihtig? Nu rihte þu gesihst hwæðer min word beo mid weorce gefilled.'

11:24 Moises com and rehte þam folce Godes word. He gegaderode hundseofontig manna of Israhela folce, þa he let standan beforan ymbe|utan þa eardungstowe. ²⁵ Drihten astah niþer þurh genip and spræc to him and nam of þam gaste þe wæs on Moise and sealde þam hundseofontigum mannum. Ða se gast gereste on him, hig witegodon and siþþan ne geswicon. ²⁶ þa belifon twegen menn on þam wicstowum, þæra oðer hatte Eldad and oþer Meldad. Ofer þa se gast gereste. Hig wæron awritene and ne eodun ut to þære eardungstowe. ²⁷ Ða hig witegodon on wicstowe, þa arn an cnapa and cwæð to Moise: 'Eldad and Meldad witegiað on wicstowun.' ²⁸ And Iosue, Nunes sunu, cwæð: 'Hlaford min, Moyses, forbeod him þæt.' ²⁹ þa cwæð Moises: 'Ne ofþince þe þæt Drihten sille his gife þam þe he wille.' ³⁰ Moises and Israheles folces ealdras cirdon to þam wicstowum.

11:31 Wind com fram Drihtne and brohte ofer sæ þa fugelas þe mann 'coturnices' hateð and sende on þa wicstowa, swa feor swa man on anum dæge gefaran mæg, on ælce healfe imbeutan þa wicstowa, hig flugon on twegra elna heahnisse bufan eorðan. ³² þa aras þæt folc and gaderode ealne dæg and ealle þa niht micle menio þæra fugela. Se þe litel gegaderode, he hæfde tyn gemetu þæs gemetes þe hig 'chorus' hateð and hig behwurfon hig buton þære wicstowe. ³³ þa git

---

11:19 tynum] tynon B   11:20 fullne monoð] fulne monað BLn   næsþyrlu] næsðyrelu Ln   weopon] weopan Ln   foron] foran Ln   11:21 þusenda] þusend BLn   flæsc] to etanne *add.* Ln   fullne] fulne BLn   11:22 hruðera] hryðera BLn   hig¹] hi BLn   habbon] habben Ln   beoþ] byð Ln   hig²] hi BLn   11:23 andwirde] andswarode BLn   Cwist] cwest Ln   gesihst] gesyxt Ln   11:24 standan] standen Ln   beforan] *om.* BLn   11:25 hig] hi BLn   11:26 menn] men BLn   Hig] hi BLn   eodun] eodon B, eodan Ln   11:27 hig] hi BLn   wicstowun] wicstowum BLn   11:30 cirdon] cyrdan Ln   11:31 mann] man BLn   feor] feorr BLn   gefaran] 'ge'faran B, gefaren Ln   hig] hi BLn   eorðan] *om.* Ln   11:32 micle] B, mid micle LLn   menio] mænigeo B, menigeo Ln   hig¹] hi BLn   hig²] hi BLn   hig buton] hi butan BLn

wæs flæsc on heora toþum, ne ateorode him þilic mete, þa wearð Drihten yrre and sloh þæt folc mid swiðe miclum wite. ³⁴ And hig nemdon þa stowe 'gewilnunga birgena'. Þær hig birgdon þæt folc and hig foron | þanon and wunedon on Asteroth. f. 75ᵛ

¹²:¹ Maria and Aaron ciddon wið Moises for his Sigelhearwenan wife, ² and cwædon: 'Segstð þu, spræc Drihten wið Moises anne? Ne spræc he eac wið us?' Ða Drihten þæt gehirde, þa yrsode he swiðe. ³ Moises wæs soðlice se bilewitusta mann ofer ealle men þe on eorðan wunedon. ⁴ And he cwæð to him and to Aarone and to Marian: 'Gaþ ut, ge þreo, to þære eardungstowe.' Þa hig wæron ut agane, ⁵ Drihten astah niðer on genipe and stod on þære stowe dura and clipode Aaron and Marian. Þa hig eodun, ⁶ þa cwæð he to him: 'Gif hwilc mann of eow bið Drihtnes witega, ic him æteowe on gesihþe oððe þurh swefne ic sprece to him. ⁷ Nis nan man Moises gelica, mines þeowes, on minum huse. Se ys me ealra getreowust. ⁸ Ic sprece to him muþe to muþe and openlice, næs þurh rædelsas ne þurh hiw. [Hwi ne] ondræde ge eow þæt ge ciddon wið Moises minne þeow?' ⁹ And he gewat yrre ongen hig ¹⁰ and þæt genip geswac. Ða ætywde hrædlice on Marian scinende hreofnis swa snaw. Þa Aaron hig beheold and geseah þæt hire lichama wæs afylled mid hreoflan, ¹¹ þa cwæð he to Moise: 'Ic bidde þe, hlaford min, þæt þu ne asette ˋo´n unc þas synne, þeah wit dislice dydon, ¹² þæt Maria uncer swustor ne forwurðe. Nu ys healf hire lichama mid hreofnisse fornumen.' ¹³ Moises þa clipode to Drihtne and cwæð: 'Drihten God, ic bidde þe, hæl hig.'¹⁴ Drihten him | andswarode and cwæð: f. 76ʳ 'Gif hire fæder spigette on hire nebb, hu ne sceolde hire, huru, þinga sceamian seofon dagas? Beo heo asin[dr]od seofon dagas fram oðrum mannum and clipige hig mann siþþan ongen.' ¹⁵ Maria wæs belocen seofon dagas butan þære wicstowe and þæt folc ne stirode h[w]æder, ær þam þe Maria wearð hal geworden.

11:33 þilic] ðyllic BLn   miclum] mycclum Ln   11:34 hig nemdon] hi genemdon BLn   stowe] stowa Ln   hig²] hi BLn   birgdon] byrigdon B   hig³] hi BLn   12:1 Sigelhearwenan] sigelhearwanan Ln   12:2 Segstð] segst BLn   anne] ænne Ln   12:3 wæs soðlice] soðlice wæs BLn   bilewitusta] bylewitesta B, bilehwiteste Ln   mann] man BLn   12:4 hig] hi BLn   12:5 hig eodun] hi eodon BLn   12:6 mann] man B   swefne] swefen BLn   12:7 þeowes] ðeowan BLn   getreowust] getreowost B   12:8 rædelsas] rædels Ln   hiw. Hwi ne] B, hiwwinge L   12:9 gewat] wat Ln   ongen hig] ongean hi B   12:10 hreofnis] hreofnysse Ln   swa snaw] swa hwit swa snaw B   hig] hi B   12:11 on] o *appar. contemp., on eras. of two letters* L   12:12 swustor] swuster Ln   12:13 hig] hi BLn   12:14 spigette] *word tampered with, probably by L'Isle, in* L *and* B   nebb] neb Ln   sceamian] sceamigean Ln   asindrod] asyndrod BLn, asingod L   clipige hig mann] clypie hi man BLn   ongen] ongean BLn   12:15 butan] buton Ln   hwæder] hræder L, nahwider BLn

NUMBERS

¹³:¹ Æfter þam þe Moises se mæra heretoga mid Israhela folce, swa swa him bebead God, ofer þa Readan Sæ ferde and Pharao adrenced wæs, and siþþan se ælmihtiga God him æ gesette hæfde, þa þa seo fyrd com to Foran þam westene, ² ða cwæð se heofonlica God to þam halgan Moise: ³ 'Ceos þe menn þæt magon sceawigean þone eard Chanaan landes, þe ic Israhela folce forgifan wille to hira gewealde, and asend twelf heafodmenn of þam twelf mægðum.' ⁴ Ða dyde Moises swa God him bebead and sende of þam westene, þe ys genemned Pharan, twelf sceaweras þe hira naman her sint awritene. ⁵ Of Ruben, Semmua, Sechores sunu. ⁶ Of Simeon, Saphat, Uries sunu. ⁷ Of Iudas, Chaleb, Ieppones sunu. ⁹ Of Effrahim, Iosee, Nunis sunu. ⁸ Of Isachar, Igal, Iosepes sunu. ¹⁰ Of Benniamin, Psalthi, Raphues sunu. ¹¹ Of Zabulon, Iedidel, Sodiis sunu. ¹² Of Iosep, Gaddi, Susiis sunu. ¹³ Of Dan, Amihel, Iemallies sunu. ¹⁴ Of Aser, Stur, Michaheles sunu. ¹⁵ Of Neptalim, Naabbi, Vaphsies sunu. ¹⁶ Of f. 76ᵛ Gad, Guhel, Mathies sunu. ¹⁷ Ðis sint þæra manna | naman þe Moises sende to sceawienne Chanaan land, ¹⁸ and þus cwæð: 'Farað geond þone suðdæl ¹⁹ and sceawiað þæt land, ²¹ hwæðer hit wæstmbære si and mid wudum gemenged, ²⁰ and þa burga, gebette oððe butan [w]eallum, ¹⁹ and hwæþer þæt landfolc si to gefeohte stranglic oððe untrumlic, feawa on getele, hwæðer þe fela. ²¹ And feriað mid eow of þære eorðan wæstmum þonne ge eft cumað.' Hit wæs þa se tima þæt winberian ripodon, ²² and hig ferdon þa sona and sceawodon þone eard ²⁶ and geond feowertig daga embferdon þone eard, ²⁴ and of þam winbogum mid berium mid eallum and æpplum and ofætum eft mid him brohton ²⁷ and comon to Moise, þær he mid þære firde wæs on Pharan þam westene, ²⁸ and þas word him to cwædon: 'We comon to þam earde þe ge us heton faran, þe flewð witodlice meolce and hunige, swa swa ge of þisum wæstmum wel

13:1 Æfter] *3-line red initial cap.* L   bebead God] god bebead BLn   Pharao] farao BLn   gesette] geset BLn   seo] se Ln   Foran] pharan BLn   13:3 þe] nu *add.* BLn   menn] men BLn   sceawigean] sceawian BLn   hira] heora BLn   heafodmenn] heafodmen BLn   13:4 þam] þa Ln   hira] heora BLn   sint] synd BLn   13:6 Saphat] sephath B   13:8–9 *verses transposed* LBLn   13:9 Effrahim] efraim B, effraim Ln   Iosee] osee BLn   Nunis] nunes BLn   13:10 Benniamin] beniamin BLn   Psalthi] pilthi (*contemp. alt. to* psalthi) Ln   13:12 Iosep] ioseph B   Susiis] susius BLn   13:15 Naabbi] naabdi BLn   13:16 Guhel] guel BLn   13:17 sint] synd BLn   þæra] ðara B   sceawienne] sceawigenne BLn   13:19–26 *Vulg. narrative reordered in the translation*   13:21 gemenged] gemencged B, gemencged Ln   13:20 weallum] BLn, eallum L   13:21 þæt] ðe BLn   winberian] winberien Ln   13:22 hig] hi BLn   13:26 embferdon] ymbferdon Ln   13:24 eallum] ealle BLn   ofætum] ofetum Ln   13:27 comon] coman Ln   13:28 comon] coman Ln   heton] hetan Ln   hunige] hunie BLn   þisum] þissum Ln

NUMBERS 145

oncnawan magon. ²⁹ Ac þa strengstan weras wuniað on þam lande and micele burga þær sint and mærlice geweallode. þær we gesawon Enachis cynryn. ³⁰ Amalech eac swilce eardað on þam suðdæle, Etheus on þam muntlandum, and Iebuseus and Amorreus, Chananeus wið þa sæ and imb þa ea Iordan.' ³¹ Hwæt þa Israhela bearn endemes hrimdon and ongean Moysen micclum ceorodon, ac [C]aleph hig gestilde and cwæð mid gebylde: 'Uton faran to þam earde and geahnian | us þæt land, for þan þe we magon mid mihte f. 77ʳ hit begitan.' ³² Ða oðre soþlice cwædon, þe mid him asende wæron: 'Ne mage we faran nateshwon to þam folce þus, for þan þe hig sind strengran þonne we, ³⁴ and we þær gesawon of þam entcynne, Enachis bearna, micelra wæstma, þam we ne sind þe gelicran þe litle gærstapan.' ³³ And hig tældon þæt land mid heora teonwordum.
¹⁴:¹ Hwæt þa eall seo meniu endemes weop sona ² and micclum ceoreddon ongean Moisen and cwædon: ³ 'We wisceað þæt we on Egipta lande wæron ær dead, and na on þisum westene, and we wisceað swiþor þæt we forwurðon her and us Drihten ne læde into þam lande þæt we þær licgon ofslagene and ure wif and ure cild wurðon gehergode. Nis us la betere þæt we bugon ongean to Egipta lande?' ⁴ And ælc cwæð to oðrum: 'Uton us gesettan efne nu heretogan and uton gecirran to Egipta lande.' ⁵ Moyses þa and Aaron micclum wurdon astirode and feollon astrehte ætforan þære meniu. ⁶ Caleph þa and Iosue ⁷ cwædon to þam folce: 'þæt land þe we sceawodon ys swiðe þearle god. ⁸ Gif Drihten us arfæst bið, he us in gelæt to þam and silþ us þa moldan þe meolce and hunige flewð. ⁹ Ne beo ge wiðerræde wið eowerne Drihten, ne ge ne ondrædon eow. Drihten ys mid us.' ¹⁰ þa hrimde eall seo meniu and mid stanum woldon hig oftorfian, ac Godes wuldor wearð sona wundorlic æteowod ofer þæt Godes scrin, þær hig on locodon. | ¹¹ And God f. 77ᵛ cwæð to Moyse: 'Hu lange tælð þis folc me and hu lange nellað hig gelyfan me on eallum þam tacnum þe ic ætforan him dyde? ¹² Ic

13:28 oncnawan] oncnawon B   13:29 strengstan] strengestan Ln   sint] synd BLn   Enachis] enac his L, enachus BLn   13:30 imb] ymbe Ln   13:31 and] *om.* B   micclum] miclum B   Caleph] BLn, aleph L   hig] hi BLn   geahnian] geagnian B   13:32 hig] hi B   13:34 Enachis] enac his L, enachys B   13:33 hig] hi BLn   14:1 eall] eal B   meniu] mæniu B   14:2 micclum ceoreddon] miclum ceorodon B   14:3 dead] deade B   ure²] *om.* B   wurðon gehergode] gehergode wurðon Ln   bugon] bugan Ln   14:4 Uton] utan Ln   14:5 micclum] miclum B   feollon] feollan Ln   meniu] mæniu B   14:8 hunige] hunie BLn   14:9 ondrædon] ondrædan Ln   14:10 hrimde] rymde Ln   eall] eal BLn   meniu] mæniu B   hig¹] hi BLn   wundorlic] wundorlice BLn   hig²] hi BLn   14:11 nellað hig gelyfan] ne gelyfað hi BLn

ofslea hig mid cwylde and fordo mid cwealme, and ic þe gesette siþþan to heretogan ofer micele þeode strengran þonne þeos.' [13] Moyses þa clipode and cwæð þus to Drihtene: 'Gif þa Egiptiscan gehirað, [14] and þa þe her eardiað abutan, [15] þæt þu þas meniu ofslihst, swa swa ænne mannan, þonne secgað hig sona [16] þæt þu ofsloge hig for þi þæt þu ne mihtest hig gelædan to þam lande þe þu him behete. [17] Ac si þin strengð gemærsod swa swa þu swore. [19] Drihten, ic þe bidde þæt þu forgife þises folces synna æfter micelnisse þinre mildheortnisse.' [20] Drihten cwæð to Moyse: 'Ic hit forgife æfter þinum worde. [22] Swa þeah soðlice ealle þa þe gesawon minne mægenþrimnisse and þa micclan tacna þe ic worhte on Egipta lande and on þisum westene, and costnodon me nu tyn siþon and mine stemne ne gehirsumodon, [23] ne geseoð hig þæt land þe ic foreswor heora fæderum, ne nan þæra þe me tælde ne gesihþ þæt land. [30] Calef and iosue cumað to þam lande. [31] Eowre bearn ic læde to þam lande soþlice, [32] and eowre lic sceolon [licgan] on þisum westene. [33] Eowre bearn beoð worigende on þisum westene feowertig wintra and eower forligr berað, oð þæt heora fædera hreaw beon fornumene. [34] Æfter þæra feowertigra daga getele, þe ge þæt land besceawodon, gear bið for dæge geteald, and on feowertigum gearum ge under|foð eowere unrihtwisnissa, þæt ge witon mine wrace.'

[14:36-7] Þa wurdon sona ofslagene on Godes gesihþe þa tyn sceaweras þe sceawodon þæt land and deade nyðer feollon, for þan þe hig þæt folc mistihton and þæt land tældon. [38] And þa twegen leofodon, Iosue and Caleph, and hi comon to þam lande. [39] Þa weop þæt folc sare [40] and sona on ærne mergen eodon gewæpnode up to ðære dune and cwædon: 'We syndon gearwe nu to gewinnenne þæt land be þam þe Drihten spræc, for þan þe we syngodon.' [41] Ða cwæð Moises to andsware: 'Hwi ofergæge ge Godes word? Hit ne becymð eow na to nanre spede. [42] Ne fare ge, ic bidde, for þan þe God nis mid eow, þæt

---

14:12 hig] hi BLn and¹] hi add. BLn micele] myccle Ln strengran] strengron Ln
14:13 cwæð þus] ðus cwæð BLn Drihtene] drihtne BLn Egiptiscan] egyptiscean B, egiptiscean Ln   14:15 meniu] mæniu B ænne] anne BLn hig] hi BLn
14:16 hig¹] hi BLn mihtest] mihtæst B hig²] hi BLn   14:19 þises] þisses Ln
14:22 minne] mine BLn mægenþrimnisse] mægnðrymnysse B micclan] miclan B
worhte] wrohte Ln   14:23 hig] hi BLn ic] ðe add. BLn (del. in B)   14:30 Calef]
caleph BLn   14:32 sceolon] sceolan BLn licgan] BLn, sweltan L   14:33 fædera]
om. Ln   14:34 getele] getæle B gear] ger B eowere unrihtwisnissa] eowre
unrihtwisnyssa B, eowre unrihtwisnysse Ln   14:36-7 feollon] fellon Ln hig] hi BLn
14:38 leofodon] leofodan B Iosue and Caleph] Caleph and Iosue Ln comon] coman Ln
14:40 mergen] merien BLn eodon] astigon B syndon] synd BLn gewinnenne] gewinnene Ln

ge ne feallon ætforan eowrum feondum.' ⁴⁴ Hig swa þeah, ablende, beotlice astigon to þæs muntes cnæppe. ⁴⁵ And þa comon heora fynd, Amalechitisc folc and Chan[an]eus samod, þe eardodon on þam munte, and hig micclum slogon and ehtende adrifon, oð þæt hig comon to Horma. ⁴⁴ And Moises wæs stille on ðære wicstowe.

¹⁵:¹⁻⁴¹ God gesette þa Moyse menigfealde beboda. ¹⁶:¹ And æfter þam færlice arison feower weras, Chore and Hon, Dathan and Abiron, ² ongean Moisen, micclum astirode, and þridde healf hund manna of þam yltsum mannum, ³ and cwædon to Moise and to Aarone þam sacerde: 'Eall þeos meniu soðlice sindon haligra bearn and God wunað on him. Hwi sind ge ahafene ofer Drihtenes folc?' ⁴ And Moyses sona feoll astreht to eorðan ⁵ and to þam folce cwæð: 'Tomergen geswutelað God hwilce he gecyst to him. ⁶ Nime eower ælc his storcillan and stere ætforan Gode, and þone þe he gecyst beo se halig.' | ¹⁸⁻¹⁹ Hig didon swa on mergen mid micclum gedwylde   f. 78ᵛ and brohton heora storcillan, standende æt þam getelde. ²⁷ Ac Dathan and Abiron stodon on heora geteldum ¹² and cwædon to Moysen mid micclum graman: ¹³ 'Is þe la litel geþuht þæt þu alæddest us of þam lande þe weoll meolce and hunie, þæt þu us ofsloge on þisum westene, buton þu eac ure gewealde? ¹⁴ Witodlice þu gelæddest us into þam lande þe eall flewð on riðum meolce and hunies and sealdest us land æhta and wineardas þær, oððe wilt þu la ut apytan ure eagan?' ¹⁹ Ða æteowde Godes wuldor, ²⁰ and God cwæð to Moisen: ²¹ 'Asindriað eow fram þisre scildigan gegaderunge, þæt ic hig færlice fordon mæge.' ³¹⁻² Hwæt þa færlice geopenode seo eorðe hig sylfe and forswealh þa weras mid wifum and cildum, Dathan and Abiron mid heora cynne and eallum æhtum, ³³ þæt hig into helle cuce siþodon mid sande ofhrorene, ³⁴ and þæt folc fleah afirht for heora hreame. ³⁵ Eac swilce færlice fyr com fram Gode and ofsloh þa oðre þe offrodon þone stor, þridde healf hund manna, þær hig heoldon þa recelsfata. ⁴¹ Eft on þam oðrum dæge eall seo meniu ceorode ongean Moisen and Aaron, cweþende: 'Ge ofslogon Godes

14:44 Hig] hi B   14:45 Chananeus] BLn, chaneus L   eardodon] eardedon B   hig micclum] hi miclum B   hig²] hi B   15:1–41 menigfealde] mænifealde BLn 16:2 micclum] miclum B   yltsum] yldstum B   16:3 meniu] mæniu B   him] Ln *ends MSS* L, B   Drihtenes] drihtnes B   16:4 sona feoll astreht] feoll astreht sona B 16:5 geswutelað] `ge´swutelað B   16:18–19 Hig] hi B   micclum] miclum B 16:12 Moysen] moyse B   micclum] miclum B   16:13 weoll] weol B   hunie] hunige B buton] butan B   16:14 hunies] hunige B   land] *and add.* B   wineardas] wingeardas B 16:20 Moisen] moyse B   16:21 hig] hi B   16:31–2 hig] hi B   cynne] geteldum B 16:33 hig] hi B   16:35 com] swilce færlice *add.* L (*later scored through*)   hig] hi B 16:41 meniu] mæniu B

folc.' ⁴²And seo sacu þa aras ⁴³and Moises and Aaron efston mid fleame to Godes getelde, and þa þa hig inn agan wæron, þa æteowde Godes wuldor. ⁴⁴And God cwæð to Moyse: ⁴⁵'Gewitað aweg fram þisre meniu. Nu ic hig adilegie.' ⁴⁶And Moises cwæð to Aarone: 'Nim þin | recelsfæt and efst to þam folce and for hig gebide, for þan þe Godes yrre ys ofer hig and his wite reþegað.' ⁴⁷Aaron þa ardlice arn to þam folce and sterde mid thimiama, standende betwinan þam cucum and þam deadum, and bæd for þæt folc. þæt wite þa geswac. ⁴⁹And þær wæron ofslagene feowertyne þusenda of þæs folces meniu and seofon hund manna, buton þam þe þær ær ofslagene wæron on Chores ceaste. ⁵⁰Aaron eode þa eft to Moise to Drihtenes getelde. ¹⁷:¹And Drihten cwæð to Moise: ²'Nim nu twelf girda æt þam twelf mægðum, fram þære mægþe ealdrum, and heora ælces nama[n] awrit on his girde, ³and Aarones nama beo on Leuies mægðe. ⁴And lege þa girde on þam getelde, þær ic þe to sprece, ⁵and þone þe ic geceose, þonne sprit his gird, and ic ges[t]ylle fram me Israhela ceorunge.' ⁶⁻⁷Moyses þa dyde swa swa him bebead Drihten ⁸and eode on ærne mergen into þam getelde and efne wæs þa growende Aarones gird on blostmum and on leafum, on hnutbeames wisan. ⁹He bær þa þa girda to Israela bearnum and hig gesawon hwæt þær geswutelod wæs. Ælc nam þa his girde. ¹⁰And God cwæð eft to Moise: 'Ber Aarones girde into þam getelde, þæt heo si gehealden þær, Israele to tacne, and heora ceorung geswice, þæt hi ne swelton.' ¹¹And Moises dyde swa swa him Drihten bebead. ¹⁸:¹God geceas Aaron him to sacerde and of his ofspringe to his offrunge simle, ²and of Leuies mægðe manega to leuitan, Aarone to fylste to þam | ælicum onsægednyssum. ³⁻¹⁹And God sylf him sealde þa gesetnissa. ²⁰:¹Æfter þisum comon Israhela bearn to þam westene Sin, and þær sweolt Maria, Aarones swuster, and ys þær bebirged. ²Ða næs þær nan wæter on þam westene þam folce ³and hig þa ciddon swiþe wið Moisen. ⁶He clipode þa to Gode ⁷and God cwæð him to: ⁸'Gang þu and Aaron and gegaderiað þis folc geond to þam stane

---

16:43 hig inn] hi in B   æteowde] ætywde B   16:45 meniu] mæniu B   hig adilegie] hi adylgie B   16:46 hig¹] hi B   hig²] hi B   16:47 cucum] cucuan B   16:49 meniu] mæniu B   buton] butam B   ær] *om.* B   ceaste] ceastre LB   16:50 Drihtenes] drihtnes B   17:2 mægþe] mægða B   naman] B, nama L   17:4 girde] gyrda B   17:5 sprit] sprytt B   gestylle] B, gesylle L   17:6–7 him bebead Drihten] drihten him bebead B   17:8 mergen] merien B   wæs þa] þa wæs B   17:9 Israela] ysrahela B   hig] hi B   17:10 þær] *om.* B   Israele] israhele B   18:1 ofspringe] ofsprincge B   18:2 leuitan] leuita B   20:1 swuster] swustor B   20:3 hig] hi B   20:7 him to] to him B   20:8 and²] B, and and L

and se stan eow sylþ wæter.' ¹⁰ Hig comon to þam flinte ¹¹ and he ætforan him eallum sloh mid þære girde tuwa þone flint and þær fleow sona of þam flinte wæter, swa genihtsumlice þæt heora nytena druncon, and eall Israela folc, of þære anre riðe. ¹⁴ Ða sende Moyses ærendracan to Edom þam cyninge, ¹⁷ bæd þæt he moste faran forð ofer his land be rihtum wege and ne hreppan his nan þing. ¹⁸ Edom þa andwirde þam ærendracum and cwæð: 'Ne fare ge þurh me.' ²⁰ And he ferde þa sona mid eallum his folce to gefeohte gearu, ²¹ and forwyrnde Israela þæt oferfæreld þurh his land. Hig gewendon þa aweg ²² and gewicodon wið þone munt þe ys Or gehaten. ²⁸⁻⁹ þær Aaron forðferde and Eleazarus his sunu wæs sacerd for hine. ³⁰ And hi ealle beweopon Aarones forðsiþ, geond þritig [daga] geomeriende swiðe.

²¹:¹ Chananeus þa wann wið Israela bearn and sige on him gewann. ² Ac hig wendon to Gode mid ealre heortan ³ and hig gehirde God and him sige forgeaf, þæt hig ofslogon þone cyning and his folc samod mid swurdes ecge and heora burga towendon, ⁴ and gewendon | him þanon ofer langne weg, þæt hig þæt land f. 80ʳ embferdon. Ðæt folc þa wearð þrit and þearle geswenct mid þam siðfæte ⁵ and ceorodon ongean God and ongean Moysen micclum, and cwædon: 'Hwi læddest þu la us of Egipta lande þæt we swulton on þisum westene? We nabbað naðor ne hlaf ne [wæter] and us wlatað nu for þisum leohtostan mete.' ⁶ For þam þingum, þa sende him God to fyrene næddran and hig þæt folc totæron and manega adyddon. ⁷ And hig to Moyse cwædon: 'We singodon swiðe, for þan þe we swa spræcon ongean God and þe, ac gebide nu for us þæt he afirsie fram us þas fyrenan næddran.' Moises þa gebæd for þæt folc ⁸ and God cwæð to him: 'Wirc ane ærenan næddran and sete up to tacne, and se þe tosliten beo, beseo upp to þære næddran and he leofað, sona swa he besihþ on hig.' ⁹ Moises þa worhte þa ærenan næddran and sette to tacne, and þa þe toslitene wæron, beheoldon to þære næddran and wurdon gehælede. ¹⁰ Hig ferdon þa þanon mid

20:10 Hig] hi B   comon] ða add. B   20:11 eallum] eallon B   tuwa] tua B   flint] e add., appar. by later hand L   Israela] israhela B   20:14 cyninge] cynincge B   20:17 hreppan] reppan B   þing] þingc B   20:20 eallum] eallon B   20:21 Israela] israhele B   Hig] hi B   20:30 daga] B, wintra L   geomeriende] geomriende B   21:1 Israela] israhela B   21:2 hig] hi B   21:3 hig¹] hi B   hig²] hi B   cyning] cynincge B   21:4 him] ham add. B   hig] hi B   þa wearð þrit] wearð ða aðryt B   21:5 God] godd B   micclum] miclum B   wæter] B, win L   21:6 þingum] ðingon B   þa] sona add. B   him God] god him B   hig] hi B   21:7 hig] hi B   spræcon] spæcon B   nu] om. B   afirsie] afyrsige B   þas fyrenan] ða fyrene B   21:8 ærenan] ærene B   up] upp B   leofað] leofoð B   hig] hi B   21:10 Hig] hi B

heora firdwicum. ²¹ And Moyses sende þa to Seon þam cyninge Amorreiscre þeode þisum wordum and cwæð: ²² 'Ic bidde þæt þu me lyfe ofer þin land to færenne. Ne hreppe we þine æceras oððe wineardas ne eower wæterpyttas ac swa swa se weg lið, we farað, gif we moton, forð ofer þin land.' ²³ Ða nolde Seon se cyning nateshwon him tiðian þæt Israel ferde forð ofer his gemæru ac gegaderode his folc and ferde him togeanes and feaht swiðe ongean, ²⁴ oð þæt he feoll | ofslagen and his folc samod mid swurdes ecge. ²⁵ Hig geeodun þa his land and ealle his burga and Israhel wunode þa on þam widgillan lande. ³² Moyses þa sende and het sceawian Azer; þære wic hig geeodun and ahton þone eard. ³³ Hig gewendon þonne and woldon to Basan, ac Og se cyning com him togeanes mid eallum his folce to gefeohte ge`a´ru. ³⁴ Drihten cwæð to Moise: 'Ne ondræd þu hine. Ic hine sealde to þinum gewealde and eall his folc and land.' ³⁵ And hig fuhton þa swiþe and Israhel ofsloh Og þone cyning and his suna and his folc eall to forwyrde, and geahton his land and ealle his burga.

²²:¹ Moises þa ferde to Moab mid þam folc[e]. ² And se cyning Balac ⁴ cwæð to his leode: 'Swa adilegað þis folc mid heora firdcræfte ealle þa þe eardiað on urum gemærum, swa swa oxa gewunað to awestenne gærs oð þa wirttruman eorðslihtes mid toðum.' ⁵ He sende þa his bodan to Balaam þam witegan, Beores suna, ⁶ and bæd þæt he come to awirigenne þæt folc þe fundode wið his, and cwæð: 'Ic wat þæt se bið gebletsod þe þu gebletsast and se bið awirged þe þu awirgest.' ⁷ Þa bodan þa comon to Balaam mid sceattum. ¹⁸ Balaam andwirde þam ærendracum and cwæð: 'þeah Balac me sille goldes and seolfres an hus full, ic ne mæg awendan Godes word, ¹⁹ ac beoð her to niht and abidað andsware.' ²⁰ Ða com God on niht to Balaam and cwæð: 'Nu þas menn þe feccað, far mid him swa þæt þu do þæt ic þe bebeode.' ²¹ Balaam þa ferde forð mid þam bodum, on assan ridende, ²² and efne Godes engel forstod | þone weg þær he wolde ridan mid atogenum swurde, swilce he hine slean wolde. ²³ Se assa geseah þone engel standende and Balaam ne geseah. þa forbeah se

21:21 Amorreiscre] amoreiscre B   21:22 færenne] farene B   hreppe] reppe B   ne] *om.* B   eower] eowwer B   21:23 Seon] *om.* B   cyning] cyningc B   Israel] israhel B   togeanes] togenes B   21:24 feoll] feol B   21:25 Hig geeodun] hi geeodon B   21:32 hig geeodun] hi geeodon B   21:33 Hig] hi B   þonne] ða ðanon B   21:35 hig] hi B   Og] B, oge L   cyning] cyningc B   22:1 folce] B, folc L   22:2 cyning] cyningc B   22:4 wirttruman eorðslihtes] wyrttruman eorðflihtes B   22:6 awirigenne] wyrigenne B   awirgest] wyrigst B   22:7 Balaam] balaan B   22:18 Balac] balaac B   22:19 abidað] bidað B   22:20 menn] men B   22:22 engel] encgel B   swurde] sweorde B   22:23 engel] encgel B

assa þæs engles swurd and eode of þam wege. Hwæt þa Balaam beot þone assan, wolde þæt he eode innan þone weg. ²⁵ Þa fleah se assa git forht for þam engle and þidde his hlafordes fot þearle to þam hege. Balaam þa git beot þone assan. ²⁶ And se engel eode into anum nyrwette, þe he ne mihte forbugan on naðere healfe, for þam þe þær nan bige næs. ²⁷ Ða feoll se asse adune, afirht for þam engle, and Balaam wearð yrre and beot hine swiðor. ²⁸ Ða geopenode Drihten þæs assan muð and he cwæð: 'Hwi beatst þu me swa swiðe?' ²⁹ And Balaam andwirde: 'For þan þe þu me beswice, and ic þe ofslean wolde gif ic swurd hæfde.' ³⁰ Ða sæde se assa: 'Ne eom ic la þin assa þe þu on ritst simle? Sege hwænne ic æfre ær þillic þe gebude.' ³¹ God þa geopenode Balaames eagan, þæt he geseah þone engel þe se assa forbeah mid nacedum swurde, and he hnah to eorðan, aleat wið þæs engles. ³² And se engel cwæð: 'Hwi beote þu þæne assan efne [n]u þriwa? ³³ Ic þe ofsloge sona and se assa leofode, gif he ne forbuge me.' ³⁴ And Balaam cwæð: 'Ic singie nitende, niste þæt þu stode ongean me, and gif þe min færeld ænig þing mislicað, ic fare eft ongean.' ³⁵ Se engel cwæð to him: 'Far mid þisum mannum and warna þæt þu nan þing elles ne sprece, buton þæt ic þe bebeode.' And Balaam þa rad forð. ³⁶ Se cyning | þa, Balac, com him togeanes. f. 81ᵛ

²³:¹ And he arærde sona seofon weofoda and þær lac geoffrode on þa ealdan wisan, ⁸ and cwæð to Balac: 'Hu mæg ic awirgan ðone þe God bletsode?' ⁹⁻¹⁰ And he witegode þa swa him wissode God and bletsode Israhel. ¹¹ And Balac cwæð to him: 'Ic þe fette for þi þæt þu mine fynd wirigdest, and þu hig bletsast.' ¹² Balaam cwæð þa: 'Cwist þu, mæg ic oðer sprecan, buton þæt Drihten hæt?' ¹³ Ða cwæð Balac him to: 'Cum to oðre stowe mid me.' ¹⁴ And he eft arærde oðre seofon weofoda and bletsode Israhel. ²⁵ And Balac cwæð: 'Ne þu hine wirige, ne þu hine bletsa.' ²⁶ Þa cwæð Balaam to Balace þus: 'Hu, ne sæde ic þe þæt swa hwæt swa God me bebude, þæt ic þæt dide?' ²⁷ And Balac cwæð: 'Cum, ic þe læde to oðre stowe, gif Gode swa gelicie þæt þu hig þanon wirige.' ²⁸ Hig eodon þa begen up to þam munte and he sona arærde seofon weofoda and lac geoffrode. ²⁴:¹ And

22:23 innan] innon B   22:25 engle] encgle B   þidde] ðyde B   22:26 engel] encgel B   naðere] naðre B   þam] ðan B   22:27 feoll] feol B   asse] assa B   hine] gyt add. B   22:29 þan] ðam B   22:30 la] na B   ritst simle] ridst symble B   þe²] B, þe þe L (*2nd* þe *del.*)   22:31 eagan] eagon B   nacedum] nacodum B   aleat] and aleat B   22:32 engel] encgel B   þæne] þinne B   nu] B, þu L   22:33 leofode] ne leofode B   22:34 singie] syngode B   ænig þing] *om.* B   22:35 engel] encgel B   Far] farr B   þing] þinc B   23:8 awirgan] awyrian B   23:11 hig] hi B   23:12 hæt] het B   23:14 seofon] seofan B   23:26 Balace] balaace B   23:27 hig] hi B   wirige] gewyrige B   23:28 Hig] hi B   seofon] seofan B

Israel bletsode and þa þing witegode þe him gewissode God. ²He mihte geseon Israel of þam munte þanon. ¹⁰ Ða yrsode Balac wið Balaam and cwæð: 'Ic þe het feccan þæt þu mine fynd wirigdest and þu nu þriwa hig bletsodest. ¹¹ Far þe nu ham. Ic hæfde gemynt þe to arwurðienne on æhtum and on feo, ac God þe benæm[d]e þæs wurðmintes.'

Hit stent on oðrum bocum þæt Balaam tæhte swa þeah þam cyninge, hu he cuman mihte þæt he hig beswice, and he eac swa dyde. He beswac hig swa þæt he sette wifmenn æt his hæþengilde gehende þam folce þær hig on locodon.

f. 82ʳ   ²⁵:¹ And hig eodon þa to manega of þam | folce to þam miltistrum and wið hig hæmdon ² and to þam hæðengilde bugon. ³ God wearð þa yrre Israhela bearnum ⁴ and het Moyses ahon þa þe þæt man dydon. ⁵ Moyses þa het þa manfullan ofslean, ealle þa þe bugon to Belphegor. ⁸⁻⁹ And þær wurdon ofslagene mid swurdes ecge feower and twentig þusenda of þæs folces meniu, and Godes yrre geswac and he him syððan miltsode. ¹⁶ God bebead siþþan Moyse and cwæð: ¹⁷ 'Wrec Israela bearn on þam Madianitiscum and ofsleað hig, ¹⁸ for þan þe hig beswicon eow.' ³¹:⁵⁻⁶ Moyses þa sende sona twelf þusenda gewæpnodra manna to þam wige caflice. ⁷ And hig þa ferdon and þæt folc ofslogon, ⁸ and þone cyning Balac and Balaam samod, ⁹⁻¹⁰ and þæt land awestan and þa wif heoldon, ¹¹⁻¹² and comon to Moyse mid micelre huðe. ¹⁴ Moises þa yrsode ¹⁵ and axode hwi hig heoldon þa wifmenn to life þe hig forlærdon ær æt þam hæþengilde, ¹⁷ and het hig þa acwellan ealle þa wif þe weras hæfdon, ¹⁸ and het healdan þa mædena. Hig didon þa swa and sige hæfdon siþþan and comon to þam lande þe hig to gelædde God, þe he Abrahame behet and his ofspringe.

²⁶:² Moises getealde þæs folces meniu þe on þam westene wæron acennede, wigendra manna, fram twentigwintre and sume eac yldran. ²⁶:⁵¹ And þær soþlice wæron six hund þusenda and feower and twentig þusend and seofon hund manna and þrittig manna.

24:1 Israel] israhel B   þing] ðingc B   24:2 Israel] israhel B   24:10 hig] hi B
24:11 benæmde] B, benæmbe L   *Summary* tæhte swa þeah] swa ðeah tæhte B   þam²]
B, mid þam L   cyninge] cyningce B   hig¹] hi B   hig²] hi B   wifmenn] wifmen B   hig³]
hi B   25:1 hig¹] hi B   hig²] hi B   25:8–9 twentig] twenti B   meniu] mæniu B
miltsode] mildsode B   25:17 Israela] israhela B   Madianitiscum] madiatiscum B   hig]
hi B   25:18 þan] ðam B   hig] hi B   31:7 hig] hi B   31:8 cyning] cyningc B
31:15 hig¹] hi B   wifmenn] wifmen B   hig²] hi B   31:17 hig] hi B   31:18 and het
. . . sige hæfdon] *om.* B   hig²] hi B   gelædde] lædde B   ofspringe] ofsprincge B
26:2 meniu] mæniu B   acennede] accennede B   26:51 þusend] ðusenda B

⁶⁴ Heora fæderas ealle forðferdon on þam westene, ⁶⁵ buton Caleph and Iosue. Hig comon to þam lande | and mid Israhela bearnum f. 82ᵛ þone eard geeodon and him betwinan dældon, swa swa him dihte Iosue. FINIT.

26:65 Hig] hi B   FINIT] *much faded but appar. by orig. scribe* L, *om.* B

[DEUTERONOMY]

Her onginð seo boc þe is genemned on Ebreisc '[H]elleadabarim' and on Grecisc 'Deuteronomium' and on Lyden 'Secunda lex' and on Englisc 'seo æftre æ'.

^{1:1} ÐIS SINT ÐA WORD ÐE MOISES SPRæc to eallum Israhela folce begeondan Iordane on þam feld westene wið þa Readan Sæ, betwix Pharan and Thophel and Laban and Aseroh, þær micel gold ys, ²endleofon daga færeld on Choreb þurh Seyr dune weg oð Cadesbarne. ³On þam feowerteoðan geare, on þam endlyftan monðe, on þam forman dæge þæs monþes, he spræc to him ealle þa þing þe Drihten him bebead. ⁴Syþþan he sloh Seon, Amorrea cyng se wunode on Essebon, and Og, cyning on Basan se wunode on Aseroth and on Edrai, ⁵beiundan Iordane on Moab lande, Moyses geswutelude þa æ and cwæð: ⁶'Drihten ure God sprecð to us on Oreb and cweð, "Genoh lange ge wunodon on þisse dune. ⁷Cirrað and farað to Amorrea dune and to oþrum feldlandum and dunlandum and to unheheran landum on suðhealfe wið þa sæ, Chanaan landes and Libani, oð þæt miccle flod Euphraten." ⁸Be þam lande Drihten cwæð, "Nu ic hit hire sealde eow. Farað inn and habbað þæt þæt Drihten foreswor eowrum fæderum Abrahame and Isaace and Iacobe þæt he hit sealde him and hira ofspringe æfter him." ⁹And ic cwæð to eow on þære tide, ¹⁰"Ne mæg ic ana eow acuman, for þam | þe Drihten eow gemænigfilde and eowre ys todæg swa fela swa steorrena. ¹¹Drihten eowre fædera God geice fela þusenda to þison ge[tele] and bletsie eow swa he eow behet. ¹²Ne mæg ic ana eowre gemang acuman, and eowre swarnissa and eowre saca." ¹³And ic cwæð to eow, "Ceosað eow wise menn [of] eowrum cynne, and glæwe, and þa þe hira drohtnung si afandud, and ic

f. 83ʳ

MSS L, B   Rubric in 3 lines, alternately metallic red and red. In B (f. 128ᵛ) rubric in red rustic caps.   Rubric Helleadabarim] B, belleadabarim L   Lyden] leden B   1:1 ÐIS] *3-line red initial cap.* L   SINT] synd B   betwix] betwux B   1:2 endleofon] endleofan B   1:3 feowerteoðan] feowerteoþam B   þing] ðingc B   1:4 cyng] cyningc B   Essebon] esebon B   cyning] cyningc B   1:5 beiundan] begeondan B   geswutelude] geswutelode B   1:6 wunodon] wunedon B   1:7 unheheran] unhehrum B   miccle] micele B   Euphraten] eufraten B   1:8 hire] *om.* B   ofspringe] ofspringce B   1:10 þam] ðan B   gemænigfilde] gemænifylde B   eowre] eower B   1:11 eowre] eower B   getele], ?geale L (*alt. by late hand to* geatel)   bletsie] bletsige B   1:12 Ne] næ B   eowre¹] eower B   eowre²] eower B   1:13 menn] men B   of] B, *om.* L   glæwe] gleawe B   hira] heora B   afandud] afandod B

gesette hig eow to ealdrum". ⁱ⁴ Ða andswarodon ge me and cwædon, "Wel þu sprecst". ¹⁵ And ic nam wise menn and wel borene and sette hig to ealdrum and to hundredmannum and to fiftigesmennum and to teoþingmannum, þe eow lærdon ælc þing. ¹⁶ And ic bebead him and cwæð, "Demað ælcon men riht, si hit burga man, si hit utacymene. ¹⁷ Demað þam rican swa þam heanan, and þam litlan swa þam micla[n], for þam þe hit ys Godes dom. Gif eow ænig þing þince earfoðlice, secgað hit me and ic hit bete."
¹:²⁰ 'Ic cwæð to eow, ²¹ "Farað to þam lande þe God behet eowrum fæderum and habbað hit. Ne ondræde ge eow, ne nan þing ne forhtgeað." ²² And ge andswarodun me and cwædon, "Uton sendan sceaweras þæt sceawion þæt land and cyðon us on hwilcne weg we faran sceolon and to hwilcon burgum." ²³ And ic sende .xii. men of eow, ²⁴ and hig foron and þæt land sceawodon ²⁵ and us þæs landes wæstmas brohton and cwædon, "God is þæt land þe God us syllan wyle". ²⁶ Ða noldon ge faran, for eowre mægðe ungeleafulnysse, and ne gelyfdon Drihtenes spræce ²⁷ and ge murcnodon and cwædon, "Drihten us hatað and for þam he alædde us ut of Egipta lande to þam | þæt he us sealde [o]n Amorreiscra hand to ofsleanne. f. 83ᵛ ²⁸ Hwider fare we? Ða bodan us færdon and cwædon: þær ys micel folc and maran menn þonne we, micle burga and oð heofun fæste; þær we gesawon Enachis suna." ²⁹ And ic cwæð to eow, "Ne forhtiað and ne ondrædað hig. ³⁰ Drihten eowre God þe eowre lateow ys, he fiht for eow, swa he dyde on Egipta lande beforan eallum folce ³¹ and ge sylfe on westene gesawon. Drihten eowre God eow bær eallum þam wegum þe ge foron, swa mann byrð litle cild, oð þæt ge comon to þisse stowe." ³² And ge furþon ne gelyfdon Drihtne eowrum Gode, ³³ se eode beforan eow on wege and mearcode þa stowa þe ge eowre geteld on slean sceoldon. On niht he tæhte eow þurh fyr and on dæg þurh genip. ³⁴ And þa Drihten eowre spræca gehirde, he wæs swiþe yrre and swor and cwæð, ³⁵ "Ne sihþ nan man of þisse wirestan cneoresse þæt gode land þe ic mid aðe behet eowrum fæderum, ³⁶ buton Chaleb, Iepones sunu; he hit gesihð and

1:15 menn] men B   hig] hi B   fiftigesmennum] fiftigesmannum B   þing] ðingc B
1:16 man] mann B   1:17 miclan] B, miclam L   þing] ðingc B   earfoðlice] earfoðlic B
1:21 þing] ðingc B   forhtgeað] forhtiað B   1:22 And] 2-line 7 mostly in marg. L, om. B
(add. by late hand)   andswarodun] andswaredon B   cyðon] cyðan B   hwilcon] hwylcum B
1:23 .xii.] twelf B   1:24 hig] hi B   1:26 mægðe ungeleafulnysse] geleaflyste B
Drihtenes] drihtnes B   1:27 on] B, an L   Amorreiscra] amoreiscra B   1:28 menn]
men B   micle] preceded by short eras. L, and micla B   1:29 hig] hi B   1:30 eowre¹]
eower B   eowre²] eower B   1:31 eowre] eowerne B   mann] man B   1:33 se] s on
eras. L   1:35 wirestan] wyrrestan B   1:36 Chaleb] c'h'aleb B   gesihð] þæt add. LB

ic hit sylle him and his bearnum, for þam þe he filide me". ³⁷ Næs þæt nan þing wundor þæt Drihten wæs þam folce gram, þonne he wæs me yrre fore [eowre] scilde and cwæð to me, "Ne færst þu þider, ³⁸ ac Iosue, Nunis sunu þin þen, he færð þyder inn for þe. Minga hine and gestranga hine and he todælþ þæt land Israela folce. ³⁹ Eowre litlingas and þa cild þe niton nanes þinges nan gescead, ne godes ne yfeles, hig farað inn and ic him sylle þæt land. ⁴⁰ Ge cirrað and farað on þæt westen þurh þa Readan Sæ ⁴¹ and þoliað þæs þe
f. 84ʳ eow God | behet for eowre ungehirsumnisse and eowre geleaflæaste."

³:²³ 'Ic bæd Drihten on þa tid and þus cwæð, ²⁴ "Drihten God, þu þe ongunne ætywan þinum þeowe þine mærðe and þinne strengestan hand, nys soðlice nan oðer God ne on heofene ne on eorðan þe mæge wircean þ`ine´ weorc þe þu wircst and beon wiðmeten þinre strengþe. ²⁵ Alife me to farenne and to geseonne þæt seloste land begeondan Iordane and þa gecorenistan dune and Libanum." ²⁶ And Drihten me wæs yrre for eowre scilde and cwæð to me, "Genoh hi[t] ys nu. Ne sprec þu natoþæshwon leng to me imbe þis þing. ²⁷ Astih on Fasgan muntes cnæpp and beseoh to westdæle and to norðdæle [and to suðdæle and to eastdæle]. Ne oferfærst þu soðlice Iordane. ²⁸ Bebeod Iosue and gestranga hine, for þam þe he stæpð beforan þison folce and todælþ him þæt land þæt he geseon sceal." ²⁹ And we wunedon on þære dene wið Phogores templ.

⁴:¹ 'L`a´ Israhel, gehir nu bebodu and domas þe þe ic lære and do þa þæt þu si langlife and fare inn and hæbbe þæt land þæt Drihten eowre fædera God eow wyle syllan. ² Ne ice ge nan þing to þam word þe ic to eow sprece. Ne ge wanion of þam. Gehealdað Drihtnes bebodu eowres Godes þe ic eow beode. ³ Ge gesawon ealle þa þing þe Drihten dyde ongen Belfegor, hu he forbritte ealle his bigengan beforan eow. ⁵ Ge witon þæt ic lærde bebodu and rihtwisnissa, swa Drihten God me bebead. ⁸ Hwilc oðer þeod is swa mære, þæt hæbbe

1:36 filide] fyligde B 1:37 þing] *om.* B fore] for B eowre] *om.* LB
1:38 Nunis] nunes B inn] in B Israela] israhela B 1:39 hig] hi B 1:40 þurh] ður B 1:41 geleaflæaste] geleafleaste B 3:24 þinne strengestan] ðine strengstan B God] godd B heofene] heofone B wircean] weorcean B þine] ine *on eras., probably contemp.* L, ða B 3:25 gecorenistan] gecorenustan B 3:26 hit] B, his L natoþæshwon leng] nateshwon lengc B þing] ðingc B 3:27 and to suðdæle and to eastdæle] B, *om.* L 3:28 Bebeod] beod B sceal] sceall B 4:1 La] a *over eras.* L þe²] *om.* B eowre] eower B wyle syllan] syllan wile B 4:2 þing] ðingc B word] worde B to eow] eow to B Ne ge] ne *add.* B of þam] B, of þa L beode] bebeode B 4:3 þing] ðingc B Belfegor] belphegor B forbritte] forrbrytte B bigengan] biggengan B 4:8 þæt] ðe B

laga and rihte domas and ealle æ, þe ic | todæg foresette beforan f. 84ᵛ
eow? ⁹ Gehealdað eow sylfe and eowre sawla geornlice. Ne cumon
eow þas word of gemynde swa lange swa ge lybbon. Lærað eowre
suna and eowre magas þæt hig healdon þa bebodu þe ic eow bebead.
¹⁵ Ne gesawe ge nane andlicnisse on þam dæge þe Drihten spræc to
eow on Oreb on fyres midlene. ¹⁶ Ne wirce ge eow þe ma nane
andlicnissa, ne wæpmannes [ne wifmannes], ¹⁷ ne nanes nytenes ne
fugeles ¹⁸ ne wurmes ne fisces. ¹⁹ Ne behealdon ge heofenan, ne
sunnan ne monan ne steorran, þe læs þe ge þurh gedwyld on hig
gelyfon. God hig gesceop eallum mannum to brice. ²⁰ Soðlice
Drihten eow alædde of Egipta lande to þam þæt he hæfde eow to
agenum folce.'

⁴:²¹ Eft he cwæð: 'Drihten me wæs yrre for eowrum spræcum and
swor þæt ic ne oferfore Iordane, ne ne come on þam selustan lande
þe Drihten eow sillan wile. ²² Nu swelte ic her on lande; ne fare ic
ofer Iordane ac ge farað and agað þæt gecorene land. ²³ Warniað eow
þæt ge næfre ne forgiton Drihtnes wedd eowres Godes þe he eow
behet. ²⁵ Gif ge þonne minum worde ne gelyfað and Drihtenes
bebodu forhogiað, ²⁶ ic hæbbe todæg to gewitnisse heofen and
eorþan þæt ge [for]wurðað raþe on þam lande þe Drihten eow to
gelæt. Ne beo ge þæron nane hwile, ²⁷ ac Drihten eow todrifð geond
ealle þa þeoda, þæt eowre bið feawa on þam lande to lafe, ²⁸ and ge
þeowiað fremdum godum, manna handgeweorc, treowene and
stænene, þa ne geseoð ne ne gehirað, ne hig | ne etað ne hig ne f. 85ʳ
drincað. ²⁹ And þonne ge gemunað Drihten eowerne God and hine
secað, þonne gemete ge hine gif ge hine mid inweardre heortan
seceað and mid ealre mihte. ³⁰ On þære ytemistan tide ge beoð
gecyrrede to Drihtne eowrum Gode and ge gehirað his stefne. ³¹ For
þam þe he ys mildheort God. Ne forlæt he eow, ne he eallinga ne
adiligað eow, ne he ne forgit his wedd on þam he swor eowrum
[fæderum]. ³² Ahsiað be ealdum dagum þa wæron ær þonne ge, of
þam dæge þe Drihten mann gesceop ofer eorðan, fram ufeweardum
heofone and oð his ende, hwæðer æfre gewurde þus gerad þing,

4:9 cumon] cuman B   hig] hi B   bebead] bead B   4:15 andlicnisse] anlicnesse B
4:16 andlicnissa] anlicnyssa B   ne wifmannes] B, *om*. L   4:18 wurmes] wyrmes B
4:19 heofenan] heofonan B   hig¹] hi B   hig²] hi B   4:21 me wæs] wæs me B
4:25 Drihtenes bebodu] drihtnes beboda B   4:26 to] *om*. B   heofen] heofon B
forwurðað] B, wurðað L   gelæt] gelet B   4:27 þa] *om*. B   eowre] eower B
4:28 hig¹] hi B   hig²] hi B   4:29 seceað] secað B   ealre] ealle B   4:30 ytemistan]
ytemestan B   stefne] stemne B   4:31 eallinga] eallunga B   adiligað] adylgað B
fæderum] B, *om*. L   4:32 Ahsiað] axiað B   ealdum dagum þa] ealdon dagon ðe B
mann] man B   þing] ðingc B

[33] oþþe hwæðer ænig mann gehirde Godes stefne and his word swa swa ge gehirdon and gesawon. [39] Ongitað eornostlice todæg on eowre heortan þæt Drihten silf ys God and nis nan oðer, ne uppe on heofone ne niþer on eorðan. [40] Gehealdað his bebodu and domas þe ic eow beode, þæt eow si wel and eowrum bearnum æfter eow and þæt ge þurhwunion lange on þam lande þe Drihten eowre God eow sillan wile.'

[4:44] Ðis ys seo æ þe Moises foresette beforan Israela folce, [45] and laga and domas, þus cweþende: [5:1] 'La Israel, gehir nu godcunde domas and leorniað þa and eac wirceað. [2] Drihten God behet us wedd on Oreb. [3] Ne sealde he wedd urum fæderum ac us þe nu git libbað. [4] Ansine to ansine he spræc to us on þam munte, of þæs fyres midlene. [5] Ic wæs dælere betwix Gode and eow on þa tide, þæt ic cyþe eow his | word. And he cwæð, [6] "Ic eom Drihten eowre God þe eow ut alædde of Egipta lande of þeowette. [7] I. Nafa þu fremde Godas beforan me. [8] II. Ne wirce þu græftgeweorc, ne nanes cynnes anlicnyssa, ne þa ne wurða. [9] Ic eom Drihten eower God þe wrece fædera unrihtwisnissa on hira bearnum [10] and miltsie þam þe me lufiað and mine bebodu healdað. [11] III. Ne nemne ge Drihtnes naman on idel, for þam þe ne bið he unscildig se þe for idelum þinge his naman nemð. [12] IIII. Heald þone restedæg, þæt þu hine halgige swa Drihten þe bebead and þus cwæð: [13] Wirc six dagas [14] and freolsa þone seofoðan; [15] gemunað þæt ge silfe wæron þeowe on Egipta lande and ic eow alisde. [16] V. Arwurða þinum fæder and þine modur, þæt þu si langlife and þæt þu si welig on þam lande þe God þe sillan wile. [17] VI. Ne beo þu manslaga. [18] VII. Ne unrihtæme þu. [19] VIII. Ne stel þu. [20] IX. Ne sege þu lease gewitnissa. [21] X. Ne girn þu þines neahstan wifes, ne his huses ne his landes, ne nan þæra þinga þe his beoð."

[5:22] 'Ðis synd þa word þe Drihten spræc to eallum Israela folce on þam munte, of þæs fyres midlene and þæs genipes micelre stefne, and wrat þa on twam stænenum tabulon and sealde me. [23] Æfter þam þe ge gehirdon his word and gesawon þone munt birnan, þa cwædon

---

4:33 mann] man B 4:39 eowre] eower B heofone] heofonum B
4:40 Gehealdað] geh'e'aldað B bebodu] beboda B wel] well B þurhwunion] ðurhwunian B eowre] eower B 4:44 Israela] israhela B 5:1 Israel] israhel B
5:5 dælere betwix] dælre betwux B cyþe] cuð B eow] and *add.* B 5:6 eowre] eower B þeowette] ðeowte B 5:7 I] *this and subsequent numerals in red or metallic red, text continuous* L 5:10 miltsie] miltsige B 5:11 þinge] ðincge B 5:12 Heald] healdað B restedæg] restendæ B halgige] halgie B 5:16 þinum] ðinne B modur] modor B 5:20 gewitnissa] gewitnessa B 5:21 neahstan] nextan B beoð] beo B
5:22 Israela] israhela B of] on B tabulon] tabulum B

to me þa ealdras and þa betst borenan men, [24] "Nu we gesawon
Godes mægenþrim and his micelnisse, we|gehirdon his stefne on
fyrynes midlene and we ongeaton todæg þæt God spræc wið menn,
and se leofað. [25] Hwi swelte we and forwurðaþ on þison mæstan fyre?
Witodlice gif we leng gehirað Drihtnes stefne ures Godes, we
forwurðaþ. [26] Hu mæg ænig man lifiendes Godes stefne gehiran
and eac libban? [27] Ga þu and gehir þa þing þe Drihten ure God þe
secge and sege us, and we gehirað þe and doð þa." [28] Ða Drihten þæt
gehirde, þa cwæð he to me, "Ic gehirde þises folces word þe hig
spræcon wel. [29] Hwanon cymð him swilc geþanc þæt hig ondredon
me and healdon mine wisan bebodu, þæt him si wel on ecnisse and
hira bearnum? [30] Sege him þæt hig faron to hira geteldum. [31] Stand
þu her mid me and ic secge þe ealle bebodu and godcunde æ and
domas. Lære hig þæt hig don þa on þam lande þe ic him to æhte
sille." [32] Healdað þa þing þe Drihten eower God eow bebead. Ne
ahilde ge naþer ne on þa wynstran healfe ne on þa swiðran. [33] Ac gað
rihte on þone weg þe Drihten eow bebead, þæt ge lybbon and eow si
well and eowre dagas sin gelengede on þam lande þe ge agan sceolon.

6:4 'Gehire Israel: Drihten ure God ys an God. [5] Lufa þinne
Drihten mid ealre þinre heortan and mid eallum mode and mid
eallum mægne, [6] and heald þa word þe ic þe bebeode. [7] And lære 'þa'
þinum bearnum þonne þu sitte on þinum husum [9] and write þa on
þinum þerscolde and on þines huses durum. [10] And þonne Drihten
eowre God eow in gelæt on þæt land þe he foreswor eowrum
fæderum Abrahame and Isaace | and Iacobe, and he eow sylþ
micle burga and þa selustan gebytlu, [11] and fulle hus ælces welan,
þa þe ge ne worhton, and wæterpyttas þe ge ne dulfon, wineardas
and elebeamas þe ge ne plantudon. [12] And ge etað and beoð gefyllede.
[13] Warniað geornlice þæt ge ne forgiton Drihten þe eow ut alædde of
Egipta lande of þeowetes huse. Geeaðmede Drihten þinne God and
þeowa him anum and swera on his naman. [14] Ne far þu æfter
fremdum godum, þe læs þe God yrsie ongen þe. [16] Ne fanda þu

    5:24 micelnisse] micelnyssæ B   fyrynes] fyrrines B   God] godd B   menn] men B
5:25 þison] ðisum B   leng] lengc B   5:26 lifiendes] lyfiende B   5:27 þing] ðingc B
5:28 hig spræcon wel] hi spæcon well B   5:29 þæt] þa`e´t B   hig] hi B   wisan] *om.* B
hira] heora B   5:30 hig] hi B   hira] heora B   5:31 hig[1]] hi B   hig[2]] hi B
5:32 þing] ðingc B   eower] eowwer B   5:33 gelengede] gelencgede B   agan] agon B
6:4 Israel] israhel B   6:5 mode and mid eallum] *om.* B   6:6 heald] healdað B
6:7 husum] huse B   6:9 write] writ B   þerscolde] þærscwolde B   6:10 eowre
God] eower godd B   micle] miccle B   6:11 wineardas] wingeardas B   plantudon]
plantodon B   6:14 þe[1]] ði B   ongen] ongean B

þines Godes swa þu didest on þære costnungstowe. [7:11] Gehealdað eornostlice þa bebodu and þa godcundan æ and domas þe ic eow sylle todæg [and] bebeode þæt ge don. [12] Gif þu hig gehiltst Drihten, þin God ge[h]ealt þæt wedd and þa mildheortnysse þe he swor eowrum fæderum. [13] And he lufað and gemenigfylt and he bletsað eow and eowre wæstmas on þam lande þe he foreswor eowrum fæderum. [14] Ge beoð gebletsod toforan eallum oðrum mannum. Ne bið mid eow nan þing unberendes, ne on mannum ne on nytenum. [15] Drihten adrifð fram eow ælc yfel and wyrpð ongen eowere fynd. [8:19-20] Gif ge þonne forgimeleasiað Drihtnes bebod eowres Godes and filiað fremdum godum, ic secge eow to soþum þæt ge forwurðaþ mid ealle, gif ge beoð ungehirsume Drihtnes beboda.

[9:4-5] 'Ne wene ge na þæt Drihten eowre God fordyde eowre fynd and sealde eow þæt seluste land for eowre rihtwisnisse, ac he hig fordyde for hira arleasnisse and þæt þæt word | wære gefylled þe he mid aðe behet eowrum fæderum, Abrahame and Isaace and Iacobe. [6] Wite ge to soþum þingum þæt God ne sealde eow for eowre godnisse þæt seluste land to æhte, for þan þe ge sind ealra folca ungeleafulluste and heardheorteste. [7] Gemunað and ne forgitað hu swiðe ge gremedon Drihten on þam westene. Of þam dæge þe he eow ut alædde of Egipta lande oð þisne dæg, æfre ge fliton and wunnon ongean Drihten. [8] On Oreb ge hine gremedon and he wæs yrre and wolde eow fordon. [9] Þa astah ic on þone munt and bær þa stænenan bredu on þam wæs þæt wedd þe Drihten wið eow gecwæð, and ic þurhwunode on þam munte .xl. daga and .xl. nihta, swa 'þæt' ic ne æt ne ne dranc. [10] And Drihten me sealde twa stænene tabulan mid Godes fingre awritene. [11] And þa .xl. daga and efenfela nihta agane wæron, Drihten me sealde þa bredu [12] and cwæð to me, "Aris and gang niþer, for þam þe þin folc þe þu ut alæddest of Egipta lande forleton raðe mine bebodu and þone weg þe þu him geswutelodest and hig guton him hæþenne God". [13] And Drihten cwæð eft to me, "Ic geseo þæt þis folc ys heardheort and ungeleaffull. [14] Læt me þæt ic hig fordo and adilgie hira naman under heofone and ic gesette þe ofer þa þeode þe ys mare þonne þeos

---

7:11 þe ic eow sylle todæg] ðe eow todæg B and³] om. LB 7:12 hig] hi B gehealt] B, gegealt L 7:13 gemenigfylt] gemænifylt B 7:14 þing] ðingc B 7:15 ongen eowere] ongean eowre B 8:19 soþum] soðan B 9:4-5 eowre¹] eower B rihtwisnisse] rihtwisnyssae B hig] hi B hira] heora B 9:6 þan] ðam B ungeleafulluste] ungeleaffulluste B 9:7 Gemunað] gemunat B dæg] an'd'weardan dæg B 9:9 .xl.¹] feowertig B .xl.²] feowertig B 9:11 .xl.] feowertig B 9:12 hig] hi B 9:14 hig] hi B hira] heora B

DEUTERONOMY

and strengere." ¹⁵ Þa ic niðer eode of þam byrnendan munte and hæfde þa twa bredu on twam handum, ¹⁶ and ic geseah þæt ge singodon beforan Gode and worhton eow gegoten cealf and wurðodon hit for God | and forleton raðe þone weg þe Drihten eow f. 87ᵛ ætywde, ¹⁷ ic wearp þa bredu of minum handum and tobræc hig beforan eow. ¹⁸ And ic feoll beforan Drihtne swa ic ær dyde, .xl. daga .xl. nihta; ne æt ic ne ne dranc for eallum [eowrum] synnum þe ge dydon ongen God and hine gremedon. ¹⁹ Ic ondred soþlice his graman and his yrre for þam þe he wæs astirod ongen eow and wolde eow fordon, and Drihten me gehirde and tiþode me. ²⁰ He wæs yrre wið Aaron and wolde hine fordon and ic gebæd for hyne. ²¹ Eowerne gylt þe ge worhton, þæt wæs þæt cealf, ic nam and forbærnde hit [and brytte] to duste and wearp on þa burnan þe of þam munte scytt. ²² On bryne and on costunge and on gewilnunge birgenum ge gremedon Drihten. ²³ Ða he sende eow of Cadesbarne and þus cwæð, "Farað and habbað þæt land þe ic eow sealde", and ge forhogedun Drihtnes gebod and ge noldon him gelyfan ²⁴ ac wæron æfre wiðerwearde o[f] þam dæge þe ic eow cuþe. ²⁵ Ic læg beforan Drihtne .xl. daga .xl. nihta, on þam ic hine bæd eadmodlice þæt he eow ne fordyde swa he cwæð þæt he don wolde, ²⁶ and ic cwæð, "Drihten God, ne forspil þu þin folc and þine yrfeweardnysse þe þu alysdest, þa þu hig ut alæddest of Egipta lande. ²⁷ Gemun þinra þeowa, Abrahames and Isaaces and Iacobes. Ne beheald þu þises folces heardnisse and arleasnisse, ²⁸ þæt þæs landes menn þe þu hig of alæddest ne secgeon: Drihten hi ne miht[e] gelædan on þæt land þe | he him behet ac he hig hatode and for þam he hig lædde ut f. 88ʳ þæt he hig ofsloge on þam westene."

¹⁰:¹ 'On þære tide Drihten cwæð to me, "Wirce þe twa stænene tabulan swilce þa ærran wæron and astih to me on þone munt and wirce treowene earce, ² and ic write on þam bredum þa word þe wæron on þam þe þu ær bræce, and lege þa on þa earce". ³ Ic worhte earce of sethim treowum and stænene tabulan swilce þa ærran wæron and ic astah on þone munt and hæbbe hig on minum handum, ⁴ and

9:14 strengere] strengre B   9:16 ætywde] æteowde B   9:17 hig] hi B
9:18 .xl. daga .xl.] feoworti daga and feoworti B   eowrum] B, *om.* L   ongen] ongean B
9:19 ongen] ongean B   9:21 hit] *om.* B   and brytte] B, *om.* L   scytt] scyt B
9:22 costunge] costnunge B   9:23 forhogedun] forhogodon B   9:24 of] on LB
9:25 .xl. daga .xl.] feowortig daga and feowortig B   eadmodlice] eaðmodlice B
9:26 hig] hi B   9:27 heardnisse] heardheortnysse B   9:28 hig¹] hi B
alæddest] alæddost B   secgeon] secgon B   mihte] B, miht (*eras. aft.* t) L   hig²] hi B
hig³] hi B   hig⁴] hi B   10:1 wirce²] wyrc B   10:3 hæbbe hig] hæfde hi B

DEUTERONOMY

he wrat on þam bredum þa tyn word þe on þam oðrum awritene wæron, and sealde hig me. ⁵ And ic eode nyþer of þam munte and lede þa bredu on þa earce þe ic worhte, þær hig sind o[þ] þisne dæg, swa Drihten me bead. ⁸ On þa tide he bead þæt Leuies mægð bære þa earce and stode beforan him on þenunge and bletsode Godes naman oð þysne andweardan dæg. ¹⁰ Ic stod on þam munte swa ic ær dyde .xl. daga and .xl. nihta and Drihten [m]e gehirde and nolde eow fordon. ¹¹ And he cwæð to me, "Ga beforan þison folce to þam lande þe ic behet hira fæderum to syllanne". ¹² La Israhel, ne bitt God þe nanes þinges buton þæt þu ondræde Drihten þinne God and lufie hine and þeowie him mid eallum mægne and mid eallum mode, ¹³ and gehealde Drihtnes bebodu and his æ þe ic þe todæg bebeode. ¹⁴ Heofon and heafuna heofun and eorðe and ealle þa þing

f. 88ᵛ þe sind on him sind Drihtnes eowres Godes. | ¹⁷ Drihten sylf ys goda God, mære God and mihtig and egefull. Ne wandað he for ricum ne for heanum. ¹⁸ He demð steopcilde and wydewan. He lufað fordrifene and sylþ him andlyfene and scrud. ¹⁹ Lufiað fordrifene, for þam þe ge sylfe wæron fordrifene and utancymene on Egipta lande. ²² Hundseofontigra sum wæron eowre fæderas þa hi foron on Egipta land and Drihten eower God eow gemænigfilde swa heofenes tungla.

¹¹:¹ 'Lufiað Drihten eowerne God and wircað his bebodu and his æ and his domas on ælcne timan. ² Oncnawað todæg þa þing þe eowre bearn nyton, þa þe ne gehirdon Drihtenes lare eowres Godes and his mærða and his strengþa, ³ and þa tacn þe he worhte on Pharaone cinge onmiddan Egipta lande ⁴ and on eallum Egipta here and on horsum and on cratum. Hu þære Readan Sæ wæteru hig adrencton, þa hig eow drifon, and Drihten hig adilgode oð þisne andweardan dæg. ⁵ And gemunað hwæt he eow dide on þam westene oþ ge comon to þisse stowe, ⁶ and hu seo eorðe forswealh Dathan and Abiron mid husum and geteldum and mid eallum hira spedum þe hig hæfdon onmiddan Israela folce. ⁷ Ge gesawon ealle þa mæran Drihtnes weorc

---

10:4 hig] hi B   10:5 hig] hi B   oþ] of LB   10:10 .xl.¹] feowertig B   .xl.²] feowertig B   Drihten me] B, drihtene L   10:11 hira] heora B   syllanne] syllenne B   10:12 bitt] bit B   God²] godd B   þeowie] ðeowige B   10:14 and heafuna heofun] om. B   þing] ðingc B   sind on him] syndon hi B   10:17 and²] om. B   egefull] egesful B   10:18 steopcilde] steopcildum B   wydewan] wudewum B   10:19 on] of B   10:22 wæron eowre fæderas] eowre fæderas wæron B   þa hi foron] om. B   land] lande B   heofenes] heofonas B   11:1 wircað] wyrceað B   11:2 þing] þingc B   Drihtenes] drihtnes B   11:3 tacn] tacnea B   cinge] cinincge B   11:4 Sæ] B, sæs L   hig¹] hi B   hig²] hi B   hig³] hi B   11:6 hig] hi B   Israela] israhela B   11:7 gesawon] gesawen (2nd e on eras.) B

DEUTERONOMY

þe he worhte ²⁵ and gehirdon his word, þus cweþende, ²⁶ "Nu todæg ic sette beforan eow bletsunga and wirginissa: ²⁷ Bletsunge gif ge gehirsumiað Drihtnes bebodum eowres Godes þe ic eow todæg bebeode; ²⁸ wirginissa gif ge ne gehirað Drihtnes bebodum þe he eow bebead | and gað æfter fremdum godum þe ge ne cunnon." ²⁹ þonne Drihten eow gelæt on þæt land þe ge to farað on to eardienne, þonne sette ge bletsunga uppan Garizim dune and awirgnisse uppan Hebal dune. ³⁰ þa synd beiundan Iordane be þam wege þe lið to sunnan setlgange on Chananeus lande, se eardað on feldlandum wið Galgalam and wið þa langan dene.

^{12:32} 'Wirceað ealle þa þing þe Drihten eow bebead and ne ice ge nan þing þærto, ne ne waniað. ^{13:1} Gif ænig witega arise betwinan eow and secge þæt him mæte swefen and secge tacna and forebeacnu, ² and hit agæþ eall swa he spricð, and he cwið to eow, "Uton gan and filigean fremdum godum þe ge ne cunnon and uton þeowian him", ³ ne hliste þu his worda, for þam þe Drihten fandaþ eowre, hwæþer ge hine lufigeon mid eallum mode. ⁴ Filigeað Drihtne eowrum Gode and ondrædað hine and healdaþ his bebodu and gehirað hine and þeowiað him. ⁵ Slea man þone leasan witegan, for þam þe he awende eow fram Drihtne eowrum Gode, þe eow ut alædde of Egipta lande, and for þam þe he dyde þæt ge dwelodon of þam wege þe Drihten eow bebead, þæt ge adrifon yfel fram eow. ⁶ Gif þin broþor þe lære dearnunga, oþþe þin sunu oþþe þin dohtor oððe þin wif oþþe þin freond, and þus cweðe, "Uton gan and þeowian fremdum godum", ⁸ ne hire þu him, ne þu him ne ara þæt þu him gemiltsie and hine bediglige, ⁹ ac ofsleh hine þærrihte ¹⁰ and oftorfa þu and eall þæt folc hine mid stanum, for þam þe | he wolde ateon þe fram Drihtne þinum Gode, þe þe ut alædde of Egipta lande of þeowettes huse, ¹¹ þæt eall Israela folc ondrede, þonne hig þæt gehirað, and natoþæshwon nan þing ne don eft swilces.

^{14:1} 'Beoþ Drihtnes bearn eowres Godes. Ne efesiað eow, ne eowre hær ne sciron, ² for þam þe Drihten eow geceas him to sindrium

11:26 wirginissa] wyrignysse B   11:27 gehirsumiað] hyrsumiað B
11:28 wirginissa] wyrignyssa B   gehirað] hyrað B   11:29 eardienne] eardigenne B
sette ge] set he B   awirgnisse] awyrignysse B   Hebal] hebald B   11:30 beiundan] begeondan B   12:32 þing¹] ðingc B   þing²] þingc B   13:1 eow] *om.* B   him] hine B   tacna] tacnu B   13:2 filigean] fylian B   13:3 þam] ðan B   eowre] eower B   lufigeon] lufian B   13:4 Filigeað] fyliað B   13:5 dwelodon] dweledon B
13:6 dearnunga] dearninga B   sunu] suna B   13:8 gemiltsie] gemiltsige B   bediglige] bedyhlige B   13:9 ofsleh] ofsleah B   13:10 þeowettes] ðeowetes B   13:11 eall Israela] eal israhela B   ondrede] ondræde B   hig] hi B   natoþæshwon] nateshwon B   þing] ðingc B   14:1 sciron] scerað B   14:2 sindrium] syndrigum B

folce ofer ealle oþre folc. ²² Syle þone teoðan dæl ealra þinra wæstma ælce geare Drihtne þinum Gode, ²³ on þære stowe þe he gecist þæt man his naman on nemne, and leorna þæt þu ondræde Drihten on ælce tid. ²⁴ Gif se weg swa lang beo þæt þu þine þing [ðyder] bringan ne mage, ²⁵ þonne syle þu hig wið wurþe and bring þæt wurð to þære stowe. ²⁶ And bige þær mid þam ylcan feo swa hwæt swa þe licige, hryþera and sceap and win and beor and eall þæt þe licie, and et þær beforan Drihtne, þu and þin hiwræden ²⁷ and se sacerd þe binnan þinre birig beo. ¹⁵:⁷ Gif ænig þinra freonda beon binnan þinre birig on þam lande þe Drihten þin God þe sillan wile, and him gelimpe þæt he þearfa beo, ne beo þu swa heardheort þæt þu him þines Godes wyrne, ⁸ ac syle him to læne swa hwæt swa he beþurfe and he þe bidde, ⁹ þe læs he wrege þe to Drihtene and hit wurðe þe to hearme. ¹⁰ Ne wanda þu þæt þu þinum frynd ne helpe þær he beþurfe, þæt Drihten eower God eow bletsie on æclne timan. ¹¹ Ne beo ge butan þearfum on þam lande þær þu on wunie, for þam | þe ic bebead þæt þu dohtest þinum breþer and wædlan and þearfan. ¹² Gif þu gebicge ænigne man, þeowie [he] þe six gear and freo hine on þam seofoþan. ¹³ And þænne þu hine freoge, ne læt þu hine gan idelhende fram þe ¹⁴ ac sile him formete on hlafe and on sufle and on wine, þæt Drihten þin God þe bletsie. ¹⁵ Gemun þæt þu sylf wære þeow on Egipta lande and Drihten þe alysde. ¹⁶ Gif se þeowa þonne cweþe þæt he nelle fram þe faran, for þam þe he lufað þe and þine hiwrædenne, ¹⁷ nim þonne anne æl and þurhsting his eare æt þines huses dura and beo he þe syþþan þeow on ecnysse.

¹⁶:¹⁸ 'Sete deman and lareowas þæt hig demon rihtne dom ¹⁹ and ne wendon ne hider ne þider. Ne wanda þu for ricum ne for heanum ne for nanum scette, for þam medsceattas ablendað wisra manna geþancas and wendað rihtwisra word. ²⁰ Filige rihtlice þam rihte, þæt þu lybbe lange on þam lande þe Drihten þin God þe sylþ. ¹⁷:²⁻⁵ Gif ænig man þeowie fremdum godum and geeaðmede hine to sunnan and to monan, and hit man to soþe ongite, oftorfige hine man

---

14:24 þing] þingc B   ðyder] B, *om*. L   mage] mæge B   14:25 hig] hi B
14:26 licige] licie B   eall] eal B   15:7 ænig þinra freonda beon] þinra freonda ænig beo B   15:9 þe¹] þæ B   Drihtene] drihtne B   15:10 þæt²] and B   God] godd B
15:11 þearfum] ðearfan B   15:12 ænigne man þeowie] ænne mann ðeowige B   he] B, *om*. L   seofoþan] seofoðam B   15:13 þænne] þonne B   15:15 sylf] *om*. B
15:16 hiwrædenne] hiwrædene B   15:17 æl] æll B   16:18 hig] hi B   16:19 Ne wanda ... word] *Cf. Cotton Vespasian D. xiv, f. 11ᵛ (see pp. lxviii–lxix)*: Ne nym þu medsceattes for heo ablændeð wisra manna geðancas and wændeð rihtwisra word   ricum] rican B   scette] sceatte B   wendað rihtwisra] awendaþ rihtwisnessa B   17:2–5 man þeowie] mann ðeowige B   soþe] soðan B   oftorfige] oftorfie B   man³] mann B

mid stanum. [15] Ne ceos þu þe cining of nanre oþre þeode mannum buton of þinum agenum cynne. [18:10] And warna þe þæt þu ne gime drycræfta, ne swefena ne hwatena ne idelra galdra. [11] Ne ne axa nane wicca rædes ne sece þu riht æt deadum. [12] Soþlice Drihten onscunað ealle þas þing and for þilcon gylte he eow fordeð. [17] Drihten cwæþ, "Gif ge nellað þa word | gehiran þe eow bebodene synd on minum naman, ic hit wrece on eow". [19:16] Gif ænig mann oþerne wrege, and him hwilcne gilt onsecge, [18] smeage man geornlice hwæþer hit soð si and gif hit þonne leas bið, [19] beo se leasa gewita þæs ilcan wyrþe þe he wolde þæt se oþer wære. [20:10] Gif þu wille ænige buruh oferwinnan, beod him ærest sibbe. [11] Gif hig þonne on hand gað and þa gatu undoþ, þonne beon hig ealle gesunde and þeowion þe and beon þine gafolgildan. [12] Gif hig þonne þæt nellað and willað ongean þe feohtan, [13] ofsleh ælcne wæpnedman, [14] buton wifum and cildum. [21:18] Gif ænig man hæbbe modigne sunu and rancne, þe nelle hiran his fæder and his meder, [19] þonne nymon hig hine and lædon to þære burge deman, [20] and cweþon to him, "þis is uncer ungehirsuma sunu. He forhogað þæt he hire uncre lare. He begæð unætas and oferdrincas and galscipe." [21] Oftorfie eall seo buruhwaru hine mid stanum to deaðe. [22] Đonne mann biþ deaþes scildig and hine mann on gealgan ahehð, [23] birge man hine þæs ilcan dæges, þe læs þe þæt land si besmiten þuruh hine. [22:5] Ne scride nan wif hig mid wæpmannes reafe, ne wæpman mid wifmannes reafe. [22] Gif ænig man hæme mid oþres wife, swelton hig buta. [28] Gif ænig man ofernyme unbeweddod mæden and hit wirð cuþ, [29] sylle hire fæder fiftig yntsena seolfres and hæbbe hig æfre siþþan to wife swa lange swa he libbe.

[23:19] 'Ne læne þine breþer nan þing | to hire [20] ac fremdum menn. [21] þonne þu behat be[h]ætst Drihtene þinum Gode, ne wanda þu þæt þu hit ne gelæste, for þam þe he hit wile habban and gif þu dead bist

---

17:15 cining] cyningc B   18:10 swefena] swefna B   18:11 Ne ne axa ... deadum] *Cf. Cotton Vespasian D. xiv, f. 11ᵛ*: ne acse þu nanre wicce rædes. ne sech þu riht æt deaden   wicca] wiccean B   18:12 Soþlice ... þas þing] *Cf. Cotton Vespasian D. xiv, f. 11ᵛ*: soðlice god ascuneð swylce þing   þing] ðingc B   19:16 mann] man B   20:11 hig¹] hi B   undoþ] ondoð B   hig²] hi B   20:12 hig] hi B   ongean] ongen B   20:13 ofsleh] ofsleah B   20:14 buton] butan B   20:19 hig] hi B   20:20 uncre] uncer B   oferdrincas] oferdrynceas B   20:21 buruhwaru] burhwaru B   20:22 mann¹] man B   mann²] man B   20:23 man hine] hine man B   þe¹] ði B   þuruh] ðurh B   22:5 hig] hi B   22:22 hig] hi B   22:28 wirð] wurð B   22:29 hig] hi B   23:19 þine] ðinum B   þing] ðingc B   23:20 menn] men B   23:21 behætst] B, ?belætt (h *and* st *add. by late hand over eras.*) L   Drihtene] drihtne B   dead] LB (*erroneous translation of* moratus)

þu bist scildig. ²² And gif þu nan þing behætst, þu byst clæne. ²⁴ Gif þu gange binnan þines freondes wineard, et þæra bergena swa fela swa þu wylle and ne ber þu na ma ut mid þe. ²⁵ And gif þu gange ofer his æcer, brec þa ear and gnid, and ne rip þu na mid sicele. ²⁴:⁵ Ðonne man niwan wif nymð, ne fare he ut to gefeohte, ne him nan man utfæreld openlice beode, ac beo him æt ham butan gilte on his huse, þæt he geblissie an gear mid his wife. ⁷ Gif ænig man sylle his broþor wið wurþe, si he ofslagen. ¹² Nafa þu nanes þearfan wedd mid þe nihtlangne fyrst, ¹³ ac agif hit him sona ær sunnan setlgange, þæt he bletsie þe þonne he gerest on his reafe and þæt þ`u´ hæbbe rihtwisnisse. ¹⁶ Ne slea man fæderas for suna gylton, ne suna for fædera gilton, ac swelte anra gehwilc for his agenum gilte. ²⁵:⁵ Gif twegen gebroðra eardiað ætsomne and hira oþer biþ dead butan bearnum, ne nime þæs forðfarenan laf nanne oþerne man buton his broþur, þæt he awecce his broþur sæd. ⁶ And nemne man þone frumcennedan sunu be þæs deadan naman, þæt his nama ne beo adilgod of Israela folce. ⁷ Gif he þonne nelle nyman his broþur lafe þe him seo æ bebyt to hæbbenne, fare þæt | wif to þam portgate and cyþe hit þam yldestan mannum. ⁸ Clipie hine man þider and axie hine be þam þingum. Gif he þonne cwið, "Nelle ic hig habban to wife", ⁹ ga þæt wif to him and nyme his gescy of his fotum beforan þam ealdrum and spæte on his nebb, ¹⁰ and nemne hine ælc man on Israela folce "unsceoda". ¹³⁻¹⁵ Hæbbe ælc man rihtne anmittan and rihte wægan and rihte gemetu on ælcum þingum, þæt hig naþær ne sin ne læssan ne maran þonne hit riht sig, ¹⁶ for þam þe Drihten ascunað ælce unrihtwisnysse.'

²⁷:⁹ Moises and þa sacerdas of Leuies cynne cwædon to eallum Israela folce: 'La Israel, ongit þæt þu eart Drihtnes folc þines Godes. ¹⁰ Gehir his word and his bebodu and his rihtwisnysse þe ic eow bebeode.' ¹¹ And Moises cwæþ to þam folce: ¹² 'Ðis sint þa þe sceolon standan and bletsian Drihten uppan Gazarim dune, þonne hig habbað Iordane oferfarene: Simeon and Leui, Iudas and Isachar,

---

23:22 þing] ðingc B   23:24 wineard] wingeard B   bergena] nim *add.* L (*later del.*)
24:5 openlice] *om.* B   beode] ne beode B   geblissie] geblissige B   24:13 þu] u *appar.*
on eras. L   25:5 ætsomne] ætsamne B   broþur¹] broðor B   broþur²] broðor B
25:6 adilgod] adylegod B   Israela] israhela B   25:7 broþur] broðor B   25:8 hig]
hi B   25:9 ga] and ga LB   25:10 Israela] israhela B   25:13-15 wægan] wæga B
þingum] þincge B   hig naþær] hi naðer B   sig] sy B   25:16 þam] ðan B
unrihtwisnysse] unrihtwisnyssae B   27:9 Israela] israhela B   Israel] israhel B
27:10 bebodu] beboda B   rihtwisnysse] rihtwisnyssa B   27:12 sint] synd B   sceolon]
sculon B   hig] hi B

Ioseph and Beniamin. ¹³ And þas sceolon standan on Hebal dune to wirgienne: Ruben and Gad, Aser and Sabulon, Dan and Neptalim. ¹⁴ And þa sacerdas of Leuies kynne cweþað to Israela folce hluddere stefne, ¹⁵ "Beo se mann awirged þe wirce agrafene Godas oþþe gegotene and on diglum sette", and eall þæt folc cweþe amen. ¹⁶ "Beo se man awirged þe ne arwurðað his fæder and his modor", and eall folc cwið amen. ¹⁷ "Si se man awirged þe forhwyrfe his freondes landgemæro", and eall folc cwið amen. ¹⁹ "Beo se man awirged þe deme unriht|ne dom steopcildum and wydewum", and cweþe eall folc amen. ²⁰ "Si se awirged, se þe hæme mid his fæder wife", and eall folc cwið amen. ²¹ "Beo se man awirged þe hæme wið nyten", and cweþe eall þæt folc amen. ²² "Si se awirged, se þe hæme wið his swustor ²³ oþþe wið [his] swegere", and eall folc cwið amen. ²⁴ "Si ælc morðslaga awirged", and eall folc cwið amen. ²⁵ "Si se awirged þe unscildigne man belæwe wiþ medscette", and eall folc cwið amen. ²⁶ "Beo se awirged ðe [ne] wunað on þisse æ and hi mid spræcon and mid wordum gefylð and nele mid worcum", and eall folc cwið amen.

²⁸:¹ 'Gif þu þonne Drihtne gehirsumast and his beboda healtst þe ic þe bebeode, Drihten þin God þe gedeð heahst and mærost ealra þæra þeoda þe on eorþan wuniað. ² Ealle þas bletsunga cumað ofer þe gif þu healtst his beboda. ³ Beo þu gebletsod on birig and beo þu gebletsod on lande. ⁴ Beo þine[s] innoþes wæstm gebletsod and þines landes wæstm and þinra nytena wæstm. ⁵ Beon þine bernu gebletsode and eac þine lafa. ⁶ Beo þu gebletsod ingangende and utgangende. ⁷ Drihten afylþ þine fynd beforan þe; on anne weg hi gað ongen þe and on seofon wegum hig fleoð fram þe. ⁸ Drihten sent bletsunga ofer þine heddern`u´ and ofer ealle þine weorc þe þu wircst and he bletsað þe on þam lande þe þu underfehst. ⁹ Drihten þe gecist to halgum folce, swa swa he swor, gif þu geheald st Drihtnes bebodu. ¹⁰ And ealle men geseoþ þæt þu Drihten lufast: him stent ege | of þe. ¹¹ Drihten gedeð þæt þu hæfst ælces godes genoh, swa he swor

27:13 wirgienne] wyrgenne B   Sabulon] zabulon B   27:14 kynne] cynne B   Israela] israhela B   hluddere] hludre B   27:15 mann] man B   eall] eal B   27:17 landgemæro] landgemæru B   27:19 unrihtne dom] unrihte domas B   cweþe eall] cwyðe eal B   27:20 eall] eal B   cwið] cweðe B   27:22 Si se] sy ðe man B   27:23 his] B, *om.* L   swegere] swegre B   eall] eal B   27:24 eall] eal B   27:25 man] mann B   medscette] metsceatte B   eall] eal B   27:26 ne] *om.* LB   spræcon] spæcon B   worcum] weorcum B   eall] eal B   cwið] cweð B   28:1 gehirsumast] hyrsumast B   wuniað] wunað B   28:2 healtst] gehealtst B   28:3 and] *om.* B   28:4 þines¹] B, þine L   þinra] ðinre B   28:7 ongen] ongean B   hig] hi B   28:9 halgum] halegum B   geheald st] gehealtst B   28:11 swa] swa swa B

DEUTERONOMY

þinum fæderum. ⁱ²He geopenað heofunan, his selustan goldhord, and sent tidrenas on þin land. He bletsaþ ealle þine weorc. Þe biddað manega þeoda þines þinges to læne and þu ne bitst nanne. ¹³Drihten þe gesett simle on foreweard and na on æfteweard and þu bist æfre bufan and na benið an, gif þu Drihtenes bebodum hirsumast swa ic þe bebeode.'

²⁸:¹⁵ Moises cwæð eft to Israela folce: 'Gif þu nelt gehiran Drihtnes bebod þines Godes, þe ic þe todæg bebeode, ealle þas wirignyssa cumaþ ofer þe and þe fordoð. ¹⁶Beo þu awirged binnan birig and butan. ¹⁷Si þin bern awirged and þine lafa. ¹⁸Si þines innoþes wæstm awirged and þines landes wæstm and þinra nytena. ¹⁹Beo þu awirged ingangende and utgangende. ²⁰Sende Drihten hunger and yrmþe ofer þe, oþ [he] þe fordo, for þam þu hine forlete. ²¹Sende Drihten cwealm on þe. ²²Slea þe Drihten mid feforadle and mid cile and mid hætan and mid swoluþan, oþ þu forwurðe. ²³Si þe heofene swilce ar and eorþe swilce isen. ²⁴Sende Drihten dust ofer þin land for ren and feallon axan of heofene ofer þe, þæt þu si forbryt. ²⁵Do Drihten þæt þu fealle beforan þinum feondum and þonne þu fare on anne weg ongen hig, þæt þu fleo on seofon wegas fram him, þæt þu si todrifen geond ealle eorðricu ²⁶and þæt þin lichama si eallum fugelum to mete and wilddeorum. ²⁷Slea þe | Drihten mid þam Egiptiscan witon þæt þu hal ne wurþe. ²⁸Sende þe Drihten on ungewitt and blindnisse, ²⁹þæt þu grapie on midne dæg swa se blinda deþ on þistrum, and þæt þu ne mæge þine wegas aredian and þolie bysmor on ælcne timan and næbbe þone þe þe werie. ³⁰þu nimst wif and oþer man liþ mid hire. þu rærst hus and ne eardast þæron. þu plantast wineard and ne bricst his. ³¹Mann slihþ þinne oxan beforan þe and þu his ne abitst. Nime man þinne assan beforan þe and hine na ne ongife. Nimon þine fynd þin orf and nafa þu nanne fultum. ³²Sin þine suna and þine dohtra geseald oþrum folce þær þu on locie and ne si nan strencþ on þinre handa. ³³Ete ælþeodig folc þine tilinga and þe mid bismore ofsitton ealle þine

28:12 heofunan] heofun B   selustan] selesta B   þinges] ðincges B   28:13 gesett] geset B   Drihtenes] drihtnes B   28:15 Israela] israhela B   28:16 awirged] awyriged B   28:17 bern] bearn B   28:18 wæstm²] awirged *add.* L   28:20 hunger] hungor B   oþ he þe] B, oþþe þe L   þam] ðe *add.* B   28:22 swoluþan] swoleðam B   28:23 heofene] heofune B   28:24 heofene] heofone B   28:25 þonne] þone B   ongen hig þæt þu] ongean hi and ðu B   28:27 Egiptiscan] egyptiscean B   28:28 ungewitt] ungewit B   28:29 werie] werige B   28:30 þu¹] and þu B   wineard] wingeard B   28:31 Mann slihþ] man slicð B   Nimon] niman B   28:32 locie] locige B   strencþ] strengð B   28:33 ælþeodig] elðeodig B   tilinga] tilunga B   ofsitton] ofsittan B

DEUTERONOMY

dagas, ³⁴þæt þu gange wa[f]iende for hire þinge and ege. ³⁵Slea þe Drihten mid þam wirstan yfele on cneowum and on spearlirum, þæt þu næbbe nan þing hales fram þam fotwolmum o[þ] þone hneccan. ³⁶Drihten sent uncuþe þeode ofer eow, þa þe ge ne cunnon, and ge þeowiað fremdum godum, stoccum and stanum. ³⁷And ge forwurþað þurh bigspell and bigcwidas. ³⁸Ge sawað micel sæd and ripað litel, for þam gærstapan hit fretað eall. ³⁹Ge plantiaþ wineardas and delfað and ge ne drincað þærof, for þam þe wurmas hine fretaþ. ⁴⁰Ealle eowre elebeamas forwurþað. ⁴¹Ge strinað suna and dohtra and ne brucað hira, for þam | þe hig man læt to oþrum lande. ⁴²Ragu and meos fornymð ealle eowres landes wæstmas. ⁴³Utancumene men eardiað on eowrum lande and beoþ wildra þonne ge and eow genyþriað. ⁴⁴Hig lænaþ eow and ge ne lænað him. Hig beoð on forwearde and ge on æfteweard.

²⁸:⁴⁵'Ealle þas wirignyssa cumað ofer eow and eow fordoþ, for þam ge oferhogodon Drihtnes beboda and þa æ þe he bebead, ⁴⁶and tacnu and forebeacnu wurþaþ on eow and on eowrum ofspringum. ⁴⁸And ge þeowiað eowrum feondum and Drihten asent hungor on eow and þurst and næcede and ælce wædlan. Drihten sett isen geoc on eowerne swuran o[þ] ge forwurþað. ⁴⁹And he asent þeoda ofer eow of feorwegum, þare spræce ge ne cunnon. ⁵³Ge beoþ swa lange inne besette þæt ge etað eowre agene suna and eowre dohtra. ⁵⁸Buton ge healdon þisse æ word þe her on þisse bec awritene sint and ondredon Drihtnes wurþfullan naman eowres Godes, ⁵⁹Drihten geeacnað eowre wito and eowres cinrenes wito. Þa wirstan untrumnissa and þone mæstan hete he sent on eow. ⁶¹And þær toeacan, ealle þa adla þe [ne] sint awritene on þisse bec he sent ofer eow, þæt ge forwurþon. ⁶²And eowre wurþaþ feawa to lafe, þe ær wæron swa fela swa heofenes tungla, for þam þe ge ne gehirdon Drihtnes word. ⁶³And swa Drihten eow ær gemiltsode and eow gemenigfilde, swa he eow fordeþ and genyðraþ and forhwyrfð eow of þam lande þe ge inn

f. 93ᵛ

28:34 wafiende] wasiende L, wasigende B   hire] hyra B   þinge and] *om*. B
28:35 þing] ðincg B   oþ] of LB   28:37 bigspell] bygspel B   28:41 hira] heora B
hig] hi B   28:43 Utancumene] Utancymene B   men] *om*. B   lande] lande (*corr. by orig. scribe fr.* landum) B   wildra] wyldran B   genyþriað] genyþeriað B   28:44 Hig¹] hi B   Hig²] hi B   forwearde] foreweard B   28:45 þam] ðe *add*.   oferhogodon] forhogedon B   28:46 ofspringum] ofspryngce B   28:48 wædlan] wædle B   oþ] LB   of   28:49 þare spræce] ðæra spræca B   28:53 besette þæt] besetene oð B   eowre²] *om*. B   28:58 sint] synd B   ondredon] ondrædan B   28:59 geeacnað] geeacnoð B   cinrenes] cynrynes B   hete] ece B   eow] *om*. B   28:61 adla] adlu *corr. to* adla B   ne] *om*. LB   forwurþon] forwurðan B   28:62 eowre] eower B   heofenes] heofones B   28:63 gemenigfilde] gemænifylde B   genyðraþ] genyðerað B

f. 94ʳ farað to agenne. ⁶⁴ Drihten eow todrifþ geond ealle | þeoda oþ eorþan endas and ge þeowiað þar godum þe ge ne cunnon, stoccon and stanon. ⁶⁵ Witodlice ne gereste ge on nanum earde. He sent on eow forhte heortan and geteoriende eagan and modes gnornunge, ⁶⁶ and eow biþ eowre lyf æwene. Ge ondrædað eow deaþ, dæges and nihtes. ⁶⁷ On ærne mergen ge cweþað, "Hwa hilpþ us þæt we æfenes gebidon?", and on æfen ge cweþaþ, "Hwa fylst us þæt we dæges gebidon?", for eowre forhtnysse and yrhþe þe eow eglað. ⁶⁸ Sciphere eow nymð and sylþ eow eowrum feondum to cepe, and eow ne alyst nan mann.'

²⁹:¹ Ðis sint þa word þe Drihten bebead Moise þæt he bude Israela folce on Moab lande, butan þam wedde þe he him behet on Oreb. ² And Moises clipode eall Israela folc and cwæþ to him: 'Ge gesawon ealle þa þing þe Drihten worhte beforan eow on Egipta lande on Pharaone and on eallum his þeowum, ³ and hu micle costunge on eallum his lande ge gesawon, þa tacn and þa forebeacn, ⁴ and Drihten eow ne sealde undergitende heortan, ne eagan to geseonne ne earan to gehirenne, oþ þisne andweardan dæg. ⁵ He lædde eow .xl. wintra geond þæt westen. Næron eowre reaf forwerede, ne eowre gesci mid ylde fornumene. ⁶ Ne æte ge hlaf, ne druncon ge win ne beor, þæt ge wiston þæt he ys Drihten eowre God. ⁷ And ge comon to þisse stowe. And Seon cing for ut of Esebon and Og cing of Basan for ongen us to gefeohte and we ofslogon hig ⁸ and namon hira land and sealdon hit
f. 94ᵛ Rubene to æhte and Gade and healfre Mannases mægþe. ⁹ Heal|daþ eornostlice ealle þisse æ word and gefyllað hig, þæt ge undergiton ealle þa þing þe ge doþ. ¹⁰ Ge standaþ todæg ealle beforan Drihtene eowrum Gode, eowre mægþa ealdras and þa betstborenan and þa lareowas and eall Israela folc, ¹¹ bearn and wif, and ealle utankymene þe mid eow eardiaþ, buton wuduheawerum and þam þe wæter berað, ¹² and gaþ on Drihtenes bebodum eowres Godes, ¹³ þæt he gelæste eow þæt he mid aþe swor eowrum fæderum Abrahame and Isaace and Iacobe. ¹⁴ Ne beode ic þas bebodu eow anum ¹⁵ ac eallum mannum, þam þe nu sint and þam þe toweaarde sint.

28:64 todrifþ] adrifð B   þar] ðam B   stanon] stanum B   28:66 eowre] eower B
28:67 æfenes gebidon] æfnes gebidan B   28:68 cepe] ceape B   mann] man B
29:1 sint] synd B   Israela] israhela B   29:2 Israela] israhela B   þing] ðingc B
29:3 hu] om. B   micle costunge] micele costnunga B   29:5 .xl.] feowertig B
forwerede] forwerode B   gesci] gescyg B   29:6 druncon] drunce B   eowre] eower B
29:7 for ut of Esebon] of esebon for ut B   ongen] ongean B   hig] hi B   29: 9 hig] hi B
þing] ðingc B   29:10 Drihtene] drihtne B   eowre] eowra B   ealdras] eardas B
Israela] israhela B   29:11 bearn] om. B   utankymene] utancymene B   buton] butan B
29:12 Drihtenes] drihtnes B   29:15 sint¹] synd B   sint²] synd B

DEUTERONOMY

^{30:15} Ongitaþ þæt God sette todæg beforan eow lif and god, and þær ongen deað and yfel, ¹⁶ þæt ge lufion Drihten eowerne God and healdon his bebodu, þæt ge libbon and sin gemenifilde. ¹⁷ Soþlice gif eowre heorte bið fram awend and nele gehiran, and ge beoþ mid gedwolan beswicen and lufiað fremde godas, ¹⁸ ic secge eow to soþe þæt ge forwurðaþ and sweltaþ on litlere hwile. ¹⁹ Ic clipie me todæg to gewitnysse heofonan and eorþan þæt ic eow sette beforan lif and god, bletsunga and wirinysse. Geceosað lif, þæt ge libbon, and eowre ofspring. ²⁰ Lufie Drihten. He ys soþlice lif and eowre daga langnis, þæt ge eardion on þam lande þe Drihten foreswor eowrum fæderum Abrahame and Isaace and Iacobe, þæt he hit sealde him.'

^{31:1} Witodlice Moises spræc ealle þas word to eallum Israela folce, ² and cwæð to him: 'Ic eom todæg hundtwentigwintre. Ne mæg ic leng faran ut and inn, and eac Drihten cwæþ to me, | "Ne oferfærst f. 95^r þu Iordane". ³ Eornustlice Drihten eower God færþ beforan eow and gewylt eow ealle þeoda to handa, and Iosue færð beforan eow swa God spræc. ⁶ Onginnaþ esnlice and beoþ staþulfæste. Ne ondrædað eow, ne ge ne onforhtion, for þam Drihten eower God eow læt and eow ne forlæt.' ⁷ Moises þa cwæð to Iosue beforan eallum Israela folce: 'Beo strang and staþulfæst. Soþlice þu lætst þis folc on þæt land þe Drihten swor þæt he sillan wolde hira fæderum and þu hit todælst mid hlyte. ⁸ And Drihten, þe eower lateow ys, biþ mid þe. Ne forlæt he þe na. Ne ondræd þu þe, ne þu ne forhta.' ⁹ Witodlice Moises awrat þas æ and sealde hig þam sacerdum, Leuies bearnum, and eallum Israela ealdrum, ¹⁰ and cwæþ to him: ¹¹ 'Ðonne eall Israela folc ætgædere sig, þonne geræde ge þas word þisse æ beforan him, ¹² þæt hig gehiron and leornion and ondrædon Drihten eowerne God and healdon and gefille ealle þisse æ word.'

^{31:14} And Drihten cwæþ to Moise: 'Nu sint þines deaþes dagas gehende. Clipa Iosue and standað on þære halgan stowe, þæt ic spece wiþ hine.' Moises and Iosue foron and stodon on þære halgan stowe, ¹⁵ and Drihten him ætiwde on genipe on þære halgan stowe ingange.

30:15 ongen] ongean B   30.16 gemenifilde] gemænifylde B   30.17 eowre] eower B   30:19 heofonan] heofon B   wirinysse] wyrignyssa B   eowre ofspring] eower ofspringc B   30:20 eowre] eower B   langnis] langnyss B   31:1 Israela] israhela B   31:2 hundtwentigwintre] hundtwelftiwintrae B   leng] lengc B   oferfærst þu] oferfærsðu B   31:3 Eornustlice] eornostlice B   31:6 staþulfæste] staðolfæste B   onforhtion] forhtion B   31:7 Israela] israhela B   staþulfæst] staðolfæst B   lætst] lædst B   31:8 eower lateow] eowwer latteow B   na. Ne] nane (*with* ne *del.*) B   31:9 awrat] wrat B   hig] hi B   Israela] israhela B   31:11 Israela] israhela B   ætgædere sig] togædere sy B   geræde] ræde B   31:12 hig] hi B   gefille] gefyllon B   31:14 sint] synd B

¹⁶ And Drihten cwæþ to Moise: 'Nu þu scealt restan mid þinum fæderum, and þis folc arist and syngað and folgaþ fremdum godum on þam land[e] þe hit to færð and oneardaþ. þær hig forlætað me and doþ for naht þæt wedd þe ic him sealde. ¹⁷ And min yrre onrist ongen hig on þam | dæge and ic forlæte hig and behide me fram him and hig beoþ fordone. Him cumaþ to ealle yfela and geswencednessa, swa þæt hig cweþaþ on þam dæge, "þas yfelu sind becumen on us for þam þe God nys mid us". ¹⁸ Soþlice ic me hide on þam dæge fram him for eallum þam yfelum þe hig didon and for þam þe hig filigdon fremdum godum. ¹⁹ Writaþ eow nu þisne cantic and læraþ Israela bearn, þæt hig hine gemyndelice singon, and si me to tacne þis leoð gemang Israela folce. ²⁰ Soþlice ic hig in gelæde on þæt land þe ic foreswor hira fæderum, þæt ys wæst[m]bære land, ægðer ge on meoluce ge on hunige. And þonne hig etaþ and fulle beoþ and fætte, þonne forlætað hig me and cirraþ to fremdum godum and þeowiaþ him and tellaþ min wedd for naht. ²¹ Siþþan hig gemetaþ manega yfelu and geswencednyssa, þis leoþ him andswaraþ for gewitnysse, and þæt leoþ ne adiligað nan man of þines ofspringes muþe. Ic wat soþlice þæs folces geþanc, hwæt hig todæg don willað ær þam þe ic hig in gelæde on þæt land þe ic him behet.'

³¹:²² Moises wrat þone cantic and lærde Israela folc, ²³ and bead Iosue, Nunis suna, and cwæþ: 'Beo strang and staþulfæst. þu gelætst Israela folc on þæt land þe ic him behet and ic beo mid þe.' ²⁴ Æfter þam þe Moises wrat þisse æ bebodu and þa gefilde, ²⁵ he bebead Leuies kynne, þe bæron þa earce þe | Drihtnes wedd on wæs, and þus cwæþ: ²⁶ 'Nimað þas boc and lecgaþ hig be þære earce sidan þe Drihtnes wedd on ys, þæt heo si þær ongen eow to gewitnysse. ²⁷ Ic can eowre geflit and eowre heardheortnisse. On minum life, þa hwile þe ic mid eow ferde, æfre ge fliton ongen God and ge doþ micle swiþor syþþan ic dead beo. ²⁸ Gegadriaþ to me ealle þa betstborenan

---

31:16 lande] B, landum L   hig] hi B   31:17 onrist] arist B   hig¹] hi B   hig²] hi B   hig³] hi B   yfela] yfelu B   geswencednessa] geswencednyssa B   hig⁴] hi B   þam dæge] fram him *add.* L *(later scored through)*   31:18 hide] behyde B   þam yfelum] *om.* B   hig¹] hi B   hig²] hi B   31:19 eow] *om.* B   Israela] israhela B   hig] hi B   to tacne þis leoð] ðis leoð to tacne B   Israela] israhela B   31:20 hig¹] hi B   wæstmbære] B, wæstbære L *(susp. mark for m add., prob. by late hand)*   meoluce] meolce B   hig²] hi B   hig³] hi B   31:21 hig¹] hi B   adiligað] adylegað B   ofspringes] ofspringces B   hig²] hi B   hig³] hi B   31:22 Moises] *3-line green initial cap.* L   þone] *om.* B   Israela] israhela B   31:23 staþulfæst] staðolfæst B   gelætst Israela] gelædst israhela B   31:24 Æfter þam] *repeated* L   31:25 kynne] cynne B   31:26 hig] hi B   ongen] ongean B   31:27 eowre¹] eower B   ongen God] ongean godd B   micle] miccle B   31:28 Gegadriaþ] gegaderiað B

on eowrum cinne and lareowas þæt hig gehiron mine word and ic clipie heofon and eorþan to gewitnysse. ²⁹ Ic wat þæt ge unrihtlice libbað æfter minum deaþe and ge sona forlætaþ þa þing þe ic eow bebead and becumað on micle yfele on þære itemestan tide, þonne ge unriht wirceaþ beforan Drihtenne and hine gremiaþ mid eowrum handgeweorce.' ³⁰ Moises spræc þas word beforan Israela folce and hig fyllde oþ ende, and þus cwæþ:
³²:¹ 'Gehiraþ heofenas þa þing þe ic sprece and gehire eorþe min word. ² Weaxe min lar swa ren. Flowe min spræc swa deaw and swa smilte ren and swa dropan ofer gærsa ciþas, ³ for þam þe ic clipie Drihtnes naman. Sillaþ mærþe urum Gode. ⁴ Godes weorc sint fullfremede and ealle his wegas sint domas. God ys getreowe and, butan ælcre unrihtwisnisse, rihtwis. ⁵ Him singodon unrihtwise and na his gecorenan bearn. La, yfele cneores, ⁶ agiltst þu Drihtene þas þing, stunt folc and unwis. Secge ge, nis he eowre fæder þe eow ahte and worhte and gesceop? ⁷ Gemunaþ ealdra daga, geþencaþ ealle cneoressa. Axiaþ eowre fæderas and | hig kyþaþ eow, eowre yldestan f. 96ᵛ and hig secgaþ eow. ⁸ Þa se hehsta todælde þeoda, þa he ascirede Adames bearn, he geset folca gemæro æfter Israela bearna getæle. ⁹ Drihtnes dæl wæs his folc and Iacob his yrfeweardnis. ¹⁰ He funde hit on westum lande on egeslicere stowe and on widum westene. He lædde hit ymbeutan and lærde hig and heold hig, swa his eagan seon. ¹¹ Swa earn his briddas spænþ to flihte and ofer hig flicerað, swa he tobrædde his feþeru and nam eowre kynren and bær on his exlun. ¹² Drihten silf wæs hira lateow and næs mid him nan fremde god. ¹³ He sette hig ofer heah land, þæt hig ætun þæs landes wæstmas and þæt hig sucon hunig of stane and ele of þam heardustan stane, ¹⁴ buteran of hriþera heorde and meoluc of sceapun, mid lama rysle and ramma of Basanes kynrene, and buccan and hwætes smedeman,

31:28 hig] hi B   clipie heofon] clypige heofun B   gewitnysse] gewittnysse B
31:29 þing] ðincg B   micle yfele] miccle yfelu B   on] B, and on L   Drihtenne] drihtne B
31:30 spræc] spæc B   Israela] israhela B   hig fyllde] hi fylde B   32:1 Gehiraþ]
AUDITE *add. in left margin appar. by orig. scribe* L   heofenas] heofonas B   þing] ðingc B
sprece] spece B   min] mine B   32:2 spræc] spæc B   32:4 sint¹] synd B
fullfremede] fulfremede B   sint²] synd B   God] godd B   getreowe] getrywe B   and]
om. B   ælcre] ælcere B   rihtwis] rihtwise B   32:5 unrihtwise] on unrihtwisum B
32:6 agiltst þu Drihtene] agyltsðu drihtne B   þing] ðincg B   eowre] eower B
32:7 geþencaþ] geðenceað B   hig kyþaþ] hi cyðað B   hig²] hi B   32:8 þa²] ðe B
Israela] israhela B   getæle] getele B   32:9 yrfeweardnis] yrfeweardnyss B
32:10 egeslicere] egeslicre B   ymbeutan] ymbutan B   hig¹] *om.* B   hig²] hi B
32:11 hig] hi B   eowre kynren] eower cynryn B   exlun] eaxlum B   32:12 hira lateow]
eowwer latteow B   32:13 hig¹] hi B   hig ætun] hi æton B   hig³] hi B   32:14 lama]
lamba B   kynrene] cynrene B

and þæt hig druncon hluttor win. ¹⁵ Hig wæron gemæste and wiþerodun for hira fætnisse. Hi forleton God hire scippend and gewiton fram hira halwendan Gode. ¹⁶ Hi gremedon hine mid fremdum godum. ¹⁷ Hi offrodon deoflum and na Gode, þam godum þe hi ne cuþon. Niwe comun þe hira fæderas ne wurþodun. ¹⁸ Ge forleton God þe eow gestrinde and ge forgeton Drihten eowerne scippend. ¹⁹ Þa Drihten þæt geseah, þa wearþ he yrre, for þam þe his suna and his dohtra hine gremedon. ²⁰ And he cwæþ, "Ic behide me fram him and ic besceawie hira endas. Soþlice hit ys ungeleaful cyn|ren and ungetreowe bearn. ²¹ Hig me tirigdon mid hira idelgildum and ic anyde hig ut on fremde folc and ic hig geswence mid disgere þeode. ²² Fyr ys onæled on minre hatheortnisse and byrnð oþ helle endas and fryt land mid his wæstme and forbærnþ duna staþelas. ²³ Ic gegadrie yfelu ofer hig and ic afæstnie mine flana on him. ²⁴ Hig beoþ mid hungre fornumene and fugelas hig fretaþ mid þære biterustan slitinge. Ic sende wildera deora teþ on hig, mid wurmum and næddrum. ²⁵ Ute hi reafaþ swurd and inne ege. Cniht and mædenu sucende, mid ealdum men. ²⁶ Ic cwæþ: Hwær sint hig? Ic gedo þæt hira gemynd geswicþ of eallum mannum. ²⁷ And for hira feonda yrre ic wandode, þe læs þe hira fynd ofermodegodun and cwædon: Ure hand ys heah and ne worhte Drihten þas þing. ²⁸ Þeod ys, buton geþeahte and butan gleawnisse. ²⁹ Ic wisce þæt hig wiston and undergeaton and foresceawodon hira ende. ³⁰ Hu an man drifþ þusend and twegen aflymaþ tyn þusendu? Hu nis hit for þam þe hira God hig forlæt and Drihten hi beleac? ³¹ Soþlice nis ure God swilce hira god ys, and ure fynd sint dema. ³² Hira wineard ys of Sodomwara winearde and of Gomorra underburgum. Hira winberie ys gealla and þæt biteroste clyster. ³³ Hira win [i]s dracena gealla and næddrena attor unhalwendlice. ³⁴ H[u] næron þas gesceapene mid me and geinseglude on minum

32:14 and þæt hig] and hi B   32:15 Hig] hi B   wiþerodun] wiðerodon B   hire] heora B   32:17 comun] comon B   wurþodun] wurðodon B   32:18 gestrinde] gestyrde B   forgeton] forgeaton B   eowerne] eowwerne B   32:20 besceawie] besceawige B   ungeleaful cynren] ungeleafful cynryn B   ungetreowe] ungetrywe B   32:21 Hig¹] hi B   hig²] hi B   hig³] hi B   32:23 gegadrie] gegaderige B   hig] hi B   afæstnie] afæstnige B   32:24 Hig¹] hi B   hig²] hi B   slitinge] slitincge B   wildera deora] wildeora B   hig³] hi B   32:25 reafaþ] reafoð B   32:26 sint hig] synd hi B   32:27 ofermodegodun] ofermodegodon B   þing] ðingc B   32:28 buton] butan B   32:29 hig] hi B   wiston] LB (alt. later to wisedon in L, poss. by 11/12th-c. glossator)   32:30 an man] an m partly eras. L   aflymaþ] aflymeþ B   hig forlæt] hi forlet B   32:31 sint dema] synd deman B   32:32 wineard] wingeard B   32:33 Hira] heora B   win is] B, wines L   unhalwendlice] unhalwendlic B   32:34 Hu] B, ?hi L (corr. by late hand to hu)   gesceapene] gesceape B

DEUTERONOMY

goldhordum? ³⁵ Seo wracu is min and ic hit agilde on tide, þæt hira fot ætslide. Hira forwirde dæg ys gehende and þas þing eow sint gegearwode." ³⁶ Drihten | demþ his folce and gemiltsað his þeowum. He gesihþ hig geuntrumod and þa belocenan geteoredon and þa lafa sint fornumene. ³⁷ And cweþaþ, "Hwær sint godas on þam hig truwan hæfdon? ³⁸ Of þæra offrunge ge ætun ryslas and druncon win on hire offrunge. Arison nu and fylston eow æt nydþearfe. ³⁹ Ge seoþ þæt ic ana eom and nis nan oþer God buton me. Ic ofslea and ic læte libban. Ic slea and ic hæle, and ne mæg nan man of minre handa ut alinian. ⁴⁰ Ic hebbe to heofena mine hand and ic swerie þurh mine swiþeran and ic cweþe: Ic libbe on ecnisse. ⁴¹ Ic gescirpe min swurd swa ligette and min hand demþ. Ic agilde wrace minum feondum and þam þe me hatedon. ⁴² Ic smirie mine flan on blode and min swurd fryt flæsc." ⁴³ Geblissiað heofenas mid him and arwurþion hine ealle Godes englas. Þeoda heriað his folc, for þam he wricþ his þeowas and agilt wrace hira feondum, and Drihten bið arfæst his folces lande.'

³²:⁴⁴ Moyses and Iosue, Nunes sunu, nu spræcon ealle þas word to eallum Israela folce ⁴⁶ and cwædon: 'Healdaþ ealle þas word þe ic eow nu todæg bebeode and beodað þa word eowrum bearnum to healdenne and to donne, ⁴⁷ for þam ne sint hig eow on idel beboden ac þæt ge libbon þurh hine and wunion lange tid and don þa þing on þam lande þe ge in farað to agenne, þonne ge ofer Iordane farað.'

³²:⁴⁸ DRIHTEN WÆS ÐA SPRECENDE TO MOISE, þus cweðende: ⁴⁹ 'Astih to me on þisne munt Abarim, þe ys on Ne|bo dune on þam lande Moab, ongean Iericho, and geseoh Chanaan land, þe ic forgife Israhela bearnum to agenne, and swelt on þam munte. ⁵⁰ And þu bist geþeod to þinum folcum, swa swa Aaron þin broþur wæs dead on þære dune Or and wæs gelogod to his folcum, ⁵¹ for þam þe git agilton ætforan me on Israhela bearnum middan, æt þæs wiðersæces wæterum on Chades on þam westene Sin, and ge ne

32:35 þing] ðingc B   sint] synd B   32:36 hig] hi B   geteoredon] geteorodun B
sint] synd B   32:37 sint] synd B   hig] hi B   32:38 offrunge¹] offrunga B   ætun]
æton B   hire offrunge] heora ofrungum B   32:39 buton] butan B   slea] ofslea B
32:40 hebbe] hæbbe B   heofena] heofone B   swerie] swerige B   swiþeran] swyðran B
32:42 smirie] smyrige B   32:43 heofenas] heofonas B   þam] ðe add. B
32:44 Israela] israhela B   32:46 nu] om. B   beodað] beoðað B   word²] om. B
32:47 sint hig] synd hi B   wunion] þurhwunion B   don] doð B   þing] þingc B   þonne]
þone B   ge³] om. B   farað²] om. B   32:48 DRIHTEN] 3-line green initial cap. L
32:49 þe¹] se B   swelt] swelc (with unclear alteration) B   32:50 geþeod] geðeodd B
broþur] broðor B   32:51 bearnum] bearna B

wurðedon me onmang Israhela bearnum. ⁵²Ðu scealt geseon þæt land and þu ne cymst þæron.'

³³:¹Moyses þa gebletsode ær his deaþe Israhela bearn, þa twelf mægða, ælce mid sindrigre bletsunge, ³⁴:¹and astah siþþan uppan þone munt Nebo on Fasgan cnæp, ongean þa burh Iericho, and Drihten him æteowode eall Galaad land oð Dan, ²and eall Neptalim land and Effraim and Mannassen and eall þæt land oð þa itemistan sæ, ³and þone suðdæl and þa rumnisse Iericho feldes and palmtreowa birig, oð Segor. ⁴Drihten cwæð þa to him: 'Ðis is þæt land þe ic behet Abrahame and Isaace and Iacobe, þus cweðende, "þinum ofspringe ic forgife þis land". Þu hit gesawe nu þinum eagum and þu ne færst þæron.' ⁵Moyses þa, Godes þeowa, wæs þær dead on Moab lande, swa swa Drihten het. ⁶And he gebirgde hine on þære dene Moab lande, ongean Phogor, and niste nan man his birgene oð þisne andwerdan dæg. ⁷Hundtwelftig geara wæs Moises, þa þa he gewat, and his eagan ne mistredon, ne his teð ne wagedon. ⁸And Israhela f. 98ᵛ bearn hine beweopon þritig daga | on Moabes feldum, and þa heofungdagas wæron þa gefyllede þe hig Moisen bemændon. ⁹Soðlice Iosue, Nunes sunu, wearð gefilled mid wisdomes gaste, for þan þe Moises sette his handa uppan hine, and Israhela bearn him [gehyrsumodon and] didon swa swa Drihten bebead Moyse. ¹⁰Ne aras siþþan nan witega on Israhela þeode swilce Moises wæs, þe Drihten cuðe of ansine to ansine, ¹¹on eallum tacnum and forebeacnum þe God sende þurh hine, þæt he worhte on Egipta lande Pharaone and eallum his folce and eallum his lande, ¹²and ealle þa strangan mihta and þa micclan wundra þe Moises worhte ætforan Israela folce.

32:51 wurðedon] wurðodon B   34:1 burh] buruh B   æteowode] æteowde B
34:2 Mannassen] mannasen B   itemistan] ytemestan B   34:3 palmtreowa] pamtreowa B   34:4 ofspringe] ofsprincge B   34:5 þeowa] ðeow B   het] wolde B
34:6 gebirgde] bebyrigde B   birgene] byrgenne B   andwerdan] andweardan B
34:7 mistredon] mistodon B   wagedon] wagodon B   34:8 hig] hi B
34:9 gehyrsumodon and] B, *om*. L   bebead] B, him bebead L   34:12 micclan] miclan B   Israela] israhela B

[JOSHUA]

^{1:1} Hit wæs [geworden] æfter Moyses forðsiþe, [Drihtnes ðeowan, ðæt] Drihten spræc to Iosue, Nunes suna, and cwæð him to: ² 'Moyses min þeowa forðferde. Aris þu nu and far ofer þas ea Iordanen, þu and eall þis folc mid þe, to þam lande þe ic forgife Israhela bearnum. ³ Eall þæt rymet þe eower fotswaþu on bestæpð ic eow forgife, swa swa ic spræc to Moise. ⁴ Fram þam westene and fram Libano oþ þa micclan ea Eufraten, eall þæt Ethea land oð ða micclan sæ ongean sunnan setlgang, beoþ eowre gemæru. ⁵ Ne mæg eow nan þing wiðstandan eallum dagum þines lifes. Swa swa ic wæs mid Moise, swa ic beo eac mid ðe and ic þe ne forlæte. ⁶ Beo þu nu gestrangod and ellenrof. [Soðlice ðu dælst mid hlote ðisum folce ðæt land ðe ic behet ðinum fæderum. ⁷ Beo ðu gestrangod and swyðe ellenrof,] þæt þu mid weorcum gefille ealle þa æ þe Moises min þeowa þe bebead. Ne þu ne gebuh fram þære æ on þa swiþran healfe ne on þa wynstran, þæt þu ongite | ealle þa þing þe þu dest. ⁹ Ic þe f. 99^r
bebeode þæt þu beo gestrangod and ellenrof. Ne ondræd þu þe, for þan þe ic þin Drihten and þin God beo mid þe on eallum þam þe þu to færst.' ^{10–11} Hwæt þa Iosue het þæt folc hig gearcian to þam earde to faranne, swa swa se ælmihtiga wolde, ^{16–17} and þæt folc him behet þæt hig him gehirsumian woldon on eallum his hæsum, swa swa hig gehirsumodon Moyse. Hig bædon þa georne: 'Beo huru God mid þe, swa swa he wæs mid Moyse, ¹⁸ and se man þe wiðcwið þinum bebodum ahwar, beo he deaþes scildig. Beo þu huru gehyrt and hicg þegenlice.'

^{2:1} Iosue þa sona asende twegen sceaweras digellice of Sathin and het sceawian þæt land and þa burh Hiericho, hu heo beworht wære. Hig ferdon þa and comon to anre miltistran huse, seo wæs Raab gehaten, and gereston hig þær. ² Ða wearð þam cyninge gekyd þæt

MSS L, B   *Joshua starts on new line in* L *but no division is signalled, though* ⟨I⟩NCIPIT LIBER IOSUE *in left margin may be contemp. In* B *(f. 140ᵛ), text starts at top of page with no heading.*   1:1 geworden] B, *om.* L   Drihtnes ðeowan ðæt] B, *om.* L   1:2 þu¹] *om.* B   eall] eal B   1:3 Eall] eal B   bestæpð] bestæppað B   1:4 micclan¹] miclan B   þæt] *om.* B   Ethea] eðea B   micclan²] miclan B   1:5 þing] ðingc B   eallum] on eallum B   1:6–7 Soðlice ðu . . . swyðe ellenrof] B, *om.* L   1:7 ealle¹] *om.* B   þing] ðingc B   1:10–11 hig] hi B   faranne] farenne B   1:16–17 hig¹] hi B   woldon] woldondon B (*1st* don, *at line end, partly eras.*)   Hig³] hi B   God] godd B   2:1 burh Hiericho] buruh iericho B   beworht] geworht B   Hig¹] hi B   seo] heo B   hig] hi B   2:2 gekyd] gecydd B

þær comon sceaweras of Israela bearnum, þæt hig þa burh sceaw‐
odon, ³ and sende to Raab and het þa sceaweras agifan. ⁴⁻⁶ Ac heo
hæfde hig behid, ær hire seo hæs to come, on hire upflora, and
geandwyrde þus: 'Ic andette þæt hig comon to me ac ic ne cuþe hira
fær, and hig urnon on æfnunge ut of þissere birig mid þam þe þa
burhgata belocene wurdon. Efstað nu ardlice and ge hig ofridað.'
⁷ Hig þa sona æfter ridon, idelum færelde. ⁸ And þæt wif þa spræc to
þam behiddum werum: ⁹ 'Ic wat nu to soþon þæt God eow sylð þisne
eard. Witodlice eower ege ys on us becumen and þis folc is geirged |
f. 99ᵛ and ormod ongean eow. ¹⁰ We gehirdon þæt Drihten adrigde þa
Readan Sæ, þa þa ge ferdon fram Egipta lande, and hu ge ofslogon
siððan twegen cynegas, Seon and Og, ¹¹ and aswearc ure mod and ure
gast forhtode to eowrum infærelde. Eower Drihten ys soðlice soþ
God on heofenum and on eorðan neoþan, þe ealle þing gewylt.
¹² Sweriað me nu þurh Drihten þæt ge don eft wið me swilce
mildheortnisse swa ic macode wið eow, and syllað me sum tacn
¹³ þæt ic sylf beo gehealden, and min fæder and modor and mine
gebroðra, and þa þe us to lociað, alysað fram deaþe.' ¹⁴ Ða cnihtas
hire andwirdon and mid aþe beheton: 'þonne ure Drihten us forgifð
þisne eard to gewealde, we kyðað mildheortnisse on þe.' ¹⁵ Witodlice
hire hus wæs on þam wealle fæst and heo let hig ut mid anum
langum rape þurh þæs huses egþyrl ofer þone weall, ¹⁶ and cwæð:
'Farað eow nu wærlice and gewendað to muntum and lutiaþ þær þry
dagas, þe læs þe eow gemeton þa þe eow æfter ridon, and efstað
siþþan aweg.' ¹⁷ Hig cwædon to þam wife: 'We beoð unscildige wið
þe, ¹⁸ þonne we to þisum lande cumað, gif þu lætst þisne rap hangian
on þam ehþyrle þær þu us ut alete and gelangast to þe þine leofostan
frynd, fæder and modor and þine magas in to þe. ¹⁹ And locahwa ut
gange, licge he ofslagen, and se þe on þam huse beo, hæbbe frið mid
þe. ²⁰ And gif þu abarast ure spræce, we ne beoð forsworene.' ²¹ þæt
wif him cwæð to: 'Eower cwide stande.' ²² Hig efston þa aweg, swa
f. 100ʳ þæt wif hig | lærde, and comon to Iosue and kyddon him eall þis.
²⁴ Hig sædon him: 'To soþan us sylð Drihten þis land. Ealle synd
geyrgede þe eardiað on þisum lande.'

2.2 Israela] israhela B   hig] hi B   2:4–6 hig behid] hi behydd B   andette] andytte B
hig²] hi B   hira] heora B   hig³] hi B   Efstað] ef's'taþ B   hig⁴] hi B   2:7 Hig] hi B
2:9 soþon] soðan B   2:10 cynegas] cyningas B   2:11 heofenum] heofonum B   neoþan]
om. B   þing] ðingc B   2:12 macode] mocode B   2:14 aþe] hyre add. B   kyðað] cyðað B
2:15 hig] hi B   langum] langan B   egþyrl] eahðirl B   weall] weal B   2:17 Hig] hi B
2:18 cumað] becumað B   2:19 locahwa] locehwa B   2:20 spræce] sprace B
2:22 Hig¹] hi B   hig²] hi B   kyddon] cyddon B   eall] eal B   2:24 Hig] hi B

JOSHUA

³:¹ Iosue þa aras raðe on þære nihte and astyrede his fyrdwic forð to Iordanen and wicode þreo niht wið þa ea on anbidunge, ² and sende þa bydelas ³ and bead eallum þam here: 'þonne man eowres Godes earce styrað mid þam gangendum bærmannum of Leuies cynne and ge ne cunnon þone weg, folgiað eow feorran þære halgan earce, ⁴ and nan man ne genealæce neh þam earce. ⁵ And beoð gehalgode. Betwux eow Drihten wyrcð wundra tomergen.' ⁶ And he cwæð to þam sacerdum: 'Nymað þis Godes scrin and gað ætforan þam folce,' and þa sacerdas dydon swa swa Iosue hi het. ⁷ And Drihten cwæð to Iosue: 'Nu todæg ic onginne þe to mærsigenne ætforan Israhela bearnum, þæt hi magon witan þæt ic wille mid þe beon, swa swa ic mid Moise wæs. ⁸ And þu gewissa þa sacerdas, þa þe þæt scrin berað, þæt hig gebidon on þære ea.' ⁹ Iosue þa clipode and cwæð to þam folce: ¹⁰ 'Be þam ge magon witan þæt God wunað betwux us, and þa hæþenan todræfð, þe nu habbað þisne eard, on eowre gesihþe, ¹³ for þan þe Iordan seo ea ætstent on hire ryne. Swa raðe swa þæt scrin in biþ geboren, swa ofstint se stream.' ¹⁴ þæt folc ferde þa forð to þære ea. ¹⁵ And sona swa þa bærmenn gesetton heora fotlæst on þære ea ofre, ¹⁶ swa ætstod se stream and ongan to þindenne ongean swilce hit wære an heah dun, and se æftra stream | arn ut to þære sæ. ¹⁷ Hwæt, þa sacerdas þa ætstodon on   f. 100ᵛ
þam grunde on drigre moldan on middan þære ea [and eal ðæt folc ferde forð ofer ða ea] be drium grunde.

⁴:¹ And Drihten cwæð to Iosue: 'Hat nu twelf weras of þam twelf mægðum. ³ Nyman twelf stanas on middan þære ea þær þa sacerdas stodon and habban forð mid eow to eowre wicstowe and wurpan hig þær.' ⁴ Ða dyde Iosue swa swa Drihten him bebead ⁵ and cwæð to þam folce: ⁶ 'Gif eowre bearn eow befrinað eft on uferum dagum hwæt doð þa stanas her, ⁷ þonne secge ge to andsware þæt seo ea Iordane adruwode mid þam þe ure fæderas ferdon ofer hig mid þam halgan scrine, and hig beoð her to gemynde Israela bearnum a on ecnisse.' ⁸ Ða dydon þa twelf weras swa swa Drihten him bebead and namon twelf stanas on þæs streames ryne, hæfdon forð mid him to hira fyrdwicum. ⁹ Iosue het eac ahebban oðre twelf stanas to middes þam streame, þær hig stodon mid þam scrine, and hig þær

3:1 raðe] hraðe B   astyrede] astyrode B   3:3 halgan] om. B   3:4 neh] neah B
earce] arce B   3:8 hig] hi B   3:10 us] eow B   3:13 þe] om. B   ea] alt. appar. fr.
eæ B   Swa raðe] om. B   3:15 bærmenn] bærmen B   3:16 æftra] æ't'fra B
3:17 and eal . . . ða ea] B, om. L   4:3 hig] hi B   4:6 þa] ðas B   4:7 hig¹] hi B
hig²] hi B   her] appar. orig. here with 2nd e eras. L   Israela] israhela B   4:8 hira] heora B   4:9 hig¹] hi B   hig²] hi B

þurhwuniað oð þisne andweardan dæg. ¹⁰ And þæt folc ferde forð mid gebylde. ¹⁴ On þam dæge gemærsode se mihtiga Drihten Iosue þone æþelan ætforan Israhela folce, þæt hig hine ondredon swa swa hig ondredon Moysen. ¹⁸ Mid þam þe hig ferdon fram þære ea Iordanen, þa arn se stream forð swa swa he ær dyde. ¹⁹ And hig wicodon on Galgala on easthealfe Iericho on þam teoðan dæge þæs forman monþes.

⁵:¹ Þa geaxodon þa cynegas þe eardodon on þam leodscipum þæt Drihten þa ea Iordanen adrigde ætforan Israhela bearnum. | Þa þa hig ferdon þærofer, þa wearð heora heorte toslopen and heora gast ne belaf on him, for þan þe hig ondredon Israhela tocymes. ² Drihten cwæð to Iosue on þære ylcan tide: 'Wirc þe nu stænene sex and oðre siþe ymbsnið Israhela bearn.' ³ Iosue þa dyde swa swa Drihten him bebead and Israhela bearn ealle ymbsnað uppan þam beorge þe ys gehaten Preputiorum. ⁴⁻⁵ Heora fæderas wæron ær on Egipto ymbsnidene and seo iuguð næs, þe be þam wege wæs acenned, ⁶ on þam langsuman færelde feowertig geara, and þis ys se intinga þære æftran ymbsnidennysse. ⁸ Hig wunudon þær swa on þære ylcan wicstowe oð þæt hig gehælede wurdon ⁹ and heton þa stowe Galgala. Drihten cwæð to Iosue: 'Nu todæg ic adyde þæra Egiptiscra hosp fram eowrum cynne.' ¹⁰ Hig wunudon þa on Galgala and worhton 'Phase', þæt ys 'færeldfreols', on þam feowerteoðan dæge þæs monðes on æfnunge, on Hiericho feldum, ¹¹ and æton of þæs landes wæstmum on þam oðrum dæge, þeorfe hlafas and polentan þæs ilcan geares. ¹² Æfter þam þe hig æton of þæs eardes wæstmum, him æteorode se heofonlica mete, ne hi siþþan ne onbirigdon þæs bigleofan ofer þæt, ac of þæs geares wæstmum Chanaan landes. ¹³ Mid þam þe Iosue com on Iericho lande, he geseah ænne wer wið þa fyrde standan mid atogenum swurde and he sona hine axode: 'Eart þu ures geferes þe ure wiðerwinna?' ¹⁴ Se wer him andwirde: 'Ic eom ealdor and latteow Drihtnes heres and ic hider nu com.' ¹⁵ Iosue þa | sona feoll afyrht to eorðan and cwæð: 'Hwæt sprico min hlaford to his þeowan þus?' ¹⁶ Se engel him cwæð to: 'Uncnyte þin gesci raðe of þinum fotum, for þam þe se stede ys halig þe þu on stentst.' And he swa dyde.

4:14 mihtiga] ælmihtiga B   hig¹] hi B   hig²] hi B   4:18 hig] hi B   4:19 hig] hi B   5:1 cynegas] cyningas B   hig¹] hi B   hig²] hi B   ondredon] B, hira add. L   5:2 nu] om. B   5:4–5 iuguð] iugoð B   5:6 langsuman] langsumon B   feowertig] feowerti B   5:8 Hig wunudon] hi gewunodan B   hig²] hi B   5:10 Hig wunudon] hi wurdon B   Hiericho] iericho B   5:11 polentan] and add. B   5:12 hig] hi B   æteorode] ateorode B   5:15 sona feoll] feoll sona B   5:16 raðe] hraðe B   þam] ðan B   stentst] styntst B

JOSHUA

⁶∶¹ Hiericho seo buruh wæs mid weallum ymtrymmed and fæste belocen for þæs folces tocyme, and hi ne dorston ut faran ne in faran for him. ² Drihten cwæð þa to Iosue: 'Ic do þas buruh Hiericho on þinum gewealde and þone cyning samod and þa strengstan weras þe wuniað on hire. ³ Farað nu six dagas simble ymbe þa burh, ælce dæg æne, ealle ˊ*feohtendras*ˊ, ⁴ and seofon sacerdas blawon mid bymon eow ætforan.' ⁶ Iosue þa swa dyde. ¹²⁻¹⁴ And þa sacerdas bæron þæt Godes scrin ymbe þa burh, ælce dæge æne, and oðre seofon bleowon mid sylfrenum bymon and hi ealle to fyrdwicum ferdon æfter þam. ¹⁵ On þam seofoðan dæge hig ferdon seofon siþon embe þa burh, ¹⁶ and on þam seofoðan ymbfærelde, þa þa sacerdas bleowon ²⁰ and þæt folc eall hrymde swa swa Iosue him rædde, þa burston þa weallas þe þa burh behæfdon endemes to grunde and hi þa in eodon, ælc mann swa swa he stod on þam ymbgange. ¹⁷ Iosue þa clipode and cwæð to þam folce: 'Si þeos burh amansumod and eall þæt bið on hire, buton Raab ana libbe and þa þe locyað to hire, for þan þe heo urum ærenddracum arfæstnisse cydde. ¹⁸ And ge nan þing ne hreppon on reafe ne on feo, þæt ge ne beon scildige scamlicre forgægednysse, and | Israhela fyrdwic for synne beo gedrefed. ¹⁹ Swa hwæt swa þær goldes bið, þæt beo Gode gehalgod, and on seolfre oððe on are, eall into his hordum.' ²¹ Hig ofslogon þa sona mid swurdes ecge weras and wifmen and þa wependan cild, hryðera and scep, assan and ealle þing. ²² Iosue cwæð þa siððan to þam foresædan ærendracum: 'Gað nu to þam huse þær ge behydde wæron and lædað ut þæt wif þe eowrum life geheolp, and þa þe hire to locyað lædað of þisre byrig.' ²³ Hig didon þa swa, swa swa him gedihte Iosue, and læddon hi of þære birig mid eallum hire magum, and hig siþþan leofodon mid sibbe betwux him. ²⁴ Hi forbærndon þa þa burh and þæt þe binnan hire wæs. ²⁵ And Iosue bæd þus: ²⁶ 'Beo se awirged þe æfre eft gedo edstaþeli[an] þas burh Hiericho.' ²⁷ God wæs þa mid Iosue on eallum his weorcum and his nama wearð gewidmærsod wide geond þæt land.

f. 102ʳ

6:1 buruh] burh B   ymtrymmed] ymbtrymed B   þæs] ðes B   6:3 ymbe] ymb B   ealle feohtendras] and ealle suwigende B; *in* L, feohtendras *is written on eras. appar. by the 11th/12th-c. Latin glossator (see p.* cxxxii)   6:4 blawon] blawan B   bymon] byman B   6:12–14 bleowon] blewon B   bymon] byman B   fyrdwicum] fyrdwicon B   6:15 hig] hi B   embe] ymb B   6:16 bleowon] blewon B   6:20 *verse translated out of sequence*   mann swa swa] man swa B   6:17 ærenddracum] ærendracum B   6:18 þing] ðingc B   scamlicre] sceamlicre B   6:19 þær] her B   6:21 Hig] hi B   wependan] wepende B   þing] ðingc B   6:22 foresædan] foresædum B   6:23 Hig¹] hy B   swa³] *om*. B   hig²] hi B   6:26 gedo edstaþelian] gedo edstaþelige L, geedstaðelie B   burh] buruh B

JOSHUA

7:1 Witodlice Achar, Charmies sunu, Zabdies suna, Zare suna of Iudan mægðe, behydde of þam herereafe þe him forboden wæs þe Iosue amansumode, and se ælmihtiga God yrsode sona ongean Israhela bearn. ²Ða sende Iosue sceaweras to Hai, þe þær gehende wæs, and het besceawian þa burh. Hi ferdon þa ³and comon and cwædon to Iosue: 'Ne læt þu eall þis folc to þære litlan byrig ac twa þusenda oððe þreo læt faran þærto. Hwæt sceal eall þis folc on idel beon geswenct?' ⁴Ða ferdon þreo þusenda feohtendra wera to oferwinnenne þa | burh, ac hig wurdon on fleame ⁵and sona ofslagene six and þritig fram þære buruhware, þe him on bæce filigdon. Ða wearð Iosue swiðe sarig on his mode and eall Israhela folc wurdon afyrhte for þære dæde. ⁶And Iosue feoll astreht ætforan Godes scrine and þa yl[d]ran men ealle hi astrehton, licgende swa oð æfen, and dydon dust uppan heora heafda. ⁷Iosue þa clipode and cwæð mid angsumnisse: 'Wella min Drihten God, hwi woldest þu lædan þis folc hider ofer þas ea, þæt þu us sealdest on Amorrea handum and us fordydest? ⁹Þis geaxiað Chananei and cumað hider to us and ealle þas landleoda belicgað us mid fyrde and ure naman adilegiað. And hwæt dest þu, Drihten, þinum mæran naman?' ¹⁰And Drihten him cwæð to: 'Aris nu Iosue. Hwi list þu neowel on eorðan? ¹¹Israhel syngode and þa gesetnisse gewemde. Hi ætbrudon of þam herereafe þe him forboden wæs and on hira hordfatum behiddon. ¹²Nu næfð Israhel nanne stede wið his fynd ac flihþ underbæc, for þan þe he ys besmiten mid þære amansumunge. Ne beo ic leng mid eow, buton ge þone fordon þe þises giltes ys scildig. ¹³And þu sege þam folce, "Beoð gearwe tomergen. Seo amansumung ys on eow. ¹⁴Gegaderiað eow be mægþum [and gange] þæt gehlot fram mægðe to mægðe and be manna hiwrædenum and be ænlipugum mannum. ¹⁵And beo se forbærnd, se þe befangen bið on þam fracodan gilte, mid eallum his æhtum, for þan unrihtan weorce."' | ¹⁶Hig gesamnodon hig þa be sindrigum mægðum ¹⁷⁻¹⁸and eode þæt gehlot swa lange oð hit becom to þam ylcan men þe þæt man gefremed[e], to þam foresædan Achar, Charmies suna of Iudan

---

7:1 Achar] LB; *alt. to* achan *by eras., date uncertain* L, *corr. to* achan *in a 12th-c. Latin note* B   Zare] zares B   7:3 læt] læd B   eall¹] eal B   7:4 hig] hi B   7:5 bæce] bæc B   eall] eal B   7:6 feoll] feol B   yldran] yltran L, yldestan B   7:9 ure] urne B   7:11 hira] heora B   7:12 nanne] nænne B   amansumunge] mansumunge B   leng] lengc B   ys] sy B   7:13 þu sege] ðus secge B   7:14 and gange] B, *om.* L   ænlipugum] ænlypegum B   7:15 forbærnd] forbæred B   þan unrihtan] ðam unrihtum B   7:16 Hig gesamnodon hig] hi samnodon hi B   7:17-18 gefremede] B, gefremodon L   Achar] B, *alt. to* achan *by eras.* L

mægðe, and he wearð ameldod. ²⁰ He andette þa Iosue ætforan him eallum and cwæð: 'Soðlice ic syngode. ²¹ Ic geseah betwux þam herereafum wurmreadne basing and twa hund entsena hwites seolfres and sumne gildene dalc on fiftigum en'tʹsum and ic ætbræd þæt and behidde on eorðan ætforan minum getelde.' ²² Iosue þa sende sona to his getelde and man funde þa þing, swa swa he foresæde, ²⁴ and hig læddon þa Achar to Achores dene mid wife and mid cildum and mid eallum æhtum ²⁵ and hine þær stændon and his þing forbærndon ²⁶ and worhton mid stanum anne steapne beorh him ofer. And Godes hatheortnys gecirde sona fram þam folce.

⁸:¹ Drihten cwæð þa to Iosue: 'Ne ondræt þu þe nan þing. Nym þæs folces meniu and far þe to Hai. Þa burh ic þe sylle and þa burhware samod, þone cyning and þæt land and þa þe locyað to him. ² Do ymbe þa burh swa swa þu didest ymbe Iericho. Habbað eow þa huþe and þæt orf eow gemæne. Sete nu syrwa wiðæftan þa burh.' ³ Iosue sende þa sona on þære nihte þritig þusend wera to þære searwa stowe ⁴ and het hig beon gearwe and abidan þær, ⁵ and cwæð: 'Ic fare mid þisum folce foran ongean þa burh and þonne [hig] ut farað to us, we fleoð endemes. ⁶ Þonne wenað hig soðlice þæt we sin geyrgede, ⁷ þonne fare ge to, mid þam þe we fleonde beoð, and gegað þa buruh | ⁸ and forbærnað hi sona.' ⁹ Hi didon þa swa swa him dihte f. 103ᵛ Iosue. ¹⁰ And he sylf on ærne mergen mid þam oðrum flocce to þære birig ferde, beotlice mid wige. ¹⁴ Hi geseah þa se cyning þe sæt on þære birig and gewende of þære birig mid ealre þære burhware and mid eallum his folce to gefeohte gearu and nyston þa searwe þe him sæton bæftan. ¹⁵ Iosue þa fleah swilce he afyrht wære mid eallum his here. ¹⁶ And þa oðre hrymdon, ridende him æfter andlang þas westenes. ¹⁸ Drihten cwæð þa to Iosue: 'Ahefe þinne scild up ongean þa burh Hai. Ic þe forgife hig.' ¹⁹ He ahefde sona his scild and þæt gesawon þa oðre, þe lutodon on þære digelnisse, swa swa him dihte Iosue, and arison sona and ridon to þære birig and hi ealle forbærndon buton gefeohte. ²⁰ Seo burhwaru þa beseah underbæc

7:21 wurmreadne basing] wyrmreadne basingc B   entsena] entsa B   ætbræd] atbræd B
7:22 þing] ðingc B   7:24 hig] hi B   þa] om. B   Achar] B, alt. to achan by eras. L
Achores] chores B   7:25 þing] ðingc B   7:26 anne] ænne B   8:1 þa¹] om. B
ondræt] ondræd B   þing] ðingc B   meniu] mæniu B   burh] buruh B   burhware] buruhware B   cyning] cyningc B   8:2 ymbe¹] ymb B   swa swa] swa B   ymbe Iericho] embe hiericho B   wiðæftan] wiðæften B   8:3 þære] ðæra B   8:4 hig] hi B   abidan] anbidan B   8:5 hig] hi B, ge L   8:6 hig] hi B   8:7 buruh] burh B   8:10 mergen] merigen B   8:14 cyning] cyningc B   and gewende of þære birig] om. B   þære burhware] ðare buruhware B   bæftan] bæfton B   8:16 ridende] hridende B   þas] ðæs B
8:18 þa²] ðas B   hig] hi B   8:19 lutodon] lutedon B   8:20 burhwaru] buruhwaru B

sona and gesawon þone smic swiðe heage astigan and ne mihton þanon fleon, ne forð ne underbæc. ²¹ Iosue þa geseah þæt seo burh wæs gegan and feaht him wið sona, ²² and his geferan wiðhinda[n], and ofslogon hi endemes, þæt þær an ne belaf. ²³ þone cyning hi brohton cucenne to Iosue. ²⁹ þone he het ahon on heagum gealgan. ²⁵ Twelf þusenda þær feollon on þam gefeohte ofslagene, wera and wifa. ³⁰ And Iosue worhte þa an weofod Gode ³¹ of ungeworhtum stanum and his lac þær geoffrode þam lifiendan Gode, ³²⁻⁵ and Moises æ geedniwode ætforan Israhela bearnum.

⁹:¹ þes hlisa wearð þa cuð þæra leoda cynegum þe begeondan Iordane eardiende wæron, ² and gesamnodon hi ealle anmodlice to gefeohte togeanes Iosue and Israhela | bearnum. ³ Hwæt þa þa Gabaniscean ⁴⁻⁵ gamenlice ræddon and mid geaplicre fare ferdon to Iosue, namon him ealde gescy and unornlic scrud and finie hlafas and forwerede fætelsas and geclutode bytta, ⁶ and cwædon to Iosue: 'We comon, leof, feorran of fyrlenum lande and we gewilniað friðes and freondrædene wið eow.' Him andwirde Iosue and Israhela folc þus: ⁷ 'We niton þeah [g]e wunion her on neawiste hwær, and we frið ne nymað þus færunga wið eow; [w]eald þeah eower eard us gesceote.' ⁹ Hi andwirdon Iosue and Israhela bearnum þus: 'We gehirdon eowerne hlisan, hu se lifigenda God eow sige forgeaf ¹⁰ on Seone þam cyninge and on Og, eal swa on Astaroth. ¹¹ þa cwædon ure frind þæt we comon to eowre manrædene, ¹² and we mid us namon nigbacene hlafas, þe for þam langan wege nu sind gefinegode, swa swa ge fandian magon. ¹³ Ure reaf sind forwerede siþþan we gewendon hider and ure gescy geclutode, swa swa ge geseon magon, for þam langsuman færelde siþþan we ferdon ut.' ¹⁴⁻¹⁵ Hig underfeng þa Iosue and ne befran his Drihten, and hig ealle him sworon þæt hi man slean nolde. ¹⁶ Hwæt þa ymbe þri dagas wearð heora dæd cuð, þæt hig on neawiste eardodon, and eall heora geapscipe wearð ameldod Israhela bearnum. ¹⁸ Hi ne mihton swa þeah þa menn acwellan, for heora aðsware, ac arodon heora life. ²⁶⁻⁷ And Iosue him bebead þæt hi bæron wæter to þæs folces neode and to Godes weofode and wudedon him simble on gesettum timan. Hi bugon þa to þam and him wæs geborgen | and wunodon on Israhel on þam weorce fæste.

8:22 wiðhindan] wiðhindon B, wiðhinda L 8:23 cyning] cyningc B cucenne] cucene B 8:29 gealgan] gealgum B 8:31 geoffrode] geofrode B 9:1 cynegum] cyningum B 9:3 þa¹] *om.* B Gabaniscean] gabanitiscean B 9:4–5 finie] fynige B 9:6 freondrædene] freondrædden B 9:7 ge] B, we L færunga] færinga B weald] B, eald L 9:11 comon] to eow *add.* B 9:14–15 Hig underfeng] hi undorfeng B hig²] hi B 9:16 hig] hi B 9:18 menn] men B 9:26–7 simble] symle B wunodon] wunedon B Israhel] israhela B

JOSHUA

¹⁰:³ Hwæt þa Adonisedech, se cyning on Hierusalem, sende to þam kynegum on Hebron and on Hierimoth and on Lachis and on Englon and cwæð: ⁴ 'Cumað to me, ic bidde, and bringað me fultum, þæt we magon þa burh Gabaon oferwinnan, for þan þe hi gebugon to Iosue and to Israhela bearnum.' ⁵ Ða comon þa fif cynegas mid firde to Gabaon and wicodon þær onemn, woldon hi oferwinnan. ⁶ Ða sende seo buruhwaru sona to Iosue, biddende þæt he come and þa burh geheolde. ⁷ Iosue þa ferde mid his fyrde þiderweard, ⁸ and Drihten him cwæð to: 'Ne ondræd þu þe nan þing: on þine handa ic hi betæce. Ne mæg heora nan þe wiðstandan.' ⁹ Iosue him þa feng on mid gefeohte ¹⁰ and Drihten hig aflymde fram Israhela bearnum. Hi feollon þa swiðe on þam fleame ofslagene. ¹¹ And God him sende ufan greate hagolstanas and wurdon ma manna ofslagene mid þam micclum hagolstanum þonne hig mid swurde ofslogon þæs dæges. ¹² On þam dæge bæd Iosue his Drihten and þus cwæð: 'Ne stira þu sunne of þam stede furþor ongean Gabaon and ne gang þu mona ongean Achialon anne stæpe furðor.' ¹³ Ða stod seo sunne on þam stede fæste, and se mona gelice, oð þæt hig aledon heora fynd. ¹⁴ Næs swa lang dæg ær ðan on þisum life, æfre ne syþþan on þisre worulde, for þan þe God wolde þa fylstan his cempan and feohtan for Israhel. ¹⁶ Ða fif cyningas ætburston and flugon to Maceda and behiddon hi on anum scræfe, hopodon to life. ¹⁷ Ða wearð Iosue gekydd þæt þa cynegas þær lagon behidde on þam | scræfe, ¹⁸ and he het þa sona f. 105ʳ wilian to ðam scræfe micele weorcstanas and beclysan hi þærinne, oð þæt hig comon eft, and sette him weardas ofer and gewende him forð. ²¹ Þæt folc þa hit gegaderode æfter þam gefeohte to Iosue to Maceda birig, and nan man ne dorste on eallum þam ymbwhyrfte aht cweðan ongean hig. ²² Ða cwæð Iosue: 'Teoð þa cynegas ut of þam scræfe ²⁴ and gange þa yldostan to ˋand´ ofstæppaþ heora swuran swiðe mid fotum.' Þa dydon þa ealdormen swa swa him dihte Iosue and þæra cynega swuran forcuðlice trædon. ²⁵ And Iosue cwæð eft to Israela folce: 'Ne ondræde ge eow. Þus deð ure Drihten eallum

10:3 se] *om.* B cyning] cyningc B Hierusalem] ierusalem B kynegum] cyningum B
Hebron] ebron B Englon] eglon B 10:4 Iosue] *followed by eras. of six or seven letters* L
to³] *om.* B 10:5 cynegas] cyningas B onemn] onem B 10:8 þing] ðingc B
10:10 hig] hi B 10:11 micclum] miclum B hig] hi B 10:12 stira] astyra B
Achialon anne] acheald ænne B 10:13 hig] hi B 10:14 ðan] ðam B
10:16 ætburston] ætbuˋrˊston B 10:17 gekydd] gecydd B cynegas] cyningas B
10:18 hig] hi B sette] setton B 10:21 aht cweðan] acweðan B hig] him B
10:22 cynegas] cyningas forð B 10:24 gange] gangon B yldostan] yldestan B and²]
B, *supplied by an appar. contemp. hand* L swuran¹] sweoran B þæra cynega] ðara
cyninga B 10:25 Israela] israhela B

eowrum feondum þe feohtende beoð wið eow.' ²⁶ Iosue hi ofsloh þa and siþþan up aheng on fif wacum bogum ²⁷ and het hi birgean on æfen on þam ylcan scræfe þær hi ær lutodon and lecgan him on uppan ormæte weorcstanas.

¹⁰:²⁸ On þam dæge he gewan þa burh Maceda and þone cyning ofsloh and acwealde his folc, and on hire ne belæfde nane lafe cuce. ²⁹ Ðanon he gewende mid wige to Lebna and oferwann þa burh ³⁰ and mid wige acwealde þone cyning and þæt folc, and þær furðon ne belæfde naht to lafe cucu þe ne lage ofslagen. ³¹ Fram Lebna he ferde mid his folce to Lachis. ³² Drihten him sealde on þone oðerne dæg þa burh on his handa and þa burhwara samod and he acwealde hig ealle ³³ and þone oðerne kyning, Hiram gehaten, þe onette on ðære byrig him to fultume, ac he feoll him silf and his folces nan þing ætfleon ne mihte. ³⁴ He ferde þa to Englon and ymbsæt þa burh, ³⁵ and on þam ylcan dæge | he geeode þa burh and mid wæpnum acwealde þa þe wunedon on hire. ³⁶ Fram Englon hi ferdon and fuhton on Hebron ³⁷ and þa burh oferwunnon and mid wige acwealdon eall þæt hi þær fundon þæs earman folces. ³⁸ Fram Hebron he gecirde to Dabira þære birig ³⁹ and hi aweste and oferwann þone cyning and his folc ofsloh mid swurdes ecge and ne let þær to lafe nan þing libbende. ⁴⁰ Iosue ofsloh þa mid þam sigefæstan here eall þæt mennisc þe on muntum wunode, and þa þe on þam suðdæle [syttende] wæron and on feldlicum wunungum þe he findan mihte, and Asedoch eac mid eallum heora cynegum, and ælc þing þe orðode he acwealde mid wæpnum swa swa Drihten him bebead, Israhela God. ⁴¹ On anre heregunge he aweste fram Chadesbarne oð þæt he com to Gazan, eall Gessen land oð Gabaon þa burh, ⁴² and ealle þa cynegas acwealde and heora folc. Drihten soðlice feaht for hine and Israel. ⁴³ And hi ealle gecirdon gesunde to Galgala.

¹¹:¹⁻³ Þis wearð þa gecyd þam cyninge Iabin þe rixode on Asor and he raðe sende to eallum þam cynegum þe cuce þa git wæron on eallum þam eardum þe him ymbe lagon. ⁴⁻⁵ And hi anmodlice comon

---

10:27 birgean] byrian B   lutodon] lutedon B   10:29 Ðanon] ða ðanon B   oferwann] oferwan B   10:31 folce] fyrde B   10:32 Drihten] and drihten B   burh] buruh B   burhwara] buruhwara B   acwealde hig] cwealde hi B   10:33 kyning] cyningc B   on] to B   feoll] feol B   þing] ðingc B   10:34 Englon] eglon B   burh] buruh B   10:36 Englon] eglon B   Hebron] ebron B   10:37 burh] buruh B   eall] eal B   10:39 oferwann] oferwan B   cyning] cyningc B   10:40 syttende] B, wunode L   cynegum] cyningum B   þing] ðingc B   10:41 heregunge] hergunge B   eall] eal B   10:42 cynegas] cyningas B   Israel] israhel B   11:1–3 gecyd] gecydd B   raðe] hraðe B   cynegum] cyningum B   git] om. B

ealle mid heora folcum, swa menigfealde swa swa sandceosol on
sæstrande bið, þæt hig mid þære meniu mihton oferwinnan Israela
bearn. ⁶ Ac Drihten cwæð to Iosue: 'Ne ondræt þu þas meniu. Nu
tomergen ic hig sylle on þisre ylcan tide ealle [to] gewundigeanne on
Israhela gesihþe, and þu soðlice forcirfst heora horsa hohsina and
heora cræta forbærnst.' ⁷ Iosue com þa mid gecampe to | him mid   f. 106ʳ
eallum his here ⁸ and hig hetelice sloh and nan þing ne belæfde
lybbende on him. ⁹ He forcearf þa hohsina ealra þæra horsa and
forbærnde heora cræta swa swa him bebead Drihten. ¹⁰⁻¹¹ He ferde
þa to Asor mid fyrdlicum truman and þa burh geeode and þær
binnan ofsloh þone kyning and þæt folc þe he þær funde. Seo burh
Asor wæs swiðe trum gefyrn and manegra burga heafod, ac hig
forbærnde Iosue, ¹² and ealle hire fæstenu hig fordilegodon mid fyre
swa swa Moyses him bebead, se mæra Godes mann. ¹⁴ Þissa burga
hu[ðe] hig hæfdon him gemæne and hig dældon þæt orf, ¹⁵ swa him
dihte Moises. Ne forlet Iosue nan þing his beboda. ¹⁶ Iosue þa
gewylde eall þæt widgille land manegra cynega on muntum and on
feldum ¹⁷ and þa cynegas ofsloh mid swurdes ecge. ¹⁸ Lange he wæs
feohtende on fyrlenum burgum ¹⁹ and ælc burhwaru wæs bugende to
him, buton Eueum ana, þe eardode on Gabaon. ²⁰ Drihten hig
gehyrde þæt hig gehæfton wið hine, þæt hig feollon on ðam gefeohte
ætforan Israhela bearnum and nane mildheortnisse ne begeaton, swa
swa God bead Moyse. ²¹ On þære tide com Iosue and ofsloh Enachim
on munt landum, Hebron and Dabir and Anab, and of ælcum munte
Iudan and Israel, and heora burga adilegode. ²³ Iosue þa gewann mid
wige þone eard, swa swa Drihten cwæð | to Moyse on ær, and he   f. 106ᵛ
dælde þæt land Israhela bearnum, eallum þam twelf mægðum, and
þæt gewinn þa geswac.

¹²:¹ Ðis sint þa cynegas þe Iosue ofsloh, and Israela bearn,
begeondan Iordane: ⁹ Kyning on Iericho. Kyning on Hai. ¹⁰ Kyning

11:4–5 menigfealde] mænigfealde B   sandceosol] sandceosel B   hig] hi B   meniu]
mæniu B   Israela] israhela B   11:6 ondræt] ondræd B   þu¹] ðe add. B   meniu]
mæniu B   hig] hi B   to²] B, om. L   gewundigeanne] wundienne B   11:8 hig] hi B
11:10–11 kyning] cyning B   þær] ðæ⟨r⟩ B (damage to closing pages of B, ff. 154ᵛ–155ᵛ,
renders some letters illegible)   manegra] mane⟨g⟩ra B   hig] hi B   11:12 hig
fordilegodon] hi fordylgodon B   mann] man B   11:14 þissa] ðæra B   huðe] B, hu L
hig¹] hi B   hig²] hi B   11:15 þing] ðingc B   11:16 cynega] cyninga B
11:17 cynegas] cyningas B   11:18 fyrlenum] fyrlynum B   11:19 burhwaru]
buruhwaru B   buton] butan B   eardode] eardodon B   11:20 hig¹] hi B   hig²] hi B
hig³] hi B   bead] bebead B   11:21 Israel] israhel B   11:23 gewinn] gewin B
12:1 sint] synd B   cynegas] cyningas B   Israela] israhela B   12:9 Kyning¹] þis is se
æresta cyningc B   Iericho] hiericho and ða buruh gewann B   Kyning²] cyning B
12:10 Kyning¹] cyning B

JOSHUA

on Hierusalem. Kyning on Hebron. ⁱⁱ Kyning on Hierimoth. Kyning on Lachis. ¹²⁻²³ Kyning on Englon. Kyning on Dabir. Kyning on Herma. Kyning on Lebna. Kyning on Macede. Kyning on Taphua. Kyning on Apheth. Kyning on Madon. Kyning on Someron. Kyning [on] Thenach. Kyning on Cedes. Kyning on Dor. Kyning on Galgal. Kyning on Gazer. Kyning on Gader. Kyning on Hered. Kyning on [O]dolla. Kyning on Bethel. Kyning on Afer. Kyning on Saron. Kyning on Asor. Kyning on Achsaf. Kyning on Mageddo. Kyning on Iachane. ²⁴ Kyning on Thersa. Þæt ys ealra kyninga an and þritig.

²¹:⁴¹ Drihten þa forgef Israhela bearnum eallne þone eard, swa swa he ær behet heora eald fæderum, and hig ahton hit syððan and hig þæron eardodon and heora ofspring siþþan. ⁴² God him forgeaf þa sibbe on eallum ymbhwyrfte and nan wiðerwinna ne dorste winnan wið þæt folc, ac ealle hig bugon to Israhela manrædene. ⁴³ And Drihten eall gefylde þæt he him ær behet; næs nan þing aidlod ac wæs eall gefylled. ¹⁴:² Hig dældon þa þæt land, swa swa him dihte Iosue, æfre be gehlote on eallum þam burgum | and on burhscirum þe binnan þam earde wæron, on wudum and on feldum, and feng ælc to his dæle.

²³:¹ Ða æfter langum fyrste siððan hig on [fr]iþe wunodon and Iosue ealdode, ² þa het he cuman him to Israhela bearn and þa yldostan heafodmenn ⁶ and manode hig georne þæt hig Moyses æ on eallum þingum heoldon, swa swa se ælmihtiga God him on Sinai dune gesette and dihte. ⁷ He bæd hig þa georne þæt hig bugan ne sceoldon fram Godes bigengum to þam bysmorfullum hæþengilde, on þæs folces wisan þe þær wearð ofslagen. ²⁴:¹⁶ Hig þa anmodlice cwædon þæt hig þam ælmi[h]tigan Gode æfre woldon þeowian on eallum heora life, ¹⁷ þe swilce wundra gefremod[e] on heora fæderum and on him. ³¹ Hig didon eac swa on Iosues dagum and on þæra ealdra dagum þe æfter him leofodon, þe þa wundra cuðon þe God

---

12:10 Hierusalem] ierusalem B   Kyning²] cyning B   12:11 Kyning¹] cyning B   Hierimoth] herim⟨ot⟩h B   Kyning²] cyning B   12:12–23 *From this point, the kings' names, probably in two columns in the Latin original, are misordered.*   Kyning *(all)*] cyning B   Englon] eglon B   Macede] maceda B   Taphua] tapha B   Apheth] afeht B   on Thenach] B, thenach L   Odolla] B, dolla L   12:24 Kyning] cyning B   kyninga] cyninga B   21:41 forgef] forgeaf B   ær] *om.* B   hig¹] hi B   hig²] hi B   eardodon] eardedo B   21:42 ac] and B   hig] hi B   Israhela] israhelea B   21:43 þing] ðingc B   14:2 Hig] hi B   23:1 hig] hi B   friþe] B, swiþe L   23:2 yldostan heafodmenn] yldstan heafodmen B   23:6 hig¹] hi B   hig²] hi B   dune] ðam munte B   dihte] gedihte B   23:7 hig¹] hi B   hig²] hi B   bigengum] biggengum B   24:16 Hig¹] hi B   hig²] hi B   ælmihtigan] B, ælmiltigan L   24:17 gefremode] B, gefremodon L   24:31 Hig] hi B   leofodon] leofodan B

worhte on him. ²⁹ Iosue wæs on ylde tyn geara and hundteontig and he þa forðferde ætforan his magum. ³⁰ And hig hine bebirigdon on his gehlotlande þe lið to Effraim dune fram norðdæle, Gaas dune. ³² Iosepes ban witodlice, þe Israela bearn brohton of Egipta lande, hig bebirigdon on Sichem, on þæs landes dæle þe Iacob bohte æt Emores sunum, Sichemes fæder, and hit wæs gehloten to Iosepes bearna lande. ³³ Eleazar eac swilce, Aarones sunu, forðferde on þam timan and Finees his sunu hine bebirigde on Gaab lande, þe him wæs geseald on Ephraim dune.

24:30 hig] hi B   his] ⟨his⟩ B   dune] d⟨une⟩ B   24:32 Israela] israhela B   brohton] broht⟨on⟩ B   hig] hi B   24:33 Eleazar eac swilce . . . on ephraim dune] *om.* B *(see p. xlix)*   B *ends; next page (f. 107ᵛ) blank in* L

[JUDGES]

f. 108ʳ DE LIBRO IUDICUM ANGLICE.

ÆFTER ÐAM ÐE MOYSES SE MÆRA HERETOGA þæt Godes folc gelædde of Pharaones þeowette ofer ða Readan Sæ and God him æ gesette, and æfter þam þe Iosue be Godes sylfes gewissunge þæt
5 mankyn gebrohte mid swiðe micclum sige to þam behatenan earde and hi þæron wunedon, þa wurdon hig ealles to oft on yfel awende and mid yfelum weorce þone ælmihtigan God þearle gegremedon. And God hi eac sona hæðenum leodum let to anwealde, swa þæt þa hæðenan hæfdon heora geweald swa oft swa hig abulgon þam
10 ælmihtigan Gode, oð þæt hig eft oncneowon heora yfelan dædan and gebugon to Gode, biddende his miltse. Ða funde he him sona sumne fultum æfre and he hig ahredde of þam reðan þeowte þæra hæðenra leoda þe heora hæfdon geweald. Hig næfdon nanne cyning him gecoren ne þa git, for ðam þe God sylf wæs heora wissiend þa and
15 gesette him deman þe demdon þam folce to swiþe langum fyrste, oð þæt hi sylfe gecuron Saul him to cyninge, swa swa us secgað bec, be Godes geþafunge on Samueles timan.

We willað nu secgan swutelicor be þisum, þæt þæt Israhela folc, æfter Iosuam forðsiþe þæs æþelan heretogan þe hig þider gelædde,
20 and æfter geendunge þæra ealdra manna þe Godes mihta cuðon and his wundra gesawon, ³:⁵ wunodon on þam lande betwux hæþenum
f. 108ᵛ leodum, ⁶ and gewifodon him | ongean Godes willan on þam hæðenum mædenum þæs hæðenan mancynnes, and fengon to lufienne heora fulan þeawas ⁷ and eaðelice forleton Godes gesetnysse
25 and his halgan æ mid ealle forgeaton. ⁸ God wearð him þa yrre for yfelum dædum and betæhte hig Chusam þam hæþenan cyninge, swa þæt hig þeowodon swiðe yfelum þeowte þam hæþenan cyninge to eahta geara fyrste. And he hig ofsette and geswencte forðearle. ⁹ Hig

MSS L, H   Title in metallic red in L. No heading in H (f. 108ʳ).   2 ÆFTER] 3-line red initial cap. extending into margin L   gelædde] H f. 108ᵛ   3 þeowette] þeowte H   4 gewissunge] wissunge H   5 mankyn] manncynn H   6 hig] hi H   7 weorce] weorcum H   9 hig] hi H   10 hig] hi H   dædan] dæda H   11 biddende] bidende H   12 sumne] fremsumne H   æfre] om. H   hig] hi H   13 Hig] hi H   14 ðam] ðan H   15 langum] langðum H   17 Samueles] samuheles H   18 swutelicor] swutollicor H   19 Iosuam] iosuan H   hig] hi H   23 fengon] gefengon H   24 forleton] H f. 109ʳ   gesetnysse] gesetnyssa H   25 for] heora add. H   26 hig Chusam] hi Chusan H   hæþenan] hæðenum H   27 hig] hi H   28 hig] hi H   Hig] hi H

JUDGES

þa eft clipodon to þam ælmihtigan Gode and he him asende sona his fultum, gesette him anne deman se hatte Othoniel. ¹⁰ On him wæs Godes gast and he hig þa gewissode and feaht wið þone Chusan and hine ofercom sona ðurh Godes sylfes fultum. ¹¹ And hi syððan wunedon on fulre sybbe ealles feowertig geara, and Othoniel þa geendode his dagas.

³:¹² Eft þa Israhel æfter his forðsiþe geeacnodon heora yfel and þone ælmihtigan God mid weorcum gegremodon, and gewendon heora mod fram his geleafan and his æ forsawon. Ða betæhte he hig eac Eglone þam cyninge [Mo]abiscre ðeode, ¹³ se hig ofsloh swiðe and heora burh gewann and gewilde hig ealle, ¹⁴ swa þæt hig him þeowodon on micclum geswince eahtatyne gear for heora unræde. ¹⁵ Hig clipodon þa swiðe on heora geswencednisse to þam heofonlican Gode, his helpes biddende, and he him asende sona alysednisse þurh heora agenne mæg, se hatte Aoth. Him wæs gelice gewylde his wynstre and his | swiðre. Ða gesende þæt folc sume lac þam cyninge þurh ðone Aoth. ¹⁷ And he him brohte þa lac. ¹⁹ Æfter heora spræce, cwæð se Aoth him to: 'Eala þu Engol cining, ²⁰ ic hæbbe þe to secganne ures Godes ærende. Uton gan onsundron.' And hig sona eodon into sumum diglan huse. ²¹ Ða abræd Aoth bealdlice his swurd mid his wynstran handa and hine hetelice þidde, ²² swa þæt þa hiltan eodon in to þam innoðe and þæt smeru wand ut, for ðam þe he wæs swiðe fætt. He forlet þa þæt swurd stician on him ²⁴ and gewende him ut æt sumere oþre duran, oð þæt he eft becom to his agenum geferon. ²⁵ Englon se cining læg þær swa dead, ²⁷ and Aoth bleow bealdlice his horn and ferde mid fultume to gefeohte sona ²⁹ and ofsloh tyn ðusend Englones folces. ³⁰ And he þa Moabiscan miclum geeadmette and hi underþeodde his agenum þeowte, and heora land þa wæs wuniende on sibbe æfter þisre dæde hundeahtatig geara.

⁴:¹ Æfter Aothes forðsiðe hi geeacnodon eft heora unrihtwisnysse and heora yfel ongean God, ² and he hig þa betæhte sumum gramlican cininge, Iabin gehaten. ³ And he hæfde heora geweald ealles twentig geara and hig yfele ofsette, and hig þa clipodon on hira earfoðnisse to

30 anne] ænne H   Othoniel] othonihel H   31 hig] hi H   33 Othoniel] othonihel H   37 hig] hi H   38 Moabiscre] H, abiscre (mo *add. by late hand*) L   hig ofsloh] ofsloh hi H   39 hig¹] hi H   hig²] hi H   41 Hig] hi H   swiðe] syððan H   42 asende sona] sona asende H   46 Eala] H *f. 109ᵛ*   Engol] eglon H   47 secganne] secgenne H   onsundron] onsundran H   hig] hi H   49 wynstran] wyn`s´tran Bo    þidde] þyd`d´e Bo   50 smeru] smyru H   ðam] ðan H   52 sumere] sumure H   duran] dura H   geferon] geferum H   53 Englon] eglon H   55 Englones] eglones H   miclum] micclum H   56 wuniende] wunigende H   57 þisre] þyssere H   59 he hig] god hi H   60 heora] hyra H   61 hig¹] hi H   hig²] hi H   hira] heora H

þam mildheortan Gode, his mildsunge biddende. ⁶Ða asende him
God sumne heretogan to, Barac gehaten, and he þa ferde mid tyn
þusend mannum ⁷to þære burnan Cison. And se cining Iabin sende
him togeanes anne ealdormann him swiðe getreowe, | Sisarra gehaten,
¹³mid nigon hund crætum and mid ealre his fyrde to gefeohte
gearowe. ¹⁴Hwæt þa se Barac, gebyld swiðe þurh God, feaht him
togeanes mid his fyrde swiðe. ¹⁵And God þa afærde þone forsædan
ealdorman and ealle his meniu, ¹⁶þæt hig mihtlease flugon and hig
man ofsloh þæt hig sweltende feollon. ¹⁷And se Si[si]rra arn of his
agenum cræte fram ealre þære fyrde, geegsod þurh God, oð þæt he
werig becom to anum wifmen æt nehstan þe him ær wæs cuð, Iahel
gehaten. ¹⁸And heo cwæð to him: 'Gang in, la leof, to urum getelde.
Ne ondræd þe nan þing.' He eode þa inn earhlice swiðe and seo
wimman mid hire hwitle bewreah hine sona, let hine licgan, swa
ætlutian his feondum. ¹⁹He wæs swiðe ofurnen and he eðode swiðe,
bæd him drincan, and heo him bliþelice sealde, be[helode] hine eft.
²⁰And he hire cwæð to: 'Stand nu and beheald. Gif her ænig man
cume, acsigende embe me, ðonne andswara þu sona þæt her nan man
ne come.' And he læg þær swa. ²¹Ða æfter litlum fyrste gelæhte seo
wifman an þæra teldsticcena and stop inn digollice, gesloh ða mid
anum bytle bu[f]an his þunwengan, þæt se sticca him eode ut þurh þæt
heafod into þære eorðan, and he ætforan hire spearnlode mid fotum oð
þæt he forðferde swa mid bysmorlicum deaðe. ²²And Barac com sona,
[sohte] þone Sisara, wolde hine ofslean. Ða clipode seo wimman
cuðlice him to, het hine sceawian þone þe he sohte, and he geseah | þa
hwar Sisara læg and se teldsticca sticode þurh his heafod. ²³God þa
geeadmette Iabin þone cining ætforan his folce. ²⁴And hig fæstlice
weoxon and mid strangre mihte hine ofþri[h]ton oð þæt hig mid ealle
hine adilegodon, ⁵:³²and hi þa feowertig wintra wunedon on sibbe.
We secgað nu eac þæt we singað be þisum on urum sealmsange,

62 mildsunge] miltsunge H   63 heretogan] heretoðan H   65 anne] ænne H
getreowe] getreowne H   Sisarra] sisara H   68 afærde] af`æ´rde (æ corr. fr. e) H
68–9 forsædan ealdorman] foresædan ealdormann H   69 hig¹] hi H   hig²] hi H
70 hig] hi H   se Sisirra] se sisara H, sesirra L   71 geegsod] geegesod H   þurh] H f.
110ʳ   72 wifmen] wimmen H   nehstan] nextan H   73 gehaten] alt. to gehal (appar.
by L'Isle) L   in] inn H   74–5 seo wimman] se wimman H   76 eðode] 1st e alt. to o L
77 him¹] þa add. H   behelode] H, beheold L   78 man] mann H   79 acsigende]
axiende H   me] om. H   man] mann H   80–1 seo wifman] se wimman H
82 bufan] H, bugan L   þunwengan] þunwengum H   85 sohte] H, om. L (acsigend
embe add. by L'Isle)   seo] se H   87 Sisara] se sisora H   88 geeadmette]
geeadmete H   hig] hi H   89 hine] H f. 110ᵛ   ofþrihton] H, ofþri..ton (eras.) L   hig]
hi H   91 nu eac] eac nu H   singað] H, singiað L

JUDGES

swa swa hit sang Dauid þurh þone halgan gast, God heriende þus:
'Ecce inimici tui sonauerunt et qui oderunt [te e]xtollerunt capud. Fac
illis sicut Madian et Sisare sicut Iabin in torrente Cison.' Ðæt ys on
urum gereorde, he cwæð to his Drihtene: 'Efne nu Drihten þine fynd 95
hlydað and þa þe þe hatiað ahebbað heora heafda. Do him swa swa
Madian and swa swa Sisaran and swa swa Iabin æt þam burnan
Cyson.' Hwæt sind Godes fynd buton þa fulan hæðenan and þa leasan
cristenan þe hlydað ongean God, and mid unrihtwisnisse þa earman
ofsittað and Godes lima dreccað, Gode to forsewennysse, ahebbende 100
heora heafda on healicre modignesse? Ac þes sealm us segð [hu him]
sceal getimian, swa swa ðam e[a]rgan Sisaran and þam arleasan Iabine,
þæt hi beon adilegode fram Drihtenes halgum mannum, þa þe hi
huxlice her on life gedrehton.

Ðeos racu us segð, þe we nu ær ræddon, [6:1-4] þæt þæt Israhela folc 105
þe we embe sprecað siþþan gesyngodon swiðe wið heora Drihten and
he let hi to handa þam hæþenan leodscipe, Madian gecweden. Þa hig
miclum geswencton and heora orf genamon and heora | æceras f. 110ᵛ
awestan and ealle heora bigleofan endemes ætbrudon, ða fleah þæt
earme folc to fyrlenum muntum and behiddon hig on scræfum, mid 110
hungre gewæhte, þæt hi mihton geseon þæt hig forsawon God. Hi
wurdon swa geeadmette yfele heora feondum sume seofon gear on
ðære miclan sorge, [5] and heora fynd ferdon freolice gehwær, swa þicce
swa gærstapan on ðam godan earde and þæs eardes brucon, [6] him to
bismore swa. [7] Israhela folc þa earmlice clipode to þam heofonlican 115
Gode, his helpes biddende. [14] And he him foresceawode sumne
heretogan, Gedeon gehaten, heora agenes cynnes. Þam bebead God
sylf þæt he sceolde faran and his folc ahreddan fram heora yrmðe, and
cwæð him wordum þus to: 'Wite þu þæt ic ðe asende.' [7:1] God hine þa
gestrangode and he gegaderode sona þæt earme folc þær þær [hig] 120
aflogene wæron and ferde ða mid fultume þær heora fynd wicodon,
swa swa him gewissode se welwillenda God. [2-3] Ða cwæð God sylf to
him: 'Swiðe micel folc þu hæfst on þinre firdinge to þam gefeohte.
Læt hi gecirran sume, ðe læs þe hi secgon eft þæt hi mid hira folce hig

92 heriende] herigende H   93 te extollerunt] te extulerunt H, ...xtollerunt
(*eras.*) L   95 Drihtene] drihtne H   98 buton] butan H   101 modignesse]
modignysse H   hu him] H, halum L   102 eargan] H, eorgan L   103 Drihtenes]
drihtnes H   107 gecweden] gecweðen H   107-8 hig miclum] hi micclum H
108 genamon] genaman H   109 ealle] eal (ne *add. by later hand*) H
110 muntum] H *f. 111ʳ*   hig] *om.* H   111 gewæhte] gehwæhte H   hig] hi H
113 miclan sorge] micclan sorche H   117 Gedeon] gedon (e *add. late*) H   heora
agenes] hyra hagenes H   120 hig] hi H, ... (*eras., with traces of an initial* h) L
123 þam] ðysum H   124 læs þe] læste H   hira folce hig] heora afole hi H

sylfe alysdon and mid heora fultume him gefuhton sige.' ⁴Ða geceas Gedeon, swa swa him gewissode God, þreo hund wera mid him of eallum þam werode. ⁷And God him sæde þa: 'Ic sylf nu alyse eow on ðisum þrim hundrydum and þe on hand betæ[c]e ða Madianitiscean þe eow swa miclum gedrehton.'

7:16-17 Ðam folce wæs gewunelic þæt hi weredon byman on ælcum gefeohte | and þa bleowon swiðe. þa het Gedeon his geferan habban heora byman him mid to þære blawunge and het heora ælcne geniman anne æmtigne sester oððe anne wæterbuc to þam gewinne forð, and cwæð him siþþan to: 'Swa swa ge geseoð þæt ic do, doð ealle endemes æfter me sona.' H[e] todæld[e] hi þa on þrim diglum f[loc]cum ¹⁹ and ferde nihtes to þær heora fy[n]d wicodon, begunnon to blawenne mid heora byman swiðe and slogon togædere ða æmtigan sestras and tobræcon þa bucas mid micelre brastlunge. ²¹ Wearð þa afæred eall seo hæðene fyrd þurch heora blawunge and ðæra buca sweg. ²²⁻³ And God hi geegsode þæt hi begunnon to sleanne ælc heora oðerne mid hira agenum swurde on þære sweartan nihte mid stiðlicum gefeohte. Hi flugon þa sume, ac him ferde æfter Gedeon, swiðe ofsleande æfre oð þæt þær ʽaʼfeollon fif and þrittig ðusenda, sume þurh hi silfe, sume þurh Gedeon. ²⁵ And twegen ealdormen eac, Horeb and Zeb, ðær feollon ofslagenne. ⁸:¹² And him ætflugon twegen ciningas, Zebee and Salmana, ac he sohte hi georne oð þæt he hi gelæhte and gelædde hi ongean to his agenre fyrde and heora feorh him benam. ²⁸ [And heora land] wæs þa wuniende on friðe feowertig wintra be Gedeones wissunge.

Be þisum we singað eac on þam foresædan sealme ongean Godes wiðerwinna þe willað æfre þwyres, swa swa se halga gast us sæde þurch Dauid: 'Pone principes eorum sicut Oreb, Zeb et Zebee et Psalmana.' Ðæt ys on Engliscre spræce, 'Sete ðu ure Drihten | heora ealdormen swa swa Horeb and Zeb and swa swa Zebee and Salmana.'

125 geceas] him add. H   126 gewissode] gewissodo H   128 betæce] H, betæhte L   Madianitiscean] madianitiscan H   129 miclum] micclum H   132 and het] H f. 111ᵛ   133 anne¹] ænne H   anne²] ænne H   135 He todælde] H, hig todældon L   floccum] H, folcum L   136 fynd] H, fyrd L   139 þurch] þurh H   140 hira] heora H   141 swurde] swurdum H   stiðlicum] swiðlicum H   142 Gedeon] gedon H   144 Gedeon] gedon H   145 ofslagenne] ofslagene H   Zebee] zebeae H   147-8 And heora land] H, om. L   148 wuniende] wunigende H   (Israel add. above by late hand in L)   Gedeones] gedones (e add. by later hand) H   150 Be] enlarged initial cap., no break L   151 wiðerwinna] wiðerwinnan H   152 þurch] þurh H   Zebee] zebeae H   153 Psalmana] salmana H   154 ealdormen] ealdormenn H   and Zeb] H f. 112ʳ   Zebee] zebeae H

Ðæt is on angite þæt þa yfelan heafodmen, Godes wiðerwinnan, 155
wurdon þa gescinde [and swa swa þas ealdormen wurdon þa gescinde].

¹⁰:⁶ Hwæt þa æfter fyrste þæt Israhela folc begunnon to geeacnienne
heora ealdan synna mid edniwum synnum on Godes gesihðe and his æ
forleton þe he him ær gesette on þam munte Sinai, ⁷ and hine micclum
gremedon, swa þæt he mid yrre hi on hand betæhte þam hæðenan 160
leodscip[e], se hatte Amon. ⁸ Hi wurdon ða gehergode and gehynde
forswiðe eahtatyne gear under heora handa, ¹⁰ oð þæt hig earmlice to
ðam ælmihtigan clipodon and heora synna andetton mid sorhfullum
mode. ¹¹:¹ Ða ofhearmode Gode heora yrmða sona and him foresceawode sumne heafodman, Iepthae gehaten. ²⁹ And him Godes gast 165
on wæs. ³² He ferde ða mid fultume and heora fynd ofsloh and hi God
betæhte to his anwealde, ³³ swa þæt he þa gewann heora twenti burga
and he hi geeadmette heora unðances swa. ¹²:⁷⁻¹⁴ And hi wunodon on
sibbe an and ðritig geara.

¹³:¹ Æfter þisum fyrste hig fengon eft to gremienne þone ælmihti- 170
gan God on heora ealdan wisan mid heora yfelum dædum. And he hi
eac betæhte þam hæðenan folce þe hatton Philistei, ealles feowertig
geara, for heora misræde. ² An man wæs eardigende on Israhela þeode,
Manue gehaten, of ðære mægðe Dan. His wif wæs untymende and hig
wunedon butan cilde. ³ Him com þa gangende to Godes engel | and f. 112ʳ
cwæð ðæt hi sceoldon habban sunu him gemæne. ⁵ Se bið Gode halig 176
fram his cildhade and man ne mot hine efsian oððe besciran, ne he
ealu ne drince næfre oþþe win, ne naht fules ne ðicge, for þam þe he
onginð to alysenne his folc Israhela þeode of Philistea þeowte. ²⁴ Heo
acende þa sunu, swa swa hyre sæde se engel, and het hine SAMSON. 180
And he swiðe weoxs and God hine bletsode ²⁵ and Godes gast wæs on
him. ¹⁴:⁵ And he wearð þa mihtig on micelre strengðe, swa þæt he
gelæhte ane leon be wege þe hine abitan wolde ⁶ and tobræd hi to
sticcum swilce he totære sum eaðelic ticcen.

155 angite] andgite H   heafodmen] heafodmenn H   156 þa] swa H   and swa ...
gescinde] *words fully erased in* L, *possibly by* L'Isle, *but some letters decipherable (see pp.* clxiii–
clxiv); *Crawford overlooked words in both* L *and* H   ealdormen]ealdormenn H   159 he]
ðe H   160 hæðenan] hæðenum H   161 leodscipe] H, leodscipum L   se] þe H
162 hig] hi H   164 ofhearmode] ofearmode H   164–5 foresceawode]
forsceawode H   165 heafodman] heafodmann H   165–6 Godes gast on wæs] com
godes gast on H   167 heora] *om.* H   twenti] twentig H   168 wunodon] wunedon H
169 ðritig] þrittig H   170 hig] hi H   173 man] mann H   eardigende] ða
eardienne H   174 hig] hi H   175 butan] buton H   176 Gode] H *f. 112ᵛ*
177 besciran] besceoran H   178 næfre] æfre H   þam] ðan H   179 his] þys H
181 weoxs] weox H   on] mid H, l mid *add. above by contemp. hand* L   184 totære]
totære.. (*eras.*) H

JUDGES

185   15:8 He begann þa to winnenne wið ða Philisteos and heora fela ofsloh and to sceame tucode, þeah þe hig anweald hæfdon ofer his leode. 9–10 Ða ferdon þa Philistei forð æfter Samsone and heton his leode þæt hi hine ageafon to hira anwealde þæt hig wrecan mihton heora teonræddenne mid tintregum on him. 13 Hig ða hine gebundon
190 mid twam bæstenum rapum and hine gelæddon to þam folce. 14 And ða Philisteiscan þæs fægnodon swiðe, urnon him togeanes ealle hlydende, woldon hine tintregian for heora teonrædene. Ða tobræd Samson begen his earmas ðæt þa rapas toburston þe he mid gebunden wæs. 15 And he gelæhte ða sona sumes assan cinban þe he ðær funde
195 and gefeaht wið hig and ofsloh an þusend mid þæs assan cinbane, 16 and cwæð to him sylfum: 'Ic ofsloh witodlice an þusend wera mid
f. 112ᵛ þæs assan cin|bane.' 18 He wearð þa swiðe ofþyrst for ðam wundorlican slege and bæd þone heofonlican God þæt he him asende drincan, for þam þe on ðære neawiste næs nan wæterscipe. 19 Ða arn of þam
200 ci[n]bane, of anum teð, wæter and Samson þa dranc and his Drihtene þancode.

Nu gif hwa wundrie hu hit gewurðan mihte þæt Samson se stranga swa ofslean mihte an þusend manna mid þæs assan ci[n]bane, þonne secge se mann hu þæt gewurðan mihte þæt God him sende þa wæter
205 of þæs assan teð. Nis þis nan gedwimor ne nan dwollic sagu, ac seo ealde gesetniss ys eall swa trumlic, swa swa se Hælend sæde on his halgan godspelle, þæt an stæf ne bið ne an strica awæged of ðære ealdan gesetnisse þæt hi ne beon gefyllede. Gif hwa ðises ne gelyfð, he ys ungeleafulic.
210   16:1 Æfter þisum he ferde to Philistea lande into anre birig on heora anwealde, Gaza gehaten. 2 And hi þæs fægnodon, besetton þa þæt hus þe he inne wunude, woldon hine geniman mid þam þe he ut eode on ærne mergen and hine ofslean. 3 Hwæt ða Samson heora syrwunga undergeat and aras on midre nihte tomiddes his feondum and genam
215 ða burhgatu and gebær on his hricge mid þam postum, swa swa hi belocene wæron, up to anre dune to ufeweardum þam cnolle and eode him swa orsorh of heora gesihþum. 4 Hine beswac swa þeah siððan an

    185 begann] began H   fela] feala. (eras. of one character) H   186 hig] hi H
    188 hira] heora H   hig] hi H   189 teonræddenne] teonrædene H   Hig] hi H
    190 folce] laðan flocce H   195 hig] hi H   197–8 wundorlican] H *f. 113ʳ*
    199 þam¹] þan H   200 cinbane] H, cimbane L   Drihtene] drihtne H
    203 cinbane] H, cimbane L   204 mann] man H   206 eall] eal H
    209 ungeleafulic] ungeleaffull H   211 besetton] besæton H   þa] *om.* H
    212 wunude] wunode H   213 mergen] merigen H   214 midre] middere H
    216 up] upp H   ufeweardum] uferweardan H   eode] heode H

JUDGES

wif, Dalila gehaten, of þam hæðenan folce, [5] swa þæt he hire sæde, þurh hire swicdom bepæht, on hwam his strengð wæs and his wundorlice miht. Ða hæðenan Philistei beheton | hir[e] sceattas wið þam þe heo beswice Samson þone strangan. [6] Ða ahsode heo hine georne mid hire olæcunge on hwam his miht wære. [7] And he hire andwirde: 'Gif ic beo gebunden mid seofon rapum of sinum geworhte, sona ic beo gewyld.' [8] Ðæt swicole wif þa begeat þa seofon rapas and he þurh syrwunge swa wearð gebunden, [9] and him mann cydde þæt þær comon his find. Þa tobræc he sona þa rapas, swa swa hefelþrædas, and þæt wif nyste on hwam his miht wæs. [11] He wearð eft gebunden mid eall niwum rapum and he þa tobræc swa swa þa oðre. [16] Heo beswac hine swa þeah, [17] þæt he hire sæde æt nextan: 'Ic eom Gode gehalgod fram minum cildhade and ic næs næfre geefsod ne næfre bescoren and gif ic beo bescoren, þonne beo ic unmihtig, oðrum mannum gelic.' [18] And heo let þa swa. [19] Heo þa on sumum dæge, þa þa he on slæpe læg, forcearf his seofan loccas and awrehte hine siðþan. Ða wæs he swa unmihtig swa swa oðre men, [21] and þa Philistei gefengon hine sona, swa swa heo hine belæwde, and gelæddon hine aweg and heo hæfde ðone sceatt swa swa him gewearð. Hi þa hine ablendon and gebundenne læddon on heardum raceteagum ham to heora birig and on cwearterne belucon to lang[um] firste, heton hine grindan æt hira handcwyrne.

16:22 Ða weoxon his loccas and his miht eft on him. [23-7] And þa Philistei full bliðe wæron, þancodon heora Gode, Dagon gehaten, swilce hig þurh his fultum heora feond gewildon. Ða Philistei þa micele fyrme geworhton and gesamnodon hi on sumre upflora, ealle | þa heafodmen and eac swilce wimmen, þreo þusend manna on micelre blisse. And þa þa hig bliðust wæron, þa bædon hig sume þæt Samson moste him macian sum gamen, and hine man sona gefette mid swiðlicre wafunge and heton hine standan betwux twam stænenum swerum. On ðam twam swerum stod þæt hus eall geworht. And Samson ða plegode swiðe him ætforan, [29] and gelæhte þa sweras mid swiðlicre mihte [30] and sloh hi togædere þæt hi sona toburston and þæt

---

220 hire] hyre H, hira L   Philistei] H f. 113ᵛ   221 ahsode] axode H
224 begeat] begeat .... (eras.) H   225 mann] man H   226 sona] om. H
230 næs næfre] næs H   231 bescoren¹] besceoren H   bescoren²] besceoren H
233 seofan] seofon H   234 men] menn H   237 raceteagum] racenteagum H
238 langum] H, langre L   239 hira] heora H   240 weoxon] weohson H   eft] om. H
242 swilce] H f. 114ʳ   hig] hi H   243 fyrme] feorme H   sumre] sumere H
244 þa heafodmen] heafodemenn H   245 hig bliðust] hi bliþost H   hig²] hi H
246 him macian] macian him H   248 twam] om. H

hus þa [of]feoll eall þæt folc to deaðe, and Samson forð mid, swa þæt he miccle ma on his deaðe acwealde ðonne he ær cucu dyde.

He hæfde getacnunge ures hælendes Cristes þe on his agenum deaðe þone deofol gewylde and his mihte ofeswiðde and hine mankynnes benæm[d]e. Ða Philistei, swa swa we her beforan sædon, besæton þone Samson and hine ofslean woldon on heora birig Gaza. Ac he bær ða gatu upp to anum beorge to bysmore his feondum, eall swa þa Iudeiscan þe ofslogon urne Drihten besetton his birgene sona mid wearde, ac he tobræc hellegatu mid his heofonlican mihte and of þam deofle genam þone dæl þe he wolde Adames ofspringes. And he eaðelice aras of ðam deaðe gesund on þam þriddan dæge and astah to heofenum to his halgan fæder, gewunnenum sige, to wuldre him sylfum and his halgum þegnum, þam ðe he alysde. Nelle we secgan na swiðor be þisum buton þæt se Israhel þe we embe spræcon mislice ferde oð þæt hi fengon to ciningum, | swa swa on Cininga Bocum ys full cuð be ðam.

Ða Romaniscan leoda wæron eac lange eal swa buton cynegum ær þam ðe cristendom wære, and hæfdon him 'consulas' þæt we cweðað 'rædboran'. Se consul sceolde him eallum wisian and beon heora yldost to anes geares fyrste. Feng þonne oðer to oðres geares firste to þam ylcan anwealde and eode swa abutan be heora gebyrdum and be heora geþingðum, oð þæt heora formanega oft fengon to anwealde and wunodon him on sibbe swiðe anrædlice and heold ælc oðerne on arwurðnisse swa. Hi hæfdon ða siððan 'cesares' ofer hig þæt we cweðað 'caseras', þa beoð cininga yldest, and hi mid heora wisdome gewyldon þa æt nehstan ealne middaneard to heora anwealde. Hi hæfdon ælce dæge heora witena gemot and wæron gesette synderlice to ðam þa 'senators'. Ðæt synd þeodwitan þe dæghwamlice smeadon on anum sindrian huse embe ealles folces þearfe and heora ræd kyddon siððan þam casere, and him gewearð anes. Gif ænig leodscipe wæs ungewylde þam casere, þonne sende he him to swa fela eoroda ðe mihton gebigan þæt mennisc him to, oþþe mid egsunge þæt hig bugon to sibbe, oððe mid wige þæt hi wurdon gewylde. Eft on þam

251 offeoll] H, afeoll L   eall] *om.* H   255 mankynnes] mancynnes H   benæmde] H, benæmbe L   we] *om.* H   256 ofslean] slean H   258 besetton] besæton H   262 heofenum] heofonan H   264 Nelle] H *f. 114ᵛ*   265 spræcon] sprecað H   ciningum] cynegum H   266 Cininga] cynega H   267 buton] butan H   269 wisian] wissian H   270 to²] to to H   271 abutan] abuton H   274 hig] hi H   276 nehstan ealne] nextan eallne H   278 þa] *om.* H   279 þearfe] ofer feala þeoda and embe rihtwisnisse *add.* H   280 kyddon siððan] syððan cyddon H   281 fela] feala H   282 gebigan] gewyldon H   egsunge] egesunge H   283 bugon] gebugon H

cristendome wæs Constantinus, se forma casere ðe to Criste beah, and
us secgað bec þæt he sigefæst wæs þurh þone Hælend Crist þe he 285
gecoren hæfde. Eac his æftergengan þe on God gelyfdon wæron æfre
sigefæste þurh þone soðan God, and se cristendom | weox wel on f. 114ᵛ
heora timan and þæt ealde deofolgild wearð adwæsced þurh hi.

Se yldra Theodosius swiðe oft hæfde sige on manegum gewinne for
his miclum geleafan, swa þæt on sumum gefeohte him sende God swa 290
micelne wind þæt þa wæmna flugon mid swiftum gesceote swiðe on
heora find, and his feonda wæmna wendon on hi sylfe and fylston þam
casere, oð þæt him com to fotum his wiðerwinna gewilniende friðes,
ac þa þæs caseres cempan hine acwealdon sona. Se gingra Theodosius
wæs swiðe gelyfed and he æfre his fyrde þam hælende betæhte and 295
God feaht for hine and his fyrde geheold, swa þæt on sumne sæl sum
his ealdormanna, þe him swiðe leof wæs, wearð gelæht fram his
feondum. Ða sende he sona to þæs ealdormannes sunu mid micclum
fultume and hi gemetton þærrihte Godes engel him togeanes, gang-
ende mid him, se him tæhte þone weg þe hi sylfe ne cuðon ofer anum 300
bradum fenne, ðær nan fær ær næs, and ofer þam wætere mid
wundorlicum færelde, drium fotum ealle, swa swa Moyses dyde
mid ðam ealdan Israhel ofer þa Readan Sæ, oð þæt hi becomon þær
ðær he gehæft wæs and his fynd ofslogon mid swurdes ecge and þone
ealdorman ahreddon fram heora reðnisse swa. 305

Ðæra Perscisra cyning wæs ðam casere wiðerræde. Þa sende he his
here him to and he eac gegaderode of þam Saraceniscum swiðe micele
fyrde togeanes þam casere, ac Crist him sende to swa micelne ogan
þæt hi hig sylfe adrengton an hund | ðusend manna on ðære miclan f. 115ʳ
ea, Eufrates gehaten, and he wolde þa frið. Ða ne moste he abugan for 310
his manna unræde. He hæfde on his anwealde an ðusend cempena,
swa cene to wige þæt hi wæron gehatene ealle 'inmortal[e]s', þæt
sindon 'undeadlice'. Ða cwædon þæt hi woldon cunnian heora mihte
on ðæs caseres fyrde ær þam þe hig fengon to sibbe. Hi þa ferdon to
truwiende on hi silfe and ðæs caseres fyrd feaht wið hig sona. Sume 315
foran ongean, sume ferdon hindan, oð þæt þa undeadlican lagon ealle
deade and heora cyning ða beah to þæs caseres willa. On sumne sæl

284 cristendome] H f. 115ʳ   beah] gebeah H   289 gewinne] gewinnum H
290 miclum] micclum   sende God] to add. H   291 wæmna] wæpna H
292 wæmna] wæpna H   293 gewilniende] gewilnigende H   294 þa] om. H
304 swurdes] H f. 115ᵛ   305 ealdorman] ealdormann H   306 Ðæra Perscisra] ðara
persciscra H   307 him] om. H   309 hig] hi H   adrengton] adrencton H   miclan]
micclan H   311 an] tyn H   312 inmortales] H, inmortalis L   314 hig] hi H
þa ferdon] ferdon þa H   315 hig] hi H   316-17 lagon ealle deade] deade lagon
ealle H   317 willa] willan H

woldon þa wiðerrædan hæðenan mid micelre fyrde faran on heregoð on þæs caseres anwealde on Romaniscre þeode, and ferdon ða to mid miclum gefilce. Ðis wearð þa gekydd ðam casere sona and he hine gewende to his gewunelicum gebedum and þæt gewinn betæhte þam welwillendan Hælende and him raðe becom Cristes sylfes fultum, swa þæt se heretoga þære hæðenra fyrde, Rugas gehaten, mid heofonlicum ligette wearð sona ofslagen and his geferan sume. And eac oðer fyr of heofenum þa becom and forbærnde þa herelafu, ðæt þær nan ne belaf. Swilcne fultum hæfde Theodosius þurh God.

On Englalande eac oft wæron cyningas sigefæste þurh God, swa swa we secgan gehyrdon. Swa swa wæs Ælfred cining þe oft gefeaht wið Denan, oþ þæt he sige gewann and bewerode his leode. Swa gelice Æðestan þe wið Anlaf gefeaht and his | firde ofsloh and aflimde hine sylfne and he on sibbe wunude siþþan mid his leode. Eadgar se æðela and se anræda cining arærde Godes lof on his leode gehwær, ealra cininga swiðost ofer Engla ðeode, and him God gewilde his wiðerwinnan a, ciningas and eorlas, þæt hi comon him to buton ælcum gefeohte, friðes wilniende, him underþeodde to þam þe he wolde. And he wæs gewurðod wide geond land.

We endiað nu þisne cwide, þus þanciende ðam ælmihtigan ealra his godnissa, se ðe æfre rixað on ecnisse. AMEN.

318 heregoð] heregað H   319 þeode] leode H   320 miclum] micclum H
gekydd] gecydd H   322 raðe] hraðe H   323 hæðenra] hæþenre H
324 ofslagen] H *f. 116ʳ*   325 heofenum] heofonum H   herelafu] herelafe H
328 Ælfred] ælfryd H   331 wunude] gewunode H   334 buton] butan H
337 endiað] geendiað H   þus] þuss H   338 AMEN] *The introduction to Ælfric's letter to Wulfgeat follows on the same line without a break.*

[LIBELLUS]

Incipit libellus de uʻeʼteri testamento et nouo.

Ðis gewrit wæs to anum men gediht ac hit mæg swa ðeah manegum fremian.

ÆLFRIC ABBOD GRET FREONDLICE SIGWERD æt East-heolon. Ic secge þe to soðan þæt se bið swiþe wis, se þe mid weorcum spricð, and se hæfð forþgang for Gode and for worulde, se ðe mid godum weorcum hine sylfne geglengð. And þæt is swiðe geswutelod on halgum gesetnissum þæt þa halgan weras þe gode weorc beeodon, þæt hi wurðfulle wæron on þissere worulde. And nu halige sindon on heofenan rices mirhþe and heora gemynd þurhwunað nu a to worulde for heora anrædnisse and heora trywðe wið God. Ða gimeleasan men þe heora lif adrugon on ealre idelnisse, and swa geendodon, heora gemynd is forgiten on halgum gewritum, buton þæt secgað þa ealdan gesetnissa heora yfelan dæda and þæt þæt hig fordemde sindon. Ðu bæde me foroft Engliscra gewritena and ic þe ne getiðode ealles swa timlice, ær ðam þe þu mid weorcum þæs gewilnodest æt me, þa ða þu me bæde for Godes lufon georne þæt ic þe æt ham æt þinum huse gespræce. And þu ða swiðe mændest, þa þa ic mid þe wæs, þæt þu mine gewrita begitan ne mihtest. Nu wille ic þæt þu hæbbe huru þis litle, nu ðe wisdom gelicað. And þu hine habban wilt þæt þu ealles ne beo minra boca bedæled.

God lufað þa godan weorc and he wyle hig habban æt us. And hit ys awriten witodlice be him | þæt he sylf blissað on his agenum weorcum, swa swa se sealmwirhta þus sang be him: ʻSit gloria Domini in seculum seculi, letabitur Dominus in operibus suisʼ. Ðæt ys on Engliscre spræce, ʻSi ures Drihtenes wuldor on worulda woruldum; ure Drihten blissað on his agenum weorcum.ʼ Þus cwæþ se witega. Se ælmihtiga scippend geswutelode hine sylfne þurh þa micclan weorc ðe he geworhte æt fruman and wolde þæt ða gesceafta gesawon his mærða and on wuldre mid him wunodon on ecnisse on his underþeodnisse, him æfre gehirsume, for ðam þe hit ys swiðe wolic þæt ða geworhtan gesceafta þam ne beon gehirsume þe hi gesceop and geworhte. Næs þeos woruld æt fruman, ac hi geworhte

MS L   1 Incipit . . . nouo] *rubric in red*   ueteri] *first* e *above, possibly by the copyist*
4 ÆLFRIC] *3-line red initial cap. extending into margin*

God silf, se þe æfre þurhwunode buton ælcum anginne on his miclan
wuldre and on his mægenþrimnisse, eall swa mihtig swa he nu ys, and
eall swa micel on his leohte, for ðan ðe he ys soð leoht and lif and
soðfæstnisse. And se ræd wæs æfre on his rædfæstum geþance þæt he
wircan wolde þa wundorlican gesceafta, be þan ðe he wolde þurh his
micclan wisdom þa gesceafta gescippan, and þurh his soðan lufe hig
liffæstan on þam life þe hig habbað. Her is seo halige þrinnis on þisum
þrim mannum. Se ælmihtiga fæder of nanum oðrum gecumen, and se
micla wisdom of þam wisan fæder æfre of him anum butan anginne
acenned, se þe us alisde of urum þeowte syððan mid þære menniscnisse þe he of Marian genam. Nu is heora begra lufu him bam æfre
gemæne, þæt is se halga gast þe ealle | þing geliffæst swa micel; and
swa mihtig þæt he mid his gife ealle þa englas onliht þe eardiað on
heofenum, and ealra manna heortan þe on middanearde libbað, þa þe
rihtlice gelifað on þone lifiendan God. And ealra manna synna soðlice
forgifð, þam þe heora synna silfwilles behreowsiað, and nis nan
forgifenis buton þurh his gife. And he spræc þurh witegan þe
witegodon ymbe Crist, for þan þe he ys se willa and witodlice lufu
þæs fæder and þæs suna, swa swa we sædon ær. Seofonfealde gifa he
gifð mancynne (git be þam ic awrat ær on sumum oðrum gewrite on
Engliscre spræce), swa swa ISAIAS se witega hit on bec sette on his
witegunge.

Se ælmihtiga scippend, ða ða he englas gesceop, þa geworhte he
þurh his wisdom tyn engla werod on þam forman dæge on micelre
fægernisse, fela þusenda on ðam frumsceafte, þæt hi on his wuldre
hine wurðedon, ealle lichamlease, leohte and strange, buton eallum
synnum on gesælþe libbende, swa wlitiges gecindes swa we secgan ne
magon. And nan yfel ðing næs on ðam englum þa git, ne nan yfel ne
com ðurh Godes gesceapennisse, for ðan ðe he sylf ys eall god and ælc
god cimð of him, and ða englas þa wunodon on þam wuldre mid
Gode. Hwæt þa binnan six dagum þe se soða God þa gesceafta
gesceop þe he gescippan wolde, gesceawode se an engel, þe þær

MSS L, Bo   56 Se ælmihtiga] Ðe ælmihtigæ Bo; *start of Bo, f. 129ʳ*   englas
gesceop] englæs isceop Bo   geworhte] wrohte Bo   57 engla] englæ Bo   forman] forme
Bo   57–8 micelre fægernisse] mucelre fægernesse Bo   58 þusenda] þusendæ Bo
58–9 hi on his wuldre hine] heo hine on his wuldre Bo   59 buton eallum] butan ealle
Bo   60 gesælþe] sælðe Bo   gecindes] cyndes Bo   61 ðing] *om.* Bo   næs] nes Bo
englum] englæn Bo   62 com] 'hym' *add. above later* Bo   ðurh] þurð Bo
gesceapennisse] sceapenesse Bo   ðan] þon Bo   he] him Bo   eall] eal Bo   63 cimð]
cymeð Bo   wunodon] wunedon Bo   64 se soða] þe soðæ Bo   64–5 gesceafta
gesceop] gesceafte isceop Bo   65 gescippan] scyppen Bo   gesceawode se] sceawode þe
Bo   engel] ængel Bo

LIBELLUS

ænlicost wæs, hu fæger he silf wæs and hu scinende on wuldre, and cunnode his mihte þæt he mihtig wæs gesceapen, and him wel | gelicode his wurðfulniss þa. Ðe hatte 'Lucifer', þæt ys 'leohtberend', for ðære miclan beorhtnisse his mæran hiwes. Ða þuhte him to huxlic þæt he hiran sceolde ænigum hlaforde, þa he swa ænlic wæs, and nolde wurðian þone þe hine geworhte and him þancian æfre ðæs þe he him forgeaf, and beon him underðeodd þæs ðe swiþor geornlice for þære micclan mærðe þe he hine gemæðegode. He nolde þa habban his scippend him to hlaforde, ne he nolde þurhwunian on ðære soþfæstnisse ðæs soðfæstan Godes sunu, þe hine gesceop fægerne, ac wolde mid riccetere him rice gewinnan and þurh modignisse hine macian to Gode, and nam him gegadan ongean Godes willan, to his unræde on eornost gefæstnod. Ða næfde he nan setl hwær he sittan mihte, for ðan ðe nan heofon nolde hine aberan ne nan rice næs þe his mihte beon ongean Godes willan, þe geworhte ealle ðinc. Ða afunde se modiga hwilce his mihta wæron, þa þa his fet ne mihton furðon ahwar standan, ac he feoll ða adun, to deofle awend, and ealle his gegadan of ðam Godes hirede into helle wite be heora gewirhtum.

Ða on ðam sixtan dæge siþþan ðis gedon wæs, gesceop se ælmihtiga God mannan of eorðan, ADAM, mid his | handum, and him sawle forgeaf, and EVAN eft siþþan of Adames ribbe, þæt hi sceoldon habban, and heora ofspring mid him, þa fægeran wununge þe se feond forleas, gif hi gehirsumedon heora scippende on riht. Ða beswac se deofol siððan eft þa men, þæt hi Godes bebod tobræcon forraþe and wurdon þa deadlice and adræfde butu of ðære myrhþe to ðisum

f. 122ʳ

70

75

80

f. 122ᵛ
86

90

67 gesceapen] isceapen Bo   68 gelicode] licode Bo   wurðfulniss] wurðfulnesse Bo   leohtberend] lihtberende Bo   69 ðære miclan] þare mycele Bo   mæran hiwes] mæren heowæs Bo   70 hlaforde] laforde Bo   71 geworhte] wrohte Bo   þancian] þankiæn Bo   72 forgeaf] geaf Bo   underðeodd] underþeod Bo   swiþor] swiðer Bo   72–3 for þære micclan mærðe] om. Bo   73 gemæðegode] mæðegode Bo   74 hlaforde] laford Bo   ne he nolde] at this point the copyist of L repeats 43 words, wurðian þone . . . ne he nolde (with he add. before swiþor)   þurhwunian] ðurhwuniæn Bo   74–5 ðære soþfæstnisse] ðare softnysse Bo   75 soðfæstan] soðfestæn Bo   sunu] om. Bo   gesceop fægerne ac] swa fæger isceop and Bo   76 riccetere] ricetere Bo   modignisse] modignesse Bo   macian] maciæn Bo   77 Gode] god Bo   gegadan] gadan Bo   78 gefæstnod] ifæstnod Bo   79 aberan] aberon Bo   80 geworhte] wrohte Bo   ðinc] þing Bo   80–1 afunde se modiga] funde ðe modig Bo   81 mihta] mihtæ Bo   furðon] om. Bo   81–2 ahwar standan] ahwær stonden Bo   82 feoll] feol Bo   gegadan] gadæn Bo   83 gewirhtum] wruht Bo   84 sixtan] sixten Bo   gedon] idon Bo   gesceop se ælmihtiga] sceop þe almihtigæ Bo   86 forgeaf] geaf Bo   EVAN] euam Bo   hi] heo Bo   87 habban] habben Bo   fægeran] fægra Bo   se] þe Bo   88 hi] heo Bo   riht] rihte Bo   88–9 se deofol] ðe deofel Bo   89 hi] heo Bo   bebod tobræcon forraþe] bod tobrecan fulraðe Bo   90 wurdon] wurðan Bo   butu] ba twa Bo   ðære myrhþe] ðare murhðe Bo   ðisum] ðissum Bo

LIBELLUS

middanearde and on sorhge leofodon and on geswincum siþþan, and eall heora ofsprinc þe him of com siððan, oþ þæt ure Hælend Crist ure yfel gebette, swa swa þeos racu æfter us segð.

We nymað of þam bocum þas endebyrdnysse þe Moises awrat, se 95 mæra heretoga, swa swa him God silf dihte on heora sunderspræce, þa þa he mid Gode wunode on þam munte Sinai feowertig daga on an and underfeng his lare, and he ætes ne gimde on eallum þam fyrste for ðære miclan bisnunge þæra boca lare. Fif bec he awrat mid wundorlicum dihte. Seo forme ys Genesis, þe befehð þas racu ærest 100 fram frumsceafte and be Adames synne, and hu he leofode nigan hund geara [and þrittig geara] on þære forman ylde þissere worulde and bearn gestrinde be his gebeddan Euan. And he siððan gewat mid sorge to helle. Cain wæs his sunu, se acwealde his broðor, Abel gehaten, unscildigne mannan, for his agenum andan þe he hæfde to him. And 105 Caines ofspring þe him of com siððan eall wearð adrenced on þam deopan flode þe on Noes dagum adydde eall mancinn, buton þam f. 123ʳ eahta mannum ðe binnan þam arce | wæron, and of þam yfelan teame ne com nan ðing siþþan. Ac Adam gestrinde æfter Abeles slege oðerne sunu se wæs Seth gehaten. Of ðam strenge com þæt þæt cucu belaf, 110 Noe and his wif and heora þri suna, Sem, Cham and Iafeth mid heora þrim wifum. We secgað nu mid ofste þas endebirdnisse, for þan ðe we oft habbað ymbe þis awriten mid maran andgite (þa þu miht sceawian), and eac ða getacnunga.

þæt Adam getacnude, þe on ðam sixtan dæge gesceapen wæs þurh 115 God, urne Hælend Crist, þe com to þissere worulde and us geedniwode to his gelicnisse. Eua getacnode, þe of Adames sida[n]

91 sorhge leofodon] sorege leofeden Bo   geswincum] swincum Bo   92 eall heora ofsprinc] æll heoræ ofspryng Bo   him of com] of heom com Bo   þæt] ðet Bo   93 æfter us segð] hæræfter sæð us Bo   94 nymað] nimæð Bo   endebyrdnysse] endeburdnesse Bo awrat se] wraðt þe (ð *eras.*) Bo   95 sunderspræce] sunderspæce Bo   96 daga] dagæn Bo 97 eallum] ealle Bo   98 ðære miclan bisnunge þæra boca] þare micelan bisgunge þare bocæ Bo   awrat] wrat Bo   99 wundorlicum] wundorlice Bo   Seo] þeo Bo   befehð] Bo *f.* *129*ᵛ   racu] race Bo   100 leofode nigan] leofede nigon Bo   101 geara] gearæ Bo   and þrittig geara] Bo, *om.* L   þrittig] þriˊtˊtig Bo   on þære] oð þare Bo   worulde] weorlde Bo 102 gestrinde] strunde Bo   gebeddan Euan] ibeddan euam Bo   sorge] sorege Bo 103 Cain] Caim Bo   se acwealde] þe acwalde Bo   gehaten] ihaten Bo   104 mannan] man Bo   agenum] agene Bo   105 ofspring] ofsprung Bo   106 deopan] deope Bo   eall mancinn buton] eal moncyn butan Bo   107 eahta mannum] æhtan monnum Bo   arce wæron] arche weron Bo   yfelan] yfelæn Bo   108 gestrinde] istreonde Bo   slege] slæge Bo 109 se] þe Bo   gehaten] ihaten Bo   þæt þæt cucu belaf] þet ðer cwic bilaf Bo   110 þri suna] ðreo sunæ Bo   Iafeth] iaphæt Bo   110-1 heora þrim] heoræ ðreom Bo 111-14 We secgað... getacnunga. þæt] *om.* Bo   114 getacnude] tacnode Bo   gesceapen] isceapen Bo   115 God urne] gode ure Bo   worulde] weorulde Bo   116 geedniwode] edniwode Bo   gelicnisse] licnysse Bo   getacnode] tacnode Bo   sidan] Bo, sida L

God silf geworhte, Godes gelaðunge þe of Cristes sidan siþþan wearð acenned. Abeles slege soðlice getacnode ures Hælendes slege þe ða Iudeiscan ofslogon, yfele gebroðra swa swa Cain wæs. Seth, Adames sunu, ys gesæd ærist, and he getacnode untwilice Crist, se þe of deaðe aras on ðam þriddan dæge. Enoh wæs geciged se seofoða man fram Adame. He worhte Godes willan and God hine ða genam mid ansundum lichaman of þisum life upp, and he ys cucu git, swa swa Helias se æðela witega þe wæs eal swa genumen to þam oðrum life, and hi cumað begen togeanes Antecriste, þæt hig his leasunga alecgon þurh God and beoð þonne ofslegen þurh ðone sylfan feond. And hi eft arisað swa swa ealle men doð. Noe, þe on ðam arce wæs on ðam miclum flode þe ealle woruld adrencte buton þam eahta man|num, ys gereht 'requies', þæt is 'rest' on Englisc. And he getacnode Crist, þe forð com to us þæt he us of yðum þissere worulde to reste gebrohte and to blisse mid him. And swa forð oð ende ælc halig fæder mid wordum oþþe mid weorcum cyddon urne Hælend and his fær witodlice.

Her wæs seo forme yld þissere worulde. And seo oðer yld wæs þissere worulde oð Abrahames timan, þæs ealdan heahfæderes. Nu segð us seo boc be Noes ofspringe þæt his suna gestrindon twa and hundseofontig suna, þa begunnon to wircenne þa wundorlican burh and þone heagan stipel þe sceolde astigan upp to heofenum be heora unræde. Ac God silf com þærto and sceawode heora weorc and sealde

117 geworhte] wrohte Bo   sidan] siden Bo   118 acenned] his sylfes agen bryd mid his blode aðwogen *add.* Bo   slege¹] slæge Bo   getacnode ures] tacnode ure Bo   slege²] slæge Bo   119 ofslogon] ofslogen Bo   gebroðra] broðræ Bo   Cain] caim Bo   120 gesæd] isæd Bo   getacnode] tacnode Bo   se] ðe Bo   121 þriddan] ðriddæ Bo   Enoh] enohc Bo   geciged se seofoða man fram] isæd þe seofeða mon from Bo   122 worhte] wrohte Bo   ða genam] nam ða Bo   123 ansundum lichaman] andsundum lichame Bo   þisum] þisse Bo   upp] up Bo   cucu] cwic Bo   124 se] þe Bo   genumen] inumen Bo   oðrum] oðre Bo   125 hi cumað] heo cymeð Bo   hig] heo Bo   leasunga alecgon] leasunge alecgan Bo   126 þonne ofslegen] þenne ofslægene Bo   hi] heo Bo   127 arce] arche Bo   128 miclum] miclæn Bo   ealle woruld] al weorld Bo   buton þam eahta mannum] buton æhtæ monnum Bo   129 gereht] iræht Bo   rest] ræst Bo   129–30 getacnode Crist þe forð com to us] tacnode for ði Crist ðe to us for ði com Bo   130 yðum] *om.* Bo   worulde] weorlde Bo   reste gebrohte] ræste brohte Bo   131 fæder] oððe *add.* Bo   132 urne] ure Bo   132–3 fær witodlice] fæder witolice Bo   134 Her] her to Bo   seo] þeo Bo   yld] ylde Bo   worulde] weorlde and of ðam æhta monnum com eal mon cyn syððan Bo   seo] ðeo Bo   yld] ylde Bo   135 worulde] werolde Bo   Abrahames timan] abrahame`s' timen Bo   ealdan] ealden Bo   136 segð] sæð Bo   seo] ðeo Bo   ofspringe þæt his suna gestrindon] ofsprunge þet his sunu streonedon Bo   136–7 and hundseofontig suna] ant hundseofentig sunæ Bo   137 wircenne] wurcenne Bo   wundorlican] wunderlice Bo   138 þone] þenne Bo   astigan upp] astigen up Bo   139 þærto] þerto Bo   sceawode] sceawæde Bo

140 heora ælcum synderlice spræce, þæt heora ælcum wæs uncuð hwæt oþer sæde. And hi swa geswicon sona þære getimbrunge and hi ða toferdon to fyrlenum lande on swa manegum gereordum swa þæra manna wæs. On þære ylcan ylde man arærde hæðengild wide geond þas woruld, swa swa we awriton æror on oðrum larspellum to geleafan
145 trimminge. And on þissere ylde þa yfelan leoda fif burhscira, ðæs fulan mennisces Sodomitisces eardes, mid sweflenum fyre færlice wurdon ealle forbærnde, and heora burga samod, buton Loþe anum þe God alædde þanon mid his ðrim hiwum for his rihtwisnisse. Of Noes yldstan sunu, þe wæs Sem gehaten, com þæt Ebreisce folc þe on
150 God gelifde, Abrahames forðfæderas, and his fæder wæs Tare, se
f. 124ʳ eardode | ærest on Chaldea rice, oð þæt Abraham ferde be Godes hæse to Chananeiscan earde, þær his cynn siððan wunode. Abraham se heahfæder hæfde twegen suna, Ismael and Isaac, and he wurþode God mid ealre his heortan and se heofonlica God him gelome to spræc
155 for his micclan geleafan, for þan þe he wolde offrian his agenne sunu Gode, Isaac þone leofran, to lace on his weofode on þa ealdan wisan, gif hit God swa wolde. God þa hine gebletsode and his bearn wæs gesund. And God silf him behet þæt þurh his cyn sceolde eall mannkynn beon gebletsod for his micclan geleafan and for his
160 gehirsumnisse þe he hæfde to Gode. Abraham, þe wolde Isaac geoffrian be Godes hæse, hæfde getacnunge þæs heofonlican fæder þe his sunu asende to cwale for us. And Isaac getacnode þone Hælend Crist ðe acweald wæs for us.

Seo þridde yld wæs ða wuniende oð Dauid þone mæran cyning,
165 Abrahames cynnes. Of ðam com Crist siððan, þe eall mancynn alysde.

140 spræce] spæce Bo ælcum] ælc Bo 141 hi¹] heo Bo geswicon sona þære getimbrunge] swican sonæ þare timbrung Bo hi²] heo Bo 142 fyrlenum lande] fyrlæna landum Bo manegum gereordum] moniga spæce Bo 143 manna] monna Bo þære] ðare Bo man arærde] mon arerde Bo 144 woruld] weorld Bo 144–5 swa swa we ... trimminge] *om.* Bo 145 yfelan] yfela Bo 146 fulan] fulestan Bo sweflenum] swæflene Bo 147 forbærnde] forbearnde Bo Loþe anum] loth ane Bo 148 alædde] lædde Bo hiwum] *del., with* wifum *add. above by late hand* L rihtwisnisse] rihtwisnesse Bo 149 yldstan] ealdeste Bo gehaten] ihaten Bo 150 God gelifde] gode lyfde Bo forðfæderas] forðfæderes Bo and his] Bo *f. 130ʳ* Tare se] thare þe Bo 151 Chaldea] caldea Bo þæt] ðet Bo ferde] eft *add.* Bo 152 þær] þer Bo cynn] cyn Bo 153 se] ðe Bo twegen suna] twægen sunu Bo 154 ealre] al Bo se heofonlica God him gelome to spræc] þe heofenlice fæder ilome to him spæc Bo 155 micclan geleafan] myclan leafan Bo agenne] agene Bo 157 gebletsode] bletsode Bo 158 gesund] isund Bo 158–9 eall mannkynn] al mon cyn Bo 159 gebletsod] ibletsod Bo micclan geleafan] miclan ileafan Bo 160 gehirsumnisse] hyrsumnesse Bo 161 geoffrian] offrian Bo getacnunge] tacnunge Bo heofonlican] heofonlicen Bo 162 asende] sende Bo cwale] cweale Bo getacnode] tacnode Bo 164 Seo] Ðeo Bo yld] ealde Bo wuniende] wunigende Bo cyning] kyng Bo 165 eall mancynn] eal moncyn Bo

LIBELLUS

Of Cham, Noes suna, com þæt Chananeisce folc. And of Iaphet þam gin[g]stan, þe wæs gebletsod þurh Noe, com þæt norðerne mennisc be þære norðsæ, for þan þe ðri dælas sind gedælede þurh hig: Asia on eastrice þam yldstan suna, Affrica on suðdæle þæs Chames cynne, and Europa on norðdæle Iaphepes ofspringe. And se ælmihtiga God æfter Noes flode eallum mancinne forgeaf him gemænlice fisccinn and fugolcinn and þa fiðerfetan deor and þa clænan | nytena for his micclan ciste. Ac he forbead swa þeah blod to þicgenne. Isaac þa gestrynde Esau and Iacob, twegen getwisan on micelre getacnunge, ac se gingra broðor, þe Iacob wæs gehaten, wæs Gode leofre for his godum þeawum, and for his bilewitnisse he wearð gebletsod. Se gestrynde twelf suna; þa syndon heahfæderas, namcuðe weras. And wearð þa micel hunger seofon gear on an, and hig siþodon ealle to Egipta lande, þær hi bigleofan fundon. His gin[g]sta sunu buton anum wæs Ioseph gehaten, wearð ðær hlaford on Egipta lande under þam cininge, him swiðe gecweme. And he heold his fæder on fullum wurðscipe þær mid eallum his broðrum and heora bearnum samod. And se Ioseph leofode on þam lande mærlice hundteontig geara and tin toeacan. And seo boc Genesis geendað þus her.

Seo oþer boc ys Exodus gehaten, þe Moyses awrat be þam miclum tacnum and be þam tyn witum þe wurdon þa gefremode ofer Pharao þone cining and ofer his folce þurh ðone ælmihtigan God, on Moises timan. Se wearð acenned, swa swa us kyð þeos boc, and his broðer Aaron, Amrames sunu, on Pharaones dæge, Gode swiþe dyre, swiðe

166 suna] sunu Bo   Chananeisce] cananeisce Bo   167 gingstan] Bo, ginstan L gebletsod] ibletsod Bo   norðerne mennisc] mennisc norðene Bo   168 þære] ðare Bo dælas sind gedælede] delas beoð idælede Bo   hig] heom Bo   169 yldstan suna] ealdestan sunu Bo   suðdæle þæs] suðdælæ ðes Bo   cynne] cynnes Bo   170 Iaphepes ofspringe] iapheðes ofsprunges Bo   se] þe Bo   171 eallum mancinne forgeaf heom imænelice Bo   gemænlice] ællum moncynne geaf heom imænelice Bo   172 fiðerfetan] del. in L with feower add. above by late hand   clænan nytena] clene nytenu Bo   173 micclan] myclæn Bo   blod] þet blod Bo   þicgenne] þicgene Bo   174 gestrynde] gestreonde Bo   twegen getwisan] twæge twinnes Bo   micelre getacnunge] mycele tacnunge Bo   175 se gingra] ðe gungere Bo   gehaten wæs] ihaten wearð Bo   leofre] leofræ Bo   176 godum] gode Bo   gebletsod] iblets od Bo   176-7 Se gestrynde twelf suna] ðe streonde .xii. sunæs Bo 177 syndon] beoð Bo   namcuðe weras] nomecuðe wæras Bo   178 hunger] hungor Bo hig siþodon] heo siðoden Bo   179 Egipta lande þær hi bigleofan] egypte londe þer heo bileofenæ Bo   gingsta] ginstan L, gyncestæ Bo   180 gehaten] ihaten ðe Bo   hlaford] laford Bo   181 cininge] kyninge Bo   gecweme] icwæme Bo   fullum] fulle Bo 182 eallum] ealle Bo   broðrum] ibroðrum Bo   bearnum] childran Bo   183 se] þe Bo leofode] leofede Bo   lande] londe Bo   184 tin] geara add. Bo   toeacan] om. Bo   seo] þeo Bo   geendað] ended Bo   185 Seo] Ðeo Bo   gehaten] ihaten Bo   awrat] wrat Bo miclum] micle Bo   186 wurdon] wurðon Bo   187 cining] kyng Bo   ðone ælmihtigan] ðonne almihtiga Bo   188 timan] timæ Bo   Se] þe Bo   kyð] cuð Bo broðer] broðor Bo   189 dyre] deore and Bo

190 mihtige menn on manegum wundrum. Ða wolde God habban þæt folc of ðam lande, Abrahames cynnes, eft to heora earde, ac se Pharao nolde þæt folc fram him lætan, ær þan þe God him sende swiðlice ogan tyn cinna wita for his teonræddenne. And Moises þa siððan þæt manncinn gelædde of Pharaones ðeowte, æfter feower hund gearum siþþan Iacob | þider com mid þam Ebreiscan kinne. On þære fyrde
196 wæron, þe ferdon fram Egipte, six hund þusend manna butan wifum and cildum and butan þære mægðe Leui þe næs genamod þærto. Moyses hig lædde þa þurh Godes mihte ealle ofer ða Readan Sæ, swa swa we rædað on bocum. And Pharao se kyning ferde him æthindan
200 on git, mid maran fyrde, wolde þæt folc habban ongean to his lande to his laðum þeowte. Þa geopenode seo sæ togeanes Moysen and þæt wæter him stod swilce stanweallas bufan heora heafdum and hi eodon be þam grundum oð þæt hi up comon ealle gesunde, heriende mid sange þone heofenlican God. Moyses þa sloh þa sæ mi`d´ his girde
205 and þæt wæter ða feoll ofer Pharaones fyrde, ofer his menifealdum crætum and his mærlicum riddum, and adrencte hi ealle, þæt þær an mann ne belaf. Nu segð us seo boc þæt God siððan afedde ealne þone here mid heofonlicum mete and him ælce dæg com edniwe of heofenum feowertig wintra fyrst on þam westene farende, and of
210 heardum stane him com yrnende wæter. And God him sette æ, þæt ys open lagu þam folce to steore, on þam fif bocum þe Moyses awrat, swa swa him gewissode God.

Ða twa bec we nemnodon. Leuiticus is seo þridde, Numerus feorðe, seo fifte gehaten Deuteronomium, þæt ys 'oþer lagu'. Ðas

f. 125ʳ

190 menn] mon Bo   manegum] monige Bo   habban] habben Bo   191 lande] londe Bo   se] þe Bo   192 þæt] ðet Bo   lætan ær þan] læten ær ðam Bo   swiðlice] swiðlicne Bo   193 teonræddenne] teonreddenne Bo   193–4 þæt manncinn gelædde] ðet mon cyn lædde Bo   195 kinne] cynne Bo   þære] ðare Bo   196 wæron] weron Bo   manna butan] monnæ buton Bo   197 cildum] childum Bo   butan þære] buton ðare Bo   genamod þærto] inamod þer to Bo   198 hig] heom Bo   ealle] e`a´lle Bo   Readan] readæn Bo   199 And Pharao] Bo f. 130ᵛ   se kyning] þe kyng Bo   200 maran fyrde] mare ferde Bo   habban] habben Bo   lande] and add. Bo   201 geopenode seo] openode ðeo Bo   Moysen] moyses Bo   201–2 þæt wæter] þet water Bo   202 stanweallas bufan heora heafdum] stanweallæs bufon heoræ hæfdum Bo   hi] heo Bo   203 grundum oð þæt hi up comon] grunde oððet heo up comen Bo   gesunde heriende] isunde herigende Bo   204 sange] sangum Bo   heofenlican] heofenlice Bo   205 þæt wæter] þet water Bo   feoll] feol Bo   menifealdum] manigfealde Bo   206 hi] heom Bo   þær] ðer Bo   207 mann] mon Bo   segð] sæð Bo   seo boc] ðeos botū (with boc add. above by contemp. hand) Bo   afedde ealne] fedde ælne Bo   208 heofonlicum mete] heofenlice mæte Bo   him] heom Bo   dæg] dæge Bo   209 westene] wæstene Bo   210 heardum stane him] hearde stanum heom Bo   yrnende wæter] hyrnende water (h del.) Bo   him] heom Bo   211 awrat] wrat Bo   212 gewissode] wissode Bo   213 seo] þeo Bo   214 seo] ðeo Bo   gehaten] ihaten Bo

ōreo bec us secgað hu hig siþþan ferdon ofer þæt widgille westen, þær
þær nan mann ne wunode ær, and be þam miclum wundrum þe God
worhte | on him binnan þam feowertigum gearum on ealre þare racu.
And we [hit] habbað awend witodlice on Englisc, on þam mann mæg
gehiran hu se heofonlica God spræc mid weorcum and mid wundrum
him to. And he eac þa weorc on gewritum afæstnode, mannum to
gemynde on miclum getacnungum. And Moises se mæra, mid þam þe
he wæs on ylde hundtwentig wintra, ða gewat he of life, and God silf
hine bebirigde and gesette Iosue on Moyses stede, þam mannum to
heretoga. And Moyses hæfde hine ær gebletsod and God silf him
behet þæt he wolde mid him beon swa swa he mid Moyse wæs on
miclum wundrum.

Seo boc þe he gesette, Liber Iosue, segð hu he ferde mid Israhela
folce to Abrahames earde and hu he þone eard gewann, and hu seo
sunne ætstod oð þæt he sige hæfde, and hu he þone eard ealne
todælde. Ðis ic awende eac on Englisc hwilon Æþelwerde ealdormen,
on þam man mæg sceawian Godes micclan wundra mid weorcum
gefremode. His fæder hatte Nun and he leofode hund geara and tyn
gear toeacan and he siþþan gewat æfter his micclan sige, and þæt
mennisc ðær siþþan þone eard bogodan under Moises lage. Iosue
hæfde ðæs Hælendes getacnunge, mid þam þe he gelædde to þam
lande þæt folc þe him behaten wæs, swa swa se Hælend deð þe læt to
heofenan rice þa ðe on hine gelyfað, gif hi mid godum weorcum hine
gegladiað.

Æfter þisum wæron witodlice deman on þam ylcan earde on
Israhela | þeode, þe þam folce wissodon, swa swa hit awriten ys on
Liber Iudicum, þæt ys 'demena boc'. Seo boc us segð swutollice be

215 hig] heo Bo   215–16 westen þær þær] wæsten þer ðer Bo   216 mann] mon Bo
be] bi Bo   miclum] micle Bo   217 worhte] wrohte Bo   feowertigum] feortigum Bo   racu]
fare Bo   218 hit] Bo, *om*. L   mann] mon Bo   219 gehiran] ihyran Bo   se heofonlica] þe
heofonlice Bo   spræc] þa spæc Bo   220 him] heom Bo   on gewritum afæstnode mannum]
mid write afestnode monnum Bo   221 miclum getacnungum] mycele tacnunge Bo   se
mæra] ðe mæræ Bo   222 on ylde hundtwentig wintra] .cxx.wintra on ylde Bo   gewat] ferde
Bo   223 bebirigde and gesette] burigede ant sette Bo   mannum] monnum Bo
224 heretoga] heretogan Bo   gebletsod] ibletsod Bo   226 miclum] his micele Bo
227 Seo] Ðeo Bo   gesette] sette Bo   segð] sægð Bo   Israhela] israelæ Bo   228 þone]
ðonne Bo   gewann] he wan Bo   seo] þeo Bo   229 þæt] ðet Bo   þone] þonne Bo   ealne] al
Bo   230–2 Ðis ic awende ... gefremode] *om*. Bo   232 hatte Nun] nun hatte Bo
leofode] leofede Bo   233 gear] geara Bo   micclan] miclan Bo   234 mennisc] menisc Bo
bogodan] bogodō Bo   235 getacnunge] tacnunge Bo   he gelædde] 'he' lædde Bo
236 him] heom Bo   se] ðe Bo   læt] læd Bo   237 heofenan] heofenen Bo   hine gelyfað]
him ilyfað Bo   hi] heo Bo   godum] gode Bo   238 gegladiað] glædiað Bo   239 þisum
wæron] ðissum weron Bo   240 Israhela] israele Bo   wissodon] wissoden Bo
241 demena] demere Bo   Seo] þeo Bo   segð swutollice] sæð swutellice Bo

þam folce þæt hi on sibbe wunedon swa lange swa hi wurðodon þone
heofonlican God on his bigengum georne, and swa oft swa hi forleton
þone lifiendan God, þonne wurdon hi gehergode and to hospe
gedonne fram hæðenum leodum þe him abutan eardodon. Eft
þonne hi clipodon on eornost to Gode mid soþre dædbote, þonne
sende he him fultum þurh sumne deman þe wiðsette heora feondum
and hi alisde of heora yrmðe. And hi lange swa on þam lande
eardodon. Ðis man mæg rædan, se þe his recð to gehirenne, on
þære Engliscan bec þe ic awende be þisum. Ic þohte þæt ge woldon
þurh ða wundorlican race eower mod awendan to Godes willan on
eornost; ac beo þeos boc her þus geendod. An wimman hatte Ruth þe
wæs æfter þisum, Moabiscre þeode, ac heo wearð geæwnod Iessan
ealdan fæder, and se Iiesse wæs DAVIDES fæder. Seo boc þe þis segð
hatte Liber Ruth, and heo is geendebyrd on ure bibliothecan.

Æfter þisum demum þæt Israhela folc gecuron him ciningas, swa
swa us cyð seo racu, on Samueles timan, þæs soðfæstan witegan. Be
þam sind awritene witodlice feower bec, þa sind gehatenne Liber
Regum on Leden, þæt ys 'ciniga boc' gecweden swa on an. And
Verba Dierum lið þærto ge[ic]ed. Seo ys seo fifte boc, for fela
gewissungum | þe seo an boc hæfð toforan þam oðrum, and þas
bec awriton Samuel and Malachim. On þisum bocum us segð þæt
Saul wæs gecoren ærest to cyninge on Israhela þeode, for þan þe hig
woldon sumne weriend habban þe hi geheolde wið þæt hæþene folc,
and cyddon heora willan þam witegan Samuele, þæt hig heora cynne
cining habban woldon, swa swa oðre leodscipas on eallum lande
hæfdon. Hwæt þa Samuel sæde þæt Gode and God him geþafode þæt
hig setton him to kininge Saul, Cises sunu. And he siððan rixode
feowertig geara fæc and þæt folc bewerode wið þa hæþenan leoda
heardlice mid wæmnum, þeah þe he misferde o'n' manegum oðrum
þingum. David, Iessan sunu, se deorwurða sealmwirhta of þam
firmestan kynne þe wæs gecweden Iudan, wearð þurh God gecoren
to cininge siþþan on Israhela þeode, hig to bewerienne. And he
stranglice rixode and bewerode þæt folc wið þa hæðenan leoda ðe him
on wun[n]on. And he hæfde æfre sige and ofsloh þa hæðenan on
ealcum gefeohte, for þan þe he wurðode þonne ælmihtigan God mid

242 hi¹] heo Bo   hi wurðodon] heo wurðoden Bo   243 heofonlican] heofonlice Bo
hi forleton] heo forlæton Bo   244 lifiendan] lifigendan Bo   þonne] þenne Bo   hi
gehergode] heo ihærgode Bo   245 gedonne] idone Bo   him abutan eardodon] heom
abuten eardoden Bo   246 hi clipodon] heo cleopodon Bo   247 him] heom Bo
heora] heoræ Bo   feondum] Bo f. 130ᵛ ends; next leaf lost   260 geiced] gecied L
270 heardlice] heard heardlice L   275 wunnon] wunedon L

ealre heortan, and mid godum weorcum he geglende his kynedom and
þæs kynedomes geweold feowertig geara on an, and his hlysa is ful cuð
on geleafullum bocum.

And seo feorðe yld þissere worulde stod fram Dauide oð Daniele 280
þam witegan. Dauid is gecweden 'fortis manum'; on andgitte þæt ys
'stranghynde' on Englisc, for þan þe he gewylde þone wildan beran
and his ceaflas | totær buton ælcum wæmne. And þa wildan leo he f. 127ʳ
gewylde eal swa, tobræc hire ceaflas mid his barum handum. And he
eode to anwige ongean þone ent, Goliam gehaten, þa þa he cniht wæs, 285
and mid his liðeran ofwearp þone geleafleasan ent þæt he læg
geswogen, and sloh him of þæt heafod and on fleame gebrohte þa
Philisteos ealle, þe fuhton wið Saul, and he sige þa hæfde. He hæfde
getacnunge þæs Hælendes Cristes þe ys stranghynde, þe þone hetolan
deofol eaðelice gewilde. And him of gewann ealle þa geleafullan on his 290
gelaðunge, swa swa Dauid gelæhte þæt scep of þam deorum. He ys
halig witega and he witegode fela ymbe urne Hælend Crist, swa swa us
kyþað þa sealmas þe he þurh Godes gast Gode to lofe gesang, and se
Saltere ys an boc þe he gesette þurh God betwux oðrum bocum on
þære bibliothecan. He gesette on his ylde his sunu to cininge, þone 295
snoteran Salomon. And he siþþan rixode feowertig wintra on fulre
sibbe æfre, and for his micclum wisdome hyne wurðodon ciningas and
man his wisdom sohte of fyrlenum eardum, and of gehwilcum landum
him comon lac to wurðscipe. And he his folc geheold butan ælcum
gefeohte. He arærde Gode þæt ænlice tempel binnan Hierusalem, on 300
wunderlicum cræfte swa fægere getimbrod and swa fæste getrymmed
and swa widgille hus, oferworht mid golde and mid hwitum seolfre,
swa we secgan ne magon. He gesette þreo bec þurh his snoternisse.
An ys Parabole, þæt ys 'bigspellboc', na swilce | ge secgað ac f. 127ᵛ
wisdomes bigspell and warnung wið disig and hu man selost mæg 305
synna forbugan and þone weg gefaran þe gewissað to Gode. Oþer ys
gecweden Ęcclesiastes, þæt ys on Englisc 'ealra þeoda ræd' and deaflic
to gehirenne on healicum gemote. Seo þridde ys gecweden Cantica
Canticorum, þæt segð on Englisc 'ealra sanga fyrmest'; þonc he sang
be Criste and be Cristes circean, þæt ys eall seo laþung þe gelyfð on 310
Crist. And þas bec standað nu on þære bibliotheca. Salomon ys
gecweden 'gesibsum' on Englisc and he getacnode urne Hælend Crist
þe us sibbe brohte and ys þære sibbe ealdor, se þe us geðeodde to
engla werodum and us circean arærde ðe is his gelaðung.

Nu standað manega cyningas on þæra cininga bocum, be þam ic 315

307 Ęcclesiastes] ęcclesiastices (ic *partly eras.*) L

gesette eac sume boc on Englisc. Sume hig wæron rihtwise and wurþodon a God, swa swa Ezechias wæs and siþþan Iosias, and eac sume oþre, þe sigefæste wæron and heora kynedom heoldon kenlice þurh Gode, þe hig wurðodon, and hi wunodon on friðe. Sume wæron
320 arlease and swiðe yfele ferdon, þonne hi Godes ne gimdon ne God him ne fylste, and amyrdon heora folc þurh heora mandæda and on bysmore leofdon þurh geleafleaste, and yfele geendodon on heora unhlisan, swa swa Sedechias se ungesæliga kining þe mann gelædde on bendum to Babilonian birig, and man ofsloh his twegen suna
f. 128ʳ ætforan his gesihþe and hine ablende siðða[n] | and gesette hine on
326 cweartern, and þam eardu[m] becom oðer wracu siððan. Nabochodonosor, se namcuða cining on Chaldeiscum earde, com to Hierusalem mid micelre fyrde and þæt manncyn ofsloh and þa burh towende and þæt tempel towearp, æfter feower hund gearum þæs þe hit gesett
330 wæs, for ðæra kininga geleafleaste, þe forleton heora Drihten, and þæs folces gimeleaste, þe ne gimde Godes; and gelædde þone kining to Chaldea mid him, Achim gehaten, swiðe huxlice, þæt he mihte oncnawan his manfullan dæda, huru on þam hæftnede, wið þone heofenlican God. Se Chaldea cininc com þa to his earde mid þære
335 huðe and þære herelafe, on ðære wæs Daniel se deorwyrða witega and þa þry cnihtas þe synt gehatenne þus: SIDRAC MISAAC ET ABDENAGO. And on oþre wisan hi wæron gehatene Annanias, Azarias, Misael. Ðas þri cnihtas het se cyning awurpan in to byrnendum ofne, ac heora bendas sona wurdon forswælede and hig
340 gesunde eodon, heriende mid sange þone heofenlican God þe hi swa geheold on þam hatan ofne þæt heora fex næs furðon forswæled. And se kining hi het þa gan of þam ofne.

Her ongan seo fifte yld þissere worulde. Seo stod swa astreht oð þæt Crist sylf com on þære sixtan ylde to þissere worulde on menniscum
345 gecynde of Marian innoðe, se þe æfre wæs God mid his ælmihtigan
f. 128ᵛ fæder. Seo herelaf | ða wunode þæs [gehergodan] folces on Chaldeiscum earde under þam kininge, gecnæwe heora synna wið þone ælmihtigan God. Hundseofontig geara hi wunodon þær on þeowte oð þæt Cirus cyning hi asende eft ongean to Iudea lande, þanon þe hi
350 alædde wæron, and het hig eft aræran þæt ænlice tempel, swa swa se ælmihtiga God on his mod asende þæt he his folce mildsode æfter swa

    325 siððan] siðða L   326 eardum] eardu L   346 gehergodan] heretogan L
    349 to] Bo *restarts, f. 131ʳ*   Iudea lande] chaldea londe Bo   349–50 hi alædde] heo ilædde Bo   350 hig eft aræran þæt ænlice] heom æft aræren þet ænlic Bo   350–1 se ælmihtiga] ðe almihtiga Bo

micelre yrmðe. And hi þær siþþan wunedon oð þæt Crist sylf wearð geboren. Nu sindon twa mære bec gesette on endebyrdnysse to Salomones bocum, swilce he hig gedihte; for þære gelicnisse his gelogodan spræce and for þære getingnysse, hi[g] man getitelode him, ac Iesus hi gesette, Siraces sunu. An ys Liber Sapientię, þæt ys 'wisdomes boc', seo oðer ys gecweden Ecclesiasticus, swiðe micele bec, and man hig ræt on circan to micclum wisdome swiðe gewunelice. 355

We nymað þa witegan nu, þe witegodon embe Crist þurh þone halgan gast, be þæs Hælendes tokime to þisum middanearde on soðre menniscnisse, swa swa we wyllað awritan heræfter. Isaias wæs gehaten sum halig witega on ðæra kininga timan, swa swa us kyð seo boc. Se witegode be Criste swiðe gewislice, swilce he godspellere wære, swiðe gewyr[ð]elice, and cwæð on his gesetnysse swa swa we secgað her: 'Ecce uirgo concipiet et pariet filium et uocabitur nomen eius Emmanuel', et reliqua. 'Efne mæ|den sceal geeacnian and oncennan sunu and his nama bið geciged "God sylf ys mid us".' Eft se ylca witega awrat on his gesetnysse: 'Puer natus est nobis et filius datus est nobis', et reliqua. 'Us ys cild acenned and us ys sunu forgifen, and his ealdordom ys on eaxle. And his nama bið gehaten wundorlic rædbora, witodlice strang God, and fæder towerdre worulde, soðlice sibbe ealdor. And his kynedom bið menigfeald and ne bið nan ende his ecan sibbe.' His boc ys swiðe micel and menigfeald be Criste and be Godes mærðe be eallum mancinne, on gastlicum andgitte on Godes gelaþunge. He bodode geleafan on Iudea lande and unriht forbead, 360 365 f. 129ʳ 370 375

352 micelre] mycele Bo   hi þær] heo ðer Bo   þæt] ðet Bo   353 geboren] iboren Bo   gesette] isette Bo   endebyrdnysse] endeburdnesse Bo   354 hig gedihte] heom dihte Bo   þære gelicnisse] þare gelicnesse Bo   355 spræce] spæce Bo   hig] his L, *om.* Bo   man getitelode him] heom mon titelode Bo   356 hi] heo Bo   Siraces] siraches Bo   sapientię] sapiencie Bo   357 seo] þeo Bo   gecweden Ecclesiasticus] icwæden eclesiasticus Bo   358 man hig ræt] mon heom red Bo   micclum] mycele Bo   360 nymað] nimæð Bo   witegodon] witegoden Bo   Crist] criste Bo   361 tokime] tocyme Bo   þisum] þisse Bo   362 menniscnisse] menniscnesse Bo   wyllað] willæð Bo   gehaten] ihaten Bo   363 ðæra kininga timan] þære kynega timæ Bo   kyð seo] cyð þeo Bo   Se] þe Bo   364 gewislice] wislice Bo   365 gewyrðelice] gewyrdelice L, wurðelice Bo   secgað] sæcgað Bo   367 Emmanuel] emanuel Bo   et reliqua] *om.* Bo   mæden] mægden Bo   geeacnian] eacnian Bo   oncennan] acennen Bo   368 nama] nome Bo   geciged] icwædon Bo   Eft se] Æft þe Bo   369 awrat] wrat Bo   gesetnysse] setnysse Bo   370 forgifen] igyfan Bo   371 on] his *add.* Bo   nama] nome Bo   gehaten] ihaten Bo   372 witodlice] witolice Bo   towerdre worulde] toweardre weorlde Bo   373 menigfeald] monigfeald Bo   374 menigfeald] monigfeald Bo   375 mærðe] mærðæ Bo   eallum mancinne on gastlicum andgitte] alle moncynne on gastlice andgite Bo   376 gelaþunge] laðunge Bo

oð þæt se reða kyning Mannases gehaten, Ezechian sunu, hine tocleaf on twa and hine acwealde swa.

Hieremias se witega wæs on þam lande swiðe halig witega fram his cildhade. Be þam cwæð God sylf to him: 'Ic þe gecuðe soðlice ær þan þe ic þe gesceope on þinre modor innoðe, and ic þe gehalgode ær þan þe þu acenned wurde, and ic þe gesette þeodum to witegan.' He wunode on clænnysse and he awrat ane boc þurh ðone halgan gast on his witegunge, micele and menigfealde þam mannum to lare of gastlicum andgitte, eac be þam Hælende. He wearð oft gebend and gebroht on cweartern for his halgan lare, and he heofode micclum þæs folces synna, swa swa his boc us segð. And he wearð oftorfod mid stanum æt nextan on Egipta lande for his geleafan. | Plato se uðwita, and se wisosta mann on hæðenum folce, hæfde hine gesprecen, and se witega þa hine gewissode þæt he cuðe gelyfan on þone lifiendan God, swa swa Agustinus hit on bocum gesette. And Ieremias ys ure witega synderlice.

Ezechiel se witega wearð gehergod mid þam folce, þa þa se Chaldeisca kining acwealde ða Iudeiscan and ða herelafe to his lande adraf, þa þa Daniel se witega wearð eac gelæht. And Ezechiel ða on þeowte þær wunode, and witegode þær and awrat ane boc micele on gesetnisse be þam mancynne and be urum Drihtene, swiðe deop on andgite, oð þæt se heafodman þæs gehergodan folces hine acwealde, swa swa us kyð sum lareow.

Daniel se witega wunude on Chaldea, wurðfull þam ciningum, and awrat ane boc on his witegunge þe him God sylf onwreah. And he

LIBELLUS

swutelice sæde on his gesetnisse be Cristes acennednisse, swa swa he com to mannum feower hund geara and hundnigontig geara fram Darie ðam cining, oð þæt ure Drihten com on soðre menniscnisse of Marian innoþe. His boc is swiðe micel on manegum getacnungum, langsum her to secgende be hire gesetnyssum, and hu he wæs aworpen þam wildum leonum; be þam we awriton on Englisc on sumum spelle hwilon. He næs na ofslagen ac he him sylf gewat, þa þa he hund geara wæs and tyn gear on ylde, and he wæs bebirged on Babilonia.

Twelf witega syndon toeacan þisum git, ðe twelf bec awriton on heora witegunge, be sumum | dæle læssan on gesetnysse, micele on andgitte, be Cristes menniscnysse and be Godes folce, swa swa God him onwreah, ðæra naman we willað awritan on þisum cwyde. OSEE. IOHEL. AMOS. ABDIAS. IONAS, se þe ðreo niht wæs wiðinnan þam hwale, and se hwæl hine abær to Niniuea birig, and seo dæd getacnode ures Drihtenes deað, þe læg on birgine swa langum fæce ac he aras of deaðe þurh his drihtenlican mihte. MICHEAS. NAVM. ABBACVC, se namnode þone Hælend be his naman þus: 'Ego autem in Domino gaudebo et exultabo in Deo Iesu meo.' Ðæt ys on Englisc, 'Ic blissie on Drihtene and ic fægnie on Gode minum Hælende'. Iesus wæs gehaten ure Hælend on life and swa sæde þes witega ær ðan þe he wurde acenned, and swa swa se heah engel hit sæde on þam godspelle. He ys gehaten eac Crist. Be þam cwæð sum witega for fela hund gearum ær þan þe he acenned wurde: 'Adstiterunt reges terre et principes conuenerunt in unum aduersus Dominum et aduersus Christum eius.' 'Eor[ð]lice ciningas and ealdormenn arison ongean

---

402 gesetnisse be] isetnysse bi Bo   acennednisse] acennednesse Bo   403 mannum] monnum Bo   hundnigontig] hundnigantig Bo   404 cining] kynge Bo   þæt] ðet Bo   menniscnisse] menniscnesse Bo   405 Marian] mariæ Bo   manegum getacnungum] monige tacnunge Bo   406 secgende] secgenne Bo   gesetnyssum] gesetnesse Bo   407 wildum leonum] wildan leon Bo   407–8 be þam . . . hwilon] om. Bo   409 gear] gearæ Bo   bebirged] iburiged Bo   411 witega syndon toeacan þisum] witegan beoð toecan ðissum Bo   awriton] writon Bo   412 læssan] læsse Bo   gesetnysse] gesetnesse Bo   413 andgitte] andgite Bo   menniscnysse] menniscnesse Bo   414 him onwreah ðæra naman] heom unwreah þære namæn Bo   willað awritan] wyllæð writan Bo   þisum] ðissum Bo   415 se] þe Bo   wiðinnan] innan Bo   416 hwale] hwæle Bo   se] þe Bo   abær] bær Bo   birig] burig Bo   seo] þeo (o del.) Bo   416–17 dæd getacnode] dæð tacnode Bo   417 Drihtenes deað] drinhtnes dæþ Bo   birgine] burigenne Bo   langum] lange Bo   418 drihtenlican] drihtenlice Bo   419 se namnode] þe namode Bo   421 blissie] blissige Bo   Drihtene] drihtne Bo   fægnie] fægnige Bo   minum] mine Bo   422 gehaten] ihaten Bo   423 se] ðe Bo   424 gehaten] ihaten Bo   425 gearum] gearæ Bo   427 Christum] xp̄m LBo   Eorðlice] Bo, Eornostlice L   ciningas] kyngas Bo   ealdormenn] ealdormen Bo

urne Drihten and þone Hælend Crist.' þæt wæs Herodes cining and Pilatus ealdormann, swa swa ða apostolas be þam understodon. Sophonias. Aggeus. Zacharias. Malachias.

Wæron eac oðre witegan þe ne writon nane bec, swa swa wæs Helias and Heliseus, ac heora wundra syndon awritene swa ðeah on þæra cininga | bocum on fulcuðum gemynde. Tyn mædena wæron on mislicre tide on hæþenum leodum, þa man het 'Sibillas', þæt synd 'witegestran'. And hi witegodon ealle be þam Hælende Criste and heora bec setton swiðe swutelice ðurh þone soþan God be ealre his fare mid fullum geleafan, for ðan þe God wolde him gewitan habban of hæðenum leodum and of geleafullum, ac heora bec ne synd na on ure gesetnissum on þære biblioþecan, swa swa þas oðre beoð.

Esdras se writere awrat ane boc, hu þæt folc com ongean fram Chaldea lande to Iudea lande and hi Hierusalem þa burh eft arærdon and þæt tempel þær binnan, swa swa Cirus kining him sealde leafe æfter hundseofontigon gearum þæt hi heora eard bogodon. And seo boc ys geendebyrd on þissere gesetnysse mid deopum andgitte on diglum getacnungum.

Iob wæs gehaten sum heah Godes þegen on þam lande Chus, swiþe geleafull wer welig on æhtum. Se wearð afandod þurh þone swicolan deofol, swa swa his boc us segð þe he sylf gesette siþþan he afandod wæs. Be þam ic awende on Englisc sumne cwide iu, and hit ys eac witegung witodlice be Criste and be his gelaþunge, swa swa lareowas secgað. And seo boc ys geendebyrd on þissere gesetnysse.

Sum Iudeisc man wearð eac afandod, Tobias gehaten, swiðe ælmesgeorn and swiþe gelyfed on þone lyfiendan God. Se wæs eac

428 urne] ure Bo   cining] kyng Bo   429 ealdormann] ealdormon Bo   understodon] understoden Bo   431 Wæron] weron Bo   writon] writen Bo   432 syndon awritene] wurdon iwritene Bo   433 þæra cininga bocum] þære kyngbocum Bo   fulcuðum] fulcuðe Bo   434 mislicre] mislicere Bo   hæþenum] hæðene Bo   man] mon Bo   synd] beoð Bo   435 hi witegodon] heo witegodan Bo   436 God] gast Bo   ealre] alre Bo   437 him] heom Bo   438 leodum] leode Bo   geleafullum] geleaffullum Bo   synd] beoð Bo   439 gesetnissum] gesetnysse Bo   þære biblioþecan] ðare bibliothecan Bo   440 Esdras se] Ezras þe Bo   awrat] wrat Bo   441 lande¹] londe Bo   lande²] londe Bo   hi Hierusalem] heo irlm Bo   eft arærdon] æft arærdan Bo   442 binnan] binnæn Bo   kining him] kyng heom Bo   443 hundseofontigon] hundseofontig Bo   hi] heo Bo   seo] þe Bo   444 geendebyrd] iendeburd Bo   gesetnysse] gesetnesse Bo   andgitte] andgite Bo   445 getacnungum] getacnunge Bo   446 gehaten] ihaten Bo   þegen] þægen Bo   lande Chus] londe hus Bo   447 geleafull] leafful Bo   Se] þe Bo   afandod] afondod Bo   447–8 swicolan deofol] swikele deofel Bo   448 segð] sæð Bo   gesette] sette Bo   449 Be þam... cwide iu] om. Bo   450 witegung witodlice] iwitegæd witolice Bo   gelaþunge] laðunge Bo   lareowas] larewæs Bo   451 seo] þeo Bo   geendebyrd] iendeburd Bo   452 man wearð] mon wæs Bo   afandod] afondod Bo   gehaten] ihaten Bo   453 ælmesgeorn] ealmesgeorne Bo   gelyfed] ilyfed Bo   lyfiendan] lifigendon Bo; Bo f. 132ʳ   Se] þe Bo

gehergod to Sirian lande ac he heold swa þeah his geleafan þær mid godum | weorcum. And God his afandode, swa þæt he blind wearð and swa wunode tyn gear, ac God hine gehælde eft þurh his heah engel, Raphael gehaten, swa swa seo racu us segð on his agenre bec þe he sylf awrat. And seo boc ys geteald to þisum getele, for ðan þe þæron ys eac swilce getacnung.

Hester seo cwen, þe hire kynn ahredde, hæfð eac ane boc on þisum getele, for ðan þe Godes lof ys gelogod þæron. Ða ic awende on Englisc on ure wisan sceortlice.

Iudith seo wuduwe, þe oferwann Holofernem þone Siriscan ealdormann, hæfð hire agenne boc betwux þisum bocum, be hire agenum sige. Seo ys eac on Englisc on ure wisan gesett, eow mannum to bysne þæt ge eowerne eard mid wæmnum bewerian wið onwinnendne here.

Twa bec synd gesette æfter cyrclicum þeawum betwux þisum bocum, þe gebiriað to Godes lofe, Machabeorum gehatene, for heora micclum gewinne, for ðan þe hig wunnon mid wæmnum þa swiðe wið þone hæðenan here þe him onwann swiðe, wolde hig adilegian and adyddan of þam earde þe him God forgeaf, and Godes lof alecgan. Hwæt þa Mathathias, se mæra Godes ðegen, mid his fif sunum, feaht wið þone here miccle gelomlicor ðonne þu gelyfan wylle. And hig sige hæfdon þurh þone soðan God þe hig on gelyfdon æfter Moyses æ. Hig noldon na feohtan mid fægerum wordum anum, swa þæt hi wel spræcon, and awendon þæt eft þe læs ðe him become se hefigtima

454 gehergod] ihergod Bo   geleafan þær] ileafan ðer Bo   455 godum] gode Bo   his afandode] hine fandode Bo   456 gear] gearæ Bo   gehælde eft] hælde æft Bo   457 gehaten] ihaten Bo   seo racu] ðeo race Bo   segð] sægð Bo   agenre] agene Bo   458 awrat] wrat Bo   seo] ðeo Bo   geteald] iteald Bo   þisum getele] ðissum tæle Bo   460 seo cwen] þeo cwæn Bo   kynn ahredde] cyn aredde Bo   460–1 þisum getele] ðissum tæle Bo   461 þæron] þeron Bo   461–2 Ða ic awende ... sceortlice] om. Bo   463 seo wuduwe] þeo wudewe Bo   oferwann Holofernem] oferwan holofernen Bo   464 ealdormann] ealdormon Bo   agenne] agene Bo   betwux þisum] betwyx ðissum Bo   465 agenum] agene Bo   Seo] þeo Bo   gesett] iset Bo   mannum] monnum Bo   466 eowerne] eower Bo   wæmnum bewerian] wæpnum beweriæn Bo   466–7 onwinnendne] onwinnende Bo   468 synd gesette] beoð isette Bo   cyrclicum] cirlice Bo   betwux þisum] betwyx ðissum Bo   469 gebiriað] geburiað Bo   gehatene] ihatene Bo   470 micclum] mycele Bo   hig] heo Bo   wæmnum] wæpnum Bo   471 hæðenan] hæðene Bo   him onwann] heom onwan Bo   wolde hig adilegian] woldon heom adiglian Bo   472 adyddan] adydan Bo   him] heom Bo   forgeaf] geaf Bo   473 se mæra] þe mære Bo   sunum] sunu Bo   474 miccle gelomlicor ðonne] mycele lomlucor ðone Bo   gelyfan] lyfan Bo   hig] heo Bo   475 hig] heo Bo   gelyfdon] lyfdon Bo   476 Hig] Heo Bo   feohtan] feohton Bo   fægerum] fegere Bo   anum] ane Bo   hi] heo Bo   477 spræcon] spæcon Bo   him] heom Bo   se hefigtima] þe hæfigtyma Bo

f. 131ᵛ cwyde þe se | witega gecwæð be sumum leodscipe þus: 'Et iratus est furore Dominus in populo suo et abhominatus hereditatem suam', et
480 cetera. 'Drihten wearð yrre mid graman his folce and he onscunode his yrfewerdnisse. And he betæhte hig on hæþenra handum and heora fynd soðlice hæfdon heora geweald and hig swiðe gedrehton þa deriendlica fynd, and hig wurdon geeadmette under heora handum.' Nolde Machabeus se mæra Godes cempa habban þisne
485 dom ðurh his Drihtenes yrre, ac him wæs leofre þæt he mid geleafan clipode on his eornost to Gode þisne oðerne cwyde: 'Da nobis Domine auxilium de tribulatione quia uana salus hominis', et cetera. 'Syle us, leof Drihten, þinne soðan fultum on ure gedrefednisse and gedo us strengran, for þan þe mannes fultum ys unmihtig
490 and idel, ac uton wyrcean mihte on þone mihtigan God, and he to nahte gedeð urne deriendlican fynd.' Machabeus þa gefylde ðas foresædan word mid stranglicum weorcum and oferwann his fynd, and sint forði gesette his sigefæstan dæda on þam twam bocum on bibliothecan, Gode to wurðmynte. And ic awende hig on Englisc and
495 rædon gif ge wyllað, eow sylfum to ræde. EXPLICIT DE VETERI TESTAMENTO. INCIPIT DE NOVO TESTAMENTO.

IC SECGE ÐE NV SIWERD ÐÆT ic her gesett hæbbe þas feawa bysna of ðan ealdan bocum on þære ealdan gecyðnysse under Moyses æ, and hu gi .... test ealne ðone wisdom þe on þam bocum stynt
f. 132ʳ .....e, wol|dest þu gelyfan þæt ic na ne wæge on þisum gewrite. Ic
501 wille nu secgan eft sceortlice þe be þære niwan gecyðnisse æfter Cristes tocyme, þæt þu mid ealle ne beo þæs andgites bedæled, þeah þe ðu be fullan underfon ne mage ealle þa gesetnissa þæs soþan gewrites, bist swa ðeah gebet þurh þas litlan bysne.
505 'Lex et prophete usque ad Iohannem sicut legitur in euangelio.'

478 se] ðe Bo   gecwæð] cwæð Bo   sumum] summum Bo   479 abhominatus] est add. Bo   480 graman] gramen Bo   481 yrfewerdnisse] yrfwerdnesse Bo   hig] heom Bo   482 fynd] feond Bo   hig] heom Bo   gedrehton] dræhton Bo   483 deriendlica] derigendlice Bo   hig] heo Bo   geeadmette] iætmette Bo   484 se mæra] þe mæræ Bo   habban] habben Bo   485 Drihtenes] drihtnes Bo   þæt] þet Bo   geleafan] ileafan Bo   486 his] om. Bo   488 Syle] sule Bo   leof] leofæ Bo   488–9 gedrefednisse] dræfednisse Bo   489 gedo] do Bo   mannes] monnes Bo   490 uton wyrcean] uten wurcæn Bo   mihtigan] almihtigæ Bo   491 nahte ... fynd] nohte dæð ure derigendlicæ feond Bo   492 foresædan] foresæde Bo   stranglicum] stronglice Bo   oferwann] oferwan Bo   fynd] feond Bo   493 sint] beð Bo   gesette] isette Bo   sigefæstan] sigefesta Bo   twam] om. Bo   494 wurðmynte] wurðmente Bo; Bo ends
MS L   497 IC SECGE] new line   499 gi .... test] damage to parchment; f þu wil add. by L'Isle (?) to complete phrase gif þu wiltest; some damage to next line also 500 ......e] þonn add. by L'Isle (?)

Moyses æ wæs, and witegan soþlice, oð Iohannes wearð acenned þe Crist gefullode. He ys ende þære ealdan æ and æt him ongann seo godspellbodung, and he wæs acenned on Cristes tocime. Swa swa dægsteorra on dægred upp gæð ætforan þære sunnan, swa scean Iohannes on haligre bodunge ætforan þam Hælende. And he wæs his bydel on his bodunge and mid his fulluhte kydde Cristes fulluht toweard. Crist sylf cwæð be him þæt ne come nateshwon betwux wifa bearnum nan mærra man ðonne he wæs, ac Crist næs na geteald to þissere wiðmetenysse, se þe acenned wæs of ðam clænan mædene. Ne awrat Iohannes nane boc synderlice ac his dæda sind awritene on Drihtenes godspelle, þone he gefullode, and his forerynel wæs on life ge on deaðe and his hlisa nu stynt swa hwær swa cristendom bið and þa Cristes bec cumað.

Feower Cristes bec sindon be Criste sylfum awriten. An ðæra awrat Matheus, þe mid þam Hælende wæs, his agen leorningcniht on þisum life farende, and he his wundra geseah and awrat hi on þære bec, þe him to gemynde þa mihton becuman, on Ebreiscum gereorde, | æfter Cristes þrowunge on Iudea lande, þam þe gelyfdon on God; and he ys se forma godspellere on ðære gesetnisse. Marcus se godspellere, þe wæs mid Petre on lare, his agen godsunu on Godes lare geþogen, wrat þa oðre boc be Petres bodunge, be ðam þe he geleornode of his larspellum on Romana byrig, swa swa he gebeden wæs þurh ða geleafullan þe gelyfdon on God of þare burhware þurh Petres bodunge. Lucas se godspellere awrat ða þriddan boc, se ðe fram cildhade folgode þam apostolum and mid Paule siþþan siðode on his fare and æt him leornode ða godspellican lare, on clænisse lybbende, and [awrat] þa Cristes boc on Achaian lande mid Greciscum gereorde, swa he of Paules lare and þæra apostola lare leornode. Iohannes se apostol on Asian lande, swa swa þa biscopas bædon, began þa feorðan boc be Cristes godgundnysse, on Greciscum gereorde, and be ðære deopnysse þe him Drihten awreah, þa þa he hlinode on his luflicum breoste, on þam ðe wæs behydd se heofonlica goldhord. Ðas synd þa feower ean of anum wyllspringe þe gað of paradisum ofer Godes folc wide. And þas feower godspelleras wæron gefyrn getacnode swa Ezechiel hi geseah: Matheus on mannes hiwe, Marcus on leon, Lucas on cealfes, Iohannes on earnes, for ðære 'ge'tacnunge ðe hig getacnodon. Matheus awrat be Cristes menniscnisse; and Marcus swa swa leo hludswege clipode on þam wildan mancynne, swilce on

532 awrat] om.

westene; and Lucas be þam | sacerde Zacharias ongann, þe cealf geoffrode on Godes onsægednisse; and Iohannes swa swa earn þa upplican digolnisse mid his scearpum eagum sceawode georne and be Cristes godgundnysse his godspell gesette.

Ðas feower bec kyþað hu Crist com to mannum of Marian ðam mædene, middaneardes alysend, on þære sixtan ylde þissere worulde, be þan ðe þa witegan hit gewriton on bocum, on Bethleem birig binnan Iudea, on Augustes dagum þæs æðelan caseres, and englas þa kyddon his acennednysse mid heofonlicum sange, fela þusenda. Ða comon þri ciningas to Criste mid lacum, of eastrice feorran. And Herodes acwealde ealle þa litlan cild þe on ðam lande wæron, þæt he Crist acwealde, ac he ne com him to na, for ðan ðe he mid swicdome hine swa sohte and se yfela cining on yrmþum acweal. Ða bec us secgað swutelice be Criste hu he wundra worhte and hu he wæs gefullod and hu he apostolas geceas, þæt sind ærendraca, twelf on anginne, þa þa he ærest bodode. þa sint gehatene þisum naman on bocum: Petrus and Andreas, Iacobus and Iohannes, Thomas [. . .] and se oðer Iacob, Philippus and Bartholomeus, Tatheus, [. . .] and Paulus. Ac Paulus wæs gecoren æfter Cristes upstige, and Mathias eac mann geceas for Iudan, þe Crist belæwde and þa forloren wæs. Æfter þisum he geceas twa and hundseofonti to his lareowdome, him to leorningcnihtum. þa he tosende geond eall to ælcere birig þider þe he towerd wæs, þæt mann wiste | his cyme, ac we ne afundon na awritene heora naman on bocum.

He wunode þa mid mannum on þisum middanearde þreo and þrittig geara, and sumne eacan þærto, and cristendom arærde and kydde mid wundrum, swa swa his godspell secgað, þæt he Godes sunu ys, þa þa he þa deadan menn þurh his mihte arærde and ælce untrumnysse eaðelice gehælde. And he wæter awende to winlicum drence and ofer sæ eode eall drium fotum and windas gestilde mid his wordes hæse and deofla adræfde of gedrehtum wodum and forgeaf gewitt æfter wodnysse. Eft siþþan he þrowode sylfwilles dead, on rode ahangen for ure alysednysse, and of deaðe aras on þam ðriddan dæge and astah to heofenum to his heofenlican fæder, gewunnenum sige, and gewylt ealle þing and cymð eft to demende eallum mancynne on þam micclan dæge, ælcum be his dædum. Ic secge þis sceortlice, for ðan þe ic gesett hæbbe of þisum feower bocum wel feowertig larspella

---

544 *f. 134ʳ: f. 133 is misbound and belongs after f. 138* 560 Thomas] 'Matthaeus' *supp. above by late hand* 561 Tatheus] 'Simon Cananaeus' *supp. above by late hand*

on Engliscum gereorde, and sumne eacan ðærto. Þa þu miht rædan be
þissere race on maran andgite ðonne ic her secge.

Ða apostoli gesetton eac swilce larspell to þam leodscipum þe to
geleafan bugon, þæt hi þurh ða mynegunge heora mod getrymdon on
Cristes geleafan on þam cristendome, ðe þa niwan asprang on þære 585
micclan niwan gecyðnysse. PETRVS se apostol awrat twegen pistolas
ac hig synd maran þonne man æt mæssan ræt and habbað langne tige
to geleafan trimminge, and hig synd to bocum | getealde on þære f.135ʳ
bibliothecan. Iacob se rihtwisa awrat anne pistol micelne on lare,
mannum to understandenne, þam þe æniges cristendomes cepað on 590
heora life. Iohannes se godspellere, Gode to wurðmynte, gesette ðri
pistolas; þæt syndon þreo bec mid lufe afyllede, folce to lare. Iudas se
apostol awrat anne pistol, na se forlorena Iudas þe ðone Hælend
belæwde ac se halga Iudas þe him æfre folgode, and her sind nu seofon
bec on þissere gesetnisse. Paulus se apostol awrat manega pistolas, for 595
þan þe Crist hine gesette eallum þeodum to lareowe, and on soþre
eufæstnysse he gesette ða þeawas ðe þa geleafullan folc on heora life
healdað, þa þe hig sylfe gelogiað and heora lif for Gode. Fiftyne
pistolas awrat se an apostol to þam leodscipum þe he to geleafan
gebigde. Þa syndon micele bec on þære bibliothecan and þa fremiað 600
us to ure rihtinge, gif we þæs leoda lareowes lare folgiað. He awrat to
þam Romaniscum anne, to Corinthios .ii., eac to Galathas anne, to
Ephesios anne, to Philipenses anne, to Thesalonicenses twegen, to
Colosenses anne, eac to Ebreos anne, and to his agenum discipulum
Timotheum twegen and Titum anne, to Philemonem anne, to 605
Laodicenses anne. Ealles fiftyne, swa hlude swa ðunor geleafullum
folcum.

Be þam ic wille secgan sume feawa word. Ærest be ðam Hælende,
hu he us lærde on his halgan godspelle, þa þe hine lufiað: 'Si diligitis
me mandatu mea serua[te]', et cetera. | 'Gif ge lufiað me, healdað f.135ᵛ
mine beboda. Se ðe me lufað, he healt mine spræce and min fæder 611
hine lufað and wit cumað to him and mid him wuniað witodlice
syððan. Se ðe me ne lufað ne healt he na mine spræce.' Her we magon
gehiran þæt se Hælend lufað swiþor þa dæde þonne þa smeðan word.
Þa word gewitað and þa weorc standað. Be þam cwæð Iacob se 615
rihtwisa apostol: 'Estote factores uerbi et non auditores tantum,
fallentes uosmet ipsos.' 'Beoð þæs wordes wircendras witodlice mid
dædum and eow sylfe ne bepæcað, swa þæt ge hlyston þa word ana

610 seruate] te *add. late on eras.*

butan þam weorcum.' Eall swa Iohannes us lærde þisum wordum:
620 'Filioli mei non diligamus uerbo neque lingua sed opere et ueritat[e].'
'Mine leofan bearn, ne lufige we, ic bidde, mid worde and mid tungan
ac mid weorce and soðfæstnysse.' Paulus se apostol be ðam ylcan
cwæð: 'Qui dicunt se nosse Deum, factis autem negant.' 'Hi secgað
þæt hig cunnon þone soðan God ac hig mid heora weorcum hine
625 wiðsacað.' Se man þe behet geswicennysse yfeles and his wedd to þam
sylð and awend þæt eft, hu mæg he ðonne habban þæs Hælendes
fultum, se þe gesihð and gesceawað 'his' heortan, þæt he wylle
awendan his word eft wið hine? Ac man mot on eornost motian wið
his Drihten, se þe wyle þæt we sprecon mid weorcum wið hine, for
630 þan se ðe wel spricð and þa word na gelæst, he ne deð nan þingc buton
fordemð hine sylfne.

    Lucas se godspellere, se ðe wæs læce on life, gesette twa bec urum
f. 136ʳ saulum to | hæle. An ys seo Cristes boc, oþer ys gecweden þus, Actus
Apostolorum, þæt ys on Engliscre spræce 'þæra apostola dæda', þe hi
635 dydon ætgædere, and hu 'hi' siððan toferdon to fyrlenum eardum,
swa swa se Hælend bebead on his halgum godspelle, þæt hig ealle
leoda læran sceoldon and gebigan to geleafan mid heora bodunge.
Petrus bodode on Antiochian byrig and þær wæron ærest gecwedene
'cristene' men þurh hine. And he ferde siððan swiþe fus to Rome and
640 þær bodode þære burhware geleafan fif and twentig wintra mid
wundrum and tacnum, oð þæt se casere Nero hine acwealde on
rode. Paulus ferde wide geond ðas woruld, bodiende manegum
leodscipum, oð þæt he on last becom into Rome byrig and þær eac
bodode. And Nero het þa hine beheafdian on þam ylcan dæge þe he
645 aheng Petrum. Andreas bodode on Achaian lande and on Scithian and
he syððan wearð on rode ahangen for þæs Hælendes naman. Iacob se
gingra, þe wæs Iohannes broþor, bodode þam Iudeiscum þe wæron
tostengte, þam twelf mægðum, tacna wircende, oð þæt Herodes
cyning hine beheafdode. Iohannes his broðor bodode on Asia on
650 easteweardan worulde and he ne wearð na ofslagen ac æfter manegum
wundrum he gewat to Criste, þa þa he on ylde wæs nygan and
hundnygontig wintra. Philippus bodode þam hæðenum folce wið
þære sæ sylfre and he siððan gewat to Hærapolim and wearð þa
f. 136ᵛ geendod. Thomas bodode on Parthon | and Medon and on Yrcanaim,
655 oð þæt he com to Indian and þær wearð ofslagen for þone soðan
geleafan. Bartholomeus bodode on Indian, on þære fyrran Indian, and

620 ueritate] *final e appar. add. late over* is   654 Yrcanaim] *Crawford emends to* Yrcaniam *(modern Hircania)*

þær wearð ofslagen. Matheus bodode on Ethiopian lande, þæt synd þa
Silhearwan, and se kining hine ofsloh, na se gelyfeda ac se ungeleaf-
fulla. Iacob se rihtwisa wunode on þam lande binnan Hierusalem,
bodiende geleafan, oð þæt þa Iudeiscan hine acwealdon. Simon and 660
Iudas samod wæron gemartyrode on Persida lande for Cristes
geleafan, on ðam þe hi bodedon and biscopas gehadedon on heora
twelf scirum, oð þæt man hig ofsloh. Mathias bodode on Iudea lande,
se þe wæs gecoren on Iudan stede, þæt þæra apostola getel wurde
gefylled. Ealra þissera apostola geendunge ic hæbbe awriten buton 665
Mathian anes, þe ic ofacsian [ne] mihte. Ða ge mihton rædan and eow
aræman on þam, gif ge holde wæron eowrum agenum sawlum.

    Iohannes leofode on þisum life heora lengst. And he awrat þa boc
on his wræcsiðe Apocalipsis gehaten, þæt ys 'onwrigennys', þe him
Crist geswutelode on his gastlican gesihþe be þam Hælende sylfum 670
and his gelaðunge and be domes dæge and be þam deoflican
Antecriste, and be þam æriste to þam ecan life. And þeos boc ys
æftemyst on ðære bibliothecan. Ic mæg þe secgan git sum þing be
Iohanne, þæt þu wylt gelyfan þæt he mid weorcum spræc to sumum
cnihte, swa swa us kyð seo racu, ðone he lufode and him eac swa 675
gelæste. Hieronimus se wurþfulla and se wisa | bocere, þe ure f. 137ʳ
bibliothecan gebrohte to Ledene of Greciscum bocum and of
Ebreiscum, he awrat be Iohanne þam halgan godspellere, Cristes
modrian sunu, on þære circlican bec Ecclesiastica Hystoria, þus
cweðende be him: 'Audi fabulam, non fabulam sed rem gestam de 680
Iohanne apostolo', et cetera. 'Gehyr ðu þas race, na swilce lease sagu
ac geworden þing be Iohanne ðam apostole, and swiþe gemyndelic
eallum geleaffullum þe on ealdum dagum be him gedon wæs.'
Domicianus hatte se deoflica casere þe, æfter Nerone, þa reðan
ehtnyssa besette on þam cristenum and hi acwealde mid witum. Se 685
het genyman þone halgan apostol and on weallendum ele he het hine
baðian, for ðan þe se hata ele gæð into ðam bane. And him wæs
eaðgete ele to þam baðe. Hig gebrohton þa Iohannem binnan þære
cyfe on þam weallendan ele, ac he wearð gescild þurh Godes mihte
and mid halum lichaman of þam baðe eode, swa swa he unwemme 690
wæs fram flæsclicum lustum and fulre galnysse. Æfter þisum gehet se
hetola casere, for ðan ðe Iohannes nolde his bodunge geswican, þæt
man hine gebrohte binnan anum igoðe, feor on wræcsiðe, Pathmos
gehaten. And he þær wunode oð þæt þæs caseres witan heora hlaford
ofslogon, swa swa him eallum gewearð for his wælhreownysse and his 695

    666 ne] *om.*

gewittleaste. And þa witan þa demdon þæt eall wurde aidlod and mid
ealle awend, swa hwæt swa he wolde mid his yfelan ræde ær þam
gefremman. Wearð þa eft gelangod se geleaf|fulla apostol of þam
iglande, ham to Ephesan byrig, þær þær he wununge hæfde, Godes
700 wundra wyrcende and þæt folc lærende to geleafan simble.

Ða æfter sumum fyrste ferde se apostol, swa swa he gelaðod wæs
þurh þa geleaffullan, to gehendum burgum, bodigende geleafan. And
he circean arærde on gehwilcum scirum, þær þær ær ðam næron, and
he eac þa gesette mid gehadodum preostum, be þam þe se halga gast
705 him simble gewissode, swa swa us segð seo racu. He becom þa to anre
birig, swa swa he gebeden wæs, gehende Ephesan, and þær bisceop
gehadode and þa circlican þeawas him sylf þær getæhte þam
gehadodum preostum ðe he þær gelogode, and mid micelre mærþe
þæt mennisc þær lærde to Godes geleafan mid glædre heortan.

710 Ða geseah Iohannes sumne cniht on þam folce, iunglicre ylde and
ænlices hiwes, stranglic on wæstme and wenlic on nebbe, swiðe glæd
on mode and on anginne caf, and begann to lufienne on his liðum
þeawum þone iungan cniht, þæt he hine Criste gestrynde. Ða beseah
Iohannes swa upp to þam bisceope, þe ða niwan wæs gehadod, and
715 him þus to cwæð: 'Wite þu, la bisceop, þæt ic wille þæt þu hæbbe
þisne iungan man mid þe on þinre lare æt ham, and ic hine þe befæste
mid healicre gecneordnisse on Cristes gewitnysse and þissere
gelaðunge.' Hwæt þa se bisceop bliðelice underfeng þone foresædan
cniht and sæde þæt he wolde his gimene habban mid geornfulnysse,
swa he him | bebead, on his wununge mid him. Iohannes þa eft
721 geedleahte his word and gelome bebead þam bisceope mid hæsum þæt
he þone iungan cniht gewissian sceolde to ðam halgan geleafan. And
he ham þa gewende eft to Efesan birig to his bisceopstole.

Se bisceop ða underfeng, swa swa him beboden wæs, þone iungan
725 cniht and him Cristes lare dæghwamlice tæhte and hine deorwurðlice
heold oð þæt he hine gefullode mid fullum truwan þæt he geleaffull
wære. And he wunode swa mid him on arwurðnysse, oð þæt se
bisceop hine let faran be his wille, wende þæt he sceolde on Godes gife
þurhwunian on gastlicum þeawum. He geseah þa sona þæt he his
730 sylfes geweold, on ungeripedum freodome and unstæððigum þeawum,
and begann þa to lufienne leahtras to swiðe and fela unðeawas mid his
efenealdum cnihtum, þe unrædlice ferdon on heora idelum lustum on
gewemmednyssum and woclicum gebærum. He and his geferan þa
begunnon to lufienne þa micclan druncennisse on nihtlicum ge-
735 dwylde, and hig ða hine on gebrohton þæt he begann to stelenne on

702 And] þæt *add*.

heora gewunan, and he gewenede swa hine sylfne simble to heora
synlicum þeawum and to marum morðdædum mid þam manfullum
flocce. He genam þa heardlice þurh heora lare on his orþance þa
egeslican dæda. And swa swa modig hors þe ungemidlod byð and nele
gehirsumian þam ðe him on uppan sitt, swa ferde se cniht on his   740
fracedum dædum and on morðdædum, micclum gestrangod on
orwen|nysse his agenre hæle, swa þæt he ortruwode on his Drihtnys   f. 138ᵛ
mildheortnysse and his fulluhtes ne rohte þe he underfangen hæfde.
Him þuhte þa to waclic þæt he wolde gefremman þa l[æs]san leahtras
ac he leornode æfre maran and maran on his manfulnysse and ne let   745
nanne his gelican on yfele. He ne geþafode þa þæt he underþeod wære
yfelum gegadum þe hine ær forlærdon ac wolde beon yldest on þam
yfelan flocce and geworhte his geferan to wealdgengum ealle, on
widgillum dunum on ealre hreownysse.

Eft þa æfter fyrste ferde se apostol to þære foresædan byrig, ðe se   750
bisceop on wunode þe þone cniht hæfde on his gimene æror, swa swa
Iohannes het. And he hine befæste and he swiðe bliðe wæs æt þam
bisceopstole. Syððan he gedon hæfde his Drihtenes þenunga and þa
ðing gefyllede þe he fore gelaþod wæs, he cwæð þa anrædlice: 'Eala
þu, la bisceop, gebring me nu ætforan þæt þæt ic ðe befæste on mines   755
Drihtnes truwan and on þære gewitnysse þe ðu wissian scealt on
þissere gelaðunge.' He wearð þa ablicged and wende þæt he bæde
sumes oþres sceattes oððe sumes feos, þæs þe he ne underfeng fram
þam apostole. Ac he eft beðohte þæt se eadiga Iohannes him leogan
nolde, ne hine þæs biddan þæt he ær ne befæste, and he forhtmod   760
wafode. Iohannes þa geseah þæt he sæt ablicged and cwæð him eft þus
to: 'Ic bidde æt þe nu þæs iungan cnihtes þe ic þe befæste and þæs
broþor sawle þe me besorh ys.' Ða begann se ealda | incuðlice   f. 139ʳ
siccettan and mid wope wearð witodlice ofergoten, and cwæð to
Iohanne: 'He, leof, ys nu dead.' Ða befran Iohannes færlice and cwæð: 765
'Hu ys he la dead, oððe hwilcum deaðe?' He cwæð him eft þus to
andsware: 'He is Gode dead, for þan þe he leahterfull and geleafleas
ætbærst. And he ys geworden nu to wealdgengan and þæra sccaðcna
ealdor þe he him sylf gegaderode, and wunað on anre dune mid
manegum sceaþum, þam þe he nu ys ealdor and heretoga.'   770

Hwæt þa Iohannes mid ormætre geomerunge cwehte his heafod
and cwæð to þam bisceope: 'Godne hyrde let ic þe þæt þu þæs broðor
sawle heolde, ac beo me nu gegearcod an gerædod hors and latteow
þæs weges þe lið to þam sceaðum.' And man him sona funde þæs þe

743 and his] mildheortnysse and his *add.*   744 læssan] leasan

226   LIBELLUS

775 he frimdig wæs and he fram þære ciricean sona swiðe efste, oð þæt he
geseah þæra sceaþena fær and to þam weardmannum witodlice
becom. Ða gelæhton þa weardmen his wealdleðer fæste, þæt he mid
fleame huru ne ætburste. Ac he nolde him ætfleon, ne nanes fleames
cepan, ac he clypode ofer eall: 'Ic com me sylf to eow. Alædað me nu
780 to, butan laþe, eowerne ealdor.' Hig clipodon þa mid þam þone cniht
him raðe to, þe hira heafodman wæs, and he com þa gewæmnod. And
he mid sceame wearð sona ofergoten, þa þa he oncneow þone Cristes
apostol, and began to fleonne fram his andweardnysse. Iohannes ða
heow þæt hors mid þam spuran and wearð him æfterweard and his
f. 139ʳ ylde ne gimde, clypode þa hlude and cwæð to þam fleondum: | 'Eala
786 þu min sunu. Hwi flihst þu þinne fæder? Hwi flihst ðu þisne ealdan
and ungewæpnode? Ne ondræd þe la earming; git þu hæfst lifes hiht.
Ic wille agildan gescead for þinre sawle Criste and ic lustlice wille min
lif for þe syllan, swa swa se Hælend sealde hine sylfne for us, and mine
790 sawle ic sille for þinre. Ætstand huru nu and gehyr þas word and gelyf
þæt se Hælend me asende to þe.'

Ða ætstod se wealdgenga syþþan he þas word gehirde and aleat to
eorðan mid eallum lichama and awearp his wæmna and weop swiðe
biterlice, and he bifiende feoll to Iohannes fotum mid geomerunge and
795 þoterunge, mid tearum ofergoten, biddende miltsunge be þam ðe he
mihte, and behydde his swiðran hand, ofsceamod forðearle for þære
morðdæde ðe he gedon hæfde and for þam manslihte þe he sloh mid
þære handa. Ða swor se apostol þæt he soðlice wolde him mildsunge
begitan æt þam mildheortan Hælende. And eac he sylf aleat to him
800 and gelæhte his swiþran, for ðære þe he ofdrædd wæs for his
morðdædum, and alædde aweg wepende to circean and for hine
gebæd mid broðorlicre lufe, swa swa he him behet to þam Hælende
gelome, and eac mid fæste fela daga on an, oð þæt he him mildsunge
beget æt þam mildheortan Criste. He hine frefrode eac mid his fægera
805 lare, and his afyrhte mod swiþe fægerlice mid his frofre geliðewæhte,
þæt he ne wurde ormod. And he nateshwon ne geswac ær þan þe his
sawul wæs wiðinnan gegladod þurh þone halgan gast and he |
f. 133ʳ mildsunge hæfde ealra his misdæda. He hine hadode eac to þæs
Hælendes þeowdome, ac us ne segð na seo racu to hwam he hine sette,
810 buton þæt he sealde soðe gebysnunge eallum dædbetendum þe to
Drihtene gecyrrað, þæt hig magon arisan gif hig rædfæste beoð fram

780 laþe] *Crawford and Grein emend to* late   787 ungewæpnode] *Crawford emends to*
ungewæpnodan   793 lichama] *Crawford emends to* lichaman   804 fægera] *Crawford
emends to* fægeran   808 *f. 133ʳ: leaf misplaced*

LIBELLUS

heora sawle deaþe and fram heora synn[a] bendum and heora scippend gladian mid soðre dædbote and habban þæt ece lif mid þam leofan Hælende, se þe a rixað on ecnysse. Amen.

We habbað nu gesæd be ðam circlicum bocum on þære ealdan æ and eac on þare niwan. Ða synd þa twa gecyðnyssa be Cristes menniscnysse and be þære halgan þrinnysse on soðre annysse, swa Isaias geseah on his gastlican gesihðe hu God sylf gesæt. And him sungon abutan duo seraphin, þæt sind twa engla werod: 'Sanctus, sanctus, sanctus, Dominus Deus sabaoth.' Þæt ys on Englisc, 'Halig, halig, halig, Drihten weroda God. Mid his wu[l]dre ys afylled eall eorðan bradnisse.' Ða twa seraphin soðlice getacnod[on] þa ealdan gekyðnysse and eac þa niwan, þe heriað mid wordum and mid weorcum æfre þone ælmihtigan God, se þe ana rixað on anre godgundnysse butan anginne and ende. Ða lareowas þe nellað heora lare nyman of þisum halgum bocum, ne heora gebysnunga, þa beoð swilce lareowas, swa swa Crist sylf sæde: 'Cecus si ceco ducatum prestet, ambo in foueam cadent.' 'Gif se blinda man byð þæs blindan latteow, þonne befeallað hi begen on sumne blindne seað.' Ða lareowas þe willað heora lare nyman of þisum halgum bocum, and heora gebysnunga, | ge of þære ealdan gekiðnisse ge of ðære niwan, þa beoð swilce lareowas, swa swa Crist eft sylf cwæð: 'Omnis scriba doctus in regno celorum similis est homini patri familias qui profert de thesauro suo noua et uetera.' 'Ælc gelæred bocere on Godes gelaðunge ys gelic þam hlaforde þe forlæt simble of his agenum goldhorde ealde þing and niwe.' Twa and hundseofontig boca sind on bibliothecan, for þan þe hig sume sind to sette on twa for heora langnysse on geleafulre ciricean: þæt mæg sceawian, þe ða gesetnisse cann. And swa fela þeoda wurdon todælede æt ðære wundorlican byrig, þe þa entas woldon wircean mid gebeote, æfter Noes flode, ær þan ðe hi toferdon. And swa fela leorningcnihta asende ure Hælend mancinne to bodienne þæra boca lare mid þam cristendome, þe þa com on þas woruld þurh ðone Hælend sylfne and þurh his bydelas. Syndon swa þeah gesette oðre bec ðurh halige lareowas þe man hæfð wide gehwær on cristendome, Criste to lofe.

And seo sixte yld þissere worulde stynt fram Criste astreht oþ domes dæg, eallum mannum ungewiss, ac hit wat se Hælend. Seo seofoðe yld ys þe yrnð mid þisum sixum fram Abele þam rihtwisan oð

---

812 synna] synnum   815 We] *enlarged initial cap. but no break*   821 wuldre] wundre (*corr. by late hand to* wuldre)   822 getacnodon] getacnode   841 And] *followed by eras. of two or three characters*

þissere worulde ende, na on lybbendum mannum ac on forðfarenum
sawlum on þam oðrum life, þær þær hig blissiað, andbidiende git þæs
ecan lifes þonne hig arisað, swa swa we ealle sceolon of deaðe gesunde
urum Drihtene togeanes. Seo eahteoðe yld ys se an eca dæg æfter
urum æriste, þonne | we rixiað mid Gode on sawle and on lichaman
on ecere sælþe. And ne biþ nan ende þ[æs] anes dæges, þonne þa
halgan scinað swa swa seo sunne deð nu. Hu mæg se man wel faran ðe
his mod awent fram eallum þisum bocum and bið him swa anwille þæt
him leofre bið þæt he lybbe æfre be his agenum dihte, ascired fram
þisum, swilce he ne cunne Cristes gesetnyssa? Moyses us lærde, se
mæra witega, on his gesetnissum, þus secgende eallum: 'Interroga
patrem tuum et adnuntiabit tibi maiores tuos et dicent tibi', et cetera.
Ðæt ys on Englisc, 'Acsa þinne fæder embe ðone soþan God and he
þe kyð be him. Befrin þine yldran and hig þe secgað.' Gif þu nelt
witan and beon gewissod her, þu scealt leornian ðær, þe laþre bið on
egeslicum witum, ðæt þu wite þonne hwæne þu forsawe and hwæs
gesetnysse.

Witan sceoldon smeagan mid wislicum geþ[eaht]e, þonne on
mancinne to micel yfel bið, hwilc [þæra] stelenna þæs cinestoles
wære tobrocen, and betan ðone sona. Se cinestol stynt on þisum þrim
stelum: Laboratores, bellatores, oratores. Laboratores sind þe us
bigleofan tiliað, yrðlingas and æhtemen to þam anum betæhte.
Oratores syndon þe us þingiað to Gode and cristendom fyrðriað on
cristenum folcum on Godes þeowdome, to ðam gastlican gewinne, to
þam anum betæhte, us eallum to þearfe. Bellatores sindon þe ure
burga healdað and eac urne eard wið [þ]on[e] sigendne here,
feohtende mid wæmnum, swa swa Paulus | sæde, se þeoda lareow,
on his lareowdome: 'Non sine causa portat miles gladium', et cetera.
'Ne byrð na se cniht butan intingan his swurd. He ys Godes þen, þe
sylfum to þearfe, on ðam yfelum wyrcendum to wræce gesett.' On
þisum þrim stelum stynt se cynestol, and gif an bið forud, he fylð
adun sona, þam oðrum stelum to unðearfe gewiss. Ac hwæt gebyrað
us embe þis to smeagenne, þis sceolon smeagan þe þæs giman sceolon.
Se rihtwisa God lufað rihte domas, ac medsceattas awendað wolice to
oft þa rihtan domas ongean Drihtenes willan and seo yfelnyss becymð
ofer eallum folce, þær ðær se unþeaw orsorhlice rixað. Se þe Godes
þegen bið sceolde deman rihtlice butan ælcum medsceatte mid
soðfæstnysse. þonne wurðode he God mid þam godan þeawe and

854 þæs] þas   866 geþeahte] eaht *late on eras.*   867 þæra] *late on eras.*
874 wið þone] wið on *corr. by late hand*

his med wære micel for Gode, se ðe leofað and rixað a to worulde.
Amen.

Ic wolde secgan be þam ungesæligum folce, be þam Iudeiscum, þe
urne Drihten ahengon, ac ic wolde ærest secgan þæt þæt ic gesæd
hæbbe. Manega ðær gelyfdon of þam mancinne on Crist ac se mæsta
dæl þæs mancinnes nolde on hine gelyfan and losodon forði. Him
becomon fela yrmða æfter Cristes þrowunge on eallum ungelimpum,
and ofslagenne wurdon fela þæs folces mid færlicum on ræsum. And
hi acwealdon Cristes apostolas, þone gingran Iacob and þone
rihtwisan Iacob, and Stephanum oftorfedon mid heardum stanum
and heora yfel geeacnodon, him sylfum to unþearfe, | and noldon
besargian þæs Hælendes slege, ne mid nanre dædbote his mildse
biddan. Ða sende he him to sillice tacna and siððan hergunge þurh þa
Romaniscan. Vespassianus wæs casere on þam timan. Se asende him
to his sunu Titum mid micelre fyrde þæs Romaniscan folces and
besæt heora burh, oð þæt hi swulton hungre. And mann awearp þa lic
for þan laþlican stence ut ofer ðone weall and ne mihton nateshwon
for heora mægenleaste þa meniu bewerian. Hi cuwon heora girdlas
and gærs æton georne and ælc læhte of oðrum gif he hwæt litles hæfde
and ðone mete of þam muðe, swiþe unmægðlice, and reaferas urnon
geond ealle þa burh and smealice sohton mid swiþlicum ðreate þone
behiddan mete on heora hordcleofan, and beoton ælcne man þe ænig
þing hæfde gif he heora wodnisse wolde wiðcweðan. Nys us na to
secgenne þone sceamlica morð þe þær gedon wæs, ac hi wurdon
adydde mid þam hatan hungre fela hund manna þæs ærman
mennisces, ma þonne we secgan willað, and þa reaferas siþþan
ofsloh ælc oðerne and seo burh wearð gewyld and toworpen
grundlunga, swa se Hælend sæde ær his þrowunge. Of þam iungum
cnihtum þe comon of ðam hungre on eallum þam lande, hi alæddon
aweg to wircenne godeweb, swa swa hi wæron getogenne. And of þam
cnapum ys þæt kynn git gehwær, and þis wæs þæt edlean heora yfelan
dæda, and eac helle wite, þæt þæt him hefegore ys. Nu miht þu wel
witan þæt weorc | sprecað swiþor þonne þa nacodan word, þe nabbað
nane fremminge. Is swa þeah god weorc on þam godan wordum,
þonne man oðerne lærð and to geleafan getrimð mid þære soþan lare
and þonne mann wisdom sprecð manegum to þearfe and to rihtinge,
þæt God si geherod se þe a rixað. Amen.

Ðu woldest me laðian, þa þa ic wæs mid þe, þæt ic swiðor drunce

910 sceamlica] *Crawford emends to* sceamlican   916 getogenne] *Crawford emends to* getogene

925 swilce for blisse ofer minum gewunan. Ac wite þu, leof man, þæt se þe
oðerne neadað ofer his mihte to drincenne, þæt se mot aberan heora
begra gil[t], gif him ænig hearm of þam drence becymð. Ure Hælend
Crist on his halgan godspelle forbead þone oferdrenc eallum gelyf-
edum mannum; healde se ðe wille his gesetnysse. And þa halgan
930 lareowas æfter þam Hælende aledon þone unðeaw þurh heora
lareowdom and tæhton þæt man drince swa swa him ne derede, for
ðan þe se oferdrenc fordeð untwilice þæs mannes sawle and his
gesundfullnysse. And unhæl becymð of þam drence.

Locahwa ðas boc awrite, write hig be þære bysne and, for Godes
935 lufon, hi gerihte, þæt heo to leas ne beo, þam writere to plihte and me
to tale.

927 gilt] gild

The manufacturer's authorised representative in the EU for product safety is
Oxford University Press España S.A. of el Parque Empresarial San Fernando de
Henares, Avenida de Castilla, 2 – 28830 Madrid (www.oup.es/en or product.
safety@oup.com). OUP España S.A. also acts as importer into Spain of products
made by the manufacturer.

www.ingramcontent.com/pod-product-compliance
Ingram Content Group UK Ltd.
Pitfield, Milton Keynes, MK11 3LW, UK
UKHW022152230426
12049UKWH00003BA/46